T0214356

Lecture Notes in Computer Science   11247

Commenced Publication in 1973
Founding and Former Series Editors:
Gerhard Goos, Juris Hartmanis, and Jan van Leeuwen

More information about this series at http://www.springer.com/series/7407

Tiziana Margaria · Bernhard Steffen (Eds.)

Leveraging Applications of Formal Methods, Verification and Validation

Industrial Practice

8th International Symposium, ISoLA 2018
Limassol, Cyprus, November 5–9, 2018
Proceedings, Part IV

 Springer

Editors
Tiziana Margaria
University of Limerick
Limerick, Ireland

Bernhard Steffen
TU Dortmund
Dortmund, Germany

ISSN 0302-9743 ISSN 1611-3349 (electronic)
Lecture Notes in Computer Science
ISBN 978-3-030-03426-9 ISBN 978-3-030-03427-6 (eBook)
https://doi.org/10.1007/978-3-030-03427-6

Library of Congress Control Number: 2018960393

LNCS Sublibrary: SL1 – Theoretical Computer Science and General Issues

This Springer imprint is published by the registered company Springer Nature Switzerland AG
The registered company address is: Gewerbestrasse 11, 6330 Cham, Switzerland

Preface

Welcome to ISoLA 2018, the *8th International Symposium on Leveraging Applications of Formal Methods, Verification and Validation*, that was held in Limassol (Cyprus) during November 5–9, 2018, endorsed by EASST, the European Association of Software Science and Technology.

This year's event followed the tradition of its symposia forerunners held 2004 and 2006 in Cyprus, 2008 in Chalkidiki, 2010 and 2012 in Crete, 2014 and 2016 in Corfu, and the series of ISoLA Workshops in Greenbelt (USA) in 2005, Poitiers (France) in 2007, Potsdam (Germany) in 2009, in Vienna (Austria) in 2011, and 2013 in Palo Alto (USA).

As in the previous editions, ISoLA 2018 provided a forum for developers, users, and researchers to discuss issues related to the **adoption and use of rigorous tools and methods** for the specification, analysis, verification, certification, construction, test, and maintenance of systems from the point of view of their different application domains. Thus, since 2004 the ISoLA series of events has served the purpose of bridging the gap between designers and developers of rigorous tools on one hand, and users in engineering and in other disciplines on the other hand. It fosters and exploits synergetic relationships among scientists, engineers, software developers, decision makers, and other critical thinkers in companies and organizations. By providing a specific, dialogue-oriented venue for the discussion of common problems, requirements, algorithms, methodologies, and practices, ISoLA aims in particular at supporting researchers in their quest to improve the usefulness, reliability, flexibility, and efficiency of tools for building systems, and users in their search for adequate solutions to their problems.

The program of the symposium consisted of a collection of *special tracks* devoted to the following hot and emerging topics:

- A Broader View on Verification: From Static to Runtime and Back
  (Organizers: Wolfgang Ahrendt, Marieke Huisman, Giles Reger, Kristin Yvonne Rozier)
- Evaluating Tools for Software Verification
  (Organizers: Markus Schordan, Dirk Beyer, Stephen F. Siegel)
- Towards a Unified View of Modeling and Programming
  (Organizers: Manfred Broy, Klaus Havelund, Rahul Kumar, Bernhard Steffen)
- RV-TheToP: Runtime Verification from Theory to Industry Practice
  (Organizers: Ezio Bartocci and Ylies Falcone)
- Rigorous Engineering of Collective Adaptive Systems
  (Organizers: Rocco De Nicola, Stefan Jähnichen, Martin Wirsing)
- Reliable Smart Contracts: State of the Art, Applications, Challenges, and Future Directions
  (Organizers: Gerardo Schneider, Martin Leucker, César Sánchez)

- Formal Methods in Industrial Practice—Bridging the Gap
  (Organizers: Michael Felderer, Dilian Gurov, Marieke Huisman, Björn Lisper, Rupert Schlick)
- X-by-Construction
  (Organizers: Maurice H. ter Beek, Loek Cleophas, Ina Schaefer, and Bruce W. Watson)
- Statistical Model Checking
  (Organizers: Axel Legay and Kim Larsen)
- Verification and Validation of Distributed Systems
  (Organizer: Cristina Seceleanu)
- Cyber-Physical Systems Engineering
  (Organizers: J Paul Gibson, Marc Pantel, Peter Gorm Larsen, Jim Woodcock, John Fitzgerald)

The following events were also held:

- RERS: Challenge on Rigorous Examination of Reactive Systems (Bernhard Steffen)
- Doctoral Symposium and Poster Session (Anna-Lena Lamprecht)
- Industrial Day (Axel Hessenkämper, Falk Howar, Andreas Rausch)

Co-located with the ISoLA Symposium were:

- RV 2018: 18th International Conference on Runtime Verification (Saddek Bensalem, Christian Colombo, and Martin Leucker)
- STRESS 2018: 5th International School on Tool-based Rigorous Engineering of Software Systems (John Hatcliff, Tiziana Margaria, Robby, Bernhard Steffen)

Owing to the growth of ISoLA 2018, the proceedings of this edition are published in four volumes of LNCS: Part 1: Modeling, Part 2: Verification, Part 3: Distributed Systems, and Part 4: Industrial Practice. In addition to the contributions of the main conference, the proceedings also include contributions of the four embedded events and tutorial papers for STRESS.

We thank the track organizers, the members of the Program Committee and their referees for their effort in selecting the papers to be presented, the local Organization Chair, Petros Stratis, the EasyConferences team for their continuous precious support during the week as well as during the entire two-year period preceding the events, and Springer for being, as usual, a very reliable partner in the proceedings production. Finally, we are grateful to Kyriakos Georgiades for his continuous support for the website and the program, and to Markus Frohme and Julia Rehder for their help with the online conference service (EquinOCS).

Special thanks are due to the following organization for their endorsement: EASST (European Association of Software Science and Technology) and Lero – The Irish Software Research Centre, and our own institutions: TU Dortmund and the University of Limerick.

November 2018   Tiziana Margaria
Bernhard Steffen

Organization

Symposium Chair

Bernhard Steffen   TU Dortmund, Germany

Program Chair

Tiziana Margaria   University of Limerick, Ireland

Program Committee

Wolfgang Ahrendt	Chalmers University of Technology, Sweden
Jesper Andersen	Deon Digital AG
Ezio Bartocci	TU Wien, Austria
Dirk Beyer	LMU Munich, Germany
Manfred Broy	Technische Universität München
Loek Cleophas	TU Eindhoven, The Netherlands
Rocco De Nicola	IMT School for Advanced Studies, Italy
Boris Düdder	University of Copenhagen, Denmark
Ylies Falcone	University of Grenoble, France
Michael Felderer	University of Innsbruck, Austria
John Fitzgerald	Newcastle University, UK
Paul Gibson	Telecom Sud Paris, France
Kim Guldstrand Larsen	Aalborg University, Denmark
Dilian Gurov	KTH Royal Institute of Technology, Sweden
John Hatcliff	Kansas State University, USA
Klaus Havelund	Jet Propulsion Laboratory, USA
Fritz Henglein	University of Copenhagen, Denmark
Axel Hessenkämper	Hottinger Baldwin Messtechnik GmbH
Falk Howar	Dortmund University of Technology and Fraunhofer ISST, Germany
Marieke Huisman	University of Twente, The Netherlands
Michael Huth	Imperial College London, UK
Stefan Jaehnichen	TU Berlin, Germany
Rahul Kumar	Microsoft Research
Anna-Lena Lamprecht	Utrecht University, The Netherlands
Peter Gorm Larsen	Aarhus University, Denmark
Axel Legay	Inria, France
Martin Leucker	University of Lübeck, Germany

Björn Lisper	Mälardalen University, Sweden
Leif-Nissen Lundæk	XAIN AG
Tiziana Margaria	Lero, Ireland
Marc Pantel	Université de Toulouse, France
Andreas Rausch	TU Clausthal, Germany
Giles Reger	University of Manchester, UK
Robby	Kansas State University, USA
Kristin Yvonne Rozier	Iowa State University, USA
Ina Schaefer	TU Braunschweig, Germany
Rupert Schlick	AIT Austrian Institute of Technology, Austria
Gerardo Schneider	University of Gothenburg, Sweden
Markus Schordan	Lawrence Livermore National Laboratory, USA
Cristina Seceleanu	Mälardalen University, Sweden
Stephen F. Siegel	University of Delaware, USA
César Sánchez	IMDEA Software Institute, Spain
Bruce W. Watson	Stellenbosch University, South Africa
Martin Wirsing	LMU München, Germany
James Woodcock	University of York, UK
Maurice ter Beek	ISTI-CNR, Italy
Jaco van de Pol	University of Twente, The Netherlands

Additional Reviewers

Yehia Abd Alrahman
Dhaminda Abeywickrama
Lenz Belzner
Saddek Bensalem
Egon Boerger
Marius Bozga
Tomas Bures
Rance Cleaveland
Giovanna Di Marzo Serugendo
Matthew Dwyer
Benedikt Eberhardinger
Rim El Ballouli
Thomas Gabor
Stephen Gilmore
Emma Hart
Arnd Hartmanns
Rolf Hennicker
Petr Hnetynka
Reiner Hähnle
Patrik Jansson
Einar Broch Johnsen

Neil Jones
Sebastiaan Joosten
Gabor Karsai
Alexander Knapp
Timothy Lethbridge
Chunhua Liao
Alberto Lluch-Lafuente
Alessandro Maggi
Dominique Méry
Birger Møller-Pedersen
Stefan Naujokat
Ayoub Nouri
Liam O'Connor
Doron Peled
Thomy Phan
Jeremy Pitt
Hella Ponsar
Andre Reichstaller
Jeff Sanders
Sean Sedwards
Christoph Seidl

Bran Selic
Steven Smyth
Josef Strnadel
Jan Sürmeli
Louis-Marie Traonouez

Mirco Tribastone
Andrea Vandin
Markus Voelter
Franco Zambonelli
Natalia Zon

Contents – Part IV

**Reliable Smart Contracts: State-of-the-art, Applications, Challenges
and Future Directions**

Industrial Day

Runtime Verification from the Theory to the Industry Practice

RV-TheToP: Runtime Verification from Theory to the Industry Practice (Track Introduction)

Ezio Bartocci[1]([✉]) and Yliès Falcone[2]

[1] Vienna University of Technology, Vienna, Austria
ezio.bartocci@tuwien.ac.at
[2] Univ. Grenoble Alpes, CNRS, Inria, LIG, 38000 Grenoble, France

Abstract. This paper introduces the RV-TOP track at ISoLA'18. The purpose of the track is to bring together experts on runtime verification and industry practitioners domains to (i) disseminate advanced research topics (ii) disseminate current industrial challenges and (iii) get RV more attractive to industry and usable in additional application domains. The track consists of eight contributed papers presented during three sessions.

1 Introduction

Runtime Verification (RV) [6,8] has gained much focus, from both the research community and practitioners. Roughly speaking, RV combines a set of theories, techniques and tools aiming towards efficient analysis of systems' executions and guaranteeing their correctness using monitoring techniques. Major challenges in RV include characterizing and formally expressing requirements that can be monitored, proposing intuitive and concise specification formalisms, and monitoring specifications efficiently (time and memory-wise).

RV can be employed before the deployment, for testing, verification, and debugging purposes or after deployment to trigger some system recovery actions when a safety property is violated and for ensuring reliability, safety, and security and for providing fault containment and recovery as well as online system repair. For example, one application of RV particularly studied in this track is to use it in combination with runtime enforcement.

Runtime enforcement [15,17,20] is a powerful technique to ensure that a program conforms to its specification. It has been initiated with the work of Schneider on security automata which halt the program whenever it deviates from its safety specification. Since then, several models and frameworks have been defined to augment enforcement mechanisms with new primitives [10,14, 18,21,35] or allow them to enforce more expressive specifications [19,38,41].

As a field, major strides have been made recently to make RV a full fledge verification technique:

- RV is now endowed with a competition for tools: three incarnations of the competition have been organized [2,22,40], an extensive report on the first

© Springer Nature Switzerland AG 2018
T. Margaria and B. Steffen (Eds.): ISoLA 2018, LNCS 11247, pp. 3–8, 2018.
https://doi.org/10.1007/978-3-030-03427-6_1

edition has been published [7], and a successful workshop reporting reflections on past competitions has been organized [39].

- A European COST action, ArVi[1], is ongoing with the purposes of (i) clarifying the dimensions of RV, its theory, algorithms and methods (ii) expose the landscape of formalisms and tools proposed and built for RV (iii) expose novel and challenging computational domains for RV and monitoring (iv) study potential applications of RV to important application areas beyond software and hardware reliability, including medical devices and legal contracts.
- Two successful schools dedicated to Runtime Verification have been organized and for the first time, high-quality videos of the lectures have been recorded [12,16].
- A Springer LNCS tutorial volume [6] on advanced research topics has been recently released by the organizers of the track.

Still, much effort is needed to make RV an attractive and viable methodology for industrial use. The purpose of this track and its past editions [5,24,25] is to synergize, and initiate the further studies needed to apply RV to wider application domains such as security, bio-health and the Internet of things.

The next section provides an overview of the papers presented at the track. Each paper benefitted from a friendly reviewing process and received at least two reviews.

2   Overview of the Track's Sessions

The track consists of eight contributed papers presented during three sessions. In the following we provide an overview of the topics discussed during each session.

2.1   Session 1 - Monitoring Cyber-Physical Systems and the Internet of Things

The first session presents the main challenges in monitoring Cyber-Physical Systems (CPS) and Internet of Things (IoT). CPS consist of a set of computational and physical entities tightly interacting. The computational entities are generally (spatially) distributed in a federated system-of-systems and they communicate through the IoT, a network infrastructure that enables the interoperability between the different computational devices. Examples of CPS include (semi-) autonomous driving cars, medical devices, smart grids and smart cities. The complex hybrid (discrete/analog) nature of CPS limits exhaustive formal verification of safety properties only to small model instances. A more practical approach to analyze CPS, is to monitor temporal (or spatio-temporal [3,27]) specifications [4] over the CPS behaviors at simulation time [1,26] or at runtime [33,34,44].

The first paper [11] advocates the urgency for a new paradigm shift in the software development of multi-agent CPS. In particular, they motivate the need

---

[1] www.cost-arvi.eu.

of new specification languages, monitoring and enforcement mechanisms that can address together both security and safety aspects at runtime.

The second paper [37] sketches a road map to develop secure and private monitors for IoT. In particular, the authors follow the vision in [28,29] where the use of decentralized monitors using migration [9,12] able to process locally the gathered data and/or to enforce locally certain policies. The use of these monitors introduce additional security and privacy threats to take into consideration. The authors propose and also discuss the use of Attribute-Based Encryption [43], a mechanism that can be used to ensure that monitors are executed by the right devices in a secure and private way.

The last paper of this session [45] presents an RV framework for multi-process monitoring on Android, supporting the analysis of nested indirect inter process communications (IPC) calls. The proposed approach addresses the challenge of ordering events across multiple Android processes and it allows users to specify properties for multi-process monitoring.

2.2   Session 2 - RV for Industrial and Large-Scale Systems

The second session focuses on the use of RV tools and techniques in the context of industrial and large scale systems.

The first paper [13] of this session provides useful criteria and considerations (based on the authors' experience with industrial partners) to measure the success of academia-industry projects.

The second paper [46] presents the main features of SMEDL, an RV framework that provides flexible and scalable deployment of monitors for large-scale software. SMEDL has been employed in the context of a target tracking applications, developed by BAE Systems and evolving in the last 15 years.

The third paper [42] addresses the problem of reusability of runtime enforcement strategies. In particular the authors target software components (i.e., Android apps and web applications) sharing a common life-cycle model with specific callbacks. The knowledge of these models can be exploited to develop generic runtime enforcement strategies that are not application dependent.

2.3   Session 3 - Latest Advances on Software Monitoring

The third session presents the latest advancements on monitoring software handling large amount of data or with concurrent threads.

The first paper [30] extends the recently proposed approach [31,32] for monitoring first-order temporal logic formulas over potentially large amount of data using binary decision diagrams (BDDs). The authors discuss a new feature that enables to forget data values when they no longer affect the RV verdict.

The second paper [36] provides an overview on the use of contracts that guarantee safety from high-level atomicity violation in components running concurrently.

Acknowledgements. The authors acknowledge the support of the ICT COST Action IC1402 Runtime Verification beyond Monitoring (ARVI).

References

1. Bartocci, E., Bortolussi, L., Nenzi, L.: A temporal logic approach to modular design of synthetic biological circuits. In: Gupta, A., Henzinger, T.A. (eds.) CMSB 2013. LNCS, vol. 8130, pp. 164–177. Springer, Heidelberg (2013). https://doi.org/10.1007/978-3-642-40708-6_13
2. Bartocci, E., Bonakdarpour, B., Falcone, Y.: First international competition on software for runtime verification. In: Bonakdarpour, B., Smolka, S.A. (eds.) RV 2014. LNCS, vol. 8734, pp. 1–9. Springer, Cham (2014). https://doi.org/10.1007/978-3-319-11164-3_1
3. Bartocci, E., Bortolussi, L., Loreti, M., Nenzi, L.: Monitoring mobile and spatially distributed cyber-physical systems. In: Proceedings of the 15th ACM-IEEE International Conference on Formal Methods and Models for System Design, MEMOCODE 2017, pp. 146–155. ACM (2017)
4. Bartocci, E., et al.: Specification-based monitoring of cyber-physical systems: a survey on theory, tools and applications. In: Bartocci, E., Falcone, Y. (eds.) Lectures on Runtime Verification. LNCS, vol. 10457, pp. 135–175. Springer, Cham (2018). https://doi.org/10.1007/978-3-319-75632-5_5
5. Bartocci, E., Falcone, Y.: Runtime verification and enforcement, the (industrial) application perspective (track introduction). In: Margaria, T., Steffen, B. (eds.) ISoLA 2016. LNCS, vol. 9953, pp. 333–338. Springer, Cham (2016). https://doi.org/10.1007/978-3-319-47169-3_24
6. Bartocci, E., Falcone, Y. (eds.): Lectures on Runtime Verification. LNCS, vol. 10457. Springer, Cham (2018). https://doi.org/10.1007/978-3-319-75632-5
7. Bartocci, E., et al.: First international competition on runtime verification: rules, benchmarks, tools, and final results of CRV 2014. Int. J. Softw. Tools Technol. Transf. 1–40 (2017). https://doi.org/10.1007/s10009-017-0454-5
8. Bartocci, E., Falcone, Y., Francalanza, A., Reger, G.: Introduction to runtime verification. In: Bartocci, E., Falcone, Y. (eds.) Lectures on Runtime Verification. LNCS, vol. 10457, pp. 1–33. Springer, Cham (2018). https://doi.org/10.1007/978-3-319-75632-5_1
9. Bauer, A., Falcone, Y.: Decentralised LTL monitoring. Form. Methods Syst. Des. **48**(1–2), 46–93 (2016)
10. Bielova, N., Massacci, F.: Iterative enforcement by suppression: towards practical enforcement theories. J. Comput. Secur. **20**(1), 51–79 (2012)
11. Bonakdarpour, B., Deshmukh, J., Pajic, M.: Opportunities and challenges in monitoring cyber-physical systems security. In: Margaria, T., Steffen, B. (eds.) ISoLA 2018. LNCS, vol. 11247, pp. 9–18. Springer, Cham (2018)
12. Colombo, C., Falcone, Y.: First international summer school on runtime verification - as part of the ArVi COST action 1402. In: Falcone and Sánchez [23], pp. 17–20
13. Colombo, C., Pace, G.: Considering academia-industry projects meta-characteristics in runtime verification design. In: Margaria, T., Steffen, B. (eds.) ISoLA 2018. LNCS, vol. 11247, pp. 32–41. Springer, Cham (2018)
14. Dolzhenko, E., Ligatti, J., Reddy, S.: Modeling runtime enforcement with mandatory results automata. Int. J. Inf. Secur. **14**(1), 47–60 (2015)

15. Falcone, Y.: You should better enforce than verify. In: Barringer, H., et al. (eds.) RV 2010. LNCS, vol. 6418, pp. 89–105. Springer, Heidelberg (2010). https://doi.org/10.1007/978-3-642-16612-9_9

16. Falcone, Y.: Second international school on runtime verification - as part of the ArVi COST action 1402. In: Proceedings of the Runtime Verification - 18th International Conference, RV 2018, Limassol, Cyprus, 10–13 November 2018, pp. 17–20 (2016, to appear)

17. Falcone, Y., Fernandez, J., Mounier, L.: What can you verify and enforce at runtime? STTT **14**(3), 349–382 (2012)

18. Falcone, Y., Jéron, T., Marchand, H., Pinisetty, S.: Runtime enforcement of regular timed properties by suppressing and delaying events. Syst. Control Lett. **123**, 2–41 (2016)

19. Falcone, Y., Marchand, H.: Enforcement and validation (at runtime) of various notions of opacity. Discret. Event Dyn. Syst. **25**(4), 531–570 (2015)

20. Falcone, Y., Mariani, L., Rollet, A., Saha, S.: Runtime failure prevention and reaction. In: Bartocci, E., Falcone, Y. (eds.) Lectures on Runtime Verification. LNCS, vol. 10457, pp. 103–134. Springer, Cham (2018). https://doi.org/10.1007/978-3-319-75632-5_4

21. Falcone, Y., Mounier, L., Fernandez, J., Richier, J.: Runtime enforcement monitors: composition, synthesis, and enforcement abilities. Form. Methods Syst. Des. **38**(3), 223–262 (2011)

22. Falcone, Y., Ničković, D., Reger, G., Thoma, D.: Second international competition on runtime verification - CRV 15. In: Bartocci, E., Majumdar, R. (eds.) RV 2015. LNCS, vol. 9333, pp. 405–422. Springer, Cham (2015). https://doi.org/10.1007/978-3-319-23820-3_27

23. Falcone, Y., Sánchez, C. (eds.): RV 2016. LNCS, vol. 10012. Springer, Cham (2016). https://doi.org/10.1007/978-3-319-46982-9

24. Falcone, Y., Zuck, L.D.: Runtime verification: the application perspective. In: Margaria, T., Steffen, B. (eds.) ISoLA 2012. LNCS, vol. 7609, pp. 284–291. Springer, Heidelberg (2012). https://doi.org/10.1007/978-3-642-34026-0_21

25. Falcone, Y., Zuck, L.D.: Runtime verification: the application perspective. STTT **17**(2), 121–123 (2015)

26. Gol, E.A., Bartocci, E., Belta, C.: A formal methods approach to pattern synthesis in reaction diffusion systems. In: Proceedings of 53rd IEEE Conference on Decision and Control, CDC 2014, Los Angeles, CA, USA, 15–17 December 2014, pp. 108–113. IEEE (2014)

27. Haghighi, I., Jones, A., Kong, Z., Bartocci, E., Grosu, R., Belta, C.: SpaTeL: a novel spatial-temporal logic and its applications to networked systems. In: Proceedings of the 18th International Conference on Hybrid Systems: Computation and Control, HSCC 2015, pp. 189–198. ACM (2015)

28. Hallé, S., Khoury, R., Betti, Q., El-Hokayem, A., Falcone, Y.: Decentralized enforcement of document lifecycle constraints. Inf. Syst. **74**(Part), 117–135 (2018)

29. Hallé, S., Khoury, R., El-Hokayem, A., Falcone, Y.: Decentralized enforcement of artifact lifecycles. In: Matthes, F., Mendling, J., Rinderle-Ma, S. (eds.) 20th IEEE International Enterprise Distributed Object Computing Conference, EDOC 2016, Vienna, Austria, 5–9 September 2016, pp. 1–10. IEEE Computer Society (2016)

30. Havelund, K., Peled, D.: BDDs on the run. In: Margaria, T., Steffen, B. (eds.) ISoLA 2018. LNCS, vol. 11247, pp. 58–69. Springer, Cham (2018)

31. Havelund, K., Peled, D.: Efficient runtime verification of first-order temporal properties. In: Gallardo, M.M., Merino, P. (eds.) SPIN 2018. LNCS, vol. 10869, pp. 26–47. Springer, Cham (2018). https://doi.org/10.1007/978-3-319-94111-0_2

32. Havelund, K., Peled, D., Ulus, D.: First order temporal logic monitoring with BDDs. In: Proceedings of the 2017 Formal Methods in Computer Aided Design, FMCAD 2017, pp. 116–123. IEEE (2017)

33. Jaksic, S., Bartocci, E., Grosu, R., Kloibhofer, R., Nguyen, T., Nickovic, D.: From signal temporal logic to FPGA monitors. In: Proceedings of the 13th ACM/IEEE International Conference on Formal Methods and Models for Codesign, MEM-OCODE 2015, pp. 218–227. IEEE (2015)

34. Jakšić, S., Bartocci, E., Grosu, R., Ničković, D.: Quantitative monitoring of STL with edit distance. In: Falcone, Y., Sánchez, C. (eds.) RV 2016. LNCS, vol. 10012, pp. 201–218. Springer, Cham (2016). https://doi.org/10.1007/978-3-319-46982-9_13

35. Ligatti, J., Bauer, L., Walker, D.: Edit automata: enforcement mechanisms for run-time security policies. Int. J. Inf. Secur. 4(1–2), 2–16 (2005)

36. Lourenço, J.M.: Verifying real-world software with contracts for concurrency. In: Margaria, T., Steffen, B. (eds.) ISoLA 2018. LNCS, vol. 11247, pp. 70–73. Springer, Cham (2018)

37. Pace, G., Picazo-Sanchez, P., Schneider, G.: Migrating monitors + ABE: a suitable combination for secure IoT? In: Margaria, T., Steffen, B. (eds.) ISoLA 2018. LNCS, vol. 11247, pp. 19–24. Springer, Cham (2018)

38. Pinisetty, S., Falcone, Y., Jéron, T., Marchand, H., Rollet, A., Nguena-Timo, O.: Runtime enforcement of timed properties revisited. Form. Methods Syst. Des. 45(3), 381–422 (2014)

39. Reger, G.: A report of RV-CuBES 2017. In: Reger, G., Havelund, K. (eds.) An International Workshop on Competitions, Usability, Benchmarks, Evaluation, and Standardisation for Runtime Verification Tools, RV-CuBES 2017, Seattle, WA, USA, 15 September 2017, vol. 3, pp. 1–9. Kalpa Publications in Computing, Easy-Chair (2017)

40. Reger, G., Hallé, S., Falcone, Y.: Third international competition on runtime verification - CRV 2016. In: Falcone and Sánchez [23], pp. 21–37

41. Renard, M., Rollet, A., Falcone, Y.: Runtime enforcement using büchi games. In: Proceedings of the 24th ACM SIGSOFT International SPIN Symposium on Model Checking of Software, pp. 70–79. ACM (2017)

42. Riganelli, O., Micucci, D., Mariani, L.: Increasing the reusability of enforcers with lifecycle events. In: Margaria, T., Steffen, B. (eds.) ISoLA 2018. LNCS, vol. 11247, pp. 51–57. Springer, Cham (2018)

43. Roman, R., Zhou, J., López, J.: On the features and challenges of security and privacy in distributed internet of things. Comput. Netw. 57(10), 2266–2279 (2013)

44. Selyunin, K., et al.: Runtime monitoring with recovery of the SENT communication protocol. In: Majumdar, R., Kunčak, V. (eds.) CAV 2017. LNCS, vol. 10426, pp. 336–355. Springer, Cham (2017). https://doi.org/10.1007/978-3-319-63387-9_17

45. Villazon, A., Sun, H., Binder, W.: Capturing inter-process communication for runtime verification on Android. In: Margaria, T., Steffen, B. (eds.) ISoLA 2018. LNCS, vol. 11247, pp. 25–31. Springer, Cham (2018)

46. Zhang, T., Eakman, G., Sokolsky, O., Lee, I.: Flexible monitor deployment for runtime verification of large scale software. In: Margaria, T., Steffen, B. (eds.) ISoLA 2018. LNCS, vol. 11247, pp. 42–50. Springer, Cham (2018)

Opportunities and Challenges in Monitoring Cyber-Physical Systems Security

Borzoo Bonakdarpour[1]($\boxtimes$), Jyotirmoy V. Deshmukh[2], and Miroslav Pajic[3]

[1] Iowa State University, Ames, USA
borzoo@iastate.edu
[2] University of Southern California, Los Angeles, USA
jdeshmuk@usc.edu
[3] Duke University, Durham, USA
miroslav.pajic@duke.edu

Abstract. Technological advances in distributed *cyber-physical systems* (CPS) will fundamentally alter the way present and future human societies lead their lives. From a security or privacy perspective, a (multi-agent) cyber-physical system is a network of sensors, actuators, and computation nodes, i.e., a system with multiple attack surfaces and latent exploits that originate both through software attacks and physical attacks. In this paper, we argue that we are in pressing need to bring about a paradigm shift in software development for multi-agent CPS. To this end, security and privacy policies should be made a critical ingredient of agent interfaces with a goal of ensuring both localized safety and privacy for each agent, as well as guaranteeing global system safety and security. We present our vision on new theory, algorithms, and tools to foster a culture of secure-by-design multi-agent CPS.

1 Introduction

Human societies of tomorrow will be immersed in multi-agent cyber-physical systems (CPS). Examples include autonomous and semi-autonomous cars coupled with intelligent transportation systems as well as fleets of unmanned aerial vehicles (UAVs) performing mundane jobs like package delivery, and teams of rescue robots in disaster management scenarios. A key feature of these systems is that they consist of networked *multi-agent cyber* components that interact with the *physical* environment. Informally, a CPS is a system that combines a *plant*, i.e., a mechanical, electrical or hydraulic component that has temporal behavior which follows the laws of physics, controlled by an embedded software *controller*. A multi-agent CPS consists of two or more such CPSs with the ability to communicate with each other or with a central agent. It is tempting to think of a multi-agent CPS as just a larger CPS with several plants and controllers, but what distinguishes a multi-agent CPS from an ordinary CPS is the decoupling between individual agents. Often, agents in such a multi-agent CPS are

© Springer Nature Switzerland AG 2018
T. Margaria and B. Steffen (Eds.): ISoLA 2018, LNCS 11247, pp. 9–18, 2018.
https://doi.org/10.1007/978-3-030-03427-6_2

autonomous, i.e., have some degree of freedom in controlling their behavior without the intervention from an external agent, or are semi-autonomous, i.e., they have the ability to switch control between a human operator and an embedded software controller.

In the past few years, we have seen the catastrophic levels of damage that attacks on cyber-physical systems can cause; examples include the blackout of the Ukrainian power grid in 2015 [30], and the MIRAI botnet that made use of Internet of Things (IoT) devices to launch Distributed Denial-of-Service attacks [25]. Some types of cyber-induced attacks can have physical impacts; examples include several examples where automobile security was compromised [11, 26, 37], including a wireless hack on a Jeep vehicle in a controlled setting that received attention in popular media [18]. In the domain of aerial vehicles, examples include a GPS spoofing attack that allegedly led to the abduction of a US drone [38]. It is clear that the need for security and trust in cyberspace is fast changing into a need for secure and trustworthy *cyber-physical spaces*.

As a multi-agent CPS is a network of sensors, actuators, and computation nodes linked through communication channels, from a security perspective, such a system presents a plethora of attack surfaces. Direct attacks on such systems, as well as latent vulnerabilities can attract both software as well as physical attacks. Here, by software attacks we mean traditional cyber attacks that target communication of a CPS agent with its external world by seeking to compromise its availability, corrupt its data integrity, or lead to a loss of its data confidentiality. By physical attacks, we mean an adversarial action that can either learn the internal physical state of the system by observing its input/output behavior, alter its internal physical state by injecting commands or control actions, or use actual physical phenomena to induce unsafe behavior. Note that these categories are not mutually exclusive, and often attacks can be constructed by exploiting vulnerabilities in both the software and physical domains.

Our position is based on the premise that for a multi-agent CPS, there is a pressing need to design a framework that supports a diverse collection of security and privacy policies, but more importantly, supports reasoning about the impact of such policies on the safety of each agent in isolation, and also on the safety, security and privacy of agents at the level of the multi-agent CPS as a whole. More specifically, we argue that to achieve a paradigm shift in CPS security, we need to pursue the following objectives:

- The first step for systematic and formal reasoning about security or privacy is to have a *machine-checkable* language/logic that can express complex policies such as information flow in the context of CPS.
- This language/logic can then be used to monitor and enforce policies at the level of individual agents through careful design and implementation of sensor instrumentation at system level to gather the data required to evaluate the policies.
- Monitoring and enforcement of policies also needs to be done in a compositional fashion at the level of multiple agents in the CPS to reason about the impact of such policies at the level of the entire system.

– Finally, the language and monitoring/enforcement mechanisms need to be realized in real-world scenarios and systems with an eye on the next generation of CPSs that will play a crucial life in our daily lives.

We elaborate on our position on each of these objectives and our view on addressing them in Sects. 2, 3 and 4.

2 Logic-Based Expression of Security and Privacy Policies for CPS

Signal Temporal Logic (STL) is a machine-checkable logical formalism that was first introduced in the context of specifying properties of mixed-signal circuits [31]. There has been considerable interest in the use of STL for specifying industrial-scale embedded systems and an ecosystem of monitoring and test-generation tools has evolved around the logic [2, 3, 13, 15, 20, 21, 24]. We envision two extensions to STL to express security properties on confidentiality, integrity, and availability as well as temporal constraints that counter side-channel attacks.

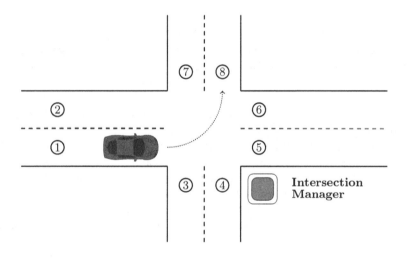

Fig. 1. Depiction of an autonomous intersection manager system.

STL Extension for Security. Our first proposed extension is *Security-Aware Signal Temporal Logic* (SA-STL), that introduces common security primitives as first-class predicates in the logic. This will allow designers to express security properties and constraints in a uniform, *machine-checkable* language. The key advantage of using SA-STL is that it inherits quantitative semantics of STL, which will allow us to quantify the *degree of security* of the system. SA-STL will also include security constraints that are stochastic in nature by allowing probabilistic predicates such as those allowed by Stochastic STL [29]. As this logic can reason over real-valued signals, it allows seamless reasoning over physical signals and quantities in a single logic. Consider for example the scenario shown in Fig. 1, where the car shown wishes to cross the intersection from the lane marked 1 to the one marked 8. The SA-STL formula (1) says that, *"if the car receives a message from the intersection manager granting permission to use the intersection, then, the car has a window of time in the future, where subject to the constraints imposed by the car's dynamics, the car can cross the intersection in a same fashion."* We can express the following property in SA-STL as follows:

$$\mathbf{G}\left(\left(\begin{matrix}\texttt{lane} = 1 \ \wedge \\ \texttt{recvEncMsg} = \texttt{granted} \ \wedge \\ \mathbf{F}_{[0,10]}\texttt{authSender} = \texttt{IntMgr}\end{matrix}\right) \implies (\texttt{accel} < 2 \ \mathbf{U}_{[3,10]} \ \texttt{lane} = 8)\right) \quad (1)$$

We remark that this is just one aspect of the security policy that specifies the timeliness of crossing and authenticity of the received message. We observe that the above security policy can be expressed as a conjunction of separate parts that monitor the transmission of the request signal, reception of the grant signal, continuous monitoring of the physical signals corresponding to acceleration and position in its control unit, and transmission of successful intersection navigation once it reaches the desired lane.

Hyper Logics. A large set of important information-flow security and privacy policies are inexpressible in trace-based variants of temporal logics (such as SA-STL). Although existing hyper logics such as HyperLTL [12] can express complex information flow policies, they currently do not allow explicit timing constraints and real-valued signals. Thus, we propose to design a new logic called *Hyper-MTL* that will allow explicit quantification over traces as well as timed temporal operators that enforce timing constraints across multiple traces. For example, we envision a timed until operator that enforces a time interval for the eventuality part of the operator as well as an error bound which allows events to happen within that bound but across multiple traces. For example, by formula $\varphi = \forall \pi. \forall \pi'. a_\pi \ \mathbf{U}_I^j \ b_{\pi'}$, we mean that in every pair of traces, b should occur within explicit time interval I, but occurrences of b in π and π' can take place in a sliding window such that occurrences are not j units apart. Thus, if $I = [0, \infty)$, then the sliding window can move at any point along the time. This will allow us to express protection policies against many side-channel timing attacks. This logic can then be extended to have predicates over real-valued signals, similar to STL, and we can formulate quantitative semantics to help obtain a notion of *robust* satisfaction.

As each agent in a multi-agent CPS is effectively a *hybrid dynamical system with inputs and outputs*, the above frameworks can employ recent research results on attack-resilient control and attack detection to synthesize observers that identify the conditions under which an agent is compromised. Thus, one can investigate mapping observers synthesized in this fashion into a SA-STL-based security or privacy policy expressed as a hyperproperty in the newly proposed hyper logic.

3   Monitor Synthesis and Resource-Aware Monitoring Algorithms

Runtime monitoring is a technique commonly used for protecting a CPS against uncertainties in its environment. Runtime monitoring enables (1) automatic identification of the minimal number of states or program variables to monitor so as to make monitoring *minimally intrusive*, (2) the use of quantitative, predictive monitoring that is resource-optimal and can prevent a security violation before it occurs, (3) the use of quantitative trust management [5,42] to dynamically monitor trust levels of agents in the multi-agent CPS, and use trust as a mechanism to synthesize distributed observations through a multiplicity of agents and sensors. Our view is to design multi-faceted algorithms to monitor complex security and privacy policies in CPS on several fronts.

Robust and Predictive Monitoring. We advocate combining robust online monitoring for STL [14] and predictive monitoring for Metric Temporal Logic [16]. We believe that robust predictive monitoring can provide nuanced information about probabilistic and quantitative information of future security risks, allowing earlier preventive actions.

Robust Monitoring of Hyper Logics. We envision algorithms for monitoring timed hyperproperties with real-valued signals. These algorithms will expand on previous efforts (e.g., [1,6,7,9,17]). Such a monitoring algorithm will take as input either (1) concurrent output traces of an instrumented running system, (2) offline logs of past executions, or (3) runtime traces and an abstract model of the system [8] as well as a set of formulas. The algorithms will evaluate the formulas and emit satisfaction/violation verdicts on the input online/offline traces. In case of violation, these verdicts will be used to take action on maintaining system safety or privacy. Following the recent trend, monitoring can be done on a GPU [4] or FPGA [19] device to minimize the impact of probe effects on the system under inspection and also achieve highly efficient resource management.

Sensor Instrumentation. Sensor instrumentation for monitoring under architectural constraints is inevitable to achieve effective CPS monitoring. One approach is to exploit logging schemes for monitoring of distributed controller networks; for a single control loop (i.e., feature), [33,34,40,41] introduce conditions that the instrumentation points need to satisfy to ensure full system observability with continuous monitoring, even in the presence of malicious components. Similarly, when intermittent monitoring is used, extensions of the techniques from [22,23,27,28] can be utilized. This would effectively also allow for attack detection and identification of compromised components.

4   Compositional Runtime Enforcement of CPS Security Policies

Multi-agent CPS are inherently component-based. Thus, it is natural to think of decompositional methods that partition the overall system security, privacy or safety into assumptions and guarantees at the level of individual agents. There are two key building blocks that give us dynamic assurance of meeting security/privacy policies at run time: (1) each agent monitors the assumptions specified by the security/privacy policy of the system on the inputs it receives from other agents or the environment, (2) a runtime enforcement system uses various techniques to enforce safe behavior of the CPS agent's actuation system, and to enforce the guarantees provided by the agent's outward communication to other agents. We discussed the first item in Sects. 2 and 3. We now focus on mechanisms for the second item.

Runtime Enforcement. In some cases, if some of the system components have been compromised, the remaining components can still be used for control with (potential) performance degradation but strong safety guarantees [35,36]. On the other hand, when some components are compromised, it is necessary to rely on architectural support to ensure safe system operation in the case of attacks [33,35] through a set of actuators. However, without architectural support, even when these actuators are identified they can continue to force the system into an unsafe state. This can be prevented with the use of secure/trusted hardware and architectural design that allows for decoupling of the attacked actuators. Similarly, if a compromised control module (e.g., a task running on an ECU) is detected, rebooting the controller and restoring it to a safe cyber-physical state could neutralize the attack; similarly, the system may decide to switch to a trusted controller that is safe, but may not be optimized for performance (e.g., as in the standard simplex architecture [32,39]). In situations where some, but not all of the control components are compromised, an interesting problem to investigate is the use of *micro-rebooting* for system recovery, which has shown to significantly reduce recovery cost, such as time to recover [10]. To design successful techniques, it is critical to have clear understanding of the underlying system architecture and how architectural support can be exploited to provide safe system performance even in the presence of attacks. Thus, one can clearly capture platform resources in the form of real-time, assume/guarantee properties of the sensor, controller and actuation modules. This will help support compositional analysis from the perspective of evolving software with runtime changes in the system configurations. In this context, a key aspect that will provide dynamic assurance is a clear formulation of various recovery and enforcement mechanisms at the level of individual agents as part of the agent's architecture. Another area to investigate is developing *repair transducers* for enforcing security policies. String transducers are automata that map input strings to output strings, and have been studied in the context of string *sanitization*.

Compositional Design. The monitoring techniques for secure and privacy-preserving CPS discussed in Sect. 3 will provide different resiliency guarantees for specific attack vectors, including claims about what attacks are detectable, identifiable, and can be attenuated through resilient control. A missing link is still providing guarantees on time-to-detection and identification, as well as potential control-performance cost degradation due to their use. One way to develop compositional design methods for combining different monitors is a hierarchical monitoring system, in order to improve system resiliency to attacks over any monitor individually. Intuitively, multiple deployed monitors can *guard* one another's blind spot or they can be activated at different time-instances due to the constrained system (e.g., computation) resources. There are multiple challenges to tackle, e.g., modeling, types of assumptions and guarantees, implementation and performance degradation costs, as well as attackers' impact over time if the security-aware module is not active. The use of logic-based modeling and reasoning should also be investigated.

5   Conclusion

In this paper, we focused on the pressing need to bring about a paradigm shift in software development for multi-agent CPS. We sketched our position on three different orthogonal fronts to tackle the problem, namely, (1) designing specification languages that can capture both security and CPS aspects of systems, (2) runtime monitoring of CPS to detect security violations and detect attackers' attempts to compromise security and/or privacy, and (3) runtime enforcement to ensure security and safety of CPS. Our view is that security and privacy policies should be made a critical ingredient of agent interfaces with a goal of ensuring both localized safety and privacy for each agent, as well as guaranteeing global system safety and security. This is especially crucial and challenging in multi-agent CPS.

Acknowledgment. This research has been partially supported by the NSF SaTC-1813388, a grant from Iowa State University, NSF CNS-1652544 and the ONR under agreements number N00014-17-1-2012 and N00014-17-1-2504.

References

1. Agrawal, S., Bonakdarpour, B.: Runtime verification of k-safety hyperproperties in HyperLTL. In: Proceedings of the 20th IEEE Computer Security Foundations Symposium, CSF, pp. 239–252 (2016)
2. Annpureddy, Y., Liu, C., Fainekos, G., Sankaranarayanan, S.: S-TaLiRo: a tool for temporal logic falsification for hybrid systems. In: Abdulla, P.A., Leino, K.R.M. (eds.) TACAS 2011. LNCS, vol. 6605, pp. 254–257. Springer, Heidelberg (2011). https://doi.org/10.1007/978-3-642-19835-9_21
3. Bartocci, E., et al.: Specification-based monitoring of cyber-physical systems: a survey on theory, tools and applications. In: Bartocci, E., Falcone, Y. (eds.) Lectures on Runtime Verification. LNCS, vol. 10457, pp. 135–175. Springer, Cham (2018). https://doi.org/10.1007/978-3-319-75632-5_5
4. Berkovich, S., Bonakdarpour, B., Fischmeister, S.: Runtime verification with minimal intrusion through parallelism. Form. Methods Syst. Des. **46**(3), 317–348 (2015)
5. Blaze, M., et al.: Dynamic trust management. Computer **42**(2), 44–52 (2009)
6. Bonakdarpour, B., Finkbeiner, B.: Runtime verification for HyperLTL. In: Falcone, Y., Sánchez, C. (eds.) RV 2016. LNCS, vol. 10012, pp. 41–45. Springer, Cham (2016). https://doi.org/10.1007/978-3-319-46982-9_4

7. Bonakdarpour, B., Finkbeiner, B.: The complexity of monitoring hyperproperties. In: Proceedings of the 31st IEEE Computer Security Foundations Symposium, CSF, pp. 162–174 (2018)

8. Bonakdarpour, B., Sanchez, C., Schneider, G.: Monitoring hyperproperties by combining static analysis and runtime verification. In: International Symposium On Leveraging Applications of Formal Methods, Verification and Validation, ISoLA (2018, to appear)

9. Brett, N., Siddique, U., Bonakdarpour, B.: Rewriting-based runtime verification for alternation-free HyperLTL. In: Legay, A., Margaria, T. (eds.) TACAS 2017. LNCS, vol. 10206, pp. 77–93. Springer, Heidelberg (2017). https://doi.org/10.1007/978-3-662-54580-5_5

10. Candea, G., Kawamoto, S., Fujiki, Y., Friedman, G., Fox, A.: Microreboot-a technique for cheap recovery. In: OSDI, vol. 4, pp. 31–44 (2004)

11. Checkoway, S., et al.: Comprehensive experimental analyses of automotive attack surfaces. In: USENIX Security Symposium, San Francisco (2011)

12. Clarkson, M.R., Finkbeiner, B., Koleini, M., Micinski, K.K., Rabe, M.N., Sánchez, C.: Temporal logics for hyperproperties. In: Abadi, M., Kremer, S. (eds.) POST 2014. LNCS, vol. 8414, pp. 265–284. Springer, Heidelberg (2014). https://doi.org/10.1007/978-3-642-54792-8_15

13. Deshmukh, J., Horvat, M., Jin, X., Majumdar, R., Prabhu, V.S.: Testing cyber-physical systems through bayesian optimization. ACM Trans. Embed. Comput. Syst. 16(5s), 170:1–170:18 (2017)

14. Deshmukh, J.V., Donzé, A., Ghosh, S., Jin, X., Juniwal, G., Seshia, S.A.: Robust online monitoring of signal temporal logic. Form. Methods Syst. Des. 51, 5–30 (2017)

15. Deshmukh, J., Jin, X., Kapinski, J., Maler, O.: Stochastic local search for falsification of hybrid systems. In: Finkbeiner, B., Pu, G., Zhang, L. (eds.) ATVA 2015. LNCS, vol. 9364, pp. 500–517. Springer, Cham (2015). https://doi.org/10.1007/978-3-319-24953-7_35

16. Dokhanchi, A., Hoxha, B., Fainekos, G.: On-line monitoring for temporal logic robustness. In: Bonakdarpour, B., Smolka, S.A. (eds.) RV 2014. LNCS, vol. 8734, pp. 231–246. Springer, Cham (2014). https://doi.org/10.1007/978-3-319-11164-3_19

17. Finkbeiner, B., Hahn, C., Stenger, M., Tentrup, L.: Monitoring hyperproperties. In: Lahiri, S., Reger, G. (eds.) RV 2017. LNCS, vol. 10548, pp. 190–207. Springer, Cham (2017). https://doi.org/10.1007/978-3-319-67531-2_12

18. Greenberg, A.: Hackers remotely kill a jeep on the highway? With me in it. Wired 7, 21 (2015)

19. Jaksic, S., Bartocci, E., Grosu, R., Kloibhofer, R., Nguyen, T., Nickovic, D.: From signal temporal logic to FPGA monitors. In: 13th ACM/IEEE International Conference on Formal Methods and Models for Codesign, MEMOCODE, pp. 218–227 (2015)

20. Jin, X., Deshmukh, J.V., Kapinski, J., Ueda, K., Butts, K.: Powertrain control verification benchmark. In: Proceedings of Hybrid Systems: Computation and Control, pp. 253–262 (2014)

21. Jin, X., Donzé, A., Deshmukh, J.V., Seshia, S.A.: Mining requirements from closed-loop control models. In: Proceedings of Hybrid Systems: Computation and Control (2013)

22. Jovanov, I., Pajic, M.: Relaxing integrity requirements for resilient control systems. CoRR, abs/1707.02950 (2017)

23. Jovanov, I., Pajic, M.: Sporadic data integrity for secure state estimation. In: 2017 IEEE 56th Annual Conference on Decision and Control, CDC, pp. 163–169, December 2017

24. Kapinski, J., Deshmukh, J.V., Jin, X., Ito, H., Butts, K.: Simulation-based approaches for verification of embedded control systems: an overview of traditional and advanced modeling, testing, and verification techniques. IEEE Control Syst. **36**(6), 45–64 (2016)

25. Kolias, C., Kambourakis, G., Stavrou, A., Voas, J.: DDoS in the IoT: mirai and other botnets. Computer **50**(7), 80–84 (2017)

26. Koscher, K., et al.: Experimental security analysis of a modern automobile. In: 2010 IEEE Symposium on Security and Privacy, SP, pp. 447–462. IEEE (2010)

27. Lesi, V., Jovanov, I., Pajic, M.: Network scheduling for secure cyber-physical systems. In: 2017 IEEE Real-Time Systems Symposium, RTSS, pp. 45–55, December 2017

28. Lesi, V., Jovanov, I., Pajic, M.: Security-aware scheduling of embedded control tasks. ACM Trans. Embed. Comput. Syst. **16**(5s), 188:1–188:21 (2017)

29. Li, J., Nuzzo, P., Sangiovanni-Vincentelli, A., Xi, Y., Li, D.: Stochastic contracts for cyber-physical system design under probabilistic requirements. In: ACM/IEEE International Conference on Formal Methods and Models for System Design (2017)

30. Liang, G., Weller, S.R., Zhao, J., Luo, F., Dong, Z.Y.: The 2015 Ukraine blackout: implications for false data injection attacks. IEEE Trans. Power Syst. **32**(4), 3317–3318 (2017)

31. Maler, O., Nickovic, D.: Monitoring temporal properties of continuous signals. In: Lakhnech, Y., Yovine, S. (eds.) FORMATS/FTRTFT -2004. LNCS, vol. 3253, pp. 152–166. Springer, Heidelberg (2004). https://doi.org/10.1007/978-3-540-30206-3_12

32. Mohan, S., Bak, S., Betti, E., Yun, H., Sha, L., Caccamo, M.: S3A: secure system simplex architecture for enhanced security and robustness of cyber-physical systems. In: Proceedings of the 2nd ACM International Conference on High Confidence Networked Systems, pp. 65–74. ACM (2013)

33. Pajic, M., Lee, I., Pappas, G.J.: Attack-resilient state estimation for noisy dynamical systems. IEEE Trans. Control Netw. Syst. **4**(1), 82–92 (2017)

34. Pajic, M., Mangharam, R., Pappas, G.J., Sundaram, S.: Topological conditions for in-network stabilization of dynamical systems. IEEE J. Sel. Areas Commun. **31**(4), 794–807 (2013)

35. Pajic, M., Weimer, J., Bezzo, N., Sokolsky, O., Pappas, G.J., Lee, I.: Design and implementation of attack-resilient cyberphysical systems: with a focus on attack-resilient state estimators. IEEE Control Syst. **37**(2), 66–81 (2017)

36. Pajic, M., et al.: Robustness of attack-resilient state estimators. In: ACM/IEEE International Conference on Cyber-Physical Systems, ICCPS, pp. 163–174, April 2014

37. Savage, S.: Modern automotive vulnerabilities: causes, disclosures, and outcomes (2016)

38. Schumann, J., Moosbrugger, P., Rozier, K.Y.: R2U2: monitoring and diagnosis of security threats for unmanned aerial systems. In: Bartocci, E., Majumdar, R. (eds.) RV 2015. LNCS, vol. 9333, pp. 233–249. Springer, Cham (2015). https://doi.org/10.1007/978-3-319-23820-3_15

39. Seto, D., Krogh, B.H., Sha, L., Chutinan, A.: Dynamic control system upgrade using the simplex architecture. IEEE Control Syst. **18**(4), 72–80 (1998)

40. Sundaram, S., Pajic, M., Hadjicostis, C., Mangharam, R., Pappas, G.: The wireless control network: monitoring for malicious behavior. In: 49th IEEE Conference on Decision and Control, CDC, pp. 5979–5984, December 2010
41. Sundaram, S., Revzen, S., Pappas, G.: A control-theoretic approach to disseminating values and overcoming malicious links in wireless networks. Automatica **48**(11), 2894–2901 (2012)
42. West, A.G., et al.: QuanTM: a quantitative trust management system. In: Proceedings of the Second European Workshop on System Security, pp. 28–35. ACM (2009)

Migrating Monitors + ABE: A Suitable Combination for Secure IoT?

Gordon J. Pace[1], Pablo Picazo-Sanchez[2], and Gerardo Schneider[2(✉)]

[1] University of Malta, Msida, Malta
`gordon.pace@um.edu.mt`
[2] University of Gothenburg, Gothenburg, Sweden
{`pablop,gersch`}`@chalmers.se`

Abstract. The rise of the Internet of Things brings about various challenges concerning safety, reliability and dependability as well as security and privacy. Reliability and safety issues could be addressed by using different verification techniques, both statically and at runtime. In particular, migrating monitors could effectively be used not only for verification purposes, but also as a way to gather information and to enforce certain policies. The addition of monitors, however, might introduce additional security and privacy threats. In this extended abstract we briefly sketch ideas on how to combine migrating monitors with a public cryptographic scheme named Attribute-Based Encryption as a way to ensure monitors are run by the right devices in a secure and private manner.

1 Introduction

The Internet of Things (IoT) is used to refer to the pervasive network of interconnected devices embedded in everyday things—sensors, actuators, devices, and applications for sharing information among them. Usual devices on the IoT include RFID (Radio Frequency IDentification) tags, smartphones, smartwatches, Implantable Medical Devices (IMD), and many other gadgets with communication capabilities.

IoT inherits most of the challenges of distributed systems due the non-locality of data collection and computation. In particular monitoring of such systems presents a wide range of challenges [4–6,20] since monitors might need information from other devices in order to duly perform their tasks.

The fact that monitoring cares about what goes on in different locations, it is clear that a monolithic local monitor is not enough. Different monitor instrumentation strategies have been proposed in the literature (e.g., [12]). The approaches can be largely split into two categories: (i) *centralised* or *orchestration approaches* in which the monitor is centrally located, receiving all relevant data and event-notification from the different nodes (e.g., [3]); and (ii) *choreography-based approaches*, in which the monitor is statically split into local parts instrumented in the different locations, and communicates only when as required (e.g., [7]). Both approaches, however, pose challenges when applied

© Springer Nature Switzerland AG 2018
T. Margaria and B. Steffen (Eds.): ISoLA 2018, LNCS 11247, pp. 19–24, 2018.
https://doi.org/10.1007/978-3-030-03427-6_3

to IoT environments. The former approach suffers from increased communication (with the central monitoring node), which grows as the number of nodes increases, resulting in slowing down of the overall system and an increase in power consumption. The major challenge with the latter approach is that for many logics, splitting the monitors in an effective manner can be difficult [4,20]. Furthermore, when nodes might be discovered at runtime, static decomposition of properties can be impossible to perform [12].

Migrating monitors is another approach proposed in the literature [11] based on dynamic choreography—instrumenting monitors locally, but giving them the ability to migrate to other locations when the need to access data or events from elsewhere becomes necessary. This last solution can be particularly suited for IoT environments where most of the correctness can be established locally. This approach avoids a blow-up in the amount of communication of generated data from IoT sensors.

Note that we have so far mentioned monitoring IoT without specifying in detail what the tasks of the monitors are. We should distinguish here three different applications of monitoring: (i) *Proper monitoring*, where the monitor collects data, possibly performing side-effect free computations (e.g., calculate an average during a specific amount of time) other than logging the information or sending it to another device, monitor or node in the network; (ii) *Runtime verification*, where the data is used for verification with respect to properties specifying what the expected behaviour of the system should be. Given the decentralised nature of IoT networks, such properties may be enacted by any of the devices or parties participating in the network, with the monitor usually being automatically generated from the property (e.g., [14]); (iii) *Runtime enforcement* takes this one step further by having the monitors carry code to be executed in the monitored system, send specific commands to control the system, in order to enforce a given property (as mentioned in *runtime verification*) by not allowing the system to act differently than the specified property (e.g., [10]).

The complexity, and degree of intrusion increase with these levels of monitoring. Since monitors can effectively leak information about the state of other entities on the system, we envisage a policy (or policies) which comes with the IoT scenario, and which specifies what types of properties can be enacted by which users e.g., a policy in a hospital context may state that no patient may enact a property that monitors events occurring on another patient's device.

Besides all the above issues, IoT monitoring is challenging due to the nature of the sensors: they are highly constrained in terms of computation, memory, battery and storage capabilities. As a consequence, monitors should be able to run under those constraints. Another challenge is that the IoT topology changes continuously over time because new sensors might be added and others are removed from the network. Migrating monitors might help here since they could automatically migrate to the new nodes when added, and they might eventually be killed when nodes disappear, without affecting the overall monitoring system.

There is, however, a problem when using migrating monitors in both orchestration and choreography-based approaches if deployed in an IoT scenario: security and privacy concerns. Migrating monitors are small software components that travel from one node to another one to either collect data and perform small computations (proper monitoring), verify some properties (runtime verification) or enforce some properties (runtime enforcement). IoT systems are networks composed of subnetworks each containing confidential local information, therefore the migrating monitors should not leak that information nor the architecture to the rest of the system.

Security and privacy concerns on IoT have been considered to be amongst the most challenging open issues nowadays (e.g., [2,15,18,21]), and *Attribute Based Encryption* (ABE) has been identified as one of the more promising cryptographic schemes to secure such systems [1,22]. ABE is a form of public key encryption where the information is encrypted under a boolean formulae (called *access policy*) which other parties must satisfy in order to decrypt the ciphertext. This cryptographic scheme is particularly useful on IoT since it simultaneously provides fine-grained access control and encryption [17]. Even though many theoretical proposals have been published in this area, only few works have deployed this cryptographic scheme on high-constrained IoT devices [13,16,22,23].

2   Combining Migrating Monitors and ABE for Secure IoT

The use of migrating monitors provides a way of augmenting IoT functionality, side-by-side with ABE which provides guarantees that there are no additional threats (in terms of security and privacy) due to the newly injected functionality.

Our proposed approach to achieve secure and private migrating monitors in IoT would work as explained below:

(i) We provide a monitoring policy specification language, which will specify which users[1] are allowed to enact what type of monitors on the network. This will be used to regulate monitors which will be enacted dynamically.

(ii) We provide a formal language to define migrating monitors integrated with ABE in such a way that it is possible to define which monitors will be executed and where. Monitors can be encrypted under certain access policies (made of attributes and represented as a boolean formulae) such that only those users in the system holding those attributes can satisfy the access policies and thus decrypt the monitors.

(iii) Monitors will be encrypted using a variant of ABE named Multi-Authority Attribute-Based Encryption (MA-ABE) [19]. With this scheme, networks and subnetworks are modelled in the MA-ABE scheme such that we can define the scope of the monitors and thus different subnetworks can share information privately and securely.

---

[1] Note that in this context, the term *user* may refer to sensors, software components or persons.

(iv) Monitors will statically be checked for the specific purpose they are created and thus identified as proper monitors, runtime verifiers or runtime enforcers. A secure runtime environment to manage monitor control-logic migrating from one IoT device to another is added to the IoT system, which also guarantees that monitors can only be executed following their main purpose. For instance, if a specification is tagged as a proper monitor (and not, for instance, as an enforcer), it will not be allowed to change the state of the devices and actuators, and will be limited to send control-flow messages to other monitor managers.

(v) By allowing users to arbitrarily create new monitors according to the monitoring policies in place, an authentication system must guarantee that only certified monitors can be run in the system.

3   Conclusions

We believe that there is great potential in using migrating monitors on IoT, combined with ABE to guarantee that monitors do not pose new security and privacy issues. In this paper, we have only presented some initial ideas and sketched a general way to achieve an IoT architecture were such monitors may run increasing functionality while not adding new security and privacy concerns. Although here we have not presented a formal argument to show that in this manner we do not introduce any new security and privacy threats, we believe that the cryptographic properties of ABE, and additional measures added at the architectural and monitoring management level, can ensure this to be the case. A more technical presentation of this work would require formal proofs to show that the combination is not vulnerable to attacks. In what concerns the practical side, we are considering the implementation of the above into the tool Larva [9], by extending DATEs [8] (the underlying automata-based specification language of Larva) with primitives from ABE. One aspect of combining migrating monitors and ABE that has not been addressed in our paper, and thus left as future work, is the use of our approach in order to provide additional security and privacy guarantees to the IoT.

Acknowledgements. This research has been partially supported by the Swedish Research Council (*Vetenskapsrådet*) under grant Nr. 2015-04154 (*PolUser: Rich User-Controlled Privacy Policies*).

References

1. AbuKhousa, E., Mohamed, N., Al-Jaroodi, J.: e-Health cloud: opportunities and challenges. Futur. Internet **4**(3), 621 (2012)
2. Atzori, L., Iera, A., Morabito, G., Nitti, M.: The social Internet of Things (SIoT) – when social networks meet the Internet of Things: concept, architecture and network characterization. Comput. Netw. **56**(16), 3594–3608 (2012)

3. Azzopardi, S., Colombo, C., Ebejer, J.P., Mallia, E., Pace, G.J.: Runtime verification using VALOUR. In: RV-CuBES, Kalpa Publications in Computing, vol. 3, pp. 10–18. EasyChair (2017)
4. Bauer, A., Falcone, Y.: Decentralised LTL monitoring. Form. Methods Syst. Des. **48**(1–2), 46–93 (2016)
5. Bauer, A., Leucker, M., Schallhart, C.: Model-based runtime analysis of distributed reactive systems. In: 17th Australian Software Engineering Conference, ASWEC 2006, 18–21 April 2006, Sydney, Australia, pp. 243–252 (2006)
6. Bonakdarpour, B., Fraigniaud, P., Rajsbaum, S., Travers, C.: Challenges in fault-tolerant distributed runtime verification. In: Proceedings of Part II Leveraging Applications of Formal Methods, Verification and Validation: Discussion, Dissemination, Applications - 7th International Symposium, ISoLA 2016, Imperial, Corfu, Greece, 10–14 October 2016, pp. 363–370 (2016)
7. Colombo, C., Falcone, Y.: Organising LTL monitors over distributed systems with a global clock. In: Bonakdarpour, B., Smolka, S.A. (eds.) RV 2014. LNCS, vol. 8734, pp. 140–155. Springer, Cham (2014). https://doi.org/10.1007/978-3-319-11164-3_12
8. Colombo, C., Pace, G.J., Schneider, G.: Dynamic event-based runtime monitoring of real-time and contextual properties. In: Cofer, D., Fantechi, A. (eds.) FMICS 2008. LNCS, vol. 5596, pp. 135–149. Springer, Heidelberg (2009). https://doi.org/10.1007/978-3-642-03240-0_13
9. Colombo, C., Pace, G.J., Schneider, G.: LARVA – safer monitoring of real-time Java programs (tool paper). In: 7th IEEE International Conference on Software Engineering and Formal Methods, SEFM 2009, pp. 33–37. IEEE Computer Society (2009)
10. Falcone, Y., Mariani, L., Rollet, A., Saha, S.: Runtime failure prevention and reaction. In: Bartocci, E., Falcone, Y. (eds.) Lectures on Runtime Verification. LNCS, vol. 10457, pp. 103–134. Springer, Cham (2018). https://doi.org/10.1007/978-3-319-75632-5_4
11. Francalanza, A., Gauci, A., Pace, G.J.: Distributed system contract monitoring. J. Log. Algebr. Program. **82**(5–7), 186–215 (2013)
12. Francalanza, A., Pérez, J.A., Sánchez, C.: Runtime verification for decentralised and distributed systems. In: Bartocci, E., Falcone, Y. (eds.) Lectures on Runtime Verification. LNCS, vol. 10457, pp. 176–210. Springer, Cham (2018). https://doi.org/10.1007/978-3-319-75632-5_6
13. Guo, L., Zhang, C., Sun, J., Fang, Y.: A privacy-preserving attribute-based authentication system for mobile health networks. IEEE Trans. Mobile Comput. **13**(9), 1927–1941 (2014)
14. Havelund, R., Roşu, G.: Runtime verification. In: Computer Aided Verification, CAV 2001 Satellite Workshop, Volume 55 of ENTCS (2001)
15. Medaglia, C.M., Serbanati, A.: An overview of privacy and security issues in the Internet of Things. In: Giusto, D., Iera, A., Morabito, G., Atzori, L. (eds.) The Internet of Things, pp. 389–395. Springer, New York (2010). https://doi.org/10.1007/978-1-4419-1674-7_38
16. Picazo-Sanchez, P., Tapiador, J.E., Peris-Lopez, P., Suarez-Tangil, G.: Secure publish-subscribe protocols for heterogeneous medical wireless body area networks. Sensors **14**(12), 22619 (2014)
17. Qiao, Z., Liang, S., Davis, S., Jiang, H.: Survey of attribute based encryption. In: 2014 15th IEEE/ACIS International Conference on Software Engineering, Artificial Intelligence, Networking and Parallel/Distributed Computing (SNPD), pp. 1–6, June 2014

18. Roman, R., Zhou, J., Lopez, J.: On the features and challenges of security and privacy in distributed Internet of Things. Comput. Netw. **57**(10), 2266–2279 (2013)
19. Rouselakis, Y., Waters, B.: Efficient statically-secure large-universe multi-authority attribute-based encryption. In: Böhme, R., Okamoto, T. (eds.) FC 2015. LNCS, vol. 8975, pp. 315–332. Springer, Heidelberg (2015). https://doi.org/10.1007/978-3-662-47854-7_19
20. Sen, K., Vardhan, A., Agha, G., Rosu, G.: Efficient decentralized monitoring of safety in distributed systems. In: 26th International Conference on Software Engineering, ICSE 2004, 23–28 May 2004, Edinburgh, United Kingdom, pp. 418–427 (2004)
21. Sicari, S., Rizzardi, A., Grieco, L., Coen-Porisini, A.: Security, privacy and trust in internet of things: the road ahead. Comput. Netw. **76**, 146–164 (2015)
22. Wang, X., Zhang, J., Schooler, E.M., Ion, M.: Performance evaluation of attribute-based encryption: toward data privacy in the IoT. In: 2014 IEEE International Conference on Communications (ICC), pp. 725–730, June 2014
23. Wu, D.J., Taly, A., Shankar, A., Boneh, D.: Privacy, discovery, and authentication for the Internet of Things. In: Askoxylakis, I., Ioannidis, S., Katsikas, S., Meadows, C. (eds.) ESORICS 2016. LNCS, vol. 9879, pp. 301–319. Springer, Cham (2016). https://doi.org/10.1007/978-3-319-45741-3_16

Capturing Inter-process Communication for Runtime Verification on Android

Alex Villazón[1], Haiyang Sun[2(✉)], and Walter Binder[2]

[1] Universidad Privada Boliviana (UPB), Colcapirhua, Bolivia
avillazon@upb.edu
[2] Università della Svizzera italiana (USI), Lugano, Switzerland
{haiyang.sun,walter.binder}@usi.ch

Abstract. Runtime verification (RV) covering the whole Android system is challenging, due to the lack of support for analyzing and monitoring events across multiple processes. Existing RV frameworks for Android, which are often built on top of RV tools for Java, only support single-process monitoring. In this paper, we describe an RV framework for Android, capable of performing RV across multiple Android components in different processes by capturing inter-process-communication events. Our approach features an extended regular expression formalism, allowing one to specify RV properties to describe event patterns across processes. We illustrate the use of our framework by detecting nested indirect service use through proxy processes, which is not possible with prevailing RV tools on Android.

1 Introduction

A core characteristic of the Android platform is its multi-process architecture. RV on Android often leverages or adapts existing RV frameworks that were designed to work only with single-process Java applications [3,6,7,10,13]. For example, detecting collusion attacks where some malwares work together to avoid security checks [2] is not possible with prevailing RV frameworks for Android [4,5], as events of interest cross their observable boundaries. A key limitation is therefore the lack of event ordering across Android processes.

In this paper we present our framework for RV across multiple processes for Android. We extend Android's inter-process communication (IPC) mechanism implemented in the "binder" library and provide a shared-memory service for event communication. The framework builds on our previous work on multi-process support for Android [11] and on ADRENALIN-RV [12], an RV framework ensuring that all events of interest originating from any executed bytecode are guaranteed to be monitored. To specify properties across multiple processes, we enhance DiSL [9], the domain-specific language (DSL) used in ADRENALIN-RV, with an extended regular-expression formalism. The user can therefore define

---

A. Villazón—Visiting researcher at Università della Svizzera italiana (USI)

T. Margaria and B. Steffen (Eds.): ISoLA 2018, LNCS 11247, pp. 25–31, 2018.
https://doi.org/10.1007/978-3-030-03427-6_4

properties over multiple processes of interest using this extended DSL, and our framework will generate and deploy the specified RV tool automatically.

We illustrate the use of our framework with a case study showing how apps use the services provided by Android via IPC, by expressing inter-process interactions revealing nested indirect communications through proxy processes, which prevailing RV tools for Android cannot detect.

2   Multi-process Support for RV

To support multi-process RV on Android, we describe how our approach ensures event order across processes, and how user-defined properties are enforced between processes.

Event Order Across Processes: We use two communication mechanisms through an extension of the binder library and a special shared memory key-value (K-V) store (see Fig. 1). The extended binder library allows each binder call to carry extra data (for control exchange) and events information is passed through our own Android service providing the K-V store (for data exchange). Thus, every binder call carries only a key with which the receiver of the binder call can retrieve the events from the K-V store. The key of a binder call expires when the binder call finishes, and the memory space for the values (events) will be reclaimed. Since the lifetime of a binder call is short, the space in the K-V store can be reused efficiently. To bridge the gap between Java and native code, we provide a callback from the binder library, such that we can track binder calls as Java-level *BinderEvent* instances.

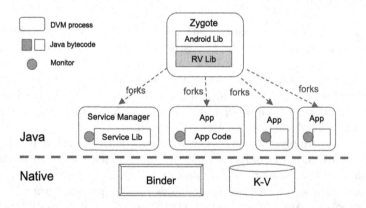

Fig. 1. Overview of our framework for RV on Android

Property Enforcement Across Processes: User-defined RV properties are specified using Multi-process Regular Expressions (MRE), our extended regular expression formalism to describe event patterns across processes (see Sect. 3).

For each user-defined property, we generate a Deterministic Finite Automata (DFA) used to match the given MRE with the event sequence including local events and events from other processes retrieved from the shared K-V store. The DFA can switch states among *matching*, *matched*, and *fail*, and a violation handler will be triggered at a predefined state.

In Android, to avoid heavy class initialization, all apps and service processes are forked from the Zygote process which includes already initialized Android libraries. We take advantage of this mechanism to instrument and load Android libraries in the Zygote process including our RV runtime library, making them available everywhere (see Fig. 1). We generate a unique monitor for each property, including the DFA terminating state defined by the user, i.e., "matched" or "fail". The app and services (libraries) are instrumented at load time according to the event generation rules defined in the instrumentation specification. At runtime, in every process under scrutiny, the corresponding monitor verifies the property. To this end, two kinds of events will be generated: (a) bytecode events from the instrumented bytecode, and (b) binder events from the modified binder library. The monitor can add events to or query the K-V store to pass or get related events for the process at the other end of the binder call. If the DFA of a monitor reaches the defined state to report, the violation handler will be called with access to the event sequence causing the violation. The violation handler may simply print a message, terminate a misbehaving app, or further explore the violation using the extra data bound to the events.

3 Multi-process Regular Expressions

Regular expression (RE) formalisms are often used in RV tools to describe a sequence of events in properties that are used to generate monitor code for validation. We introduce Multi-process Regular Expression (MRE) as an extension to a traditional RE formalism to describe event patterns across multiple processes.

$$MRE \rightarrow (RE|\_MRE\_)* \qquad (1)$$

$$\_MRE\_ \rightarrow \#process(MRE) \qquad (2)$$

In this definition, RE stands for the event pattern described using normal regular expressions. $\_MRE\_$ is used to describe one inter-process communication (IPC) interaction between the caller process starting the binder call and the receiver process, and MRE is a sequence of RE or $\_MRE\_$. $\#ProcA(...)$ allows the caller process to verify events that happened in process named ProcA during the binder call. We use process names to identify events from different apps because an Android app always uses its package name as process name, which is guaranteed to be unique at installation time.

MRE can describe event patterns across processes, including nested cases where the receiver of one binder call may start another binder call. For example, during a binder call from ProcA to ProcB, while ProcB is processing the request it may start a new binder call to ProcC before returning to ProcA. This can be specified as $\#ProcB(...\#ProcC(...)...)$. An one-level indirection matching any process can be specified with $\#(...)$, whereas $\#*(...)$ indicates an arbitrary number of levels of nested indirections matching any process.

4 Monitor Code Generation

Our RV library parses the MRE, create the DFA, and generate the monitor code. We extend DiSL [9] used in ADRENALIN-RV [12] to support our MRE formalism. DiSL allows one to define an instrumentation in Java using annotations. We use standard DiSL features for the event generation, while a new annotation "@Property" was added to support MRE expressions. The method annotated with the property acts as the violation handler. We build our work on ADRENALIN-RV using dynamic weaving to benefit from comprehensive bytecode instrumentation. This allows one to load the monitor code generated from properties into the right library or app code whenever necessary and no repackaging is needed.

5 Monitoring Indirect Service Use

In Android, apps can call system services which run in a separate *system server* process, and serve apps for different purposes, such as e.g. the Activity Manager Service (AMS) to handle activities states or the Content Provider Service to share data between apps. A service in Android is used directly if the app starts an IPC call directly to the corresponding service thread in the system server process. On the other hand, using a service indirectly means that an app accesses the service via some "proxy" processes. More specifically, the app starts an IPC to a proxy process during which the proxy starts the IPC call to the service in the system server.

Whereas detecting direct calls to services can be done by analyzing a single binder call (or to some extend, by inspecting service APIs invoked by an app), nested indirect calls cannot be monitored through single binder call analysis. Identifying such call patterns through proxies is important to detect misuse of services or other security problem caused by some malware. Existing RV tools monitoring events in only one process are not able to track such behaviors involving multiple processes due to the lack of event ordering across processes.

5.1 Property Specification

The property definition supporting MRE to monitor indirect use of services is shown in Fig. 2. The first part defines the instrumentation we need to get the events, whereas the second part adds the monitoring logic for the events and the processing logic when a violation is detected.

To analyze which service is being indirectly used, we instrument the corresponding classes in the Android library as shown in method serviceUse

```
class ServiceDiSLClass {
  final static String propertyId = "service";
  @Before(marker = BodyMarker.class, scope = "com.android.server.*Service.*")
  static void serviceUse(StaticContext dsc) {
    PropertyManager.findProcessor(propertyId)
      . newTLEvent( "use",
        dsc. className(), //service name
        dsc. methodName() //API being used
      );
  }
  @Property(id = propertyId, mre = "#*((#system_server(use+))+)", reportAt =
      "matched")
  static void violation (DynamicContext mdc) {
    ServiceAnalysis. onViolation(mdc.getEvents());
  }
}
```

Fig. 2. Definition of the service-use property

annotated with @Before. The scope com.android.server.*Service.* specifies to instrument all methods of classes whose name matches *Service in the
com.android.server package. We are able to instrument these classes inside
the Android library while other tools based on static weaving will not support
it. Any execution of the instrumented method will emit a service-use event to
the property monitor. The StaticContext is a DiSL API to provide static information about the instrumented code region. Here, we use it for the service being
used (the class name) and the API of this service (the method name).

The method violation annotated with @Property will automatically generate a monitor for this property. Events for different properties are distinguished
with the propertyId, allowing multiple properties to be monitored simultaneously. The MRE "#*((#system_server(use+))+)" reports a violation if we find
any service use(s) indirectly from any app (to the system server). Symbol "*" can
match any name and any processes and as a result, we can find nested indirect
use with an arbitrary number of intermediate processes. When an indirect violation is found, the related events are retrieved via DynamicContext.getEvents()
and processed to generate detailed reports.

5.2 Results

First, we investigate one-level indirection, using the "#_((#system_server
(use+))+)" MRE. Figure 3 shows the indirect service uses found. A dashed
line represents the IPC call from an app to the one-level proxy process (with
the number of indirect service uses), while the solid line stands for the nested
direct use of the service. The highlighted region represents the related services
in the system server process. The analysis reveals that several apps use services
with an one-level indirection. Several apps always interact with a specific proxy,

e.g., Google apps often use the process *gapps* as proxy. We can observe that *gapps* itself uses the *phone* process as a proxy (64 calls). However, the #_ one-level indirection MRE cannot tell us if any of the processes that uses *gapps* as a proxy actually triggers a second-level nested indirection to *phone*. To explore this, we use the `"#*((#system_server(use+))+)"` specification for multi-level verification. The results obtained confirm that only one-level indirection happen globally, and that no caller of the *gapps* process triggers calls to *phone*, but *gapps* itself initiates those calls. This demonstrates the power of our multi-process RV approach on Android to verify multi-level nested indirections.

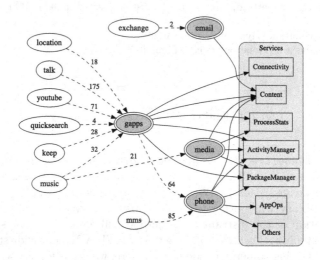

Fig. 3. Nested indirect service use in Android

6   Related Work

Static weaving is used in most of the existing instrumentation frameworks [1,4,5] for Android. However, it cannot cover library code and code loaded at runtime. In contrast, our framework leverages dynamic weaving of ADRENALIN-RV [12], enabling all instrumentation at load-time and allowing full bytecode coverage including app, library, and dynamically loaded code. This ensures that all events originating from any executed bytecode are guaranteed to be monitored.

RV tools for Android [4,5] only target single process cases and fail to analyze behaviors between multiple Android components in different processes. In [8], DroidTracer is used to monitor events to detect malware by analyzing Android's binder IPC message exchanges. Their approach does not extend the binder library, and the analysis captures raw messages and unmarshalls them using reverse engineering to identify events of interest. In contrast to our approach, RV with DroidTracer is limited to direct communications only. Based on previous work [11], we support multi-process RV with an extended regular-expression formalism and nested IPC monitoring for Android.

7 Conclusion

This paper describes our framework for multi-process RV on Android and the analysis of nested indirect IPC calls. Our approach addresses the challenge of event ordering across multiple Android processes and allows users to specify properties for multi-process monitoring with an extended multi-process regular expression formalism. We show with a case study that our tool can monitor arbitrary levels of nested indirect interactions between Android apps and services.

Acknowledgments. The work presented in this paper has been supported by Swiss National Science Foundation (scientific exchange project IZSEZ0_177215) and by Hasler Foundation (project 18012). The research was conducted while A. Villazón was with Università della Svizzera italiana.

References

1. Backes, M., Gerling, S., Hammer, C., Maffei, M., von Styp-Rekowsky, P.: App-Guard – enforcing user requirements on Android apps. In: Piterman, N., Smolka, S.A. (eds.) TACAS 2013. LNCS, vol. 7795, pp. 543–548. Springer, Heidelberg (2013). https://doi.org/10.1007/978-3-642-36742-7_39
2. Bosu, A., Liu, F., Yao, D.D., Wang, G.: Collusive data leak and more: large-scale threat analysis of inter-app communications. In: ASIA CCS, pp. 71–85 (2017)
3. Colombo, C., Pace, G.J., Schneider, G.: LARVA–safer monitoring of real-time Java programs (tool paper). In: SEFM, pp. 33–37 (2009)
4. Daian, P., et al.: RV-Android: efficient parametric android runtime verification, a brief tutorial. In: Bartocci, E., Majumdar, R. (eds.) RV 2015. LNCS, vol. 9333, pp. 342–357. Springer, Cham (2015). https://doi.org/10.1007/978-3-319-23820-3_24
5. Falcone, Y., Currea, S., Jaber, M.: Runtime verification and enforcement for android applications with RV-Droid. In: Qadeer, S., Tasiran, S. (eds.) RV 2012. LNCS, vol. 7687, pp. 88–95. Springer, Heidelberg (2013). https://doi.org/10.1007/978-3-642-35632-2_11
6. Jin, D., Meredith, P.O.N., Lee, C., Roşu, G.: JavaMOP: efficient parametric run-time monitoring framework. In: ICSE, pp. 1427–1430 (2012)
7. Kim, M., Kannan, S., Lee, I., Sokolsky, O., Viswanathan, M.: Java-MaC. ENTCS **55**(2), 218–235 (2001)
8. Küster, J.-C., Bauer, A.: Monitoring real android malware. In: Bartocci, E., Majumdar, R. (eds.) RV 2015. LNCS, vol. 9333, pp. 136–152. Springer, Cham (2015). https://doi.org/10.1007/978-3-319-23820-3_9
9. Marek, L., Villazón, A., Zheng, Y., Ansaloni, D., Binder, W., Qi, Z.: DiSL: a domain-specific language for bytecode instrumentation. In: AOSD, pp. 239–250 (2012)
10. Reger, G., Cruz, H.C., Rydeheard, D.: MarQ: monitoring at runtime with QEA. In: Baier, C., Tinelli, C. (eds.) TACAS 2015. LNCS, vol. 9035, pp. 596–610. Springer, Heidelberg (2015). https://doi.org/10.1007/978-3-662-46681-0_55
11. Sun, H., North, A., Binder, W.: Multi-process runtime verification for android. In: APSEC, pp. 701–706 (2017)
12. Sun, H., Rosà, A., Javed, O., Binder, W.: ADRENALIN-RV: android runtime verification using load-time weaving. In: ICST, pp. 532–539 (2017)
13. Xiang, C., Qi, Z., Binder, W.: Flexible and extensible runtime verification for Java (Extended Version). Int. J. Softw. Eng. Knowl. Eng. **25**, 1595–1609 (2015)

Considering Academia-Industry Projects Meta-characteristics in Runtime Verification Design

Christian Colombo[✉] and Gordon J. Pace

Department of Computer Science, University of Malta, Msida, Malta
christian.colombo@um.edu.mt

Abstract. Runtime verification, with its practical applicability and myriad of theoretical challenges it still poses, has the potential to bridge the gap between academic research in the field of formal methods with the software industry. In order to facilitate this, it is useful to extrapolate success patterns from previous projects: Are certain characteristics of an industry-academia project a determining factor in the project's success? How can runtime verification design decisions take into considerations project characteristics to improve the chances of success?

This paper attempts to shed some light on these questions by reflecting on five projects with two partners over the past ten years. A number of lessons emerge, perhaps the most poignant one being the need to think long term in setting mutually beneficial goals from which a strong working relationship can emerge.

1 Introduction

Although various underlying notions from runtime monitoring and verification, albeit in limited form, have long found themselves in standard quality assurance practice in industry, its adoption as a first class element and building block of the system being built is still rare. Much of the use of runtime verification techniques in industry, thus still stems from projects in conjunction with academic partners interested in exploring scalability and industrial-relevance of these techniques. In the literature reporting these projects, the focus is invariably the effectiveness of the techniques used on the system under scrutiny. What is usually not reported (being beyond the scientific scope of such publications), is the process of adoption, the context of the project, the logistic challenges encountered and its longer term impact in terms of adoption of techniques beyond the scope of the original project e.g. *Was it an industry- or academia-led project? Was runtime verification being engineered retrospectively on a legacy system or one being developed from scratch?* It is worth noting that some, although not all, of the observations we make are relevant to any project with partners from both industry and academia, and not limited to runtime verification.

© Springer Nature Switzerland AG 2018
T. Margaria and B. Steffen (Eds.): ISoLA 2018, LNCS 11247, pp. 32–41, 2018.
https://doi.org/10.1007/978-3-030-03427-6_5

In this paper, we present anecdote-based observations based on our experience from five academia-industry projects[1], discussing and reviewing major design decisions in runtime verification engineering. An implicit assumption throughout the paper will be that the goal of the academia-industry collaboration is the benefit to both parties. Hence, in the next section we attempt to describe success from the two points of view. In Sect. 3 we describe project meta-characteristics which might affect the engineering decisions discussed in Sect. 4. We bring everything together in Sect. 5 by reviewing our decisions in five projects and report on their success. The last section concludes with some final remarks.

2 Defining Success

Success in the context of industry-academia projects may take various forms, and defies a simple uni-dimensional metric. Instead, it makes more sense to talk of ways in which a project may have a positive impact on the industrial partner, the academic one, or the collaboration between the two.

2.1 Impact on Industrial Partners

We start by identifying different ways in which a collaborative runtime verification project may leave an impact on the industrial partners.

Direct changes within their systems: The direct way in which a project may leave impact is in resulting to changes in their actual software systems (post-project) either through (i) stronger runtime checks within the normal logic of the system to ensure higher confidence in system correctness; or (ii) changes in the system architecture, introducing separate logical units to perform runtime checks or even through the adoption of the use of a runtime verification tool thus completely separating concerns of the normal system and verification logic.

Changes to the quality assurance process: Another way in which projects may leave an impact on the system is through the quality assurance process, particularly during testing, either (i) by enabling the quality assurance team to identify further correctness elements or runtime scenarios, thus resulting in more or better test oracles and test cases; or (ii) through the adoption

---

[1] While it would have been preferable to include a wider set of projects in our analysis (including those from other research groups), we found that reporting of the "post-mortem" of such projects is sparse in the literature. Many of the observations we make in this paper are on the non-scientific aspects of the research projects (e.g. whether participation of the industrial partner in the project had an impact on the way they approached validation and verification of other systems they were developing), which are typically not discussed in scientific reports of the outcome of such projects. Therefore, while we are aware of several projects which have applied academic techniques in an industrial setting, we cannot include these in this paper due to the lack of information of what happened *after* the end of the project.

of techniques from runtime verification to support the specification of a test suite—from the oracles to test scripts and test cases e.g. moving from timeless assertion-based oracles which assert constraints on the system state at a particular point in the execution of the system, to temporal oracles each of which may refer to and compare the state of the system at various temporal points.

Indirect effects: Although the project may not result in direct changes to the current or planned future versions of the system, or to the quality assurance process, exposure to runtime verification may have indirect and longer-term effects, sometimes due to the Hawthorne effect[2] resulting from oversight by the academic partner due to the collaboration and accentuated by the domain ignorance of the oversight [12]. Two ways we have seen this happen was through exposing architects and developers (i) to alternative ways in which verification can be integrated into a system, yet keeping it in a separate component; and (ii) to the realisation of the possibility to look at different levels of failure handling at runtime going beyond class invariants and pre- and post-conditions.

Although we define the notion of success in a rather broad manner, we have witnessed projects which have partially failed to realise an impact in any of the three effects listed above, typically due to one of (i) the fact that day-to-day fire-fighting with system problems did not leave enough time and resources to consider further changes which runtime verification may require; (ii) lack of interest in immersion into deploying runtime verification due to the designers or developers involved felt that the change was imposed on them (e.g. through company policy to participate in the project) or due to being involved with a team which felt that dynamic analysis was not within their remit (e.g. developers may feel that it is an aspect which quality assurance should handle, or the quality assurance may feel that the onus should be on the developers since the checks are performed at runtime); or (iii) despite an interest to consider the use of runtime monitoring or verification, fear (rightly or wrongly) of its impact on the complexity of the system and its performance impeded its adoption.

2.2   Impact on Academic Partners

Given the different objectives of the academic partners, the impact sought is similarly different. We identify three aspects in which joint runtime verification projects with industrial partners can prove to be fruitful:

Evaluation of new techniques on real-world systems: Typically, a primary measure of success from an academic perspective in many collaborative projects is that of evaluating new techniques on a real-world system. The degree to which the proposed techniques are successfully integrated into

---

[2] Sometimes referred to as the *observer effect*, the Hawthorne effect is the phenomenon that when aware of being observed, individuals may modify aspects of their behaviour.

the system to be evaluated is a major measure of project impact from the academic side.

Application of tools to real-world systems: Many academically developed tools tend to be proof-of-concept artefacts, and mostly developed in an evolutionary manner across generations of students, mostly with little regard to software engineering practice. The experience of applying such tools on real-world systems can be a major challenge but can result in important insight on the strengths but also on design and algorithmic bottlenecks of the tools.

Understanding better the challenges to real-world adoption: The very experience of attempting to transpose runtime verification techniques to be applicable in a real-world setting is in itself a learning experience, exposing the academic partners to real-world challenges, which can lead to the development of new techniques and solutions, and establish longer-term collaboration with the industrial partners.

3   Success-Determining Factors

When considering our past projects (see Sect. 5), two common success-determining characteristics clearly emerge.

Project lead: One of the determining factors is the degree to which all the partners have at stake in the project. Particularly from the industrial side, where ongoing commercial deadlines and pressures may result in the project being put on the back burner; how central the project is to those partners immediate (or near-future) commercial objectives makes a substantial difference to the chances of success. In general, projects which are instigated, designed and/or led by these partners result in two important advantages towards achieving success:

  (i) **Priority:** In industrial settings, priorities may change easily and quickly (e.g., change in leadership, change in market, etc). When a project is low on the industrial partner's priority list, chances are that resources get allocated elsewhere. Projects which were initiated by the industry partner(s) tended to be given more priority and it was easier to obtain information and get access to resources in a timely manner.

  (ii) **Engagement:** When an industrial partner gets involved in a project without a clear direct benefit (but perhaps to start a long term research collaboration, to test what academic tools may offer, or to get in touch with students as potential employees), there is a great possibility that the academic researchers will not find much enthusiasm and engagement from the stakeholders within the company—particularly employees who do not see the value of the project.

Legacy vs. new system: A major distinction in industrial runtime verification projects is whether the effort concerns an existing legacy system or whether the system is being designed from the ground up with runtime verification in mind. This issue is particularly pronounced in runtime verification due to the desirability of extracting events non-intrusively *at runtime*. Legacy systems are typically hard to modify and interoperate with for several reasons, particularly their brittleness and sometimes poorly supported dated technologies. Furthermore, obtaining the necessary information and understanding how a legacy system works might also be significantly challenging due to unmaintained or incomplete documentation and code which has been changed and fixed over and over again.

On the other hand, a system which is being newly built and which incorporates runtime verification from the start, may provide a dedicated interface for the monitor which makes all relevant events readily available and also listens out for any incoming instructions from the monitor.

4   Design Decisions

When applying runtime verification to real-world systems, a number of design decisions have to be taken. In this section we focus on some of the most pertinent ones, particularly those which (from our experience—see the next section) may severely affect project success. It is worth noting that some of the design choices are interconnected and may influence each other.

4.1   System Feedback: Level of Runtime Intrusion

One important decision is that of how intrusive on the system the runtime analysis will be. From a most basic level in which one can merely *monitor* or *observe* a system and log information about its runtime behaviour, then moving up to *runtime verification*, in which not only is the behaviour observed, but particular behavioural patterns are identified to be undesirable and algorithmically classified to be so. This latter level of intrusion can be taken further by adding on logic to support *runtime recovery* or *reparation*, triggering in the case of undesirable behaviour being observed (to make up for it)[3]. One can also go another step further, using *runtime enforcement* [9] to ensure that the undesirable behaviour is avoided in the first place, modifying the system's behaviour to ensure it works as expected.

The higher the level of intrusion, the more difficult it is to have the runtime system to be integrated with the production-ready system. In the context of the success-determining criteria discussed in Sect. 3, intrusion beyond non-reparatory runtime verification is unlikely to be achieved on legacy systems, but this can be pushed up considerably in industry-led projects on systems still being designed and developed.

4.2   Online vs. Offline

Another fundamental design decision is whether runtime monitoring is carried out online or offline. Online monitoring interacts directly with the system at runtime while offline monitoring involves processing runtime events independently

---

[3] This is supported by typical RV tools such as JavaMOP [4] and Larva [8].

of the running system. This is a major difference from an intrusiveness point of view as in the case of online monitoring the verification software very likely interferes with the running system and typically competes for the same resources.

Considering the success-determining factors identified in the previous section, similar to higher intrusiveness, online monitoring decreases the likelihood of the project being taken onboard by the industrial partner on the live systems. Therefore, caution should be used and in the case of an academia-led legacy project, it should ideally be avoided altogether. On the other hand, when working in the context of an industry-led project where a system is being designed and developed with online runtime verification in mind, the associated risks can be minimised and catered for.

4.3   System-Monitor Communication

Once the runtime verification mode of online vs. offline is decided, one would typically decide on the communication mode; particularly how the system events are to reach the verifier. The choice is highly dependent on whether monitoring takes place online or offline. As one would expect, offline monitoring allows for communication to be significantly more loosely coupled. For example this may take the form of simply dumping a relevant part of the monitored system's database. The advantage of loose coupling is that it does not interfere with the monitored system. In the case of online monitoring, the choice between tightly and loosely coupled communication modes would typically be more constrained by the desire to have the monitor receive system events in a timely fashion. Options in this case may range from direct method calls from the system, to message transmission over a network. While all these options are possible when considerations are included in the design, more care should be taken when dealing with legacy systems due to repercussions the modifications may bring about.

4.4   Event Extraction

Legacy systems are less amenable to incorporating a clean and modular way of extracting relevant system events. It is for this reason that runtime verification is perhaps one of the best case studies for aspect-oriented programming (AOP)[10]. However, even with the sophistication of AOP, understanding which method invocations to capture and whether these provide enough context to bind the necessary data variables is a non-trivial task. Moreover, when runtime verification is also used to steer the system (as opposed to simply being a passive observer), particular care needs to be taken to ensure that bugs are not accidentally introduced. Maintenance and system updates might also result in unintended consequences in the system-monitor interaction. Another approach to extract events in a legacy system context is through the use of a proxy. This is convenient when the events of interest are visible from a communication point of view.

In contrast, when dealing with a new system, the monitoring of events can be designed as part of the system, i.e. the system proactively makes relevant events available to the monitor. When a new system is designed for an offline setting, one may still opt for a less direct way of extracting events, such as by interfacing with the database. Extracting events from the database would also probably be the most rational choice when dealing with a legacy system, albeit some database modifications might be needed.

4.5 Specification of Properties

When dynamic analysis is used to verify behaviour, the manner in which the discriminator between correct or expected behaviour from bad behaviour is written, plays an important role in determining the success of adoption of the techniques in the real-life system. Although in some projects (particularly academia-led ones) the specification language used may be determined by the objectives of the project itself (e.g. a project focussing on how overheads induced due to monitoring specifications using a particular logic or class of logics can be reduced), in many cases this choice may be flexible, ranging from one extreme of developer-friendly specifications written as observers in the same programming language as the main system, to the other extreme involving the use of complex logics which developers may require training to use in an effective manner. In between, one can find intermediate specification languages which bridge this gap e.g. the use of graph-based formalisms (e.g. automata) or regular expressions with which most developers would be familiar.

As in the other design challenges, the higher the industrial involvement, the more one can choose to identify and adopt an appropriate logic (possibly hidden beneath syntactic sugar or within a controlled natural language), while with lower industrial involvement, developer-friendly formalisms would be preferable.

5   Observations and Commentary

In order to review our past projects in the light of the above design choices, we start by describing the projects. We had five projects with two partners, with the information summarised in Fig. 1 ordered in completion date order. The first project was with one partner while the following four projects were with the second partner[4].

1. *System Feedback: Level of Runtime Intrusion.* In the majority of the projects, we opted for the least intrusive of the approaches—that of a passive observer. In the case of the first project where we had online monitoring, we could also alert the system of a violation. Further along the intrusiveness spectrum, the last project includes runtime enforcement where transactions may be stopped if they would lead to a violation. In this last project, the monitor also plays the role of an observer when collating statistics which do not involve corrective actions.

---

[4] Names of the industrial partners are left out due to information sensitivity and in order to allow us to be able to discuss project success or otherwise more freely.

2. *Online vs. Offline.* The online vs. offline choice is closely related to the intrusiveness choice before. All observer monitors were naturally offline while the rest of the options necessitated an online architecture.
3. *System-Monitor Communication.* The offline monitoring projects made use of a database dump and text files to store the observed data. The online counterparts intercepted method calls in the first case, while in the second case, used asynchronous messages to establish handshakes between the system and the monitor.
4. *Event Extraction.* The second and third projects used a database script to obtain a copy of the relevant part of the database. In the first and fourth projects, we used aspect-oriented programming since these were legacy systems, while in the last project we could construct custom events which were designed as part of the system.
5. *Specification of Properties.* In most projects we used an automata-based formalism—namely DATEs [7]. In the case of the fourth project we used assertions since these were extracted automatically from test traces. Finally, in the last project we provided a controlled natural language [11] which internally compiled to a ruled-based language.

Proj	Part	Characteristics		Decisions				
		Lead	System	Intr	On/Off	Comm	Events	Spec
1	A	Aca	Leg	RV	On	Method call	AOP	Aut
2		Aca	Leg	Obs	Off	Db dump	Db script	Aut
3	B	Ind	Leg	Obs	Off	Db dump	Db script	Aut
4		Aca	Leg	Obs	Off	Text files	AOP	Ass
5		Ind	New	Enf/Obs	On/Off	Async messaging	Custom events	CNL

Fig. 1. Summary of the collaborative runtime verification projects discussed.

Given the above design choices, we can now comment on the successes of each partnership:

Partner A (Project 1). From an academic perspective, this project provided us with the experience and case study needed to create a practical runtime verification tool. From an industry perspective, it was useful to demonstrate to the partner how checks can be embedded in a system and how they can be expressed. However, to date we are not aware of any use of explicit runtime verification technologies adopted within their system.

Partner B (Projects 2–5). The first project with this partner served mainly to prepare the way for other future ones—the next project was an initiative of a number of employees and was successfully deployed on their live data. These experiences led the way to two other projects: Projects 4 and 5. Project 4 was successful from an academic perspective in exploring new ideas however, so far it did not result in direct effects in the industrial technology used. The last project enabled us the freedom of applying the latest academically developed ideas to an industrial system with relative success from both perspectives.

Key Observations

Better chances of success when legacy systems are monitored offline:
We note that with the exception of the last project, all projects took place on legacy systems. In all cases with the exception of the first project, we applied offline monitoring when working with legacy systems. The first project which went against this pattern was not successful from an industrial perspective.

Industry-led projects more likely to succeed (industrially): Another observation is that the two industry-led projects were both very successful from an industrial perspective. From an academic perspective, it is less predictable though as the emphasis is on finding a solution to the problem at hand.

Industry-led projects on non-legacy systems give rise to win-win situations: Although the latest project has the advantage of hindsight gained from previous projects, and a well established relationship with the partner, it was also the only one which was both industry-led and dealt with a non-legacy system. We hypothesise that these latter characteristics significantly improved the chances of achieving high levels of success from the point of view of both parties.

6   Conclusions

In this paper, we have considered how poignant characteristics of a project affect the engineering choices in the context of runtime verification. Engineering design decisions are particularly delicate in the context of runtime verification since, unlike other techniques such as testing or static analysis, the generated runtime verification code typically interacts directly with the running system. Runtime verification design aspects such as whether to monitor a system online or offline have been the subject of numerous publications [2,3,5]. However, to the best of our knowledge, it is the first time that runtime verification engineering design choices were put against the backdrop of project meta-characteristics. Indisputably, there are various other variables contributing to the success (or lack thereof) of a project. In particular, the human aspects come to mind with questions such as how to build a working relationship amongst partners, how to involve the right stakeholders in the project, and how to handover the outcome of a project to the industrial partner have been tackled in [6] and more generally in [1].

Ultimately, the chance of success of an academia-industry project depends on the quality of the relationship (and the trust) between the parties. Once the parties learn to better understand each other, the chances of success increase dramatically. For this reason, a project in the early years of a collaboration might simply serve the purpose of establishing a good working relationship between the partners. Once the relationship improves, it becomes more probable that undertaken projects are of higher importance to the industrial partner. Hence, the more likely it is that a project is industry-led and concerns a non-legacy system which consequently (as we have explained throughout the paper) increase the design options dramatically.

References

1. Aksit, M., Tekinerdogan, B., Sozer, H., Safi, H.F., Ayas, M.: The DESARC method: an effective approach for university-industry cooperation, pp. 51–53. Institute of Research Engineers and Doctors, January 2015. https://doi.org/10.15224/978-1-63248-038-5-10
2. Baresi, L., Ghezzi, C.: The disappearing boundary between development-time and run-time. In: Proceedings of the Workshop on Future of Software Engineering Research, FoSER 2010, at the 18th ACM SIGSOFT International Symposium on Foundations of Software Engineering, Santa Fe, NM, USA, 7–11 November 2010, pp. 17–22 (2010)
3. Cassar, I., Francalanza, A., Aceto, L., Ingólfsdóttir, A.: A survey of runtime monitoring instrumentation techniques. In: Proceedings Second International Workshop on Pre- and Post-Deployment Verification Techniques, PrePost@iFM, pp. 15–28 (2017)
4. Chen, F., Roşu, G.: Java-MOP: a monitoring oriented programming environment for Java. In: Halbwachs, N., Zuck, L.D. (eds.) TACAS 2005. LNCS, vol. 3440, pp. 546–550. Springer, Heidelberg (2005). https://doi.org/10.1007/978-3-540-31980-1_36
5. Colombo, C., Pace, G., Abela, P.: Safer asynchronous runtime monitoring using compensations. Formal Methods Syst. Des. **41**(3), 269–294 (2012)
6. Colombo, C., Pace, G.J.: Industrial experiences with runtime verification of financial transaction systems: lessons learnt and standing challenges. In: Bartocci, E., Falcone, Y. (eds.) Lectures on Runtime Verification. LNCS, vol. 10457, pp. 211–232. Springer, Cham (2018). https://doi.org/10.1007/978-3-319-75632-5_7
7. Colombo, C., Pace, G.J., Schneider, G.: Dynamic event-based runtime monitoring of real-time and contextual properties. In: Cofer, D., Fantechi, A. (eds.) FMICS 2008. LNCS, vol. 5596, pp. 135–149. Springer, Heidelberg (2009). https://doi.org/10.1007/978-3-642-03240-0_13
8. Colombo, C., Pace, G.J., Schneider, G.: LARVA – safer monitoring of real-time java programs (tool paper). In: Seventh IEEE International Conference on Software Engineering and Formal Methods, SEFM 2009, Hanoi, Vietnam, 23–27 November 2009, pp. 33–37 (2009)
9. Falcone, Y., Mounier, L., Fernandez, J.-C., Richier, J.-L.: Runtime enforcement monitors: composition, synthesis, and enforcement abilities. Formal Methods Syst. Des. **38**(3), 223–262 (2011)
10. Kiczales, G.: Aspect-oriented programming. In: 27th International Conference on Software Engineering (ICSE 2005), 15–21 May 2005, St. Louis, Missouri, USA, p. 730 (2005)
11. Kuhn, T.: A survey and classification of controlled natural languages. CoRR, abs/1507.01701 (2015)
12. Niknafs, A., Berry, D.M.: An industrial case study of the impact of domain ignorance on the effectiveness of requirements idea generation during requirements elicitation. In: 21st IEEE International Requirements Engineering Conference, RE 2013, Rio de Janeiro-RJ, Brazil, 15–19 July 2013, pp. 279–283 (2013)

Flexible Monitor Deployment for Runtime Verification of Large Scale Software

Teng Zhang[1], Gregory Eakman[2], Insup Lee[1], and Oleg Sokolsky[1(✉)]

[1] University of Pennsylvania, Philadelphia, PA 19104, USA
{tengz,lee,sokolsky}@cis.upenn.edu
[2] BAE Systems, Burlington, MA 01803, USA
gregory.eakman@baesystems.com

Abstract. The paper presents a brief overview of the SMEDL monitoring system that provides flexible and scalable deployment of monitors for large-scale software. The SMEDL specification language expresses monitoring logic as a collection of monitoring objects and monitoring architecture as flows of information between the monitored system and monitoring objects. The system supports synchronous as well as asynchronous deployment of monitoring objects and dynamic instantiation of monitoring objects on demand. The application of the SMEDL system for the monitoring of a target tracking application is briefly discussed.

1 Introduction

Modern software systems affect all aspects of our lives, offering ever richer capabilities. This outsized role comes at a price: software keeps increasing in scale and complexity, requiring ever more effort to design, build, test, and deploy. Hardly any large-scale systems are designed from scratch today. Systems are integrated from separately developed modules, both vertically and horizontally. Concurrency and distributed computation are extensively used in the integration of modules. Modules are often developed by independent teams and incorporated as black boxes into the larger system. Moreover, over the life of the system, individual modules will be updated, so systems assembled and deployed in different time frames are likely to use different versions of the module. All of these factors allow incompatibilities between modules to slip in, in the form of communication protocol errors, broken assumptions made by developers of individual modules, etc. As a result, flaws in a software system are often discovered after the system is built and deployed.

Runtime monitoring can be used to detect and diagnose these flaws and alert system users and developers. In this paper, we will consider specification-based monitoring, where monitors detect deviation of system behaviors from the

This work is supported in part by the Air Force Research Laboratory (AFRL) and Defense Advanced Research Projects Agency (DARPA) under contract FA8750-16-C-0007 and by ONR SBIR contract N00014-15-C-0126.

T. Margaria and B. Steffen (Eds.): ISoLA 2018, LNCS 11247, pp. 42–50, 2018.
https://doi.org/10.1007/978-3-030-03427-6_6

specifications and raise alarms (or, potentially, trigger recovery). This kind of monitoring came to be known as *runtime verification* [3]. To be useful in monitoring of large-scale software systems, runtime verification needs to be supported by a flexible monitor deployment framework. The framework should allow us to specify our requirements, determine how each requirement should be monitored, which observations are needed by monitors to perform their job and how these observations should be extracted. In cases where dynamic instantiation of monitors or communication between monitors are needed, the framework should also allow us to specify when and how monitors need to be instantiated and removed, and what communication flows should be present.

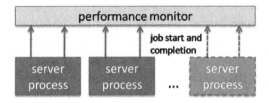

Fig. 1. Running example

Throughout the paper, we will be using a simple example of performance monitoring. Consider the setting illustrated in Fig. 1. We have a system built as a set of distributed server processes, each completing a series of jobs. A shaded process indicates that server processes can be added and shut down dynamically to satisfy demand. The monitor should calculate an average performance metric for the whole system. Such a monitor would receive timestamped observations from each process, corresponding to start and completion of each job, status of a job at completion, etc., and output alerts if performance, according to the chosen metric, falls below a threshold.

The paper is organized as follows. In Sect. 2, we give a brief introduction to runtime verification and discuss challenges of applying runtime verification techniques to large-scale software systems. Section 3 we introduce a flexible monitoring framework and discuss how it addresses the challenges. We conclude the paper with a discussion of remaining challenges and future work.

2 Background: Runtime Verification

Runtime verification is a collection of techniques for correctness monitoring of systems with respect to formally specified properties. An executable monitor is constructed for a given property and is run over a stream of observations to arrive at a conclusion, whether the property is satisfied or not. Runtime verification approaches differ in how properties are specified; how monitors are constructed; how observations are extracted; whether monitoring is performed online or over a recorded trace; if the monitoring is online, how the monitors are deployed within the running system.

2.1 Challenges

Application of runtime verification to large-scale software systems faces a number of challenges that stem from many of the same factors that make large-scale software hard in the first place. Below, we consider several of these challenges.

Multiple Properties with Different Criticality Levels. A large software system would have many different properties to monitor. Some of these properties relate to safety and security of the system and require fast response. Evaluation of others, for example performance properties, may be delayed or even performed off line. Monitors for these properties may rely on the same observations. And there can be dependencies between properties; for example, a security monitor may perform anomaly detection on a performance metric. Keeping track of properties along with their dependencies, and ensuring that deployment of monitors is appropriate for their criticality levels and preserves dependencies, is a challenge that quickly increases with the scale of the system.

Global vs. Local Properties. Some of the properties to monitor may be local to one module in the system, while others concern global behaviors of the system. In a distributed system, checking global properties may incur prohibitive overhead and interfere with the system operation. Local monitoring is usually preferable. Deciding where monitors should be placed and managing monitor placement in a large system is a challenge.

Multiple Variants of System Implementations. As discussed above, different system installations may utilize different implementations of system modules. This creates two challenges to be addressed. First, the same observation may have to be extracted differently in different versions of a module. For example, in one version of the module, an observation may be obtained by instrumenting a particular function call. In a subsequent version, the call may be renamed or eliminated through code refactoring, so that a different instrumentation needs to be introduced. Second, properties specific to the module may also change. For example, the property may reflect assumptions that the module makes about interactions with its environment. A new version of the module may make different assumptions. Maintaining multiple versions of the property is another challenge that is exacerbated by scale.

3 SMEDL Monitoring System

In order to address the above challenges, we have developed a prototype monitoring system [4] that aims to address challenges presented above. Below, we discuss several salient features of the SMEDL[1] system.

---

[1] SMEDL stands for Scenario-based Meta-Event Definition Language.

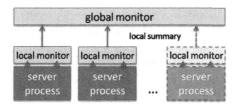

Fig. 2. Modular specification of the performance monitor

3.1 System Design

Modular Property Specification. In order to effectively monitor a property in a large-scale distributed system, SMEDL allows us to specify properties in a modular fashion. In this way, a complex property can be decomposed into a set of monitoring modules that communicate with each other and collectively implement the monitor for the overall property. A common pattern for modular specification is partitioning a global property for a distributed system into a set of locally deployed modules that operate on local observations of each process in the distributed system and convey results of local processing to the global module that computes the overall result. Consider our performance monitor example. Instead of sending all observations to a monolithic global monitor, we partition it into a set of local monitors, one for each process, and a global monitor, as shown in Fig. 2. Local monitors would calculate performance of that process and then send a summary to the global monitor that would aggregate local reports into the global value.

Monitor Coordination and Communication. Clearly, monitor modules need to communicate with each other. The flow of interactions between monitors depends on the property and how it is partitioned into modules. Specification of the monitoring architecture, described below, makes these flows explicit.

Synchronous and Asynchronous Deployment. We specify the logic of each monitor module and, separately, how this module is to be deployed. Often, the user has a choice of deploying the same module synchronously or asynchronously, so decoupling the logic of the module from its deployment strategy increases flexibility of the framework. Continuing our example, for the modular monitor shown in Fig. 2, we deploy the global monitor asynchronously, while local monitors can be deployed synchronously or asynchronously, depending on, e.g., relative overheads of the two approaches.

Dynamic Monitor Instantiation. Large-scale software systems typically contain many similar components that can be added and removed dynamically. In our example, server processes can be spun up and down to meet the demand. When this happens, local monitors are instantiated for each new server process and are connected to the global monitor.

Separation of Property Specification from Observation Extraction. A monitoring specification describes, among other things, what observations are needed by the monitor in order to do its job. In order to deploy monitors, we also need to know how to extract these observations from the target system. Extraction of observations can be performed in many different ways, for example by instrumenting source code or binaries of system components, by snooping on the system bus, or even off line, reading from a recorded trace. Over time, the target system may evolve and offer new ways of observation extraction, or different variants of system component implementations may require different placement of instrumentation probes. It is important to accommodate these changes in the monitoring setup with as little disruption as possible. SMEDL separates monitoring logic from observation extraction using an event-based API, so that events can be raised in a specified format by an appropriate extraction technology. We have experimented with several such technologies, such as AspectC [2] for instrumenting C source code and a dynamic translation tool SySense by GrammaTech for capturing observations from binary code.

3.2 Monitoring Specification

In SMEDL, monitoring specification contains two major parts: monitoring objects and monitoring architecture.

Monitoring Objects. Monitoring objects represent logic used in checking the property. Each monitoring object has an *interface*: imported events that a monitor receives from its environment and exported events that it raises. Imported events can be observations from the target system or events sent by other monitors. Similarly, exported events can be alarms that are delivered to the system operator or used to trigger recovery, or they can be sent to other monitors for processing. The logic itself is expressed using communicating finite state machines extended with local state variables. State machines take transitions in response to imported events and can raise exported events or update state variables when a transition is taken. Monitoring modules are designed to allow the use of other formalisms to express the logic.

Monitoring objects can have *identity parameters*. Choosing different parameter values allow us to have multiple instances of monitoring objects. In our running example, a natural parameter for the local monitor is the identity of a server. We note that at the specification level, we may want to abstract from the precise nature of this identity. Depending on the system implementation, a server process may be identified by a computer name, an IP address, or maybe a virtual machine identifier where the server runs.

Monitoring Architecture. Monitoring architecture is a directed graph that represents communication between monitoring objects. Nodes of the graph have ports that correspond to events that the node can consume or produce. Nodes that represent monitoring objects have ports that match the interface of the object. Nodes can also represent components of the target system. Ports of these nodes represent observations that are obtained from this component. Edges in the graph represent communication flows from exported events of one node to imported events of another node. Nodes in a monitoring architecture are partitioned into sets. Monitoring objects within a set are deployed together and are executed synchronously, using a single thread of control. When a monitoring object is placed into a set with a node representing a system component, monitor instances are running synchronously with the component, essentially becoming a part of component instrumentation. Objects in an architecture may be instantiated statically or dynamically. Statically instantiated objects are created at the beginning of a monitored run of the system. Dynamically instantiated objects are created when new values of identity parameters are discovered.

4   Case Studies

The SMEDL system is extensively used in the RINGS project, led by BAE Systems as part of the DARPA BRASS program. The goal of the program is to develop techniques to adapt a given application to changes in the application environment or the underlying execution platform. The RINGS project focuses on a target tracking application, developed by BAE Systems and continuously evolved over a period of over 15 years. The tracker receives data from a number of sensors, e.g., imaging devices, that supply information about observed objects, and contains algorithms that parse sensor inputs and compose observations into tracks, i.e., sequences of points representing position of an object over time.

Over time, both the application and its environment can change. For example, new sensors are introduced into the system, and parsers for new sensor inputs need to be added. Standards for the format of sensor data evolve, which also requires changes to parsers. Track processing algorithms may need to be updated to account for new sensors. The tracker uses a large number of tuning parameters to handle weather and other environmental conditions. Misconfiguration of parameter settings may lead to poor tracking results.

We use SMEDL monitors to detect when the application does not behave as intended. Alarms raised by monitors trigger adaptation modules that perform fault localization and generate patches that compensate for the detected changes. In this paper, we discuss only the detection aspect of the case study.

The main challenge in constructing monitors for the tracking application is that there is no ground truth about tracks available at run time. Instead, monitors have to rely on indirect evidence of misbehavior. Alternatively, monitor can focus on specific faults that are known to have caused misbehavior in the past. Both approaches are imperfect: indirect monitors may not catch all violations, while fault monitors may raise false alarms if the system tolerates the fault. Below, we discuss examples of both monitoring approaches.

Track Quality Monitors. Developers of the tracking application have identified a number of metrics that characterize track output quality. These metrics, collected using a sliding window time interval, include average duration of a track observed in a time interval and the number of *unassociated detections*, i.e., observations of objects that are not associated with any track, also in a given time interval. We can monitor these metrics at run time and raise an alarm when significant changes are observed. Note that these metrics are indirect.

Consider the design of a track duration monitor. A track is observed as a sequence of timestamped points. Each new point added to the track results in a *track report*. Each track report is delivered to the monitor as an event that carries the track identifier as attribute. We also assume that the system produces timeout events that represent boundaries of the sliding window. The monitoring architecture is very similar to the one shown in Fig. 2: there is a local monitor for each track that calculates duration of the track in the current window and, at each window boundary, sends the value to the global monitor to calculate the metric for all tracks and raise an alarm, if needed. As tracks are added by the application, new track monitors are instantiated.

To implement calculation of a quality metric over a sliding window, the window is partitioned into a series of subwindows, each represented by a separate monitor. In addition, a window manager monitor for each track handles switching of subwindows, while the aggregator monitor combined calculations from each subwindow into the overall track duration within the whole window. The architecture of the monitor is shown in Fig. 3a. Some events and auxiliary monitors are not shown for clarity. Each box represents a monitor, with types of monitor parameters shown in brackets. Edges represent events exchanged by monitors. Each edge is annotated with parameter matching that determines replication of event flows when new instances are created. Consider, for example, the `track` event raised by `WindowManager` and consumed by `Subwindow` monitor. The matching ties the first parameter of the `WindowManager` instance raising the event to the first parameter of the `Subwindow` instance receiving the event. Since `Subwindow` has the second parameter, not bound by the matching, the connection is a *fan-out*, when the `track` event is received by all instances subwindow monitors for that track. By contrast, event `metric_sub` represents a *fan-in*, when events raised by any subwindow for a track are delivered to the `Aggregator` instance for that track. Finally, `metric` events raised by any track aggregator are delivered to the same `Metric` monitor, which is not parameterized. An instance of the architecture for two tracks, and two subwindows in a window, is shown in Fig. 3b.

We illustrate a monitoring specification in SMEDL using a simplified version of the `Aggregator` monitor, shown in Fig. 4. The monitor includes a single parameter, denoted by the `identity` keyword and a number of state variables. It has two imported (input) events, one representing a report from a subwindow and the other used for initialization, and one exported (output) event, representing the track duration calculated at the window boundary. It also has a number of internal events, described below. Monitoring logic is represented by a collection of scenarios. Each scenario represents an event-driven state machine. In this example, each scenario has a single state. Each transition in a scenario is triggered by an imported or internal event and can happen only if a guard is satisfied. Guards are predicates over state variables of the monitor and attributes of the triggering events. When a transition occurs, a series of actions is executed,

a)

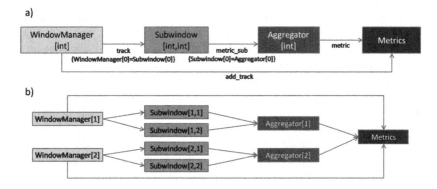

b)

Fig. 3. Monitoring architecture for the case study

each of which either updates a state variable or raises an exported or internal event. For clarity, we do not show details of the guards and elide most of the actions. We can see that each scenario performs a certain check represented as a guard. For example, the check can determine whether the track started or was dropped within the current window, and updates the state variables accordingly. Then, an internal event is raised to trigger the next check.

```
object Aggregator

identity
    int id;

state
    int msg_cnt = 0;
    int event_cnt = 0;
    float observed_time = 0;

events
|   imported initial(int, float, int, int);
    imported metric_sub(int, float, float, int);
    internal checkNum();
    internal i1( int, float, float);
    internal i2(float,float);
    internal i3(float);
    internal output();
    exported metric(int, float);

scenarios

initialization:
    init -> initial(ts, sub_w, sub_size,  prob) {...} -> init

accumulation:
    start -> metric_sub(n,ft,lt,flag) { msg_cnt ++; ...; raise i1(n,ft,lt); } -> start

chk1:
    in -> i1(n,ft,lt) when (g1) { event_cnt = event_cnt + n; raise i2(ft,lt); } -> in
    in -> i1(n,ft,lt) when (!g1) { event_cnt = event_cnt + n; raise checkNum(); } -> in

ft_chk:
    ftc -> i2(ft,lt) when (g2) { ...; raise i3(lt); } -> ftc
    ftc -> i2(ft,lt) when (!g2) { raise i3(lt); } -> ftc

lt_chk:
    ltc -> i3(lt) when (g3) { ...; raise checkNum(); } -> ltc
    ltc -> i3(lt) when (!g3) {  raise checkNum(); } -> ltc

output_chk:
    opc -> checkNum() when (g4) { observed_time = ...; raise output(); } -> opc
    opc -> checkNum() when (!g4) { observed_time = ...; raise output(); ...; } -> opc

out:
    fin -> output() { ...; raise metric(event_cnt, observed_time); ...; } -> fin
```

Fig. 4. Specification of the `Aggregator` monitor

Sensor Format Monitors. The second case study, also motivated by past experiences, concerns data interchange formats. To facilitate independent development of sensor devices and tracking applications, data interchange standards such as STANAG 4607 [1] have been introduced. Nonetheless, incompatibilities can still be encountered during missions, either because a sensor does not always follow the standard or because the parser module has not been updated to the latest version of the standard. The standard offers both a binary encoding of sensor messages and an XML encoding. We have developed monitors to detect deviations from the standard binary format. In the binary format, fields do not have explicit delimiters and their sizes are specified within the parser. If a field in the message has a different size than the parser expects, fields will be misaligned and the message will be parsed incorrectly. In our case study, we rely on the knowledge of acceptable ranges for a field in the message in order to detect and localize the problem.

5 Conclusions

We have presented challenges to monitoring of complex software system and briefly described a monitoring system that aims to address the challenges by offering flexible monitor specification and deployment. The monitoring system has been applied in a case study involving a large-scale target tracking application. In the case study, monitors have been used detect deviations from the original application intent and to trigger an automated search for repair.

References

1. NATO ground moving target indicator format - STANAG 4607, edition 2. https://standards.globalspec.com/std/1300603/nato-stanag-4607. Accessed 9 May 2018, September 2010
2. Coady, Y., Kiczales, G., Feeley, M., Smolyn, G.: Using aspectC to improve the modularity of path-specific customization in operating system code. SIGSOFT Softw. Eng. Notes **26**(5), 88–98 (2001)
3. Sokolsky, O., Havelund, K., Lee, I.: Introduction to the special section on runtime verification. Softw. Tools Technol. Transf. **14**(3), 243–247 (2012)
4. Zhang, T., Gebhard, P., Sokolsky, O.: SMEDL: combining synchronous and asynchronous monitoring. In: Falcone, Y., Sánchez, C. (eds.) RV 2016. LNCS, vol. 10012, pp. 482–490. Springer, Cham (2016). https://doi.org/10.1007/978-3-319-46982-9_32

Increasing the Reusability of Enforcers with Lifecycle Events

Oliviero Riganelli, Daniela Micucci, and Leonardo Mariani[✉]

University of Milano-Bicocca, Viale Sarca 336, 20126 Milan, Italy
{riganelli,micucci,mariani}@disco.unimib.it

Abstract. Runtime enforcement can be effectively used to improve the reliability of software applications. However, it often requires the definition of ad hoc policies and enforcement strategies, which might be expensive to identify and implement. This paper discusses how to exploit lifecycle events to obtain useful enforcement strategies that can be easily reused across applications, thus reducing the cost of adoption of the runtime enforcement technology. The paper finally sketches how this idea can be used to define libraries that can automatically overcome problems related to applications misusing them.

Keywords: Runtime enforcement · Self-healing · Proactive library

1 Introduction

Runtime enforcement techniques are effective solutions for guaranteeing that software applications satisfy certain correctness policies at runtime [17]. When using runtime enforcement, developers are typically in charge of identifying the policies that must be enforced, defining a strategy to enforce them, and finally implementing the software enforcer that applies the strategy.

The enforced policies are often *application-specific*, that is, policies are defined ad hoc for the target application. Working with application-specific policies might be quite expensive. In fact every time a new application is considered, new policies must be identified, and the modelling and implementation activities must be repeated from scratch.

Interestingly policies may also refer to libraries and components that can be reused across applications being themselves eligible for reuse. *Reusable policies* are extremely important because they can alleviate the developers from the burden of identifying both the policies to be enforced and the corresponding enforcement strategies. Developers could simply reuse policies and enforcement

This work has been partially supported by the H2020 Learn project, which has been funded under the ERC Consolidator Grant 2014 program (ERC Grant Agreement n. 646867) and the GAUSS national research project, which has been funded by the MIUR under the PRIN 2015 program (Contract 2015KWREMX).

T. Margaria and B. Steffen (Eds.): ISoLA 2018, LNCS 11247, pp. 51–57, 2018.
https://doi.org/10.1007/978-3-030-03427-6_7

strategies while they reuse libraries, de facto simplifying the application of runtime enforcement techniques.

Unfortunately, the definition of reusable policies and enforcement strategies can be challenging. Since the context of use of a library is not known a priori, a reusable policy and the corresponding enforcement strategy could be defined referring to the operations of the library only. For example, a reusable policy of a library for interacting with the file system may require that a file is opened before any content is written in the file. However, several relevant policies may depend not only on the usage of a library, but also on the behavior of the application that interacts with the library. For instance, a policy that forces an app to close a file before its execution is suspended depends on both the library and the app, and cannot be specified referring to the library only.

There is a popular class of software applications that naturally facilitate both the identification of reusable policies and the definition of enforcement strategies. We call them *life-cycle based applications*. They are applications whose units of composition are modules with an explicitly documented life-cycle model. There is a huge number of life-cycle based applications. For example, Android apps are composed of activities with a known life-cycle model and with callbacks that are invoked when there is a change in the state of the app; similarly Spring applications are composed of components with a known life-cycle model and callbacks. The same applies to many other contexts, such as Web applications, multi-threaded applications, and so on.

Life-cycle based applications have the important advantage of responding to the same life-cycle and implementing the same callbacks, regardless of what a specific application does. Thus policies and enforcement strategies can exploit this information to consider some aspects of the behavior of the application, still remaining reusable. We call these reusable policies *life-cycle based policies* and the corresponding strategies *life-cycle based enforcement strategies*.

We further elaborate the concept of life-cycle based application and policy in Sect. 2. We show how we exploited these concepts to define *proactive libraries*, a class of libraries augmented with reusable enforcement strategies, in Sect. 3. We provide final remarks in Sect. 4.

2   Life-Cycle Based Policies

The life-cycle of a software unit specifies the possible states of the unit and the events that can cause the transition between two states. Units with a non-trivial and well-defined lifecycle are typically executed and managed by a framework that explicitly controls their life, invoking callback methods when there is a state transition. For example, Android activities have callback methods that are invoked when an application is started and suspended. Similarly, Web components have callback methods that are invoked when they are created and destroyed.

These callback methods are pervasively present in life-cycle based applications. For instance, every activity in every Android application implements the same callback methods. This is an important aspect that eases the definition of both reusable policies and reusable enforcement strategies that can be generally valid for every application of a specific domain. For instance, a policy about an Android library can also refer to callback methods without any loss of generality.

Policies with life-cycle events are particularly relevant. Applications may have to implement non-trivial behaviors in reaction to state transitions [1–3,6,7,9], and this may lead to faulty applications, for instance applications with faulty library interactions [14,21].

Although these policies might be non-trivial to address, they are easy to find in the documentation of libraries and systems and can be the basis for the design of reusable policies. We report below three examples of reusable policies that can be defined for completely different life-cycle based systems.

The `onPause()` method is an Android callback that is automatically executed when a user stops interacting with an activity and is relevant to several correctness policies. For instance, an activity that is paused after acquiring the `Camera` must release it otherwise the camera might be unusable from other activities[1].

In the OSGi Java framework [4], application bundles can be started, stopped, installed, and uninstalled remotely without rebooting. The execution of these operations must obey to specific policies. For example, stopping a bundle requires unregistering every previously registered service [3].

React is a JavaScript library widely used to build encapsulated components that can be composed to create complex Web UIs [5]. Each component has several life-cycle callback methods that can be overridden to execute custom code at particular times in the component's life-cycle. For example, the method `componentWillUnmount()` is invoked immediately before a component is unmounted and destroyed. The library documentation requires applications to implement specific operations when this callback is executed, such as invalidating timers, deleting network requests, or cleaning up subscriptions [6].

Note that all these examples are cases of policies that can be arbitrarily reused across applications since they exploit information about life-cycle events and library APIs. These policies would be impossible to define without exploiting the information about life-cycle events.

In the next section, we show how we exploited this concept to define *proactive libraries*, that is, libraries equipped with life-cycle based enforcement strategies We present proactive libraries in the Android domain because it is the most popular among the application domains described above, and because it has been already used as application domain in related work [11,18,20].

3 Proactive Libraries

Let us refer to the *Plumeria*[2] app, a simple Android app, to illustrate the concept of *proactive library* [19]. *Plumeria* has a fault, that is, one of its activities does not release the camera when it is suspended, as a consequence the camera becomes

---

[1] https://developer.android.com/guide/topics/media/camera#release-camera.
[2] https://github.com/DonLiangGit/Plumeria.

inaccessible to the other apps of the device. This is a classic resource leak problem that could be avoided by enforcing the policy presented in Sect. 2. In particular, if the camera API is released as a proactive library, this problem would never show up because it would be automatically detected and fixed by the enforcement mechanism embedded in the proactive library.

Proactive libraries are standard libraries augmented with the built-in capability of enforcing reusable policies at runtime.

Figure 1 shows the generation process of proactive libraries. The process distinguishes the development and the runtime phases.

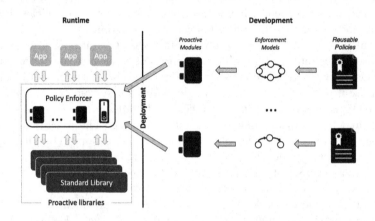

Fig. 1. The generation process of proactive libraries.

At development time, developers start from the identification of reusable correctness policies, that is, natural language statements that specify how the application should use a library according to the status of both the application, detected through the execution of its life-cycle callback methods, and the library, detected through the execution of its API methods. The reusable correctness policy that ensures the correct usage of the camera is: "*An activity that is paused while having the control of the camera must first release the camera.*"

Correctness policies are used to derive enforcement models that define how to react to correctness policies violations. We use edit automata [16] to define the enforcement models because they naturally support the definition of enforcement rules by means of events to be intercepted, inserted and suppressed, and they could be also verified [20]. The definition of an enforcement model does not require any knowledge about the app that uses the API, but it uniquely requires the knowledge of the API and of the Android callback methods, which are the same for any app.

Figure 2 shows a slightly simplified enforcement model that forces the release of the `Camera` when the activity is paused without releasing the `Camera`. The prefix r is used to distinguish the calls to the API methods from callbacks. To

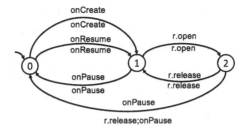

Fig. 2. Simplified enforcement model for the `Camera`.

keep the example real but small, the enforcement model does not include the part that reassigns the `Camera` to the activity once its execution is resumed.

To actually enforce the policy in the target environment, the enforcement models are turned into *proactive software modules* that intercept the execution of life-cycle callback methods and API methods, and produce additional invocations when needed, according to the enforcement model.

Since proactive modules are activated by the invocation of specific methods, their execution in the user environment is controlled by a *policy enforcer* that intercepts the events and dispatches them to the deployed proactive modules. The policy enforcer also controls the activation and deactivation of the proactive modules, which can be turned off and on by the user.

The language and frameworks to implement the proactive modules and the policy enforcer depend on the target environment. In the case of Android, we use the Java Xposed framework [8], which allows to cost-efficiently intercept method invocations and change the behavior of an Android app using run-time hooking and code injection mechanisms.

In our experience, we successfully used proactive libraries to automatically overcome several problems present in Android apps [19].

4   Conclusions

Research on runtime enforcement has already delivered both theoretical [10,12, 16,17] and practical results [11,13,15,19]. However, identifying policies, specifying enforcement strategies, and implementing the corresponding enforcers is still a difficult and time consuming task. Reusable policies, as discussed in this paper, can relieve developers from this tedious and error-prone task, facilitating reuse and easing the practical adoption of the runtime enforcement technology.

We plan to extend our work on runtime enforcement in three directions. *Automatic code generation of runtime enforcement mechanisms*: since manually implementing runtime enforcement mechanisms is particularly difficult and expensive, we plan to define a model-driven software development process and the corresponding tool chain to automatically derive enforcer code from the models. *Automatic testing of software enforcers*: To achieve highly reliable and safe enforcing mechanisms, we need techniques specifically defined to validate the behavior of software enforcers, which have the distinguishing characteristic of being designed to dynamically change the behavior of other software applications, causing hard to predict side effects. *Public repository of software enforcers*: Since life-cycle based enforcement strategies are application-independent, publishing well developed software enforcers in a public repository is important to facilitate the distribution of plug-and-play enforcement strategies that can be easily exploited by developers.

References

1. Apache Felix iPOJO - Lifecycle callbacks. http://tiny.cc/iyvoty
2. Kubernetes - Container Lifecycle Hooks. http://tiny.cc/k9voty
3. OSGi - Life Cycle Layer. http://tiny.cc/k9voty
4. OSGi Alliance - The Dynamic Module System for Java. https://www.osgi.org
5. React - A JavaScript library for building user interfaces. http://tiny.cc/iyvoty
6. React - State and Lifecycle. https://reactjs.org/docs/state-and-lifecycle.html
7. Spring - Customizing the nature of a bean. http://tiny.cc/rs2oty
8. Xposed. http://repo.xposed.info/
9. Android: The Activity Lifecycle. https://developer.android.com/guide/components/activities/activity-lifecycle.html
10. Bielova, N., Massacci, F.: Do you really mean what you actually enforced? Int. J. Inf. Secur. (IS) **10**(4), 239–254 (2011)
11. Falcone, Y., Currea, S., Jaber, M.: Runtime verification and enforcement for android applications with RV-Droid. In: Qadeer, S., Tasiran, S. (eds.) RV 2012. LNCS, vol. 7687, pp. 88–95. Springer, Heidelberg (2013). https://doi.org/10.1007/978-3-642-35632-2_11
12. Falcone, Y., Fernandez, J.C., Mounier, L.: What can you verify and enforce at runtime? Int. J. Softw. Tools Technol. Transfer **14**(3), 349–382 (2012)
13. Hallé, S., Ettema, T., Bunch, C., Bultan, T.: Eliminating navigation errors in web applications via model checking and runtime enforcement of navigation state machines. In: Proceedings of the International Conference on Automated Software Engineering (ASE) (2010)
14. Hou, D., Li, L.: Obstacles in using frameworks and APIs: an exploratory study of programmers' newsgroup discussions. In: Proceedings of the International Conference on Program Comprehension (ICPC) (2011)
15. Kumar, A., Ligatti, J., Tu, Y.-C.: Query monitoring and analysis for database privacy - a security automata model approach. In: Wang, J., et al. (eds.) WISE 2015. LNCS, vol. 9419, pp. 458–472. Springer, Cham (2015). https://doi.org/10.1007/978-3-319-26187-4_42
16. Ligatti, J., Bauer, L., Walker, D.: Edit automata: enforcement mechanisms for run-time security policies. Int. J. Inf. Secur. **4**(1), 2–16 (2005)
17. Ligatti, J., Bauer, L., Walker, D.: Run-time enforcement of nonsafety policies. ACM Trans. Inf. Syst. Secur. **12**(3), 19:1–19:39 (2009)
18. Riganelli, O., Micucci, D., Mariani, L.: Healing data loss problems in android apps. In: Proceedings of the International Workshop on Software Faults (IWSF), Co-located with ISSRE (2016)
19. Riganelli, O., Micucci, D., Mariani, L.: Policy enforcement with proactive libraries. In: Proceedings of the 12th International Symposium on Software Engineering for Adaptive and Self-Managing Systems (SEAMS) (2017)

20. Riganelli, O., Micucci, D., Mariani, L., Falcone, Y.: Verifying policy enforcers. In: Lahiri, S., Reger, G. (eds.) RV 2017. LNCS, vol. 10548, pp. 241–258. Springer, Cham (2017). https://doi.org/10.1007/978-3-319-67531-2_15
21. Wang, W., Godfrey, M.W.: Detecting API usage obstacles: a study of ios and android developer questions. In: Proceedings of the Working Conference on Mining Software Repositories (MSR) (2013)

BDDs on the Run

Klaus Havelund[1(✉)] and Doron Peled[2]

[1] Jet Propulsion Laboratory, California Institute of Technology, Pasadena, USA
klaus.havelund@jpl.nasa.gov
[2] Department of Computer Science, Bar Ilan University, Ramat Gan, Israel

Abstract. Runtime verification (RV) of first-order temporal logic must handle a potentially large amount of data, accumulated during the monitoring of an execution. The DEJAVU RV system represents data elements and relations using BDDs. This achieves a compact representation, which allows monitoring long executions. However, the potentially unbounded, and frequently very large amounts of data values can, ultimately, limit the executions that can be monitored. We present an automatic method for "forgetting" data values when they no longer affect the RV verdict on an observed execution. We describe the algorithm and illustrate its operation through an example.

1 Introduction

Runtime verification (RV) can be used to check the execution (run) of a system against a temporal property, yielding an alarm when the property is violated, so that aversive action can be taken. For each consumed event the monitor performs incremental computation, updating its internal memory, and has to decide whether the property is violated based on the finite part of the execution trace that it has viewed so far. To inspect an execution, the monitored system is instrumented to report on occurrences of events.

Runtime verification is often applied to executions that consist of events that contain data values [1–7,9–13,16–18]. A large amount of different observed data values can pose a challenge to the efficiency of RV systems, in terms of time and space, since it is essential to keep up with rapid occurrence of events in very long executions. We present the DEJAVU system and its logic QTL (Quantified Temporal Logic), which in its core supports *past* temporal properties, including existential quantification, predicates with data values and variables, the Boolean operators *and*, *not*, and the modal operators $\ominus$ for previous-time and $\mathcal{S}$ for since. Several standard operators are derived from these.

In [14] we presented an early version of DEJAVU and its algorithm based on the use of BDDs. We describe here furthermore an approach for detecting when

The research performed by the first author was carried out at Jet Propulsion Laboratory, California Institute of Technology, under a contract with the National Aeronautics and Space Administration. The research performed by the second author was partially funded by ISF grant 2239/15: "Runtime Measuring and Checking of Cyber Physical Systems".

T. Margaria and B. Steffen (Eds.): ISoLA 2018, LNCS 11247, pp. 58–69, 2018.
https://doi.org/10.1007/978-3-030-03427-6_8

data elements that were seen so far do not affect the rest of the execution and can be discarded, also referred to as *dynamic data reclamation*. As an example, consider the following formula, asserting that data can be written to a file only if it has been opened in the past, and not closed since then.

$$\forall f \left((\exists d \, write(f,d)) \longrightarrow (\neg close(f) \, \mathcal{S} \, open(f)) \right) \tag{1}$$

We can observe that if a file was opened and subsequently closed, then the property would be invalidated if a value is written to that file, just as in the case where the file was never opened. This means that we can "forget" that a file was opened when it is closed, without affecting our ability to monitor the formula. If there are no more than N files simultaneously opened at any time, then we need space for only N files for monitoring the property. This is in contrast to [14], where space for all new file names must be allocated. We present the algorithm for storing data as BDDs, and the automatic detection of data values that are not required anymore, reclaiming the space used for storing them.

The contents of the paper is as follows. Section 2 presents the syntax and semantics of QTL. Section 3 describes the basic BDD-based algorithm. Section 4 outlines the dynamic data reclamation approach. Section 5 illustrates the extended algorithm by executing a monitor on an example trace. Finally Sect. 6 concludes the paper.

2   Syntax and Semantics

Let X be a finite set of *variables*. An *assignment* over a set of variables $W \subseteq X$ maps each variable $x \in W$ to a value from its associated domain $domain(x)$. We assume that the domains (e.g., integers, strings) are infinite (see [14] for dealing with finite domains). For example $[x \rightarrow 5, y \rightarrow$ "abc"] maps x to 5 and y to "abc". Let T be a set of *predicate names*, where each predicate name p is associated with some domain $domain(p)$. A predicate is constructed from a predicate name and a variable or a constant of the same type. Thus, if the predicate name p and the variable x are associated with the domain of strings, we have predicates like $p(\text{"gaga"})$, and $p(x)$. Predicates over constants are called *ground predicates*. An *event* is a finite set of ground predicates. For example, if $T = \{p, q, r\}$, then $\{p(\text{"xyzzy"}), q(3)\}$ is a possible event. An *execution trace* $\sigma = s_1, s_2, \ldots$ is a finite sequence of events.

The formulas of the logic QTL are defined by the following grammar. For simplicity of the presentation, we define here the logic with unary predicates, but this is not due to any principle limitation, and, in fact, our implementation supports predicates with multiple arguments.

$$\varphi ::= true \mid p(a) \mid p(x) \mid (\varphi \wedge \varphi) \mid \neg \varphi \mid (\varphi \, \mathcal{S} \, \varphi) \mid \ominus \varphi \mid \exists x \, \varphi$$

The formula $p(a)$, where a is a constant in $domain(p)$, means that the ground predicate $p(a)$ occurs in the most recent event. The formula $p(x)$, for a variable $x \in X$, holds with a binding of x to the value a if a ground predicate $p(a)$

appears in the most recent event. The formula $(\varphi\ \mathcal{S}\ \psi)$ means that ψ held in the past (possibly now) and since then φ has been true. The formula $\ominus\ \varphi$ means that φ is true in the previous event. We can furthermore define the following derived operators: $false = \neg true$, $(\varphi \vee \psi) = \neg(\neg\varphi \wedge \neg\psi)$, $(\varphi \rightarrow \psi) = (\neg\varphi \vee \psi)$, $\mathbf{P}\ \varphi = (true\ \mathcal{S}\ \varphi)$, $\mathbf{H}\ \varphi = \neg\mathbf{P}\ \neg\varphi$, and $\forall x\ \varphi = \neg\exists x\ \neg\varphi$.

Let $free(\varphi)$ be the set of free (i.e., unquantified) variables of a subformula φ. Let $I[\varphi, \sigma, i]$ be the semantic function, defined below. It returns the set of assignments that satisfy φ after the ith event of the execution σ. The empty set of assignments $\emptyset$ behaves as the Boolean constant 0 and the singleton set that contains an assignment over an empty set of variables $\{\epsilon\}$ behaves as the Boolean constant 1. We define the union and intersection operators on sets of assignments, even if they are defined over non identical sets of variables. In this case, the assignments are extended over the union of the variables. Thus intersection between two sets of assignments, A_1 and A_2, is defined like a database "join" operator; i.e., it consists of assignments whose projection on the *common* variables agree with an assignment in A_1 and with an assignment in A_2. Union is defined as the operator dual of intersection. Let Γ be a set of assignments over a set of variables W; we denote by $hide(\Gamma, x)$ the set of assignments over $W \setminus \{x\}$, obtained from Γ by removing the assignment to x for each element of Γ. In particular, if Γ is a set of assignments over just the variable x, then $hide(\Gamma, x)$ is $\{\epsilon\}$ when Γ is nonempty, and $\emptyset$ otherwise. $A_{free(\varphi)}$ is the set of all possible assignments of values to the variables that appear free in φ. We add a 0 position for each sequence σ (which starts with s_1), where I returns the empty set for each formula. The assignment-set semantics of QTL is shown in the following. For all occurrences of i it is assumed that $i > 0$.

- $I[\varphi, \sigma, 0] = \emptyset$.
- $I[true, \sigma, i] = \{\epsilon\}$.
- $I[p(a), \sigma, i] = $ if $p(a) \in \sigma[i]$ then $\{\epsilon\}$ else $\emptyset$.
- $I[p(x), \sigma, i] = \{[x \mapsto a] \mid p(a) \in \sigma[i]\}$.
- $I[(\varphi \wedge \psi), \sigma, i] = I[\varphi, \sigma, i] \bigcap I[\psi, \sigma, i]$.
- $I[\neg\varphi, \sigma, i] = A_{free(\varphi)} \setminus I[\varphi, \sigma, i]$.
- $I[(\varphi\ \mathcal{S}\ \psi), \sigma, i] = I[\psi, \sigma, i] \bigcup (I[\varphi, \sigma, i] \bigcap I[(\varphi\mathcal{S}\psi), \sigma, i-1])$.
- $I[\ominus\varphi, \sigma, i] = I[\varphi, \sigma, i-1]$.
- $I[\exists x\ \varphi, \sigma, i] = hide(I[\varphi, \sigma, i], x)$.

3   An Efficient Algorithm Using BDDs

We describe here an algorithm for monitoring QTL, first presented in [14], and implemented as the first version of the tool DEJAVU. We shall represent a set of assignments as an Ordered Binary Decision Diagram (OBDD, although we write simply BDD) [8].

Recall that a BDD is a directed acyclic graph (DAG), where the non-leaf nodes represent Boolean variables. Figures 2 and 3 (to be explained) show BDDs over the BDD variables b_0, b_1, b_2, and b_3. A BDD is a compact representation of a Boolean formula over these variables, and can be used to determine, for a given assignment to the variables, whether the formula is true or not. Each non-leaf node is the source of two arrows leading to other nodes. A dotted-line arrow represents that the Boolean variable has the value 0 (false), while a thick-line arrow represents that it has the value 1 (true). The nodes in the DAG have the same order along all paths from the root. However, some of the nodes may be absent along some paths, when the result does not depend on the value of the corresponding Boolean variable. Each path leads to a leaf node that is marked by either 0 (false) or 1 (true), representing the Boolean value returned by the formula for the variable assignment corresponding to the followed path.

Assume that we see $p(\text{"ab"}), p(\text{"de"}), p(\text{"af"})$ and $q(\text{"fg"})$ in subsequent events in an execution trace, where p and q are predicates over the domain of strings. When a value associated with a variable appears for the first time in the current event (in a ground predicate), we add it to the set of values of that domain that were seen. We assign to each new value an *enumeration*, represented as a binary number, and use a hash table to point from the value to its enumeration. The least significant bit in an enumeration is represented by BDD variable b_0, and the most significant bit by the BDD variable with highest index. Using a three-bit enumeration $b_2 b_1 b_0$, the first encountered value "ab" can be represented[1] as the bit string 000, "de" as 001, "af" as 010, and "fg" as 011. A BDD for a subset of these values returns a 1 for each bit string representing an enumeration of a value in the set, and 0 otherwise. E.g. a BDD representing the set { "de", "af"} (2nd and 3rd values) returns 1 for 001 and 010. This is the Boolean function $\neg b_2 \wedge (b_1 \leftrightarrow \neg b_0)$.

When representing a set of assignments for two variables x and y with k bits each, we use Boolean BDD variables $x_{k-1}, \ldots, x_0, y_{k-1}, \ldots y_0$. A BDD will return a 1 for each bit string consisting of the concatenation of enumerations that correspond to the represented assignments, and 0 otherwise. For example, to represent the assignment $[x \mapsto \text{"de"}, y \mapsto \text{"af"}]$, where "de" is enumerated as 001 and "af" with 010, the BDD will return a 1 for 001010. The BDD that returns always 0 is denoted by $\text{BDD}(\bot)$, and the BDD that returns always 1 is denoted by $\text{BDD}(\top)$.

Given a ground predicate $p(a)$, observed in the currently monitored event of the execution, then when matching with $p(x)$ in the monitored property, let **lookup**(x, a) be the enumeration of a. If this is a's first occurrence, then it will be assigned a new enumeration. Otherwise, **lookup** returns the enumeration that a received before. The function **build**(x, V), where V is a set of values, returns a BDD that represents the set of assignments where x is mapped to (the enumeration of) a for $a \in V$. This BDD is independent of the values assigned to any variable other than x, i.e., they can have any value.

The algorithm, shown below, operates on two vectors (arrays) of values indexed by subformulas (as in [15]): pre for the state before that event, and now for the current state (after the last seen event).

---

[1] Enumerations are here selected using a counter initialized to 0, as in [14]. The data reclamation solution in Sect. 4 instead uses a SAT solver.

1. Initially, for each subformula φ, $\mathsf{now}(\varphi) := \mathrm{BDD}(\bot)$.
2. Observe a new event (as set of ground predicates) s as input.
3. Let $\mathsf{pre} := \mathsf{now}$.
4. Make the following updates for each subformula. If φ is a subformula of ψ then $\mathsf{now}(\varphi)$ is updated before $\mathsf{now}(\psi)$.
   - $\mathsf{now}(true) := \mathrm{BDD}(\top)$.
   - $\mathsf{now}(p(a)) :=$ if $p(a) \in s$ then $\mathrm{BDD}(\top)$ else $\mathrm{BDD}(\bot)$.
   - $\mathsf{now}(p(x)) := \mathbf{build}(x, V)$ where $V = \{a \mid p(a) \in s\}$.
   - $\mathsf{now}((\varphi \wedge \psi)) := \mathbf{and}(\mathsf{now}(\varphi), \mathsf{now}(\psi))$.
   - $\mathsf{now}(\neg\varphi) := \mathbf{not}(\mathsf{now}(\varphi))$.
   - $\mathsf{now}((\varphi \; \mathcal{S} \; \psi)) := \mathbf{or}(\mathsf{now}(\psi), \mathbf{and}(\mathsf{now}(\varphi), \mathsf{pre}((\varphi\mathcal{S}\psi))))$.
   - $\mathsf{now}(\ominus \varphi) := \mathsf{pre}(\varphi)$.
   - $\mathsf{now}(\exists x \; \varphi) := \mathbf{exists}(\langle x_0, \ldots, x_{k-1}\rangle, \mathsf{now}(\varphi))$.
5. Goto step 2.

At any point during monitoring, enumerations that are not used in the pre and now BDDs represent all values that have *not* been seen so far in the input. In particular, we save for that purpose the highest valued enumeration $11\ldots11$, which we denote by $\mathrm{BDD}(11\ldots11)$. This allows us to use a finite representation and quantify existentially and universally over *all* values in infinite domains.

4   Dynamic Data Reclamation

We now describe the possibility of reusing enumerations of data values, when this does not affect the decision whether the property holds or not. When a value a is *reclaimed*, its enumeration e can be reused for representing another value that appears later in the execution.

Recall that upon the occurrence of a new event, the basic algorithm uses the BDD $\mathsf{pre}(\psi)$, for any subformula ψ, representing assignments satisfying this subformula calculated based on the sequence monitored so far before the new event. Since these BDDs sufficiently summarize the information that will be used about the execution monitored so far, reclaiming data can be automated without user guidance or static formula analysis, solely based on the information the BDDs contain.

We are seeking a condition for reclaiming values of a variable x. Let A be a set of assignments over some variables that include x. Denote by $A[x = a]$ the set of assignments from A in which the value of x is a. We say that the values a and b are *analogous* for variable x in A, if $hide(A[x = a], x) = hide(A[x = b], x)$. This means that a and b, as values of the variable x, are related to all other values in A in the same way. A value can be reclaimed if it is analogous to the values not seen yet in all the assignments represented in $\mathsf{pre}(\psi)$, for each subformula ψ.

As the pre BDDs use enumerations to represent values, we find the enumerations that can be reclaimed. Then, their corresponding values are removed from the hash table, and the enumerations can later be reused to represent new values. Recall that the enumeration $11\ldots11$ represents all the values that were *not* seen so far. Thus, we can check whether a value a for x is analogous to the values not seen so far for x by performing the checks on the pre BDDs between the enumeration of a and the enumeration $11 \ldots 11$. In fact, we do not have to perform the checks enumeration by enumeration, but use a BDD expression that constructs a BDD representing (returning 1 for) all enumerations that can be reclaimed for a variable x.

Assume that a subformula ψ has three free variables, x, y and z, each with k bits, i.e., $x_0, \ldots, x_{k-1}, y_0, \ldots, y_{k-1}$ and $z_0, \ldots, z_{k-1}$. The following expression returns a BDD representing the enumerations for values of x in assignments represented by $\mathsf{pre}(\psi)$ that are related to enumerations of y and z in the same way as $11 \ldots 11$.

$$I_{\psi,x} = \forall y_0 \ldots \forall y_{k-1} \forall z_0 \ldots \forall z_{k-1} (\mathsf{pre}(\psi)[x_0 \setminus 1, \ldots x_{k-1} \setminus 1] \leftrightarrow \mathsf{pre}(\psi))$$

To take advantage of reclaimed enumerations, we represent a set of available enumerations for a variable x using a BDD $avail(x)$. Initially at the start of monitoring, we set $avail(x) := \neg BDD(11 \ldots 11)$. Let $sub(\varphi)$ be the set of subformulas of the property φ. When we are short in the number of available enumerations and thus we want to perform data reclamation, we calculate $I_{\psi,x}$ for all the subformulas $\psi \in sub(\varphi)$ that contain x as a free variable, and set:

$$avail(x) := (\bigwedge_{\psi \in sub(\varphi),\ x \in free(\psi)} I_{\psi,x}) \wedge \neg BDD(11 \ldots 11)$$

This updates $avail(x)$ to denote all available enumerations, including reclaimed enumerations. When we need a new enumeration for variable x, we just pick some enumeration e that satisfies $avail(x)$. Let $BDD(e)$ denote a BDD that represents only the enumeration e. To remove that enumeration from $avail(x)$, we update $avail(x)$ as follows:

$$avail(x) := avail(x) \wedge \neg BDD(e)$$

The formula $I_{\psi,x}$ includes multiple quantifications (over the bits used to represent the free variables other than x). Therefore, it may not be efficient to reclaim enumerations too frequently. We can reclaim enumerations either periodically or when $avail(x)$ becomes empty or close to empty.

As the BDD-based algorithm detects which enumerations e can be reclaimed, we need to identify the related data value a and update the hash table, so that a will not point to e. In particular, we need to be able to find the data that is represented by a given enumeration. To do that, one can use a *trie*: in our case this will be a trie with at most two edges from each node, marked with either 0 or 1. Traversing the trie from its root node on edges labeled according to the enumeration e reaches a node that contains the value a that is enumerated as e. The traversing and updating the trie is linear per each enumeration. The current implementation, however, uses the simpler straightforward strategy of walking though all values and removing those which point to reclaimed enumerations.

5   Example Monitor Execution

In this section we illustrate the working of the algorithm with a minimal, and yet complete, example. Specifically we execute the algorithm on formula (1) and the following trace consisting of nine events:

$\{open(f1)\},\{open(f2)\},\{open(f3)\},$
$\{close(f1)\},\{close(f2)\},\{close(f3)\},$
$\{open(f1)\},\{open(f4)\},\{write(f4,2)\}$

The formula contains two variables f and d, and we use just two bits to represent each of these, yielding four possible bit combinations per variable: 00, 01, 10, and 11. The enumeration 11, however, as has been explained, is devoted to represent *values not seen yet* in the trace during monitoring, hence with two bits we can represent three values observed in the trace at a time.

To recall previous material, the algorithm in Sect. 3 updates for each new event the now array, updating entries for innermost formulas first. References are made to the pre array when computing BDDs for subformulas containing a temporal operator at the outermost level, such as in this case the subformula $(\neg close(f) \mathcal{S} \, open(f))$. The *subformulas-first* principle is achieved by enumerating subformulas as shown in Fig. 1 (left) and use this enumeration to update the now array in the generated monitor code[2], as shown in Fig. 1 (right).

We illustrate now the BDDs generated for selected positions in the now array as the events in the above trace are submitted to the monitor. Figure 2 shows selected BDDs from monitoring the first six events, whereas Fig. 3 shows selected BDDs from monitoring the remaining three events. A BDD is either the denotation of $avail(f)$ (Sect. 4), or the contents of the now array at an index corresponding to a position in the subformula tree in Fig. 1 (left). The caption for each BDD identifies either $avail(f)$ or a subformula index, an @-sign, and the event that caused the computation of this BDD.

Recall that upon analysis of a new event, a data value in the event for a variable is mapped to one of the bit enumerations 00, 01, or 10 (in a hash table for that variable). The BDD denoted by a subformula (and stored in the now array at the appropriate index) for a single variable will represent a subset of these three enumerations, representing the set of values making the subformula true. The BDD for a variable has a unique *BDD variable* for each bit. In our case BDD variables b_0 and b_1 are used to represent the variable f, and BDD variables b_2 and b_3 are used to represent variable d. The monitoring of the trace above proceeds as follows.

Initially: Figure 2a shows the BDD representing initially available enumerations for variable f ($avail(f)$). These are all enumerations different from 11 (namely 00, 01, and 10). The enumeration 11 is the reserved enumeration representing all values not yet seen, and is the only assignment leading to leaf-node 0 (follow the fully drawn arrows).

---

[2] An additional 600+ lines of, mostly property-independent, code is generated.

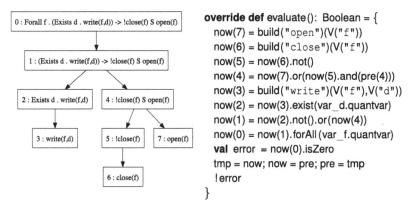

```
override def evaluate(): Boolean = {
    now(7) = build("open")(V("f"))
    now(6) = build("close")(V("f"))
    now(5) = now(6).not()
    now(4) = now(7).or(now(5).and(pre(4)))
    now(3) = build("write")(V("f"),V("d"))
    now(2) = now(3).exist(var_d.quantvar)
    now(1) = now(2).not().or(now(4))
    now(0) = now(1).forAll(var_f.quantvar)
    val error = now(0).isZero
    tmp = now; now = pre; pre = tmp
    !error
}
```

Fig. 1. Numbering of subformulas and generated monitor for property (1).

After event *open*(f1): Figure 2b shows the generated BDD for the enumeration 10 (note that the least significant rightmost bit in 10 corresponds to the BDD variable b_0 at the top of the BDD). This enumeration represents file f1, and is picked from $avail(f)$ using a SAT solver. Figure 2c shows the BDD for subformula 4 ($\neg close(f) \, S \, open(f)$). It represents the enumeration 10 for file f1, since this is the only file that has been opened so far and not closed yet, and this BDD is therefore the same as the one in Fig. 2b. Figure 2d shows the BDD denoted by $avail(f)$ thereafter, representing the set $\{00, 01\}$. Note that these are the enumerations where the leftmost (most signifiant) bit is 0, shown in the BDD as BDD variable b_1 having value 0 (the dashed line).

After event *open*(f2): Figure 2e shows the enumeration 01 allocated for file f2. $avail(f)$ is updated accordingly, subtracting 01 (now shown). Figure 2f shows the BDD for subformula 4, which now represents the set containing the two enumerations $\{10, 01\}$. This illustrates the core principle of representing a set of assignments as a BDD. This BDD is obtained by performing a BDD **or** (corresponding to a set union) on the BDDs for 10 respectively 01.

After event *open*(f3): Figure 2g shows the last available enumeration 00 allocated for file f3. $avail(f)$ is updated accordingly, subtracting 00, and now becomes BDD($\perp$) (not shown), that returns 0 for all enumerations. Figure 2h shows the BDD for subformula 4, which now represents the set containing the three enumerations $\{10, 01, 00\}$, in other words: any enumeration except 11, which is the only enumeration leading to 0.

After event *close*(f1): Figure 2i shows the BDD for node 4 after removal of the enumeration 10 representing file f1, resulting in the set: $\{01, 00\}$, which contains all enumerations where BDD variable b_1 (representing the most significant bit) is 0.

After events *close*(f2) and *close*(f3): The subsequent closing of files f2 and f3 results in a situation where node 4 is BDD($\perp$), since all files now have been

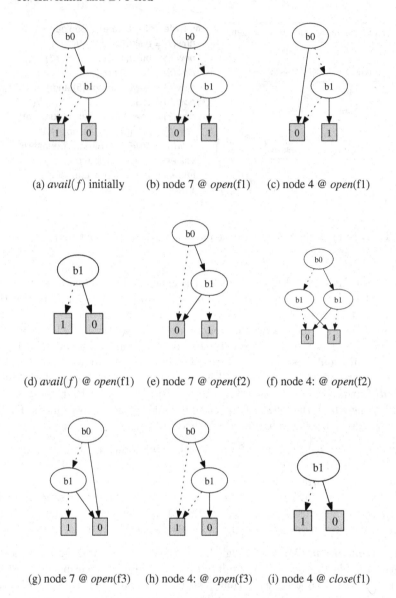

(a) *avail(f)* initially   (b) node 7 @ *open*(f1)   (c) node 4 @ *open*(f1)

(d) *avail(f)* @ *open*(f1)   (e) node 7 @ *open*(f2)   (f) node 4: @ *open*(f2)

(g) node 7 @ *open*(f3)   (h) node 4: @ *open*(f3)   (i) node 4 @ *close*(f1)

Fig. 2. Selection of BDDs computed during monitoring of first six events.

closed. Furthermore, $avail(f)$ is also still BDD($\perp$), meaning that the opening of
a new file not yet seen will cause reclamation to be initiated.

After event *open*(f1): The re-opening of file f1 is possible without data reclamation (even though $avail(f)$ is BDD($\perp$)) since the former enumeration 10 associated with f1 is still recorded in the hash table and is therefore reused. This leads
to a BDD for node 4 that is the same as in Fig. 2c. $avail(f)$ remains BDD($\perp$).

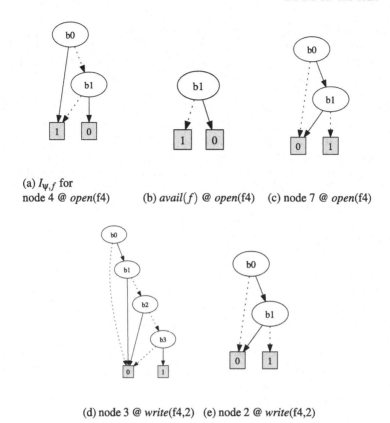

(a) $I_{\psi,f}$ for
node 4 @ *open*(f4)   (b) *avail*(f) @ *open*(f4)   (c) node 7 @ *open*(f4)

(d) node 3 @ *write*(f4,2)   (e) node 2 @ *write*(f4,2)

Fig. 3. Selection of BDDs computed during monitoring of remaining three events.

After event *open*(f4): The opening of file f4 causes data reclamation since there are no more available enumerations: $avail(f)$ is BDD($\bot$). Recall from Sect. 4 that the new value of $avail(f)$ is computed by computing the BDD $I_{\psi,f}$ of available enumerations for variable f for each subformula ψ, and **and**-ing them together with **not**(BDD(11)). We only need to compute these contributions for temporal formulas. Figure 3a shows the BDD $I_{\psi,f}$ for $\psi = (\neg close(f) \, \mathcal{S} \, open(f))$. Since file f1 was re-opened, and thereby its enumeration 10 reused, the irrelevant enumerations $I_{\psi,f}$ stemming from this subformula are all the enumerations (including the special value 11, which will be subtracted later) that are different from 10, which here is the only enumeration leading to a 0-leaf. Figure 3b shows the value of $avail(f)$ after these computations have been performed, resulting in the BDD representing all enumerations different from 10 and 11. These are the enumerations $\{01, 00\}$ (BDD variable b_1, representing the most significant bit, is 0), which now can be allocated again for new data. Specifically, Fig. 3c shows the BDD for the allocation of enumeration 01 for the new file f4.

After event *write*(**f4,2**)**:** Above we have seen examples of how a set of assignments to a single variable (f) is represented as a BDD. The writing of the datum 2 to file f4 illustrates how assignments to multiple variables, in this case f and d, are represented. Writing 2 to file f4 invokes the just allocated enumeration 01 for f4 and a new enumeration 10 for d (same procedure as for f). Figure 3d shows the BDD representing the juxtaposition of these two enumerations. BDD variables b_0 and b_1 (representing f) denote the enumeration 01, and BDD variables b_2 and b_3 (representing d) denote the enumeration 10. This BDD therefore represents the assignment $[f \mapsto f4, d \mapsto 2]$. Finally, Fig. 3e shows the BDD in node 2 of Fig. 1 after performing existential quantification over d on the 4-variable BDD in Fig. 3d. The result is obtained by removing BDD variables b_2 and b_3, and repointing BDD variable b_2's incoming arrow to leaf-node 1.

6   Conclusion

We described a BDD-based algorithm for monitoring executions of a system against first-order past time temporal logic properties. The algorithm supports automated dynamic data reclamation, removing data values when they no longer affect the verdict. The BDD data structure appears to offer advantages for runtime verification w.r.t. efficiency of monitoring, but also w.r.t. expressiveness of the logic. Although not discussed in this paper, DEJAVU supports numerical relations between variables, and, in addition to quantification over all possible values in an infinite domain, also quantification only over values seen in the trace. Future work includes support for real-time constraints, and functions applied to data values.

References

1. Allan, C., et al.: Adding trace matching with free variables to AspectJ. In: OOP-SLA 2005, SIGPLAN Notes, vol. 40, no. 10, pp. 345–364. ACM (2005)
2. D'Angelo, B.: LOLA: runtime monitoring of synchronous systems. In: TIME 2005, pp. 166–174. IEEE Computer Society (2005)
3. Barringer, H., Goldberg, A., Havelund, K., Sen, K.: Rule-based runtime verification. In: Steffen, B., Levi, G. (eds.) VMCAI 2004. LNCS, vol. 2937, pp. 44–57. Springer, Heidelberg (2004). https://doi.org/10.1007/978-3-540-24622-0_5
4. Barringer, H., Havelund, K.: TraceContract: a Scala DSL for trace analysis. In: Butler, M., Schulte, W. (eds.) FM 2011. LNCS, vol. 6664, pp. 57–72. Springer, Heidelberg (2011). https://doi.org/10.1007/978-3-642-21437-0_7
5. Barringer, H., Rydeheard, D., Havelund, K.: Rule systems for run-time monitoring: from Eagle to RuleR. In: Sokolsky, O., Taşıran, S. (eds.) RV 2007. LNCS, vol. 4839, pp. 111–125. Springer, Heidelberg (2007). https://doi.org/10.1007/978-3-540-77395-5_10
6. Basin, D.A., Klaedtke, F., Müller, S., Zalinescu, E.: Monitoring metric first-order temporal properties. J. ACM **62**(2), 1–45 (2015)
7. Bauer, A., Küster, J.-C., Vegliach, G.: From propositional to first-order monitoring. In: Legay, A., Bensalem, S. (eds.) RV 2013. LNCS, vol. 8174, pp. 59–75. Springer, Heidelberg (2013). https://doi.org/10.1007/978-3-642-40787-1_4

8. Bryant, R.E.: Symbolic Boolean manipulation with ordered binary-decision diagrams. ACM Comput. Surv. **24**(3), 293–318 (1992)
9. Colombo, C., Pace, G.J., Schneider, G.: LARVA - safer monitoring of real-time Java programs (Tool Paper). In: SEFM 2009, pp. 33–37. IEEE Computer Society (2009)
10. Decker, N., Leucker, M., Thoma, D.: Monitoring modulo theories. Int. J. Softw. Tools Technol. Transf. **18**(2), 205–225 (2016)
11. Goubault-Larrecq, J., Olivain, J.: A smell of ORCHIDS. In: Leucker, M. (ed.) RV 2008. LNCS, vol. 5289, pp. 1–20. Springer, Heidelberg (2008). https://doi.org/10.1007/978-3-540-89247-2_1
12. Hallé, S., Villemaire, R.: Runtime enforcement of web service message contracts with data. IEEE Trans. Serv. Comput. **5**(2), 192–206 (2012)
13. Havelund, K.: Rule-based runtime verification revisited. Int. J. Softw. Tools Technol. Transf. **17**(2), 143–170 (2015)
14. Havelund, K., Peled, D., Ulus, D.: First-order temporal logic monitoring with BDDs. In: FMCAD 2017, pp. 116–123. IEEE (2017)
15. Havelund, K., Roşu, G.: Synthesizing monitors for safety properties. In: Katoen, J.-P., Stevens, P. (eds.) TACAS 2002. LNCS, vol. 2280, pp. 342–356. Springer, Heidelberg (2002). https://doi.org/10.1007/3-540-46002-0_24
16. Kim, M., Kannan, S., Lee, I., Sokolsky, O.: Java-MaC, a run-time assurance tool for Java. In: RV 2001, ENTCS, vol. 55, no. 2, pp. 218–235. Elsevier (2001)
17. Meredith, P.O., Jin, D., Griffith, D., Chen, F., Rosu, G.: An overview of the MOP runtime verification framework. Int. J. Softw. Tools Technol. Transf. **14**(3), 249–289 (2012)
18. Reger, G., Cruz, H.C., Rydeheard, D.: MarQ: monitoring at runtime with QEA. In: Baier, C., Tinelli, C. (eds.) TACAS 2015. LNCS, vol. 9035, pp. 596–610. Springer, Heidelberg (2015). https://doi.org/10.1007/978-3-662-46681-0_55

Verifying Real-World Software with Contracts for Concurrency

João M. Lourenço[✉]

NOVA LINCS—NOVA Laboratory for Computer Science and Informatics,
Departamento de Informática, Faculdade de Ciências e Tecnologia,
Universidade Nova de Lisboa, 2829-516 Caparica, Portugal
joao.lourenco@fct.unl.pt

Abstract. In this paper we present *Contracts for Concurrency*. A contract for concurrency specifies the protocol to access the services provided by a software module or library. A program that respects a (well-defined and complete) contract for a module is safe from high-level atomicity violations with respect to that module. On the other hand, violations of a contract may denote errors in the program, and the application of contracts for concurrency to some real-world open source software packages did uncover a few latent bugs.

1 Introduction

The encapsulation of a set of services as software module offers strong advantages in the software development process, since it promotes the reuse of code and eases the maintenance efforts. If unacquainted with the implementation details of a particular set of services provided by a software module, the programmer may fail to identify correlations that exist across those services, such as data and code dependencies, and misuse the services and introduce bugs in the program. This is particularly relevant in a concurrent setting, where it is hard to account for all the possible interleavings between threads and their effects in the module's internal state when its services are used.

When using a (third-party) software module, a program must follow its *protocol*, which defines the legal sequences of invocations of its methods. For instance, a module that offers an abstraction to deal with files will typically demand the programmer to start by calling the method open(), followed by an arbitrary number of read() and write() operations, and concluding with a call to close(). A program that does not follow this protocol is incorrect and should be fixed. A way to enforce a program to conform to such well defined behaviours is to use the design by contract methodology [5], and specifying contracts that regulate the module's protocol. Contracts serve as useful documentation and may be automatically verified, thus ensuring the program obeys the protocol [1,3].

Concurrency brings new challenges to the definition of module protocols, as it also brings additional requirements such as ensuring the atomic execution of sequences of calls that are susceptible of causing atomicity violations. Some of these (high-level) atomicity violations are possible even when the individual methods of the module are protected by some concurrency control mechanism.

T. Margaria and B. Steffen (Eds.): ISoLA 2018, LNCS 11247, pp. 70–73, 2018.
https://doi.org/10.1007/978-3-030-03427-6_9

Figure 1 shows part of a program that suffers from a high-level atomicity violation. The schedule() method gets a task from a queue and executes it only if it is ready to run. This program contains a potential high-level atomicity violation since the method may end executing a task that was not marked as ready. This may happen when another thread concurrently schedules the same task, despite

```
void schedule() {
    Task t=taskQueue.next();

    if (t.isReady())
        t.run();
}
```

Fig. 1. Program with a atomicity violation.

the fact the methods of Task are atomic. In this case the isReady() and run() methods should be executed in the same atomic context to avoid atomicity violations. Atomicity violations are one of the most common source of bugs in concurrent programming [4], and are particularly susceptible to occur when composing calls to an external module whose implementation details are unknown.

In this paper we describe *Contracts for Concurrency* [2,6], which improves the correctness of concurrent programs by extending module usage protocols with a specification of the sequences of calls that should be executed atomically.

2   Contract Specification

The contract of a module is a protocol, and this protocol specifies which sequences of calls of the non-private methods of that module are to executed atomically. In the spirit of the *programming by contract* methodology, the specification of the terms of the contract, including the identification of the sequences of methods that should be executed atomically, is a responsibility of the module's developer.

The *Contract for Concurrency* of a module with public methods $m_1, \cdots, m_n$ is a set of clauses, each clause c_i is described by e_i, a star-free regular expression over the alphabet $\{m_1, \cdots, m_n\}$. Star-free regular expressions are regular expressions without the Kleene star, using only the alternative (|) and the (implicit) concatenation operators.

Each sequence defined in e_i must be executed atomically by the program using the module, otherwise there is a violation of the contract. Our verification analysis assumes that the contract defines a finite number of call sequences.

Example.   Consider the array implementation as offered by the *Java* standard library, java.util.ArrayList. For simplicity we will only consider the methods add(obj), contains(obj), indexOf(obj), get(idx), set(idx,obj), remove(idx), and size().

The following contract defines some of the clauses for this class.

1. contains indexOf
2. indexOf (remove | set | get)
3. size (remove | set | get)
4. add (get | indexOf)

Clause 1 of the above contract denotes that the execution of contains() followed by indexOf() should be atomic, otherwise the client program may confirm the existence of an object in the array, but fail to obtain its index due to a concurrent modification. Clause 2 represents a similar scenario where, in addition, the position of the object is modified. Clause 3 deals with the common situation where the program verifies if a given index is valid before accessing the array. To make sure the size obtained by size() is valid when accessing the array, these calls must be atomic. Clause 4 maps scenarios where an object is added to the array and then the program tries to obtain information about that object by querying the array.

Another relevant clause is "contains indexOf (set | remove)", but the contract's semantic already enforces the atomicity of this clause as a consequence of the composition of clauses 1 and 2, as they overlap in the indexOf() method.

2.1 Extending Contracts with Parameters

Basic contracts may be too restrictive because they enforce methods to always be executed atomically. However, frequently two methods may have to be executed atomically if they refer to the same data and my be executed concurrently otherwise. To incorporate this concept, Contracts were extended with parameters [2, 6].

Example. When including symbolic parameters, the above contract may be refined as:

1. contains(X) indexOf(X)
2. X=indexOf(_) (remove(X) | set(X,_) | get(X))
3. X=size() (remove(X) | set(X,_) | get(X))
4. add(X) (get(X) | indexOf(X))

This contract uses the underscore as a free variable, and captures in detail the dependencies between method calls, expressing the relations that are problematic and excluding those that do not cause atomicity violations, hence allowing for more concurrency without compromising correctness.

2.2 Extending Contracts with Spoilers

Some sequences of method calls from the module's API may need to be executed atomically with respect to some well identified methods, while with some others they do not. For example, the clause contains indexOf states that this sequence of calls must always be executed atomically (w.r.t. methods of the given module), regardless of which methods the other threads are executing. Interleaving a thread executing this sequence with another one is thus a contract violation regardless of whether the other thread executes remove or get, not distinguishing that the former is harmful while the latter is not.

Contract spoilers [2] address the above problem by allowing to express in which context the contract clauses shall be enforced. For that, each clause of the basic contract (a *target*) is coupled with a set of *spoilers* that restrict its application. A spoiler represents a set of sequences of methods that may violate its target. Client programs must then ensure that each target is executed atomically w.r.t. its spoilers, whenever executed on the same object. For the target clause contains indexOf, a possible spoiler is remove, and the extended clause would be: contains indexOf ⤳ remove.

Example. The basic contract for `java.util.ArrayList` extended with parameters and spoilers is:

1. `contains(X) indexOf(X)` ⤳ `remove(_)`
2. `X=indexOf(_) ( remove(X) | set(X,_) | get(X) )` ⤳ `remove(_) | add(_) | set(X,_)`
3. `X=size() ( remove(X) | set(X,_) | get(X) )` ⤳ `remove(_)`
4. `add(X) ( get(X) | indexOf(X) )` ⤳ `remove(_) | set(X,_)`

3 Conclusions

The *Contracts for Concurrency* may be validated statically or dynamically [2,6]. Experiments with applying these Contracts in real-world programs resulted in identifying multiple atomicity violations in production open-source softwares such as Tomcat[1], Derby[2], Cassandra[3], Chromium-1 (version 6.0.472.35). Both, the automatic generation of Contracts for Concurrency and their extension to address other concurrency issues are current ongoing work.

Acknowledgments. This paper describes work that was developed in collaboration with other colleagues from NOVA University Lisbon and Brno University of Technology [2,6]. This work was partially supported by NOVA LINCS (UID/CEC/ 04516/2013) and the National Science Foundation (FCT/MEC) in the framework of the HiPsTr research project (02/SAICT/2017–032456).

References

1. Cheon, Y., Perumandla, A.: Specifying and checking method call sequences of Java programs. Softw. Qual. Control. **15**(1), 7–25 (2007)
2. Dias, R.J., et al.: Verifying concurrent programs using contracts. In: 2017 IEEE International Conference on Software Testing, Verification and Validation (ICST), pp. 196–206, March 2017
3. Hurlin, C.: Specifying and checking protocols of multithreaded classes. In: Proceedings of the 2009 ACM Symposium on Applied Computing, SAC 2009, pp. 587–592. ACM, New York (2009)
4. Lu, S., Park, S., Seo, E., Zhou, Y.: Learning from mistakes: a comprehensive study on real world concurrency bug characteristics. SIGPLAN Not. **43**(3), 329–339 (2008)
5. Meyer, B.: Applying "design by contract". Computer **25**(10), 40–51 (1992)
6. Sousa, D.G., Dias, R.J., Ferreira, C., Lourenço, J.M.: Preventing atomicity violations with contracts. arXiv preprint arXiv:1505.02951, May 2015

---

[1] https://issues.apache.org/bugzilla/show_bug.cgi?id=56784.

[2] https://issues.apache.org/jira/browse/DERBY-6679.

[3] https://issues.apache.org/jira/browse/CASSANDRA-7757.

Formal Methods in Industrial Practice - Bridging the Gap

Formal Methods in Industrial Practice - Bridging the Gap (Track Summary)

Michael Felderer[1,2], Dilian Gurov[3], Marieke Huisman[4(✉)], Björn Lisper[5], and Rupert Schlick[6]

[1] University of Innsbruck, Innsbruck, Austria
[2] Blekinge Institute of Technology, Karlskrona, Sweden
[3] KTH Royal Institute of Technology, Stockholm, Sweden
[4] University of Twente, Enschede, The Netherlands
m.huisman@utwente.nl
[5] Mälardalen University, Västerås, Sweden
[6] AIT Austrian Institute of Technology, Seibersdorf, Austria

1 Motivation and Goals

Already for many decades, formal methods are considered to be the way forward to help the software industry to make more reliable and trustworthy software. However, despite this strong belief, and many individual success stories, no real change in industrial software development seems to happen. In fact, the software industry is moving fast forward itself, and the gap between what formal methods can achieve, and the daily software development practice does not seem to get smaller (and might even be growing).

In the past, numerous recommendations have already been made and studies performed on how to develop formal methods research in order to close the gap (e.g., [3,5–7,9,13,17]) between research and industrial practice, which also exists in other areas of software engineering like testing [10]. This track had the goal to investigate why the gap between research and industrial practice nevertheless still exists for formal methods, and what steps can be taken by the formal methods research community to bridge it.

The track consisted of three sessions of three speakers of 30 min each, followed by a 90 min closing discussion. We invited speakers that have collaborated with industry, and asked them for their experiences and recommendations on what should be done to close the gap. We also invited industrial speakers who have collaborated with academia, so as to learn from their experiences. Finally, the 4th session presented the idea to have a repository with formally verified benchmarks, to foster the industrial adoption of formal methods. During the closing discussion, we discussed the set up of such a benchmark. In addition, we also investigated if there are shared recommendations, and how we can put these recommendations into practice.

The track was in part a continuation of a Lorentz workshop in 2015, titled *Verification of Concurrent and Distributed Software: Towards Industrial Use.*

© Springer Nature Switzerland AG 2018
T. Margaria and B. Steffen (Eds.): ISoLA 2018, LNCS 11247, pp. 77–81, 2018.
https://doi.org/10.1007/978-3-030-03427-6_10

2 Contributions

2.1 Session 1: Testing and Requirements in Industrial Practice

The first session investigated current practices in testing and requirements engineering in industrial practice, and how formal techniques can help. During this session, the following papers were presented.

Peleska et al. [15] (*Model-based Testing for Avionic Systems Proven Benefits and Further Challenges*) report on the transition of model-based testing (MBT) from a widely discussed research discipline to an accepted technology that is currently becoming state of the art in industry, and in particular, in the field of safety-critical systems testing. They review how focal points of MBT-related research in the past have "survived" and found their way into today's commercial MBT products. The authors describe the benefits of MBT that are – from their experience – most appreciated by practitioners. Moreover, some interesting open challenges are described, and potential future solutions are presented. Their material is based on practical experience with recent MBT campaigns performed for Airbus in Germany.

Bardin et al. [2] (*Test Case Generation with PathCrawler/LTest: How to Automate an Industrial Testing Process*) consider automatic white-box testing based on formal methods as a relatively mature technology for which operational tools are available. Despite this, and the cost of manual testing, the technology is still rarely applied in an industrial setting. The authors describe how the specific needs of the user can be taken into account in order to build the necessary interface with a generic test tool. They present PathCrawler/LTest, a generator of test inputs for structural coverage of C functions, and describe the essential participation of the research branch of an industrial user in bridging the gap between the tool developers and their business unit and adapting PathCrawler/LTest to the needs of the latter.

Alzuhaibi et al. [1] (*Pitfalls upon Applying Model Learning to Industrial Legacy Software*) address refactoring of legacy software as one of the most common struggles of the current software industry, being costly and yet essential. They tackle this problem by applying model learning with the aim of understanding the observable behaviour of legacy components. The used technique interacts with a component in runtime and extracts abstract models that lead to better informed development decisions. The authors describe their experience in applying model learning to legacy software, aiming to prepare the newcomer for what shady pitfalls lie therein, as well as to provide the seasoned researcher with concrete cases and open problems. They narrate their experience in analysing certain legacy components at Philips Healthcare describing challenges faced, solutions implemented, and lessons learned.

2.2 Session 2: Software Verification in Industrial Practice

The second session then took the point of view of people working in software verification, and how they considered that their techniques could be used in industrial practice. During this session, the following papers were discussed.

Nyberg et al. [14] (*Formal Verification in Automotive Industry: Enablers and Obstacles*) describe and summarize their experiences from six case studies in applying formal verification techniques to embedded, safety-critical code. The studies have been conducted at Scania over the period of eight years. Despite certain successes, the authors admit to have so far failed to introduce formal techniques on a larger scale. Based on their experiences, they identify and discuss some key obstacles to, and enabling factors for, the successful incorporation of formal verification techniques into the software development and quality assurance process.

Knüppel et al. [11] (*Scalability of Deductive Verification Depends on Method Call Treatment*) address the problem of treating method calls in the context of deductive verification of safety-critical and security-critical applications applied in industry. During verification, a method call can either be replaced by an available method contract (called contracting) or by inlining the method's implementation. The authors argue that neither approach alone is feasible for verifying real-world software systems: Only relying on method inlining does not scale, as the number of inlined methods may lead to a combinatorial explosion; on the other hand, contracting is notoriously hard and time-consuming, making it economically unrealistic to be used exclusively. The authors discuss circumstances in which one of the two approaches is preferred. They evaluate the program verifier KeY with large programs varying in the number of method calls of each method and the maximum depth of the stack trace. Their analyses show that specifying 10% additional methods in a program can reduce the verification costs by up-to 50%, and, thus, an effective combination of contracting and method inlining is indispensable for the scalability of deductive verification.

Cok [8] (*Java Automated Deductive Verification in Practice: Lessons from industrial proof-based projects*) considers automated proof-based deductive verification used in industry to give confidence in the security and correctness of libraries and applications. The author presents various observations on current tools and processes based on recent experience with verification projects on industrial software, related to scalability, breadth, specification language expressibility and semantics, capabilities of underlying SMT tools, and integration into industrial build and continuous integration processes.

2.3   Session 3: Application Areas

The 3rd session investigated how focusing on specific application areas could help to make the use of formal verification techniques more feasible. During this session, the following papers were presented.

Bolignano and Plateau [4] (*Security Filters for IoT Domain Isolation*) consider network segregation as the key to the security of the Internet of Things, but also to the security of more traditional critical infrastructures or SCADA systems that need to be more and more connected and allow for remote operations. The authors believe that traditional firewalls or data diodes are not sufficient, considering the new issues at stake and that a new generation of filters is needed to replace or complement existing protections in these fields.

Larsen et al. [12] (*20 Years of Uppaal Enabled Industrial Model-Based Validation and Beyond*) review how the Uppaal Tool Suite served in industrial projects and was both driven and improved by them throughout the last 20 years. They show how the need of industry for model-based validation, performance evaluation and synthesis shaped the tool suite and how the tool suite aided the use cases it was applied in. The authors highlight a number of selected cases, including success stories and pitfalls, and discuss the important roles of both basic research and industrial projects.

Zakharov and Novikov [18] (*Verification of Operating System Monolithic Kernels without Extensions*) observe that operating systems and, in turn, applications strongly depend on monolithic kernels, and so the requirements for functionality, security, reliability and performance of the latter are ones of the highest. Currently used approaches to software quality assurance help to reveal quite many defects in monolithic kernels, but none of them aims at detecting all violations of checked requirements and providing some guaranties that target programs always operate correctly. The authors present a new method which is based on software verification and which enables thorough checking and finding complicated faults for various versions of monolithic kernels. One of its most important features is that it is not necessary to spend considerable effort for configuring tools and developing specifications to obtain valuable verification results, but one is able to steadily improve their quality. The authors implemented the suggested method within the software verification framework Klever and evaluated it on subsystems of the Linux monolithic kernel.

2.4   Session 4: A Repository of Formal Methods Examples and Experiments

Schlick et al. [16] (*A Proposal of an Example and Experiments Repository to Foster Industrial Adoption of Formal Methods*) observe that formal methods have been around almost since the beginning of computer science. Nonetheless, the perception in the formal methods community is that pickup by industry is rather low, measured by the potential benefits. As one approach to address this issue, they sketch the setup of a repository of software development problems and an accompanying open data storage to document, disseminate and compare solutions from formal model based methods. The purpose of this is to allow the industry to better understand the available solutions and more easily select and adopt one fitting their needs. At the same time, it should foster the adoption of open data and good scientific practice in the research field.

References

1. Alzuhaibi, O., Mooij, A., van Wezep, H., Groote, J.F.: Pitfalls upon applying model learning to industrial legacy software. In: Margaria, T., Steffen, B. (eds.) ISoLA 2018. LNCS, vol. 11247, pp. 121–138. Springer, Heidelberg (2018)

2. Bardin, S., Kosmatov, N., Marre, B., Mentré, D., Williams, N.: Test case generation with PathCrawler/LTest: how to automate an industrial testing process. In: Margaria, T., Steffen, B. (eds.) ISoLA 2018. LNCS, vol. 11247, pp. 104–120. Springer, Heidelberg (2018)
3. Bicarregui, J., et al.: Formal methods into practice: case studies in the application of the B method. IEE Proc.-Softw. **144**(2), 119–133 (1997)
4. Bolignano, D., Plateau, F.: Security filters for IoT domain isolation. In: Margaria, T., Steffen, B. (eds.) ISoLA 2018. LNCS, vol. 11247, pp. 194–211. Springer, Heidelberg (2018)
5. Bowen, J.P., Hinchey, M.G.: Ten commandments of formal methods. Computer **28**(4), 56–63 (1995)
6. Bowen, J.P., Hinchey, M.G.: Ten commandments revisited: a ten-year perspective on the industrial application of formal methods. In: Proceedings of the 10th International Workshop on Formal Methods For Industrial Critical Systems, pp. 8–16. ACM (2005)
7. Clarke, E.M., Wing, J.M.: Formal methods: state of the art and future directions. ACM Comput. Surv. (CSUR) **28**(4), 626–643 (1996)
8. Cok, D.: Java automated deductive verification in practice: lessons from industrial proof-based projects. In: Margaria, T., Steffen, B. (eds.) ISoLA 2018. LNCS, vol. 11247, pp. 176–193. Springer, Heidelberg (2018)
9. Davis, J.A., et al.: Study on the barriers to the industrial adoption of formal methods. In: Pecheur, C., Dierkes, M. (eds.) FMICS 2013. LNCS, vol. 8187, pp. 63–77. Springer, Heidelberg (2013). https://doi.org/10.1007/978-3-642-41010-9_5
10. Garousi, V., Felderer, M.: Worlds apart: industrial and academic focus areas in software testing. IEEE Software **5**, 38–45 (2017)
11. Knüppel, A., Thüm, T., Padylla, C., Schaefer, I.: Scalability of deductive verification depends on method call treatment. In: Margaria, T., Steffen, B. (eds.) ISoLA 2018. LNCS, vol. 11247, pp. 159–175. Springer, Heidelberg (2018)
12. Larsen, K.G., Lorber, F., Nielsen, B.: 20 years of Uppaal enabled industrial model-based validation and beyond. In: Margaria, T., Steffen, B. (eds.) ISoLA 2018. LNCS, vol. 11247, pp. 212–229. Springer, Heidelberg (2018)
13. Margaria, T., Steffen, B.: Agile IT: thinking in user-centric models. In: Margaria, T., Steffen, B. (eds.) ISoLA 2008. CCIS, vol. 17, pp. 490–502. Springer, Heidelberg (2008). https://doi.org/10.1007/978-3-540-88479-8_35
14. Nyberg, M., Gurov, D., Lidström, C., Rasmusson, A., Westman, J.: Formal verification in automotive industry: Enablers and obstacles. In: Margaria, T., Steffen, B. (eds.) ISoLA 2018. LNCS, vol. 11247, pp. 139–158. Springer, Heidelberg (2018)
15. Peleska, J., Brauer, J., ling Huang, W.: Model-based testing for avionic systems proven benefits and further challenges. In: Margaria, T., Steffen, B. (eds.) ISoLA 2018. LNCS, vol. 11247, pp. 82–103. Springer, Heidelberg (2018)
16. Schlick, R., Felderer, M., Majzik, I., Nardone, R., Raschke, A., Snook, C., Vittorini, V.: A proposal of an example and experiments repository to foster industrial adoption of formal methods. In: Margaria, T., Steffen, B. (eds.) ISoLA 2018. LNCS, vol. 11247, pp. 249–272. Springer, Heidelberg (2018)
17. Woodcock, J., Larsen, P.G., Bicarregui, J., Fitzgerald, J.: Formal methods: practice and experience. ACM Comput. Surv. (CSUR) **41**(4), 19 (2009)
18. Zakharov, I., Novikov, E.: Verification of operating system monolithic kernels without extensions. In: Margaria, T., Steffen, B. (eds.) ISoLA 2018. LNCS, vol. 11247, pp. 230–248. Springer, Heidelberg (2018)

Model-Based Testing for Avionic Systems Proven Benefits and Further Challenges

Jan Peleska[1,2(✉)], Jörg Brauer[1], and Wen-ling Huang[2]

[1] Verified Systems International GmbH, Bremen, Germany
{peleska,brauer}@verified.de
[2] Department of Mathematics and Computer Science, University of Bremen,
Bremen, Germany
{peleska,huang}@uni-bremen.de

Abstract. In this article, we report on the transition of model-based testing (MBT) from a widely discussed research discipline to an accepted technology that is currently becoming state of the art in industry; in particular, in the field of safety-critical systems testing. It is reviewed how focal points of MBT-related research in the past have found their way into today's commercial MBT products. We describe the benefits of MBT that are – from our experience – most appreciated by practitioners. Moreover, some interesting open challenges are described, and potential future solutions are presented. The material presented in this paper is based on our practical experience with recent MBT campaigns performed for Airbus in Germany.

Keywords: Model-based testing · Avionic systems
HW/SW integration testing · Scenario-based testing

1 Introduction

1.1 Motivation

Though the industrial applicability of formal verification methods has been continuously improved during the last decade, standards for safety-critical systems development – for example, the avionic standard RTCA DO-178C [31] – insist on performing tests on target hardware, in particular, HW/SW integration tests. This is well-justified, because implicit assumptions made during formal software verification about the underlying hardware and firmware may not be fulfilled by the target computer. As of today, there are no trustworthy and comprehensive formal models of complete control computers. Promising approaches cover, for example, CPU, cache, and interface bus models for the purpose of worst-case execution time calculation [17], or complex CPU models for general verification

The work presented in this contribution has been partially funded by the German Federal Ministry for Economic Affairs and Energy (BMWi) in the context of project STEVE, grant application 20Y1301P.

© Springer Nature Switzerland AG 2018
T. Margaria and B. Steffen (Eds.): ISoLA 2018, LNCS 11247, pp. 82–103, 2018.
https://doi.org/10.1007/978-3-030-03427-6_11

objectives [11], but none of them provides a *complete* computer model. Therefore, a formal treatment of HW/SW integration allowing to forgo HW/SW integration testing will remain infeasible for at least another decade.

As a consequence, methods improving the effectiveness of HW/SW integration testing are of considerable importance. According to our assessment of current trends in cyber-physical systems, the growing application complexity will make it impossible in the near future to perform trustworthy test campaigns without automating several of the crucial testing activities. Automation should apply to test case identification, requirements tracing, test procedure generation, execution, and evaluation.

We consider model-based testing (MBT) as one of the most promising methods allowing for this higher degree of test automation. At the same time, we deem MBT to be able to maintain adequate test strength in presence of increasing application complexity.

1.2 Contributions

In this paper, we review some of the most important research areas of MBT during the last decade and point out how they have become key enablers for tool-supported MBT in practice. It is a suitable point in time for such a review, because several major key players in several application domains currently shift their development, verification, and validation processes towards model-based systems engineering (MBSE). This assessment is based on our own experiences with verification and validation of safety-critical systems in the avionic, automotive, and railway domains.

We describe several aspects of MBT that are regarded to be the main benefits from the practitioner's perspective. Moreover, an open problem is described, concerning the automated model-based construction of effective test cases for given requirements. A solution to this challenge is proposed, and we expect that this will help to make MBT even more effective for industrial application in the future.

Examples are provided from "real-world" projects performed by Verified Systems International for Airbus during HW/SW integration test campaigns for the cabin communication system and the smoke detection control system.

Technical, tool-related aspects are highlighted using our MBT product RT-Tester. Following the taxonomy proposed in [33], this tool operates with deterministic, timed, discrete, transition-based input-output model specifications represented in SysML [24]. The test generation can be based on model coverage criteria, requirements coverage, as well as on user-defined symbolic test cases specified as LTL formulas. Concrete test data for symbolic test cases is calculated using an SMT constraint solver [28]. Test execution is offline, this means that the test data to be passed to the SUT is calculated before the test execution. This is adequate for SUTs from the safety-critical systems domain, where deterministic behavior is expected and tests need to be repeatable without changing the data between executions.

It should be emphasized that there is a growing number of MBT tools whose maturity is adequate for practical application in an industrial context: in several aspects, RT-Tester competes with tools like Rational Test Conductor and Automated Test Generator[1], the TGV tool integrated with TORX [4], and UppAal-TRON [19]. Each of these tools has its unique selling points, but they adhere to the same model-based testing paradigm, where models specify the expected behavior of the SUT, test cases are identified in the model using some auxiliary information, and concrete test data are calculated using model checking methods for witness generation or SMT constraint solvers. We have named these three tools explicitly, because we are aware of their functionality and of their suitability for application in industrial-scale projects[2].

1.3   Terminology

When using the term MBT in the context of this paper, this is understood in the following sense. A *test model* is developed specifying the expected behavior of the SUT, as far as observable on the interfaces of a *hardware-in-the-loop (HiL)* testing environment. The tests are black-box, so the internal model structure will just represent a functional decomposition of the applications to be tested and not necessarily reflect the internal SUT design. The test model is used to automatically identify test cases, calculate concrete test data, and generate test procedures running the test cases against the SUT. This includes the generation of *test oracles* checking the SUT responses observed against the expected behavior encoded in the model.

It should be noted that MBT also comprises a complementary approach, where models represent testing activities and/or test cases and steps to be performed against an SUT. We refer to [21,22] as an example of an industrial-strength tool following this paradigm. This paradigm, however, will not be considered further for the rest of this paper.

Following the terminology of the avionics software development standard RTCA DO-178C [31, p. 117], *a test case is a set of test inputs, execution conditions, and expected results developed for a particular objective, such as to exercise a particular program path or to verify compliance with a specific requirement.* Note that in our context, test inputs are usually traces of input vectors to be passed to the SUT at specific points in time during the test execution. Furthermore, the expected results are typically not specified on a per-test case basis, because an executable version of the test model can be run as a test oracle in back-to-back fashion to the SUT during test execution, checking the SUT reactions in dependency of the inputs.

Just as software test case executions result in a certain code coverage, we use the term *model coverage* to be achieved by an MBT test case execution.

---

[1] See https://www.ibm.com/support/knowledgecenter/SSB2MU_8.2.1/com.btc.tcatg. user.doc/topics/com.btc.tcatg.user.doc.html and ftp://public.dhe.ibm.com/software/ uk/itsolutions/innovate2013/12.00_Udo_Brockmeyer-003.pdf.

[2] A more extensive list of MBT tools is given in http://mit.bme.hu/~micskeiz/pages/ modelbased_testing.html#tools.

The timed trace of input vectors associated with a test case, when simulated in the test model, leads to a model execution covering certain external and internal model interfaces, as well as states and transitions in concurrent timed state machines. Formally, mode executions can be interpreted as the computations of Kripke structures [25]. Each computation step consists of a state valuation function indicating the values of interfaces and internal model variables and specifying the state machine control states each concurrent machine resides in. In analogy to code coverage metrics, various measures for *model coverage* exists. As an example, we mention *transition coverage* which gives the percentage of state machine transitions covered by a test suite, when executing its test cases against the model. A detailed overview of coverage metrics for models can be found in [25, 35].

A *test procedure* is an executable unit in the HiL environment which drives one or more concrete test cases against the SUT, at the same time checking the SUT responses against the expected ones specified in the test model.

1.4   Overview

A case study derived from a real-world test model is presented in Sect. 2; this will be used in the subsequent sections to illustrate various aspects of MBT for HW/SW-integration testing of avionic systems. The case study is a revised version of the one originally presented in [26]. In Sect. 3, some crucial MBT-related research results of the past are reviewed. Using RT-Tester as a reference tool, it is explained how these results have found their way into today's tools that are capable of handling industrial-scale MBT campaigns. Section 4 reviews the main benefits of MBT in practice, as perceived by our customers and by the MBT specialists at Verified Systems. In Sect. 5, one of the most important open MBT challenges is discussed: the problem to generate meaningful test cases for given requirements from a test model, without having to supply too much and too complex information in a manual way about how the requirement is encoded in the model. A solution for this challenge is proposed in Sect. 6. Section 7 presents a conclusion. We refer to related work throughout the text where appropriate.

2   Case Study – Fasten Seatbelt Sign Control

To illustrate various aspects of MBT for avionic systems, a case study concerning the control of fasten seatbelt (FSB) signs is presented in this section. The study has been derived from the real FSB control function as used in today's aircrafts, but it has been reduced with respect to the input and output interfaces to be handled, and the control logic has been simplified to facilitate the presentation of various MBT features.

2.1   Interfaces

The input and output interfaces of the FSB control function, parameters, and internal model variables are listed in Table 1.

Table 1. Variables used in state machine diagrams.

Symbol	I	M	O	Meaning
p_a	p			FSB AUTO condition variant, range 1, 2, 3
p_{ea}	p			Excessive altitude (EA) handling variant for FSB signs, range 0 (no EA handling for FSB signs), 1 (FSB signs are switched on when EA is active)
C	•			Cockpit switch for FSB signs, range 0 (FSB signs OFF), 1 (ON), 2 (AUTO)
EA	•			Excessive altitude (i.e., cabin decompression) is active, range 0 (false), 1 (true)
EM	•			Emergency mode active (normal power unavailable), range 0 (false), 1 (true)
ESG	•			Engine shutdown & aircraft on ground, range 0 (false), 1 (true)
L	•			Nose landing gear down & locked, range 0 (false), 1 (true)
S_1	•			Slats 1 extended, range 0 (false), 1 (true)
S_2	•			Slats 2 extended, range 0 (false), 1 (true)
a		•		AUTO condition active, range 0 (false), 1 (true)
f		•		FSB ON condition active, range 0 (false), 1 (true)
SC			•	System startup completed, range 0 (false), 1 (true)
F			•	Fasten seatbelts signs are switched on, range 0 (off), 1 (on), 2 (undefined)

I: p = configuration parameter (regarded as constant input)
I: • = Input variable
M: Internal model variable
O: Output variable

The main input is the FSB cockpit switch C which is used to switch the signs on (switch position 1) or off (position 0). In switch position 2 (so-called AUTO position), the FSB signs are switched automatically on or off, depending on further inputs L, S_1, S_2, and ESG signaling the status of the nose landing gears, slats 1 and 2, and the engine status in conjunction with on-ground status of the aircraft, respectively. The normal control logic can be overridden by the occurrence of the excessive altitude condition (input EA) or by the loss of normal power (input EM).

The SUT outputs considered during FSB-related tests are represented by variables SC indicating that the SUT is in the operative state and F indicating whether the FSB signs are to be switched on. Output F is an abstraction of the status of all FSB signs which are connected to a peripheral bus and need to be controlled by sending ON/OFF commands to all device addresses where FSB signs are deployed. Since all FSB signs are switched synchronously, the test model just uses one variable aggregating their state. A subordinate software layer of the test engine monitors the individual device states and aggregates the concrete bus commands associated with FSB devices to outputs 0 (all FSB signs off), 1 (all on), or to value 2 (undefined) as long as the FSB signs are in inconsistent states.

The control logic for FSB signs depends on two configuration parameters p_a and p_{ea} which may be set only once at system startup and remain constant during the whole SUT execution. Parameter p_a has 3 different values determining the variant how FSB signs are automatically switched on or off while the cockpit switch is in the AUTO position. Boolean parameter p_{ea} indicates whether the occurrence of the excessive altitude state affects the FSB control logic or not.

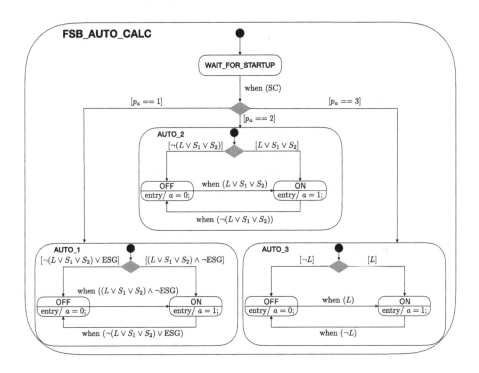

Fig. 1. State machine calculating the auto condition.

2.2 Functional Model

The FSB control functionality is modeled by three concurrent, interacting state machines depicted in Figs. 1, 2, and 3. The first machine decides whether the condition for switching signs automatically on holds and records the decision in internal variable a (see Table 1). The second decides whether FSB signs should be switched on and records this decision in the model variable f. The decision is based on inputs C and EA, and on the AUTO condition a. The third machine actually writes to the FSB control output F; the output value depends on the current value of f and the state of the EM input.

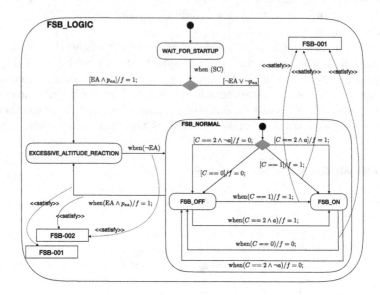

Fig. 2. State machine modeling the FSB ON/OFF logic.

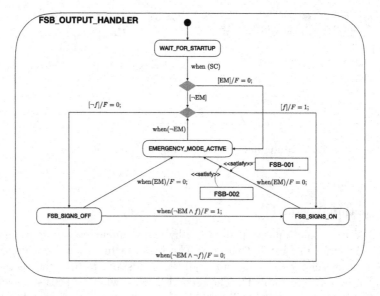

Fig. 3. State machine modeling the FSB output handler logic, taking the emergency mode into account.

The state machines shown adhere to UML/SysML syntax as defined in [24]. The *change event* when(c) occurs when a Boolean condition c switches from `false` to `true`. The transitions emanating from transient choice pseudo states are labelled with *guard conditions* in square brackets, determining the transition to be followed.

FSB AUTO Function. The FSB AUTO condition depends on a parameter p_a, since different airlines prefer specific variants of the automatic switch function; this is modeled by the state machine shown in Fig. 1. The machine sets the internal model variable a to 1 if and only if the AUTO condition holds. When p_a equals 1, signs shall be automatically switched on if the aircraft is not on ground with engines switched off (ESG = 0), and the nose landing gear is down and locked or at least one of the slats is extended. With parameterization $p_a = 2$, the AUTO condition only depends on nose landing gear and slats, and for $p_a = 3$, it depends on the nose landing gears alone.

FSB Control Logic. The central control logic setting the FSB on flag f is shown in Fig. 2. If the excessive altitude state EA has no influence on the FSB control logic (this is reflected by parameter setting $p_{ea} = $ `false`), control of the FSB signs is specified completely by submachine FSB_NORMAL: the signs are switched on if the cockpit switch is in position 1, or if it is in position 2 and the AUTO condition a holds. Otherwise the FSB signs are switched off.

If the FSB control logic should take the excessive altitude state into account ($p_{ea} = $ `true`), occurrence of this state forces the signs to be switched on, regardless of the cockpit switch position and the state of the AUTO condition. When the excessive altitude state is no longer active, the FSB signs are switched again according to the rules of the FSB_NORMAL submachine.

The state machine in Fig. 2 also exemplifies how model elements can be traced back in SysML to the requirements they help to realize. In the example shown here, only two requirements (**FSB-001** and **FSB-002**) are referenced. The first one is defined as follows (the second requirement is discussed below in Sect. 5).

FSB-001. The FSB signs shall be switched on if the cockpit switch C is in position 1, and they shall be switched off if C is switched back to 0. This holds as long as the sign state is not overridden by the excessive altitude condition or the emergency mode.

Obviously, all transitions setting f to 1 or 0 due to cockpit switch changes between $C == 1$ and $C == 0$ contribute to modeling this requirement. Therefore, the transitions triggered by $C == 1$ and $C == 0$ conditions are connected to the requirement by means of a *satisfy relationship*. Its interpretation is that every model computation triggering one of these three transitions is a witness for requirement FSB-001. Moreover, the transition from FSB_NORMAL to EXCESSIVE_ALTITUDE_REACTION and a transition in Fig. 3 are linked to FSB-001, because they specify how the effect of the switch C can be overridden by inputs EA and EM.

FSB Output Handler. The state machine depicted in Fig. 3 performs the actual writes to the output interface F. As long as normal power is available (EM = `false`), output F is switched consistently with internal variable f. The occurrence of a power loss (EM = `true`) forces the FSB signs to be switched off.

3   Key Enablers for MBT in Practice

The comprehensive research on MBT performed during the last decades has provided a tremendous amount of results of high practical relevance. In this section, just four of these are discussed, because they have been most valuable for building today's MBT tools that are able to cope with industrial-scale MBT campaigns.

Symbolic Model Coverage Test Cases. Test cases are designed to investigate specific SUT properties. Since the expected SUT behavior is encoded in the test model, each test case is reflected by a model property, i.e., a (possibly infinite) set of model executions. Recall from Sect. 1.3 that an execution is interpreted as a sequence of states in a Kripke structure, each state characterizing the current value of each model interface and each internal variable, as well as the control states each state machine resides in. Model execution sets can be characterized by temporal logic formulas. For the purpose of testing, we are only interested in safety properties, because their violation can be detected by finite prefixes of infinite computations. For the RT-Tester tool, Linear Temporal Logic (LTL) is used for this purpose [9]. As a consequence, all practically relevant test cases can be represented symbolically as safety formulas from temporal logic [32]. A concrete test case is just a finite solution of such a formula. The admissible solutions need to fulfill the side condition that they must be extensible to infinite executions of the model. This induces a symbolic representation of each test case as a formula

$$\text{TestCase} \equiv I(s_0) \wedge \bigwedge_{i=1}^{k} \Phi(s_{i-1}, s_i) \wedge G(s_0, \ldots, s_k) \tag{1}$$

which is well-known from bounded model checking [3]. Here, $I(s_0)$ specifies the initial model state, and Φ is the model's transition relation. $G(s_0, \ldots, s_k)$ is a first-order representation of the LTL formula φ specifying the property to be tested and interpreted on the finite state sequence $s_0, \ldots, s_k$ as described in [3].

Model coverage test cases specify conditions to cover a certain model element during a test execution. Though we will discuss in Sect. 5 below that these test cases do not always result in tests of satisfactory strength, they have the considerable advantage that they can be automatically derived from the model.

Example 1. The model coverage goal *"cover the transition from* FSB_ON *to* FSB_OFF *labelled by change event* $C == 0$*"* in submachine FSB_NORMAL can be specified in LTL as

$$\mathbf{F}\big(\text{FSB\_ON} \wedge C = 0 \wedge (\neg \text{EA} \vee \neg p_{ea})\big)$$

The finally operator **F** admits any computation that visits state FSB_ON and lets condition $C == 0$ become true while in this state. Note that state FSB_ON can never be entered while condition $C == 0$ is fulfilled. Therefore, $\mathbf{F}(\text{FSB\_ON} \wedge C = 0)$ really specifies the occurrence of the change event *"while in* FSB_ON, *C changes from a non-zero value to zero"*.

The condition $(\neg EA \vee \neg p_{ea})$ ensures that the transition is really taken and not overridden by the occurrence of excessive altitude, leading to a high-level transition into EXCESSIVE_ALTITUDE_REACTION.   □

Automated Test Data Calculation. From a solution of (1), the sequence of input vectors $s_i(\boldsymbol{x}), i = 0, \ldots, k$, together with their input time stamps $s_i(t), i = 0, \ldots, k$ is extracted. Model parameters are encoded in the transition relation as special inputs p satisfying $s_i(p) = s_{i-1}(p), i = 1, \ldots, k$. This implies that they can be set only once as the very first input and remain constant throughout the remaining execution. For the solution of formula (1), RT-Tester uses an SMT solver that is capable of handling transition relations of typical test models as they occur in avionic systems [28]. Other tools obtain concrete test data by means of the witness generators of global model checking tools [10].

Automated Test Procedure Generation. The concrete test data obtained when solving the constraints specified by a symbolic test case can be executed against the SUT by means of a test procedure. Using typical model-to-text transformations which are well-known from code generation in model-driven development (see, e.g., [2]), one or more concrete test cases can be transformed into a test procedure to be executed against the SUT. In RT-Tester, the procedure also executes the test oracles obtained from the model as separate threads, such that all SUT responses are continuously checked against the responses expected according to the model.

Replay. With a test model at hand, it is helpful to be able to compare an *observed* test execution to the *expected* execution specified by the model. During such a *replay*, the inputs of the test execution are used as inputs to a model simulation, and the outputs observed are compared to the outputs expected according to the simulation. The replay function provides several important capabilities. (1) It supports debugging of failed test executions by allowing to compare the observed data to the computation expected according to the model. (2) It supports tool qualification (see [5] for more details about this topic). (3) It allows for the identification of additional test cases that have been covered during the test execution, without specifying them explicitly as a test objective. This is achieved in the RT-Tester tool by checking whether the model executions obtained during the replay are also solutions of other symbolic test cases which had not been specified when generating the test procedure.

Test Oracles as Passive Testers. Since the test model encodes the expected behavior of the SUT, it can be transformed into a *passive tester* providing a test oracle continuously checking all SUT reactions for compliance with the expected behavior. In RT-Tester, this is achieved by generating code from the state machines of the model which runs in back-to-back fashion with the SUT during the test execution. Every input sent to the SUT is also consumed by these executable machines, and they communicate via the shared model variables. Every SUT output, however, is compared by these machines against the expected output they have calculated before, taking into account admissible latency in SUT outputs and admissible deviations of floating point data. More details about the test oracle generation process have been described in [25].

4   MBT Benefits in Practice

In our discussions with verification and validation experts from Airbus, the following characteristics of Verified's MBT technology were considered as the main advantages, in comparison to conventionally programmed test procedures.

Automated Requirements Tracing. The MBT approach allows for automated creation of traceability information, linking requirements to test cases (see more about this aspect in the sections below), test cases to test procedures, and test procedures to test results.

Automated Identification of Implicitly Covered Test Cases. When running a test procedure to execute one or more test cases, some other test cases are covered as well, because the SUT passes through states where other properties could also be checked. In RT-Tester, the replay function described above records these additional test cases and stores the coverage and PASS/FAIL information in a test management database system.

150% Models. Most avionic systems are parameterized by configuration data influencing their behavior. A so-called *150% model* covers the expected SUT behavior for *all* admissible parameterizations. RT-Tester supports the identification of SUT configurations that need to be considered in different tests and automatically generates test procedures for the required parameter combinations (see [26] for a more detailed description of this feature).

Advantages During Regression Testing. When test procedures are programmed in the conventional way, *all* of them need to be analyzed when a new release of the SUT is created due to updated and added requirements. In contrast to this, the MBT approach allows us just to change the test model. Then the test procedures are re-generated automatically for the new SUT behavior.

Efficient Verification of Verification Results. Since RT-Tester can be qualified according to the requirements of RTCA DO-178, it is no longer necessary to verify the test procedures with respect to correct implementation of test cases and checks against expected results.

Test Suite Validation in Simulation Mode. With a test model at hand, many MBT tools allow for generating a simulation of the SUT. This is exploited by RT-Tester, so that the effectiveness of a test suite can be evaluated even *before* the SUT is available. Only the requirements specifications are needed, so that the test model can be created. By creating an executable simulation from the model and injecting errors into the simulation, it is possible to assess the test suite strength by checking which of the errors are detected by the generated procedures.

Efficient Failure Analysis. Advanced MBT tools allow for an intuitive and detailed comparison of the SUT behavior observed against the behavior expected according to the model. This facilitates the analysis of failed test executions in a considerable way. In RT-Tester, this feature is provided by the replay function described above.

The MBT benefits listed in this section have been discussed in more detail in [26].

5   Challenges

A Summary of Open Problems Affecting MBT in Practice. From our practical experience, the open problems listed in Table 2 present major challenges to be overcome in order to raise the efficiency of MBT for embedded control systems in the avionic domain to the next level.

Problems 1 and 2 stated in Table 2 are well-known and have been extensively addressed in the MBT literature. It is interesting to note, however, that Problem 3 has not been identified in the survey articles [23, 30, 33]: there, the problem of finding constraint solvers or counter example generators with sufficient performance has been regarded as the main challenge. From our experience, however, the latter problem can be regarded to be solved for a large portion of today's test models typically encountered in embedded systems testing. Moreover, the Problems 4 and 5 have not been addressed in any of these surveys. Our interpretation of this fact is that now, since more feedback from industrial-scale MBT projects is available, new challenges become visible. Finally, it is very encouraging to note that several risks and open problems listed in [23, 30] have been adequately solved during the last years.

Problem Statement. In the remainder of this paper, we will discuss Problem 3 (*Meaningful test scenarios*) in more detail. This challenge is induced by the necessity to perform selective, requirements-based testing in most testing campaigns, instead of executing *all* tests suggested by an MBT strategy. Though a complete model encodes all functional requirements by structural and behavioral model elements, the identification of requirements in models is a non-trivial matter. In particular, conventional model coverage criteria (e.g., transition coverage) result in test strength that strongly depends on the syntactic model representation [14]. As a consequence, their requirements coverage may be very weak, if the model

Table 2. Open problems affecting MBT for embedded control systems in practice.

No.	Problem	Description	See
1.	Efficient and correct modeling	Creating test models with sufficient detail to serve as a basis for both test data generation and verification of expected results requires considerable effort. Moreover, the quality of the models is crucial for the quality of the test suites to be generated. Finally, the creation of good test models requires higher expertise than, for example, programming simple test procedures in a script language	[23,30]
2.	Configuration testing	Selection of meaningful parameter settings for testing configurable embedded control systems presents a big challenge, because the parameter space is usually too big to be enumerated for all possible combinations. This problem is often discussed in the context of product line testing and combinatorial testing	[18,20,26,33]
3.	Meaningful test scenarios	Calculating concrete test data by means of constraint solvers or as counter-examples from a model checker does not necessarily lead to timed input traces for the SUT which are considered as "typical normal behavior". On the contrary, without further guidance, generators will often produce test data that rather represent robustness tests or lack test strength (see Example 2 below). Therefore, methods to provide guiding constraints without unduly increasing the manual test data generation effort are required	[6,26]
4.	Interface abstraction	If the SUT controls a very large number of peripheral elements (e.g., all fasten seatbelt signs in an aircraft), it is cumbersome to represent all of these interfaces explicitly in the test model. Instead, *interface abstractions* are needed to represent classes of peripherals with equivalent state. For test oracles generated from the model, this introduces further complications if the abstraction is a *relation* between concrete interfaces states and abstracted ones, and not a simple mapping. In the case of a relation, a concrete state can be associated with several abstract interface states, and the oracle needs additional guidance about which abstract state to expect	[6]
5.	Oracles for hybrid systems	For systems combining time-discrete with time-continuous behavior, test oracles need to take into account admissible deviations which may occur both in the time and in the value domain	[1]

has an unsuitable syntactic representation. Only the so-called *complete* testing strategies[3] guarantee adequate requirements coverage, at the cost of large test suite sizes [13].

To illustrate this challenge, consider the following example. It shows that tests generated to achieve model coverage may result in weak test cases for the associated requirements, because the choice of test data made by the constraint solver to cover the required model elements will not always be the best for checking the associated requirements.

Example 2. Consider the requirement

FSB-002. Whenever excessive altitude occurs (EA = 1) and the excessive altitude reaction for FSB has been configured (p_{ea} = 1), the FSB signs are activated until the excessive altitude situation no longer applies or the emergency mode (EM = 1) is entered.

Formally, this requirement may be adequately captured by the LTL formulas

$$\mathbf{G}\big(\mathrm{SC} \wedge \mathrm{EA} \wedge p_{ea} \Rightarrow \mathbf{X}(f\mathbf{W}\neg\mathrm{EA})\big) \tag{2}$$

$$\mathbf{G}\big(f \Rightarrow \mathbf{X}(F\mathbf{W}(\mathrm{EM} \vee \neg f))\big) \tag{3}$$

Formula (2) states that if the FSB controller is active and excessive altitude occurs and is configured, the model variable f will be set to 1 and keep this value at least until the excessive altitude situation no longer applies.[4] Formula (3) states that whenever f is 1, the FSB signs will be switched on ($F = 1$) until the emergency mode occurs (EM = 1) or f is set back to 0.

If a test is generated from the model which just covers the transitions between EXCESSIVE_ALTITUDE_REACTION and hierarchic state FSB_NORMAL in state machine FSB_LOGIC, the constraint solver may come up with the following solution.

1. Set EA = 1; p_{ea} = 1; C = 1; EM = 0;
2. After some wait time, set EA = 0;

This test is certainly valid for the excessive altitude reaction, but it is quite weak because the cockpit switch C is kept in the ON position throughout the test: It cannot be decided whether the occurrence of excessive altitude or the FSB ON command from the cockpit has caused the activation of FSB signs.   □

---

[3] A test suite is complete with respect to a given reference model M, conformance relation $\leq$, and fault domain $\mathcal{D}$, if (1) every implementation conforming to M passes all test cases, and (2) every implementation whose behavior is reflected by a model M' in the fault domain $\mathcal{D}$ fails at least one test case in the suite if M' does not conform to M. The fault domain $\mathcal{D}$ contains a (possibly infinite) set of models that may or may not conform to the reference model. In black-box testing, completeness can only be guaranteed under the assumption that the true SUT behavior is captured by one of the models in $\mathcal{D}$.

[4] Formula $\psi_1\mathbf{W}\psi_2$ uses the *weak until operator* which states that ψ_1 will hold until ψ_2 holds, but it is not guaranteed that ψ_2 will ever become true. In this case, ψ_1 will always hold, so $\psi_1\mathbf{W}\mathtt{false} \equiv \mathbf{G}\psi_1$.

Discussion of Existing Solutions. The challenge stated above is quite well-known, and several solutions have been suggested and also implemented in tools.

Observer State Machines. Safety requirements may be expressed by so-called *observers* (also called *test automata*) that are inserted into the model as concurrent components. They monitor inputs, outputs and internal state changes and transit to a final state COVERED indicating requirements coverage, as soon as the model executions observed are suitable witnesses for the requirements [16]. With the help of an observer, requirements coverage has been transformed into a reachability problem, and test generation for a requirement can always be expressed by the goal $\mathbf{F}(\text{COVERED})$.

The test generation technique based on observers is well-established, and it is integrated in many model checking and testing tools, including RT-Tester. However, the creation of the test automata requires additional effort, on top of the effort required for developing the original test model.

Fine-Grained Requirements Specification by Temporal Logic. Since requirements are reflected by subsets of model executions, they may be specified by temporal logic formulas, referring to inputs, outputs, internal model variables and control states. This has been illustrated in Example 2 above. Finding a finite witness computation for such a formula results in a test case for the requirement. By adding conjuncts to the original formula specifying the requirement, unwanted test case solutions can be ruled out. The unwanted solution with $C = 1$ in Example 2 could be avoided, for example, by adding the condition $\mathbf{G}(C = 0)$ to the formulas (2) and (3).

This technique is also well-stablished and supported by many tools, including RT-Tester. Again, the effort for characterizing each requirement as a temporal logic formula can be quite high, in particular, when it comes to excluding unwanted solutions.

Test Scenario Specifications. A third option to create requirements-specific tests is to specify *test scenarios*[5], where test engineers use their expertise to restrict the potential solutions for covering a requirement to the "expressive and interesting" ones. As a result, the constraint solver's degrees of freedom are restricted, so that it comes up with appropriate solutions.

Again, this technique is supported by tools like RT-Tester, but it should only be used for situations where special expertise suggests that some "hand-crafted" test cases could be valuable. For general requirements-based testing, it is again desirable to avoid the additional effort for manual scenario development.

These considerations have led to a novel approach to requirements-based testing which is described in the next section and currently implemented in RT-Tester.

---

[5] We use the term *test scenario* to denote a composite test case, exercising a larger fragment of SUT functionality in end-to-end fashion. Typically, a test scenario comprises several model coverage test cases in a specific order.

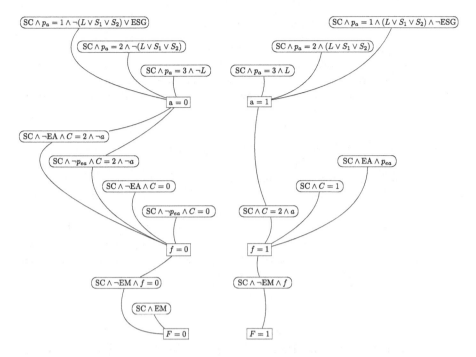

Fig. 4. Data flow analysis graph derived from the FSB application model.

6   A New Approach to Automated Requirements-Based Test Generation

As described in Sect. 2, requirements can be linked to SysML model elements with low effort. Just covering the model elements associated with each requirement, however, will often lead to weak test cases for the requirement under consideration, as illustrated in Example 2. In this section, it is explained how an approach based on static model analysis enables us to produce effective test scenarios for a given requirement *in an automated way*, exploiting the use-definition chain information and knowledge about conditional assignments obtained during the static analysis.

Static Analysis. By traversing the abstract syntax sub-tree of each state machine, the static analysis identifies all conditions leading to writes to internal model variables and outputs. This is a conventional static use-definition chain analysis across several concurrent test model components. It can be performed with well-established methods, see, e.g. [7]. For the FSB controller case study, the resulting graph is depicted in Fig. 4. Every internal variable and every output variable is listed in square boxes, together with their possible assignment expressions. In this paper's case study, the assignment are just $a = 0, a = 1, f = 0, f = 1, F = 0, F = 1$; in the general case, all assignments expressions

$$\texttt{variable} = \text{expression}(\texttt{variable}_1, \dots, \texttt{variable}_k) \qquad (4)$$

are collected. In rounded boxes, the conditions for executing such assignments are listed. For example, the condition SC $\land$ EM is sufficient to perform a write $F = 0$ or to ensure that F stays at that value. Note that in more complex models, these condition expressions may also refer to control states and timing conditions.

Requirements Annotation. Instead of using observers or temporal logic formulas to capture requirements in the model, we just need requirements annotations containing the variables (inputs, outputs, parameters, internal variables) referenced in the requirements specification. If the textual requirements specification already uses a dictionary of uniquely specified identifiers, these symbols can be directly used in the model, and the identifier extraction can be made in an automated way. Otherwise, the extraction needs to be performed manually. This however, certainly requires much less effort than creating observers or requirements specifications in temporal logic.

Example 3. For requirement **FSB-002** in Example 2, the symbols involved are EA, EM, p_{ea}, f, F.   □

Automated Requirements-Based Test Scenario Generation. We present an algorithm for calculating test scenarios that are suitable for testing a given requirement.

Inputs. As input for the automated test scenario generation, the original test model, the static analysis graph illustrated in Fig. 4, and the symbols associated with a given requirement are used as inputs.

Outputs. A collection of one or more test scenarios.

Parameter Settings. In the first step, the values of all parameters referenced by the requirement are enumerated; each enumeration induces a separate test.

Example 4. For requirement **FSB-002** from Example 2, one test is produced for $p_{ea} = 1$ and one for $p_{ea} = 0$. Unreferenced parameters can be instantiated with any value, because they occur nowhere in the use-definition chain; we choose $p_a = 3$ for these tests. In [26], a more detailed discussion of systematic configuration testing is presented. In Fig. 5, the data flow analysis graph for parameter setting $p_a = 3, p_{ea} = 1$ is presented.   □

Negation of Unrelated Conditions. In the data flow graph, unrelated conditions inducing writes to symbols associated with the requirement are negated, so that they will not affect the test of the requirement under consideration.

Example 5. For requirement **FSB-002** from Example 2, conditions containing none of the symbols EA, EM, f, F are unrelated. This leads to a further reduction of the graph displayed in Fig. 5 to the one shown in Fig. 6.   □

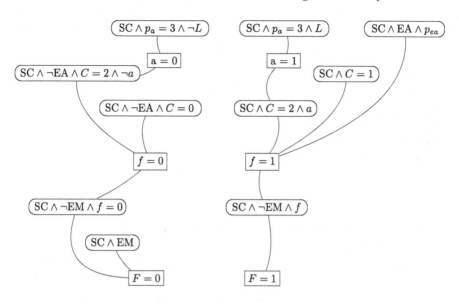

Fig. 5. Reduced data flow analysis graph for parameters $p_a = 3, p_{ea} = 1$.

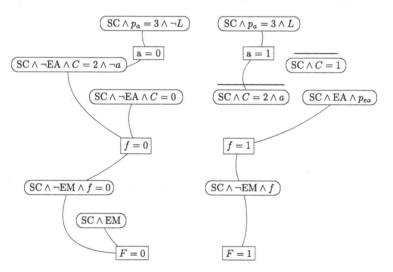

Fig. 6. Reduced data flow analysis graph, where conditions unrelated to requirement **FSB-002** have been negated (marked by a line above the predicate's rounded box).

Association of Constraints with Output Valuations. For every combination of output assignments according to Eq. (4), the applicable conditions inducing these assignments are extracted from the reduced data flow graph.

Example 6. From Fig. 6, the following constraints inducing $F = 0$ are extracted.

OFF(1) SC $\wedge$ EM
OFF(2) SC $\wedge \neg$EM $\wedge \neg$EA $\wedge C = 2 \wedge \neg L$
OFF(3) SC $\wedge \neg$EM $\wedge \neg$EA $\wedge C = 0$

Output valuation $F = 1$ induces the following constraints.

ON(1) SC $\wedge \neg$EM $\wedge$ EA $\wedge C = 0$
ON(2) SC $\wedge \neg$EM $\wedge$ EA $\wedge C = 2 \wedge \neg L$

□

Scenario Construction. Finally, the scenario is constructed by creating sequences of constraints inducing the different assignments to each output variable.

Example 7. From the formulas in Example 6, we derive a test scenario covering the conditions

$$\textbf{OFF(1)} \rightarrow \textbf{ON(1)} \rightarrow \textbf{OFF(2)} \rightarrow \textbf{ON(2)} \rightarrow \textbf{OFF(3)} \rightarrow \textbf{ON(1)}$$

Obviously, this covers all aspects of **FSB-002**.   □

7   Conclusion

In this paper, model-based testing has been reviewed from today's application perspective in the avionic systems domain. Essential research results enabling the construction of effective tools have been discussed. The main benefits of MBT, as perceived by practitioners, were described. A new solution for a major open MBT challenge concerning the automated generation of requirements-based test cases has been proposed.

We expect that in the safety-critical systems domain, there will be a growing need for novel testing strategies with guaranteed fault coverage in the near future. These so-called *complete* strategies are currently still considered as an important research field, but deemed not yet to be fit for practical application. This is due to the enormous number of test cases to be performed when using the original complete methods, as described, for example, in [8,34]. This, however, has changed during recent years with the introduction of equivalence classes and symbolic methods into complete testing methods [12,13,29]. This enables to decrease the number of tests needed to guarantee complete fault coverage in a significant way. First experiments have shown that these new complete methods are already capable to handle real-world applications in several domains [15,27].

References

1. Araujo, H.L.S., Carvalho, G., Mohaqeqi, M., Mousavi, M.R., Sampaio, A.: Sound conformance testing for cyber-physical systems: theory and implementation. Sci. Comput. Program. **162**, 35–54 (2018). https://doi.org/10.1016/j.scico.2017.07.002
2. Banci, M., Fantechi, A., Gnesi, S., Lombardi, G.: Model driven development and code generation: an automotive case study. In: Gaudin, E., Najm, E., Reed, R. (eds.) SDL 2007. LNCS, vol. 4745, pp. 19–34. Springer, Heidelberg (2007). https://doi.org/10.1007/978-3-540-74984-4_2
3. Biere, A., Heljanko, K., Junttila, T., Latvala, T., Schuppan, V.: Linear encodings of bounded LTL model checking. Log. Methods Comput. Sci. **2**(5) (2006). arXiv:cs/0611029
4. Du Bousquet, L., Ramangalahy, S., Simon, S., Viho, C., Belinfante, A., de Vries, R.G.: Formal test automation: the conference protocol with TGV/TORX. In: Ural, H., Probert, R.L., v. Bochmann, G. (eds.) Testing of Communicating Systems. IAICT, vol. 48, pp. 221–228. Springer, Boston, MA (2000). https://doi.org/10.1007/978-0-387-35516-0_14
5. Brauer, J., Peleska, J., Schulze, U.: Efficient and trustworthy tool qualification for model-based testing tools. In: Nielsen, B., Weise, C. (eds.) ICTSS 2012. LNCS, vol. 7641, pp. 8–23. Springer, Heidelberg (2012). https://doi.org/10.1007/978-3-642-34691-0_3
6. Brauer, J., Schulze, U.: Model-based testing for avionics systems. In: Havelund, K., Peleska, J., Roscoe, B., de Vink, E. (eds.) FM 2018. LNCS, vol. 10951, pp. 657–661. Springer, Cham (2018). https://doi.org/10.1007/978-3-319-95582-7_40
7. Cavarra, A.: Data flow analysis and testing of abstract state machines. In: Börger, E., Butler, M., Bowen, J.P., Boca, P. (eds.) ABZ 2008. LNCS, vol. 5238, pp. 85–97. Springer, Heidelberg (2008). https://doi.org/10.1007/978-3-540-87603-8_8
8. Chow, T.S.: Testing software design modeled by finite-state machines. IEEE Trans. Softw. Eng. **SE–4**(3), 178–186 (1978)
9. Clarke, E.M., Grumberg, O., Peled, D.A.: Model Checking. The MIT Press, Cambridge (1999)
10. Hessel, A., Larsen, K.G., Mikucionis, M., Nielsen, B., Pettersson, P., Skou, A.: Testing real-time systems using UPPAAL. In: Hierons, R.M., Bowen, J.P., Harman, M. (eds.) Formal Methods and Testing. LNCS, vol. 4949, pp. 77–117. Springer, Heidelberg (2008). https://doi.org/10.1007/978-3-540-78917-8_3
11. Hou, Z., Sanán, D., Tiu, A., Liu, Y.: A formal model for the SPARCv8 ISA and a proof of non-interference for the LEON3 processor. Archive of Formal Proofs 2016 (2016). https://www.isa-afp.org/entries/SPARCv8.shtml
12. Huang, W., Peleska, J.: Complete model-based equivalence class testing. Softw. Tools Technol. Transfer **18**(3), 265–283 (2016). https://doi.org/10.1007/s10009-014-0356-8
13. Huang, W., Peleska, J.: Complete model-based equivalence class testing for nondeterministic systems. Formal Aspects of Comput. **29**(2), 335–364 (2017). https://doi.org/10.1007/s00165-016-0402-2
14. Huang, W., Peleska, J.: Model-based testing strategies and their (in)dependence on syntactic model representations. Int. J. Softw. Tools Technol. Transf. **20**, 441–465 (2017). https://doi.org/10.1007/s10009-017-0479-9
15. Hübner, F., Huang, W., Peleska, J.: Experimental evaluation of a novel equivalence class partition testing strategy. Softw. Syst. Model. (2017). https://doi.org/10.1007/s10270-017-0595-8

16. Jensen, H.E., Larsen, K.G., Skou, A.: Modelling and analysis of a collision avoidance protocol using spin and UPPAAL. In: Grégoire, J., Holzmann, G.J., Peled, D.A. (eds.) The Spin Verification System, Proceedings of a DIMACS Workshop, New Brunswick, New Jersey, USA, August 1996. DIMACS Series in Discrete Mathematics and Theoretical Computer Science, vol. 32, pp. 33–50. DIMACS/AMS (1996). http://dimacs.rutgers.edu/Volumes/Vol32.html

17. Kästner, D., et al.: Timing validation of automotive software. In: Margaria, T., Steffen, B. (eds.) ISoLA 2008. CCIS, vol. 17, pp. 93–107. Springer, Heidelberg (2008). https://doi.org/10.1007/978-3-540-88479-8_8

18. Kuhn, D.R., Kacker, R.N., Lei, Y.: Introduction to Combinatorial Testing. CRC Press, Boca Raton (2013)

19. Larsen, K.G., Mikucionis, M., Nielsen, B., Skou, A.: Testing real-time embedded software using UPPAAL-TRON: an industrial case study. In: Proceedings of the 5th ACM International Conference on Embedded Software, EMSOFT 2005, pp. 299–306. ACM, New York (2005). http://doi.acm.org/10.1145/1086228.1086283

20. Lee, J., Kang, S., Lee, D.: A survey on software product line testing. In: Proceedings of the 16th International Software Product Line Conference, SPLC 2012, vol. 1, pp. 31–40. ACM, New York (2012). http://doi.acm.org/10.1145/2362536.2362545

21. Mohacsi, S., Felderer, M., Beer, A.: A case study on the efficiency of model-based testing at the European space agency. In: 8th IEEE International Conference on Software Testing, Verification and Validation, ICST 2015, Graz, Austria, 13–17 April 2015, pp. 1–2. IEEE Computer Society (2015). https://doi.org/10.1109/ICST.2015.7102618

22. Mohacsi, S., Felderer, M., Beer, A.: Estimating the cost and benefit of model-based testing: a decision support procedure for the application of model-based testing in industry. In: 41st Euromicro Conference on Software Engineering and Advanced Applications, EUROMICRO-SEAA 2015, Madeira, Portugal, 26–28 August 2015, pp. 382–389. IEEE Computer Society (2015). https://doi.org/10.1109/SEAA.2015.18

23. Neto, A.C.D., Travassos, G.H.: A picture from the model-based testing area: concepts, techniques, and challenges. Adv. Comput. **80**, 45–120 (2010). https://doi.org/10.1016/S0065-2458(10)80002-6

24. Object Management Group: OMG Systems Modeling Language (OMG SysML), Version 1.4. Technical report, Object Management Group (2015). http://www.omg.org/spec/SysML/1.4

25. Peleska, J.: Industrial-strength model-based testing - state of the art and current challenges. In: Petrenko, A.K., Schlingloff, H. (eds.) Proceedings Eighth Workshop on Model-Based Testing, Rome, Italy, 17th March 2013. Electronic Proceedings in Theoretical Computer Science, vol. 111, pp. 3–28. Open Publishing Association (2013)

26. Peleska, J.: Model-based avionic systems testing for the airbus family. In: 23rd IEEE European Test Symposium, ETS 2018, Bremen, Germany, 28 May–1 June 2018, pp. 1–10. IEEE (2018). https://doi.org/10.1109/ETS.2018.8400703

27. Peleska, J., Huang, W., Hübner, F.: A novel approach to HW/SW integration testing of route-based interlocking system controllers. In: Lecomte, T., Pinger, R., Romanovsky, A. (eds.) RSSRail 2016. LNCS, vol. 9707, pp. 32–49. Springer, Cham (2016). https://doi.org/10.1007/978-3-319-33951-1_3

28. Peleska, J., Vorobev, E., Lapschies, F.: Automated test case generation with SMT-solving and abstract interpretation. In: Bobaru, M., Havelund, K., Holzmann, G.J., Joshi, R. (eds.) NFM 2011. LNCS, vol. 6617, pp. 298–312. Springer, Heidelberg (2011). https://doi.org/10.1007/978-3-642-20398-5_22

29. Petrenko, A.: Checking experiments for symbolic input/output finite state machines. In: Ninth IEEE International Conference on Software Testing, Verification and Validation Workshops, ICST Workshops 2016, Chicago, IL, USA, 11–15 April 2016, pp. 229–237. IEEE Computer Society (2016). https://doi.org/10.1109/ICSTW.2016.9

30. Petrenko, A., Simao, A., Maldonado, J.C.: Model-based testing of software and systems: recent advances and challenges. Int. J. Softw. Tools Technol. Transf. **14**(4), 383–386 (2012). https://doi.org/10.1007/s10009-012-0240-3

31. RTCA SC-205/EUROCAE WG-71: Software Considerations in Airborne Systems and Equipment Certification. Technical report, RTCA/DO-178C, RTCA Inc, 1140 Connecticut Avenue, N.W., Suite 1020, Washington, D.C. 20036, December 2011

32. Sistla, A.P.: Safety, liveness and fairness in temporal logic. Formal Aspects Comput. **6**(5), 495–511 (1994)

33. Utting, M., Pretschner, A., Legeard, B.: A taxonomy of model-based testing approaches. Softw. Test. Verif. Reliab. **22**(5), 297–312 (2012). https://doi.org/10.1002/stvr.456

34. Vasilevskii, M.P.: Failure diagnosis of automata. Kibernetika (Transl.) **4**, 98–108 (1973)

35. Weißleder, S.: Test models and coverage criteria for automatic model-based test generation with UML state machines. Ph.D. thesis, Humboldt University of Berlin (2010). http://d-nb.info/1011308983

Test Case Generation
with PathCrawler/LTest: How
to Automate an Industrial Testing Process

Sébastien Bardin[1], Nikolai Kosmatov[1(✉)], Bruno Marre[1], David Mentré[2],
and Nicky Williams[1]

[1] CEA, List, Software Reliability and Security Lab, PC 174, Gif-sur-Yvette, France
{sebastien.bardin,nikolai.kosmatov,bruno.marre,nicky.williams}@cea.fr
[2] Mitsubishi Electric R&D Centre Europe (MERCE), Rennes, France
d.mentre@fr.merce.mee.com

Abstract. Automatic white-box testing based on formal methods is now a relatively mature technology and operational tools are available. Despite this, and the cost of manual testing, the technology is still rarely applied in an industrial setting. This paper describes how the specific needs of the user can be taken into account in order to build the necessary interface with a generic test tool. We present PathCrawler/LTest, a generator of test inputs for structural coverage of C functions, recently extended to support labels. Labels offer a generic mechanism for specification of code coverage criteria and make it possible to prototype and implement new criteria for specific industrial needs. We describe the essential participation of the research branch of an industrial user in bridging the gap between the tool developers and their business unit and adapting PathCrawler/LTest to the needs of the latter. We present the excellent results so far of their ongoing adoption and finish by mentioning possible improvements.

1 Introduction

In current software engineering practice, testing [3,25,27,34] is the primary approach to find errors in a program. Testing all possible program inputs being intractable in practice, the software testing community has long worked on the question of *test selection*: which test inputs to choose in order be confident that most, if not all, errors have been found by the tests. This work has resulted in proposals of various *testing criteria* (a.k.a. *adequacy criteria*) [3,34], including *code-coverage criteria*. A coverage criterion specifies a set of *test requirements* or *test objectives*, which should be fulfilled by the *test suite* (i.e., the set of test-cases). Typical requirements include for example covering all statements (statement coverage) or all branches (decision coverage) in the source or compiled code. Code coverage criteria present two advantages. Firstly, the obtained coverage can be quantified. Secondly, code coverage criteria facilitate automated testing: they can be used to guide the selection of new test inputs, decide when

T. Margaria and B. Steffen (Eds.): ISoLA 2018, LNCS 11247, pp. 104–120, 2018.
https://doi.org/10.1007/978-3-030-03427-6_12

testing should stop and assess the quality of a test suite. This is notably the case in *white-box* (a.k.a. *structural*) software testing, in which the tester has access to the source code—as is the case, for example, in unit testing. Tools for the generation of test input values for code coverage are often based on *program analysis and formal methods* for reasoning about the structure and semantics of the source code.

Code coverage criteria are widely used in industry. In regulated domains such as aeronautics, code coverage criteria are strict normative requirements that the tester must satisfy before delivering the software. In other domains, they are recognized as good practice for testing.

However, automatic tools for the generation of test inputs to satisfy code coverage criteria have not yet made it into widespread industrial use. This despite the maturity of the underlying technology and the promise of significant gains in time, manpower and accuracy. This reticence is probably cultural in part: an automated test process can be very different to a manual one and test engineers who are used to functional testing have to accept the idea that an automatic tool can generate test inputs to respect a code coverage criterion but cannot provide the oracle. It can no doubt also be explained by the very importance of the test process: businesses may be reluctant to conduct experiments in such a crucial part of the development cycle. Finally, we have to suppose that existing test tools do not correspond closely enough to the needs of industrial users and cannot easily be integrated into existing processes.

This is the gap which has to be closed in order for automatic structural testing tools to be used in an industrial setting and this paper describes how one such tool is currently being integrated into industrial practice thanks to a successful experience of collaboration between academia and industry. The present work was done in collaboration between CEA List, a research institute, and MERCE, a research center of Mitsubishi Electric. First, we describe the functionality of the main components of the tool, resulting from several years of academic research and selected by the industrial user as being the most appropriate for its needs. Then we describe the crucial role played by the research branch of the industrial user in refining the definition of the needed functionality and building the interface between the tool and the end users in the business unit. Finally, we present the benefits of the proposed solution and provide some lessons learnt from this experience.

2 Overview of the Tool Architecture

The structure of the complete business-oriented test solution is illustrated by Fig. 1. The generic test generation tool PATHCRAWLER/LTEST provided by the CEA List institute contains three main ingredients. A concolic testing tool, PATHCRAWLER, is used to generate test-cases for a given C program. The generation of concrete test inputs for a given program path relies on a constraint solver, COLIBRI. The specification mechanism of *labels* and a specific label-oriented strategy allow an efficient support of a desired test coverage criterion expressed as labels.

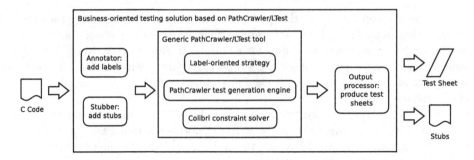

Fig. 1. Tool architecture

To adapt PATHCRAWLER/LTEST for a specific industrial context, additional modules were developed by MERCE, the research branch of the industrial partner. They include ANNOTATOR (that expresses the specific target criterion in terms of labels), STUBBER (that produces necessary stubs) and OUTPUT PROCESSOR (that creates the required test reports).

The paper is organized as follows. First, Sect. 3 presents the PATHCRAWLER testing tool and its main features. Then, Sect. 4 presents the COLIBRI constraint solver used by the considered testing tool. Next, Sect. 5 introduces the notion of labels, a recent specification mechanism for coverage criteria, and describes their benefits. Section 6 presents the support of labels in the LTEST toolset developed on top of PATHCRAWLER. The ongoing adoption of PATHCRAWLER/LTEST by an industrial partner is described in Sect. 7. Finally, Sect. 8 provides a conclusion and future work.

3   PATHCRAWLER Test Generation Tool

PATHCRAWLER [10,32] is a test generation tool for C programs which was initially designed to automate structural unit testing by generating test inputs for full structural coverage of the C function under test.

PATHCRAWLER has been developed at CEA List since 2002. Over the years it has been extended to treat a larger subset of C programs and applied to many different verification problems, most often on embedded software [14,28,33,35]. In 2010, it was made publicly available as an online test server [1], for evaluation and use in teaching [19].

PATHCRAWLER is based on a method [32] which was subsequently baptized *concolic* or *Dynamic Symbolic Execution* [11,31], i.e. it performs symbolic execution along a concrete execution path. The user provides the compilable files containing the complete ANSI C source code of the function under test, f, and all other functions which may be directly or indirectly called by f. He also selects the coverage criterion and any limit on the number of loop iterations in the covered paths as well as an optional precondition to define the test context. He may finally provide an oracle in the form of C code or annotate the code with assertions. Test generation is then carried out in two major phases.

In the first phase, PATHCRAWLER extracts the inputs of f and creates a *test harness* used to execute f on a given test-case. The test harness is basically an instrumented version of the code that outputs a trace of the path covered by each test-case. The extracted inputs include the formal parameters of f and the non-constant global variables used by f. Each test-case will provide a value for each of these inputs. This phase uses the FRAMA-C platform [18], developed at CEA List.

The second phase generates test inputs to respect the selected coverage criterion. This phase is based on symbolic execution, which generates constraints on symbolic input values, and constraint solving to find the solution, in the form of new concrete input values, to a new set of constraints. Indeed, symbolic execution is used to analyse the trace of the execution path followed when the harness executes f on the concrete input values of each generated test-case, and produce the *path predicate* defining the input variables which cause that path to be covered.

PATHCRAWLER differs in two main ways from other tools based on this concrete/symbolic combination.

Like other tools, PATHCRAWLER runs the program under test on each test-case in order to recover a trace of the execution path. However, in PATHCRAWLER's case actual execution is chosen over symbolic execution merely for reasons of efficiency and to demonstrate that the test does indeed activate the intended execution path. Unlike tools designed mainly for bug-finding, PATHCRAWLER does not use actual execution to recover the concrete results of calculations that it cannot treat. This is because these results can only provide an incomplete model of the program's semantics and PATHCRAWLER aims for complete coverage of a certain class of programs rather than for incomplete coverage of any program.

Indeed, even with incomplete coverage many bugs can often be detected, but PATHCRAWLER was designed for use in more formal verification processes where coverage must be quantified and justified so that and it can also be used in combination with static analysis techniques [12,29]. If a branch or path is not covered by a test, then unreachableness of the branch or infeasibility of the path must be demonstrated. Soundness and completeness are necessary for 100% satisfaction of a coverage criterion. Test-case generation is *sound* when each test-case covers the test objective for which it was generated, and *complete* when absence of a test-case for some test objective means this objective is infeasible or unreachable.

The soundness of the PATHCRAWLER method is verified by concrete execution of generated test-cases on the instrumented version of the program under test. The trace obtained by the concrete execution of a test-case confirms that this test-case really executes the path for which it was generated.

Completeness can only be guaranteed when the objectives can all be covered by a reasonable number of test-cases, symbolic execution correctly represents the semantics of C and constraint solving (which is combinatorially hard) always terminates in a reasonable time. Note that completeness and the verification of soundness on the instrumented code actually require symbolic execution of program features to be adapted to the target platform (compiler optimisations, libraries, floating-point unit, etc.) and also PATHCRAWLER's execution of the tests on the instrumented code to be carried out in the same environment. PATHCRAWLER is currently only adapted to a Linux development environment and Intel-based platform. The search strategy of the PATHCRAWLER method ensures iteration over all feasible paths of the program, which is necessary for completeness, for all terminating programs with finitely many paths. Programs containing infinite loops cannot be tested in any case in the way we describe here, as the execution of the program on the test inputs would never terminate. Any infinite loop which has been introduced as the result of a bug can only be detected by a timeout on the execution of each test-case on the instrumented code. Terminating programs with an infinite number of paths must have an infinite number of inputs and this is another class of programs that cannot be tested using the PATHCRAWLER method.

The second main difference between PATHCRAWLER and other similar tools is that PATHCRAWLER is based not on a linear arithmetic or SMT solver but on the finite domain constraint solver COLIBRI, also developed at CEA List (see Sect. 4). PATHCRAWLER and COLIBRI are both implemented in Constraint Logic Programming, which facilitates low-level control of constraint resolution and the development of specialized constraints, as well as providing an efficient backtracking mechanism. Within PATHCRAWLER, specialized constraints have been developed to treat bit operations, casts, arrays with any number of variable dimensions and array accesses using variable index values. The attempt to correctly treat all C instructions is ongoing but PATHCRAWLER can already treat a large class of C programs.

PathCrawler outputs detailed results in the form of XML files. These include overall statistics on the test session, including results in terms of coverage, whether the session ended normally or timed out or crashed and start and end times. For each test-case, the input values, result (according to the user's oracle or assertions, if provided, or run-time error, timeout or detection of an unitialised variable), covered path and concrete output values are provided. The result is either the verdict according to the user's oracle or assertions, if provided, or maybe a run-time error, timeout or detection of an unitialised variable. The symbolic (i.e. expressed as a formula over input variables) output values are also given. Moreover, for each path prefix which could not be covered, the reason is given: demonstration of infeasability, constraint resolution timeout, limit on the number of loop iterations, or untreated C language construction. The predicate on the input variables of each covered path and uncovered prefix is also given. In the case of path prefixes found to be infeasible, the predicate can be used to explain the infeasibility to the user and in the case of constraint resolution timeout, it can be used to determine manually the feasability of the path.

4 COLIBRI Constraint Solver

Constraint solving techniques are widely recognized as a powerful tool for Validation and Verification activities such as test data generation or counter-example generation from a formal model [23], program source code [15, 16] or binary code [7]. A constraint solver maintains a list of posted constraints (*constraint store*) over a set of variables and a set of allowed values (*domain*) for each variable, and provides facilities for constraint propagation (*filtering*) and for instantiation of variables (*labeling*) in order to find a solution.

In this section we present the COLIBRI library (COnstraint LIBrary for veRIfication) developed at CEA List since 2000 and used inside the PATHCRAWLER tool for test data generation purposes. The variety of types and constraints provided by COLIBRI makes it possible to use it in other testing tools at CEA List like GATeL [23], for model based testing from Lustre/SCADE, and Osmose [7], for structural testing from binary code.

General Presentation. COLIBRI provides basic constraints for arithmetic operations and comparisons of various numeric types (integers, reals and floats). Cast constraints are available for cast operations between these types. COLIBRI also provides basic procedures to instantiate variables in their domains making it possible to design different instantiation strategies (or *labeling procedures*). These implement specific heuristics to determine the way the variables should be instantiated during constraint resolution (e.g. a particular order of instantiation) and the choice of values inside their domain (e.g. trying boundary or middle values first). Thus the three aforementioned testing tools have designed their own labeling procedures on the basis of COLIBRI primitives.

The domains of numerical variables are represented by unions of disjoint intervals with finite bounds: integer bounds for integers; double float bounds for reals; and double/simple float bounds, infinities or NaNs for double/simple floating point formats. These unions of intervals make it possible to accurately handle domain differences. For each numeric type and each basic unary/binary operation or comparison, COLIBRI provides the corresponding constraint.

Moreover, for each arithmetic operation, additional filtering rules apply algebraic simplifications, which are very similar for integer and real arithmetics, whereas floating arithmetics uses specific rules.

Bounded and Modular Integer Arithmetics. COLIBRI provides two kinds of arithmetics for integers: bounded arithmetics for ideal finite integers and modular arithmetics for signed/unsigned computer integers.

Bounded arithmetics is implemented with classical filtering rules for integer interval arithmetics. These rules are managed in the projection functions of each arithmetic constraint. Moreover, a congruence domain is associated to each integer variable. Filtering rules handle these congruences in order to compute new ones and maintain the consistency of interval bounds with congruences (as in [20]). The congruences are introduced by multiplications by a constant and propagated in the projection functions of each arithmetic constraint.

Modular arithmetics constraints are implemented by a combination of bounded arithmetics constraints with modulus constraints as detailed in [17]. Thus they benefit from the mechanisms provided for bounded integer arithmetics. Notice that using unions of disjoint intervals for the domain representation makes it possible to precisely represent the domain of signed/unsigned integers.

Real and Floating Point Arithmetics. Real arithmetics is implemented with classical filtering rules for real interval arithmetics where interval bounds are double floats. In real interval arithmetics each projection function is computed using different rounding modes for the lower and the upper bounds of the resulting intervals. The lower bound is computed by rounding downward, towards $-1.0Inf$ (i.e. $-\infty$), while the upper bound is computed by rounding upward, towards $+1.0Inf$ (i.e. $+\infty$). This enlarging ensures that the resulting interval of each projection function is the smallest interval of doubles including all real solutions.

Floating point arithmetics is implemented with a specific interval arithmetics as introduced by Michel in [26]. Notice that properties like associativity or distributivity do not hold in floating point calculus. The projection functions in this arithmetics have to take into account *absorption* and *cancellation* phenomena specific to floating point computations. These phenomena are handled by specific filtering rules allowing to further reduce the domains of floating point variables. For example, the constraint $A +_F X = A$ over floating point numbers means that X is absorbed by A. The minimal absolute value in the domain of X can be used to eliminate all the values in the domain of A that do not absorb this minimum. Thus, in double precision with the default rounding mode (called *nearest to even*), for $X = 1.0$ the domain of A is strongly reduced to the union of two interval of values that can absorb X:

$$[MinDouble\,..\,-9007199254740996.0,\ 9007199254740992.0\,..\,MaxDouble].$$

COLIBRI uses very general and powerful filtering rules for addition and subtraction operations as described in [24]. For example, for the constraint $A + B = 1.0$ in double precision with the *nearest to even* rounding mode, such filtering rules converge to the same interval for A and B

$$[-9007199254740991.0\,..\,9007199254740992.0].$$

Implementation Details. COLIBRI is implemented in ECLiPSe Prolog [30]. Its suspensions, generic unification and meta-term mechanisms make it possible to easily design new abstract domains and associated constraints. Incremental constraint posting with on-the-fly filtering and automatic backtracking to a previous constraint state provided by COLIBRI are important benefits for search-based state exploration tools, and in particular, for test generation tools.

To conclude this short presentation of COLIBRI, let us remark that the accuracy of its implementation relies a lot on the use of unions of intervals and the combination of abstract domain filtering rules with algebraic simplifications. Experiments in [4,9,13] using SMT-LIB benchmarks show that COLIBRI can be competitive with powerful SMT solvers. In 2017 and 2018, COLIBRI was the winner of the floating point category at the 12th and 13th International Satisfiability Modulo Theories Competitions (SMT-COMP 2017 and 2018).

5 Generic Specification of Coverage Criteria with Labels

In 2014, a previous paper introduced *labels* [8], a code annotation language to encode concrete test objectives, and showed that several common coverage criteria can be simulated by label coverage. In other words, given a program P and a coverage criterion $\mathbf{C}$, the concrete test objectives instantiated from $\mathbf{C}$ for P can always be encoded using labels. In this section, we recall some basic results about labels.

Labels. Given a program P, a *label* ℓ is a pair (loc, φ) where loc is a location of P and φ is a predicate over the internal state at loc, that is, such that:

- φ contains only variables and expressions (in the same language as P) defined at location loc in P, and
- φ contains no side-effect expressions.

There can be several labels defined at a single location, which can possibly share the same predicate. More concretely, our notion of labels can be compared to labels in the C language, decorated with a pure C expression. Some examples of labels (named $l_1, \ldots, l_4$) are given in Fig. 2.

```
1  statement_1;
2  // l1: x==5
3  // l2: x==y && a<3
4  statement_2;
5  // l3: x==5
6  // l4: x!=y && a>=b
7  statement_3;
```

Fig. 2. Examples of labels

We say that a test datum t *covers a label* $\ell = (loc, \varphi)$ in P, denoted $t \overset{\text{L}}{\leadsto}_P \ell$, if the execution of P on t reaches loc on some program state s such that s satisfies φ. For example, for the program given in Fig. 2, label l_1 is covered by test datum t if the execution of the program for this test datum reaches line 2 (or, more precisely, the program location between statements 1 and 2) with a program state in which $x = 5$. If statement 2 does not modify variable x and its execution does not change control flow, label l_3 will be covered by the same test datum. However, if statement 2 can modify x or change control flow, a simultaneous coverage of both labels is not guaranteed.

An *annotated program* is a pair $\langle P, L \rangle$ where P is a program and L is a set of labels defined in P. Figure 2 shows an example of an annotated program with four labels.

Given an annotated program $\langle P, L \rangle$, we say that a test suite TS satisfies the *label coverage criterion* **LC** for $\langle P, L \rangle$ if TS covers every label of L, that is, for any label ℓ in L, there is a test-case t in TS such that $t \overset{L}{\leadsto}_P \ell$. This is denoted $TS \overset{L}{\leadsto}_{\langle P,L \rangle}$ **LC**.

Criterion Encoding. We say that label coverage *simulates a given coverage criterion* **C** if any program P can be *automatically* annotated with a set of labels L in such a way that any test suite TS satisfies **LC** for $\langle P, L \rangle$ if and only if TS covers all the concrete test objectives instantiated from **C** for P. We call *annotation* (or *labeling*) *function* such a procedure automatically adding test objectives to a given program for a given coverage criterion.

It is shown in [8] that label coverage can notably simulate basic-block coverage (**BBC**), branch coverage (**BC**) and decision coverage (**DC**), function coverage (**FC**), condition coverage (**CC**), decision-condition coverage (**DCC**), multiple condition coverage (**MCC**), **GACC** [2], as well as the side-effect-free fragment of weak mutations (**WM'**) in which the considered mutation operators are not allowed to introduce side-effects. Moreover, these encodings can be fully automated: the corresponding labels can be inserted automatically into the program under test. Similarly, labels can be used to encode other, more specific criteria.

Figure 3 illustrates the simulation of some common criteria with labels on sample code. The resulting annotated code is automatically produced by the corresponding annotation functions. For example, consider decision coverage (**DC**). It is easy to see that a test suite covers **DC** for the initial program (on the left) if and only if this test suite covers **LC** for the annotated program produced for the **DC** criterion. It is ensured by the systematic insertion of labels for all branches of the code. The encoding of **GACC** (General Active Clause Coverage) [2] is shown in Fig. 4. In **GACC**, each clause in a decision should become true for some test-case and false for some test-case. In addition, the clause should affect the decision: changing the value of this clause should change the whole decision. For example, labels named l_1, l_2 in Fig. 4 simulate these requirements for the first clause x==y: label l_1 ensures that it can become true, while label l_2 ensures it can become false. The second part of the predicates of these labels ensures that changing only the first clause would indeed change the decision.

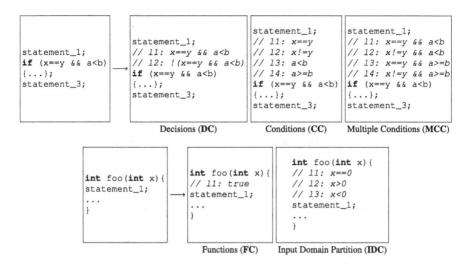

Fig. 3. Simulating standard coverage criteria with labels

Fig. 4. Simulating the GACC coverage criterion with labels

6   Efficient Test-Case Generation for Labels in LTEST

Labels appear to be not only convenient to express various testing criteria, but
also amenable to efficient support in various testing tasks. Previous efforts [6,8,
21] showed that labels can be efficiently supported during test-case generation,
coverage evaluation and detection of polluting (e.g. infeasible) test objectives.
This support was originally implemented in 2013–2014 in the LTEST toolset [5].
In this section, we detail the label-oriented strategy for test-case generation used
in the PATHCRAWLER/LTEST tool and implemented in top of PATHCRAWLER.

The label-oriented strategy is based on two main principles, *tight instrumentation* and *iterative label deletion*. They can be implemented in a dedicated
manner or used in a black-box manner on top of a Dynamic Symbolic Execution
(DSE) tool. We follow the second approach to present them here, and assume
we have an existing DSE tool used to cover program paths.

Let us illustrate tight instrumentation in comparison with a simple approach,
referred to as direct instrumentation (cf. Fig. 5). In direct instrumentation the

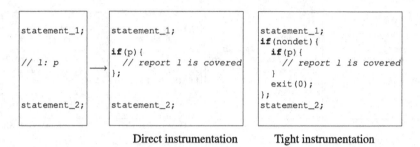

Fig. 5. Two ways to instrument a label: direct and tight instrumentation

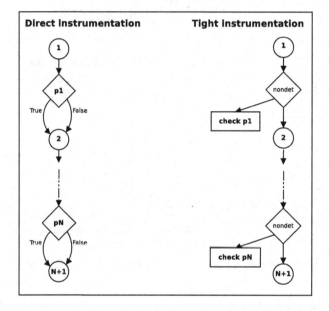

Fig. 6. Comparison of direct and tight instrumentation for a sequence of N labels

label is replaced by a conditional statement that checks the label predicate p and reports that the label is covered whenever the predicate is satisfied. In tight instrumentation, the conditional statement is reached only when a nondeterministic operation **nondet** returns true. Moreover, the execution exits after the evaluation of the label predicate, whenever it is true or not. Note that any DSE engine can simulate non-deterministic choices via an additional input array of (symbolic) boolean values.

In the resulting instrumented program, direct instrumentation leads to creating two paths[1] for each path in the non-instrumented program, while tight instrumentation makes DSE consider only one additional program path each

---

[1] And sometimes even more, if the label was inside a loop or a function called several times.

time a label is traversed. This situation is schematically illustrated for a sequence of N labels in Fig. 6. We see that tight instrumentation leads to $N + 1$ paths to be considered by DSE, while direct instrumentation results in 2^N paths.

Along with a smaller number of paths to consider, tight instrumentation brings another benefit: conditions coming from labels are added to path predicates only during the evaluation of the label predicate, while in direct instrumentation path predicates always contain conditions on previously traversed labels. Thus, tight instrumentation yields only a linear growth of the path space without any complexification of path predicates.

The main idea behind iterative label deletion is to ignore a label that has been covered while continuing the test generation session. It can be easily implemented by introducing a status for each label and considering that the nondet operation never returns true for an already covered label. The label-oriented test generation strategy is further detailed in [8].

7   Ongoing Adoption of PATHCRAWLER/LTEST in an Industrial Setting

Mitsubishi Electric is a global group having a wide range of activities from Home Products to Space Systems including Automotive Equipment, Transportation Systems, Energy Systems and many others. A lot of those products are software intensive, are developed in C language and are safety critical, like train control systems or automotive components. They thus require a high quality level, typically meeting railway EN 50128 SIL4 or automotive ISO 26262 ASIL D certification criteria. To reach such quality, extensive and diverse testing is needed. This testing is very costly, due to the effort needed to reach such very stringent testing criteria: design adequate test sheets satisfying the criteria with adequate test-cases, fill inputs and expected outputs of those test-cases, apply those test sheets on the developed code, compare actual and expected outputs, determine actual coverage, compare actual results to expected one, determine missing coverage and rework the test sheets and the code accordingly. On a typical safety critical software, 65% of the cost is due to testing and associated rework.

Mitsubishi Electric R&D Centre Europe (MERCE) is the advanced European research laboratory of Mitsubishi Electric group. From MERCE knowledge of business unit test process, MERCE identified that PATHCRAWLER/LTEST could accelerate it. More specifically given a C source code as input, PATHCRAWLER/LTEST can automatically produce a set of test-cases satisfying a coverage criterion, thus opening the door to automatic structural test generation. The only manual step is to encode as labels the coverage criterion through annotation on the tested source code. MERCE knows that to be usable by engineers, a new technology should be as automated and as integrated as possible within the existing development process. Thus MERCE decided to focus on unit testing which seems amenable to full automation. Therefore, the question studied by MERCE was simple: is it possible to design a fully automatic structural unit test generation tool that can be easily integrated into the current development process used in the business unit?

To answer this question MERCE started to evaluate PATHCRAWLER/LTEST technology, first on a few examples provided by the business unit. MERCE manually encoded a business unit coverage criterion by adding labels on the source code samples, a few functions ranging from a few hundreds to one thousand lines of code. PATHCRAWLER/LTEST was able to successfully cover all the labels, in a few seconds for small functions to a few tens of minutes for the biggest one having 2^{145} paths[2]. One interesting outcome of PATHCRAWLER technology is that it is possible to determine when a test objective (i.e. a label) is *impossible* to cover due to the structure of the code, which seemed a quite important feedback to give to the tester and potentially a crucial information to be used in a certification process.

From this first very positive step, MERCE decided to start the design and the implementation of the desired test generation solution. This solution works as follows (cf. Fig. 1): take as input the original, unmodified source code, automatically add labels satisfying the business unit coverage criterion through ANNOTATOR, automatically produce stubs suitable for unit testing through STUBBER, find actual test-cases using PATHCRAWLER/LTEST, process its output in OUTPUT PROCESSOR to produce final test sheets in Excel and CSV (Comma Separated Value) formats for human and machine use in the remaining part of the test process. MERCE developed an OCaml plug-in of about 1,500 lines within FRAMA-C to do the annotation and stub generation parts, reusing FRAMA-C capabilities to parse and modify C source code. An additional program of 2,000 lines was also written to coordinate the call to the annotation plug-in, the call to PATHCRAWLER, the parsing of PATHCRAWLER's output and production of ready-to-use test sheets.

MERCE conducted experiments with this new tool on real industrial code. This code is about 80,000 lines of C code (without headers), making about 1,300 functions to unit test distributed over about 150 files. The MERCE tool was able to parse and annotate 100% of the files, and to successfully apply PATHCRAWLER/LTEST for generating test sheets for 86% of the functions and covering about 14,000 test objectives, of which 17% are structurally impossible test objectives. The total test generation time is about 8 h on a regular PC, i.e. less than a day, taking on average 26 s per function. MERCE roughly estimated the total manual generation of those tests to 230 work days[3], therefore bringing an effective benefit factor of more that 230 for test input generation. Those very good results are very encouraging for pushing the technology in business units.

Developing such a tool requested a non negligible engineering effort from MERCE. Despite FRAMA-C providing all the needed framework, understanding and applying the FRAMA-C toolbox, moreover in the non mainstream OCaml

---

[2] Recall that path exploration stops as soon as all labels are covered.

[3] This time does not include the time to elaborate an oracle whose elaboration remains manual.

language, took some time. On the benefit side, PATHCRAWLER provides all the information needed to produce the test sheets and thus creating them was relatively easy.

8 Conclusion and Future Work

We have described an example of how to transfer new technology based on formal methods to industrial use. PATHCRAWLER is a mature test generation tool and *labels* offer an easy way to adapt it to the user's own code coverage criterion.

Several lessons can be learned from this experience. First of all, this work demonstrates that *a close collaboration between the tool developers and the industrial user* is vital. Having an efficient tool developed by a research laboratory is necessary, but often not sufficient for its integration into an industrial testing process. The role of MERCE in adapting the tool to the specific needs of the business units has been crucial.

Changing habits in an industrial process is always difficult and that is why, when trying to industrialize PATHCRAWLER/LTEST technology, MERCE focused on *a fully automated tool* that would integrate well in the current testing process. Of course such automation is done at the expense of richer functionalities: in this case MERCE focused on unit testing (while PATHCRAWLER/LTEST could probably handle more elaborate testing). And beyond the technological core, there is still a lot of mundane integration work to adapt the tool to the real process (e.g. with other tools or legacy test material) and let testers be at ease with it.

An important factor is related to *the completeness of the tool,* or its capacity to justify the absence of a test input for a given test objective. This feature can be particularly appreciated in an automated testing process since it can be very difficult (or even impossible) to achieve manually. *Soundness and completeness of the tool* are also particularly important in the context of certification. They help to rigorously justify the coverage of each test-case and the whole test suite, and to provide the certification authority with a proof of best-achievable coverage.

The performance of the tool is another crucial factor for its integration. While current speed of PATHCRAWLER/LTEST has already shown an astonishing possible increase in productivity (a factor of 230 on a real-life example), having even higher performance would allow interactive use and direct integration into developers' IDE, thus allowing even greater productivity by merging the testing phase into the development phase.

Regarding future work, extension of PATHCRAWLER/LTEST to currently unhandled coverage criteria (like MCDC) is certainly a strong requirement as those criteria are requested by standards like ISO 26262. Other examples of test criteria of interest are related to rigorous boundary testing and coverage of function outputs. Efficient support of hyperlabels [22], a recent generalization of labels to a larger class of criteria, is another future work direction.

References

1. The PathCrawler online test generation service (2010–2018). http://pathcrawler-online.com/
2. Ammann, P., Offutt, A.J., Huang, H.: Coverage criteria for logical expressions. In: Proceedings of the 14th International Symposium on Software Reliability Engineering (ISSRE 2003), pp. 99–107 (2003)
3. Ammann, P., Offutt, J.: Introduction to Software Testing, 1st edn. Cambridge University Press, Cambridge (2008)
4. Bardin, S., Herrmann, P., Perroud, F.: An alternative to SAT-based approaches for bit-vectors. In: Esparza, J., Majumdar, R. (eds.) TACAS 2010. LNCS, vol. 6015, pp. 84–98. Springer, Heidelberg (2010). https://doi.org/10.1007/978-3-642-12002-2_7
5. Bardin, S., Chebaro, O., Delahaye, M., Kosmatov, N.: An all-in-one toolkit for automated white-box testing. In: Seidl, M., Tillmann, N. (eds.) TAP 2014. LNCS, vol. 8570, pp. 53–60. Springer, Cham (2014). https://doi.org/10.1007/978-3-319-09099-3_4
6. Bardin, S., et al.: Sound and quasi-complete detection of infeasible test requirements. In: Proceedings of the 8th IEEE International Conference on Software Testing, Verification and Validation (ICST 2015), pp. 1–10. IEEE (2015)
7. Bardin, S., Herrmann, P.: Structural testing of executables. In: Proceedings of the First International Conference on Software Testing, Verification, and Validation (ICST 2008), pp. 22–31. IEEE (2008)
8. Bardin, S., Kosmatov, N., Cheynier, F.: Efficient leveraging of symbolic execution to advanced coverage criteria. In: Proceedings of the 7th IEEE International Conference on Software Testing, Verification and Validation (ICST 2014), pp. 173–182. IEEE (2014)
9. Bobot, F., Chihani, Z., Marre, B.: Real behavior of floating point. In: Proceedings of the 15th International Workshop on Satisfiability Modulo Theories (SMT 2017), Part of CAV 2017 (2017)
10. Botella, B., et al.: Automating structural testing of C programs: experience with PathCrawler. In: Proceedings of the 4th International Workshop on the Automation of Software Test (AST 2009), Part of the 31st International Conference on Software Engineering (ICSE 2009), pp. 70–78. IEEE (2009)
11. Cadar, C., Dunbar, D., Engler, D.R.: KLEE: unassisted and automatic generation of high-coverage tests for complex systems programs. In: Proceedings of the 8th USENIX Symposium on Operating Systems Design and Implementation (OSDI 2008), pp. 209–224. USENIX Association (2008)
12. Chebaro, O., Kosmatov, N., Giorgetti, A., Julliand, J.: Program slicing enhances a verification technique combining static and dynamic analysis. In: Proceedings of the 27th Annual ACM Symposium on Applied Computing, Software Verification and Testing Track (SAC-SVT 2012), pp. 1284–1291. ACM (2012)
13. Chihani, Z., Marre, B., Bobot, F., Bardin, S.: Sharpening constraint programming approaches for bit-vector theory. In: Salvagnin, D., Lombardi, M. (eds.) CPAIOR 2017. LNCS, vol. 10335, pp. 3–20. Springer, Cham (2017). https://doi.org/10.1007/978-3-319-59776-8_1
14. Dierkes, M., Faivre, A., Le Guen, H., Williams, N.: Completion of test models based on code analysis. In: Proceedings of the Conference on Embedded Real Time Software and Systems (ERTS2 2014) (2014)

15. Gotlieb, A.: Euclide: a constraint-based testing platform for critical C programs. In: Proceedings of the Second International Conference on Software Testing Verification and Validation (ICST 2009), pp. 151–160. IEEE (2009)

16. Gotlieb, A., Botella, B., Watel, M.: INKA: ten years after the first ideas. In: Proceedings of the the International Conference on Software and Systems Engineering and their Applications (ICSSEA 2006) (2006)

17. Gotlieb, A., Leconte, M., Marre, B.: Constraint solving on modular integers. In: Proceedings of the Workshop on Constraint Modelling and Reformulation (ModRef 2010), Part of CP 2010 (2010)

18. Kirchner, F., Kosmatov, N., Prevosto, V., Signoles, J., Yakobowski, B.: Frama-C: a software analysis perspective. Formal Asp. Comput. **27**(3), 573–609 (2015)

19. Kosmatov, N., Williams, N., Botella, B., Roger, M.: Structural unit testing as a service with pathcrawler-online.com. In: Proceedings of the 7th IEEE International Symposium on Service-Oriented System Engineering (SOSE 2013), pp. 435–440. IEEE (2013)

20. Leconte, M., Berstel, B.: Extending a CP solver with congruences as domains for software verification. In: Proceedings of the Workshop on Constraints in Software Testing, Verification and Analysis (CSTVA 2006), Part of CP 2006 (2006)

21. Marcozzi, M., Bardin, S., Kosmatov, N., Papadakis, M., Prevosto, V., Correnson, L.: Time to clean your test objectives. In: Proceedings of the 40th International Conference on Software Engineering (ICSE 2018), pp. 456–467. ACM (2018)

22. Marcozzi, M., Delahaye, M., Bardin, S., Kosmatov, N., Prevosto, V.: Generic and effective specification of structural test objectives. In: Proceedings of the IEEE International Conference on Software Testing, Verification and Validation (ICST 2017), pp. 436–441. IEEE (2017)

23. Marre, B., Blanc, B.: Test selection strategies for Lustre descriptions in GATeL. Electron. Notes Theor. Comput. Sci. **111**, 93–111 (2005)

24. Marre, B., Michel, C.: Improving the floating point addition and subtraction constraints. In: Cohen, D. (ed.) CP 2010. LNCS, vol. 6308, pp. 360–367. Springer, Heidelberg (2010). https://doi.org/10.1007/978-3-642-15396-9_30

25. Mathur, A.P.: Foundations of Software Testing. Addison-Wesley Prof (2008)

26. Michel, C.: Exact projection functions for floating point number constraints. In: Proceedings of the 7th International Symposium on Artificial Intelligence and Mathematics (AIMA 2002) (2002)

27. Myers, G.J., Sandler, C., Badgett, T.: The Art of Software Testing, 3rd edn. Wiley, Hoboken (2011)

28. Park, J., Pajic, M., Lee, I., Sokolsky, O.: Scalable verification of linear controller software. In: Chechik, M., Raskin, J.-F. (eds.) TACAS 2016. LNCS, vol. 9636, pp. 662–679. Springer, Heidelberg (2016). https://doi.org/10.1007/978-3-662-49674-9_43

29. Petiot, G., Kosmatov, N., Giorgetti, A., Julliand, J.: How test generation helps software specification and deductive verification in Frama-C. In: Seidl, M., Tillmann, N. (eds.) TAP 2014. LNCS, vol. 8570, pp. 204–211. Springer, Cham (2014). https://doi.org/10.1007/978-3-319-09099-3_16

30. Schimpf, J., Shen, K.: ECLiPSe - from LP to CLP. Theory Pract. Log. Program. **12**(1–2), 127–156 (2011)

31. Sen, K., Marinov, D., Agha, G.: CUTE: a concolic unit testing engine for C. In: Proceedings of the 5th Joint Meeting of the European Software Engineering Conference and ACM SIGSOFT Symposium on the Foundations of Software Engineering (ESEC/FSE 2005), pp. 263–272. ACM (2005)

32. Williams, N., Marre, B., Mouy, P., Roger, M.: PathCrawler: automatic generation of path tests by combining static and dynamic analysis. In: Dal Cin, M., Kaâniche, M., Pataricza, A. (eds.) EDCC 2005. LNCS, vol. 3463, pp. 281–292. Springer, Heidelberg (2005). https://doi.org/10.1007/11408901_21
33. Williams, N., Roger, M.: Test generation strategies to measure worst-case execution time. In: Proceedings of the 4th International Workshop on Automation of Software Test (AST 2009), pp. 88–96 (2009)
34. Zhu, H., Hall, P.A.V., May, J.H.R.: Software unit test coverage and adequacy. ACM Comput. Surv. **29**(4), 366–427 (1997)
35. Zutshi, A., Sankaranarayanan, S., Deshmukh, J.V., Jin, X.: Symbolic-numeric reachability analysis of closed-loop control software. In: Proceedings of the 19th International Conference on Hybrid Systems: Computation and Control (HSCC 2016), pp. 135–144 (2016)

Pitfalls in Applying Model Learning to Industrial Legacy Software

Omar al Duhaiby[1(✉)], Arjan Mooij[2], Hans van Wezep[3], and Jan Friso Groote[1]

[1] Eindhoven University of Technology, 5612AZ Eindhoven, The Netherlands
{o.alduhaiby,j.f.groote}@tue.nl
[2] ESI (TNO), Eindhoven, The Netherlands
arjan.mooij@tno.nl
[3] Philips Healthcare, Best, The Netherlands
hans.van.wezep@philips.com

Abstract. Maintaining legacy software is one of the most common struggles of the software industry, being costly yet essential. We tackle that problem by providing better understanding of software by extracting behavioural models using the *model learning* technique. The used technique interacts with a running component and extracts abstract models that would help developers make better informed decisions. As promising in theory, as slippery in application it is, however. This report describes our experience in applying model learning to legacy software, and aims to prepare the newcomer for what shady pitfalls lie therein as well as provide the seasoned researcher with concrete cases and open problems. We narrate our experience in analysing certain legacy components at Philips Healthcare describing challenges faced, solutions implemented, and lessons learned.

Keywords: Model learning · Active learning · Legacy software

1 Introduction

As software evolves over years and decades, its very architecture starts to change. And with the original developers unavailable anymore, and the documentation outdated, it becomes increasingly difficult to maintain that software. That is what legacy software is [19]. Not only does maintenance become a more pressing matter, but also a costly and even risky endeavor. As legacy software that has been running a business successfully for decades, refactoring it without complete understanding might lead to unexpected and severe impediments. To achieve that level of understanding, different techniques have been deployed to analyse legacy software, such as process mining [1], static code analysis [9], and our method of choice, active model learning [19].

These techniques aim to model legacy software. With accurate readable abstract models, developers can improve the software in less time, discover hidden behaviour, and generate documentation. Active model learning is a technique that aims to build a finite-state model of a system from observed input and output [19].

© Springer Nature Switzerland AG 2018
T. Margaria and B. Steffen (Eds.): ISoLA 2018, LNCS 11247, pp. 121–138, 2018.
https://doi.org/10.1007/978-3-030-03427-6_13

In practice, however, active model learning is not at all an easily realisable endeavour. As many success stories there are [2,17,18], as many pitfalls we faced in our experience applying it—pitfalls such as dealing with obscure proprietary interfaces, unclear code, and lacking documentation; ensuring the accuracy of the learning outcome; interpreting unexpected behaviour; avoiding state space explosion; and a variety of technical problems. Our contribution lies in

- identifying the pitfalls in applying active model learning,
- detailing how they manifested in our industrial setting,
- providing lessons on how to deal with them,
- and suggesting future research directions.

This work is based on our experience with applying model learning to parts of the X-ray imaging software at Philips Healthcare. We use LearnLib [7] as the core learning engine combined with necessary complementary software that we detail in Sect. 2. We first explain the theory in a simple manner, then describe our target system and the learning setup. Section 3 lays out our main contribution describing the practical experience through lessons learned and challenges faced. Then in Sect. 4, we reflect on the practical challenges with suggested future research directions and open questions. We finally conclude with Sect. 5.

2 Background

In this section, we describe the learning method and the component being learned as well as a few relevant technicalities.

2.1 LearnLib, L* and Mealy Machines

As mentioned before, LearnLib [7] is our learning tool. LearnLib houses a few learning algorithms, the most prominent of which is L*, first introduced by Dana Angluin in 1986 [3]. L* learns regular languages by asking whether certain strings belong to that language. This type of querying is not suited for reactive systems such as the ones we mostly face in the industry. To tackle that, Niese in [15] introduced a variant of L* called L^*_{Mealy} which outputs a Mealy machine such as that shown in Fig. 2.

We shall explain some basic concepts, followed by the algorithm and then Mealy machines. Refer to Fig. 1 showing the learning setup. The learner is internally composed of a model builder and a model tester. We assume that the *System under Learning (SuL)* responds to every action. The learner can send *actions* as input to the SuL and receive *responses* as output, making a sequence of action/response pairs, called a *trace*. The learner has the ability to *reset* the SuL back to its initial state and thus terminate the current trace. The learning algorithm can be summarised in the following iterative steps:

1. Building: the builder sends/receives action/response traces to/from the SuL, each trace followed by a SuL reset, to build a hypothesis model (as a Mealy machine).

2. Testing: the tester tests the hypothesis model against the SuL similarly through action/response traces.
3. Feedback: if the tester discovers an action/response pair that is not consistent with the hypothesis model, then return to step 1 (building) while using that pair as a counter example to refine further queries; otherwise, the model is verified and the learning is complete.

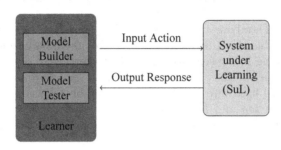

Fig. 1. High-level overview of the learning setup.

This technique requires the input actions to be defined beforehand as well as the SuL's reset routine. We call the set of all admissible input actions the *input alphabet* or the *action set*. The set of all responses is similarly called the *output alphabet*. It is not strictly necessary for the output alphabet to be known beforehand.

Refer to Fig. 2 showing an example Mealy machine produced by this learning technique and describing the following simple behaviour. Suppose that the SuL admits actions: *Init(X)*, which initialises an object *X*; and *Use(X)*, which uses that object. Both actions give a *Succ* or *Fail* response. The simple behaviour shown in this model is that an object X cannot be used successfully before being initialised.

Fig. 2. Example Mealy machine.

2.2 Description of the Legacy Component

Our case study is a software driver for the electrical generator of an X-ray machine responsible for powering the X-ray tube. The driver sets the correct

parameters for electrical requirements depending on the type of X-ray exposure desired. The driver also monitors the hardware's sensors for any necessary
intervention. It is called GS for Generator Service. The reasons it was chosen
for study were: (1) its reasonable size of 15,000 effective lines of code as measured by TICS[1], (2) the expectation that it can be adequately described by a
state machine, (3) that it had undergone recent refactoring which meant that
more knowledge was available, (4) an interest in revealing any missed refactoring
opportunities or missed behaviour, and (5) that it was relatively easy to isolate
and communicate with.

The first step of studying this component as a black box was gaining as much
knowledge as possible about its interfaces and a bit about its inside architecture.
The ease of isolating it is resembled by the fact that it had only two interfaces
as seen in Fig. 3 one interface to the application layer (shown on the top side),
and another to the hardware layer (shown on the bottom side). We may refer
to them simply as *top* and *bottom* layers, respectively. The bottom interface
communicating with the hardware requires a certain HW interface adapter.

Fig. 3. Interface schematic of the GS component.

The behaviour we aimed to learn was essentially the one shown in Fig. 2,
where the component needs to be properly initialised in order to be used. The
reason behind learning such seemingly simple behaviour was (1) to confirm that
the learned behaviour is equivalent to our expectation (Sect. 3.4 uncovers this
result), and (2) to explore the result of learning with a lower-level action set,
discussed in Sect. 3.2. Our Experiments showed that the initialisation procedure
of our legacy component, as simple as it seems, is not straightforward and would
not be learned smoothly. In fact, all the experiments of this paper are merely
exploring the GS's initialisation procedure.

Before we take the reader through our model learning experience addressing
individual learning experiments, we dive into the practical setup of the learning
environment.

---

[1] TICS (TIOBE Software Quality Framework; www.tiobe.com/tics/tics-framework).

2.3 Practical Learning Setup

The first step of setting up the learning experiment is to determine the interfaces on the SuL, and then, for each interface, to determine the following:

- The input alphabet, which in practice would be the list of functions calls provided by the interface.
- Means for sending actions to the SuL.
- Means for receiving or retrieving responses from the SuL.

We left out the output alphabet as we mentioned earlier that pre-defining it is not absolutely necessary. The only requirement is reading the output regardless of its type; the means of reading should be generic enough.

Note from Fig. 3 that we have two interfaces. This means that we need to identify inputs and outputs through each of these two interfaces. On the top side lies the application layer. In the real environment, commands are sent from the application layer into the GS, which can result in output through any of the two interfaces. We needed to replicate exactly that in order to send our actions. So, we wrote our own component that acts as the application layer. We call that component the *action executer* and it is part of the learning driver.

Note also from Fig. 3 that the bottom component is a hardware device. In our setup, communicating with that device involved many low-level details that were not possible to replicate through the action executer. Therefore we chose to use an abstraction that is the hardware interface adapter.

In such a case, the natural question is how to run the SuL without the actual hardware. Luckily, we had a test environment that provided the answer, namely that the aforementioned hardware interface adapter supported a testing mode where it would also act as a replacement for the real hardware through a test stub. This posed a peculiar case discussed in Sect. 3.5. The action executer communicates with that stub.

Refer to Fig. 4 showing the implemented learning setup. It essentially shows the learning driver being hooked up to the SuL from Fig. 3. The action executer connects to the SuL on the aforementioned interfaces and is responsible for the following:

- Communicating with the Learner. It receives input actions from the learner as strings and sends back responses as strings over a TCP socket connection.
- Translating input actions from strings into executable code. It can call functions that the SuL provides on its interfaces.
- Receiving the relevant response, for each action, from the SuL and translating it into a string.
- Resetting the SuL.

On the left side of Fig. 4 lies the LearnLib client which uses the LearnLib library and is responsible for setting parameters of LearnLib, e.g. selecting a learning algorithm and a testing algorithm, setting testing parameters, as well as fetching the input alphabet, and producing graphs of learned automata. The source code of the LearnLib client is available online[2]. The LearnLib client and the action executer combined make up what we call the learning driver, shown in Fig. 4, whose main role as a whole is to provide a wrapper around the SuL that acts as Mealy view for LearnLib.

For more information on the requirements and implementation of a learning driver, we refer the reader to the work of Merten et al. [14].

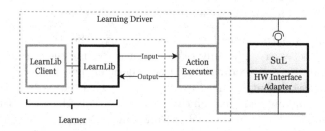

Fig. 4. Implemented learning setup.

3 Lessons Learned from the Case Study

This section details our experience with the case study through individual lessons learned.

3.1 Utilising the Test Environment

The availability of a test environment for the SuL is very valuable for the purpose of model learning. In our case, unit tests are conducted using the CppUnit testing framework [12] and they initially provided insight on how to run the GS without its hardware as mentioned in Sect. 2.3. In a similar use case, Hungar et al. [10] utilised an integrated test environment in their learning setup that is described in detail by Niese et al. in [16]. A major benefit of building such a test environment is having tests of different levels of abstraction from as high as the whole SuL to as low as the lowest subcomponents. In our case, this was achievable with manual work of dissecting the tests into smaller units as discussed in Sect. 3.3. An additional benefit we gained was the ability to extract information about the SuL's interface from individual tests. This point is significant in the case of legacy software, and particularly in our case, where APIs were not well documented. Luckily, the tests had high coverage and their functions acted as an abstraction layer on the SuL's lower-level interface. Moreover, the tests were written in a rather consistent fashion and were quite readable.

Unit tests have a linear structure consisting of three stages: (1) setting preconditions, (2) testing the outcome (usually with an assert statement), and (3)

---

[2] https://gitlab.science.ru.nl/ramonjanssen/basic-learning.

resetting the environment. This can be mapped to the structure of learning experiments, explained in Sect. 2.3, in the following way. From stage 1, we can extract two things: the initialisation actions and the input actions. It is worth mentioning that classifying a test's pre-conditions into initialisation actions and input actions is a matter of experiment design that we shall revisit in Sect. 3.2. Next, from stage 2, we extract the relevant output which must be configured as the SuL's response to the input actions from stage 1 (to satisfy the Mealy view). Finally, from stage 3, we learn how to undo the initialisation actions of stage 1. Once again, by looking at multiple tests, we extract the requirements for a global (SuL) reset which we configure the learner to perform at the end of each trace. Table 1 summarises this mapping.

Table 1. Mapping elements from unit tests into the learning experiment.

Test structure	Information extracted
Pre-conditions	Initialisation actions
	Input actions
Outcome test	SuL response/output
Reset	Uninitialisation
	Global (SuL) reset

Utilising the test environment is certainly a convenience, but we need to keep a few issues in mind:

- The tests may not cover every possible action. Functions and special arguments that are never used in the tests must be extracted from the SuL's code.
- The tests abstract from certain details. We may fine-tune our level of abstraction as covered in Sect. 3.2.
- Tests are context-specific. We may want to combine different contexts to conduct experiments with more actions. But is learning with more actions always a better idea? We address this question in Sect. 3.4.
- The nature of the learning process—where actions are executed in different possible orders and with different frequencies—can often lead to traces that are not covered in tests or ones that are not even achievable in normal use. A test environment is probably not built to handle such scenarios and will thus cause errors. We allude to this issue in Sect. 4.2.
- One more issue that is rather specific to our environment is the test stub attached to the SuL and the particular challenge of separating the two in regards of actions as well as learned models. This issue is discussed in Sect. 3.5.

We utilise the test environment in experiments of the following subsections, and reuse excerpts of code directly taken from unit tests as we address the challenges mentioned above.

3.2   Fine-Tuning the Level of Abstraction of the Alphabet

When composing an alphabet from code, a level of abstraction must be determined. Consider the actions of the model in Fig. 2. Each of these actions encloses multiple lower level actions that contain lower-level details which we simply hide by choosing the higher level action set. This yields a more abstract and readable model yet linear and without much variety to explore. On the other hand, however, let us explore the result of choosing the lowest level of abstraction. Consider the code from Listing 1.

```
Listing 1: Top activates GS

1 GS = CreateInstance();
2 F = GS.GetFrontalFactory();
3 L = GS.GetLateralFactory();
4 FOp = F.GetOperationalInterface();
5 LOp = L.GetOperationalInterface();
6 FOp.Activate();
7 LOp.Activate();
```

This excerpt is a precondition for most tests in our environment. For the lowest level of abstraction, we chose to set each line of code as a single input action. So this is our fine-grained action set. We set the response for each action to be a simple success/failure check on the call. This setup yields the model in Fig. 5 where transition labels correspond to line numbers in the code, all shown transitions have the output *success* which is omitted, and failed calls are self-loop transitions which are also omitted. We can clearly see the interleaving pattern created by independent actions.

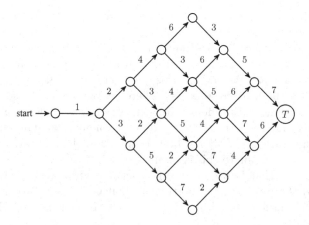

Fig. 5. Learned model of activation with fine-grained actions. Transition labels correspond to the line numbers in Listing 1.

The reason they are independent is because they activate independent components, and that can be done in arbitrary order. So, we can combine actions to yield a more readable model. Action 1 will remain the same and be labelled a_1, while the sequence of actions 2 to 7 will be combined into action a_{2-7}. Then we reach the model in Fig. 6. We simply eliminate interleaving through abstraction.

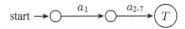

Fig. 6. The learned model of activation with coarse-grained actions.

Practical Results. We conducted two learning experiments, one with six input actions for learning one of the two independent components, and the other with 12 input actions for learning both components together. The first experiment took less than an hour and produced an eight-state model, and the second one lasted 6.5 h and produced a 64-state model. These numbers depend on many factors and are only given for the reader to get a sense of the cost of such an experiment.

Step-Wise Action Refinement. It is not possible to determine which actions are independent without either prior knowledge or experimentation. In the case where domain knowledge is not available, we resort to a technique called stepwise refinement [20]. It simply means we run the experiment with a minimal alphabet, and incrementally increase the size of the alphabet; as soon as interleaving is observed on two actions, such as 2 and 3 from Fig. 5, we abstract those into one single action, and so on. The downside of this technique is that earlier parts of the model will be learned again and again, which is clearly inefficient. Suppose we are only interested in behaviour that occurs at some state R onwards. Then to overcome the aforementioned inefficiency, we configured the learning driver such that every time the SuL is started, a certain action sequence is executed that transitions the state of the SuL to state R, which effectively makes the learning begin from state R. Currently, LearnLib does not have the feature of resuming learning from a certain state it has learned before. This is part of our future work as it will make stepwise refinement much more efficient.

The lesson we learn here is that the objective of a learning experiment decides which details to abstract. More fine-grained actions naturally yield more information in the learned model. On top of that, in this particular experiment, it provided a clue for one more property about the components labelled F and L (Listing 1), namely that they are symmetric, which we explore in the next subsection.

3.3 Exploiting Symmetry

Different patterns of symmetry are observed in software systems [6]. The pattern we refer to is when a certain component can be replaced by another one without resulting in an observable change in behaviour. Refer to the experiment of the previous section and to Listing 1. We learn from the domain expert that the components labelled F and L are symmetric. So we conduct the same experiment but excluding actions of the L component and we find that the new action set suffices to reach a state we call T_F (Fig. 7) which marks the F component active and ready for executing further actions successfully.

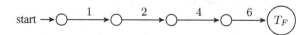

Fig. 7. Learned model of activation with actions of only one of the two symmetric components.

Thus we do not need to repeat the experiment for a certain component once we have already done so on a behaviourally equivalent one. This assumption of symmetry needs to be tested, however. So far, it is verified up to state T, but as we expand our alphabet to learn further parts of the software, we need to repeatedly verify that assumption. Doing so through matching traces from one component against the other is much more efficient than repeating the learning experiment altogether for the other assumed-symmetric component. In other words, the learned model of one component can be used as a hypothesis to be tested against the other symmetric model. We call this initial hypothesis a conjecture and we discuss it in Sect. 4.

So far, we learned that we can reduce our models by abstracting independent actions and by excluding one of two symmetric components from the action set. We continue on learning the next activation procedure and learning more lessons.

3.4   Faster Learning vs. Thorough Testing

Besides L^*_{Mealy} [15], LearnLib offers a faster variant of the L* algorithm, called TTT, introduced by Isberner [11]. Learning with TTT is more efficient simply because it produces a final model sooner. However, it goes through many more iterations and produces many more intermediate hypotheses, which requires more rigorous testing. Thus, optimising the learning process also requires optimising the testing algorithm.

Schuts et al. [17] provide experimental results on learning a small model with TTT combined with various testing algorithms. They conclude that TTT is faster than L* by a factor of 3 regardless of the testing method used. However, producing a correct model is as significant a concern, if not more significant, as speeding up the process. In our experiment, we contrasted between two learning algorithms, L* and TTT, and two testing methods, the W-method [5] and a simple random-walk test that LearnLib provides. The random walk tests random paths in the hypothesis against the SuL. It requires a maximum number of input actions and a probability of resetting the SuL after each action. The more rigorous W-method requires a parameter that effectively sets an upper bound on the length of the tests. Therefore in both tests, an estimate on the size of the target model must be made. This is quite problematic for the reason made clear by the next experiment.

In this experiment, we have only two actions: *Activate*, which abstracts the SuL activation procedure detailed in Sect. 3.2; and *GetLogicalResource*, which returns a logical resource object to access the hardware. We shorten these two actions as A and B respectively. The output of both actions is an S or F response standing for success and failure respectively. The expected behaviour is exactly that shown in Fig. 2 (if *Init* and *Use* are renamed to A and B respectively) where action B's success depends on action A's success. With this expectation in mind, estimating an upper bound on the number of states to eight, four times larger than the expected model, should be rigorous enough. And indeed we get the expected two-state model. However, with the cheaper random walk testing method, we set the maximum number of actions to 1000, and discover that our previous hypothesis was false and that a more accurate model is the ten-state model of Fig. 8. The model shows that the action *GetLogicalResource* succeeds after *Activate* but calling it eight times fills a certain hidden buffer and causes any subsequent calls to fail, even though *Activate* still succeeds.

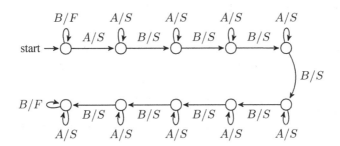

Fig. 8. A learned model showing the hidden buffer of size eight. Input actions are A: *Activate*, and B: *GetLogicalResource*; outputs are S: Success, and F: Fail.

Clearly, we would not want to discover such behaviour in a larger experiment. Such behaviour expands a two-state model to a ten-state model; and in a setup with one more input action, it expanded four states to 28 states. However, we would like to be aware of such behaviour and find a way to abstract from it. For this particular case, such a sequence will never be executed in practice and is therefore deemed uninteresting to learn. Not only that, but it is also expensive to learn and test, and therefore we would like to avoid observing it altogether. We call this an unduly complex model and we discuss it in Sect. 4.2.

Moreover, the bigger the action set, the lower the chance of discovering such behaviour. Thus it is wiser to experiment with a smaller action set before expanding.

We learned that faster learning comes with drawbacks. It comes at the expense of the accuracy of the learned model. We showed a case where not only would faster learning yield a less accurate model, but even slower learning with wrong assumptions can do the same.

3.5   Utilising the Test Stub

Recall from Sect. 2.3 that the HW interface adapter shown in Fig. 4 supports a testing mode where a built-in test stub would act as a replacement for the real hardware. This subsection contains multiple experiences and multiple lessons in utilising the test stub. We start with a piece of code taken directly from a test case, Listing 2, a procedure called *ToStandby* which runs after the activation procedure of Listing 1.

Listing 2: ToStandby()

```
1 stub.NotifyGS(On);
2 stub.IsRequested(Idle);
3 stub.SetState(Idle);
4 stub.NotifyGS(Idle);
5 stub.IsRequested(Standby);
6 stub.SetState(Standby);
7 stub.NotifyGS(Standby);
```

The goal of the code is to activate the stub and make it reach a standby state. It shows us the proper order of guiding the bottom layer (the stub) to a Standby state. First, the stub notifies the GS that it is powered on and awaits a request to go to an *Idle* state. Once it receives that request, the stub's state is set to Idle, it notifies the GS of that, and awaits the request to go to *Standby*. Again, once it receives the request, the stub is set to Standby and it notifies the GS of that.

Note the calls to IsRequested on line 2 and line 5 marked in boldface. These two calls are blocking, i.e. they wait for the output which means we are forced to implement a timeout. In the real setting which uses actual hardware, such calls are asynchronous, but in a testing environment, we are forced to make them synchronous.

When forming the action set out of Listing 2, lack of domain knowledge forced us to take the crude method of making each line of code into a single input action, while configuring the output read to be the success or failure of that particular call; in case of the call IsRequested, we get an additional output which is also a boolean value. Additionally, some actions that were added to the setup such as NotifyGS(Off) are not part of this particular unit test but were extracted from other tests and from the SuL's source code.

Inseparable Components. The stub is part of HW interface adapter (Fig. 4) and is thus inseparable from the SuL. While learning the SuL, it is probable that part of the learned behaviour is due to the stub. This is not to say that the stub is an undesired component. On the contrary, it provides great benefit in abstracting away all the obscure low-level communication details necessary in the real hardware connection. Eliminating the stub enforces a greater task which is to reverse engineer this low-level communication and incorporate it into our input and output alphabets, after which we can choose whether to learn it or to abstract away from it; the latter will, in turn, take us back to the situation we are currently in. Moreover, there is no accessible interface between the SuL and the interface adapter, which forces us to learn the combination of these two components rather than the SuL alone. This problem is revisited in Sect. 4.4.

Nondeterminism and Timing. Continuing with the stub experiment and the described alphabet, we discuss a certain problem we faced. As we ran the learner a few times with this setup, it started complaining about nondeterministic behaviour. It would report traces such as the following:

```
Listing 3: Trace showing nondeterminism

1 stub.NotifyGS(Idle);
2 stub.NotifyGS(Idle);
3 stub.NotifyGS(Standby);
4 stub.NotifyGS(On);
5 stub.SetState(Standby);
6 stub.SetState(Idle);
7 stub.SetState(Standby);
8 stub.IsRequested(Standby); -> True/False
```

The arrow at the last line indicates output. The learner here is complaining that the output for this trace is not deterministic, i.e., sometimes true and other times false. In such a setting where blocking is forced on an otherwise-asynchronous communication, we learn from Schuts et al. [17] that simply inserting time pauses after each message is a viable solution. The reason is that the SuL needs time to process and respond to messages. Through trial and error, we were able to determine the shortest pause duration necessary for a deterministic-output run. For this specific environment, the duration was 100 ms. A lesson learned here is that reported nondeterminism may not be so for as simple a reason as needing a time pause.

Expanding the Scope of the Output. A separate attempted solution to solve the nondeterminism problem was applying an abstraction on the actions by grouping them as follows:

```
1 stub.NotifyGS(On);          ⎫
2 stub.IsRequested(Idle);     ⎬ — b_1
3 stub.SetState(Idle);        ⎫
4 stub.NotifyGS(Idle);        ⎬ — b_2
5 stub.IsRequested(Standby);  ⎭
6 stub.SetState(Standby);     ⎫
7 stub.NotifyGS(Standby);     ⎬ — b_3
```

This setup did eliminate the need for inserting time pauses, but it yielded neither new states nor new transitions in the learned model, which pointed our attention to the output. Note that even though we abstracted actions, the scope of the output has not changed. Thus, we decided to revert from the abstraction solution back to the time-pause solution, and in addition do the following: to read the output of both IsRequested(Idle) and IsRequested(Standby) after each action and remove these two calls from the action set. In other words, we moved them from the input alphabet to the output alphabet. We were able to read both outputs because they were stored as flags in the HW interface adapter. This yields the model in Fig. 9. Output flags are represented by a dash if read *false* and by the first initial of the flag name if read *true*. And to save space, the action names were shortened.

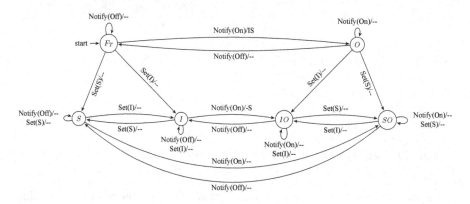

Fig. 9. The learned model of the *ToStandby* procedure with fine-grained actions and aggregated output.

Aggregating output and reading it globally revealed that both flags could be set as response to a single action, a fact that contradicts the implicit assumption of our previous output-reading setup. A more general benefit of aggregating output is that it removes the nondeterminism resulting from the common ambiguity of which output arrived first. The lesson learned here is that the scope of the output should be expanded, i.e. by reading more output, especially if at little or no extra cost.

The model in Fig. 9 also reveals that some actions, namely NotifyGS(Idle) and NotifyGS(Standby), have no effect on either the output or the state, which is why they are omitted from the figure. This raises the question: do they cause no change at all; or is the change simply hidden from our view due to this peculiar test stub?

We still do not know the answer but the sure lesson is that in some cases we cannot effectively learn the isolated target system and we are forced to utilise auxiliary components such as the test stub.

4   Future Work

In this section we discuss future solutions to the challenges seen in this case study.

4.1   Learning with Conjectures

We have seen a case in Sect. 3.3 where we use the knowledge that two components are symmetric. To ensure the accuracy of the learned model, we would like to treat this piece of knowledge as an assumption or a conjecture. We were able to verify the symmetry by learning each of the two components separately and finding that they are strongly bisimilar. However, there are two problems with this: first is the obvious unnecessary expense of learning the same behaviour twice, and second is that this only verified symmetry up to state T. Adding further actions to the experiment will require redoing the learning and the verification. So we would like to keep this conjecture of symmetry for all future experiments. When starting a new experiment, the learner would start with the conjecture and test it. Recall the three steps of the learning algorithm explained in Sect. 2.1. Step 2 was testing the already built hypothesis model. Our future direction is that we would like the conjecture to be an initial hypothesis model and that in the first iteration of the loop, we start with step 2, i.e. testing the hypothesis/conjecture.

Symmetry is one property that can be represented as a conjecture. There are certainly other properties that fit into a conjecture, including undesired sequences, explained in Sect. 4.2. This solution was mentioned in [13] as presenting an abstract model to the learner before starting the experiment.

Furthermore, we need a formalism for conjectures such that a property can be uniquely expressed and then translated into a hypothesis model. The output learned model should abstract away unwanted details to produce a more readable model just as Fig. 6 is compared to Fig. 5, while still keeping the information of the expanded model as a formalised property.

In summary, we would like to research the theory necessary to express conjectures, translate them into hypotheses, start learning with a hypothesis as a starting point, and output an abstract readable learned model.

4.2   Avoiding Illegal/Undesired Sequences

Because of the nature of the learning process where actions are executed in different possible orders and with different frequencies, it can often lead to traces that are not covered in tests or ones that are not even allowed in normal use. An example is turning on a device that is already on. A test environment is probably not built to handle such scenarios and will thus cause errors. In such a case, we would like to specify two subsequent *turn on* actions as an illegal sequence. This research direction investigates how to formulate such illegalities and how to keep the learner's traces within certain boundaries.

Another example is the one seen in Sect. 3.4, where eight *Activate* actions in a run is an undesired sequence because it explodes the state space and thus we would like to avoid observing it altogether. This problem can fall under illegalities but we would like to investigate whether such a sequence can be expressed as a conjecture and thus fall under the problem discussed in Sect. 4.1.

4.3   Avoiding Repetition of Traces

In the current learning implementation, every new trace starts from the initial state. In many cases, however, we are interested in a certain state and would like to run multiple traces from that state without repeating the sequences that leads to it after each reset. Bauer et al. [4] introduce the idea of reusing previous traces in what they call the Reuse algorithm. The reuse algorithm acts as an intermediate layer between the learner and the SuL. It would respond to the learner with a previously known response instead of running it explicitly on the SuL, which obviously saves time. They keep the information of previous runs in a reuse tree.

As mentioned in Sect. 4.1, we would like to start learning from a hypothesis. And we see in this context one way to implement this, namely that LearnLib would use the hypothesis as a reuse tree. We believe that this is a more generic approach, but the question remains about which approach is more efficient.

4.4   Composition and Decomposition of Models

Looking at the case of Sect. 3.5 and the learned model of Fig. 9, a pressing question is: what does the model say about the real behaviour of the SuL, and what does it say about the combination of the SuL and its interface adapter? Is there a way to correctly decompose the learned model to deduce one describing the behaviour of the SuL alone? Such a scenario can be seen in practice and the question invites theoretical research. Moreover, the more complex the auxiliary component is, the more difficult it will be to analyse the learned model.

On the other hand, we would like to investigate composition of models. Consider the models of Figs. 7 and 9. The latter model starts at state F_T where the former model ends. Both have different sets of actions and different scopes. We can make the assumption that the action set from one model has no effect on the states of the other model. Based on this assumption, we can take the union of these two models and present the resulting model as a conjecture for further experiments, which would also serve in testing the assumption. Composing models that learn different parts of a system into one that describes the complete behaviour is a problem that relates directly to the scalability of model learning techniques and the efficiency of learning large systems.

4.5   Automating the Learning Setup

Automation is essential for growing the model learning technique into an industrial-scale application. There are certain parts in the learning setup process that can be automated. For instance, Howar et al. [8] modified their LearnLib driver such that it automatically applies an abstraction on the alphabet when non-determinism is faced, whereas Merten et al. [14] automate the process of setting up the learner with input alphabet and other parameters. The latter is especially viable in our environment for the availability of consistent unit tests.

5   Conclusion

We narrated our experience in applying model learning to industrial legacy software. We faced interleaving, discovered hidden behaviour unintentionally, and dealt with an auxiliary component. We provided lessons about abstracting actions, exploiting symmetry, thoroughly testing the learned models, dealing with asynchronous communication, expanding the scope of read output, and carefully treating auxiliary components. Finally, we discussed future research directions, including learning with conjectures, and learning given an initial hypothesis.

Acknowledgement. We would like to thank Joshua Moerman and Ramon Janssen for their help with LearnLib and several related concepts, and Mathijs Schuts for sharing his knowledge about model learning.

References

1. Van der Aalst, W.M.P., Weijters, A.: Process mining: a research agenda. Comput. Ind. **53**(3), 231–244 (2004). https://doi.org/10.1016/j.compind.2003.10.001
2. Aarts, F., De Ruiter, J., Poll, E.: Formal models of bank cards for free. In: 2013 IEEE Sixth International Conference on Software Testing, Verification and Validation Workshops, pp. 461–468, March 2013. https://doi.org/10.1109/ICSTW. 2013.60
3. Angluin, D.: Learning regular sets from queries and counterexamples. Inf. Comput. **75**(2), 87–106 (1987). https://doi.org/10.1016/0890-5401(87)90052-6
4. Bauer, O., Neubauer, J., Steffen, B., Howar, F.: Reusing system states by active learning algorithms. In: Moschitti, A., Scandariato, R. (eds.) EternalS 2011. CCIS, vol. 255, pp. 61–78. Springer, Heidelberg (2012). https://doi.org/10.1007/978-3-642-28033-7_6
5. Chow, T.S.: Testing software design modeled by finite-state machines. IEEE Transactions on Software Engineering **SE-4**(3), 178–187 (1978). https://doi.org/10. 1109/TSE.1978.231496
6. Coplien, J.O., Zhao, L.: Symmetry breaking in software patterns. In: Butler, G., Jarzabek, S. (eds.) GCSE 2000. LNCS, vol. 2177, pp. 37–54. Springer, Heidelberg (2001). https://doi.org/10.1007/3-540-44815-2_4
7. Howar, F., Isberner, M., Merten, M., Steffen, B.: LearnLib tutorial: from finite automata to register interface programs. In: Margaria, T., Steffen, B. (eds.) ISoLA 2012. LNCS, vol. 7609, pp. 587–590. Springer, Heidelberg (2012). https://doi.org/ 10.1007/978-3-642-34026-0_43

8. Howar, F., Steffen, B., Merten, M.: Automata learning with automated alphabet abstraction refinement. In: Jhala, R., Schmidt, D. (eds.) VMCAI 2011. LNCS, vol. 6538, pp. 263–277. Springer, Heidelberg (2011). https://doi.org/10.1007/978-3-642-18275-4_19

9. Huang, Y.W., Yu, F., Hang, C., Tsai, C.H., Lee, D.T., Kuo, S.Y.: Securing web application code by static analysis and runtime protection. In: Proceedings of the 13th International Conference on World Wide Web, WWW 2004, pp. 40–52, ACM, New York (2004). https://doi.org/10.1145/988672.988679

10. Hungar, H., Margaria, T., Steffen, B.: Test-based model generation for legacy systems. In: 2003 Proceedings of the International Test Conference, ITC 2003, vol. 2, pp. 150–159, September 2003. https://doi.org/10.1109/TEST.2003.1271205

11. Isberner, M., Howar, F., Steffen, B.: The TTT algorithm: a redundancy-free approach to active automata learning. In: Bonakdarpour, B., Smolka, S.A. (eds.) RV 2014. LNCS, vol. 8734, pp. 307–322. Springer, Cham (2014). https://doi.org/10.1007/978-3-319-11164-3_26

12. Madden, B.: Using CPPunit to implement unit testing. In: Game Programming Gems, vol. 6 (2006)

13. Margaria, T., Niese, O., Raffelt, H., Steffen, B.: Efficient test-based model generation for legacy reactive systems. In: Proceedings of the Ninth IEEE International High-Level Design Validation and Test Workshop (IEEE Cat. No. 04EX940), pp. 95–100, November 2004. https://doi.org/10.1109/HLDVT.2004.1431246

14. Merten, M., Isberner, M., Howar, F., Steffen, B., Margaria, T.: Automated learning setups in automata learning. In: Margaria, T., Steffen, B. (eds.) ISoLA 2012. LNCS, vol. 7609, pp. 591–607. Springer, Heidelberg (2012). https://doi.org/10.1007/978-3-642-34026-0_44

15. Niese, O.: An integrated approach to testing complex systems. Ph.D. thesis, Technical University of Dortmund, Germany (2003)

16. Niese, O., Steffen, B., Margaria, T., Hagerer, A., Brune, G., Ide, H.-D.: Library-based design and consistency checking of system-level industrial test cases. In: Hussmann, H. (ed.) FASE 2001. LNCS, vol. 2029, pp. 233–248. Springer, Heidelberg (2001). https://doi.org/10.1007/3-540-45314-8_17

17. Schuts, M., Hooman, J., Vaandrager, F.: Refactoring of legacy software using model learning and equivalence checking: an industrial experience report. In: Ábrahám, E., Huisman, M. (eds.) IFM 2016. LNCS, vol. 9681, pp. 311–325. Springer, Cham (2016). https://doi.org/10.1007/978-3-319-33693-0_20

18. Smeenk, W., Moerman, J., Vaandrager, F., Jansen, D.N.: Applying automata learning to embedded control software. In: Butler, M., Conchon, S., Zaïdi, F. (eds.) ICFEM 2015. LNCS, vol. 9407, pp. 67–83. Springer, Cham (2015). https://doi.org/10.1007/978-3-319-25423-4_5

19. Vaandrager, F.: Model learning. Commun. ACM 60(2), 86–95 (2017)

20. Wirth, N.: Program development by stepwise refinement. Commun. ACM 14(4), 221–227 (1971)

Formal Verification in Automotive Industry: Enablers and Obstacles

Mattias Nyberg[1,2(✉)], Dilian Gurov[1], Christian Lidström[2],
Andreas Rasmusson[2], and Jonas Westman[1,2]

[1] KTH Royal Institute of Technology, Stockholm, Sweden
[2] Systems Development Division, Scania AB, Södertälje, Sweden
mattias.nyberg@scania.com

Abstract. We describe and summarize our experiences from six industrial case studies in applying formal verification techniques to embedded, safety-critical code. The studies were conducted at SCANIA over the period of eight years. Despite certain successes, we have so far failed to introduce formal techniques on a larger scale. Based on our experiences, we identify and discuss some key obstacles to, and enabling factors for the successful incorporation of formal verification techniques into the software development and quality assurance process.

1 Introduction

Formal methods are making their way only slowly into industrial practice for quality assurance of general software (SW). Their adoption in the domain of embedded, safety-critical systems, however, has seen much progress over the last years, as evidenced by the industrial case studies reported in the literature, e.g. see [18]. One reason for this development, from an industrial perspective, is the increased analysis effort advocated by various standards to achieve functional safety of such systems. The automotive functional safety standard ISO 26262, for instance, recommends formal verification for higher levels of criticality. Another reason is related to feasibility: the relatively smaller size of embedded code as compared to arbitrary applications, and the constraints on how such code is structured in order to safeguard against potential unwanted behaviours, make the application of formal analysis and verification techniques a viable complement to the traditional testing approaches. One example of a company developing embedded SW is SCANIA, a leading manufacturer of commercial vehicles, and specifically heavy trucks and buses. A large part of the embedded C-code developed at SCANIA is safety-critical, and a considerable effort during code development and deployment is spent on quality assurance. On top of the traditional testing methods, SCANIA is exploring the possibility for integrating various formal methods, such as deductive verification and model checking, into the code design and quality assurance process. The main motivation for this is the increased safety requirements resulting from innovative trucking solutions such as platooning and autonomous driving.

T. Margaria and B. Steffen (Eds.): ISoLA 2018, LNCS 11247, pp. 139–158, 2018.
https://doi.org/10.1007/978-3-030-03427-6_14

In the present paper, we present a summary of our experiences with applying formal verification techniques to a number of industrial case studies at SCANIA. The first three studies concern the deductive verification of requirements on C-code modules by means of semi-automated annotation of the code (for the given requirements), and the use of an off-the-shelf verification tool, VCC[6], to statically check the annotations. The fourth study investigates the application of two popular model checkers, the Simulink Design Verifier and UPPAAL, to verify requirements formalized as Simulink models. The fifth study evaluates the application of learning-based testing, a form of black-box testing executed in a virtualization environment, for checking requirements expressed in temporal logic. The last of these studies concerns the verification of correctness of the requirement breakdown of top-level requirements down to component-level requirements, following an hierarchical architectural description of the system.

Based upon the industrial case studies, but also considering other important aspects affecting the industrial usability of formal verification methods, the main contributions of the paper are to (*i*) summarize and generalize the observations and experiences from the conducted case studies, (*ii*) identify and discuss factors that *enable* wide-scale adoption of formal verification techniques, and tools supporting these, in the software development and quality assurance process within the automotive industry, (*iii*) identify and discuss factors that are *obstacles* to this development, and (*iv*) propose a roadmap of tasks to facilitate a near-time widespread usage of formal verification in industry. With this, our work contributes to the wider, ongoing discussion on how to facilitate the transfer of verification technology from academic research to industrial practice (see, e.g., [2,18] among many others).

Structure of the Paper. The remainder of the paper is organized as follows. In Sect. 2 we describe the industrial context in which we strive to apply formal methods, while Sect. 3 describes our case studies and identifies enablers and obstacles related to these. In Sect. 4, we discuss other industrial factors, not exposed in the case studies, but still related to the adoption of formal verification. In Sect. 5, we summarize and generalize our observations and experiences, and we discuss how enablers can be utilized and obstacles overcome to reach a successful adoption of formal methods in the automotive industry. Section 6 concludes the paper.

2   Context of Study

This section describes the industrial context in which the case study was conducted. As described in the introduction of the paper, SCANIA is a leading manufacturer of heavy trucks and buses. The R&D department consists of roughly 4000 engineers and, of these, about 1000 are working on the development of the electrical system in the truck. This includes design of electronic control units (ECUs) but the main effort is the development of embedded SW.

Most parts of the software are safety critical, i.e. a bug has the potential to cause accidents, and in many cases with fatal consequences. In alignment with the general trend in the automotive area, a substantial part of the current development efforts are related to ADAS (Advanced Driver Assistance Systems) and Autonomous Driving (AD) [16]. This involves a huge amount of safety critical software. To support the development of safety-critical systems, SCANIA applies the automotive functional-safety standard ISO26262 [10].

In comparison with other automotive companies, SCANIA relies to a very high degree on in-house development. As a consequence, SCANIA has developed in-house expertise in SW development. Also, it has been possible to optimize SW with respect to specific SCANIA needs, for example resulting in higher execution performance, fewer line of codes, and lower complexity.

SCANIA has adopted the principle of evolving product lines. This means that there is only one product line, with e.g. an 8-wheel drive mining truck and a city bus representing just two different configurations. The product line is evolving, in the sense that some parts of the construction going into production, typically SW, are changed every week. As a consequence, there are no 'model years'. Furthermore, SCANIA vehicles are connected, so SW updates can be managed 'over-the-air' and be initiated at any time. All these circumstances sum up to a need for highly competent product-data and configuration-management systems, with the ability to track the exact set of parts and configuration of each SCANIA vehicle ever produced and over its lifetime. In fact, such highly competent product-data and configuration-management systems do not exist commercially, so SCANIA has been forced to also develop this in-house. Yet another consequence of the evolving product line, is that a large part of the software is legacy; each single update typically introduces only a small part of completely new SW. Most SW remains the same or is the result of minor incremental improvements.

Regarding processes and organization, SCANIA has since long adopted the principles of lean and agile. The adoption is general, covering development, production, and after market support, but is particularly articulated in the area of SW development. Focus is not on documentation, for example of requirements, but instead on the people involved and their knowledge and competence. Each developer has the responsibility to understand customer needs, and develop the product according to these needs. Other companies often split the development in 'layers' with different responsibilities such as requirement elicitation, high level design, low level design, implementation (programming), and testing. In contrast, SCANIA generally adopts a flatter structure where the same engineer may be responsible for all these tasks, but only for their part of the construction. As a result of these principles, SCANIA is able to obtain an industry-leading product [1] in spite of a lack of heavy documentation.

Lastly, the engineers developing embedded systems at SCANIA, including programmers, come from a variety of backgrounds. Most common education is mechanical engineering followed by electrical engineering or applied physics. Engineers with computer science background are rare. This means that engineers learn the practice of software engineering and programming, not from state-of-the-art university courses, but from other practicing engineers.

3 Industrial Case Studies

Several studies have been performed at SCANIA, evaluating the incorporation of different forms of formal verification into parts of the embedded systems development process. The case studies are sorted into 4 groups according to the method of formal verification used. The case study groups are described in Sects. 3.1, 3.2, 3.3 and 3.4, which includes the conclusions drawn for each specific method.

In Sect. 3.5 we summarize the enablers and obstacles identified in the different case studies, and in Sect. 3.6 the results are discussed more generally.

The purpose of the industrial case studies was to evaluate the suitability of different verification techniques for general-purpose use within the automotive industry. The cases were chosen based on criticality to safety, generality, and availability.

In all cases the verification was performed by people with some experience with formal methods but who cannot be considered experts within the respective areas, with the assistance of researchers familiar with the topics. Much of the work was performed within MSc theses, and as such the effort required in terms of time was several months.

3.1 Deductive Verification of C Code

Evaluating and improving upon methods for deductive verification of C code has been an ongoing project at SCANIA. This section describes three case studies, and the different tools and methods used and developed for this purpose.

Tool Support. The primary tool used in the three studies is VCC [6]. Other tools have also been experimented with, most prominently FRAMA-C [7] with a plugin called WP. Both of these tools use deductive reasoning to prove properties of C code. The verification is function-modular, meaning that functions are verified independently, relative to the specifications of the other functions. These specifications are given in the form of function *contracts*, which are provided in the source code by means of annotations, and for which each tool has its own annotation language.

Each of the tools has its advantages and disadvantages. For example, while VCC supports more fine-grained reasoning about concurrency and complex data structures, compared to FRAMA-C it appears less mature and does not support verification of floating-point arithmetic. More details about the tools and our reasoning for choosing them can be found in [12].

In addition to the tools performing the actual verification, we have developed our own prototype tool to automate parts of the annotation process, which we call *Annotation Weaver*. This tool automatically inserts into the code so-called *auxiliary annotations*, which are annotations that are needed independently of the functional requirements, and that can be generated by combining analysis of the source code and data from an interface specification (defining e.g. the types and ranges of input/output variables). Examples include ensuring the validity and separation of pointers.

Industrial Cases. Three different software modules have been used in the context of deductive verification.

The first of these modules is called STEE, which is a C module of the embedded system that controls the dual-circuit steering system in vehicles. The initial work was performed in two MSc projects [8,12], and a report on our continued experiences was published in [9], which we summarize here. This module has an associated specification document, describing 27 requirements on the software. The requirements were stated informally, and some of them were safety-critical. The case study focused on requirements that were strictly *functional*, i.e., requirements that define output values as a function of the input values. In the existing requirements this functional relation was often described by means of intermediary requirement variables (variables that are neither input nor output variables and that might not be represented in the software). A formal requirements model that captured these properties was defined, according to which the module requirements were formalized. We also found that this model allows the set of requirements to be understood and visualized as a combinational logic circuit. A visualization of all case study requirements affecting the output variable SCHS is shown in Fig. 1.

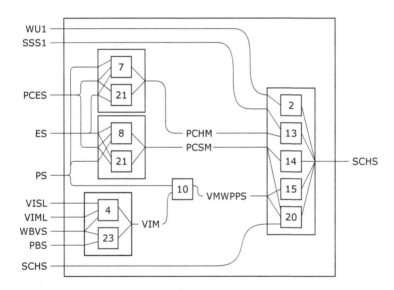

Fig. 1. Combinational logic circuit of case study requirements.

In the report, a process was described for the manual annotation and verification of the C module with respect to the formalized requirements. The C module consisted of 10 functions in total, of which one acted as an entry-point function. Thus, the formal requirements could be converted into a contract for this function, which then had to be decomposed through the function hierarchy.

The next case was a C module called VLTQ. This module is responsible for calculation of torque losses. Compared to the module addressed in the previous case study, VLTQ uses more complex programming constructs (such as loops, which are completely absent in STEE, to perform interpolation), and performs floating-point arithmetic.

The specification for this module was given as a flow chart, with a small part of the module specified in more detail in the form of a finite-state machine. The purpose of the case study was two-fold: to continue the exploration of automating the verification process, and to manually verify a single safety-critical aspect of the module. The property to be verified was one stating that the summation of several contributions to the total torque loss should be within a given interval.

The most recent case is the C module UAPC (Unintended Activation of Planetary Clutch), which is a module monitoring a safety-critical output value of another module. The module has a single requirement, which is not strictly functional as it is both temporal and stateful.

Results. Out of the 27 existing STEE requirements, 14 were identified as functional and specific to the case study module. Of these, 10 were successfully verified, and a possible inconsistency was identified between two of the requirements. The remaining 4 requirements were not verified because of lack of time. Verification of the entire annotated module took 165 s, and the function which required the most time took 65 s. The case study also resulted in the identification of guidelines for writing code and requirements that facilitate formal verification, as well as descriptions of several common obstacles and solutions for dealing with them.

We also experimented with inlining functions to avoid having to solve the problem of decomposing function contracts. However, inlining just a few functions of the STEE module resulted in the verification time of VCC increasing to unreasonable levels, in some cases not terminating within hours.

In the VLTQ case we never managed to verify the desired property. One of the reasons for this was the fact that VCC lacks certain fundamental features such as reasoning about floating point arithmetic, something which is commonly found in the C code developed at SCANIA. Another reason was the lack of specification, both in terms of precise description of the wanted functionality, as well as in description of the interface.

One outcome from the latter case studies was the above-mentioned *Annotation Weaver* prototype tool for automatic generation and insertion of auxiliary annotations. More restrictions on the source code were also identified, in order to ease automation of the verification process.

Conclusions. In our experience report [9], we concluded that deductive verification of embedded C code is a viable option, but requires rigorous formalization and deep understanding of the tools and processes. We also noted that automation of large parts of the process is a requirement for more widespread use, and described possible paths towards this goal.

Our belief in the value of automation of the verification process has since been reinforced. Even with the help of a tool for inserting auxiliary annotations, and with built-up expertise from previous experiences, successfully verifying properties of complex code is still a laborious task.

We also conclude that putting restrictions on the C code is a necessity. This is particularly true for the automated decomposition of contracts, since generating specifications is very hard in the general case. A possible solution to this is the use of smaller scale monitors, such as UAPC, that validate the safety-critical outputs of larger modules. Such constructs may even enable the use of inlining of functions for verification purposes.

The evaluated verification tools also lack certain fundamental features, such as reasoning about floating points in the case of VCC. The use of floating point arithmetic cannot simply be restricted, instead such shortcomings in tools need to be worked around.

Finally, formalizing the requirements involved resolving inconsistencies and ambiguities that are not apparent in informal requirements, but which makes successful verification impossible. Even worse, one module lacked even informal requirements.

3.2 Model Checking of Simulink Models

Another technique for formal verification of requirements that has been explored is model checking, and more details about our experiences can be found in [3].

Tool Support. In this case study the model checkers Simulink Design Verifier (SDV)[1] and UPPAAL [5] were compared qualitatively, with respect to their ability to be used in an actual industrial process for formal verification of requirements. SDV was chosen since it is an embedded model checker in Simulink, which is nowadays a de facto standard for design and evaluation of embedded systems. UPPAAL was chosen since it is a popular and well documented model checker, and has been successfully applied to problems of similar characteristics.

The model checker of SDV is called Prover Plug-In. Given a Simulink model, a requirement specification is expressed as a combination of *Proof objectives* and *Proof assumptions* that define a relation between the inputs and the outputs of the model. Proof objectives and assumptions can be modelled by logical and relational operators, MATLAB functions, or Stateflow graphs. A Proof objective is proven valid if there does not exist any state of the model that violates the Proof objective, given restrictions on the inputs, as specified by Proof assumptions. When a violation is detected, SDV generates a test vector that can demonstrate the violation in simulation.

UPPAAL is a model checker based on the theory of timed automata [5] that allows symbolic representation of time. UPPAAL provides a graphical editor, a simulator and a verifier. The verifier verifies properties that are defined as a subset of TCTL (Timed Computation-Tree Logic) and whenever a property is

---

[1] http://www.mathworks.se/products/sldesignverifier/.

not satisfied, it provides a counter example in the form of a trace that can be explored with the help of the simulator.

Industrial Case. The case study target was the Fuel Level Display (FLD) SW component, whose purpose is to provide an estimate of the total fuel level using a Kalman filter.

A subset of the specification consisting of 7 functional requirements was chosen for verification. Out of these requirements, 5 of them were dependent on time, while the other 2 were not. The emphasis was not placed on proving correctness of the system design, nor on the computational efficiency of the tools, but on the ability of the tools to be used within the organization in an actual process, in order to identify the problems faced by regular engineers performing model checking.

Results. The formalization of the requirements with SDV seemed fairly easy to grasp for the engineers, since it is based on function blocks and this is a well-known concept in systems and control engineering. Moreover, since SDV uses the original Simulink model, the interfaces between the submodules are clearly defined. This becomes very helpful because system requirements are typically defined in terms of these submodules/interfaces.

Table 1 shows the time needed for each verification. It is remarkable that some of the proofs needed a substantial amount of time, despite the simplicity of the system. This raised concerns about the scalability of this technique.

Table 1. SDV verification results.

Req.	Time (s)	Req.	Time (s)
AER201-12	2	AER202-2	3
AER201-13	238	AER202-3	25
AER201-14	238	AER202-2	1
AER201-15	24		

Using UPPAAL, the engineers first had to manually construct a model of the FLD component based on timed automata, and subsequently formalize the requirements into TCTL properties. These manual activities required extra supervision, and needed much more time than initially expected. The first problem was associated with the fact that UPPAAL has no support for using fixed and floating point numbers in the models. A solution to this is to scale such numbers up to integers, which for complex systems requires certain expertise. Second, due to the degree of abstraction, the engineers had some difficulties with mapping the elements of the timed automata with the real elements of the system.

Due to this, and because of the strict time requirements of the project, not all of the requirements in Table 1 were verified with UPPAAL. For the requirements that were verified, the verification time was substantially lower than for SDV, e.g. the verification time of AER202-2 was 0.2s.

Conclusions. The insights gathered from the case study is that SDV offers key features, such as the support for fixed point and floating point numbers and clearly defined interfaces, which appeal to the typical engineer. As an embedded feature of Simulink, which is widely used in industry, it eliminates the problem of having to transform the system to be verified into a formal model. Instead the requirements can be formalized as Simulink models, which the engineers found easy because of their familiarity with Simulink.

UPPAAL, on the other hand, offers high performance as compared to SDV, and relies on well-founded theories for handling complexity. UPPAAL requires the model to be transformed into timed automata, which is a relatively unknown concept to a typical engineer. As such, the formalization of the system to be verified requires considerable expertise and constitutes a real obstacle for its integration with current industry practices. This process would itself need to be verified or automated.

3.3   Learning-Based Testing

Our next case study evaluated the use of learning-based testing, a form of black-box testing, as a means for quality assurance of embedded safety-critical code.

Tool Support. LBTest [14] (see Fig. 2) is an automated, combined test-stimuli generator and evaluator that implements the methodology of learning-based testing [13]. LBTest is used to generate test-stimuli and evaluate responses from the system-under-test (e.g. an ECU). LBTest receives requirements as input, but has no model of the system-under-test. Instead, LBTest incrementally learns a model of the black-box system by issuing sequences of input and updating its learned model. The learning algorithm generally explores the state-space in a breadth-first manner, and a model checker receives the tentative models learned. Each such tentative model is checked against the requirements and, if the model is non-compatible, the model checker produces a concrete counterexample input/output sequence. This counterexample is sent to the system-under-test for validation. Most often, executing the counterexample will mispredict the output of the system-under-test and this will lead to amendments to the learned model, but when the prediction is correct, a true requirements violation has been detected.

Industrial Case. To evaluate the feasibility of learning-based testing for automotive applications, a benchmark experiment was performed [4,11], comparing LBTest to an existing test-suite on the Dual Circuit Steering (STEE) application, a sub-system of the ECU software.

As LBTest expects requirements formulated in PLTL (Propositional Linear-time Temporal Logic), the set of existing, informal requirements first had to be translated into PLTL. Out of the original 32 informal requirements, 11 could not be formalized in PLTL since some were not describing any actual relation between inputs and outputs and others referred to a specific platform for hardware-in-the-loop (HIL) testing. This ratio seems to be on par with other

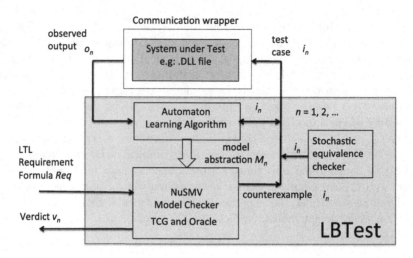

Fig. 2. LBTest architecture

similar studies [4]. The remaining 21 requirements could be formalized in PLTL, although they required extensive reformulation since they made use of variables denoting assumed internal states and internal signals. Also, the informal requirements did not always systematically model all the corner cases necessary for an unambiguous translation into formal requirements.

Results. To estimate the strength of LBTest to an existing test-suite (piTest), 10 errors were manually injected into the system-under-test and the recalls of the errors for each test-tool were compared. LBTest failed to detect 2 of 10 injected errors whereas piTest failed to detect 3 of 10 injected errors [4]. The types of errors that were detected or missed by the two tools may give an indication of their respective strengths and weaknesses. The errors not detected by LBTest were both changes to boundary values, whereas the errors not detected by piTest where changes to output values. No conclusive analysis was made for the missed errors. One integration of the testing procedure took about 7 h to terminate for an empirically estimated final model coverage at 97%. There are many potential ways to improve the performance of LBTest, but at the time of the experiment, the long turnaround time was an impediment to more extensive mutation testing.

Conclusions. Having performed the case study, we believe that empirical black-box methods, where tests are automatically generated from formal requirements, add testing-value since they should be less likely to miss errors due to feature interactions. Also, black-box testing puts minimal constraints on how the actual software is produced (i.e., what languages, tools or processes are used to produce the software), and does not even require access to the source code. However, as indicated by the 3 out of 10 missed injected errors, empirical methods can never conclusively prove the absence of bugs, and also, no amount of testing will automatically generate high quality software-design.

3.4   Verification of Requirements and Variability

At SCANIA, an in-house tool for specification, structuring, and verification of requirements has been developed for research purposes [17]. This section describes a case study where this in-house tool was used to perform a breakdown of a top-level safety requirement (a safety goal) all the way down to requirements on software modules.

Tool Support. In the in-house tool, requirements can be specified and linked together across different abstraction levels, forming a hierarchical breakdown of top-level requirements down to low-level requirements on software and hardware. The tool also integrates with other parts of the SCANIA toolchain by fetching data that various other tools have made available in a central database. This database contains information about internal software variables, CAN signals, truck configuration parameters (such as names, ranges, and types) and other data that has proven valuable for formal reasoning about specifications.

The tool supports formal specification of requirements in a simple logic language, as well as assigning validity of requirements in terms of production dates and truck configurations. These features enable simple sanity checks such as syntactic validation of requirements, and whether two linked requirements are ever valid in the same configuration or at the same production date, as well as checks of more complex properties such as completeness and consistency. Utilizing the data from other tools, we can semantically check whether values used in requirements and configuration specifications are in the actual range of the referenced signals or parameters. Combining these formal aspects, it is possible to verify, for example, whether a high-level requirement is fulfilled (i.e. semantically entailed) by its linked lower level requirements at a certain production date for all configurations in which the high-level requirement is valid. All checks and verification are performed on-the-fly, using the SMT solver Z3 [15].

Industrial Case. The case study target was the dual-circuit steering system, already described in Sect. 3.1. In the case study, a safety goal for the dual-circuit system was formalized and broken down in several levels until requirements could be allocated to the STEE module. Verification was performed at each level to check that every requirement was entailed by its linked requirements at the lower level.

Results and Conclusions. An experience gathered from the case study was that the task of formalizing and structuring requirements to be able to verify entailment is truly difficult. Especially when working with the high-level requirements, despite appearing easy to formulate in concept, many ambiguities and unclarities arose when trying to formalize them. One reason for this difficulty with formalizing the requirements was the low quality of the existing informal requirements, which in turn suggests that writing requirements in general is hard. A feature of the tool that gave support during the formalization was the on-the-fly check/verification of requirement conditions. The fact that the feedback was provided almost immediately was critical since it was then in most cases clear what action caused the violation of a condition. It was even found that getting such immediate feedback was so important that it could be beneficial to even increase performance at the cost of added false-negatives.

3.5 Summary of Enablers and Obstacles

A comprehensive summary of the enablers and obstacles identified in the different industrial case studies is shown in Table 2, listed in the order they are discussed below.

In all of the case studies problems with performance and scalability were encountered. This can to some extent be mitigated by taking verification into account both when formalizing the requirements (so that they can be efficiently verified) as well as during development of the application, whether it is written in C or modelled in Simulink (e.g. by putting restrictions on the allowed constructs). In any case, a deep understanding of the relevant tools is necessary.

Another common thread is that formalization and (in the case of deductive verification) annotation of requirements is a very time-consuming and complex task. As such, this process needs to be automated as far as possible, and for tasks that cannot be automated, as much support (e.g. feedback) as possible needs to be provided by tools. Because of the complexity, formalization is also prone to being erroneous, and one solution to this are tools supporting the validation of requirements.

In several case studies the formalization was even found to be impossible due to ambiguities and contradictions in the requirements, which suggests that formalization is a valuable task in itself since it exposes such deficiencies.

3.6 Discussion

In order to formally verify a system/SW against its requirements, both the system/SW and its requirements first need to be formalized, i.e. described mathematically. Formalizing complex system or SW properties is indeed difficult, and an observation from working with the presented case studies is that this difficulty seems to grow with the level of abstraction. That is, it is part of every-day development to engineer formal products, e.g. code. Reasoning about what the code does is hard, but feasible. Formalizing what the code does, e.g. in terms of pre- and post-conditions, is very hard. Formalizing the overall property that the code is intended to do is even harder. What is most difficult is formalizing and structuring requirements to be able to verify relations between requirements.

This difficulty is reflected in the quality of engineering artifacts at these abstraction levels. This was an issue in all of the case studies: the high-level engineering artifacts that we were supposed to verify against were highly ambiguous and the only artifact that could truly be trusted was the code (*"code is king"*) or the model that the code was generated from. Thus, we had to look into the code/model to resolve the ambiguities and 'understand' what the high-level artifacts were expressing. Naturally, we could claim that we had good judgment

Table 2. Identified *enablers* (E) and *obstacles* (O) in each case study group using methods: (1) deductive verification, (2) model checking, (3) learning-based testing, and (4) requirements verification.

ID	Conclusion	E/O	CS Group 1	2	3	4
1	Deep understanding of tool and method required	O	✓	✓		✓
2	Restrictions on code	E	✓			
3	Tool lacks capabilities (e.g. floats)	O	✓	✓		
4	Automation	E	✓	✓	✓	✓
5	Inefficiency/scalability issues	O	✓	✓	✓	
6	Monitor small parts of code	E	✓			
7	Low-quality informal requirements	O	✓	✓	✓	✓
8	Lack of requirements	O	✓			
9	Formalization of requirements is hard	O	✓	✓		✓
10	Formal modeling of the code is hard	O		✓		
11	Time-consuming manual work	O	✓	✓		
12	Familiar requirement formalization	E		✓		
13	Feedback to users	E	✓			✓

when doing this; however, the question still stands if we simply verified that the implementation does what it expresses rather than what it is intended to do.

One difference that might contribute to this discrepancy in quality between high-level artifacts and code is that when working with the latter, one receives almost immediate feedback from the tools operating on it. In contrast, when working with structuring high-level requirements, there is little to no feedback support provided by tools. Working towards providing such support in the requirements and variability case study, we indeed found that it was critical that a user gets immediate feedback when violating a requirement condition, so that it becomes evident which action caused the violation. We even found that getting such immediate feedback was so important that it could be beneficial to increase performance at the cost of increased false-negatives.

Another observation is that the difficulty in formalizing grows if the formalization is to be done by someone who is not an expert in the chosen formalism. This was observed in the case study comparing UPPAAL and SDV where a big obstacle for the integration of UPPAAL with current industry practices is the fact that the user is forced to formalize a system and its requirements as timed automata and CTL formulas, which are relatively unknown formalisms to a typical engineer. UPPAAL also does not provide support for fixed and floating point numbers, which means that it requires scaling up to integer numbers, which requires some expertise. In contrast, using SDV requires only knowledge in modelling using Simulink blocks, a formalism used daily by many engineers.

However, as shown in the case study, SDV does not scale very well, and thus, cannot be used to verify an arbitrary model; knowing which models can and which cannot be verified (due to, e.g., scaling issues) requires experience and inside-knowledge of the underlying theory and applied algorithms.

Thus, both SDV and UPPAAL suffer from critical drawbacks with respect to being applied in practice. Most notably, their usage is rather restricted to people with expertise and in-depth understanding of the tools and their underlying theory. This observation is common for all of the tools used in the case studies. E.g. when using VCC understanding the underlying theory of the tool is essential to writing annotations that may be successfully verified and, perhaps more importantly, to avoid writing annotations specifying an incorrect behaviour of the code that is then successfully verified because of software bugs.

In addition to this similarity, VCC suffers from the same problem with scalability, which was made evident when trying to inline the helper functions of the STEE module in order to avoid the manual decomposition of top-level function contracts.

Using exhaustive, formal methods in parallel with developing the software is more likely to ensure that good software development practices will be used (e.g. designs with minimal amounts of undefined internal state).

4   Other Factors

In Sect. 3, we draw conclusions of enablers and obstacles based upon solely the case studies. In the present section, we try to add the perspective of other factors, namely management and SW architecture.

Management Commitment. In general, engineers and management are typically positive to, and understand, the benefits from using formal verification such as higher confidence, automation, etc. However, there is often a lack of understanding of what is actually needed to make these methods work in practice. This includes not understanding the level of effort and competence needed to formalize the systems and requirements to be analyzed.

Formal verification is not yet state-of-practice in the automotive industry. This means that to start practicing formal verification, new costly resources and competences need to be added. In a cost-aware development department, any new cost needs to be strongly motivated. To motivate a recruitment in the area of formal verification, upper management needs to be convinced about the benefits. However, as observed in the case studies, it is not at all clear that formal verification is technically ready for general automotive industrial practice. Furthermore, management decisions are often sensitive to general trends; i.e. if it is known that other companies are practicing formal verification or are planning to do so, it is easier to motivate recruitment. However, currently, formal verification is not part of a general automotive trend.

Having safety critical software should increase the need for formal verification. However, ISO26262 *recommends* but does not *require* the usage of formal verification. So there has to be reason to go beyond what is required in ISO26262. One reason could be that the cost or time required of verifying a system with formal methods is lower than for traditional methods. This should be more articulated for parts of the vehicle that are more safety critical, i.e. having the highest safety integrity level. Since ADAS and AD involves more safety critical components, this trend might very well reach a turning point when the amount of verification of highly critical components is so large that the limitations of current testing methods become a blocker for introducing this new technology into the vehicles.

Legacy Systems. Formal verification comes with restrictions on the code and requirements having certain structures and being written following certain principles. Having systems consisting of large amounts of legacy code with legacy requirements often implies that these restrictions are not respected. Thus formal verification can not be used or the SW and requirements need to be rewritten, making formal verification harder to justify from a cost perspective.

Architecture and SW Complexity. The fact that embedded systems are developed in-house, may have both positive and negative effects on architecture and code complexity. A software tailor made for only one use case, is likely to have the consequence of a less general architecture. This stands in contrast to SW developed by suppliers, that are mandated to follow industry standards, such as AutoSAR, and provide a general architecture possible to adapt to all its customers. The comparably smaller focus on SW architecture makes systematic usage of formal verification difficult, especially using compositional verification.

On the other hand, a more streamlined and less general SW is likely to also have a positive effect on SW complexity. An example is the execution model used at SCANIA. Since it is known exactly when and which code is needed to be executed, relying on a general-purpose operating system is unnecessary, and a very simple real time scheduling principle can be used, for example relying to a high degree on fixed time scheduling, avoiding many issues associated with concurrency.

Product line principles have likely a negative effect on SW complexity. A similar negative effect may be seen in the requirements. For example, to support many product variants, requirements need in general to be parameterized or instantiated into many variants. This combined with the need for keeping requirements decomposition consistent is a substantial challenge.

In addition to architecture, a general adoption of formal methods and tools requires a high degree of information consistency across the organization. For example if an effort is made to prove the correctness of a system producing a signal X, but then the system consuming the signal has a different interpretation of the same signal X, a correctness proof of the second system will not help to guarantee correctness of the total combined system. To avoid this situation, general cross-system usage of formal verification needs to be backed up by a formal data-model, and in turn an information model.

4.1   Summary of Enablers and Obstacles

In accordance with Sect. 3, we summarize in Table 3 the enablers and obstacles
identified above.

Table 3. Identified *enablers* (E) and *obstacles* (O) related to other factors.

ID	Conclusion	E/O
14	Methods are efficient for at least some cases	E
15	Resistance to process and methodology changes	O
16	Evidence of method matureness and efficiency is missing	O
17	Method usage requires new recruitement	O
18	Not required by the process standards	O
19	Many upcoming safety critical applications	E
20	Unnecessarily complex software	O
21	Bad system and SW architecture	O
22	Legacy SW	O
23	Generic parameterized software	O
24	Standardized architectural frameworks	E
25	Complex variability	O

5   Exploiting Enablers and Overcoming Obstacles

Tables 2 and 3 summarize 25 enablers and obstacles found in the case studies and
the analysis of business-related factors inherent to the automotive industry. As a
next step, we analyze the obstacles to identify remedies, and analyze the enablers
to identify means through which they can be exploited. This is presented below,
by grouping together similar remedies and exploitations. Based on this, we then
suggest a roadmap of concrete tasks to be performed.

Improvement of Formal Verification Tools (3, 4, 5, 10, 11, 13). Tools
need to be improved to add capabilities, e.g., handling of floats. Tools also need
to be largely automated, especially concerning annotation of the code to be
verified. Tools need to become more efficient for larger problems, i.e., scalability
needs to be addressed. Tools need to have immediate and informative feedback
to the user. If the target language of the verification tool is different from the
implementation language of the code, then automated transformation from code
to the verification target language is needed. Alternatively, tools need to be
developed such that they can handle the implementation language of the code.

Improvement of Methodology on SW and Architecture (1, 2, 17).
Restrictions on code for verification tools to be efficient need to be identified.
Also, patterns of code, where formal verification is likely to work well, need to be
defined. In general, the methodology has to be simple, and education material for
engineers has to be developed. The aim should be a methodology that does not
require deep expert knowledge. As part of the methodology improvement, general
requirements on the code, SW and system architecture need to be identified.

Improvement of SW and Systems (6, 20, 21, 22, 23, 25). Development
of new SW and systems need to follow the general requirements on the code,
SW and system architecture identified above in the remedy on SW and architecture methodology. This includes structuring the code into highly safety-critical
components, to be formally verified, and non- or less safety-critical components,
that do not need to be verified formally. To avoid complex verification tasks,
complex SW has to be avoided. In addition, legacy SW and systems need to be
refactored using the same principles.

**Improvement of Tools and Methodology for Requirements Engineer-
ing (7, 8, 9, 12, 13, 24).** Engineers writing requirements, informal or formal,
need knowledge of how to write good requirements. It is the authors' observation
that existing books and industrial courses in requirements engineering are not
at all sufficient to make engineers produce requirements of high enough quality
to be formalized. The problem is that requirements engineering researchers, who
are typically authors of books, and experienced industrial practitioners, who are
typically the teachers in courses, have no or very little experience in writing
formal requirements used in formal verification. So what is needed is a collaboration between requirements engineering researchers, industrial practitioners,
and researchers in formal verification, to produce new books and courses.

Unfortunately, raising the stringency of requirements will often make it
harder to write the requirements. This in turn will reduce the willingness to at
all write requirements. A big part of the solution can be requirements-authoring
tools with excellent support for the user. A source of inspiration could be SDV
with their formal requirement language that is very intuitive to the engineers.
Another part of the solution can be a tight connection to the SW architecture
(with formal references to component interfaces), as we demonstrated in [17].

Another complementary direction is to rely on requirements patterns, and
make them highly accessible to the user. This is more likely to succeed if an architectural framework is assumed, and even more so if standardized architectural
frameworks, such as AutoSAR, are considered.

Technology Transfer (14, 15, 16, 18, 19). The key to technology transfer
are successful pilot projects using the new methodologies and tools. These success stories need also to be shared across companies. When successful projects
can be demonstrated, confidence in formal verification as an efficient method

will grow. This then lays the ground for more strongly recommended or even demanded formal verification in revised process standards, such as future editions of ISO26262.

5.1 Suggested Roadmap

As can be noted, many of the remedies are in control of, and can be solved within, the research community. However, several of the remedies can only be implemented with help from industry. Also, to maximize the likelihood of a near-time widespread usage of formal verification in industry, the order of the remedies should be carefully chosen. Below we provide a roadmap, with a suggested order of remedies, and also a suggested allocation of tasks to the research community and industry, respectively.

Task 1. Improvements of the formal verification tools. This is a task that the research community needs to take.

Task 2. Along with Task 1, the general requirements on the code, SW and system architecture need to be identified. This task needs to be taken by the research community, but in collaboration with industry.

Task 3. Improvement of tools and methodology for requirements engineering. Researchers from the areas of requirements engineering and formal verification need to collaborate. Also, a close collaboration with industry is needed.

Task 4. Technology transfer. When tools and methodology for requirements authoring and tools for formal verification are ready, they need to be applied in real industrial pilot projects developing new systems. Industry will need to lead this task, but researchers should be involved in coaching.

Task 5. Improvement of legacy SW and systems to meet the requirements identified in Task 2 on general requirements on the code, SW and system architecture. After having completed Task 4, industry should be ready to take on this task by itself.

6 Conclusion

Despite providing a straightforward way towards applying formal verification, the suggested roadmap requires considerable work and dedication over an extended period of time. Without realizing this, it is easy to get caught in a typical Catch 22 of formal methods: on the one hand, to truly make such methods work requires significant effort and resources (for education, development, organization, etc.), while on the other hand, industry wants to see proof that they really work before putting such an amount of effort and resources in realizing them.

It is therefore important to emphasize that a move towards a more formalized way of working, despite requiring a lot of effort, could actually be beneficial regardless of whether formal methods end up being used or not, since it forces an organization to establish a more rigorous and structured development. At that point, then, actual usage of formal methods can be considered a bonus from this effort.

References

1. Scania tops prestigious European truck test for the second year running. http:// news.cision.com/scania/r/scania-tops-prestigious-european-truck-test-for-the-second-year-running,c2460100. Accessed 22 Apr 2018
2. Alglave, J., Donaldson, A.F., Kroening, D., Tautschnig, M.: Making software verification tools really work. In: Bultan, T., Hsiung, P.-A. (eds.) ATVA 2011. LNCS, vol. 6996, pp. 28–42. Springer, Heidelberg (2011). https://doi.org/10.1007/978-3-642-24372-1_3
3. Ali, S., Sulyman, M.: Applying model checking for verifying the functional requirements of a Scania's vehicle control system. Master's thesis, Mälardalen University (2012)
4. Bäckström, S.: Learning-based testing of automotive ECUs. Master's thesis, KTH Royal Institute of Technology, School of Computer Science and Communication (2016)
5. Behrmann, G., David, A., Larsen, K.G.: A tutorial on UPPAAL. In: Bernardo, M., Corradini, F. (eds.) SFM-RT 2004. LNCS, vol. 3185, pp. 200–236. Springer, Heidelberg (2004). https://doi.org/10.1007/978-3-540-30080-9_7
6. Cohen, E., et al.: VCC: a practical system for verifying concurrent C. In: Berghofer, S., Nipkow, T., Urban, C., Wenzel, M. (eds.) TPHOLs 2009. LNCS, vol. 5674, pp. 23–42. Springer, Heidelberg (2009). https://doi.org/10.1007/978-3-642-03359-9_2
7. Cuoq, P., Kirchner, F., Kosmatov, N., Prevosto, V., Signoles, J., Yakobowski, B.: Frama-C: a software analysis perspective. In: Eleftherakis, G., Hinchey, M., Holcombe, M. (eds.) SEFM 2012. LNCS, vol. 7504, pp. 233–247. Springer, Heidelberg (2012). https://doi.org/10.1007/978-3-642-33826-7_16
8. Eriksson, J.: Formal requirement models for automotive embedded systems. Master's thesis, KTH Royal Institute of Technology (2016)
9. Gurov, D., Lidström, C., Nyberg, M., Westman, J.: Deductive functional verification of safety-critical embedded C-Code: an experience report. In: Petrucci, L., Seceleanu, C., Cavalcanti, A. (eds.) FMICS/AVoCS -2017. LNCS, vol. 10471, pp. 3–18. Springer, Cham (2017). https://doi.org/10.1007/978-3-319-67113-0_1
10. ISO26262: Road vehicles - functional safety. Standard ISO26262, International Organization for Standardization (2011)
11. Khosrowjerdi, H., Meinke, K., Rasmusson, A.: Learning-based testing for safety critical automotive applications. In: Bozzano, M., Papadopoulos, Y. (eds.) IMBSA 2017. LNCS, vol. 10437, pp. 197–211. Springer, Cham (2017). https://doi.org/10.1007/978-3-319-64119-5_13
12. Lidström, C.: Verification of functional requirements of embedded automotive C code. Master's thesis, KTH Royal Institute of Technology (2016)
13. Meinke, K.: Automated black-box testing of functional correctness using function approximation. In: Proceedings of the ACM/SIGSOFT International Symposium on Software Testing and Analysis, ISSTA 2004, 11–14 July 2004, pp. 143–153, Boston, Massachusetts, USA (2004)

14. Meinke, K., Sindhu, M.: LBtest: A learning-based testing tool for reactive systems. In: Sixth IEEE International Conference on Software Testing, Verification and Validation, ICST 2013, Luxembourg, Luxembourg, 2013, pp. 447–454 (2013)
15. de Moura, L., Bjørner, N.: Z3: an efficient SMT solver. In: Ramakrishnan, C.R., Rehof, J. (eds.) TACAS 2008. LNCS, vol. 4963, pp. 337–340. Springer, Heidelberg (2008). https://doi.org/10.1007/978-3-540-78800-3_24
16. Watzenig, D., Horn, M.: Automated Driving: Safer and More Efficient Future Driving. Springer, New-York (2016). https://doi.org/10.1007/978-3-319-31895-0
17. Westman, J., Nyberg, M.: Providing tool support for specifying safety-critical systems by enforcing syntactic contract conditions. Requirements Engineering (2018)
18. Woodcock, J., Larsen, P.G., Bicarregui, J., Fitzgerald, J.S.: Formal methods: practice and experience. ACM Comput. Surv. 41(4), 19:1–19:36 (2009)

Scalability of Deductive Verification Depends on Method Call Treatment

Alexander Knüppel$^{(\boxtimes)}$, Thomas Thüm, Carsten Padylla, and Ina Schaefer

TU Braunschweig, Braunschweig, Germany
{a.knueppel,t.thuem,carsten.burmeister,i.schaefer}@tu-bs.de

Abstract. Today, software verification is vital for safety-critical and security-critical applications applied in industry. However, specifying large-scale software systems for efficient verification still demands high effort and expertise. In deductive verification, design by contract is a widespread software methodology to explicitly specify the behavior of programs using Hoare-style pre- and postconditions in a modular fashion. During verification, a method call can either be replaced by an available method contract or by inlining the method's implementation. We argue that neither approach alone is feasible for verifying real-world software systems. Only relying on method inlining does not scale, as the number of inlined methods may lead to a combinatorial explosion. But specifying software is in itself notoriously hard and time-consuming, making it economically unrealistic to specify large-scale software completely. We discuss circumstances in which one of the two approaches is preferred. We evaluate the program verifier KeY with large programs varying in the number of method calls of each method and the maximum depth of the stack trace. Our analyses show that specifying 10% additional methods in a program can reduce the verification costs by up-to 50%, and, thus, an effective combination of contracting and method inlining is indispensable for the scalability of deductive verification.

Keywords: Deductive verification · Design by contract
Method inlining · Method contracting · KeY · Method call treatment

1 Introduction

A challenging task in software engineering is to reason about the correctness of large programs [32]. *Deductive verification* is a technique focusing on formal program verification by generating proof obligations based on implementation and a formal specification [1,22]. Such proof obligations can then be proved to be correct by interactive and automated program provers [1,26] to ensure that a software system behaves as explicitly specified. In *design by contract*, specifications are typically provided in the form of code annotations [4,17,38]. A developer following this methodology annotates part of the source code, such as methods, with *contracts*. Contracts are inspired by the theory of Hoare triples [31]. That

© Springer Nature Switzerland AG 2018
T. Margaria and B. Steffen (Eds.): ISoLA 2018, LNCS 11247, pp. 159–175, 2018.
https://doi.org/10.1007/978-3-030-03427-6_15

is, contracts specify *preconditions* that need to be satisfied by callers and *post-conditions* that callers can then rely on. Moreover, contracts can have additional information, such as *frame conditions*, which express explicitly what locations (i.e., program variables) a method is allowed to modify [10].

However, deductive verification combined with design by contract is not a widespread methodology in industry. Despite its various advantages, such as an increased trust in the program's correctness, industry sees little benefit in it compared to less demanding approaches (e.g., unit testing). One reason is that it is regareded as cost-ineffective. Indeed, the specification effort is high and error-prone [5] and verification tasks are time-consuming.

In this regard, method call treatment is one critical aspect in the discussion about scability of deductive verification. Generally, there exist three strategies to handle method calls. The first strategy is to always *inline* methods [1]. That is, each method call in the method under verification is replaced by its respective implementation. However, method inlining is often infeasible due to two reasons: (1) it fails per definition in case of recursion or unavailable source code and (2), based on large call stacks, it often results in larger and more complex proof obligations, which are too costly to verify. The second strategy is *method contracting* [35], where we exploit the contract of a called method if available. In this case, the verification consists of checking the preconditions at call-site and abstracting the call by its postcondition. If the implementation of a method specified with a contract changes, and the contract holds after the change, only the method itself had to be verified again. With pure method inlining, always all callers need re-verification. One problem is that not all methods can be specified, as the specification effort is typically too high for large-scale software systems. The third strategy is to use both, method inlining and method contracting, in combination.

Surprisingly, method inlining and method contracting seem to be used interchangeably in research. Numerous evaluations simply use one or the other without justification and often not even let readers *explicitly* know which one was applied (e.g., [1,2]). This is problematic, as research prototypes are typically applied to tiny examples only, where the verification effort is not high enough to see a difference. Hence, when aiming to apply such approaches to large-scale programs in industry, where the specification and verification effort is indeed high, applicability may be unclear.

In this paper, we investigate method call treatment and its scalability in the context of deductive verification empirically to discuss on how to improve the cost-effectiveness of this methodology to become more effective in industrial applications. As a starting point, we employ KeY [1], a static verifier for JAVA programs with an active community. In KeY, a user either applies pure method inlining or replaces methods with their respective contract (i.e., applying inlining only when no contract is available). To measure the verification effort in a controlled evaluation setting, we generate large, fully specified artificial programs that vary in the number of method calls within each method and the maximum depth of the stack trace. We justify the generation of artificial programs based on three reasons: (1) to the best of our knowledge, no fully-specified real software systems exist that provide a large enough call depth necessary for our evaluation, (2) the specification effort of such systems is too large for us to specify them ourselves, and (3) generating such programs gives us confidence in the correctness of the implementation and specification. In summary, we make the following contributions:

- We discuss method inlining and method contracting for their advantages and limitations in deductive verification and propose to use an effective mixture of both approaches.
- We introduce an artificial benchmark for JML-based verification tools.
- We evaluate our proposal on large generated programs with KeY empirically by measuring the verification effort in different scenarios. Our empirical investigation is a stepping stone towards automated deductive verification and better applicability for industrial use cases.

2   Method Call Treatment in Deductive Verification

Deductive verification is a formal approach to reason about logical properties of programs [43]. Properties such as *"does not crash"*, *"has no arithmetic overflows"*, and even more complex behavioural properties such as *"sorts an array"* are possible. Program verifiers translate these properties and the program to different flavors of first-order logic to reason about their conformance and to become amenable for proof automation [1, 4, 26]. Deductive program verification is often based on one of two approaches to transform implementation and specification into provable verification conditions, namely *weakest precondition calculus* and *symbolic execution*. Following the original formulation of Floyd-Hoare logic [27, 31], Dijkstra suggested the weakest precondition calculus to compute the weakest conditions that must hold at the initial state of the program for given postconditions [22]. Symbolic execution follows a forward manner. Here, all possible execution paths for all possible input data are explored, which can be exploited for program verification against functional properties [15]. Program verification is often not fully automatic due to the undecidability of the underlying verification problem. User interaction, such as providing loop invariants, becomes necessary when proofs exist but cannot be found automatically.

The program verifier KeY allows practitioners to verify that a given Java program (or parts thereof) adheres to its contracts written in the Java Modeling Language (JML). Figure 1 illustrates how JML is used to specify the intended behavior of a Java program in terms of method contracts. Here, method `maxInArray` returns the maximum integer in an integer array and `max` the maximum of two integers. The keyword **requires** represents the precondition that must be fulfilled. The keyword **ensures** represents the postcondition that all callers of that method can rely on when the precondition is fulfilled.

Method `maxInArray` calls method `max` when the size of the array exceeds one. To verify that `maxInArray` indeed conforms to its contract, we must verify that all invoked methods behave correctly as well. Otherwise, we cannot ensure

```
 1  /*@ public normal_behavior
 2    @ requires array.length >= 1;
 3    @ ensures \result =
 4            (\max int j; 0 <= j && j < array.length; array[j]);
 5    @*/
 6  public int maxInArray(int array[]){
 7      int tmp = array[0];
 8      for(int i = 1; i < array.length; ++i) {
 9          tmp = max(array[i], tmp);
10      }
11      return tmp;
12  }
13  /*@ public normal_behavior
14    @ ensures   a <= b ==> \result = b
15    @           && a > b ==> \result = a
16    @*/
17  public int max(int a, int b){
18      return a > b ? a : b;
19  }
```

Fig. 1. Specification of Methods `maxInArray` and `max`

that the method returns the maximum integer in the given array. Typically, two options exist to treat method calls in deductive program verification: *method inlining* and *method contracting*. In this regard, we can either inline the implementation of method `max` into method `maxInArray` at invocation time or we can use the method contract instead.

When verifying a specified method, method contracting only focuses on the first level of method calls, whereas in method inlining the whole call stack of a method is of interest. In our experience, real programs have stack sizes of 20 and beyond. A considerable consequence is thus the increase in size and complexity of the respective proof obligations when method inlining is used, potentially rendering the verification effort infeasible. However, defining strong enough contracts for automated verification is notoriously hard and requires numerous iterations. Even when methods are already specified by developers, a lot of time is spent on refining dependent contracts to make them sufficient for method contracting.

Although examples of real-world software as subject to deductive verification exist in the literature (e.g., TimSort [21] or JavaCard [48]) where a combination of method inlining and contracting was used, the difference in verification effort between both approaches is negligible, because of their comparably small call stacks. To the best of our knowledge, verification effort for either approach of larger programs has not been evaluated empirically before. In the next section, we first discuss under which circumstances method inlining or contracting is preferred.

3   Criteria for Method Call Treatment

Method inlining and method contracting have both their place in deductive verification. In this section, we discuss advantages and drawbacks of both strategies. To this end, we chose criteria important for software engineering and deductive verification involving specification correctness, specification effort, information hiding, unbounded loops, unbounded recursion, verification effort, and incremental verification. In the following discussion, we further distinguish two types of criteria. First, *hard criteria*, where only one approach is applicable in a verification attempt. Second, *soft criteria*, where both approaches are applicable but with varying degrees of success.

3.1   Hard Criteria for Method Call Treatment

Specification Effort. Baumann et al. [5] already argued that writing adequate specifications is the hardest part in formal verification. Typically, developers specify methods concurrently. As a consequence, insufficient specifications or even unspecified methods during the early verification attempts are inevitable. In our experience, writing specifications that are sufficient for method contracting requires numerous iterations over a method itself and its called methods. Moreover, not each developer that specifies contracts is also involved in the verification itself, making it almost impossible to come up with a sufficient method contract for complex behavior from the beginning. Hence, invocations of insufficiently specified methods can only be dealt with through method inlining, when there are no resources available for improving the specification.

Incomplete Implementation. A concern with method inlining when proving correctness of a method is that the implementation of all called methods must be accessible. If source code is unavailable, as often is the case for calls to APIs (e.g., Java's Collection API), or a method is not yet implemented, inlining will fail and correctness cannot be ensured. An exception to the case when source code is unavailable constitutes techniques regarding the verification of bytecode [40]. However, bytecode verification is limited to languages executed by a virtual machine (e.g., Java). Method contracting omits the implementation, as the contract makes the intended behavior of a method explicit. If we assume that all called methods adhere to their respective contract, we can prove correctness with method contracting even when source code is unavailable by providing adequate contracts.

Unbounded Loops and Unbounded Recursion. Dealing with loops and recursion in deductive verification is typically difficult. Bounded loops and bounded recursive calls can be unrolled [1]. When the stop criterion is indefinite at compile-time, loop invariants must be specified and used during verification. For instance, the length of the input array of `maxInArray` is not necessarily known before run-time. If the array's length cannot be determined statically, the `for`-loop becomes unbounded (e.g., the size of the input array is determined at run-time). Inlined methods depending on unbounded loops or recursion may therefore result in a time out and consequently fail. A good choice is to use method contracting instead if a contract is available. In the aforementioned example, when `maxInArray` is called in a method that we want to prove correct, method contracting or an additional loop invariant is the preferred choice to automatically ensure that `maxInArray` does not violate any stated properties. The call could also provide concrete bounds, but would deteriorate software evolution and maintainability.

3.2 Soft Criteria for Method Call Treatment

Verification Effort. Verification effort is typically either measured in terms of *proof steps* of a found proof [1] or in total execution time. Here, we focus on the former measurement, as it is independend of external factors, such as computational power. In particular, reasons for a large number of proof steps are manifold, such as the size and complexity of the program and specification that are subject to verification. For instance, symbolic execution in KeY leads to a step-wise unfolding of Java source code. In case of dynamic dispatch, additional case distinctions have to be made during verification [1]. Unlike method contracting, pure method inlining may lead to a combinatorial explosion in the verification effort, as each method can invoke methods itself that must be also inlined. Nevertheless, there exist cases where sufficient method contracts may also result in larger predicates than the actual implementation. In our evaluation, we aim at empirically investigating the verification effort for method inlining and method contracting in more detail.

Re-verification Effort. When software evolves, each modification may solve prior defects or lead to the introduction of new defects and, thus, re-verification becomes necessary. Because verification is expensive, it is desirable to save verification effort once a program is proved by only re-verifying the parts affected by a change. If the implementation of a specified method changes, only the contract has to be re-established for contracting, whereas for method inlining all callers must be re-verified. If the specification of a method changes, however, only contracting is affected. In this case, the method itself and all of its callers must be re-verified. Moreover, this may involve an adaption of multiple depending contracts. Method inlining is unaffected in this regard, because specifications of inlined methods are ignored. To conclude, we state the hypothesis that the re-verification effort is less with method contracting than with method inlining.

3.3 Summary

Table 1 summarizes our insights of the previous discussion. A "+" means that the respective approach usually performs better and a "−" means that the respective approach fails or performs poorly in that category. The first three rows represent the hard criteria for method call treatment. When dealing with insufficient specifications, only method inlining allows us to verify the correctness of a method.

In case of incomplete implementations and unbounded loops and recursion, however, only method contracting suffices. For the soft criteria, we see verification effort and re-verification effort after a change in the implementation in favor of method contracting. If the specification of a called method changes and method inlining is used, re-verification is not needed. However, if the specification of a proven method changes, method inlining should perform worse depending on call width and call depth of the method. Our goal of the next section is to investigate verification effort under change empirically.

Table 1. Comparison of method contracting and method inlining based on chosen criteria

Criteria	Contracting	Method inlining
Specification effort	–	+
Incomplete implementation	+	–
Unbounded loops and recursion	+	–
Verification effort (initial phase)	+	–
Re-verification effort (change in implementation)	+	–
Re-verification effort (change in specification)	–	+

4   Scalability of Method Call Treatment

We conducted a controlled experiment to measure the effect of method inlining and method contracting on scalability for deductive verification. According to our experience, it is untypical to verify a software system all at once. Hence, we are particularly interested in the effort needed for re-verification of small changes in implementation and specification of single methods. The two independent variables are (a) the *call width* representing the number of method calls within a method body and (b) the *call depth* representing the maximum stack trace of a method call. Both variables allow us to increase the program complexity in a comprehensible and controllable way.

For proving methods in realistic software systems, two problems arise. On the one hand, due to our interest in the verification effort under change, each method needs to be specified with strong enough contracts. The demand in specification effort is, thus, high and not manageable by us for research projects of this scope. On the other hand, for call depths of 20–30, the verification effort becomes infeasible with method inlining. Our solution is therefore to generate artificial programs, varying in call width and call depth, for which we can ensure correct implementations and specifications such that all proofs can be closed automatically.

The rationale behind excluding user interaction is twofold. First, developers need to know how to formally specifiy software, but they should not need to have expertise in proof theory [4]). This, however, is necessary to work with verification systems interactively. Second, the increased expense does not justify the additional insights we may get and is probably unmanageable for us with respect to our experiments.

For the comparison between method inlining and method contracting, we (a) evaluate the root method and a leaf method under change, which gives us indirectly upper and lower bounds for the verification effort of an arbitrary method in-between the call hierarchy, and (b) evaluate the verification effort of ten randomly chosen scenarios, where specifications are sufficient for method contracting in 0%, 10%, ..., 100% of the total number of methods. We address the following research questions.

- **RQ1.1:** What is the re-verification effort if the root method's implementation is changed?
- **RQ1.2:** What is the re-verification effort if the root method's contract is changed?
- **RQ2.1:** What is the re-verification effort if a leaf method's implementation is changed?
- **RQ2.2:** What is the re-verification effort if a leaf method's contract is changed?
- **RQ3:** Given a partially specified program, to what extend does the distribution of contracts impact the verification effort?

Our generators produce Java programs with JML specifications for a given call width and call depth. We analyzed these programs using the program verifier KeY in version 2.6. With the exception to the treatment of method calls, all parameters are set to their respective default. All generators, implementation artifacts, and experimental results can be found online.[1]

4.1   Benchmark for JML-Based Verification

Sorting algorithms are typical in software systems and should ideally be verified to ensure their intended behavior [21]. They are particularly interesting for an evaluation, as they embody real use cases with typical language constructs such as arrays or loops. We therefore decided to implement a sorting algorithm close to bubble sort called *circuitous sorting*, where we are able to specify a variable call width and call depth. However, writing generators with variable call width and call depth to produce verifiable programs with moderate complexity is non-trivial. For the circuitous sorting program we needed countless iterations until all generated method contracts including loop invariants were strong enough for the successful verification with method contracting. Consequently, we decided to write a generator for a simpler program first, namely a program with variable call width and call depth that performs an addition called *circuitous addition*. Our generators together with their respective results may serve as benchmarks

---

[1] https://www.github.com/AlexanderKnueppel/MethodCallTreatment.

for upcoming techniques that aim at reducing verification effort. In the following, we briefly describe both generators.

Generator for the Circuitous Addition: We built a generator for programs that count and return the number of total method calls plus some input i. The control flow of these programs with call width n and call depth m for the root method a1 is as follows. First, the method a1 takes an integer as input and invokes n methods. Each of these methods invokes n methods itself. This procedure goes on until the depth size m is reached. Leaf methods return input i. As depicted in Fig. 2, a1's method contract ensures in its ensures statement that i is incremented by 2. In the example, the call depth is set to 1, so b1 is a leaf method returning input i.

```
1  /*@ public normal_behavior          /*@ public normal_behavior
2  @ requires i < 2147483608-2;        @ requires i < 2147483608;
3  @ ensures \result==\old(i)+2;       @ ensures \result==\old(i);
4  @*/                                  @*/
5  public int a1(int i){                public int b1(int i){
6      int j = b1(i); i = j+1;              return i;
7      j = b1(i); i = j+1;              }
8      return i;
9  }
```

Fig. 2. Root method a1 and leaf method b1 of generated circuitous addition program with call width = 2 and call depth = 1.

Generator for Circuitous Sorting: The root method a1 of the generated circuitous sorting program for call width $n = 2$ is depicted in Fig. 3. Usually, bubble sort is formulated using two nested loops. To integrate call width and call depth, we decomposed the original algorithm into numerous methods accordingly. The leaf method brings exactly one element to its correct sorting position in the input array. The methods on the layer above are calling the leaf method n times and are also bringing one element to the correct position themselves.

Code Optimization. Our generators produce very large programs with many methods for high call widths and call depths. For instance, the add program with call width 9 and call depth 9 allocates approximately 10GB of hard drive. As a result, a huge amount of time is spent in the parsing process of the program in KeY for such programs. We thus simplified our programs such that only one method is created for each layer. The examples in Figs. 2 and 3 are already optimized such that they call method b1 two times instead of calling a method b1 and then a method b2, both having an equivalent implementation and specification. We checked that the verification effort in KeY is the same for both approaches, which is why we kept this optimization for **RQ1** and **RQ2**. For **RQ3**, we use the former approach, as otherwise we would not be able to have specified and non-specified methods at the same time on the same layer.

```
1   /*@ public normal_behavior
2   @ requires p >= 0 && p + 7 < a.length;
3   @ requires (p > 0 ==>(\forall int y; 0 <= y &&
4       y < a.length - p; a[y] <= a[a.length - p]));
5   @ requires (\forall int z; a.length - p <= z &&
6       z < a.length -1; a[z] <= a[z+1]);
7   @ ensures (\forall int o; 0 <= o &&
8       o < a.length - (7+p); a[o] <= a[a.length - (7+p)]);
9   @ ensures (\forall int pos; a.length - (7+p) <= pos &&
10      p < a.length-1; a[p] <= a[p+1]);
11  @*/
12  public void a1(int[] a, int p){
13      b1(a,p+0);
14      b1(a,p+3);
15      int b = 0;
16  /*@ loop_invariant
17  @ 0 <= b && b < a.length - (p + 6) &&
18  @ (\forall int k; 0 <= k && k < b; a[k] <= a[b]) &&
19  @ (\forall int l; a.length - (p + 6) <= l &&
20      l < a.length -1; a[l] <= a[l+1]) &&
21  @ ((p + 6) > 0 ==> (\forall int m; 0 <= m &&
22      m < a.length - (p + 6); a[m] <= a[a.length - (p + 6)]));
23  @ decreasing a.length - b;
24  @ assignable a[*];
25  @*/
26      while(b < a.length-(1+(p + 6))){
27          if(a[b] > a[b+1]){
28              int x = a[b];
29              a[b] = a[b+1];
30              a[b+1] = x;
31          }
32          b++;
33      }
34  }
```

Fig. 3. Root method a1 of the circuitous sorting program for call width = 2.

4.2   Empirical Comparison of Method Call Treatment

We now present the results of our study for circuitous addition and circuitous sorting. We decided to use KeY, since a user can choose between the options *method expand* (i.e., method inlining) and method contracting. We conducted all experiments on an infrastructure with two virtual servers, each constituting 16 cores and an assigned RAM of 48 GB. We limited the number of proof steps to 500,000 per experiment, after which we could not observe anymore progress in the verification phase.

RQ1.1: What is the re-verification effort if the root method's implementation is changed? If the root method's body is changed, only the root method must be verified again, because the root method has no callers. Figure 4a and b depict the number of proof steps needed to verify the root method of the circuitous addition and circuitous sorting programs for method inlining and method contracting. Y-axes of (a)–(c) have logarithmic scale. The call depth for both programs reaches from 1 to 10. The call width is 5 for the circuitous addition program and 1 for the circuitous sorting program. In our experience, 5 is a realistic number of method calls for good-structured Java programs. However, circuitous sorting was not verifiable anymore for larger call widths. The result were either timeouts or OutOfMemory-exceptions. As expected, changing the root method's implementation results in exponential verification effort for method inlining, because every method in the call stack is inlined. For method contracting, we have linear verification effort.

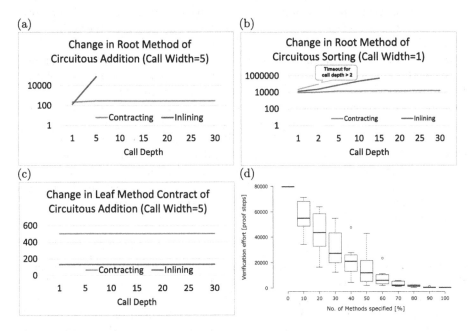

Fig. 4. Empirical results of our evaluation for various change scenarios with respect to call width and call depth.

RQ1.2: *What is the re-verification effort if the root method's specification is changed?* Likewise to RQ1.1, if the root method's specification is changed, only the root method must be verified again. Hence, the result is the same as for *RQ1.1*.

RQ2.1: *What is the re-verification effort if a leaf method's implementation is changed?* For method inlining, every method that inlines the respective leaf method must be verified again. In this case, the verification effort becomes exponential, as every method is inlined at each layer above their own layer exactly once. For method contracting, only the leaf method must be verified and, thus, only a constant number of proof steps is required, independent of the call depth. This case is identical to *RQ2.2* in terms of verification effort.

RQ2.2: *What is the re-verification effort if a leaf method's contract is changed?* If the contract of a leaf method is changed, we have constant verification effort for method inlining and proportional effort to the number of callers for method contracting (cf. Fig. 4c). However, for method inlining we only need to re-verify the leaf method, whereas for method contracting, we need to re-verify the leaf method and every caller of it exactly once, independent of our optimization. The re-verification effort is thus higher with method contracting.

RQ3: *Given a partially specified program, to what extend does the distribution of contracts impact the verification effort?* We evaluated ten scenarios, where the circuitous addition program was specified iteratively. In each iteration, 10% additional randomly-chosen methods are specified. Subsequently, the verification effort of the root method is measured to control call width and call depth. Since KeY does not support a mixture of method contracting and method inlining natively, this way we simulate a combination of both approaches. The box plot in Fig. 4d illustrates the results, where 0% represents method inlining (i.e., only the root method is specified) and 100% represents method contracting (i.e., every method is specified). The analysis emphasizes that strategically specifying an additional 10% of all methods inside the call hierarchy can reduce the verification effort by up-to 50% on average (cf. the median on 20% and 30%). Moreover, there is a wide range in verification effort on numerous iterations. Hence, it matters which parts are specified with respect to the verification effort and, thus, there seems to be potential for a guiding specification process to further support developers.

Threats to Validity. We generated programs ourselves, which threatens internal validity, as we might have chosen unrealistic specifications or implementations. However, the sorting program exhibits that writing generators for specified source code – even for small programs – sufficient for method contracting and automated verification is non-trivial. Moreover, we focused on controlling call width and call depth to investigate the scalability of method call treatment approaches, which otherwise would not have been possible. In this regard, we mostly depicted results for a call width of five, as long methods are considered a bad smell anyway [28]. Moreover, we specified all loops in the sorting program with a loop invariant. Even for method inlining, loop invariants are necessary to find proofs automatically.

An external threat is the choice of KeY as the only verification system. In fact, our evaluation revealed a bug in the implementation leading to an increased garbage collection, which deteriorated the verification time needed. Yet, KeY is one of the most mature verification systems for Java programs with a dedicated community. Moreover, we were not interested in the total number of proof steps needed for either method inlining or method contracting, but how both approaches influence deductive verification in relation. Finally, we generated programs with exactly one class, as we did not want to measure the influence of classes on the verification effort, but only changes in specification and implementation of methods directly.

5   Related Work

Method call treatment is only one parameter of many in the verification of programs. For instance, other parameters in KeY include the treatment of loops (i.e., loop unrolling or using a specified invariant), strategies for proof splitting, and also how arithmetic or quantifiers are treated [1]. However, we were particularly interested in the differences between method inlining and method contracting, which is why we set all other parameters to their defaults.

To give a feeling on how research on deductive verification is considering the treatment of method calls, we inspected numerous publications. In particular, we looked at publications containing empirical evaluations and verification measurements, as well as publications contributing conceptual ideas based upon method contracts. To briefly summarize, we found eight publications that use method contracting [5, 16, 17, 23, 24, 39, 44, 49] and seven publications that use method inlining [7, 18, 20, 34, 37, 42, 47]. Numerous other publications we investigated do not give information about the used approach [1, 2, 6, 9, 11, 13, 25, 46]. Our evaluation shows that method call treatment is not yet another parameter, but greatly affects the performance of evaluations significantly. Essentially, inlining allows us to trade human time for an increase in machine time. To put claimed evaluation results into perspective, the respective approach to method calls should thus be indicated.

A survey on different languages for behavioral contracts was done by Hatcliff et al. [30]. Besides JML, there are alternatives for specifying Java source code, such as C4J [14] or Contract4J [50]. Other examples of tools for deductive program verification include Dafny [36], VCC [19], Verifast [33], Spec# [4], KIV [41], Why3 [8], and F* [45]. We plan to investigate those tools with respect to method call treatment in the future.

A further abstraction on contracts is provided by means of abstract contracts [29]. Method inlining is prone to changes in the implementation, whereas method contracting is prone to changes in the specification. Abstract contracts delay reasoning about changes of method contracts to the latest stage and, thus, enable sophisticated proof reuse by being less prone to changes.

There exist also alternatives to human-written contracting that were not discussed here. Algorithmic techniques aim at extracting contracts for helper procedures, such as logical abduction [3] or logical interpolation based on Horn clauses [12]. Such techniques can help to achieve efficiency and scalability of verification without significantly increasing the required human specification effort, potentially reducing the latter to human inspection of machine-produced specifications.

6   Conclusion and Future Work

Deductive verification has not found its way into industry yet due to issues with the scalability in specification and verification. We investigated method call treatment, which is an important parameter that needs to be considered when working with deductive verification. Our discussion on the differences between method inlining and method contracting reveals that neither approach is superior in all aspects. Surprisingly, an empirical comparison with respect to the verification effort and specification effort has not been made before. We filled that gap by conducting experiments using the program verifier KeY, in which we used artificial programs varying in the number of method calls of each method and the maximum depth of the stack trace.

A sufficient specification for method contracting demands high effort. The study of the circuitous sorting program showed that even specifying small programs to be sufficient for method contracting is hard. However, mainly relying on method inlining in the verification process leads to scalability problems. In this case, our benchmark revealed that inlining over numerous layers is ineffective for re-verification (i.e., time out for the circuitous addition program over a call depth of five). We thus advocate to use an efficient mixture of both, method inlining and method contracting; putting too much work on less impacting specifications may impair the verification effort significantly, whereas a better prioritization is indispensable when programs are specified and verified incrementally (cf. Fig. 4d).

To make deductive verification scalable, we need to develop strategies for identifying specifications of prime importance that reduce the accumulated verification effort. To investigate how such strategies may look like, it is necessary to verify more fully-specified programs with respect to the number of proof steps needed, and also to evaluate how other parameters and other verifiers influence the verification effort. In particular for KeY, an additional annotation in the source code to indicate method calls that should be inlined (i.e., even in the presence of a contract) could be integrated to allow for a explicit mixture of method inlining and method contracting. To cope with high specification effort in general, stronger tool support is needed for guiding less experienced developers in the specification process.

Acknowledgments. This work was supported by the DFG (German Research Foundation) under the Researcher Unit FOR1800: Controlling Concurrent Change (CCC). We gratefully acknowledge Richard Bubel for fruitful discussions and valuable feedback throughout this work.

References

1. Ahrendt, W., Beckert, B., Bubel, R., Hähnle, R., Schmitt, P.H., Ulbrich, M.: Deductive Software Verification – The KeY Book: From Theory to Practice, vol. 10001. Springer, Heidelberg (2016). https://doi.org/10.1007/978-3-319-49812-6
2. Ahrendt, W., Dylla, M.: A system for compositional verification of asynchronous objects. Sci. Comput. Program. **77**(12), 1289–1309 (2012)
3. Albarghouthi, A., Dillig, I., Gurfinkel, A.: Maximal specification synthesis. ACM SIGPLAN Not. **51**, 789–801 (2016)
4. Barnett, M., Fähndrich, M., Leino, K.R.M., Müller, P., Schulte, W., Venter, H.: Specification and verification: the Spec# experience. Comm. ACM **54**, 81–91 (2011)

5. Baumann, C., Beckert, B., Blasum, H., Bormer, T.: Lessons learned from micro-kernel verification-specification is the new bottleneck. SSV, pp. 18–32 (2012)
6. Beckert, B., Grebing, S., Böhl, F.: How to put usability into focus: using focus groups to evaluate the usability of interactive theorem provers. In: Workshop on User Interfaces for Theorem Provers (UITP) (2014)
7. Beckert, B., Klebanov, V.: A dynamic logic for deductive verification of concurrent java programs with condition variables. In: Satellite Workshop at CONCUR, p. 3 (2007)
8. Bobot, F., Filliâtre, J.-C., Marché, C., Paskevich, A.: Why3: shepherd your herd of provers. In: Proceedings of International Workshop on Intermediate Verification Languages, pp. 53–64 (2011)
9. Boldo, S.: Deductive formal verification: how to make your floating-point programs behave. Ph.D. thesis, Université Paris-Sud (2014)
10. Borgida, A., Mylopoulos, J., Reiter, R.: On the frame problem in procedure specifications. IEEE Trans. Softw. Eng. (TSE) **21**(10), 785–798 (1995)
11. Braibant, T., Jourdan, J.-H., Monniaux, D.: Implementing and reasoning about hash-consed data structures in Coq. J. Autom. Reason. **53**(3), 271–304 (2014)
12. Brillout, A., Kroening, D., Rümmer, P., Wahl, T.: An interpolating sequent calculus for quantifier-free presburger arithmetic. In: Giesl, J., Hähnle, R. (eds.) IJCAR 2010. LNCS (LNAI), vol. 6173, pp. 384–399. Springer, Heidelberg (2010). https://doi.org/10.1007/978-3-642-14203-1_33
13. Bruns, D., Klebanov, V., Schaefer, I.: Verification of software product lines with delta-oriented slicing. In: Beckert, B., Marché, C. (eds.) FoVeOOS 2010. LNCS, vol. 6528, pp. 61–75. Springer, Heidelberg (2011). https://doi.org/10.1007/978-3-642-18070-5_5
14. Buchwald, H., Meyerer, F.: C4J: Contracts, Java und Eclipse. Eclipse Mag. **13**(3), 64–69 (2013)
15. Burstall, R.: Program Proving as Hand Simulation with a Little Induction. North-Holland, Amsterdam (1974)
16. Charguéraud, A.: Characteristic formulae for the verification of imperative programs. In: Proceedings of International Conference Functional Programming (ICFP), vol. 46, pp. 418–430. ACM (2011)
17. Cok, D.R.: OpenJML: JML for Java 7 by extending OpenJDK. In: Bobaru, M., Havelund, K., Holzmann, G.J., Joshi, R. (eds.) NFM 2011. LNCS, vol. 6617, pp. 472–479. Springer, Heidelberg (2011). https://doi.org/10.1007/978-3-642-20398-5_35
18. Cok, D.R., Johnson, S.C.: SPEEDY: an eclipse-based IDE for invariant inference. In: Workshop on Formal Integrated Development Environment (F-IDE), 149 (2014)
19. Dahlweid, M., Moskal, M., Santen, T., Tobies, S., Schulte, W.: VCC: contract-based modular verification of concurrent C. In: Companion International Conference Software Engineering (ICSEC), pp. 429–430. IEEE (2009)
20. de Gouw, S., de Boer, F., Ahrendt, W., Bubel, R.: Integrating deductive verification and symbolic execution for abstract object creation in dynamic logic. Softw. Syst. Model. **15**, 1–24 (2014)
21. de Gouw, S., Rot, J., de Boer, F.S., Bubel, R., Hähnle, R.: OpenJDK's Java.utils.Collection.sort() is broken: the good, the bad and the worst case. In: Kroening, D., Păsăreanu, C.S. (eds.) CAV 2015. LNCS, vol. 9206, pp. 273–289. Springer, Cham (2015). https://doi.org/10.1007/978-3-319-21690-4_16
22. Dijkstra, E.W.: A Discipline of Programming, 1st edn. Prentice Hall PTR, Upper Saddle River (1976)

23. El Ghazi, A.A., Ulbrich, M., Gladisch, C., Tyszberowicz, S., Taghdiri, M.: JKelloy: a proof assistant for relational specifications of java programs. In: Badger, J.M., Rozier, K.Y. (eds.) NFM 2014. LNCS, vol. 8430, pp. 173–187. Springer, Cham (2014). https://doi.org/10.1007/978-3-319-06200-6_13
24. Engel, C.: Deductive verification of safety-critical Java programs. Ph.D. thesis, Karlsruhe Institute of Technology (2009)
25. Filliâtre, J.-C.: Deductive program verification. Ph.D. thesis, Université Paris (2011)
26. Filliâtre, J.-C., Marché, C.: The why/krakatoa/caduceus platform for deductive program verification. In: Damm, W., Hermanns, H. (eds.) CAV 2007. LNCS, vol. 4590, pp. 173–177. Springer, Heidelberg (2007). https://doi.org/10.1007/978-3-540-73368-3_21
27. Floyd, R.W.: Assigning meanings to programs. Math. Aspects Comput. Sci. **19**, 19–32 (1967)
28. Fowler, M.: Refactoring: Improving the Design of Existing Code. Addison-Wesley, Boston (2000)
29. Hähnle, R., Schaefer, I., Bubel, R.: Reuse in software verification by abstract method calls. In: Bonacina, M.P. (ed.) CADE 2013. LNCS (LNAI), vol. 7898, pp. 300–314. Springer, Heidelberg (2013). https://doi.org/10.1007/978-3-642-38574-2_21
30. Hatcliff, J., Leavens, G.T., Leino, K.R.M., Müller, P., Parkinson, M.: Behavioral interface specification languages. ACM Comput. Surv. **44**(3), 16:1–16:58 (2012)
31. Hoare, C.A.R.: An axiomatic basis for computer programming. Comm. ACM **12**(10), 576–580 (1969)
32. Hoare, T.: The verifying compiler: a grand challenge for computing research. In: Böszörményi, L., Schojer, P. (eds.) JMLC 2003. LNCS, vol. 2789, pp. 25–35. Springer, Heidelberg (2003). https://doi.org/10.1007/978-3-540-45213-3_4
33. Jacobs, B., Smans, J., Philippaerts, P., Vogels, F., Penninckx, W., Piessens, F.: VeriFast: a powerful, sound, predictable, fast verifier for C and Java. In: Bobaru, M., Havelund, K., Holzmann, G.J., Joshi, R. (eds.) NFM 2011. LNCS, vol. 6617, pp. 41–55. Springer, Heidelberg (2011). https://doi.org/10.1007/978-3-642-20398-5_4
34. Ji, R., Bubel, R.: PE-KeY: a partial evaluator for Java programs. In: Derrick, J., Gnesi, S., Latella, D., Treharne, H. (eds.) IFM 2012. LNCS, vol. 7321, pp. 283–295. Springer, Heidelberg (2012). https://doi.org/10.1007/978-3-642-30729-4_20
35. Leavens, G.T., Cheon, Y.: Design by Contract with JML, September 2006
36. Leino, K.R.M.: Dafny: an automatic program verifier for functional correctness. In: Clarke, E.M., Voronkov, A. (eds.) LPAR 2010. LNCS (LNAI), vol. 6355, pp. 348–370. Springer, Heidelberg (2010). https://doi.org/10.1007/978-3-642-17511-4_20
37. Leino, K.R.M.: Automating induction with an SMT solver. In: Kuncak, V., Rybalchenko, A. (eds.) VMCAI 2012. LNCS, vol. 7148, pp. 315–331. Springer, Heidelberg (2012). https://doi.org/10.1007/978-3-642-27940-9_21
38. Meyer, B.: Object-Oriented Software Construction, 1st edn. Prentice-Hall Inc., Upper Saddle River (1988)
39. Mostowski, W.: Fully verified Java card API reference implementation. Verify, 7 (2007)
40. Posegga, J., Vogt, H.: Byte code verification for Java smart cards based on model checking. In: Quisquater, J.-J., Deswarte, Y., Meadows, C., Gollmann, D. (eds.) ESORICS 1998. LNCS, vol. 1485, pp. 175–190. Springer, Heidelberg (1998). https://doi.org/10.1007/BFb0055863

41. Reif, W.: The Kiv-approach to software verification. In: Broy, M., Jähnichen, S. (eds.) KORSO: Methods, Languages, and Tools for the Construction of Correct Software. LNCS, vol. 1009, pp. 339–368. Springer, Heidelberg (1995). https://doi.org/10.1007/BFb0015471

42. Schreiner, W.: Computer-assisted program reasoning based on a relational semantics of programs. In: First Workshop on CTP Components for Educational Software (2012)

43. Schumann, J.M.: Automated Theorem Proving in Software Engineering. Springer, Heidelberg (2001). https://doi.org/10.1007/978-3-662-22646-9

44. Suter, P., Dotta, M., Kuncak, V.: Decision procedures for algebraic data types with abstractions. Proc. Symp. Princ. Program. Lang. (POPL) **45**(1), 199–210 (2010)

45. Swamy, N., et al.: Dependent types and multi-monadic effects in F*. In: Proceedings of Symposium Principles of Programming Languages (POPL), vol. 51, pp. 256–270. ACM (2016)

46. ter Beek, M.H., de Vink, E.P., Willemse, T.A.: Towards a feature mu-Calculus targeting SPL verification. In: Proceedings of International Workshop Formal Methods and Analysis in Software Product Line Engineering (FMSPLE), pp. 61–75 (2016)

47. Thüm, T., Schaefer, I., Apel, S., Hentschel, M.: Family-based deductive verification of software product lines. In: Proceeding of International Conference Generative Programming and Component Engineering (GPCE), vol. 48, pp. 11–20. ACM (2012)

48. Trentelman, K.: Proving correctness of JavaCard DL Taclets using Bali. In: Proceedings of International Conference Software Engineering and Formal Methods (SEFM), pp. 160–169. IEEE (2005)

49. Walter, D.: A formal verification environment for use in the certification of safety-related C-programs. Ph.D. thesis, Bremen, University, Dissertation (2010)

50. Wampler, D.: Contract4J for design by contract in Java: design pattern-like protocols and aspect interfaces. In: Fifth AOSD Workshop on ACP4IS, pp. 27–30. Citeseer (2006)

Java Automated Deductive Verification in Practice: Lessons from Industrial Proof-Based Projects

David R. Cok[✉]

CEA, LIST, Software Safety and Security Laboratory,
PC 174, 91191 Gif-sur-Yvette, France
david.r.cok@gmail.com

Abstract. Formal methods in the form of automated proof-based deductive verification is increasingly used in industry to give confidence in the security and correctness of libraries and applications. This paper presents observations on current tools and processes based on recent experience with verification projects on industrial software: scalability, breadth, specification language expressibility and semantics, capabilities of underlying SMT tools, and integration into industrial build and continuous integration processes.

1 Introduction

Automated deductive, static analysis of software has been increasing in capability over the past decade. This trend was initially fueled by performance and feature improvements in SMT solvers and has now reached the point that software verifications of industrial software in practical use are being executed. As capability has improved and the kinds of problems being tackled have changed, the challenges for deductive verification have also changed. In this paper I present some of those challenges as experienced in recent industrial verification projects.

Automated deductive verification follows the following paradigm: the intent of the software under study (the 'target software') is expressed in machine-readable specifications; both these specifications and the target software are translated into a logical form; a logical proof tool then determines, if possible, whether the logical representations of the specifications and the implementation are consistent. If so, then the implementation is considered *verified*, that is, to be consistent with the specifications; if not, then either the implementation or the specifications (or both) have some fault to be found and corrected. Automation is critically important for the technique to become widespread and for efficiency in application. Thus we do not consider tools that translate into interactive proof environments.

The observations reported in this paper are largely the result of projects that used the Java Modeling Language (JML) and the OpenJML program verification tool. However, these observations are also informed by experience with and

© Springer Nature Switzerland AG 2018
T. Margaria and B. Steffen (Eds.): ISoLA 2018, LNCS 11247, pp. 176–193, 2018.
https://doi.org/10.1007/978-3-030-03427-6_16

discussions about the KeY tool, ACSL and Frama-C, Ada and SPARK, C# and Spec#, Dafny, and designing specification languages for C++ and Fortran.

2   Specification Languages and Tools

JML [6,31] is a language for specifying behavior of (non-concurrent) Java source code. Its syntax and semantics are similar to its host programming language, Java, with extensions appropriate to expressing assertions in a typed first-order logic appropriate to reasoning about software. JML is largely method-centric, with syntax to write pre-, frame- and post-conditions for each method, along with object invariants and other advanced features. JML is widely used in education about software specification and as a platform for research and experimentation in specification and reasoning about software.

JML is similar in purpose and structure to other *Behavioral Interface Specification Languages* [18]. Other examples are later languages such as ACSL for C programs [5], Spec# for C# [35], SPARK for Ada [3], and Dafny [23]. JML was designed using experience with the Larch tools [17] and with Eiffel [24]. The Key tool [2] is also a program verification tool for Java, but addresses only the pre-generics (Java 4) subset of Java. In contrast to BISLs are specification languages such as Z [29] and the B-method [1] that are more mathematical, are programming-language independent, and are refined, with accompanying proofs, to implementations in specific programming languages.

OpenJML [8–10,13,33] is a tool built on the OpenJDK [32] Java compiler. It translates both Java and JML into a logical form. This logical form contains a (large) number of specific assertions (a.k.a verification conditions); if all of the assertions are true, then the Java implementation is consistent with the given specifications. The logical form is translated into SMT-LIB [4,34] and then back-end logical solvers check whether the verification conditions are true and hence whether method implementations and specifications are consistent. Like most of the tools mentioned above, OpenJML uses an SMT solver (in our case, Z3 [16]) to check the logical verification conditions. Each of the specification languages above has corresponding tools to generate verification conditions and manage back-end tools that check those conditions. An example is the Frama-C [30] toolkit for ACSL. Some proof systems, such as Coq and Isabelle, are partially interactive, whereas OpenJML and most SMT-based tools aim for full automation, given program annotations.

An example of JML is given in Fig. 1. Syntactically, JML specifications are written as structured Java comments (beginning with //@ or /*@). The method specification is expressed as a sequence of *clauses*: the **requires** clause is a precondition, **assignable** denotes a frame-condition, **ensures** a post-condition, and **signals** the post-condition on throwing an exception. Frame conditions state what memory locations may be assigned by the method; any memory location not mentioned can be assumed to be unchanged by the actions of the method. Not shown are **invariants**, which state consistency properties of data structures that are expected to always hold (except perhaps during manipulation).

Accompanying tools perform both static checking and runtime assertion checking using the JML specifications. Other specification languages use similar keywords, language structure, and architecture, differing mainly in the specification language constructs needed for various individual aspects of the different programming languages.

Applying logical reasoning tools to prove the consistency of implementation and specification without executing the program is called static deductive verification (DV). Our focus is on automated tools, which need the user to provide specifications of functional behavior, but then carry out a proof of the implied assertions automatically. Other tools may use interactive proof tools, implement runtime assertion checking, or apply other less-logically-founded static checking techniques.

```
1 //@ requires i != Integer.MIN_VALUE;
2 //@ assignable \nothing;
3 //@ ensures \result >= 0 && (\result == i || \result == -i);
4 //@ signals (Exception e) false;
5 int abs(int i);
```

Fig. 1. Example JML specification of an absolute-value method

3   Target Projects

The primary project on which the observations in this paper are based is a case study [15] of an implementation of a secure streaming communication protocol that underpins much of the communication between distributed components in Amazon and AWS (e.g., AWS's Kinesis service). The software was a useful case study because it was developed without deductive verification as a concern, and consequently it is an instance of legacy code implementing a design that was not affected by any constraints of a verification system and was the subject of specification and verification only after being written. It is also highly important to Amazon and its customers and so worth the effort of specification and verification. This code is not yet publicly available, as it is Amazon proprietary code, but AWS is considering open sourcing this code, as it has with some other critical software. The open sourcing is driven in part by security-conscious customers who are requesting publication of the code with verification proofs, to help them understand and audit how security is established on their behalf.

Additional insight into the specification needs of large-scale software comes from verification projects on other proprietary software, on the development of various specification tools for US-government-funded research contracts [11,12], and on case studies performed during current development of a specification language for C++ [36].

4   Observations

Industrial-scale software differs significantly from challenge problems posed in competitions or as published exercises that demonstrate particular proof techniques. The latter often focus on particular means to verify the implementation of algorithms or design patterns. Industrial-scale software by contrast is much larger in scale. Intricate algorithms are limited to small corners of the software. Instead the concerns are ones of data representation, data movement, abstraction, and large state spaces. Consequently the abilities needed of proof tools and SMT solvers are different. The implications for tools are more ones of engineering and representation than of logical capability.

The following subsections discuss a variety of issues encountered during our case study.

4.1   Scale

A significant industrial software system can be quite large. Even when well-designed and modular, the state space is large and the dependencies among modules are significant. Consider what is needed to verify a method of a class with a large internal state, that is, with many data fields. First, each data field may have associated invariants. These may be implicit invariants such as the numerical range of primitive types or explicit invariants distinguishing legal states from illegal. These explicit invariants may be class (in the Java sense) invariants for the type of the data field. Thus there are dependencies on all of the types of the data fields and formal parameters. Those dependencies may propagate recursively. In addition, there are relationships among Java types to be represented: which types are derived from others and which are not. For example, even if a class is itself quite simple, every Java class derives ultimately from `Object`, which includes a `toString` method, and so includes `String`, `CharSequence`, `StringBuffer`, `CharBuffer`, `StringBuilder`, sequences, arrays, and the like. Interfaces add more complexity because an object of (static) class `A` may indeed be an instance of interface `I` if the object happens to be an instance of some (unseen) class `D` derived from `A` that also implements interface `I`.

Consequently the collection of all the facts that might be relevant to a method (the prelude) is quite large, even if the body of the method itself is very simple. The proof of the assertions required to verify the method may require only a small number of facts from the prelude. However, a proof tool needs to wade through all of these facts to find the relevant ones. At best a large prelude will only cause the proof attempt to take more memory or more time; but it might also cause an unknown result because of inadequate time or memory.

One way to address this situation is to rely on well-engineered SMT solvers to sort through all the chaff. In this approach, the translation of the verification problem to SMT would include all the facts of the prelude. The SMT solver would need to parse this large prelude and maintain an internal representation of it all. The SMT solver then executes a search through these facts to find a chain of inferences that leads to a contradiction. A well-engineered solver will not select possible next facts in its search by random, but rather will base its search at least in part on common variables and the like. Such a search ought to remove or at least deprioritize facts unlikely to be relevant to the desired proof. This does not reduce the size of the fact set, but does rely on the SMT tool to handle large fact sets well.

A second approach is for the translation tool to be somewhat selective in its choice of facts to include in the prelude. For example, suppose a method's implementation calls a method m in another class B. That will create dependencies on invariants of B and on any classes or methods mentioned in the specification of m. But it need not create dependencies on other methods of B or their specifications. Similarly, suppose that a method being verified has a formal parameter b of type B. If fields or methods of b are used, then the specifications of b and any invariants of B become possibly relevant. However, if the value b is simply copied into a field of type B, then no properties of b or B are relevant, other than, possibly, whether b is permitted to be null or not.

Thirdly, after generating a set, even a fully complete set, of prelude facts, the translation tool could do its own exploration of the web of dependencies among the facts themselves, discarding any that do not appear to be connected to the assertions to be proved. Recall that the SMT prover is attempting to establish a contradiction; removing a logical fact will never cause a contradiction where there was none with the fact included. That is, removing facts will at worst cause the inability to establish a desired assertion, never establish one unsoundly. This approach simplifies the logical problem presented to the SMT solver, at the cost of doing some work that the solver may well be able to do itself.

It is an open research question in the design of program verification translation tools and of SMT solvers to what extent pre-processing of the input assertions for the purpose of removing irrelevant facts is best done by the SMT solver or as part of translation to SMT, or a combination.

4.2 Writing Specifications

It is well-known that a core problem of scale when applying deductive verification is that specifications need to be written for each method. The effort to write and check these specifications is still considerable. Thus the cost of such projects could be reduced, and consequently the breadth of application increased, by having practical specification inference and other means of lessening specification writing. Specification inference is a large, active area of research. One endeavor to include inference as part of verification tools is [28].

4.3 Specifications of Libraries

Another common aspect of large-scale software is heavy use of library routines. In fact, the absence of broadly applicable libraries is seen as an impediment to adoption of a new programming language—the experience of C++, Java and Python are examples. Verifications of individual algorithms or demonstrations of proof techniques are much less likely to use library routines.

To prove facts about code that uses library methods requires that those methods have specifications documenting their effects. Separately, the implementations of the library routines should be verified against the specifications, but for clients of the library it is the presence of the specifications that is important. This raises the question: who is to write and review the specifications of such libraries? If deductive verification were part of common practice (or when it is) it will be seen as part of the development of a library to write (and verify) the specifications also. But we are not yet at that point in accepted practice. It remains an open piece of work, for example, to write specifications for the ever-growing Java system library. (Some specifications are part of the OpenJML release, on the public OpenJML github site [33].) Similarly, the ACSL specifications for the C standard libraries as used by the Frama-C tool have much to be added.

This problem is accentuated by the fact that there may be more than one set of specifications needed. The specifications for runtime-assertion checking for example need to be executable, while those used for static verification need to be amenable to deductive verification tools. Even within the use of static verification, in some situations light-weight specifications are sufficient for assuring a lack of runtime errors while in others carefully detailed behavioral specifications are needed to prove behavioral properties of client programs. Different tools for the same specification language may have differing success with different ways of formulating equivalent specifications.

Thus, along with generating an initial set of specifications for commonly used libraries, it is an open research question as to how much customization of the form of the specifications is necessary to accommodate the variety of anticipated applications. Would a well designed specification language accommodate all uses? Is some sort of macro facility needed to enable or disable different parts of a specification for different applications? Or does there need to be wholly different sets of specifications perhaps in quite different specification languages?

4.4   Verification of Libraries

As noted in the last subsection, clients of libraries need specifications for those libraries if they are to perform DV on code using those libraries. Perhaps the clients are producing software libraries of their own and need to generate specifications for them. Writing specifications for libraries has some unique challenges. A method in an application or a library that is used within the application or library must be specified in a way that (a) permits the implementation of the method to be proved consistent with the specification and (b) permits clients (callers) of the method to know what the method does. Overly weak specifications make (a) easy but (b) impossible; strong specifications make (b) possible but (a) more challenging. Thus many methods have a natural check: the specifications must be correctly strong enough or something will not verify in the system as a whole.

However, the methods at the public API of a library do not have this check, because they are not necessarily called by the library itself. It is easy for methods at the top of the call tree to have specifications that are too weak: easily proved against their own implementations, but inadequate to prove the behavior of their callers. A solution for this problem is for the library developers to also create a set of example programs that exercise the public API *and are proved correct against the specifications of the API*. In fact, these example programs could be part of the library's (dynamic) test suite. Even further, it could be a requirement that all of the (dynamic) test cases in the library's test suite should also be statically verified to succeed. Constructing a test suite suitable for both static and dynamic testing requires a bit of creative generalization: for static verification, we would state that a test should hold for the complete range and combinations of legal parameters; for dynamic testing, we would choose some subset of the range and combinations of parameters to exercise.

An important aspect of these tests of the public API is that *combinations* of the public API methods work together as expected. For example, a test of a Stack library would check that a push followed by a pop gives expected results. Although the specifications for individual methods might be correct, proving that combinations work as expected ensures that the methods' specifications are strong enough to prove client programs. As a simple example of this approach, consider the implementation of a Stack class in Fig. 2. Here Stack may be an abstract class of an interface; that is, it may not have a concrete implementation; even a concrete implementation may be private, and not to be exposed to the user to ensure information hiding. So model variables are used to represent the intent of the specification; here the stack is modeled as an array and a size (whether or not the actual implementation uses a corresponding concrete representation).

These specifications are correct (according to informal expectations of a Stack) and consistent with a (not-shown) implementation. They are also sufficient to show that an assertion such as push(i); int j = pop(); //@ assert i == j; is true. However, they cannot show that the assertion in push(i); push(ii); int jj = pop(); int j = pop(); //@ assert i == j; is true. The problem is that the methods are under-specified: for example, push should also ensure that the elements in the stack before the push operation are still present in the same order after the push operation. Verifying example uses such as the second example above do not guarantee that the specifications are always adequately strong, but are a help.

```
1 public class Stack {
2 //@ model public int size;   public invariant size >= 0;
3 //@ model public Integer[ ] stack; public invariant stack.length >= size;
4
5 //@ requires size > 0;
6 //@ assignable \nothing;
7 //@ ensures \result == stack[size-1];
8 Integer top();
9
10 //@ assignable stack, size;
11 //@ ensures top() == a && size == \old(size) + 1;
12 void push(Integer a);
13
14 //@ requires size > 0;
15 //@ old int topvalue = top(); // Value before removing it
16 //@ assignable stack, size;
17 //@ ensures topvalue == \result && size == \old(size) - 1;
18 void Integer pop();
19 }
```

Fig. 2. Stack methods with weak specifications

4.5   Continuous Integration

It is now standard practice in software development to implement a dynamic test suite that is run regularly: certainly for each release, but better each night, or continuously if it is large, or even on each commit to the source code repository. The same discipline should be adopted for static verification. This is generally a straightforward process. It requires that proof attempts be recheckable automatically. For SMT-based proofs, this means simply re-attempting the proof. For interactive proofs, this means capturing the proof steps as a script and replaying the proof, checking that it is still valid. When SMT solvers are able to record proofs, it will perhaps be possible to replay those as well, saving considerable time over re-finding the proof.

Verifying a large system can be very time-consuming. In our case study a full run of 5K lines of code took about 16 h. However, the proof system is modular and hence highly parallelizable. Proof attempts of each of the 700 or so methods in our case study could have been executed independently and in parallel, limiting the wall clock time to about 60 min for the longest proof and much less for most proofs.

A related challenge is engaging the software developers responsible for code development directly in the specification and verification process. Currently it is much more common for formal methods experts to complete verifications as a separate project. Even if verification remains a specialty, as dynamic testing often is, having the static verification aspect be a first-class, fully-integrated aspect of the development process is the goal.

4.6   Verifying Security

Software safety and correctness require proving that the actual behavior includes the intended behavior. Security on the other hand requires in part that no unintended behaviors can happen as a by-product of intended behaviors. That is, verification only establishes the properties that are stated; there may be other necessary properties that have been forgotten. To avoid unintended behaviors, the concept of code coverage as a quality metric for dynamic testing can be extended to static verification. Various degrees of code coverage are well known in dynamic testing: all statements are executed, all branch possibilities are taken, all possible paths are exercised, etc. Static verification by design already considers all of these possibilities and checks for correct behavior for each combination. However, the range of possibilities considered is constrained by a method's preconditions and the properties established are limited to the stated postconditions. That leaves open the following possibility: a method performs its expected functionality but also some additional functionality; the precondition of the method is written to preclude that extra functionality, that is, the extra functionality appears to be dead code; an application calls the method, ignoring the precondition's constraint, and exercises the extra functionality (which might have some nefarious intent). The same result can be obtained by a weak postcondition that does not say anything about the extra functionality. In these cases, the static verification will succeed and dynamic testing may also.

Accordingly, we would like a measure of *static* code coverage. Such a measure could work as follows.

- To measure the quality of preconditions, the verification system can check that given the stated preconditions all basic code blocks of the method's implementation are feasible and all branches and switches can take on any of the implemented values. That is, there is no dead code and no trivial branch conditions. It is also possible to measure whether all preconditions are needed by selectively eliminating each top-level conjunct and testing whether the implementation is still verifiable.
- For frame conditions, the system should check that the set of modifiable locations is no larger than necessary.
- For postconditions, the verification system can check that each modifiable location in the frame condition is constrained by the postcondition.

```
1
2  //@ requires (* array a big enough for all accesses, indices in range *);
3  //@ assignable a[*];
4  //@ ensures a[i] == \old(a[j]) && a[]j] == \old(a[i]);
5  void swap(int[] a, int i, int j) {
6      int k = i == 23456 ? 23456 : 23457;
7      a[k] = a[i];
8      a[i] = a[j];
9      a[j] = a[k];
10 }
```

Fig. 3. Swap function with unspecified functionality

For example, the implementation in Fig. 3 is consistent with the specification and (mostly) with what would be expected of a swap procedure. However, the implementation has some extra functionality in that it modifies location a[23456] (or 23457), possibly leaking information. Note that the frame condition allows modifying any array location but the postcondition does not express any properties of array locations other than i and j. This underspecification can be detected by tools (though not all underspecifications can be). Either the frame condition should be modified to be more restrictive, such as assignable a[i], a[j] or the postcondition should express additional properties, such as

```
ensures (\forall int i; 0 <=k && k<a.length;
                       k!=i && k!=j ==> a[k] == \old(a[k])));
```

In either case, the proof would now fail; alternately, if the new specifications accurately reflected the implementation, the extra functionality of modifying the extra array location would be apparent in the specifications.

It might also be possible to check that the implementation is minimal in some sense. In the course of translating specifications and implementation into logic, each condition and statement of the specification and implementation becomes part of the overall logical condition to be checked. What is important then is that each logical term arising from the specification or implementation be essential in establishing the proof of consistency. We can omit from this requirement any background axioms that do not explicitly stem from the code and its specifications. Imagine omitting each program statement in turn, or alternately, each logical assertion in the translation, and then rechecking whether the proof is still successful. A single extraneous assignment could be omitted and the proof successful, indicating that it is irrelevant to the specifications. However, this concept needs considerable expansion to detect cases in which multiple statements work in concert to produce the extra functionality; it also relies on having a complete functional specification of the target software.

4.7   Expressiveness of Specification Languages

Specification-based software verification is capable of verifying the functional behavior of software. Without specifications, tools can only check that software does not violate internal properties of the programming languages themselves, such as not dereferencing null pointers and not indexing arrays out of bounds. The functional behavior specification need not be complete. For example, one might specify and verify only key security or information flow properties that one expects the target software to obey. In verifying such properties one is determining that no security boundary is violated, but it still is possible that, for example, the target software does nothing at all, which would include not violating security properties.

So, verification systems aspire to being able to verify fairly complete specifications of the functional behaviors of a system. But verification systems can only check that the specifications and the target software are consistent. Even if they agree, *both may be wrong in the sense that neither represents what the author or a user actually want the system's behavior to be*. A specification and the target software implementation are two different representations of what the software does. There is some merit in simply having a second representation to double-check that the human intent for the software is what is desired. However, it is much better if the specification is written in a form in which it is much more obvious than in the code itself what the software is intended to do. If the specification is as verbose and difficult to understand as the code, then not much is gained. In any case, it is clear that the specifications must undergo human review for correctness; the verification system must be designed so that such human review is likely to find specification errors and omissions.

So a first goal is conciseness and readability. Can an appropriate combination of defaults, readable syntax and clear expression enable specifications that are concise, readable, and correctly understood by humans. Current specification languages of the BISL variety express specifications in a variant of sorted first-order logic with a syntax and semantics close to the target programming language. By using syntax like the target programming language, as opposed to, for example, a programming-language independent mathematical language, the learning barrier is lowered: software engineers using the target programming language will be familiar with the syntax of the specification language. And, by using a form of sorted first-order logic, the meaning of and translation to a logical form is unambiguous and straightforward.

But such a syntax may not be the best one for expressing the desired behavior or for human review of whether the specified behavior matches the desired behavior. Consider some examples. How would one specify the behavior of a tool that parsed a text input and produced an abstract syntax tree? The standard means in computer science for describing the behavior of a parser is a BNF specification of the intended grammar. One might combine that in this case with a library of tree operations.

Consider a second example: how would one specify the desired behavior of a continuously operating IoT device? One means is a state table: a table showing the appropriate action for each combination of input and environmental conditions. Such tables were promoted at least as far back as [27] as a specification that was more understandable by domain experts than purely logical representations.

Both of these examples are instances of DSLs – domain-specific languages – geared to the problem domain at hand. The advantage of DSLs is that they can be tailored to the concepts and syntax of the problem domain. The disadvantage is that each DSL must be accompanied by tools that convert instances of the DSL to a logical form that appropriate, e.g., SMT, tools can reason about. And this conversion, as one more step in the tool chain, must itself be verifiably correct. This disadvantage, however, needs to be addressed once, by tool-building experts. The advantage is gained each time the DSL is used to specify an appropriate system.

Thus our observation on this point is the following. Specification languages tied to programming languages have been good for development of specification methodology by programmers, logicians and verification experts. They are still an appropriate foundation for specification. As we move from verifying algorithms to verifying applications and systems, we should now explore adding capabilities appropriate to the domains being specified. Some research questions are these:

- What DSLs have general utility and understandability by experts across a number of domains?
- Can there be a meta-DSL framework that simplifies the work of creating a new DSL for a domain and the work of (verifiably) correctly translating that DSL into a checkable logical representation?
- What new theories should be built into SMT solvers to improve the runtime performance and the proof success rate in reasoning about assertions that originally came from DSLs?

4.8   Specification Language Features

The previous subsection described a general approach for future specification languages—domain specific specification languages. There are also a number of smaller-scale features needed in current languages or that need semantic clarity. An interesting comparison on this point is the set of challenges evaluated a dozen years ago in [21] (see Sect. 5 below), which reacted to challenges enumerated prior to that, in [19].

Mathematical Concepts. A common underpinning to many abstraction and modeling problems is basic mathematical concepts such as sets and sequences. In one sense these are the most basic domain-specific specification languages. Their use was anticipated in [21] Sect. 2.1.4. Moving toward incorporating mathematical types into the specification language is a step away from BISLs and toward language-independent modeling. Nevertheless, at least if the built-in mathematical types are restricted to concepts that are broadly known, such types supply a ready-to-hand set of basic concepts. Furthermore such types can be purely mathematical, value-based types, so reasoning about them is much simpler, as there are no concerns about mutable values or aliasing or program state. The experience of the case studies reported here is that a robust set of mathematical types would simplify both modeling and reasoning about software.

In static deductive verification, the question arises as to whether such types are (a) simply axiomatized within a theory of uninterpreted functions or (b) built-in to SMT solvers as theories with their own decision procedures. The point of using specialized decision procedures in SMT solvers is to improve proof performance, so one should expect that if supported by the SMT solver, mathematical types in the specification languages should be mapped to the corresponding concepts in SMT-LIB. For example, SMT-LIB has long included arrays, integers and reals and is in the process of defining strings, sets and sequences.

For runtime assertion checking, mathematical types in the specification language will need executable representations. This is generally straightforwardly feasible with some restrictions. For example, unbounded quantification is generally not supported in runtime assertion checking.

Once the representation of these modeling types is defined, there still remains the task of defining and axiomatizing a suitable set of such constructs.

Invariants. Invariants state properties of data representations that define the permitted states of that representation. As distinguished in ACSL, some invariants are *strong*, meaning that they always hold; an example is requiring that a reference field be never null. Other invariants may be *weak* meaning that they need hold only at function call and return points. The latter form is necessary to be able to modify data structures, allowing invariants to be violated temporarily. However, as discussed in [22] and elsewhere, strictly requiring invariants to hold at procedure call boundaries is often impractical and can be non-modular. Specification writers need more fine-grained control over which invariants hold at given program points. Spec#, for example, required explicit opening and closing of representations (and their invariants). Research such as [25] and [21] (and citations therein) propose disciplines for tree-structured ownership-based control of invariants. However, no proposed solution is without its difficulties and no solution has been widely adopted and implemented. This also is very much still an open research issue.

Abstraction and Refinement. Large software systems rely on abstraction and modularity to be comprehensible. In object-oriented programming, a base class can be used to represent some abstract behavior, which is then concretely implemented in derived classes. Clients use the base class without knowing the specifics of the implementation. The behavior of the base class is known through its specification. That specification must be written in terms of abstractions, as there are no public concrete fields in the base class to which to refer. Then the derived class implementation must be connected to the base class abstractions in a way that the derived class implementations will satisfy the base class specifications. This connection is expressed as a definition that functions as an axiom. For example, JML declares `model` fields in the base class and defines them with a `represents` clause in the derived class.

The semantics of these model fields and representational definitions must be considered carefully. For example, at what program points does the definition hold? Ideally it always holds even at program points that class invariants do not hold. For that to be true the definition cannot depend on weak invariants.

A second point to note is that the specification of the abstraction should be expressed in terms appropriate to the abstraction. Thus the desire for mathematical data types in the specification language (Sect. 4.8) or even full-fledged, user-defined specification language extensions appropriate to the domain (Sect. 4.7).

A third point relates to management of definitions and axioms. Mathematical concepts use both theorems about the concepts and definitions relating the concepts to simpler component properties. A student of mathematical proof needs to develop an intuition as to when proofs can be accomplished using theorems alone and when the definitions need to be 'unfolded' and the proof expressed in terms of the elements of the definition. Similarly, the translation of specifications and implementations into logic needs to include both axiomatizations of properties of abstraction concepts and their definitions. But proof tools need the intuition to know when and when not to unfold the definitions as part of the search process.

Finally, the specification relationship between abstract and concrete is similar to the relationships between different levels of refinement in refinement-based design. It would be desirable to have the same concepts and methodologies for both.

Quantification. SMT solvers were originally designed to work on sets of ground formulae, without quantification. Though quantified formulae are now an essential part of SMT-LIB, their use can often lead to unknown results from a solver rather than a clear result of validity or invalidity. Theories including quantified formula rely on heuristics to determine when and how to instantiate a quantification; performance problems can arise from recursive or infinite matching loops in the solvers.

On the other hand, research in automated first-order theorem proving (ATP) as used in the TPTP project and the CADE ATP system competition are built to handle quantified formulae from the start, with the specific theories that SMT solvers incorporate being a much later addition. Consequently there would appear to be much to learn and much practical gain for software verification by cross-pollinating and uniting these two fields of research.

Hidden State and Observational Purity. Sound reasoning about programs with state (i.,e., most imperative programs) requires stating *frame conditions*— specifications about the set of non-local memory locations that might be changed by a method. Such specifications propagate up the call tree, recursively. Even with means to abstractly represent sets of locations, a substantial degree of information hiding and abstraction is lost. What is needed is a means to allow internal state changes within a method without needing to mention them in a frame condition, as long as such changes are not observed outside the method. This property is called *observational purity*.

An example is a method that caches the result of a computation, so that the result can be returned quickly if the same computation is requested again. The internal state (the cache) is not visible (except by runtime performance); the method returns the same result whether or not the cache is populated. We would like to specify the action of the method, including its frame conditions, without having to mention the cache.

Observational purity has been the subject of a variety of research [7,14,26]. The problem principally affects large-scale systems, where information hiding and abstraction are particularly important. Perhaps as a result, the theory has not yet been completely worked through and tools do not implement syntax to accommodate observational purity.

Understanding and Debugging Proof Failures. In a verification project, by far the bulk of time is spent understanding why proof attempts fail. The reasons can be any combination of faulty specifications, faulty implementation, inadequacies in the logical representations of specification or implementation, or lack of capability in the underlying solver. Even if the reasons are just in the first two categories, it can be quite difficult to determine the cause and fix of the problem. Over time the situation has improved. For example, IDEs now typically represent counterexample information in source code terms and the execution path of the counterexample overlaid on the source code (cf. OpenJML [8], Dafny, and the Why3 IDE as examples).

However, there are still significant improvements to be made. Legitimate counterexamples are concrete; better would be symbolic counterexamples—for example, that the proof fails if x is negative, not just when x is -2. Furthermore, the engineer is often trying to determine what information is *missing*, a difficult question for a reasoning system to answer. In other situations a set of specifications is *infeasible*, meaning it contains a contradiction; in that case, it would be helpful to provide the user with a minimal set of logical formulae that create the contradiction.

4.9   Concurrency

Specifying and verifying programs using concurrently executing threads or processes is still an open area of research. The case study prompting this paper used quite a bit of multi-threading, which had to be simply ignored, leaving a partial verification of the software package. Multi-threaded programs are harder to write and thus stand to benefit more from verification. Consequently practical specification and verification techniques for concurrent software would be very timely.

5   Related Work

Considerable progress has been made in specification theory and implementation over the past decade, to the point where the principal problems encountered in our case study had to do with the scale of industrial software and the work of writing functional specifications rather than the lack of specific verification techniques. Nevertheless, on reviewing past compilations of verification challenges, it is clear that many significant problems have remained either unsolved or unimplemented. As evidence, Table 1 lists the challenges documented in the 2012 assessment of the state of specification [21], with a brief comment on the current state.

Table 1. Specification challenges as listed in [21]

Challenge (section numbers from [21])	Current state (section numbers in this paper)
Section 2.1 Specifying modeling types	Still an issue, as discussed in Sect. 4.8
Section 2.2 Comprehensions	Still an issue, though not discussed here
Section 3.1 Method calls in specifications	Largely solved in OpenJML and Dafny, though convenient handling of frame conditions (e.g., Sect. 4.8) needs improvement and implementations of **reads** clauses are still needed
Section 3.2 Frame conditions for static fields	Largely still open
Section 3.3 Class initialization	Largely still open
Section 4.1 Semantics of invariants	Though partially solved there are still significant open questions (cf. Sect. 4.8)
Section 4.2 Specifying finalizers	Not yet addressed
Section 5.1 Specifying uses of function objects	Theory presented in [20]; evaluation and implementation underway in OpenJML and ACSL++
Section 5.2 Specifying invocations of function objects	
Section 6.1 Library specifications	Still an issue as discussed in Sect. 4.3
Section 6.2 Multiple tools	An open issue as discussed in Sect. 4.3

6 Conclusion

The scale and scope of realistic, industrial software makes demands of specification languages that are different from those needed to verify algorithms and small demonstration programs. They include managing complexity, appropriately specifying abstractions, including mathematics and DSL concepts in the specification language, additional techniques for verifying libraries, and the need for full-fledged specification of system libraries. In addition, though progress has been made in recent years in understanding and improving specification languages and tools, revisiting previously published compilations of challenges reveals many areas that still need better semantics and more thorough implementations. At industrial scale, a core problem is still the work required to write functional specifications for a large software system, so successful specification inference that reduces this burden is essential (cf. [28]). Nevertheless, despite the research and implementation work yet to be completed, successful deductive verifications of industrially-relevant software is beginning to be possible, practical, and even welcomed by developers.

References

1. Abrial, J.R., Hoare, A., Chapron, P.: The B-Book: Assigning Programs to Meanings. Cambridge University Press, Cambridge (1996)
2. Ahrendt, W., Beckert, B., Bubel, R., Hähnle, R., Schmitt, P.H., Ulbrich, M. (eds.): Deductive Software Verification - The KeY Book - From Theory to Practice. LNCS, vol. 10001. Springer, Heidelberg (2016). https://doi.org/10.1007/978-3-319-49812-6
3. Barnes, J.: Spark: The Proven Approach to High Integrity Software. Altran Praxis, UK (2012). http://www.altran.co.uk
4. Barrett, C., Stump, A., Tinelli, C.: The SMT-LIB standard: version 2.0. In: Gupta, A., Kroening, D. (eds.) Proceedings of the 8th International Workshop on Satisfiability Modulo Theories, Edinburgh, England (2010)
5. Baudin, P.: ACSL: ANSI C Specification Language. http://frama-c.com/download/acsl_1.4.pdf
6. Burdy, L., et al.: An overview of JML tools and applications. In: Arts, T., Fokkink, W. (eds.) Eighth International Workshop on Formal Methods for Industrial Critical Systems (FMICS 2003). Electronic Notes in Theoretical Computer Science (ENTCS), vol. 80, pages 73–89. Elsevier, June 2003
7. Cok, D.R.: Observational purity by underspecification (and separation logic?). In Dagstuhl Conference, Typing, Analysis and Verification of Heap-Manipulating Programs (2009)
8. Cok, D.: Improved usability and performance of SMT solvers for debugging specifications. STTT **12**, 467–481 (2010)
9. Cok, D.R.: OpenJML: JML for Java 7 by extending OpenJDK. In: Bobaru, M., Havelund, K., Holzmann, G.J., Joshi, R. (eds.) NFM 2011. LNCS, vol. 6617, pp. 472–479. Springer, Heidelberg (2011). https://doi.org/10.1007/978-3-642-20398-5_35
10. Cok, D.R.: OpenJML: software verification for Java 7 using JML, OpenJDK, and Eclipse. In: Workshop on Formal Integrated Development Environment (F-IDE 2014). EPTCS, vol. 149, pp. 79–92, Grenoble, France, 06 April 2014 (2014)

11. Cok, D.R.: Specification editing and discovery assistant for C/C++ software development. In: Nguyen, H., Steele, G. (eds.) SBIR Advanced Technologies in Aviation and Air Transportation System 2016 (2017)
12. Cok, D.R., Johnson, S.C.: SPEEDY: an eclipse-based ide for invariant inference. In: Electronic Proceedings in Theoretical Computer Science (EPTCS) (2014)
13. Cok, D.R., Kiniry, J.R.: ESC/Java2: uniting ESC/Java and JML. In: Barthe, G., Burdy, L., Huisman, M., Lanet, J.-L., Muntean, T. (eds.) CASSIS 2004. LNCS, vol. 3362, pp. 108–128. Springer, Heidelberg (2005). https://doi.org/10.1007/978-3-540-30569-9_6
14. Cok, D.R., Leavens, G.T.: Extensions of the theory of observational purity and a practical design for JML. In: Seventh International Workshop on Specification and Verification of Component-Based Systems (SAVCBS 2008), pp. 43–50, November 2008. CS-TR-08-07 (2018)
15. Cok, D.R., Tasiran, S.: Practical Methods for Reasoning about Java 8's Functional Programming Features. VSTTE 2018 (2018)
16. de Moura, L., Bjørner, N.: Z3: an efficient SMT solver. In: Ramakrishnan, C.R., Rehof, J. (eds.) TACAS 2008. LNCS, vol. 4963, pp. 337–340. Springer, Heidelberg (2008). https://doi.org/10.1007/978-3-540-78800-3_24
17. Garland, S.J., Guttag, J.V.: A guide to LP, the larch prover. Technical report 82, Digital Equipment Corporation, Systems Research Center, 130 Lytton Avenue, Palo Alto, CA 94301, December 1991. Order from src-report@src.dec.com
18. Hatcliff, J., Leavens, G.T., Leino, K.R.M., Müller, P., Parkinson, M.: Behavioral interface specification languages. Technical report CS-TR-09-01, School of EECS, University of Central Florida, Orlando, March 2009
19. Jacobs, B., Kiniry, J., Warnier, M.: Java program verification challenges. In: de Boer, F.S., Bonsangue, M.M., Graf, S., de Roever, W.-P. (eds.) FMCO 2002. LNCS, vol. 2852, pp. 202–219. Springer, Heidelberg (2003). https://doi.org/10.1007/978-3-540-39656-7_8
20. Kassios, I.T., Müller, P.: Modular specification and verification of delegation with SMT solvers. Technical report, ETH Zurich (2011)
21. Leavens, G.T., Leino, K.R.M., Müller, P.: Specification and verification challenges for sequential object-oriented programs. Form. Asp. Comput. 19(2), 159–189 (2007)
22. Leavens, G.T., et al.: JML Reference Manual. Department of Computer Science, Iowa State University (2013). http://www.jmlspecs.org
23. Leino, K.R.M.: Dafny: an automatic program verifier for functional correctness. In: Clarke, E.M., Voronkov, A. (eds.) LPAR 2010. LNCS (LNAI), vol. 6355, pp. 348–370. Springer, Heidelberg (2010). https://doi.org/10.1007/978-3-642-17511-4_20
24. Meyer, B.: Object-Oriented Software Construction. Prentice Hall, New York (1988)
25. Müller, P., Poetzsch-Heffter, A., Leavens, G.T.: Modular invariants for layered object structures. Sci. Comput. Program. 62(3), 253–286 (2006)
26. Naumann, D.A.: Observational purity and encapsulation. Theor. Comput. Sci. 376(3), 205–224 (2007)
27. Parnas, D.L.: Tabular representation of relations. Technical report (1992)
28. Singleton, J.L., Leavens, G.T., Rajan, H., Cok, D.R.: Poster: an algorithm and tool to infer practical postconditions. In: 2018 IEEE/ACM 40th IEEE International Conference on Software Engineering Software Engineering (ICSE). IEEE (2018)
29. Spivey, J.M.: The Z Notation: A Reference Manual. Prentice Hall International (UK) Ltd., London (1992)

30. https://frama-c.com
31. Many papers regarding JML can be found on the JML. http://www.jmlspecs.org
32. OpenJDK. http://www.openjdk.org
33. http://www.openjml.org
34. http://www.smtlib.org
35. The Spec# web site gives code, documentation and papers. http://research.microsoft.com/SpecSharp/
36. The work on C++ specification is part of the VESSEDIA project. The VESSEDIA project has received funding from the European Union's Horizon 2020 research and innovation programme under grant agreement No. 731453. https://vessedia.eu

Security Filters for IoT Domain Isolation

Dominique Bolignano$^{(\boxtimes)}$ and Florence Plateau

Prove & Run, Paris, France
dominique.bolignano@provenrun.com

Abstract. Network segregation is key to the security of the Internet of Things but also to the security of more traditional critical infrastructures or SCADA systems that need to be more and more connected and allow for remote operations. We believe traditional firewalls or data diodes are not sufficient considering the new issues at stake and that a new generation of filters is needed to replace or complement existing protections in these fields.

Keywords: Internet of Things · Firewalls · Filters · Data diodes
Security · Formal methods · Embedded devices · Connected car

1 Introduction

Modern IoT (i.e. Internet of Things) security architectures generally make use of partitions to define security domains and try to impose strict information-flow policies on the messages that transit from one domain to another. Typically, this is achieved by forcing all messages to transit through dedicated filters. The correct implementation of such filters is essential for the whole security of the system as the only path available to hackers to perform remote attacks, when the architecture is well designed, is to send triggering messages through these filters. Gateways in new automotive architectures are representative example of devices that implement filters. They are typically used to control the information flows between various security domains, such as the powertrain domain, the infotainment domain, the comfort domain, etc.

The proposed approach is meant to be applied to filters but only in situations where it is possible to explicitly identify and characterize commands and responses that are allowed to go through a given filter. As we will see, this is a sensible requirement to answer to the new security concerns arising in various contexts like: when connecting critical systems (e.g. Cyber Physical Systems), when connecting SCADA[1] systems (e.g. Operational Technology Systems connected to the IT infrastructure), in embedded automotive, aeronautic, or railway equipment, and more generally the IoT. For the IoT, this is mainly due to the fact that the large volume of connected devices creates huge opportunities and extremely good business models for hackers.

In this paper we will first explain why there is a new challenge. We will then explain how this new challenge can be addressed in general, and then show how the security of the more demanding filters can be achieved.

---

[1] SCADA: Supervisory Control And Data Acquisition, a type of industrial control system.

T. Margaria and B. Steffen (Eds.): ISoLA 2018, LNCS 11247, pp. 194–211, 2018.
https://doi.org/10.1007/978-3-030-03427-6_17

2   The New Challenge with Remote Attacks

In this section we will show that the new challenge is mainly due to the existence of new business models for hackers. In the past, reaching an acceptable level of security mainly boiled down to implementing a few basic ingredients: cryptographic algorithms and protocols (such as digital signatures and encrypted communications), secure elements, etc. However, the advent of the IoT and the need to connect remotely to SCADA and critical systems are changing the security paradigm. There is now a real business model for hackers and organized crime syndicates in performing remote attacks. By investing a few millions of euros, they are now indeed almost sure to be able to identify potential large-scale remote attacks in current connected architectures with potentially a very high return on investment. In the IoT industry hackers can for example send a few devices to "reverse-engineering consultants" located in countries where this can be done legally or without too much risk. With the proper reconstructed documentation, they can then ask "creative" hacking consultants to prepare an attack. With such a budget at hand it is almost always possible to identify dramatic large-scale attacks, at least by exploiting bugs and errors that always exist in the OS and protocol stacks that are included in the Trusted Computing Base (TCB) of a device. Such errors can usually be found in the software architecture, or in the design, implementation or configuration of a device. The business model is usually quite obvious to find as in most situations such attacks make it at least possible to block the normal operation of the targeted infrastructure, causing damages that are way beyond the investment. In many cases such attacks could even create more dramatic situations that might lead to loss of life. An attack similar to the well-publicized Jeep attack [4] would correspond roughly to an investment of less than half a million of dollars (an estimate based on the detailed description of the identification phase of the attack by the authors), and if performed on a massive scale by criminal organizations could have led to the death of a very large number of people. These new business models (which in the case of the IoT is exploiting the combination of high volume and potentially physical impact) are bringing unpreceded security needs on the resistance to logical attacks and this is clearly a disruption in the security needs.

Security for high volume transactions (such as in payment systems) were (and are) mitigated by the use of proper risk management. Such risk management techniques are a lot less efficient (and in some cases not applicable) when it comes to IoT systems, as actions cannot be delayed or canceled as financial transactions can be. It is for example not practically possible to detect and block in real time an attack that would make all cars of a certain model turn right at a given time.

In the next subsection, we try to give more accounts on the fact that it is always possible to use the weaknesses of the OSs or protocol stacks that are part of the TCB.

2.1   The Challenge of Securing OSs, Kernels and Protocol Stacks

Various public databases (such as [2]) provide statistics on public bugs or vulnerabilities on all kinds of software. These databases clearly show that current OSs and kernels suffer from a great number of errors and weaknesses, no matter who writes them, and no matter how long they have been in the field. For example, new errors are still reported in the thousands every year on "well-known" systems such as Linux.

This situation is basically due to the inherent complexity of such OSs and kernels, which rely more and more on complex and sophisticated hardware. OSs and kernels are by nature concurrent and very complex because of the need to support various kinds of peripherals (interruption handling becomes more and more difficult), the performance objectives (e.g. complexity of cache management), the resource consumption issues (e.g. need for a sophisticated power management), etc. This complexity increases with time, increases with new IoT architectures and increases when it comes to microprocessors (as opposed to microcontrollers).

Even Trusted Execution Environments (TEEs), i.e. small security OSs that were introduced to very significantly reduce the size of the TCB, are regularly attacked [9, 10, 13]).

The real challenge (and only known solution) is to produce and demonstrate that the OSs, kernels and software stacks that are part of the TCB are as close as possible to "zero-bug" i.e. are free from errors (in their design and implementation) that could be potentially exploited for logical attacks.

Traditional software engineering techniques such as exhaustive testing or code inspections are clearly not sufficient anymore to bring the level of assurance that is needed to secure complex OSs. This is due to the fact that there are too many different situations to consider for a kernel designer or tester and no real methods to review the quality of such kernel code in a systematic way, beside the use of proof techniques.

Instead we believe the only valid response to such complexity is a special class of formal methods, which are known as deductive techniques or proof techniques. Even other formal methods such as static analysis or model checking are not fully addressing the problem at hands. More details are presented in [1].

2.2 Limitations of Traditional Firewalls

The firewall is the right concept for controlling and building the segregation of an architecture but it has two significant drawbacks (1) the configuration of a firewall is usually done on low level protocol concepts such as ports, IP addresses, etc., and making sure that such configuration implements the correct high-level security policy is difficult and very error prone at best (2) most importantly the TCB of a firewall includes at least its OS as well as its protocol stacks. Both are very error prone. In practice the complexity of the attack surface forbids this architecture from meeting the highest level of security, which is a must for the use-cases at hand. The first drawback can be avoided using applicative firewalls. This kind of firewalls allows to use higher level concepts to implement the security policy, which reduces the gap between the security policy and its implementation and hence the risk of error.

The second drawback is not only much more difficult to cope with, it is also very general: it applies to standard packet filter firewalls, to applicative firewalls, whether they use so-called "protocol break" or not. In all these firewalls there is at least an OS as part of the TCB and this OS is very error prone (i.e. the TCB is complex and not formally proven as it should be). The only exception, besides the new approach we are presenting in this paper is when a dedicated filtering hardware is used instead of an OS, but as of now such dedicated hardware are either too simple to address the need or too complex and error prone to be brought to the right level of security and of certification.

The attack surface of a traditional firewall is indeed unnecessarily large. In order to better understand this, let us consider an extremely simple (and unrealistic) security policy which is meant to impose that only the text command "set" can be sent remotely and that this command has a single mandatory parameter whose values can be only "on" or "off". Let us consider here that these commands are sent using TCP/IP on an Ethernet network and let us consider in a first step, for the sake of simplicity, that we are not using a VPN or more generally that messages are not signed or encrypted. We implicitly assume here in this illustrative example a firewall that is based on a standard secure OS (i.e. not based on a micro-kernel), but similar examples could be shown for other architectures.

Even if this security policy is only to accept two possible commands: "set on" and "set off", the degrees of freedom for the attacker are huge, and hence the surface of attack. First at the lexical level, the attacker could insert spaces in the text command (or other allowed delimiters such as tabs) in an attempt to exploit, for example, implementation bugs they have found in the lexical analyzer. They could in the same way exploit bugs in the syntactic analyzer (typically after reverse engineering it). The chances that they find problems that lead to real attacks there are limited because lexical and syntactic analysis is a well-understood software engineering problem with lots of available scientific know-how and tools. However, such weaknesses may still exist anyway (inadequate grammar type, buffer overflow due to improper memory configuration, etc.). What is important in this case is that such degrees of freedom will typically exist within each layer of the protocol stack (e.g. application layer, host-to-host transport layer, internet layer, network interface layer), which enlarges the attack surface, increasing the possibility of finding an exploitable bug. Wireless communication links are more exposed to these issues compared to wired ones because radio technologies (i.e. GSM, WiFi, Bluetooth, ZigBee, etc.) are usually complex and very error prone. In addition, in an OS such as Linux, protocols stacks are part of the kernel, which makes the attacks even simpler. In any case attackers will have an extremely large surface of attack (i.e. many degrees of freedom) to try to exploit bugs in the various protocol layers or in the OS itself.

2.3 Some Representative Attacks

Many attacks on IT systems are reported every day. Here we present some attacks of diverse kinds as a matter of illustration. The first one is the so-called 2015 attack on the Ukrainian power grid [12]. It is quite representative of weaknesses coming from the complexity of the general architecture of large-scale IT systems and their configuration. In the case of this attack, it appears that only a weak security policy was enforced, i.e. users with only a low-level credential could still send any commands and receive any response from critical systems. In their comprehensive report Booz-Allen-Hamilton recommends among other measures (1) to install a stateful firewall or data diode, (2) to use a stronger authentication mechanism (such as two-factor authentication) for some of the accesses. Using a stateful applicative firewall would allow to enforce a proper security policy but the security level of existing firewalls[2] is not sufficient to cope with potential attacks (considering the level of return of investment that could be obtained by organized criminal organizations). A data diode is simpler and therefore can be brought to the right level of security (for example some data diodes have obtained an EAL7 Common Criteria certification) but can only make sure that the flow of information goes in a single direction: it cannot selectively block some commands and allow other. In addition, such systems usually require bidirectional communications, so data diodes are not adequate for this purpose. The filter we propose in this paper brings the benefits of both, i.e. the resistance of a data diode with the selectivity and programmability of an applicative firewall.

A second attack is the so-called Heartbleed attack which is one of the many attacks and vulnerabilities that were found on SSL/TLS overtime [11]. This latter attack is very representative of attacks that exploit the complexity of the software itself. Such bugs are very similar to the bugs that can be found in error-prone software components such as OS kernels or communication stacks.

Errors are not only found in software. They can also happen at the hardware level and lead to logical and remote attacks such as the recently announced Meltdown [5] and Spectre [6] attacks. Other cache attacks had been demonstrated in the past [7, 8] and new ones will probably be found in the future. We believe that hardware design should also be formally proven eventually, at least for their TCB part (MMU, ARM TrustZone mechanism, etc.). This will not prevent non-logical attacks such as the Rowhammer attack presented in [3], but it would prevent at least a large majority of logical attacks. However, errors in hardware that can be exploited for large scale remote attacks are very rare (one or two are found every year as of now) and they can usually be addressed by proper software countermeasures. Prove & Run has developed ProvenCore [15], a formally proven OS kernel that rely only on a few simple hardware mechanisms and to implement a very secure firmware update mechanism so that not only the risks from such hardware attacks are minimized but also that when they happen such problems can be easily fixed by a very robust over the air firmware update mechanism.

2.4   Addressing the New Challenge

The proposed approach to design an extremely secure filter builds on the approach we presented in [1]. We recall here briefly this approach before presenting new ideas that can be used to develop this filter. Some of these ideas are patent pending.

First it is important to use state-of-the-art security methodologies such as the one proposed by the Common Criteria framework. In particular we assume that for each architecture and use case a proper risk analysis and threat model are made available, and that a proper security target has been defined and is used to guide the security architect, the developers, the testers and the security evaluator. It is worth noticing that such documents can be reused from one evaluation to another so as to further reduce costs.

---

[2] See the list of existing certified firewalls https://www.commoncriteriaportal.org/pps/.

We also recommend as described in [1] to explicitly describe a clear "security rationale" that fully explains the hypotheses, conditions and reasons why the security architecture meets the desired security level. The security rationale should not only describe the countermeasures used to address each threat but also provide a detailed rationale as detailed and convincing as an informal mathematical proof.

The last step of the approach is to define an architecture that is based on a TCB that contains only formally proven kernels and protocol stacks. So, in the end the security rationale for the most complex parts of the TCB must rely on formally proven software (and using a tool is necessary to check that the proof is itself free of errors) whereas the other, simpler parts of the security rationale are presented as an informal proof which can be easily audited by experts. Now instead of formally verifying large OSs and kernels such as Linux or Android where new features and drivers are added on an ongoing basis so as to address new requirements, we propose to use a separate formally proven secure OS kernel, i.e. in our case ProvenCore, to address peripherals that need be secured and to run secure applications, in a way that allows us to:

- Retain the normal OS (for example Linux, Android or any other proprietary OS or RTOS) and thus benefit from all its features,
- Push the normal OS outside of the TCB, so that any error in the normal OS cannot be used to compromise the TCB,
- Use a proven OS to perform security functions.

Our formally proven kernel, ProvenCore, was designed in a way that makes it generic enough to be used as COTS (Commercial Off-the-Shelf) in virtually any IoT architecture.

We describe here how this can be done on ARM architectures that account for the vast majority of the IoT market, but the same approach can be transposed to other CPU architectures.

On ARM architectures and in particular on the Cortex-A and Cortex-M families of ARM microprocessors and microcontrollers, a security mechanism called TrustZone provides a low-cost alternative to adding a dedicated security core or co-processor, by splitting the existing processor into two virtual processors backed by hardware-based access control mechanisms. This lets the processor switch between two states, i.e. two worlds, typically the "Normal World" on one side and the "Secure World" on the other side. Therefore, TrustZone can be used as an extremely small and security-oriented asymmetric hypervisor that allows:

- The so-called Normal World to run on its own, potentially oblivious of the existence of the Secure World and,
- The Secure World to have extra privileges such as the ability to have some part of the memory, as well as some hardware peripherals, exclusively visible and accessible to itself.

In the proposed architecture the proven secure OS kernel, i.e. ProvenCore in our case, runs in the Secure World, and the rich but error-prone OS (Linux, Android, etc.) runs in the Normal World.

3 Proposed Approach and Solution

Here the key assumption (or in other words the requirement that is to be met for the proposed solution to be applicable) is that the list of commands and arguments that we want to allow in each direction can be made explicit and fully characterized. In other words, the security architect or administrator must be able to express a precise filtering security policy on the commands and arguments that must go across the filter from one security domain to the other. This may be difficult to do so within a standard information system: when security is not considered a high priority, the administrator is often not in a position to fully characterize all the commands and arguments in use nor even to identify all information flows. However, defining such a filtering security policy is a must as soon as a high level of security is needed e.g. for connected SCADA and critical systems. If a filtering security policy goes beyond a few trivial commands taking no arguments, then the implementation of this policy as a filter must be formally proven. In the next part we will explore how formally proven filters can address the challenge of critical IoT systems.

Connected Critical Systems and SCADAs

In the case of critical or SCADA systems it is usually necessary to accept incoming commands sent through a VPN by authorized remote agents either to perform routine maintenance and configuration or to exert manual control, at least in the case of an emergency situation where some remote administrators or decision makers need to take action quickly. In this case it is quite easy to identify and characterize the list of allowed incoming commands and outgoing responses[3]. The filtering security policy may be stateless or state-based. For example, an authorized user might be required to authenticate itself before issuing a command that modifies the configuration of the system. In this case the corresponding filtering security policy will obviously be state-based (i.e. identification and authentication are required before accepting a given command).

In the case of the Ukrainian critical infrastructure we would have proposed to clearly identify the list of remote commands that where acceptable for each authorized (and authenticated) user. This list could have been used as the base of a filtering security policy.

Embedded Devices and the IoT

In the case of embedded automotive, aeronautic, or railway connected equipment, or more generally any equipment part of the IoT, such filters will for example be placed in the gateways that exist for most of these systems, but may also be placed elsewhere (e.g. within the Telematic Control Unit of a car).

In the automotive industry, this approach could be used to filter incoming V2X[4] alerts coming from the car gateway. Today these alerts are delivered to the driver only through the dashboard, but in the very near future these alerts might be forwarded

---

[3] The control of outgoing responses is less sensitive but still makes attacks more difficult and is also useful in case confidentially is at stake.

[4] V2X: Vehicle-to-everything communication.

directly to the brake-control system, forcing the car to slow down. Filtering security policies may for example apply to data exchanged between the OEM and the car, and/or commands between various domains inside the car (such as chassis, engine or infotainment domains).

Because of the new business models available to enterprising hackers, high level security policies need to be expressed and enforced by the gateways. It is not easy (i.e. at the very best error prone and in some cases impossible with the right level of precision) to express such policies on the low-level objects (such as IP packets) that firewalls normally use. The administrator in charge of configuring such firewalls or the security architect defining the gateway has to use low level concepts such as ports whereas they would like to implement a high-level security policy where they could precisely specify and restrict the type of high level commands or responses that gets in or out.

As we have seen in Sect. 2.2, the resistance of such implementations is not high enough to cope with the remote attacks at stake. Thus, even if the firewalls are properly configured, hackers will still have many ways to attack such entry points. They will typically bypass information-flow policies by exploiting bugs and errors commonly found in protocol stacks and OSs used to implement such firewalls. In fact, the security level reached by the most secure firewalls is usually very limited. In addition, the most secure ones have an expensive bill of material, which does not fit well with embedded systems requirements.

3.1 Proposed Architecture

Instead of filtering low-level packets we propose to filter high-level commands and arguments directly. We also propose to use a protocol break and to implement the filter as a formally proven (or at least highly secure) application (stateful or stateless, depending on the requirements of the task) that only operates on high-level commands and arguments, running on a formally proven and secure OS. This OS will have to guarantee a number of security properties (such as separation, integrity, ...) and which in addition will have to enforce configurable information-flow policies between its components. This information-flow policy will make sure that communication flows coming from the outside (e.g. incoming commands) go through the filtering application which is the one applying the filtering security policy.

In Fig. 1 we present an example of such an architecture in which we use ProvenCore to guarantee the security properties required to host the filtering application such as isolation, confidentiality and integrity [1]. ProvenCore also enforces a (programmable) information-flow policy between the various security applications and between the hardware peripherals and the corresponding drivers and other security applications. This policy ensures that there is no possibility for an incoming command or outgoing response to somehow bypass the filtering application. In the figure, it is materialized by the black arrows that represent the only authorized communication channels.

Since ProvenCore is a micro-kernel that guarantees the integrity and separation of the processes/applications it executes, even a severe problem within the hardware

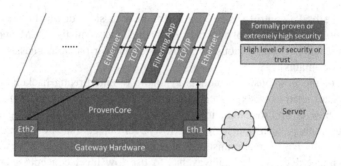

Fig. 1. Proposed architecture

drivers or in the protocols stack themselves will not lead to any security problem besides a lack of availability[5].

In the example above the filtering application implements two filtering security policies: one on incoming commands, one on outgoing responses. More than one filtering applications can be used with more complex topologies in which ingoing (resp. outgoing) messages are routed to different filters according to their nature, but the overall principles remain unmodified.

Such an architecture allows us to design a filter that can be formally proven or more generally brought to the highest level of certification. We have summarized our architecture in Fig. 2.

The TCB is composed of (1) a formally proven kernel, here ProvenCore which is the very first formally proven kernel on the market with the proper security features to support this filtering architecture, and (2) a formally proven filtering application (see Sect. 4), which is by itself a very simple application, even if it includes the filtering per se but also the command and data lexical and syntactic analysis. This architecture thus allows us to obtain a filter (i.e. a particular applicative firewall) whose TCB is entirely formally proven to satisfy the given filtering policy expressed in a simple and high level formal language.

The fact that we use a protocol break on such a secure micro-kernel allows us to put all the protocol stack outside of the TCB. The separation properties of the OS, coupled with the access control mechanism between applications forces the information flow to go through the filtering applications(s). In this architecture the twin protocol stacks used to support the protocol break execute as distinct processes on the same instance of ProvenCore, but in two separate security domains on each side of the filtering application(s) as displayed in Fig. 2.

With traditional firewalls we had to cope with a very error prone TCB with a large attack surface, not surprisingly inadequate to meet the highest level of security. With

---

[5] The lack of availability that would result from a successful attack on the protocol stacks can be mitigated by adding complementary security applications running in parallel to detect such attacks (such as a specialized IDS, i.e. Intrusion Detection System) and providing a security application in charge of reloading a new update over the air (or even inspect and repair the other software components). This is not featured here as it is out of scope of the current paper.

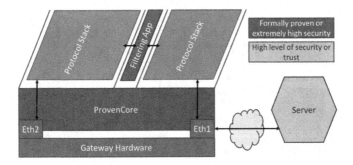

Fig. 2. Proposed architecture, simplified view

this new kind of filter, we are relying on a bullet proof formally proven TCB, which in addition can be proved to exactly implement the intended filtering function. Non-surprisingly such a formally proven TCB can be brought to the very highest levels of security.

But there is more to it. Even with a bullet proof filter there is still the problem that we might be forced to authorize potentially damaging commands (i.e. it is very likely that we have to accept as part of the filtering security policy some commands that are dangerous but necessary). So the remaining problem is not about tampering with the filter (or the security policy) but with the fact that some valid commands may be used to attack the receiving side. Going back to our artificially simple "set on"/"set off" example of a filtering security policy illustrates in an obvious way the fact that the attackers have almost no degree of freedom left to perform an attack on the receiving side. The only commands that can be sent are "set on" and "set off" as planned and the filtering application will leave absolutely no degree of freedom in the way any of them can be expressed. The situation would be exactly the same for more complex and realistic filtering security policies: the only degree of freedom left is indeed the one allowed by the filtering policy itself. But the commands that are defined as being acceptable by the filtering security policy could be dangerous by themselves. For example, most embedded devices will need a "firmware_update" command to manage the firmware update process for the whole platform. For this reason, it is usually also important to make sure that incoming commands have not been tampered with and have been issued by authorized and trusted persons. In other words, it is necessary to add proper authentication, and also guarantee the integrity and potentially the confidentiality of the commands. Guaranteeing these security properties is typically the role of a proper VPN. Here we propose to integrate a VPN application that can be brought to the same level of security as the filtering application(s). This will give the simplified architecture presented in Fig. 3.

Using a proper highly secure VPN thus further reduces the attack surface and shows the benefit that can be obtained by the use of these new generation of filters. Our artificially simple filtering security policy makes it easy to see that an attacker would have only one degree of freedom left: the possibility of (either) slowing down (or theoretically accelerating although this would be much harder) the reception of ingoing commands. Attackers would have no other degree of freedom and thus the attack

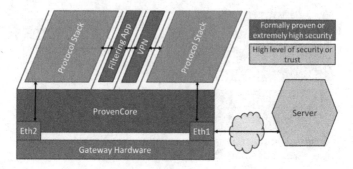

Fig. 3. Proposed architecture, with authentication

surface for performing any attack would be almost nil. Here the fact that TCB is formally proven and can be brought to the highest levels of security is key. It allows the filtering application itself to be brought to the highest level of security and we believe that such a possibility is a real breakthrough in the firewalling/filtering world.

3.2   A Practical Implementation

In practice, the architecture presented above can be easily implemented on an ARM processor using the architecture presented in Fig. 4.

Now the same benefits can be achieved for any kind of (stateful or stateless) filtering security policy. Another significant advantage is that this can be achieved without any impact on the bill of materials and therefore at very little cost. Therefore, such filters are not only much more secure than existing ones, but this architecture is applicable to cost-sensitive devices sold in large volumes. The only costly investment was the design, implementation and formal proof of the security of ProvenCore, an investment which has been done once and for all and can benefit to the huge volumes of compatible devices from various market segments. Depending on the situations these filters can be used to replace existing filters or to complement them (to be put in sequence with another firewall or an IPS[6]).

4   Focus on the Filtering Application

The filtering application (named FilteringApp in figures) is specific to each application domain and security policy, but it can also be implemented and formally proven at little cost, using Prove & Run's formal language and dedicated environment, respectively named Smart and ProvenTools (and described in [15], Sect. 3).

---

[6] IPS : Intrusion Prevention System.

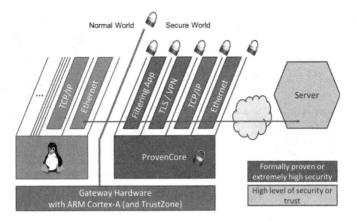

Fig. 4. Practical implementation

Classically, we decompose the filtering application in two main components:

1. a parser, that checks that commands are syntactically correct w.r.t the list of allowed commands, awaited arguments and options. This parser also translates the input string into a structured version, the Abstract Syntax Tree (AST),
2. a validator, that receives this AST and analyses it to check that semantic constraints of the security policy are met (e.g. some command options that cannot be used together).

These two components are described in more details respectively in Sects. 4.1 and 4.2. They can be combined following two distinct architectures, depending on the needs.

The first one, depicted in Fig. 5A, is the less intrusive. When both filtering components accept the data, the filtering application outputs to the server the exact value of the input. This guarantees that, when the security policy is satisfied, the presence of the filtering application doesn't change at all the behavior of the overall system: it may only block some data, but never alters it.

The second architecture, depicted in Fig. 5B, provides maximal security. It prints back the AST on its output. Thus, the data received by the server is as close as possible to the abstract version of the data on which the semantic checks have been performed. It can differ from the input in aspects which have no semantic impact, as the formatting (e.g. the number of spaces between a command and its argument). As these aspects are a degree of freedom, transmitting a normalized version is a plus.

4.1 Proven Parser Generation

The parser, the printer and the AST shape definition are automatically generated from the commands' syntax definition. Associated specifications are also automatically generated and proven, giving an extremely high confidence in these components. In addition of being extremely reliable, these components are inexpensive to develop and to maintain: the only piece of work is to settle and maintain the high-level specification

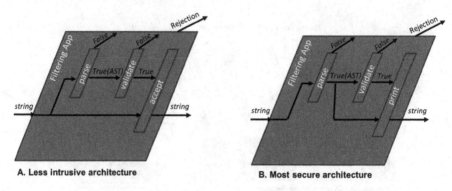

Fig. 5. Focus on the FilteringApp

of the syntax, which is used by ProventTools to generate the executable code, its specifications and proofs.

Let us consider a very simple example of security policy to provide a complete picture of the parser design and generation process. The filter application should accept only the following set of commands (named `shell_micro`):

- `ls [-ltS] [filename]`, where `[-ltS]` is an optional options block introduced by a dash followed by one or more options (among `l`, `t` and `S`); and `[filename]` is an optional argument indicating about which direct folder the information is requested
- `exit` with no option and no argument

The security policy additionally contains semantic constraints on `ls` options block, that are described in Sect. 4.2.

The grammar of accepted commands is defined using a subset the Parsing Expressions Grammars (PEG) formalism [14], that we'll name PEG⁻. A PEG⁻ grammar is a set of rules, each rule consisting of a name, followed by a ←, then a definition body (where a special syntax # marks the presence of mandatory spacing):

This formalism looks similar to context-free grammars (CFGs), but has a different interpretation: in PEG, the choice operator (/) selects the first match and the option (?) and repetition (+) operators are greedy (whereas all these operators are ambiguous in CFG). This interpretation guarantees grammar unambiguity by construction, makes suitable the expression of both lexical and syntactical rules in a unified way, and allows to generate a top-down parser which closely mimics the structure of the grammar.

Executable Code Generation

From a grammar G, we generate the following executable `Smart` code:

1. one type AST_r per rule r of the grammar, defining the shape of the produced AST. These types definitions are inferred as follows:

   - non-constant characters and strings are stored in standard library *character* and *string* types. For instance, the type generated to store the `filename` of Fig. 6 is an alias to the string type: *type filename = string*.

```
command ← ls_cmd / exit_cmd

ls_cmd ← "ls" # ls_options? filename?
ls_options ← "-" ls_option+ #
ls_option ← "l" / "t" / "S"
filename ← ['a'-'z' 'A'-'Z' '_' '.']+ #

exit_cmd ← "exit" #
```

Fig. 6. Definition of `shell_micro` in PEG⁻

- a sequence is stored in a structure, with one field per non-constant sequence element, where repetitions and options are stored in standard library *list* and *option* types. For instance, the type generated to store an ls_cmd is *type ls_cmd = {ls_options_opt: option < ls_options > , filename_opt: option < filename > }*, where *"ls_options_opt"* and *"filename_opt"* are the fields names, followed by a ":" introducing the associated field types.
- a choice is stored in a variant[7], with one constructor per branch of the choice, allowing to store the non-constant content associated to the branch. For instance, the type inferred to store a command is: *type command = Ls_cmd(ls_cmd) | Exit_cmd*, where *Ls_cmd* and *Exit_cmd* are the variant constructors names[8], *ls_cmd* is the type of the content of values belonging to the *Ls_cmd* case, and values belonging to the *Exit_cmd* case have no content.

2. one parse function *parse_r* per grammar rule *r*:

$$parse\_r : string \rightarrow [True(string, AST\_r) \mid False]$$

It takes a *string* as input, and either successes (*True* case) and returns the unconsumed suffix of the input along with the AST node of type *AST_r* (built with the consumed prefix of the input); or fails (*False* case). Smart is very well suited to express, manipulate and specify such functions having named exit statuses (describing the internal execution case) associated to distinct sets of return values: here the unconsumed suffix and the built AST node are returned in the successful case, and no return value is available in the failure case.

These parse functions are unsurprisingly defined as follows:

- parsing a character, or a string (as a keyword or a pattern) is done calling library parsers defined once and for all;

---

[7] That is, a disjoint union of types, each one being introduced by a constructor.

[8] Constructor names are in particular used to define some operations depending on which constructor case a variant value belongs to.

- parsing a reference to another rule is done calling this rule's parse function;
- parsing a sequence consists in parsing each element in order and returning in a structure the aggregation of called parse functions results (which must all be successful);
- parsing a choice consists in trying in order each choice branch and returning a variant wrapping with the appropriate constructor the first successful parse result.

3. the entry point parser (*parse_G: string* → *[True(AST_r$_0$)* | *False]*) which simply calls the parser of the first rule r_0 and checks that the remaining suffix is empty.
4. one printer function per grammar rule *r* (*print_r: AST_r* → *string*) which prints into a string the content of the AST node, conforming to the syntax defined by the associated rule (including the constant content, as keywords and delimiters, which is not stored in the AST).
5. the entry point printer (*print_G: AST_ r$_0$* → *string*) which simply calls the printer associated to the grammar's first rule r_0.

Specification and Proofs Generation
More interestingly, three theorems are also generated along with their proof: the parser correctness and completeness, and a characterization of the AST content.

The formalization generated for the parser correctness and completeness relies on a shallow embedding of PEG⁻ into a Smart library, written once for all, providing:

- a type *grammar* allowing to define a PEG⁻ grammar in Smart (relying on a type *rule* which allows to define a PEG⁻ rule's definition body);
- a relation *recognizes(grammar, string)* which is true if an input *string* is conform to a given *grammar* (and thus defines the meaning of each PEG grammar's construct: sequences, ordered choices/, greedy repetition +, etc.). This relation's definition relies on a more basic relation, *denote(rule, string, Success(string)|Reject)*, which tells if a grammar rule succeeds in recognizing an input string (*Success* case, which takes in parameter the unconsumed suffix string) or if it rejects this input (*Reject* case).

Using the above described library, from a grammar *G*, we generate a Smart definition, named *grammar_G* and of type *grammar,* which embeds *G* in Smart (and consists of a set of objects *rule_r* of type *rule* embedding each rule). The correctness and completeness of the parser are expressed with respect to *grammar_G*.

Theorem (Parser Correctness)

$$\forall\ input,\ parse\_G(input) \Rightarrow recognizes(grammar\_G, input)$$

This theorem states that the parser is correct with respect to the grammar: all inputs accepted by the parser are conform to the grammar.

Proof. The generated proof uses lemmas generated (along with their proof) for each rule *r*:

$$\forall \ input, \ \forall \ suffix,$$
$$parse\_r(input) = True(suffix, \_) \Rightarrow denote(rule\_r, input, Success(suffix))$$

Leafs of the proof tree use library lemmas stating the correctness of library parsers.

Theorem (Parser Completeness)

$$\forall \ input, \ \neg parse\_G(input) \Rightarrow \neg recognizes(grammar\_G, input)$$

This theorem states that the parser is complete with respect to the grammar: none of the inputs rejected by the parser is conform to the grammar.

Proof. Similarly to the correctness proof, this proof relies on lemmas stating the property on unit parsers (and on library lemmas lifting the property on library parsers):

$$\forall \ input, \ \neg parse\_r(input) \Rightarrow denote(rule\_r, input, Reject)$$

Parser Correctness and Completeness theorems provide the guarantee that the parser component of the filtering application does the awaited syntactic filtering. As the parser is also responsible of building the AST processed by the semantic validator component, it is worth specifying the content of the produced AST. This is done thanks to the *print_G* function, which is thus useful for the sake of the specification, even if the chosen architecture doesn't use it (like in Fig. 5A).

Theorem (AST Content)

$$\forall \ input, \forall \ ast, \ parse\_G(input) = True(ast) \Rightarrow print\_G(ast) \approx input$$

This theorem shows that the *ast* produced by the parser doesn't lose meaningful information contained in the *input* string, by stating that printing the *ast* produces a string which is equivalent modulo spacing ($\approx$) to the parsed one. This can be better understood thanks to the following diagram:

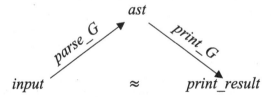

Proof. Same pattern as preceding proofs, using the following expression of the property on all kind of AST nodes:

$$\forall \, prefix, suffix, ast\_r,$$
$$parse\_r(append(prefix, suffix)) = True(suffix, ast\_r)$$
$$\Rightarrow print\_r(ast\_r) \approx prefix$$

4.2 Semantic Validator

The semantic validator is implemented as a regular Smart program, allowing to handle arbitrarily complex security policies. In our shell_micro security policy, we could imagine the following semantic constraints on ls command options: absence of duplicates, and mutual exclusion between options t and S.

If the security policy is complex, we encourage the use of ProvenTools to also specify the awaited behavior and prove the correspondence with the validator implementation. For instance, in our toy example, the formal specification of what "absence of duplicates" means is simpler (thus less error prone) than the implementation of the associated validator, hence proving that the validator implementation is conform to the specification of the constraint is a plus.

Finally note that, as for syntactic constraints, a specific language could be designed to declare some kind of semantic constraints (as here constraints on lists: absence of duplicates, mutual exclusion, elements enabling other ones, etc.), allowing to automatically generate a proven validator.

5 Conclusion

In this paper we have shown why it is very difficult (or even impossible) to bring traditional firewalls and filters to the required level of security. We have proposed an approach that allows us to build new filters based on protocol breaks where the software TCB is made very simple and is just composed of a formally proven kernel, namely ProvenCore here (which is currently seeking a Common Criteria EAL7 certification), and a few security applications that can also be easily formally proven. The other parts of the software stack which normally compose a firewall, such as the drivers, the protocol stack, and the normal OS are here kept outside of the TCB. This is why such filters can be brought to levels of security that only simple physical data diodes could previously meet.

Acknowledgments. The authors would like to thank Érika Baëna and Horace Blanc for their valuable contribution to the work presented in Sect. 4.1.

References

1. Bolignano, D.: Proven security for the internet of things. In: Proceedings of the Embedded World Conference 2016, February 2016
2. National Vulnerability Database. In: NIST. https://web.nvd.nist.gov/view/vuln/search. Accessed 15 Jan 2016

3. Seaborn, M., Dulien, T.: Project zero: exploiting the DRAM rowhammer bug to gain kernel privileges (2015). http://googleprojectzero.blogspot.fr/2015/03/exploiting-dram-rowhammer-bug-to-gain.html. Accessed 15 Jan 2016
4. Miller, C., Valasek, C.: Remote exploitation of an unaltered passenger vehicle. Technical report, IOActive, Seattle, WA (2015). http://www.ioactive.com/pdfs/IOActive_Remote_Car_Hacking.pdf. Accessed 15 Jan 2016
5. Lipp, M., et al.: Meltdown. https://arxiv.org/abs/1801.01207. Accessed 11 Jan 2018
6. Kocher, P., et al.: Spectre attacks: exploiting speculative execution. https://arxiv.org/abs/1801.01203. Accessed 11 Jan 2018
7. Osvik, D.A., Shamir, A., Tromer, E.: Cache attacks and countermeasures: the case of AES. In: Pointcheval, D. (ed.) CT-RSA 2006. LNCS, vol. 3860, pp. 1–20. Springer, Heidelberg (2006). https://doi.org/10.1007/11605805_1
8. Lipp, M., Gruss, D., Spreitzer, R., Maurice, C., Mangard, S.: ARMageddon: cache attacks on mobile devices. In: 25th USENIX Security Symposium (USENIX Security 2016). USENIX Association, Austin, August 2016
9. Cohen, C.: AMD-PSP: fTPM Remote Code Execution via Crafted EK Certificate. http://seclists.org/fulldisclosure/2018/Jan/12. Accessed 11 Jan 2018
10. Beniamini, G.: Trust issues: exploiting TrustZone TEEs. https://googleprojectzero.blogspot.com/2017/07/trust-issues-exploiting-trustzone-tees.html
11. TLS/SSL Explained – Examples of a TLS Vulnerability and Attack, Final Part. https://www.acunetix.com/blog/articles/tls-vulnerabilities-attacks-final-part/. Accessed 11 Jan 2018
12. When The Lights Went Out - A Comprehensive Review of the 2015 Attacks On Ukrainian Critical Infrastructure. https://www.boozallen.com/content/dam/boozallen/documents/2016/09/ukraine-report-when-the-lights-went-out.pdf. Accessed 11 Jan 2018
13. Beniamini, G.: Extracting Qualcomm's KeyMaster Keys - Breaking Android Full Disk Encryption. http://bits-please.blogspot.fr/2016/06/extracting-qualcomms-keymaster-keys.html. Accessed 15 Jan 2018
14. Ford, B.: Parsing expression grammars: a recognition based syntactic foundation. In: Proceedings of the 31st ACM SIGPLAN-SIGACT Symposium on Principles of Programming Languages (2004). https://doi.org/10.1145/964001.964011
15. Lescuyer, S.: ProvenCore: towards a verified isolation micro-kernel. In: MILS-Workshop (2015). http://www.provenrun.com/wp-content/uploads/2015/01/Prove-Run-ProvenCore-Towards-a-Verified-Isolation-Micro-Kernel.pdf. Accessed 03 Aug 2018

20 Years of UPPAAL Enabled Industrial Model-Based Validation and Beyond

Kim G. Larsen$^{(\boxtimes)}$, Florian Lorber, and Brian Nielsen

Department of Computer Science, Aalborg University, Aalborg, Denmark
{kgl,florber,bnielsen}@cs.aau.dk

Abstract. In this paper we review how the UPPAAL Tool Suite served in industrial projects and was both driven and improved by them throughout the last 20 years. We show how the need of industry for model-based validation, performance evaluation and synthesis shaped the tool suite and how the tool suite aided the use cases it was applied in. The paper highlights a number of selected cases, including success stories and pitfalls, and we discuss the important roles of both basic research and industrial projects.

1 Introduction

Within the last 20 years, the tool UPPAAL, originally purely a model-checker for timed automata, has come a long way. It has expanded into a full-grown tool suite that covers a number of different areas, including verification, testing, scheduling and controller synthesis. From the very beginning in the year 1995 [32], the development of UPPAAL was driven by industrial cases. Some of these were founded by research projects, others in direct collaboration with various companies. In this paper we will present an overview of these cases, and focus on how the industrial need for new features drove our research and tool development to all these different ares and on how the different UPPAAL tools could satisfy those needs. This paper is strongly related to another recent overview paper [27], however, in the current paper we put strong emphasis on the impact of research projects on our research and tool development.

An overview of the most important case studies and the correlating projects which will be discussed within this paper can be found in Fig. 1.

The UPPAAL *Tool Family.* In this paragraph we will give a short overview over UPPAAL and its branches, as they developed over time. The core functionality of UPPAAL [4], which was released in 1995, is model-checking of hard real-time properties on timed automata models, supported by a simulation tool which enables manual and random tracing through the model. The first branch of UPPAAL was UPPAAL CORA, which adds support for priced timed automata to the UPPAAL tool family, to address the need for (optimal) usage of resources [28].

Work supported by Innovation Center DiCyPS, DFF project ASAP, and the ERC Advanced Grant Project Lasso.

T. Margaria and B. Steffen (Eds.): ISoLA 2018, LNCS 11247, pp. 212–229, 2018.
https://doi.org/10.1007/978-3-030-03427-6_18

Usecase	Tool	Goal	Projects	Outcome
PACP	UPPAAL	Verification	collaboration w. Philips	Significant tool improvement
BRP	UPPAAL	Verification	collaboration w.Philips & Twente University	Protocol verified
BOP	UPPAAL	Verification	BRICS	Bug found and corrected
BOPC	UPPAAL	Verification	BRICS	Frequency limits identified
FR	UPPAAL	Verification	AVACS (external)	Improved fault-tolerance guarantees
FW	UPPAAL	Verification	collaboration w. Radboud University	Sound timing restrictions identified
GC	UPPAAL	Verification	ARTES (external)	Several requirements verified
HPS	UPPAAL	Verification	DaNES	Schedulability of task-set established
NMN	UPPAAL	Verification	Reachi	Energy performance of protocol
D	UPPAAL TRON	Testing	MoDES	Demonstration of feasibility of online testing
NN	UPPAAL YGGDRASIL UPPAAL CORA	Testing	DaNES	Two times industrial takeup
G	UPPAAL YGGDRASIL	Modelling, Testing	DiCyPS	Interest provoked - new collaboration
M	UPPAAL YGGDRASIL	Modelling, Testing	MBAT	Refactoring of UPPAAL YGGDRASIL
S	UPPAAL TIGA	Controller Synthesis	DaNES	Synthesis of zone-based controller
H	UPPAAL TIGA	Controller Synthesis	QUASIMODO	Improved controller
BPNS	UPPAAL STRATEGO	Scheduling	SENSATION	Battery life improvement of a satellite
HA	UPPAAL STRATEGO	Controller Synthesis	CASSTING & CASSEK	Intelligent floor heating
ICTL	UPPAAL STRATEGO	Controller Synthesis	DiCyPS	Efficient traffic controller

Fig. 1. UPPAAL used in industrial and research projects.

Shortly after that, the branch UPPAAL TRON was introduced, which offers the possibility of performing on-line conformance testing of *real* real-time systems with respect to timed input-output automata [30,34]. In 2005, UPPAAL TIGA was added to the tool family, allowing for control strategies to be synthesized from timed games, i.e. two-player games played on a timed automaton [3,8]. The tool was developed within the project QUASIMODO and implements an efficient symbolic on-the-fly algorithm for synthesizing winning strategies for reachability, safety as well as Büchi objectives and taking possible partial observability into account [9]. In 2007 UPPAAL YGGDRASIL, an off-line test case generator, was developed. Later, in the project MBAT, it was re-factored and integrated into the main UPPAAL component. It aims at creating a test suite for edge coverage and enables the user to associate test code with transitions and locations, which is integrated into the test case whenever a trace traverses them. In 2010 the branch ECDAR was introduced supporting a scalable methodology for compositional development and stepwise refinement of real-time systems [17–19]. One of the most recent branches of the UPPAAL tool suite is UPPAAL SMC, which was introduced in 2011. It allows for performance evaluation of the much richer formalisms of stochastic hybrid automata and games [15,16]. For a full account of UPPAAL SMC we refer the reader to the recent tutorial [14]. The latest branch is UPPAAL STRATEGO. The idea behind UPPAAL STRATEGO [11,12] came up in the CASSTING project in 2014. The branch allows to generate, optimize, compare and explore consequences and performance of strategies synthesized for stochastic priced timed games (SPTG) in a user-friendly manner. In particular, UPPAAL STRATEGO comes with an extended query language, where strategies are first class objects that may be constructed, compared, optimized and used when performing (statistical) model checking of a game under the constraints of a given synthesized strategy.

2   Verification

The early development of UPPAAL was highly driven by colleagues in the Netherlands using the tool for automatic verification of industrial protocols. The basic research done in those early years received funds by the research projects BRICS and VHS and resulted in a huge performance improvement reducing both time- and space-consumption by over 99%. In this section we will present some of the cases where UPPAAL was used for verification.

Philips Audio Control Protocol (PACP). Before the release of UPPAAL, Bosscher, Polak and Vaandrager had in 1994 modelled and verified a protocol developed by Philips for the physical layer of an interface bus that connects the various devices of some stereo equipment (tuner, CD player,...). Essentially – after a suitable translation – the model of the protocol is a timed automata. Whereas the first proof in [7] was manual, the first automated verification of the protocol was done using the tool HyTech. Later, automated – and much faster – verifications were obtained using UPPAAL and Kronos. However, all these proofs were based on a simplification on the protocol, introduced by Bosscher et.al. in 1994, that only one sender is transmitting on the bus so that no bus collisions can occur. In many applications the bus will have more than one sender, and the full version of the protocol by Philips therefore handles bus collisions. Already in the autumn of 1995 an automatic analysis of a version of the Philips Audio Control Protocol with two senders and bus collision handling was achieved using UPPAAL 0.96. To make the analysis feasible a notion of *committed location* was introduced (to remove unnecessary interleavings) and the analysis was carried out on a super computer, a SGI ONYX machine [5]. The total verification time was 8.82 h using more 527.4 MB. It is interesting to note that using UPPAAL 3.2 the same verification was reduced to only 0.5 s using 2.5 MB of memory. In any case, the success in 1996 was a true milestone in the development of UPPAAL as this version of the protocol was orders of magnitude larger than the previously considered version with only one sender, e.g. the discrete state-spaces was 10^3 times larger and the number of clocks and channels in the model was also increased considerably.

Bounded Retransmission Protocol (BRP). In parallel with the collaboration with the group of Vaandrager, D'Argenio, Katoen, Reus and Tretmans from Twente University were also applying – and seriously testing – the first versions of UPPAAL. In particular, they successfully modelled and verified the Bounded Retransmission Protocol, a variant of the alternating bit protocol introduced by Philips. In [10] it is investigated to what extent real-time aspects are important to guarantee the protocol's correctness and using UPPAAL and the Spin model checker.

B&O Protocol (BOP). In 1996, we were ourselves approached by Bang & Olufsen with a request of "analysing their proprietary IR Link protocol". The protocol, about 2800 lines of assembler code, had been used in products from the audio/video company Bang & Olufsen throughout more than a decade, and its purpose was to control the transmission of messages between audio/video components over a single bus. Such communications may collide, and one essential purpose of the protocol is to detect such collisions. The functioning is highly dependent on real-time considerations. Though the protocol was known to be faulty in that messages were lost occasionally, the protocol was too complicated in order for the company to locate the bug using normal testing. However – after 4-5 inaccurate models of the protocol – an error trace was automatically generated using UPPAAL and confirmed in the actual implementation of the protocol. Moreover, the error was corrected and the correction was automatically proven correct, again using UPPAAL [24].

B&O Powerdown Control (BOPC). [23] Our first collaboration with Bang & Olufsen were very much characterized as a reverse engineering exercise of an existing protocol: the only documentation of the protocol was the 2800 lines of assembler code together with 3 flow-charts and a (very) knowledgeable B&O

engineer. In our second collaboration with the company, modelling and verification in UPPAAL was carried out in parallel with the actual implementation of a new real-time system for power-down control in audio/video components. During modeling, 3 design errors were identified and corrected, and the following verification confirmed the validity of the design and additionally revealed the necessity for an upper limit of the interrupt frequency. The resulting design was later (seamlessly) implemented and incorporated as part of a new product line.

Whereas the above collaborative projects with B&O were very successful, neither UPPAAL nor model-driven development were taken-up in the company. An obvious reason could be the immaturity (and lack of GUI) of the tool back then. However, in retrospect, an other equally likely reason is the fact that we were spending (all) our effort in collaborating with technicians in the company and not on marketing our tool and "disruptive" methodology to decision-makers in the company.

Flexray (FR). As part of the German DFG project AVACS[1] the FlexRay protocol was modeled and verified using UPPAAL. Flexray is a standard, developed by a cooperation of leading companies in the automotive industry, as a robust communication protocol for distributed components in modern vehicles. Developed by the FlexRay Consortium, a cooperation of leading companies including BMW, Bosch, Daimler, Freescale, General Motors, NXP Semiconductors, and Volkswagen, FlexRay was first employed in 2006 in the pneumatic damping system of BMW's X5, and fully utilized in 2008 in the BMW 7 Series. The FlexRay specification was completed in 2009 and is widely expected to become the future standard for the automotive industry. In [22] a timed automata model of its physical layer protocol is presented, and UPPAAL is used to automatically prove fault tolerance under several error models and hardware assumptions. In particular, it is shown that the communication system meets, and in fact exceeds, the fault-tolerance guarantees claimed in the FlexRay specification.

Firewire (FW). The IEEE 1394-1995 serial bus standard defines an architecture that allows several components to communicate at very high speed. Originally, the architecture was designed by Apple (FireWire), with more than 70 companies having been involved in the standardisation effort. In [39] a timed automata model of the leader election protocol is presented and its correctness is established using UPPAAL. In particular, it is shown that under certain timing restrictions the protocol behaves correctly. The timing parameters in the IEEE 1394 standard documentation obey the restrictions found in this proof.

MECEL Gear Controller (GC). In [33] an application of UPPAAL to the modelling and verification of a prototype gear controller was developed in a joint project between industry and academia. In particular, the project was carried out in collaboration between Mecel AB and Uppsala University. In particular, the (timely) correctness of the controller was formalized (and verified) in 47 logical formulas according to the informal requirements delivered by industry.

---

[1] http://www.avacs.org.

Herchel and Planck Schedulatilibity (HPS). In the danish project DaNES, we collaborated with the company Terma on using timed automata model checking as a more exact method for establishing schedulability of a number of periodic tasks executing on a single CPU under a given scheduling policy. In particular a fixed priority preemptive scheduler was used in a combination with two resource sharing protocols and in addition voluntary task suspension was considered. In [35] schedulability was established under the assumption of exact computation times of the tasks. In [13] non-deterministic computations times was considered; depending on the size of the computation time interval schedulability was either verified (using UPPAAL) or refuted (using the concrete search engine of UPPAAL SMC).

3 Testing

Our research on model-based test generation for timed (event recording) automata started with the thesis work around 1996–2000 in [36]. The approach aimed at covering timed equivalence classes defined through the clock guards of the timed automata. It assumed strictly deterministic systems, and its scalability was limited by the analysis techniques of the time. It thus had limited industrial applicability [37,38].

Later (2002–2004), inspired by [20,41], we developed the on-line testing tool UPPAAL TRON [1]. This approach could effectively handle non-determinism in both the specification (due to abstraction) and system under test (due to uncertainties in scheduling, execution times, timing, etc.), scaled to large models, and provided response times low enough for many practical cases [2,31,40]. On-line testing generate effective randomized long tests, but coverage must be evaluated post-mortem and cannot be guaranteed a priori. Moreover, it is difficult to repeat the precise same test and inspect the set of test cases (might be required by certification bodies).

Our first work on offline test-case generation (with Uppsala University) appeared [25] in 2003. Here we showed how to interpret witness traces generated by the UPPAAL model-checker as test cases for the sub-class deterministic output urgent timed automata. Specifically, we showed how to generate the test cases with the minimum duration that satisfied a given test purpose formulated as a reachability property by exploiting UPPAAL's fastest witness trace generation feature. We furthermore formulated coverage as a reachability question, giving the ability to generate (time optimal) tests that guarantee meeting common coverage criteria. This work led to the UPPAAL COVER tool (no longer developed) and UPPAAL YGGDRASIL.

In the time between 2006 and 2014 our work on testing heavily was driven by the projects MoDES, DaNES and MBAT where we evaluated and enhanced our tools.

The Danfoss Case (D). We applied and evaluated UPPAAL TRON on embedded controller supplied by the company Danfoss' Refrigeration Controls Division

around year 2003–2004 [31]. The target device was a stable product for refrigerator controller for industrial and large supermarket installations. As computer
scientist we did not have domain expertise, and it soon became clear that the supplied documentation (high-level requirements and user manuals) was insufficient
for us to build accurate models. Hence, we ended op formulating a hypothesis
model, running the test, and refining the model when the test failed. The final
model consisted of 18 concurrent components (timed automata), 14 clock variables, and 14 discrete integer variables, and is thus quite large for the time. When
confronting the refined model with Danfoss engineers, they too were surprised
about certain aspects of its behavior, and needed to have that confirmed by
other developers. Although we found no confirmed defects, the case showed that
our technique were practically applicable, and effective in finding discrepancies
between specified and observed behavior. Encouraged by these results, both parties continued the collaboration on automated testing. At the end, our testing
approach was not included in their new test setup that emphasized a new test
harness for automated executing of manually defined scripts. Retrospectively,
the gap between our method and their established development processes and
tools was too big.

The Novo Nordic Case (NN). The first version of UPPAAL YGGDRASIL was
developed in 2007–2009 specifically to support an collaboration with Novo Nordic
for model-based GUI testing for medical devices. This version used UPPAAL
CORA as back-end, and operate in a 3 step process inspired by the company's
needs: (1) A separate test sequence is generated for each user defined (supposedly
critical) test purposes, (2) using UPPAAL's search heuristics for optimizing model
(edge) coverage considering constraints on the maximum lengths of the test
cases, and (3) generating targeted test cases for each of the remaining uncovered
transitions. The actual test case code was generated from model-annotations
that the test engineers added to the model issuing appropriate GUI commands
and assertions. Initially, the models were made using UML state-charts (and then
translated into the UPPAAL syntax) due to the engineers familiarity with this
notation. It is important to remark that the engineers had no prior experience
with formal modelling, and models were made for illustrative purposes using
Microsoft Visio. Even then, making models that now had a tangible and formal
meaning required a substantial training period. First the models were jointly
developed assisted by the tool developer, and later only by company engineers
with ordinary support.

This approach reduced the time used on test construction from upwards of 30
days to 3 days spent modelling and then a few minutes on actual test generation.
At the same time, coverage was easier to establish that in the manual approach,
and script maintenance greatly reduced. Later again, the company started using
the UPPAAL-editor directly, circumventing a heavy (and costly) UML tool. The
approach was thus successfully embedded within the company. Unfortunately,
that development team was dissolved as part of a company restructuring a year
later, and the competence was no longer used.

MBAT (M). Since the original UPPAAL YGGDRASIL was tailormade for this collaboration, and since it used a the UPPAAL CORA engine that is also no longer being developed, it ended up in a non-usable state. Recently, as part of the EU Artemis MBAT (Combined Model-based Testing and Analysis) project, we re-architected the tool, and integrated it into—and shipped with—the main branch of UPPAAL, such that it now (1) uses the normal search engine, and (2) uses the graphical editor to create the needed annotations, and (3) provides a GUI widget for creating the test case configurations.

UPPAAL YGGDRASIL was applied to a case-study [26], and evaluated positively by a few consortium member companies. However, the collaboration did not result in commercial exploitation, partly because the project came to an end, and partly because we did not have an established company that could sell the licenses, and required maintenance, training, and consultancy.

MBAT also facilitated further developments for tool interoperability that is seen as crucial for large companies owning hundreds of various software development tools. That included prototyping of Open Services for Lifecycle Collaboration (OSLC)[2] adaptors for UPPAAL, and prototyping of Functional Mock-up Interfaces (FMI)[3] co-simulation interfaces. So it is regretful that this source of funding for Artemis/ECSEL industrial collaboration at a European scale ceased, as the Danish government halted national co-funding.

Grundfos (G). Grundfos is a major Danish company and world renowned for its pump products. In a recent meeting in the context of the DiCyPS project[4], we discussed different possible topics for further evaluation, including model-based testing. Based on our positive experiences with Danfoss (whose refrigerator controllers at an abstract level is similar to Grundfos pump controllers) we presented all the benefits/strengths of online model-based tested. However, it was when we presented off-line testing that their interest was really triggered. They in particular liked our idea of modelling each of their requirements, using this (combined) model to automatically generate test scripts, and executing these on their existing test harness. Hence, there is a strong fit with their existing testing process and equipment. Also they believed that the (formalized) requirement models could be a valuable documentation complementing the existing design documentation. Hence, we decided to focus the collaboration on this approach, and postpone on-line testing.

In the first phase, we (university/tool provider/academic) perform the modelling and test case generation in order to prepare the tool and evaluate the method, for this particular case. We have identified an interesting, non-trivial subsystem of a newly developed pump controller exhibiting core functionality. If this stage is successful we plan to train selected Grundfos engineers and evaluate their experiences.

Since the collaboration is ongoing, we cannot report on the outcome here.

---

[2] https://open-services.net/.

[3] http://fmi-standard.org/.

[4] National Innovation Found Supported project on Data-Intensive Cyber-Physical Systems.

4   Planning, Scheduling and Synthesis

Within its newer branches, the UPPAAL tool suite allows for the usage of prices and stochastic elements, in order to enable various features, such as cost-optimal reachability, optimal scheduling or synthesis of strategies. The first practical step in this direction was made in 2002, with the initial release of UPPAAL CORA. UPPAAL CORA was developed as part of the VHS and AMETIST projects, and uses *linear priced timed auomata* (LPTA) for reachability problems, searching for paths with the lowest accumulated costs. The idea behind UPPAAL STRATEGO came up in the CASSTING project. It was released in 2014, and facilitates the generation, optimization, comparison as well as consequence and performance exploration of strategies for /em stochastic priced timed games (SPTGs) in a user-friendly manner. The tools were since applied in several case studies, such as optimal planning of missions for battery-powered nano-satellites [6], efficient heating in home automation [29] or traffic light scheduling [21]. Below we will give an overview of the three mentioned case studies.

Battery-Powered Nano-Satellites (BPNS). This case study focused on the battery consumption of a GOMX-3 satellite built by the company GomSpace. It contains several antennas, solar panels and a battery. Depending on the scheduling of the different tasks of the satellite, the deterioration of the battery may vary significantly, depending on, for instance, the depth the battery is discharged to before reloading it. UPPAAL STRATEGO was used to analyze different battery usage profiles, to optimize the lifetime of the satellite. This was done via a wear score function, which ranked the profiles according to their impact on the battery life. Additionally, the satellite was modelled as an SPTG in an abstract way. It could choose between the four different experiment types with different strains on the battery. Using the reinforcement learning approach implemented in UPPAAL STRATEGO we could near-optimize the scheduling of the experiments with respect to both the battery life and the number of experiments performed.

Home Automation (HA). In [29] we collaborated with the Danish company Seluxit within the European project CASSTING. Our focus was on using timed games to synthesize a controller for a floor heating system of a single family house. Each room of the house has its own hot-water pipe circuit, which is controlled based on the room temperature. The original system used a simple "Bang-Bang"-like strategy. Our goal was to use weather forecast information to synthesize an improved control strategy. Due to the state-space explosion caused by the number of control modes, we could not apply UPPAAL STRATEGO directly. To cope with this, we proposed a novel on-line synthesis methodology, which is periodically called and learns an optimal controller for a limited timeframe. We further improved this approach by applying compositional synthesis, making it scalable enough for the study. The controller could access the weather forecast for the next 45 min, and used that information to shut down or start the valves much earlier than other controllers, resulting in substantial energy savings and increased comfort.

Intelligent Control of Trafic Light (ICTL). Within the Innovation Center DiCyPS we used UPPAAL STRATEGO for the synthesis of an efficient traffic control strategy. The controller gains information about the traffic via radar detectors and aims at optimizing the total traffic flow in a given traffic light junction. The strategy optimizes the total delay, the queue length and the number of times the vehicles have to stop. Again the synthesis is done on-line, this time in 5 s intervals, during which the next operation of the traffic light is calculated. We investigated an existing intersection in the municipality of Køge, Denmark, and simulated it with the open source tool SUMO and the commercial tool VISSIM. The strategy computed by UPPAAL STRATEGO could be integrated into these tools, to analyze the behaviour based on randomly generated traffic szenarios. We evaluated the strategies in comparison to a static controller and a so called Loop controller, under three types of traffic szenarios with low, medium and maximal traffic. For low traffic, all controllers performed very similar, with the Loop controller showing the best results and for medium traffic, all performed equally. However, for high traffic, UPPAAL STRATEGO outperformed both other controllers significantly, essentially halving the expected waiting time [21].

5 Projects

In this section we will give an overview of the different projects we were involved in, which financed, drove and benefited from the development of the different tool components. An overview of the projects and the developed tool components and their entangled time lines can be seen in Fig. 2.

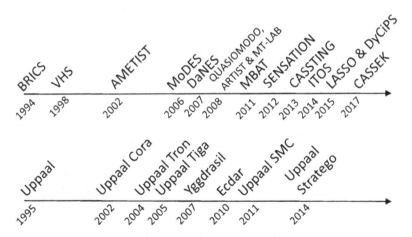

Fig. 2. Time lines of the starting dates of different projects, and the developed tool extensions.

BRICS

- **Type:** Basic research funded by Danish National Research Foundation
- **Period:** 1994–1998
- **Goal:** Establishing important areas of basic research in the mathematical foundations of Computer Science, notably Algorithmics and Mathematical Logic.
- **Partners:** Aarhus University
- **Development of** UPPAAL: BRICS supported the development of the first UPPAAL version and the improvement of algorithms for model-checking timed automata.

VHS

- **Type:** ESPRIT-LTR Project
- **Period:** 1998–2000
- **Goal:** Verification of hybrid systems
- **Partners:** Sidmar, Nystral, Krup Uhde, Verimag, Dortmund, Nijmegen
- **Development of** UPPAAL: In VHS we focused on the application of UPPAAL to scheduling problems, which (together with the work done in AMETIST) led to the development of UPPAAL CORA. The basic research done here also resulted in a huge performance improvement of the runtime and space consumption of UPPAAL's model checking algorithms.

AMETIST

- **Type:** IST project
- **Period:** 2002–2005
- **Goal:** Modelling and analysis of complex, distributed real-time systems with resource allocation.
- **Partners:** AXXOM, Bosch, Cybernetix, Terma
- **Development of** UPPAAL: In AMETIST we first introduced priced timed automata to UPPAAL via UPPAAL CORA, allowing us to perform verification of resource dependent systems.

MoDES

- **Type:** Basic research funded by Danish National Research Foundation
- **Period:** 2006–2009
- **Goal:** Developing, evaluating and disseminating concepts, methods and tools that can be used to design dependable embedded systems that meet their requirements in a controlled and resource-efficient way using model-driven approaches.
- **Partners:** DTU, SDU, Hardi International, Danfoss, Skov, Reactive Systems, CSI Center for Software Innovation, PAJ
- **Outcome:** Methods and tools for embedded systems were aligned among many leading Danish companies. The evaluations showed that model-driven development leads to better performing products in less time and that *standardization* of methods, models and tools will increase industrial take-up.

QUASIOMODO

- **Type:** IST FP7 project
- **Period:** 2008–2010
- **Goal:** Theory, techniques and tool components for handling quantitative (e.g. real-time, hybrid and stochastic) constraints in model-driven development.
- **Partners:** Terma, Chess, Hydac
- **Development of** UPPAAL: In QUASIMODO we introduced and developed UPPAAL TIGA, which we then used to improve controller synthesis for Hydac.

DANES

- **Type:** Danish Advanced Technology Foundation
- **Period:** 2008–2011
- **Goal:** Establishing, developing and testing a model-driven and component-based development process for the implementation of the intelligent embedded systems of the future.
- **Partners:** DTU, SDU, ICEpower, Novo Nordisk, PAJ Systemteknik, Prevas, Skov, Terma
- **Outcome:** The company Terma used UPPAAL to achieve an improved schedulability analysis and NOVO Nordic vastly improved their testing methodology using UPPAAL YGGDRASIL. However, we had to learn that organizational changes makes sustainable impact difficult, as in NOVO Nordic the particular software group we were working with was laid down, and replaced by outsourcing.

ARTIST

- **Type:** FP7
- **Period:** 2008–2012
- **Goal:** Integrate topics, teams, and competencies, through an ambitious and coherent research program of research activities which are grouped into 4 Thematic Clusters: "Modelling and Validation", "Software Synthesis, Code Generation, and Timing Analysis", "Operating Systems and Networks", "Platforms and MPSoC".
- **Partners:** 31 partners
- **Outcome:** Methods and tools for embedded systems were aligned at a European level. As in the previous MoDES project we saw the willingness of industrial take-up increase with standardization of methods, models and tools.

MT-LAB

- **Type:** Basic research: basic research funded by Danish National Research Foundation
- **Period:** 2008–2013

- **Goal:** Development of research results and knowledge that will eventually be utilized in application-oriented research and projects in business through front research in IT Modeling.
- **Partners:** Danmarks Tekniske Universitet
- **Development of** UPPAAL: Improved algorithms for model-checking timed automata.

MBAT

- **Type:** ARTEMIS project
- **Period:** 2011–2014
- **Goal:** Combining Model-based Analysis and Testing of Embedded Systems
- **Partners:** 39 partners
- **Development of** UPPAAL: Refactoring of UPPAAL YGGDRASIL and integrating it into the main UPPAAL tool.

SENSATION

- **Type:** IST FP7
- **Period:** 2012–2015
- **Goal:** Increase the scale of systems that are self-supporting by balancing energy harvesting and consumption up to the level of complete products.
- **Partners:** RWTH Aachen University, INRIA, University of Saarland, University of Twente, GOMSpace, Recore Systems
- **Outcome:** We learned that the model-based approach to planning scales to industrial usage, and could actually be applied to satellites. However, constant interaction with companies is needed to ensure sustainability, especially in a fast-growing company as GOMSPACE.

CASSTING

- **Type:** FP7
- **Period:** 2013–2016
- **Goal:** Developing a novel approach for analysing and designing collective adaptive systems in their totality, by setting up a game theoretic framework.
- **Partners:** CNRS, Université de Mons, Université Libre de Bruxelles, RWTH Aachen, Seluxit, Energi Nord
- **Outcome:** We showed that the model-based approach to optimal synthesis scales to industrial usage. An interesting observation was that small companies are more agile in adapting new methodologies (e.g. model-based approaches). In fact Seluxit is now taking up the methodology in the CASSEK project.

ITOS

- **Type:** Danish industry foundation
- **Period:** 2014–2016

- **Goal:** Creating knowledge and enhancing skills and techniques used to develop embedded technologies.
- **Partners:** 15 partners
- **Outcome:** Four involved companies applied model-based development for a substantial time. We saw first hand, that the model-based approach to formal methods fits very well the methodologies of several companies within embedded systems. Various types of models (e.g. MATLAB/Simulink) were already in heavy use.

LASSO

- **Type:** ERC Grant
- **Period:** 2015–2020
- **Goal:** Developing a new generation of scalable tools for cyber-physical systems through combining advanced model-checking techniques with machine learning.
- **Partners:** -
- **Outcome:** Lasso is a basic research project, were we improve and expand our algorithms and implementations. We hope the advancement in basic research may lead to disruptive industrial solutions.

DiCyPS

- **Type:** Danish Innovation Fund
- **Period:** 2015–2021
- **Goal:** Utilize software and data from IT management of complex physical systems to create smarter and more user-friendly solutions to society and individuals.
- **Partners:** Balsgard Norgard, Blip Systems, Danfoss, Energi Styrelsen, Flex-Danmark, Huge Lawn, Lærerstandens Brandforsikring, Neogrid Technologies, Nyfors, Ramboll, Region Nordjylland, Rejsekort, Scada, Seluxit, Aalborg Kommune, ScaDS, Estasys, UCL
- **Development of** UPPAAL: Improvement to algorithms and implementations of various branches of UPPAAL, to demonstrate their capability in the presented industrial cases.

CASSEK

- **Type:** Eurostars Project
- **Period:** 2017–2018
- **Goal:** Accelerate developments in IoT through a sustainable marketplace model and an IoT app store.
- **Partners:** Seluxit
- **Outcome:** We will demonstrate how UPPAAL can be integrated and used to improve IoT scheduling.

Reachi

- **Type:** Eurostars Project
- **Period:** 2017–2019
- **Goal:** Development of disaster-proof communication devices that send data from device to device until it reaches its destination, thereby connecting first responders and relief coordinators.
- **Partners:** Attensys.io Gmbh, Neocortec, Linkaiders Aps
- **Outcome:** We will improve algorithms in UPPAAL SMC to enable massive simulations of mesh networks and model and verify the developed device.

6 Discussion and Conclusions

We learned countless lessons throughout the presented projects. We would like to summarize the most important ones below:

- **Formal method tools need to adapt to industrial needs!** This holds true in multiple directions. They need to be user friendly in order for engineers to apply them (for instance, we got great feedback on the fact that UPPAAL provides simulation to manually step through the system and check whether it behaves as intended), they have to fit into the development methodology and connect to the tools in use, and they need to comply to safety certification standards to not be perceived as additional overhead. While the learnability and scalability in terms of size and features of our methodologies and tools have improved hugely over the years, they remain challenges that we will continually address.
- **Model-based verification requires models!** And thus, new industrial collaboration projects usually require a two step phase, where first we produce models to demonstrate the capabilities of model-based verification, and then we train the engineers at creating meaningful and efficient models. Embedding this modelling (implicitly or explicitly) in the industrial development process such that it is not an extra overhead is still a topic for research.
- **One project is rarely enough!** Within the first project, the involved companies get to know the tool and its advantages, but will not incorporate it into their day to day use. But after knowing the tool they can think of suitable applications and apply the tool within designated follow-up projects.
- **The trend goes towards automation!** While our early projects were mainly about verification of models, this changed into many projects on automated test-case generation, and finally into projects on the automatic synthesis of optimized and correct-by-construction controllers. This trend reflects the need of industry, to integrate formal methods into their automated production processes.

Our experiences throughout the projects showed that basic research is absolutely necessary in order to achieve mathematically sound, effective and efficient formal methods tools, while applied research led us towards industrially interesting and challenging new areas. Altogether, the variety of different projects was what enables us to develop UPPAAL, sustain it over the years, expand it to different areas, and, ultimately, integrate it into industrial use. To maintain UPPAAL for the coming 20 years, we plan on following this path further by constantly getting in touch with new companies, assessing the current needs of industry and applying for joint industrial projects.

References

1. Mikucionis, M., Larsen, K.G., Nielsen, B.: T-UPPAAL: online model-based testing of real-time systems. In: Grunbacher, P. (ed.) 19th IEEE International Conference on Automated Software Engineering (ASE 2004) Proceedings, United States, pp. 396–397. IEEE Computer Society Press (2004). ISSN 1068–3062
2. Asaadi, H.R., Khosravi, R., Mousavi, M.R., Noroozi, N.: Towards model-based testing of electronic funds transfer systems. In: Arbab, F., Sirjani, M. (eds.) FSEN 2011. LNCS, vol. 7141, pp. 253–267. Springer, Heidelberg (2012). https://doi.org/10.1007/978-3-642-29320-7_17
3. Behrmann, G., Cougnard, A., David, A., Fleury, E., Larsen, K.G., Lime, D.: UPPAAL-Tiga: time for playing games!. In: Damm, W., Hermanns, H. (eds.) CAV 2007. LNCS, vol. 4590, pp. 121–125. Springer, Heidelberg (2007). https://doi.org/10.1007/978-3-540-73368-3_14
4. Behrmann, G., et al.: UPPAAL 4.0. In: 2006 Third International Conference on Quantitative Evaluation of Systems. QEST 2006, pp. 125–126. IEEE (2006)
5. Bengtsson, J., et al.: Verification of an audio protocol with bus collision using UPPAAL. In: Alur, R., Henzinger, T.A. (eds.) CAV 1996. LNCS, vol. 1102, pp. 244–256. Springer, Heidelberg (1996). https://doi.org/10.1007/3-540-61474-5_73
6. Bisgaard, M., Gerhardt, D., Hermanns, H., Krčál, J., Nies, G., Stenger, M.: Battery-aware scheduling in low orbit: the GOMX–3 case. In: Fitzgerald, J., Heitmeyer, C., Gnesi, S., Philippou, A. (eds.) FM 2016. LNCS, vol. 9995, pp. 559–576. Springer, Cham (2016). https://doi.org/10.1007/978-3-319-48989-6_34
7. Bosscher, D., Polak, I., Vaandrager, F.: Verification of an audio control protocol. In: Langmaack, H., de Roever, W.-P., Vytopil, J. (eds.) FTRTFT 1994. LNCS, vol. 863, pp. 170–192. Springer, Heidelberg (1994). https://doi.org/10.1007/3-540-58468-4_165
8. Cassez, F., David, A., Fleury, E., Larsen, K.G., Lime, D.: Efficient on-the-fly algorithms for the analysis of timed games. In: Abadi, M., de Alfaro, L. (eds.) CONCUR 2005. LNCS, vol. 3653, pp. 66–80. Springer, Heidelberg (2005). https://doi.org/10.1007/11539452_9
9. Cassez, F., David, A., Larsen, K.G., Lime, D., Raskin, J.-F.: Timed control with observation based and stuttering invariant strategies. In: Namjoshi, K.S., Yoneda, T., Higashino, T., Okamura, Y. (eds.) ATVA 2007. LNCS, vol. 4762, pp. 192–206. Springer, Heidelberg (2007). https://doi.org/10.1007/978-3-540-75596-8_15
10. D'Argenio, P.R., Katoen, J.-P., Ruys, T.C., Tretmans, J.: The bounded retransmission protocol must be on time!. In: Brinksma, E. (ed.) TACAS 1997. LNCS, vol. 1217, pp. 416–431. Springer, Heidelberg (1997). https://doi.org/10.1007/BFb0035403
11. David, A., et al.: On time with minimal expected cost! In: Cassez, F., Raskin, J.-F. (eds.) ATVA 2014. LNCS, vol. 8837, pp. 129–145. Springer, Cham (2014). https://doi.org/10.1007/978-3-319-11936-6_10

12. David, A., Jensen, P.G., Larsen, K.G., Mikučionis, M., Taankvist, J.H.: UPPAAL STRATEGO. In: Baier, C., Tinelli, C. (eds.) TACAS 2015. LNCS, vol. 9035, pp. 206–211. Springer, Heidelberg (2015). https://doi.org/10.1007/978-3-662-46681-0_16

13. David, A., Larsen, K.G., Legay, A., Mikucionis, M.: Schedulability of Herschel revisited using statistical model checking. STTT **17**(2), 187–199 (2015)

14. David, A., Larsen, K.G., Legay, A., Mikucionis, M., Poulsen, D.B.: UPPAAL SMC tutorial. STTT **17**(4), 397–415 (2015)

15. David, A., et al.: Statistical model checking for networks of priced timed automata. In: Fahrenberg, U., Tripakis, S. (eds.) FORMATS 2011. LNCS, vol. 6919, pp. 80–96. Springer, Heidelberg (2011). https://doi.org/10.1007/978-3-642-24310-3_7

16. David, A., Larsen, K.G., Legay, A., Mikučionis, M., Wang, Z.: Time for statistical model checking of real-time systems. In: Gopalakrishnan, G., Qadeer, S. (eds.) CAV 2011. LNCS, vol. 6806, pp. 349–355. Springer, Heidelberg (2011). https://doi.org/10.1007/978-3-642-22110-1_27

17. David, A., Larsen, K.G., Legay, A., Nyman, U., Traonouez, L., Wasowski, A.: Real-time specifications. STTT **17**(1), 17–45 (2015)

18. David, A., Larsen, K.G., Legay, A., Nyman, U., Wąsowski, A.: ECDAR: an environment for compositional design and analysis of real time systems. In: Bouajjani, A., Chin, W.-N. (eds.) ATVA 2010. LNCS, vol. 6252, pp. 365–370. Springer, Heidelberg (2010). https://doi.org/10.1007/978-3-642-15643-4_29

19. David, A., Larsen, K.G., Legay, A., Nyman, U., Wasowski, A.: Timed I/O automata: a complete specification theory for real-time systems. In: Johansson, K.H., Yi, W. (eds.) Proceedings of the 13th ACM International Conference on Hybrid Systems: Computation and Control. HSCC 2010, 12–15 April 2010, pp. 91–100. ACM, Stockholm (2010)

20. de Vries, R.G., Tretmans, J.: On-the-fly conformance testing using SPIN. STTT **2**(4), 382–393 (2000)

21. A.B. Eriksen, et al.: Uppaal stratego for intelligent traffic lights. In: ITS European Congress (2017)

22. Gerke, M., Ehlers, R., Finkbeiner, B., Peter, H.-J.: Model checking the FlexRay physical layer protocol. In: Kowalewski, S., Roveri, M. (eds.) FMICS 2010. LNCS, vol. 6371, pp. 132–147. Springer, Heidelberg (2010). https://doi.org/10.1007/978-3-642-15898-8_9

23. Havelund, K., Larsen, K.G., Skou, A.: Formal verification of a power controller using the real-time model checker UPPAAL. In: Katoen, J.-P. (ed.) ARTS 1999. LNCS, vol. 1601, pp. 277–298. Springer, Heidelberg (1999). https://doi.org/10.1007/3-540-48778-6_17

24. Havelund, K., Skou, A., Larsen, K.G., Lund, K.: Formal modeling and analysis of an audio/video protocol: an industrial case study using UPPAAL. In: Proceedings of the 18th IEEE Real-Time Systems Symposium (RTSS 1997), 3–5 December 1997, San Francisco, CA, USA, pp. 2–13. IEEE Computer Society (1997)

25. Hessel, A., Larsen, K.G., Nielsen, B., Pettersson, P., Skou, A.: Time-optimal test cases for real-time systems. In: Larsen, K.G., Niebert, P. (eds.) FORMATS 2003. LNCS, vol. 2791, pp. 234–245. Springer, Heidelberg (2004). https://doi.org/10.1007/978-3-540-40903-8_19

26. Kim, J.H., Larsen, K.G., Nielsen, B., Mikučionis, M., Olsen, P.: Formal analysis and testing of real-time automotive systems using uppaal tools. In: Núñez, M., Güdemann, M. (eds.) Formal Methods for Industrial Critical Systems. pp, pp. 47–61. Springer International Publishing, Cham (2015)

27. Kim, F.L., Larsen, G., Nielsen, B.: 20 years of real real time model validation (2018, under submission)
28. Larsen, K., et al.: As cheap as possible: effcient cost-optimal reachability for priced timed automata. In: Berry, G., Comon, H., Finkel, A. (eds.) CAV 2001. LNCS, vol. 2102, pp. 493–505. Springer, Heidelberg (2001). https://doi.org/10.1007/3-540-44585-4_47
29. Larsen, K.G., Mikučionis, M., Muñiz, M., Srba, J., Taankvist, J.H.: Online and compositional learning of controllers with application to floor heating. In: Chechik, M., Raskin, J.-F. (eds.) TACAS 2016. LNCS, vol. 9636, pp. 244–259. Springer, Heidelberg (2016). https://doi.org/10.1007/978-3-662-49674-9_14
30. Larsen, K.G., Mikucionis, M., Nielsen, B.: Online testing of real-time systems using UPPAAL. In: Grabowski, J., Nielsen, B. (eds.) FATES 2004. LNCS, vol. 3395, pp. 79–94. Springer, Heidelberg (2005). https://doi.org/10.1007/978-3-540-31848-4_6
31. Larsen, K.G., Mikucionis, M., Nielsen, B., Skou, A.: Testing real-time embedded software using UPPAAL-TRON: an industrial case study. In: Wolf, W.H. (ed.) 5th ACM International Conference On Embedded Software, Proceedings. EMSOFT 2005, 18–22 September 2005, Jersey City, NJ, USA, pp. 299–306. ACM (2005)
32. Larsen, K.G., Pettersson, P., Yi, W.: UPPAAL in a nutshell. STTT 1(1–2), 134–152 (1997)
33. Lindahl, M., Pettersson, P., Yi, W.: Formal design and analysis of a gear controller. STTT 3(3), 353–368 (2001)
34. Mikucionis, M., Larsen, K.G., Nielsen, B.: T-UPPAAL: online model-based testing of real-time systems. In: 19th IEEE International Conference on Automated Software Engineering (ASE 2004), 20–25 September 2004, Linz, Austria, pp. 396–397. IEEE Computer Society (2004)
35. Mikučionis, M., et al.: Schedulability analysis using Uppaal: Herschel-Planck case study. In: Margaria, T., Steffen, B. (eds.) ISoLA 2010. LNCS, vol. 6416, pp. 175–190. Springer, Heidelberg (2010). https://doi.org/10.1007/978-3-642-16561-0_21
36. Nielsen, B.: Specification and test of real-time systems. Ph.D. thesis, Aalborg University (2000)
37. Nielsen, B., Skou, A.: Automated test generation from timed automata. In: Margaria, T., Yi, W. (eds.) TACAS 2001. LNCS, vol. 2031, pp. 343–357. Springer, Heidelberg (2001). https://doi.org/10.1007/3-540-45319-9_24
38. Nielsen, B., Skou, A.: Test generation for time critical systems: tool and case study. In: 13th Euromicro Conference on Real-Time Systems, Delft, June 2001, The Netherlands, pp. 155–162 (2001)
39. Romijn, J.: A timed verification of the IEEE 1394 leader election protocol. Formal Methods Syst. Des. 19(2), 165–194 (2001)
40. Rütz, C.: Timed model-based conformance testing - a case study using tron: testing key states of automated trust anchor updating (RFC 5011) in autotrust. B.Sc. thesis (2010)
41. Tretmans, J.: A formal approach to conformance testing, C-19, pp. 257–276 (1993)

Verification of Operating System Monolithic Kernels Without Extensions

Evgeny Novikov[✉] and Ilja Zakharov

Ivannikov Institute for System Programming of the Russian Academy of Sciences,
Moscow, Russia
{novikov,ilja.zakharov}@ispras.ru

Abstract. Most widely used, general-purpose operating systems are
built on top of monolithic kernels to achieve maximum performance.
These monolithic kernels are written in the C/C++ programming language primarily and they may exceed one million lines of code in size
even without optional extensions or loadable kernel modules such as
device drivers and file systems. In addition, they evolve rapidly for supporting new functionality and due to continuous optimizations and elimination of defects. Since operating systems and, in turn, applications
strongly depend on monolithic kernels, requirements for their functionality, security, reliability and performance are ones of the highest. Currently used approaches to software quality assurance help to reveal quite
many defects in monolithic kernels, but none of them aims at detecting
all violations of checked requirements and alongside providing guarantees that target programs always operate correctly. This paper presents
a new method that is based on the software verification technique and
that enables thorough checking and finding hard-to-detect faults in various versions of monolithic kernels. One of its key features is the possibility to avoid considerable efforts for configuring tools and developing
specifications to obtain valuable verification results while one still can
steadily improve their quality. We implemented the suggested method
within software verification framework Klever and evaluated it on subsystems of the Linux monolithic kernel.

Keywords: Formal verification · Software verification
Deductive verification · Formal specification · Program decomposition
Environment model · Operating system · Monolithic kernel

1 Introduction

An architecture of most widely used, general-purpose operating system kernels
is either completely or mostly monolithic [1]. Like tiny microkernels, monolithic
kernels usually implement such main facilities as scheduling, memory management and interprocess communication. Besides, unless specially configured, they

The reported study was partially supported by RFBR, research project No. 16-31-
60097.

T. Margaria and B. Steffen (Eds.): ISoLA 2018, LNCS 11247, pp. 230–248, 2018.
https://doi.org/10.1007/978-3-030-03427-6_19

also have a built-in support for low-level network protocols, security modules, servers or monitors, the cryptography API, underlying abstraction layers for different device classes and so on. One can further extend a set of monolithic kernel facilities by enabling various optional extensions or loadable kernel modules such as device drivers and file systems. There may be available thousands of such extensions but as a rule each monolithic kernel of a particular operating system instance has several dozens of them at a time. It is possible to add new extensions and remove existing ones either by recompiling monolithic kernels or loading and unloading them dynamically.

The paper focuses on verification of monolithic kernels without extensions, since many other works already address the latter [2–7]. Below for brevity we refer to monolithic kernels without extensions as *monolithic kernels*.

Sizes of typical monolithic kernels may exceed one million lines of code in the C/C++ programming language primarily. In addition, they evolve rapidly for supporting new functionality, e.g. to support new device classes or a new security model, and due to continuous improvements like optimizations and elimination of defects. For instance, from 2009 to 2016 the size of the Linux monolithic kernel grew in more than 2 times and now it exceeds 1.4 million lines of code [8].

During the boot process a monolithic kernel is loaded into memory and then it operates completely in the same address space having a full direct access to all its internal data structures as well as to all hardware. This is the main reason why the given architecture allows reaching maximum performance. As a huge drawback, even minor faults in monolithic kernels can lead to an incorrect operation, data corruption and considerable performance degradation of operating system components including monolithic kernel extensions, and, in turn, applications. Critical faults can lead to privilege escalations and confidential data breaches.

Challenge. Operating systems based on monolithic kernels operate on billions of devices[1]. That makes monolithic kernels one of the most critical software in computer systems, thus, requirements for their functionality, security, reliability and performance are ones of the highest.

To identify defects in monolithic kernels developers and quality assurance engineers from different organizations use various methods and tools like code review, testing and static analysis [9]. However, none of these approaches aims at detecting all violations of checked requirements and providing some guarantees that target programs always operate correctly. Considering a very high importance of monolithic kernels, industry is eager for additional software quality assurance methods and tools. In some cases, e.g. for checking safety-critical computer systems based on monolithic kernels, certification authorities can specify quite rigorous requirements for such the tools [10]. However, there is a lack of available tools and evaluations of their applicability to fulfill such the requirements.

---

[1] https://www.computerworld.com/article/3050931/microsoft-windows/windows-comes-up-third-in-os-clash-two-years-early.html.

Below we present various formal verification methods and tools that meet the challenge.

Related Work. *Deductive verification* tends to prove the complete formal correctness of target programs. There are several quite successful projects devoted to deductive verification of microkernels [11–13]. Few works address deductive verification of small parts of special purpose and monolithic kernels [14–16]. In both cases authors show that it is necessary to do an enormous amount of manual work to develop models and specifications. Therefore, it is extremely hard to use existing specification languages, methods and tools of deductive verification for large-scale verification of target monolithic kernels since their typical sizes exceed ones of microkernels and special purpose kernels by 2–3 orders. Moreover, monolithic kernels constantly evolve that hinders deductive verification especially if yielded proofs are complex and rely on many factors.

Many researchers suggest using special programming languages and even special hardware for designing more safe and secure software, in particular operating system kernels [17–20]. This substantially simplifies formal verification but these approaches can not help for formal verification of existing general-purpose monolithic kernels.

Promising and outstanding results in formal verification of software have been achieved using *software model checking* [21] which today is often called *software verification* [22]. This technique provides a higher level of automation relatively to deductive verification. Software verification already has many successful applications regarding operating system monolithic kernels and their extensions including:

- Verification of operating system device drivers [2–7].
- Verification of network protocols [23].
- Verification of file systems [24,25].
- Verification of a Linux kernel memory management subsystem [26].

Contribution. Thus far researchers focus on verification of specific subsystems of monolithic kernels providing appropriate specifications and tools that do not suit for other subsystems. Moreover, nobody takes care of reusing and updating tool configurations and specifications for different versions of monolithic kernels.

This paper presents a new method that is based on the software verification technique and that enables thorough checking and finding hard-to-detect faults for various versions of monolithic kernels. The method allows avoiding considerable efforts for configuring tools and for developing specifications to obtain valuable verification results by means of:

- Verification of monolithic kernel subsystems together with extensions that use their interfaces.
- Reusing specifications developed for verification of monolithic kernel extensions.

– A high level of automatization of routine operations at various steps of the software verification workflow.

Besides, the suggested method remains room for improving verification results quality, i.e. for reducing the number of false alarms and the number of missed faults of various kinds. Primarily one can achieve that by means of developing specifications. Sometimes it may be necessary to adjust tool configurations.

Paper Outline. Before proceeding to the suggested method we give more details on monolithic kernel internals and on capabilities of software verification methods and tools (Sect. 2). In Sect. 3 we present a new method for verification of monolithic kernels. Section 4 describes the implementation of the suggested method. Its evaluation on subsystems of the Linux monolithic kernel is given in Sect. 5. Section 6 presents conclusions and future works.

2   Background

Both operating system monolithic kernels and software verification methods and tools are extremely wide areas of research and development. In this section we consider only those aspects that are vital for verification of operating system monolithic kernels.

2.1   Operating System Monolithic Kernels

Traditionally one considers monolithic kernels as several abstraction layers which often are referred to as subsystems. An actual implementation of these layers often does not fit well their abstract representations. Monolithic kernel subsystems can be tangled in an intricate way since this may be more efficient from the practical point of view and easier for development.

In this study we rely on the fact that target monolithic kernels are developed over decades and their current code bases are already mature and well organized. In particular, most likely developers already put closely related functionalities, that form subsystems, into corresponding groups of source files and perhaps directories. For instance, some group of source files constitutes a memory management subsystem, other source files are responsible for a particular network protocol, all source files from some directory form a subsystem for supporting some class of devices, and so on.

Each monolithic kernel subsystem has an API decorating implementation details. For instance, top-level subsystems define system calls that applications invoke for using facilities of monolithic kernels and underlying hardware. As a rule, at the bottom there is a hardware abstraction layer that introduces a uniform API for various devices for the rest monolithic kernel subsystems and extensions.

Middle-level subsystems implement either a number of interfaces, such as helper functions used in other subsystems and extensions, or event-driven APIs by registering event handling callbacks. Such events include software and hardware interrupts. Also, callbacks can be invoked in more implicit ways, e.g. on expiration of timers or during execution of queued works. It is worth noting that monolithic kernel extensions are similar to middle-level subsystems, but their APIs and interrelations are usually simpler than subsystem ones. In particular, mechanisms for defining, registering and unregistering callbacks in subsystems are the same as in extensions [27].

In order to allocate required resources and to subscribe for handling events, monolithic kernels initialize all subsystems in an appropriate order on loading into memory. This process is not so straightforward due to the necessity to ensure that event handlers are registered in advance to invocation:

– There are subsystems or some parts of subsystems to be initialized first of all. This is the case for, say, memory management and scheduling. Usually monolithic kernels perform such initialization in startup functions such as *start_kernel* in the Linux kernel and *init386* in the FreeBSD kernel.
– Most subsystems and subsystem parts are initialized in accordance with their levels. For instance, the Linux monolithic kernel of version 3.14 has 19 such the levels[2]. Initialization of its subsystem for supporting PCI devices leverages 6 of them starting from registering a PCI bus and finishing by registering file attributes for PCI devices. Monolithic kernels provide different mechanisms to set initialization levels for particular subsystem interfaces There are dedicated macros often, e.g.:
  • in the Linux kernel macros *postcore_initcall, arch_initcall, subsys_initcall,* etc. take corresponding initialization function names, e.g.:
```
postcore_initcall(pci_driver_init);
arch_initcall(acpi_pci_init);
subsys_initcall(pci_slot_init);
fs_initcall_sync(pci_apply_final_quirks);
device_initcall(pci_proc_init);
late_initcall(pci_resource_alignment_sysfs_init);
```
  • in the BSD based kernels such as FreeBSD, NetBSD and Darwin there is macro *SYSINIT* that takes corresponding initialization function names, their levels and orders within levels, e.g.:

---

[2] One can see files *include/linux/init.h* and *init/main.c* for details.

```
enum sysinit_sub_id {
    ...
    SI_SUB_VNET_PRELINK = 0x1E00000, /* vnet init before modules */
    ...
    SI_SUB_VNET         = 0x21E0000, /* vnet 0 */
    ...
    SI_SUB_VNET_DONE    = 0xdc00000, /* vnet registration complete */
    ...
}
enum sysinit_elem_order {
    SI_ORDER_FIRST      = 0x0000000, /* first*/
    SI_ORDER_SECOND     = 0x0000001, /* second*/
    ...
    SI_ORDER_ANY        = 0xfffffff  /* last*/
};
SYSINIT(vnet_init_prelink, SI_SUB_VNET_PRELINK, SI_ORDER_FIRST, ...);
SYSINIT(vnet0_init, SI_SUB_VNET, SI_ORDER_FIRST, ...);
SYSINIT(vnet_init_done, SI_SUB_VNET_DONE, SI_ORDER_ANY, ...);
```

- Some subsystems trigger initialization of parts of other subsystems or even their complete initialization. Usually this is the case when subsystems depend on each other.

Monolithic kernels invoke callbacks when corresponding events happen after completing initialization and even during it. In turn, callbacks can refer to interfaces provided by other subsystems, e.g. for allocating and freeing resources or for acquiring and releasing locks. Each event handling execution path can pass through many subsystems and even several extensions.

Monolithic kernel subsystems operate until either normal or abnormal operating system reboot unlike extensions that can be loaded and unloaded dynamically. In particular, subsystems do not need a final clean-up, e.g. to free resources and release locks, at the end of their work.

There are many diverse requirements for monolithic kernel subsystems. In this paper, we do not consider functional requirements since one has to spend too much efforts on developing models and specifications to check them. As for nonfunctional requirements, monolithic kernel subsystems should invoke used interfaces properly and obey generic rules of safe programming such as an absence of null pointer dereferences or buffer overflows.

2.2   Software Verification Methods and Tools

The method suggested in the following section is based upon methods for software verification [21,22]. In the previous work [28] we already described an interface, features and requirements of modern software verification tools like SLAM [5] and CPAchecker [29]. The fundamental limitation of these tools is the possibility to check programs of thousands or dozens of thousands of lines of code in size at most depending on the number of conditions. Thus, one needs to decompose monolithic kernels into moderate-sized subsystems to verify them independently.

An experience of leveraging software verification tools demonstrated the necessity of modeling a target program environment in a rather accurate way [2–7,27,30]. Software verification tools may produce false alarms at checking spurious scenarios of interactions between the program and its environment and miss faults if some paths possible during the program execution are forbidden by the environment model. Regarding monolithic kernel subsystems, their environment mainly consists of other subsystems, various extensions, hardware and applications. The environment model should initialize subsystems, invoke registered subsystem callbacks and provide models of used interfaces which implementations are out of verification scope but which significantly influence verification results.

Software verification tools are capable to check satisfiability of safety and liveness properties. Sometimes these properties explicitly match requirements, e.g. this is the case for memory safety. Otherwise, it is necessary to formulate specific requirements as a property supported by tools. For instance, one represents rules of correct usage of a particular API as a reachability problem usually. Software verification tool can both miss faults and obtain false alarms in case of imprecise formalization of requirements.

In contrast to methods and tools for deductive verification [11–16], the software verification technique does not require developing complete models and formal specifications covering all functional and high-level requirements. It is possible to detect faults of particular kinds as well as to prove correctness under certain assumptions even having inaccurate models and specifications. This stems from the following factors:

- One does not prove the complete formal correctness of target programs but searches for violations of quite widespread non-functional requirements using software verification methods and tools. We gave examples of such requirements for operating system monolithic kernels at the end of the previous subsection.
- Software verification tools automatically build models for all functions from target programs. These models are accurate enough for checking specified requirements.
- Software verification tools make certain assumptions either by default or being configured appropriately. For instance, tools can ignore the inline assembler. One should not expect many related problems since in monolithic kernels there are not many such statements and they are concentrated in architecture dependent subsystems [8]. Otherwise, one can develop corresponding models in the C/C++ programming language.
- Researches suggest new software verification methods and optimize the implementation of existing ones. Thanks to that today tools can automatically build accurate models and check satisfiability of specified properties for medium-sized programs using reasonable computational resources.

2.3   Klever Software Verification Framework

It is hardly possible to use software verification tools out of the box for industrial programs [28]. Fortunately, there are higher-level methods and frameworks that considerably automate the entire software verification workflow [2–7,28]. Most existing software verification frameworks target specific software like operating system device drivers [2–7]. In contrast, Klever is an extensible framework for checking various GNU C programs by design [28].

At the moment Klever is capable to thoroughly check Linux device drivers. It includes a set of specifications allowing both to generate rather accurate environment models for invoking most popular device driver APIs and to check various requirements. These specifications are also applicable at verification of the Linux monolithic kernel after slight customizations.

3   Verification of Monolithic Kernels

Following subsections consider adaptations of the common method for verification of GNU C programs [28] that we suggest for verification of monolithic kernels. Because of the limited space, we do not provide details like formats and samples of tool configurations and specifications.

3.1   Decomposing Monolithic Kernels into Subsystems

We suggest treating all source files from specified directories built into a monolithic kernel for a specified architecture and configuration as subsystems. This simplifies updates of tool configurations for new versions of monolithic kernels since developers rarely modify directories. Provided source files of different subsystems belong to the same directory, one should divide them between these subsystems explicitly.

The approach allows obtaining quite compact subsystems. If some subsystem is too complex for software verification tools at checking particular requirements, we suggest doing an additional decomposition using the same approach. One can expect several hundreds of subsystems for each monolithic kernel assuming a mean size of a subsystem to be about several thousands of lines of code.

However, our assumption that developers strictly follow separation of concerns is wrong sometimes. For instance, the same source file can contain functionalities of several subsystems. It is possible to extend a decomposition level further, e.g. by enabling enumeration of particular subsystem functions. But one has to provide and maintain different function name lists for various versions of monolithic kernels because developers change function names rather frequently. To avoid such difficulties we suggest considering source files shared by different subsystems indivisibly.

3.2   Verifying Monolithic Kernel Subsystems with Extensions

We suggest verifying monolithic kernel subsystems together with extensions that use their interfaces to avoid development of specifications considering corresponding interaction scenarios. There are several related assumptions:

- There should be environment model specifications for selected extensions to cover execution paths invoking target subsystem interfaces.
- Extensions should use subsystem interfaces correctly. Correctness of extensions is within the scope of other works [2–7].

One can select extensions using subsystem interfaces in different ways. If there is enough time and computational resources, we suggest taking all relevant extensions since this helps to cover all possible interaction scenarios. Otherwise, we propose to follow the algorithm:

- Obtain function coverage when verifying target monolithic kernel subsystems without extensions.
- Determine what subsystem functions are not covered and which of them are invoked by extensions.
- Obtain a minimal number of extensions invoking all uncovered subsystem functions or gather extensions in a greedy way.

3.3   Generating Environment Models for Monolithic Kernel Subsystems

We base the approach for generating environment models for monolithic kernel subsystems on the method we developed for modeling environment for Linux device drivers [27]. The method suggests specifying callbacks using a special domain specific language (DSL). Also, it has a hardcoded algorithm for initializing and exiting extensions occurring after loading and before unloading them respectively. Using environment model specifications and target extensions an environment model generator produces an extra C code to be verified together with a source code of these extensions.

To cope with monolithic kernel subsystems that have more complex APIs we suggest extending the existing method to support a number of DSLs for developing specifications and a corresponding number of environment model generators. These generators should prepare a final environment model as a parallel composition of its fragments generated independently for each DSL and the target program. Below we consider 3 such DSLs and environment model generators for monolithic kernel subsystems.

Modeling Initialization of Monolithic Kernel Subsystems and Extensions. It is vital to perform accurate initialization since during it resources are allocated and callbacks are registered. We suggest supporting a corresponding environment generator for specifying initialization of monolithic kernel subsystems and extensions as well as exit of extensions. It allows setting:

- Initialization levels and sublevels together with mechanisms to relate them with concrete initialization functions without referencing names of the latter.
- Initialization levels and sublevels for concrete initialization functions using their names (this is necessary for invoking those initialization functions for which initialization levels and sublevels are not set within target subsystems).
- Mechanisms to obtain exit functions for extensions without referencing names of the latter.

An environment model generator responsible for initializing subsystem and extensions and for exiting extensions:

- Obtains all initialization and exit functions defined by target subsystems and extensions with help of specified mechanisms.
- Properly orders obtained functions together with ones specified explicitly in accordance with respective levels and sublevels.
- Generates C code invoking initialization and exit functions in the calculated order taking into account failures of initialization functions if necessary[3].

Modeling Invocations of Monolithic Kernel Subsystem Callbacks. Regarding callbacks we propose to use the same approach to environment model generation for monolithic kernel subsystems as applied for verification of their extensions [27]. Often subsystems implement the same event-driven APIs as extensions, so, one can reuse existing environment model specifications.

Modeling Remaining Environment of Monolithic Kernel Subsystems. Sometimes nothing suggested above helps to cover subsystem interfaces, e.g. when they are invoked just by other subsystems or not invoked anywhere in a target monolithic kernel or considered extensions. To cover them we suggest to manually extend an intermediate environment model which is prepared at the previous stage since it is hard to suggest appropriate top-level specifications.

It may be necessary to develop models of interfaces invoked by target subsystems but which implementations are out of verification scope unless existing environment model specifications contain them. For these models we suggest using the C programming language with special expressions. The most important such expressions are functions which return non-determined values of their return value types. By using them one can force software verification tools to consider various paths, e.g. when functions both succeed and fail.

3.4   Checking Requirements for Monolithic Kernel Subsystems

We suggest checking those requirements for monolithic kernel subsystems that are vital but do not require much time for developing corresponding specifications. These requirements include memory safety and relevant for subsystems

---

[3] For instance, for the Linux kernel initialization functions can fail and return error codes. In this case, the environment model generator should not invoke exit functions if so, but can try to invoke failed initialization functions again.

rules of correct usage of monolithic kernel subsystem interfaces that are traditionally checked at verification of monolithic kernel extensions [2–7]. Unlike extensions one should not check that subsystems perform a final clean up since they can not be unloaded on demand.

3.5 Improving Verification Results

Generated environment models and requirement specifications may be imprecise. As we discussed in the previous section it can lead to missed faults, which is extremely undesirable, and false alarms substantially complicating verification results analysis. In addition, considering subsystems with or without extensions may be too hard for software verification tools at checking particular requirements. To improve verification results we suggest:

- To adjust tool configurations describing target subsystems and extensions verified together with them.
- To refine environment model and requirement specifications step by step until one obtains a reasonable coverage and an acceptable number of false alarms.

This process can be hardly formalized. There are strict deadlines usually, so one has to balance time spent on setting tool configurations, developing specifications, verification results analysis and preparing final accounts.

4 Implementation

We implemented the suggested method within the Klever software verification framework [28]. The implementation employs all existing Klever components and specifications intended for verification of Linux device drivers. At the moment it aims at thorough checking subsystems of the Linux monolithic kernel but it can be extended for other monolithic kernels as well.

For decomposing the Linux monolithic kernel into subsystems we allowed specifying directories and particular source files belonging to subsystems. Also, we extended a Klever component responsible for program decomposition so that it automatically triggers required build actions and filters out all required subsystem source files. Moreover, this component started to generate program fragments incorporating both subsystems and device drivers together.

We considerably extended the corresponding Klever component to generate environment models for monolithic kernels. The new version supports additional kinds of specification DSLs and generates corresponding environment model parts on their basis. In addition, we implemented a common environment model specification taking care of multilevel initialization for Linux monolithic kernel subsystems. We allowed disabling checking a final state since monolithic kernel subsystems do not need that.

5   Evaluation

For evaluating the suggested method we considered 3 subsystems of the Linux monolithic kernel that was built for architecture *x86_64* and configuration *allmodconfig* (Table 1). We limited the number of target subsystems as we did a thorough analysis of results to investigate various aspects of verification quality while analyzing only found violations does not take much time.

All experiments were conducted on OpenStack virtual machines each with 8 virtual cores of the Intel Xeon E312xx (Sandy Bridge) CPU, 64 GB of memory and Debian 9 (Stretch) on board[4]. We used Klever Git branch *kernel-verification* [28], CPAchecker Subversion revision *trunk:27583* [29] and, unless particularly pointed, those specifications and tool configurations that are used in Klever by default. In particular, CPAchecker could spend 15 min of CPU time and 10 GB of memory for checking each subsystem against any requirements specification. Earlier in Subsect. 2.2 we discussed major limitations of CPAchecker and other software verification tools as well as how these tools operate.

Table 1. Target Linux monolithic kernel subsystems (numbers of source files and lines of code are given for Linux 3.14)

Subsystem name	Directory	Source files	Lines of code
Character devices support (*CHAR*)	drivers/char	5	4194
General-Purpose I/O (*GPIO*)	drivers/gpio	6	4472
Terminal devices support (*TTY*)	drivers/tty	11	12129

5.1   Verification of Linux Monolithic Kernel Subsystems

To confirm that the suggested method meets one of its major expectations we verified target subsystems for all major versions of the Linux kernel issued from 2013, April 28 (version 3.9) to 2015, February 8 (version 3.19). This period covers almost 2 years of development and includes 11 major versions. Table 2 provides generic information on changes made in target Linux monolithic kernel subsystems.

To launch Klever we used the same tool configuration and specifications for all treated versions of the Linux kernel. To get better function coverage and to get rid of annoying false alarms we made following improvements in environment model specifications that are specific for Linux monolithic kernel subsystems:

– Explicitly specify initialization levels for two initialization functions from the *CHAR* and *TTY* subsystems.

---

[4] http://www.bigdataopenlab.ru/about.html.

Table 2. Changes of target Linux monolithic kernel subsystems (percentages were calculated relatively Linux 3.14)

Subsystem name	Source files added/removed	Lines of code added/removed
CHAR	+0/−1 (+0%/−20%)	+950/−712 (+23%/−17%)
GPIO	+2/−3 (+33%/−50%)	+5074/−3079 (+113%/−69%)
TTY	+1/−0 (+9%/−0%)	+4012/−3221 (+33%/−27%)

- Develop a model for function *panic* that abnormally terminates kernel operation.
- Place memory allocated in environment models into global lists to avoid detection of memory leaks after termination of subsystems.

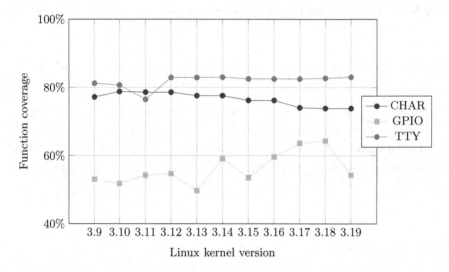

Fig. 1. Function coverage for target subsystems of the Linux monolithic kernel

Function Coverage. Figure 1 demonstrates function coverage for target subsystems of the Linux monolithic kernel. One can see that for *CHAR* and *TTY* subsystems function coverage changes rather slightly except for Linux 3.11. In this version developers added to the *TTY* subsystem a new source file defining specific semaphores but there were no users of an introduced API at that time yet.

Function coverage for the *GPIO* subsystem changes more often and more significantly because this subsystem is relatively new. It was introduced in 2008[5]

---

[5] https://lkml.org/lkml/2008/1/5/137.

while other target subsystems have been developing from the nineties of the previous century. One can see that this correlates with numbers of added and removed source files and lines of code from Table 2.

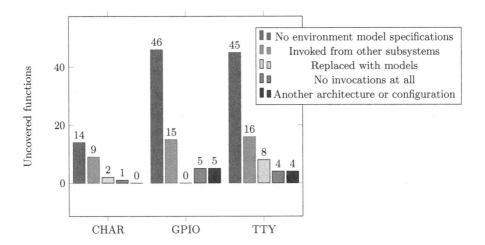

Fig. 2. Reasons of an absence of function coverage for target subsystems of the Linux monolithic kernel (for Linux 3.14)

Figure 2 demonstrates reasons why remaining functions of target subsystems of the Linux monolithic kernel are not covered. In the most cases it is necessary to develop additional environment model specifications to invoke specific callbacks.

Verification Results. We verified all target subsystems of the mentioned versions of the Linux kernel against the most relevant requirement specifications, namely, *generic:memory*, *linux:{alloc:{irq, spinlock}, arch:io, drivers:base:{class, dma-mapping}, fs:sysfs, kernel:locking:{mutex, rwlock, spinlock}, kernel:{module, rcu:update:lock}}* (12 specifications in total).

Figure 3 shows a dependency of obtained verdicts for each Linux kernel version. The *Safe* verdict means that the software verification tool was able to prove the absence of violations of checked requirements. The *Unsafe* verdict corresponds to a violation. The *Unknown* verdict means that the software verification tool was not able to issue either *Safe* or *Unsafe*, e.g. because of it needed more CPU time than it had. All subsystems were verified with different numbers of extensions depending on a Linux kernel version. To place plots for all subsystems in one figure, we provide average numbers of verdicts by dividing absolute ones on corresponding numbers of extensions.

One can see that *CHAR* and *TTY* subsystems are quite stable while there are several jumps on plots for the *GPIO* subsystem. Here there are additional reasons of these deviations than for function coverage at Fig. 1. For instance,

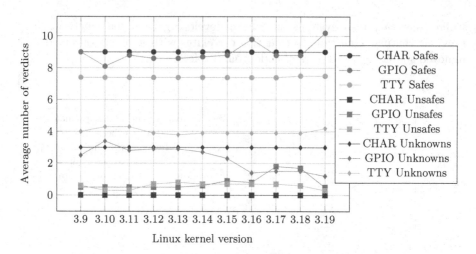

Fig. 3. Average number of verdicts for target subsystems of the Linux monolithic kernel

in Linux 3.17 and Linux 3.18 developers violated requirements specification *linux:kernel:locking:spinlock* that was detected by Klever.

We could not find any faults for *CHAR* and *TTY* subsystems that confirms their maturity. For the *TTY* subsystem about 62% of false alarms are relevant to the subsystem itself and 38% ones are relevant to device drivers verified together with it. All false alarms issued for the subsystem are due to inaccurate specifications. For the *GPIO* subsystem about 51% of *Unsafes* correspond to faults. One fault is in the subsystem. We already mentioned it, it was introduced in Linux 3.17 and fixed in Linux 3.19. Other 2 faults were detected at error paths in device drivers and they still exist in the newest versions of the Linux kernel. Regarding *GPIO* 59% of false alarms are for the subsystem and 41% are for device drivers. To get rid of about 86% of false alarms in the subsystem it is necessary to fix existing specifications and to develop new ones. Remaining 14% ones were reported due to inaccuracies of CPAchecker.

There are several directions of development to improve verification results. The first direction is an improvement of specifications to mitigate false alarms. The second one is to simplify target subsystems by replacing complex functions with models or by splitting them into several subsystems for independent verification. This can help obtaining more *Safes* and *Unsafes* instead of *Unknowns* (timeouts).

5.2   Finding Known Faults in Linux Monolithic Kernel Subsystems

We tried to find already fixed faults in target Linux monolithic kernel subsystems for estimating the suggested method ability to perform thorough checking. We analyzed manually all commits except merging ones made to the mainline Git repository[6] between tags *v3.9* and *v3.19* to source files of target subsystems. In total 488 commits matched these conditions. Among them we chose commits that fix violations of requirements for which there are corresponding specifications in Klever. There were fixes of 8 such faults (Table 3).

Table 3. Faults fixed in target Linux monolithic kernel subsystems

Subsystem name	Commit hash	Requirements specification	Detection status
CHAR	08d2d00b291e	*generic:memory*	✗ (another architecture)
	b5325a02aa84	*generic:memory*	✓ (extra source files)
	61c6375d5523	*generic:memory*	✗ (another configuration)
GPIO	e9595f84a627	*generic:memory*	✓ (extra source files)
	00acc3dc2480	*linux:kernel:locking:spinlock*	✓
TTY	b216df538481	*generic:memory*	✗ (needs specification)
	07584d4a356e	*linux:kernel:module*	✓ (dead code)
	1d9e689c934b	*generic:memory*	✗ (too complex)

A fault fixed in commit *00acc3dc2480* was already considered in the previous subsection. Klever could find it without additional efforts. We analyzed target subsystems together with those parts of other subsystems that define several helper functions to detect faults fixed in commits *b5325a02aa84* and *e9595f84a627*. Klever could not find a fault fixed in commit *07584d4a356e* since it proved that corresponding code is dead.

To reveal a fault fixed in commit *08d2d00b291e* it is necessary to verify the *CHAR* subsystem for architecture *x86_32*. For a fault fixed in commit *61c6375d5523* a corresponding source file is built for another configuration rather than for *allmodconfig*. For detecting a fault fixed in commit *b216df538481* one should develop an environment model specification for work queues. We could not find out a fault fixed in commit *1d9e689c934b* because of it turned out to be too complex for the software verification tool.

6   Conclusion

Researchers and proof engineers verify formally either special purpose operating system kernels or relatively small parts of large monolithic kernels that form a basis of most widely used, general-purpose operating systems. Therefore, there is still a huge gap between one of the most critical software used by billions of people and formal verification methods and tools. As a step towards closing this gap, this paper introduces a new method that enables rather thorough checking and finding hard-to-detect faults for various versions of monolithic kernels without requiring considerable efforts for configuring tools and developing specifications. Also, the method allows improving verification results step by step.

---

[6] https://git.kernel.org/pub/scm/linux/kernel/git/torvalds/linux.git.

Evaluation of the suggested method on subsystems of the Linux monolithic kernel showed that the same tool configurations and specifications are suitable for verifying subsystems of a large range of Linux kernel versions. We could detect one fault in one of target subsystems, but there is room for improvement primarily by means of developing specifications. Also, we found 2 unknown faults in device drivers analyzed together with target subsystems. Regarding known faults, we were able to reveal 4 of 8 of them after slight adjustments. For finding the remaining faults it is necessary to perform verification for other architecture and configuration and to develop an additional environment model specification.

We encourage researchers to adapt the suggested method and its implementation for verification of other operating system monolithic kernels. But one should clearly realize that it will be necessary to spend quite a long time for developing models and specifications unless some of them were developed in advance like for operating system device drivers [2–7].

References

1. Silberschatz, A., Galvin, P.B., Gagne, G.: Operating System Concepts, 9th edn. Wiley, Hoboken (2012)
2. Zakharov, I.S., Mandrykin, M.U., Mutilin, V.S., Novikov, E.M., Petrenko, A.K., Khoroshilov, A.V.: Configurable toolset for static verification of operating systems kernel modules. Program. Comput. Soft. **41**(1), 49–64 (2015)
3. Lal, A., Qadeer, S.: Powering the Static Driver Verifier using Corral. In: Proceedings of the 22nd ACM SIGSOFT International Symposium on Foundations of Software Engineering, FSE 2014, pp. 202–212. ACM, New York (2014)
4. Beyer, D., Petrenko, A.K.: Linux driver verification. In: Margaria, T., Steffen, B. (eds.) ISoLA 2012. LNCS, vol. 7610, pp. 1–6. Springer, Heidelberg (2012). https://doi.org/10.1007/978-3-642-34032-1_1
5. Ball, T., Levin, V., Rajamani, S.K.: A decade of software model checking with SLAM. Commun. ACM **54**(7), 68–76 (2011)
6. Post, H., Sinz, C., Küchlin, W.: Towards automatic software model checking of thousands of Linux modules - a case study with Avinux. Softw. Test. Verif. Reliab. **19**(2), 155–172 (2009)
7. Witkowski, T., Blanc, N., Kroening, D., Weissenbacher, G.: Model checking concurrent Linux device drivers. In: Proceedings of the 22nd International Conference on Automated Software Engineering, ASE 2007, pp. 501–504. ACM, New York (2007)
8. Novikov, E.: Evolution of the Linux kernel. Trudy ISP RAN/Proc. ISP RAS **29**(2), 77–96 (2017)
9. Novikov, E.: Static verification of operating system monolithic kernels. Trudy ISP RAN/Proc. ISP RAS **29**(2), 97–116 (2017)
10. Black, P., Ribeiro, A.: SATE V Ockham sound analysis criteria. NIST Interagency/Internal Report **8113**, 1–31 (2016)
11. Gu, R., et al.: Deep specifications and certified abstraction layers. In: Proceedings of the 42nd Annual ACM SIGPLAN-SIGACT Symposium on Principles of Programming Languages, POPL 2015, pp. 595–608. ACM, New York (2015)
12. Klein, G., et al.: Comprehensive formal verification of an OS microkernel. ACM Trans. Comput. Syst. **32**(1), 1–70 (2014)

13. Alkassar, E., Paul, W.J., Starostin, A., Tsyban, A.: Pervasive verification of an OS microkernel. In: Leavens, G.T., O'Hearn, P., Rajamani, S.K. (eds.) VSTTE 2010. LNCS, vol. 6217, pp. 71–85. Springer, Heidelberg (2010). https://doi.org/10.1007/978-3-642-15057-9_5

14. Efremov, D., Mandrykin, M.: Formal verification of Linux kernel library functions. Trudy ISP RAN/Proc. ISP RAS **29**(6), 49–76 (2017)

15. Ferreira, J.F., Gherghina, C., He, G., Qin, S., Chin, W.N.: Automated verification of the FreeRTOS scheduler in HIP/SLEEK. Int. J. Softw. Tools Technol. Transf. **16**(4), 381–397 (2014)

16. Gotsman, A., Yang, H.: Modular verification of preemptive OS kernels. In: Proceedings of the 16th ACM SIGPLAN International Conference on Functional Programming, ICFP 2011, pp. 404–417. ACM, New York (2011)

17. Azevedo de Amorim, A., et al.: A verified information-flow architecture. In: Proceedings of the 41st ACM SIGPLAN-SIGACT Symposium on Principles of Programming Languages, POPL 2014, pp. 165–178. ACM, New York (2014)

18. Leino, K.R.M.: Developing verified programs with Dafny. In: Proceedings of the 2013 International Conference on Software Engineering, ICSE 2013, pp. 1488–1490. IEEE Press, Piscataway (2013)

19. DeHon, A., et al.: Preliminary design of the SAFE platform. In: Proceedings of the 6th Workshop on Programming Languages and Operating Systems, PLOS 2011, pp. 1–5. ACM, New York (2011)

20. Yang, J., Hawblitzel, C.: Safe to the last instruction: automated verification of a type-safe operating system. In: Proceedings of the 31st ACM SIGPLAN Conference on Programming Language Design and Implementation, PLDI 2010, pp. 99–110. ACM, New York (2010)

21. Jhala, R., Majumdar, R.: Software model checking. ACM Comput. Surv. **41**(4), 1–54 (2009)

22. Beyer, D.: Software verification with validation of results. In: Legay, A., Margaria, T. (eds.) TACAS 2017. LNCS, vol. 10206, pp. 331–349. Springer, Heidelberg (2017). https://doi.org/10.1007/978-3-662-54580-5_20

23. Musuvathi, M., Engler, D.R.: Model checking large network protocol implementations. In: Proceedings of the 1st Conference on Symposium on Networked Systems Design and Implementation, NSDI 2004, pp. 12–12. USENIX Association, Berkeley (2004)

24. Galloway, A., Lüttgen, G., Mühlberg, J.T., Siminiceanu, R.I.: Model-checking the Linux virtual file system. In: Jones, N.D., Müller-Olm, M. (eds.) VMCAI 2009. LNCS, vol. 5403, pp. 74–88. Springer, Heidelberg (2008). https://doi.org/10.1007/978-3-540-93900-9_10

25. Yang, J., Twohey, P., Engler, D., Musuvathi, M.: Using model checking to find serious file system errors. ACM Trans. Comput. Syst. **24**(4), 393–423 (2006)

26. Liakh, S., Grace, M., Jiang, X.: Analyzing and improving Linux kernel memory protection: a model checking approach. In: Proceedings of the 26th Annual Computer Security Applications Conference, ACSAC 2010, pp. 271–280. ACM, New York (2010)

27. Khoroshilov, A., Mutilin, V., Novikov, E., Zakharov, I.: Modeling environment for static verification of Linux kernel modules. In: Voronkov, A., Virbitskaite, I. (eds.) PSI 2014. LNCS, vol. 8974, pp. 400–414. Springer, Heidelberg (2015). https://doi.org/10.1007/978-3-662-46823-4_32

28. Novikov, E., Zakharov, I.: Towards automated static verification of GNU C programs. In: Petrenko, A.K., Voronkov, A. (eds.) PSI 2017. LNCS, vol. 10742, pp. 402–416. Springer, Cham (2018). https://doi.org/10.1007/978-3-319-74313-4_30

29. Beyer, D., Keremoglu, M.E.: CPACHECKER: a tool for configurable software verification. In: Gopalakrishnan, G., Qadeer, S. (eds.) CAV 2011. LNCS, vol. 6806, pp. 184–190. Springer, Heidelberg (2011). https://doi.org/10.1007/978-3-642-22110-1_16

30. Engler, D., Musuvathi, M.: Static analysis versus software model checking for bug finding. In: Steffen, B., Levi, G. (eds.) VMCAI 2004. LNCS, vol. 2937, pp. 191–210. Springer, Heidelberg (2004). https://doi.org/10.1007/978-3-540-24622-0_17

A Proposal of an Example
and Experiments Repository to Foster
Industrial Adoption of Formal Methods

Rupert Schlick[1]([✉]), Michael Felderer[2,3], Istvan Majzik[4], Roberto Nardone[5],
Alexander Raschke[6], Colin Snook[7], and Valeria Vittorini[5]

[1] Center for Digital Safety and Security,
AIT Austrian Institute of Technology GmbH, Vienna, Austria
`rupert.schlick@ait.ac.at`
[2] Department of Computer Science, University of Innsbruck, Innsbruck, Austria
`michael.felderer@uibk.ac.at`
[3] Department of Software Engineering, Blekinge Institute of Technology,
Karlskrona, Sweden
[4] Department of Measurement and Information Systems,
Budapest University of Technology and Economics, Budapest, Hungary
`majzik@mit.bme.hu`
[5] Department of Electrical Engineering and Information Technology (DIETI),
University of Naples Federico II, Naples, Italy
`{roberto.nardone,valeria.vittorini}@unina.it`
[6] Institute of Software Engineering and Programming Languages, Ulm University,
Ulm, Germany
`alexander.raschke@uni-ulm.de`
[7] Electronics and Computer Science, University of Southampton, Southampton, UK
`cfs@soton.ac.uk`

Abstract. Formal methods (in a broad sense) have been around almost
since the beginning of computer science. Nonetheless, there is a perception in the formal methods community that take-up by industry is low
considering the potential benefits. We take a look at possible reasons
and give candidate explanations for this effect. To address the issue,
we propose a repository of industry-relevant example problems with an
accompanying open data storage for experiment results in order to document, disseminate and compare exemplary solutions from formal model
based methods. This would allow potential users from industry to better
understand the available solutions and to more easily select and adopt
a formal method that fits their needs. At the same time, it would foster
the adoption of open data and good scientific practice in this research
field.

Keywords: Formal models · Formal methods · Benchmarks
Industrial adoption

© Springer Nature Switzerland AG 2018
T. Margaria and B. Steffen (Eds.): ISoLA 2018, LNCS 11247, pp. 249–272, 2018.
https://doi.org/10.1007/978-3-030-03427-6_20

1 Introduction

There is a perception in the formal method (FM) community that, with all the possible gains of FM use, their adoption in industry is quite low. This is not a new thing, it accompanies the development of FM for quite some time and has lead to several studies trying to clarify what is holding FM back, e.g. [11,16,50]. It is hard to establish concrete market numbers about the adoption of FMs, but the low number and size of companies selling tooling for FM alone gives a clear hint that it cannot be high. On the academic side, FM courses are rarely mandatory for computer science students and only a small share of students attends them, limiting transfer of the know-how to industry.

Another indicator that FM did not arrive at the masses is that the European Shift2Rail funding scheme[1] has started a work package *Formal Methods and Standard Interfaces for Smart Signalling* in September 2017 to compare and select FMs for application in the rail signalling domain. This is a very welcome initiative. But it is also revealing. After all, the railway and particularly the signalling domain is one of the driving and most cited applications of FM. So if even for that know-how seems to be missing which methods, formalisms and tools are there and how they can be used best, how would someone from a less (safety) critical domain know how to choose and use a FM?

In our opinion, to a substantial degree, the low pickup of FM can be attributed to low awareness of the potential and properties of and missing comparability between the methods. This includes information about positive effects, side effects, needed effort for adoption and use, ease of application, and understandability of both process and results. Consequently, in this paper we propose to make this information more accessible by establishing a repository of examples and experiments, documenting the opportunities and strengths of FM and making methods and tools better comparable.

The remainder of the paper starts with an overview of pre-requisites to adoption (Sect. 2) and of obstacles hampering adoption (Sect. 3) of FM. It is followed by a presentation of similar approaches for benchmarks, competitions and repositories in Sect. 4. Section 5 details the vision of the examples and experiments repository and how we expect it to take effect and Sect. 6 gives more detail how we want to approach this and what needs to be done. Finally, a conclusion is drawn and the next steps to bring the proposed repository to life are sketched in Sect. 7.

2 Formal Methods Adoption

The term *formal methods* is not strictly defined and common understanding includes a large variety of approaches and methods. They are considered the 'mathematics of software engineering' [12] as they rely upon the usage of formal languages, i.e. rigorous mathematical notations having a formal syntax and a formal semantics. What we propose in this paper focuses on methods that build

---

[1] https://shift2rail.org/.

on the use of some form of *formal model*, expressed in a formal language, in contrast to e.g. software verification tools that work directly on code.

For tools working on code, comparison of approaches and tools is much more straight-forward. If you already have the code to work on, an interested user only needs to figure out the best parametrization/configuration and can run the tools applicable to the language used for development. If the problem at hand needs to be expressed in some formalism first, for adopting a formal method, not only methods and tools, but also formalisms need to be compared.

There is a grey area around this differentiation between formal model based and code based, because even e.g. for code based model checkers, there is a need to express verification properties by e.g. LTL, which is again a formalism where multiple options are available.

Formal models can be used for specification purposes only, or to perform several kinds of proofs and analysis: from proving consistency and integrity through model checking or theorem proving to the assessment of functional and non-functional properties. Formal models are also used to automatically generate test cases in model-based testing approaches, or to build simulators [32,49]. They can also be used in broader contexts which are out of the scope of this work, for example to cope with planning or synthesis problems [50].

2.1   Availability and Maturity of Tools

An initial analysis on the current state of tools is represented by the work shown in [3]. The authors discuss on the availability and the maturity of verification tools, in the perspective of their integration in software development lifecycles. Mainly, they identified two significant barriers in the development of robust tools and environments from academics: (1) *it is difficult to obtain research funding for tool development*, and (2) *the priorities of publication venues are a disincentive to building robust tools*. These two points open a discussion on the responsibilities of academics about the development of robust tools. In fact, as shared by researchers, it is not in the interests and responsibilities of researchers to develop industrial-strength tools, but it is important to highlight that minimal prototypes and/or small case studies playing the role of proof-of-concept are not enough for the industrial adoption of formal methods and techniques.

An important measurement system recently adopted also by several funded Research Programmes is the Technology Readiness Level (TRL) [34]. TRL is a scale system introduced by NASA for assessing the maturity level of a technology and consisting of nine growing levels from the beginning of a scientific research (TRL1) to a technology used at least in one successful mission (TRL9). A mature technology or tool should have TRL greater than six, this guarantees that it is more than a fully functional prototype. Several well-known tools supporting formal modeling and analysis can be considered mature according to this scale. Nonetheless, the low adoption of FMs in industrial settings with respect to their potential suggests that FMs need to be supported by a technology whose maturity is over TRL9 for industrial pickup. The difference seems to be the capability of achieving a seamless integration of a formal approach into the development process, in fact FMs are successfully used when they are *embedded* in frameworks or platforms supporting the software development process in whole or in part. A non-exhaustive list of such frameworks includes SCADE, Simulink design verifier and Polyspace, Atelier-B and B-toolkit, Spark ADA, and Escher Verification Studio.

2.2 Industrial Pickup

In a recent paper Newcombe et al. describe the successful experience at Amazon Web Services in using formal specification and model checking to verify the design of complex distributed systems [41]. In a previous paper Newcombe reports the evaluation and comparison of FMs performed at Amazon, also presenting a list of requirements for FMs to be successfully adopted in an industrial setting [40]. These works point out several industry needs that we have also experienced in other domains [5]. The needs can be summarized as follows: (a) being able to handle the problem at all; (b) minimizing the effort; and (c) return on investment.

In fact, a common perception is that FMs work on ad-hoc built examples under simplifying assumptions, so that evidence is needed that they are able to work on real-world systems. Hence, on the one hand formal languages need to be expressive enough to cope with the complexity of systems; on the other hand, a FM should be easy to learn and apply, so that the software engineers are not burdened by a further weight. In addition, the introduction of FMs should be worth the effort in terms of time-to-market, quality and correctness of the system, while limiting the impact on the industrial processes.

A relevant industry sector for FMs adoption is the sector of safety-critical systems. FMs are particularly desirable in safety-critical applications in different domains such as aerospace, railway, health-care and automotive. They are recommended in specific activities of the development lifecycle by the international norms and standards (regulating the system certification). FMs are sometimes addressed as mandatory in safety-related evaluations and suggested to specify or to prove what has been clearly stated in requirements at sub-system level. The practice is to determine the critical parts of the system and apply FMs during their design and validation.

As an example, CENELEC EN 50128 specifies the process and technical requirements for the software development of programmable electronic systems to use in European railway control and protection applications. Modeling is a major technique mentioned by this standard and the adoption of FMs is explicitly addressed. In particular, the usage of FMs is *highly recommended* for safety-critical sub-systems. In this context, a presentation has been published by Esterel Technologies (aquired by ANSYS) [39] in which guidelines to apply the SCADE solution in the railway domain are provided for CENELEC EN 50128. SCADE provides a formal verifier able to prove properties on models written using its synchronous formalism. By applying certified compilers from SCADE to programming languages these properties are preserved on the concrete system. The presentation explains which techniques and steps are covered by the SCADE

Suite, concluding that its model-based design approach helps save up to 45% of the total design costs. Similarly, in [10] the authors present the usage of the Ada-Core's technology based on Ada and SPARK. The SPARK tool-set uses theorem proving to verify properties that can be expressed as program pre-conditions, post-conditions, type invariants and sub-type predicates, so enabling the usage of FMs to check architectural properties.

These cases seem to confirm that the effective usage of FMs in industry requires to go beyond the simple availability of tools supporting modelling and analysis and that TRL is a useful mean to evaluate them if the level of integration of tools and methods into the existing industrial processes is also considered.

Another necessity for increased adoption of a modelling language is to be *as simple as possible and as rich as needed* [24]. In other words, an adequate system specification language should provide a sufficiently rich set of primitive constructs to allow for a natural modelling of the system of interest, and to capture and describe specific features of the system in a natural way, without introducing unnecessary difficulties in learning or modelling. Proper guidelines are also necessary to cope with a problem that cannot be easily overcome by other means: models of systems are not the systems themselves. Thus, to be useful, models must capture the significant aspects of the real system, but the capability of abstracting is a special skill, that requires experience.

3   Adoption Obstacles

Besides the pick-up of FMs in some particular niches, different obstacles hamper industry to adopt FMs in many cases. In this section, we want to discuss some of these obstacles and their causes resp. consequences.

3.1   Change in Industry

Successful introduction of a FM in a company does not only depend on the FM itself but on the involved necessary changes regarding established processes or knowledge. Even with semi-formal methods like model-based engineering, it needs special care to change the course of action [45].

Unless the company is very progressive and tries to be on the leading edge as a principle, changes are usually driven by lost money or contracts. If a lack of efficiency is not causing pressing problems, change is mostly delayed in favour of daily business. Though, if a company considers to have a closer look at new methods, the following questions are typically asked: (a) Does it work at all? (b) Does it fit my problem? and (c) are the benefits worth the efforts and costs?

The answers are not obvious and very difficult to find. And there is a long list of different FMs to choose from. Currently, there is no trusted source for these answers for any method. This makes it necessary for the company to do some investment in evaluating different methods. Evaluating a single, highly promising method is usually doable. But if there are several methods and tools, the evaluation effort quickly becomes prohibitive and the investment for one method cannot be reused across the evaluations of different methods.

Similar to an evaluation of a programming language or a framework, a trustworthy evaluation has to be done by an expert who is able to understand the underlying concepts, who might not be available within the company. Even if the evaluation includes only minimal pilot projects, they require people sufficiently trained in applying the methods.

Since they are competing with productive work, evaluation projects quite often fail with causes not related to the nature and properties of the evaluated method or tool, but due to business priorities favouring paid projects.

3.2 Comparability, Reproducibility and Evaluation of Applicability

On the academia side there are also some reasons for the absent adoption of FMs in industry. First of all, there are plenty of different FMs with diverse syntaxes and semantics. Each of these is mainly invented by researchers with only little focus on the usability in practice. Instead, formal techniques are evaluated typically by their inventors and developers (i.e., expert researchers) using a small set of examples which are rarely used by others. These academic examples often focus on the understanding of the approach's concepts or emphasize the advantages of the applied FM. This makes it even harder for industrial experts to decide if the problem they have falls into the class of problems where the method performs well. Conclusions drawn from these selected models might not be generalizable to real-world examples from industry.

Besides this "method bias" researching the scalability of a new approach is sometimes just omitted and if it is done, the artificial blow-up used to increase the examples complexity does not necessarily allow to decide if a real application would also benefit from the approach.

As mentioned by Newcombe from Amazon [40] "[they] preferred candidate methods that had already been shown to work on problems in industry [...]". That means, academic researchers should use industrial examples to evaluate their methods. Unfortunately, industrial examples are very often not shared since they contain trade secrets of the industrial partner (intellectual property (IP)).

Sometimes industry provides e.g. in the context of funded projects a shareable "almost-real" example, where IP sensitive information is removed. But even those models are very often not published in detail, mainly because they are much too large to fit in a conference article; in general, papers about real-world applications tend to get penalized – either the examples are not sufficiently described or they take too much room away from the scientific content. Also failed attempts are rarely published. Thus, an interested party gets no information that something they want to do has already been tried and failed for possibly even well-known reasons.

Similar to the model-driven software engineering approaches, FM research focuses on developing the concepts and not necessarily the tools. There have been a lot of improvements regarding performance and supporting complex systems in the last years, but usability and integration into an existing tool landscape are usually either not considered at all or only secondary goals for research implementations of methods and concepts.

4 Benchmarks, Model Repositories and Competitions

In this section we present notable examples of benchmarks, model repositories, and tool competition related problem suites (without any claim of completeness). These examples help us identifying those key properties that have to be fulfilled by our proposed FM repository for a successful adoption. These properties must be taken into account from the beginning of the design of the repository and drive its maintenance after the initial period of its operation.

4.1 Success Stories and Lessons Learnt from Other Domains

The concept of a benchmark traditionally means a widely accepted (standard) procedure aiming at evaluating and comparing different systems or solutions with regard to specific measures. Accordingly, benchmarks shall contain definitions of the measures for evaluation (what to measure) as well as the procedures how to determine these measures in a valid and comparable way (how to measure). The procedures typically need predefined inputs (e.g., a workload to apply in case of benchmarking performance) that form part of the benchmark; when the context (measures and procedures) are clear these are called the benchmark suite.

Performance benchmarking is the most successful area as it has contributed to improve successive generations of computer systems and led to benchmarking organizations such as SPEC (Standard Performance Evaluation Corporation) [43] and TPC (Transaction Processing Performance Council) [48]. Dependability benchmarking (to compare different systems or components from a dependability point of view) was also subject of research, having led to the proposal of several dependability benchmarks [29]. In case of security, a well-known example is the benchmark suite provided by the CIS (Center for Internet Security) [14], although not explicitly designed for systems' comparison.

In general computer science, comparability via benchmarks has fostered competition and progress in several domains. Just to name a few, e.g. for computer vision, [51] lists 24 data sets for stereo computer vision, the first going back until 2002. The robust vision challenge[2] includes 6 of those data sets with publicly maintained result lists. The development of SMT-solvers has greatly benefited from the SMT-COMP[3] competition and the common input language and benchmarks defined in SMT-LIB[4].

Several publications analysed the success criteria of benchmarks. In [28], it is stated that good benchmarks are relevant, repeatable, fair, verifiable, and economical. The authors of [7] focused on repeatability and reliability (to ensure high accuracy and sufficient precision). Benchmarks in [29] were designed

---

[2] http://www.robustvision.net.

[3] http://www.smtcomp.org.

[4] http://smtlib.cs.uiowa.edu.

for representativeness, portability, repeatability, scalability, simplicity and non-intrusiveness (this latter was important in case of fault injection experiments). On the basis of these studies, we can conclude that to achieve acceptance by its user community a good benchmark should fulfill the following set of key properties:

- *Representativeness*: The benchmarks should resemble relevant (and preferably realistic) problems of its user community – typically based on known examples and case studies from industry or academia.
- *Diversity*: To avoid bias, the benchmark shall include a balanced set of examples covering many different classes of problems that are relevant to evaluation.
- *Portability*: The benchmark suite and the measures should be defined in a format that is widely understood and supported.
- *Repeatability* (reproducibility): Enough public information shall be provided to enable benchmarking several times with the same result.
- *Scalability*: The benchmark suite and the related procedures shall support a wide range of measurement result values.
- *Simplicity of use*: The benchmarks shall be understandable.

In software engineering methods research, the need for sharing data and estimation models has recently become more urgent and researchers have started to investigate and address it systematically [38]. It has especially been pointed out that transferability of estimation models between companies or different domains, is a critical issue. In general, openly sharing research data is only common in few areas of research. It is increasingly asked for by research funding agencies, in the interest of good scientific practice, to enable reproducibility of results. Zenodo[5] is a platform to share research data and software from all research fields aiming at supporting open data and open science. But reproducibility of results does not necessarily produce or support comparability of approaches.

The tera-PROMISE Repository [37] is a research dataset repository specializing in software engineering research datasets. Its goal is to provide a long term storage facility for software engineering data. Amongst others, it contains defect, effort, performance, requirements and maintenance data including for instance data from NASA projects. Finally, it also contains models, which are in that case mainly prediction models, for instance for defect and effort prediction [6]. While it contains meta-data and links for several data sets, they are mixed across software related methods. There were many submissions in 2015 and 2016, but input seems to have dried up beginning of 2017. Since several data sets simply link to an entry at zenodo, it could be that the added value of the classification of data sets was not enough to motivate people to submit their data.

In general, curated data sets are common in several domains and they are very helpful for research working with data analysis. For methods research and method comparison, also the reproducibility of experiments and the reuse of

---

[5] https://zenodo.org/.

inputs is important. The Qualitas Corpus [47] is a "Curated Collection of Java Code for Empirical Studies" and provides code examples for empirical software engineering research. It is actively used since 2010, although several of the currently 261 citations according to GoogleScholar and 171 citations according to semanticscholar.org are not using the data set, but refer to it because they introduce a data set for another language or another purpose, or extended with additional data.

4.2   FM Related Problem and Model Repositories

In the area of model based design and FMs, there were several proposals for benchmark models and model repositories.

The *Embedded Systems Testing Benchmarks Site*[6] was initiated on the basis of [42] that presented benchmark goals and described an UML model with the purpose of offering a real-world benchmark for model based testing in the automotive domain. To support portability, the model was made available in several file formats. As a reference for comparing alternative solutions, the test procedures and an initial test suite were described, but unfortunately it was rarely used by competing solutions. An additional example from the railway domain and two examples for controlled natural language requirements have been added, but otherwise the suite did not grow.

Another related family of benchmarks is the challenge of *Rigorous Examination of Reactive Systems* (RERS) [23]. It provides generated and tailored benchmarks suited for comparing the effectiveness of automatic software verifiers. RERS is the only software verification challenge that features problems with linear temporal logic (LTL) properties in larger sizes that are available in different programming languages. In 2016, the competition comprised 18 sequential and 20 parallel benchmarks. The 20 benchmarks from the new parallel track feature LTL properties and a compact representation as labeled transition systems and Promela code.

The *Repository for Model Driven Development* (ReMoDD)[7] aims to support the sharing of example models, case studies, descriptions of methodologies and experiences. It is mostly used as a source of models for the research community, but not as a shared basis for comparing and evaluating methods and solutions.

Tool developers often collect models to demonstrate the capabilities of their tools. For example, the *UPPAAL Benchmarks* page[8] lists 9 timed automata based models and presents run-time data of their formal verification with the UPPAAL tool; this suite is often re-used by researchers developing related algorithms. A typical drawback of the tool-related collections is the lack of information characterizing the models (e.g., with metadata) and descriptions that could support understanding and mapping the models to other formalisms. In [19] the characteristics of the model collections of 9 model checker tools were

---

[6] http://www.informatik.uni-bremen.de/agbs/testingbenchmarks/.

[7] http://www.cs.colostate.edu/remodd/.

[8] https://www.it.uu.se/research/group/darts/uppaal/benchmarks/.

analysed and it turned out that only a portion of the models can be considered as scalable; in several cases properties to check are not provided; and sufficient documentation (e.g., references to publications) are missing. Representativeness and diversity are typically not among the goals of these model collections.

The *Archive of Formal Proofs*[9] is a very active repository of examples and proof libraries for the theorem prover Isabelle. The organisation as a scientific journal makes contributions easily citable and ensures the quality of contributions through refereeing. Other than the title and abstract, there is no mandatory, explanatory text or other natural language documentation of the entries in the archive.

The VerifyThis database[10] (emerging from COST Action IC0701[11]) has unfortunately become unavailable. It seems that, after the end of the COST action, when some of the used hosting infrastructure reached its end of life, nobody felt responsible to keep the service alive or migrate it to another host.

4.3 Competitions Related to FMs

The competitions organized typically in the frame of FM related conferences are successful in collecting and regularly maintaining a relevant and widely accepted suite of problems, this way fostering the development of better algorithms and tools. Examples in the area of model checking are the *Hardware Model Checking Competition* (HWMCC)[12] for hardware models, the *Competition on Software Verification* (SV-COMP)[13], and the *Model Checking Contest* for Petri net models (MCC)[14]. The verification problems are well-defined and the examples are available to download and re-use by the competitors. Organizers devoted efforts to have (as far as possible in the context of the competition) diverse and scalable problems, and enforce repeatability. Unfortunately, the problems are only stated in a form that can be used by the model checkers. If they are not purely academic in the first place, they have lost their connection back to the original industrial problem description. They are not very representative for actual needs from systems and software engineering industry. The MCC does have a separation of models into academic and industrial, but there are also no natural language descriptions available that would allow reproducing the examples in a different formalism without influence from concessions made to the formalism of Petri-Nets.

The VerifyThis competition[15] has challenges given in pseudo-code and natural language. The formalism and tool to actually verify the properties of the algorithms can be chosen freely. Since the challenges are to be solved within

---

[9] https://www.isa-afp.org/.
[10] http://verifythis.cost-ic0701.org/.
[11] http://www.cost-ic0701.org/.
[12] http://fmv.jku.at/hwmcc17/.
[13] https://sv-comp.sosy-lab.org/.
[14] https://mcc.lip6.fr/.
[15] http://www.pm.inf.ethz.ch/research/verifythis/Archive.html.

90 min during the competition, they are quite small in relation to full blown industrial software systems.

The following group of competitions is closer related to problems from industry. In 1995, the Dagstuhl Seminar "Methods for Semantics and Specification" [1] was conducted in form of a "competition". Several experts of a particular FM presented their solutions regarding the *Steam Boiler Control Specification* [2] which was published almost one year in advance.

In 2005, a Verified Software Grand Challenge was proposed [27], and in its context a Verified Software Repository (VSR) [8]. Although a workshop produced several new publications related to the Mondex case study [44] and the site proposed the POSIX file store and a pacemaker as additional examples, there was not a lot of follow-up activity after that. Meanwhile the VSR web page[16] suffers from severe link rot and the example solutions seem not to be accessible anymore.

The idea of a "competition" among FMs was revived on the occasion of the ABZ conference 2014 by introducing a *case study track*. Starting with a landing gear system [9], in 2016 a Hemodialysis Machine case study [35], and in 2018 a part of the European Train Control System (ETCS) [26] were presented. For each of these case studies several solutions exist modeled in FMs like ASMs, B, or Event-B. Currently, there is a discussion in the ABZ community to extend the case study track towards larger systems and a longer period of time for processing.

Although these (real world) case studies modeled with different methods allow for an overview of the different approaches, a structured repository with easy access to all available data (executable models, proofs, etc.) and valuable meta information is still missing.

A first step into this direction is given in [20]. In this book, 18 FMs are presented by each answering 24 questions related to a given case study. This book distinguishes between state-based, event-based, and other formal approaches. The editors give a brief summary and comparison of the presented approaches, but again, also with that book it is still not easy for a software engineer in the industry to choose the right method that will help solving the current problem.

4.4 Desirable Repository Properties

Without going into a detailed analysis of the success or failure of the mentioned repositories and benchmarks, we can still draw the following conclusions:

- A collection of examples or benchmarks should not depend on a single person or a small group - neither for maintenance nor for making decisions.
- To enable good benchmarking, a collection of inputs should be representative, diverse, portable, repeatable, scalable, and simple. In order to foster industrial adoption of methods, representativeness is the most important. For formal methods using different formalisms, portability is very hard to achieve.

---

[16] http://vsr.sourceforge.net/.

- "Drop off only" repositories, where the contributor has no effort with preparing the contribution, tend to suffer from the *attic effect* - lots of stuff, hard to find it once you need something, lots of garbage there, some things become valuable to the second-next generation, if they can find it.
- If there is any additional preparative work needed to contribute, there needs to be some incentive for the contributor. If the benefit is only on the repository's user's side, the repository will stay empty. Participating in a competition or otherwise producing citable artefacts, works for academic research, but not necessarily for people from industry.
- Curated collections provide quality control and tend to be more useful. But spending the effort for quality assurance needs to be compensated somehow.

5   Vision of a FM Experiment Repository

During researching and writing a publication on formal models based techniques, methods and tools, among others the following work results are typically produced: (1) descriptions of (the requirements of) the examples used for explanation and evaluation, (2) formal models, (3) experimental results, and (4) the published article itself.

We believe that items (1) and (2) are prime candidates for re-use between researchers, methods/tools and of course publications. Therefore, we propose to establish a web-based repository for these two groups of items, the data of the related experiments and the links between them and links to the used tools and to the resulting publications.

Below, we sketch the benefits we would expect from such a repository. There are three groups of stakeholders that would benefit from the repository: (1) researchers (2) industry in the role of tool vendors and (3) industry in the role of method users.

5.1   Benefits for Research and Researchers

Focus on Solutions. For researchers, the open availability of a representative set of industrial sized problems provides a touchstone for newly developed methods and approaches. Well developed requirements for the example applications let the researcher focus on the core competence of finding a good solution instead of finding out if the problem actually fits the current direction of work.

Recognition and Honouring of Contributions. Sufficiently working out the requirements of an industrial sized problem is a lot of effort in itself. In a publication about working on the problem, this effort is often not honoured by the review process. Review rightfully focuses on the scientific contribution and page limits force the authors to limit the description of the problem and also the formal model in favour of the description of their new or improved solution.

Work can be split up and submitted to the repository (and publication) in separate steps: (a) describing the example application itself, (b) describing the problem to solve, e.g. demonstrating consistency of requirements, (c) modelling the example in a certain formalism, and (d) when preparing the related publication itself, formalizing and solving the problem and running experiments for validation. This way, all parts of the work can be sufficiently honoured and contribute to the reputation of the authors. Even more important, it eases reuse of the results of the first three steps in this process for different publications.

Open Data. Publishing the formal models as well as the result data in the repository helps both researchers and publishers to fulfil open data requirements. Funding authorities are increasingly making open data a recommendation or even a precondition for funding.

Open data in itself is a good thing, because experimental parts of computer science, especially related to software engineering, are particularly bad with respect to reproducibility of results. Openly available input and output data allow other researchers to verify, discuss and extend the results of others. This could even lead to a more comparative style of publications, where research reports on which approaches (own ones or from other researchers) work better or worse on certain groups of example applications. By that, also the effect of publication bias, i.e. favoring positive over negative results in the publication process, could be reduced.

Easier Review. By using established sets of examples and refering to them, publication reviewers depend less on the problem description from the authors and can also focus on evaluating the solution proposed, instead of the quality and understandability of the description of the example.

Visibility and Traceability of Work. The relation between papers using certain examples and models can be tracked both in the repository and via having examples and models documented as citable work, thereby leveraging on infrastructure for handling citations that is already in place in publication databases. Not only can researchers find related work using the same examples they use, it also adds visibility to their own work to other researchers.

5.2   Benefits for Tool Vendors

Focus on Solutions. With the development of more example models over time, academic tool developers can focus on the improvement of tools instead of putting effort into finding good and representative examples.

Selection of Features to Develop. For commercial tool vendors and commercialised academic tools, ongoing research becomes much easier to compare. Thereby, picking new techniques from research to integrate into a tool becomes much more straight forward.

Advertising. Through the comparability of tools, both academic and commercial, both sides can win. Academic tools can demonstrate how a certain new technique solves a certain problem superior to others. Commercial tools can demonstrate how well their tool does for several different types of problems and how well their implementation of a technique scales on industry sized examples. Whoever accesses the repository, will see which tools were used on different examples and with which results. If sufficient visibility of the repository can be reached, this visibility transfers also to the tools.

5.3   Benefits for Tool and Method Users

The main benefit for tool and method users is to enable them to find the best candidates for closer evaluation. Thereby, they can avoid sinking costs into an evaluation project of a method or tool that was selected because there was not sufficient accessible data to make the right choice. This is made possible by:

Realistic Examples. The separation of example development, model development and research, as well as the re-use of the former two, makes it easier for researchers to work on larger, more realistic examples. Interested users from industry can even propose their own examples (cleaned up regarding company secrets and other intellectual properties) for inclusion in the repository. From the larger, more realistic examples industry can draw conclusions that predict the usability of an approach much better.

Documented Applicability. Openly available, sufficiently large examples allow potential tool and method users to compare their problems to examples in the repository. It allows them to recognize example properties they have in the systems they work on and select methods that perform well on these types of systems.

Evaluated Scalability. The examples in the repository will have different levels of size and complexity. If evaluations in publications use a sufficiently large set of examples, potential users will get a much better impression of the scalability of a certain tool or approach for a certain type of system.

Visible Versatility. With examples classified according to certain properties, a potential user can find out, how diverse the set of examples is that were used to evaluate a method or tool. It becomes visible if something works perfectly, but only on a small group of examples or if it does work reasonably well on many diverse examples.

Traceable Activity. Given that the repository provides search features for that, potential users can find out how actively a certain tool is extended with new features and analysed by the community.

5.4   Outlook, Long Term Vision

The combination of the effects on all three groups will foster both the improvement of methods and their transfer into industrial application. Mid to long term, we imagine the following things could develop:

Established Use. If the community accepts and embraces the use of the repository, it could become common practice to use examples from the repository for method and tool evaluation papers. Some conferences might even make the use of examples from the repository compulsory for a certain submission type or track. Once there are enough experiments in the repository, this can be used as basis for meta-studies and new research, utilizing data mining and automated analysis of requirements and models. Furthermore, publishing the examples and cases developed within funded projects to the repository might earn project proposals additional points in the evaluation or also become common practice.

Benchmarks. Leveraging on the increased comparability of methods and tools, selected groups of examples or models in the repository could be used in newly defined benchmarks. This could lead to positive effects in the development of tools as they were observed e.g. for SMT solvers with the establishment of SMTlib.

Platform for Competition and Case Study Reviews. The repository needs infrastructure for submitting, classifying and reviewing artefacts (example descriptions, models and experimental results). External tools like EasyChair provide support for this on the level of articles, but are not necessarily well-suited to do it for models, data and tools. Since the repository needs it anyway, not only the examples but also the submission and review infrastructure could be made available for tool competitions and case study tracks of conferences.

The repository could thereby collect even more example descriptions, formal models and experiment data sets.

Automation. The repository could offer options to also enter tool snapshots, to allow others to repeat the experiments. If this is done with a fitting virtualisation or container approach, even more possibilities open up: certain experiments can be automatically repeated with newer versions of formalizations and tools; the repository could volume-buy and re-sell (cloud) computation power to researchers, at the same time ensuring documented, comparable and reproducible hardware configurations.

Generalisation Towards Software Engineering Research in General. Use of the repository examples will probably start with core techniques and methods from FMs, like formal modeling itself, model checking, refinement checking and proving. But we imagine this to quickly extend to things like model based testing, interface compatibility checking, model well-formedness checking and model transformation like discussed eg. in [46]. In addition, (empirical) software engineering research shares a need addressed by the repository: to have comparable examples and cases that can be applied in different application areas and contexts [13]. Examples that can be replicated in different contexts form a basis for meta analysis and could allow the vision of evidence-based software engineering [31] coming to life even in the very context of FMs.

Business Data. In the long run, the repository could even include complexity metrics for examples and models and effort numbers for certain tasks, like building the model in the first place. These data sets could be extracted from publications from empirical software engineering research. Sufficiently prepared, they would allow users from industry to use them in their return-of-investment estimations. In addition, the repository can also help to unify the terminology used and the problems considered relevant in industry and academia, which often differs significantly [21,22]. Return on investment investigations can play an important role for communication between industry and academia and increase awareness about the relevance and applicability of specific methods both in both worlds.

6   Needed Ingredients and Open Questions

In order to make this vision come to live and stay alive over an extended time, we believe that a couple of topics need to be taken care of. They are sketched and discussed in this section and take the conclusions drawn at the end of Sect. 4 into account.

6.1   Structure of the Repository

The structure of the Repository should support the benchmarking goals, i.e., documenting, evaluating and comparing the usage of FM (formal languages and related techniques) according to different characteristics (e.g., performance, scalability, resource needs) in case of various software engineering problems. It needs to be oriented on what can be considered different, reusable work results as sketched in Sect. 5.1.

The proposed repository structure is inspired by the so-called *star schema* used in data warehousing [15] and already applied in similar repositories, like the one designed for dependability evaluation experiments [33]. Here the star schema consists of (1) a central fact table that stores factual data about experiments and links to the dimensions of the experiment, and (2) separate dimension tables that characterize the re-usable context of the benchmarking.

In our case, the central element stores experiment results (of using a FM), while dimensions are formed by the target application (case study), the related problem (to be solved by a FM), their formalization, the applied FM usage pattern, and the applied tool. The structure of the repository is presented as a class diagram in Fig. 1. Instances of classes are the entities stored in the repository. The attributes of classes represent the related fields and metadata (we present only the most important attributes in the figure). Note that each class has common attributes as a unique ID, name, author (with contact), version, and date; these common attributes are omitted from the figure.

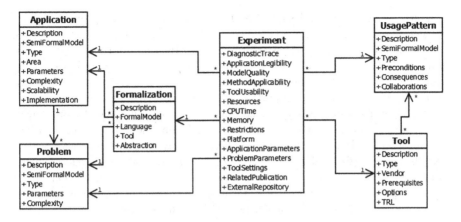

Fig. 1. The structure of the repository.

In more detail, the repository consists of the following parts:

- The central class of the structure is the *Experiment*. It stores the results of applying a FM in a given context (identified by links to context elements described in the sequel). The first group of its attributes includes the diagnostic trace (e.g., model checking result, generated test cases), the qualitative assessment results (legibility of the application description , model quality, method applicability, flexibility, tool usability, experience needed, etc. with ratings and comments), the quantitative measurement results (resources, CPU time, memory needed, manual effort needed . . .), and general restrictions (e.g., marking incomplete results). The second group of attributes describes the experiment platform and characterizes the experiment by the concrete values for application parameters, problem parameters, and tool settings. The third group includes related publications and external repository that may also be referenced. Note that the first group of attributes forms typically the basis of method/tool evaluation and comparison.
- A FM is applied in case of an *Application*. The related entity contains a mandatory informal (natural language) description of an industrial case study (e.g., the design of a communication protocol, an algorithm to solve certain tasks etc.), or an academic study created directly for evaluation purposes. An optional part is a set of semi-formal representations (models). Related attributes are the application type (industrial or academic, widely used benchmark or only a candidate), application area (communication networks, factory automation, railway control etc.), parameters (like the number of participants in a protocol), complexity, scalability, issues, (optional) link to implementation, and related test suite. Further context parameters that take, for instance, the applied development process and the required knowledge level of the involved stakeholders into account, can be added on demand.
- An application is associated with several *Problems* that are to be solved by FMs. Problems may include the checking of generic characteristics (like unam-

biguity, consistency of a design) as well as application-specific properties (e.g., absence, existence, deadline of specific behaviour), or comprise process-related tasks (e.g., to generate test cases for a design). Here an informal (natural language) description is included with an optional semi-formal representation. Related attributes are problem type (e.g., formalizing a specification, verification of state reachability properties, concurrency, or timeliness), parameters (e.g., potential restrictions), and complexity (estimated when the problem is described). Note that problems are separated from the applications as different problems related to the same application may need different FMs.

– Applications and problems are formalized using formal languages, resulting in *Formalizations* where each formalization captures an application and a related problem. Attributes of a formalization are the formal language(s) used, the modelling tool(s), and the applied abstractions.

– Solving a problem is based on a *Usage Pattern*. Each pattern is a generic description of the procedure of applying a FM to solve a problem type. The natural language description may be extended with semi-formal representation (e.g., using activity diagrams). Patterns can be considered as an adaptation and refinement of the idea of process patterns, known in the field of software development [4]. Attributes of a pattern are its type (essentially based on the purpose of the pattern), preconditions, consequences (benefits, trade-offs, drawbacks, outcome), and collaboration needs. Note that referring to a pattern documents a way of performing the experiment, thus providing an important aspect of the repeatability of experiments.

– The usage of a FM according to a pattern may be supported by a *Tool*. Note that for simplicity reasons tool-chains formed by a sequence of tools are considered as composite tools. Attributes of tools include its description, tool type (e.g., model checker, test case generator, SMT solver), vendor, prerequisites, configuration options (for potential settings), and TRL.

Some attributes are mandatory (e.g., description of an application) while others are optional (e.g., link to an implementation). The values of non-numerical attributes may originate from a predefined taxonomy, but also open to unconstrained entry (to form input for the extension of the corresponding taxonomy during regular maintenance of the repository). Especially the types (problem type, tool type, pattern type) may be selected from a related taxonomy. The initial taxonomies can be constructed on the basis of existing categorization of patterns (developed in research projects like MBAT [36] and ENABLE-S3 [18]), problems (e.g., using classification of behavioural properties [17]), and tools.

According to this structure, an example of an Experiment entity is the following. The linked context includes as Application instance the "Bang & Olufsen Collision Detection Protocol" [25], the related Problem is "Checking undiscovered collisions", the Formalization is a timed automaton model "bopdp.xml" including the temporal logic formalization of the checked problem, the applied Pattern is "Model checking timed automata models", and the related tool is "UPPAAL verifyta v4.1.3". The concrete tool setting is the verifyta option "-C -y", result attributes are the CPU time and the memory needed for model checking.

Although already very detailed, this structure proposal is considered to be more a starting point for discussion than a finished specification. A balance needs to be found to have the structure applicable to many different methods, while still ensuring that the purpose of easy re-use of information and artefacts can be made. By providing a set of attributes we tried to highlight the need of proper metadata and description that support understanding and comparison of results.

6.2   Community Buy-In and Incentives

To ensure take-up of the repository by the scientific community, a broad basis of researchers shall be invited to contribute to and comment on the planned repository. Organisers of competitions and challenges will be approached and invited to contribute their new target examples to the repository.

By making the different artefacts in the repository citable, researchers shall be encouraged to sufficiently package work results (example descriptions, formalisations) they need anyway to do their research, but often cannot publish as a self-contained work item.

By promoting the repository at various conferences, researchers developing new methods shall be encouraged to use examples from the repository. Instead of studying example requirements and building formalisations, the effort reduces to selecting already formalised examples. The saved effort can be used to try out the new method on a larger set of examples.

On occasion, companies define shareable example problems. They take particular care to get the examples free of any protected or protectable IP, trade secrets or other confidential information. These examples strive to represent the real-world problems the company encounters in their daily business. We will invite the companies to contribute their example into the repository. Hopefully, once the repository is sufficiently known, companies will contribute such models on their own.

6.3   Rules and Processes

Quality of the content of the repository is important to be of value to its users. Therefore, defined rules that a contribution should comply to and a form of quality assurance process are needed. The latter should define how an artefact becomes part of the repository and who is checking that all rules are followed (mandatory parts are given, level of quality of verbal descriptions as well as formalizations, etc.). It also needs to take care of maintenance, i.e. correction and extension of already included artefacts.

One option would be to use peer review as it is done for the papers about the respective experiments anyway. But if it is not possible to directly connect a contribution of artefacts to a publication and join the review processes into one, this might not succeed due to a lack of reviewers. Alternatives are paid editors or a community rating. An interesting approach for an improved peer review approach, sketched by Kaplan in [30], involves making the reviewer's names public, providing both recognition for the reviewer on a good paper and an incentive to do good and constructive reviews.

The repository part for *Applications* could be split into a recommended core, core candidates, additional submissions, and sections related to events like conferences, challenges or competitions. There would be different inclusion process variants for these parts. The recommended core would provide a reference set, grouped by applicable methods; comparative research would be encouraged to use a representative subset of the applicable groups from the core. For the sections related to events, the review would be in part delegated to the event organizers.

6.4 Repository Maintenance and Governance

The discussed rules and processes need to be defined and maintained over time by somebody. In the beginning, this could be done informally, similar to the steering committee of a conference series.

Mid-term, we envision the set-up of a non-profit association taking care of this. The governing body for the repository would be a steering committee that is selected by the general assembly of the association. In order to involve all the stakeholders and respect their interests, the association should be open to research, tool industry and industrial end-users of the tools and methods. In case that there is an imbalance in the number of members of the groups, votes could be weighted to give the three groups an equal level of influence.

6.5 Financial Support

The cost of hosting the repository itself are negligible and could probably be taken over by an arbitrary institution. But establishing it needs effort, including the initial structure definitions and specifications, developing a sufficient software solution and setting it up for operation. Said software needs to be maintained and extended. On top of that, as incentive to get the repository filled faster, it might make sense to offer rewards for submissions and reviews in some form.

Distributing costs among as many stakeholders as possible would keep costs low for the individual institution. At the same time, this would help keeping the repository independent and impartial. One option to achieve this would be membership fees in the association. Part of the fees could be paid by in-kind contributions, e.g. universities could contribute to the software development for the portal.

Accepting sponsoring money from industry (if offered at all) is tempting. It needs to be done in a way that avoids suspicion of the repository being controlled by the sponsors exceeding their influence as members of the association.

7   Conclusion and Outlook

We have described some of the problems for industrial adoption of FMs and sketched how knowledge transfer from research to industry could be supported by an example and experiments repository for FMs.

We have discussed existing repositories, benchmarks and archieves and described how a repository matching the goal of having comparisons based on realistic examples could look like.

In order to go forward and actually build the repository, we will seek support and buy in from FM researchers, FM tool developers and existing and future FM users. This can utilize working sessions at related conferences, a survey collecting input from said stakeholders and dedicated follow-up events. Also starting a new *COST action*[17] focusing on FM comparability, usability and training would be an option.

Once a core team has been built out of these groups of stakeholders, development of the repository rules, processes and web portal can start. Growing the governing body out of the core team can be started in parallel, including clarification of legal aspects, like licensing and IPR rules.

It would be great if a prototype could already be used in connection with events like the next ABZ conference's case study track 2020 or in connection with a dedicated track within ISoLA's next doctoral symposium.

Acknowledgments. The authors thank Wolfgang Herzner for his valuable feedback on the content of this paper.

The work of Istvan Majzik was supported by the BME - Artificial Intelligence FIKP grant of EMMI (BME FIKP-MI/SC). The work of Roberto Nardone and Valeria Vittorini has been partially supported by MIUR within the GAUSS project (CUP E52F16002700001) of the PRIN 2015 program. And by DIETI within the project MODAL (*MOdel-Driven AnaLysis of Critical Industrial Systems*). The work of Rupert Schlick has received funding from the EU (program H2020) and national Austrian funding from BMVIT (program ICT of the future) in ECSEL project AutoDrive (Grant No. 737469).

References

1. Abrial, J.R., Börger, E., Langmaack, H.: Methods for Semantics and Specification, vol. 117. Dagstuhl Seminar No. 9523, Schloss Dagstuhl, International Conference and Research Center for Computer Science (1995)
2. Abrial, J.R., Börger, E., Langmaack, H.: Formal Methods for Industrial Applications: Specifying and Programming the Steam Boiler Control. LNCS, vol. 9. Springer, Heidelberg (1996). https://doi.org/10.1007/BFb0027227
3. Alglave, J., Donaldson, A.F., Kroening, D., Tautschnig, M.: Making software verification tools really work. In: Bultan, T., Hsiung, P.-A. (eds.) ATVA 2011. LNCS, vol. 6996, pp. 28–42. Springer, Heidelberg (2011). https://doi.org/10.1007/978-3-642-24372-1_3
4. Ambler, S.W.: Process Patterns. Cambridge University Press, Cambridge (1998)
5. Benerecetti, M., et al.: Dynamic state machines for modelling railway control systems. Sci. Comput. Programm. **133**, 116–153 (2017)
6. Bettenburg, N., Nagappan, M., Hassan, A.E.: Think locally, act globally: improving defect and effort prediction models. In: Proceedings of the 9th IEEE Working Conference on Mining Software Repositories, pp. 60–69 (2012)

---

[17] http://www.cost.eu.

7. Beyer, D., Löwe, S., Wendler, P.: Reliable benchmarking: requirements and solutions. Int. J. Softw. Tools Technol. Transf. 1–29 (2017)
8. Bicarregui, J., Hoare, C., Woodcock, J.: The verified software repository: a step towards the verifying compiler. Formal Aspects Comput. **18**(2), 143–151 (2006). https://doi.org/10.1007/s00165-005-0079-4
9. Boniol, F., Wiels, V., Ait-Ameur, Y., Schewe, K.D. (eds.): ABZ 2014: The Landing Gear Case Study. Communications in Computer and Information Science, vol. 433. Springer, Cham (2014). https://doi.org/10.1007/978-3-319-07512-9
10. Boulanger, J.L., Ochem, Q.: AdaCore Technologies for CENELEC EN 50128: 2011 (2015)
11. Bowen, J.P., Hinchey, M.G.: The use of industrial-strength formal methods. In: Proceedings of The Twenty-First Annual International Computer Software and Applications Conference, COMPSAC 1997, pp. 332–337 (1997)
12. Bowen, J.P., Hinchey, M.G.: Ten commandments of formal methods... ten years later. Computer **39**(1), 40–48 (2006)
13. Briand, L., Bianculli, D., Nejati, S., Pastore, F., Sabetzadeh, M.: The case for context-driven software engineering research: generalizability is overrated. IEEE Softw. **34**(5), 72–75 (2017)
14. Center for Internet Security: CIS Benchmarks (2018). https://www.cisecurity.org/cis-benchmarks/
15. Chauduri, S., Dayal, U.: An overview of data warehousing and OLAP technology. ACM SIGMOD Rec. **26**, 65–74 (1997)
16. Davis, J.A., et al.: Study on the barriers to the industrial adoption of formal methods. In: Pecheur, C., Dierkes, M. (eds.) FMICS 2013. LNCS, vol. 8187, pp. 63–77. Springer, Heidelberg (2013). https://doi.org/10.1007/978-3-642-41010-9_5
17. Dwyer, M.B., Avrunin, G.S., Corbett, J.C.: Patterns in property specifications for finite-state verification. In: Proceedings 1999 International Conference on Software Engineering, pp. 411–420. IEEE (1999)
18. ENABLE-S3 Consortium: V&V Methodology. Project deliverable D3.2.2 v1 (2017). https://www.enable-s3.eu/media/deliverables/
19. Farkas, R., Bergmann, G.: Towards reliable benchmarks of timed automata. In: Proceedings of the 25th PhD Mini-Symposium, pp. 20–23. Budapest University of Technology and Economics (2018)
20. Frappier, M., Habrias, H.: Software Specification Methods. ISTE Ltd. (2006)
21. Garousi, V., Felderer, M.: Worlds apart: industrial and academic focus areas in software testing. IEEE Softw. **34**(5), 38–45 (2017)
22. Garousi, V., Felderer, M., Kuhrmann, M., Herkiloğlu, K.: What industry wants from academia in software testing?: hearing practitioners' opinions. In: Proceedings of the 21st International Conference on Evaluation and Assessment in Software Engineering, pp. 65–69. ACM (2017)
23. Geske, M., Jasper, M., Steffen, B., Howar, F., Schordan, M., van de Pol, J.: RERS 2016: parallel and sequential benchmarks with focus on LTL verification. In: Margaria, T., Steffen, B. (eds.) ISoLA 2016. LNCS, vol. 9953, pp. 787–803. Springer, Cham (2016). https://doi.org/10.1007/978-3-319-47169-3_59
24. Glinz, M.: Statecharts for requirements specification-as simple as possible, as rich as needed. In: Proceedings of the ICSE2002 Workshop on Scenarios and State Machines: Models, Algorithms, and Tools (2002)
25. Havelund, K., Skou, A., Larsen, K.G., Lund, K.: Formal modelling and analysis of an audio/video protocol: an industrial case study using UPPAAL. In: Proceedings of 18th IEEE Real-Time Systems Symposium, pp. 2–13. IEEE CS (1997)

26. Hoang, T.S., Butler, M., Reichl, K.: The hybrid ERTMS/ETCS level 3 case study. In: Butler, M., Raschke, A., Hoang, T.S., Reichl, K. (eds.) ABZ 2018. LNCS, vol. 10817, pp. 251–261. Springer, Cham (2018). https://doi.org/10.1007/978-3-319-91271-4_17

27. Hoare, T., Misra, J.: Verified software: theories, tools, experiments vision of a grand challenge project. In: Meyer, B., Woodcock, J. (eds.) VSTTE 2005. LNCS, vol. 4171, pp. 1–18. Springer, Heidelberg (2008). https://doi.org/10.1007/978-3-540-69149-5_1

28. Huppler, K.: The art of building a good benchmark. In: Nambiar, R., Poess, M. (eds.) TPCTC 2009. LNCS, vol. 5895, pp. 18–30. Springer, Heidelberg (2009). https://doi.org/10.1007/978-3-642-10424-4_3

29. Kanoun, K., Spainhower, L.: Dependability Benchmarking for Computer Systems. Wiley - IEEE Computer Society Press (2008)

30. Kaplan, D.: How to Fix Peer Review, June 2005. https://www.the-scientist.com/? articles.view/articleNo/16474/title/How-to-Fix-Peer-Review/

31. Kitchenham, B.A., Dyba, T., Jorgensen, M.: Evidence-based software engineering. In: Proceedings of the 26th International Conference on Software Engineering, pp. 273–281. IEEE Computer Society (2004)

32. Kunzli, S., Poletti, F., Benini, L., Thiele, L.: Combining simulation and formal methods for system-level performance analysis. In: Proceedings of Design, Automation and Test in Europe, DATE 2006, vol. 1, pp. 1–6. IEEE (2006)

33. Madeira, H., Costa, J., Vieira, M.: The OLAP and data warehousing approaches for analysis and sharing of results from dependability evaluation experiments. In: Proceedings of IEEE 2003 International Conference on Dependable Systems and Networks, DSN 2003, pp. 22–25. IEEE CS (2003)

34. Mankins, J.C.: Technology readiness levels. White Paper, 6 April 1995

35. Mashkoor, A.: The hemodialysis machine case study. In: Butler, M., Schewe, K.-D., Mashkoor, A., Biro, M. (eds.) ABZ 2016. LNCS, vol. 9675, pp. 329–343. Springer, Cham (2016). https://doi.org/10.1007/978-3-319-33600-8_29

36. MBAT Consortium: MBAT Analysis and Testing Patterns (2014). http://mbat-wiki.iese.fraunhofer.de/index.php/MBAT_Analysis_and_Testing_Patterns

37. Menzies, T., Krishna, R., Pryor, D.: The Promise Repository of Empirical Software Engineering Data (2015). North Carolina State University, Department of Computer Science. http://openscience.us/repo

38. Menzies, T., Kocaguneli, E., Turhan, B., Minku, L., Peters, F.: Sharing Data and Models in Software Engineering. Morgan Kaufmann, Burlington (2014)

39. Morin, G.: EN 50128:2011 – what's new and applying it to your development and verification process (2014). http://www.esterel-technologies.com/wp-content/uploads/2014/10/Webinar-EN-50128-2011-Wha-is-New.pdf. Accessed 17 May 2018

40. Newcombe, C.: Why Amazon chose TLA+. In: Ait Ameur, Y., Schewe, K.D. (eds.) ABZ 2014. LNCS, vol. 8477. Springer, Heidelberg (2014). https://doi.org/10.1007/978-3-662-43652-3_3

41. Newcombe, C., Rath, T., Zhang, F., Munteanu, B., Brooker, M., Deardeuff, M.: How Amazon web services uses formal methods. Commun. ACM 58(4), 66–73 (2015)

42. Peleska, J., et al.: A real-world benchmark model for testing concurrent real-time systems in the automotive domain. In: Wolff, B., Zaïdi, F. (eds.) ICTSS 2011. LNCS, vol. 7019, pp. 146–161. Springer, Heidelberg (2011). https://doi.org/10.1007/978-3-642-24580-0_11

43. Standard Performance Evaluation Corporation: SPEC's Benchmarks (2018). http://spec.org/benchmarks.html
44. Stepney, S., Cooper, D., Woodcock, J.: An electronic purse: specification, refinement, and proof. Technical monograph PRG-126, Oxford University Computing Laboratory, July 2000
45. Stieglbauer, G., Roncevic, I.: Objecting to the revolution: model-based engineering and the industry - root causes beyond classical research topics. In: Pires, L.F., Hammoudi, S., Selic, B. (eds.) Proceedings of the 5th International Conference on Model-Driven Engineering and Software Development, MODELSWARD 2017, pp. 629–639. SciTePress (2017)
46. Szárnyas, G., Izsó, B., Ráth, I., Varró, D.: The train benchmark: cross-technology performance evaluation of continuous model queries. Softw. Syst. Model. **17**(4), 1365–1393 (2017)
47. Tempero, E., et al.: The qualitas corpus: a curated collection of java code for empirical studies. In: Proceedings of the 2010 Asia Pacific Software Engineering Conference, APSEC 2010, pp. 336–345. IEEE Computer Society, Washington, DC (2010). https://doi.org/10.1109/APSEC.2010.46
48. Transaction Processing Performance Council: Active TPC Benchmarks (2018). http://www.tpc.org/information/benchmarks.asp
49. Utting, M., Legeard, B.: Practical Model-Based Testing: A Tools Approach. Morgan Kaufmann, Burlington (2010)
50. Woodcock, J., Larsen, P.G., Bicarregui, J., Fitzgerald, J.: Formal methods: practice and experience. ACM Comput. Surv. **41**(4), 1–36 (2009)
51. Zendel, O., Honauer, K., Murschitz, M., Humenberger, M., Domínguez, G.F.: Analyzing computer vision data — the good, the bad and the ugly. In: 2017 IEEE Conference on Computer Vision and Pattern Recognition (CVPR), pp. 6670–6680, July 2017

Reliable Smart Contracts: State-of-the-art, Applications, Challenges and Future Directions

Reliable Smart Contracts: State-of-the-Art, Applications, Challenges and Future Directions

César Sánchez[1]([⊠]), Gerardo Schneider[2]([⊠]), and Martin Leucker[3]([⊠])

[1] IMDEA Software Institute, Madrid, Spain
cesar.sanchez@imdea.org
[2] University of Gothenburg, Gothenburg, Sweden
gerardo@cse.gu.se
[3] University of Lübeck, Lübeck, Germany
leucker@isp.uni-luebeck.de

Abstract. The popularization of blockchain technologies have brought a sudden interest in software that executes on top of blockchain, the so called smart contracts, with many potential applications, from financial contracts to unforgeable elections. Smart contracts are pieces of software that manipulate the shared data stored in the blockchain, with the promise that no central authority can forge or manipulate the execution or its results. This promise also involves an important risk, as well-intentioned users cannot easily roll-back undesired effects due to errors, or prevent other users from finding and exploiting loop-holes in deployed smart contracts. In this ISoLA track we seek to attract a variety of experts in the different aspects of smart contract reliability, discuss the state of the art and explore avenues for future research.

1 Blockchains and Smart-Contracts

Blockchain is a global distributed ledger, or database, running on millions of devices where not just information but anything of value (money, music, art, intellectual property, votes, etc.) can be moved and stored with a certain level of security and privacy. The blockchain trust is established through mass (distributed) collaboration. Blockchain has the potential to change in a fundamental way how we deal, not only with financial services, but also with more general applications, improving transparency and regulation. Many applications of blockchain have been proposed, starting with cryptocurrencies like *Bitcoin* [5], and more sophisticated programmable behaviors based on smart contracts, as introduced in Ethereum [1].

Smart contracts are software programs that, once deployed, execute autonomously on a blockchain. Smart contracts are openly stored in the blockchain (they can be read and used by anyone), and—as everything else in blockchains—they are permanent and cannot be altered, not even by their creator. The execution of smart contract is performed in the blockchain network

© Springer Nature Switzerland AG 2018
T. Margaria and B. Steffen (Eds.): ISoLA 2018, LNCS 11247, pp. 275–279, 2018.
https://doi.org/10.1007/978-3-030-03427-6_21

by "workers" (commonly known as miners) that earn some crypto money in return for the execution of a smart contract. A smart contract typically offers several functions which can be invoked by anyone via the Internet's API of the blockchain. As part of this functionality, users can transfer (crypto) value and any other kind of information, to other users via the contract. The contract will manage these invocations and execute the corresponding instructions that manipulate the local book-keeping of data (including the cryptocurrency) and can transfer data or value to the corresponding users. Underlying to the smart contract's idea is the description, and prescription, of an agreement between different parties in order to automate the regulated exchange of value and information over the internet. Given their implementation over a blockchain, these smart contracts are immutable and openly checkable.

The promise of smart contract technology is to diminish the costs of contracting, enforcing contractual agreements, and making payments, while at the same time ensuring trust and compliance, all in the absence of a central authority. It is not clear, however, whether this promise can be delivered given the current state-of-the-art and state-of-practice of smart contracts. In particular, some recent multi-million Ethereum bugs [3,4,6] just witness some the risks involved in any kind of software and that the community were afraid of. It is not clear what contracts mean and how to ensure that they are reliable and error free, which are incarnations in the smart contract world of classical issues in software reliability. This calls for better programming languages specifically for smart contracts with stronger security and privacy guarantees, or to develop mechanisms for the verification of smart contracts to guarantee reliability, security and privacy concerns.

In the track we have collected new results and discussions related to:

- Research on different languages for smart contracts (e.g., Solidity [2]), including their expressivity and reasoning methods.
- Research on the use of formal methods for specifying, validating and verifying smart contracts (both statically and at runtime).
- Surveys and state-of-knowledge about security and privacy issues related to smart contract technologies.
- New applications based on smart contracts.
- Description of challenges and research directions to future development for better smart contracts.

2 Summary of Selected Articles

In this section, we briefly summarize the articles invited to the track "Reliable Smart Contracts: State-of-the-art, Applications, Challenges and Future Directions".

- **Smart Contracts and Opportunities for Formal Methods,** by Andrew Miller, Zchicheng Cai and Somesh Jha, provides a background on smart contracts and surveys existing smart contract languages and verification tools.

The paper also present some verification challenges for the formal methods community.

- **Contracts over Smart Contracts: Recovering from Violations Dynamically,** by Gordon Pace, Christian Colombo and Joshua Ellul, discuss the problem of checking and ensuring correctness of smart contracts, which is a challenging problem as smart contracts cannot easily be changed once in the blockchain. A variety of runtime monitoring, verification, recovery, enforcing as well as design patterns are discussed to achieve correct behaviour.
- **Security Analysis of Smart Contracts in Datalog,** by Petar Tsankov, briefly introduces *Securify*, a fully automated security analyzer for Ethereum smart contracts. Securify symbolically encodes relevant control- and data-flow dependencies in stratified Datalog and uses scalable Datalog solvers to derive relevant semantic facts about the smart contract. It allows the possibility to check compliance and violation patterns to capture sufficient conditions for proving if a given security property holds or not.
- **Temporal Properties of Smart Contracts,** by Ilya Sergey, Amrit Kumar and Aquinas Hobor attacks the static verification of smart contracts using theorem proving. The approach consists on using an intermediate representation language, called Scilla, specifically designed for verification. Scilla borrows well-known abstractions from static verification like communicating automata state-transition systems and temporal property templates, and separate the functional computation from the effects on the state of the contract and the underlying blockchain. Verification activities are ultimately carried out as proofs written in the Coq proof system.
- **Temporal Aspects of Smart Contracts for Financial Derivatives,** by Christopher Clack and Gabriel Vanca, presents the problem of modeling over-the-counter financial derivative contracts. The paper first introduces terminology to differentiate the different uses of the term "contract" (smart legal contract vs smart contract code), and then argue that a formal language that handles over-the-counter financial derivatives must include temporal, deontic and operational aspects and sketches a potential direction for such a formalism.
- **Marlowe: Financial Contracts on Blockchain,** by Simon Thompson and Pablo Lamela Seijas, explores the design of a DSL, called Marlowe, targeted at the execution of financial contracts on blockchains. Domain Specific Languages, compared to general languages, have the potential of being simpler for humans to comprehend programs, and to prevent ambiguities and incomprehensible behaviors. The paper presents an executable semantics of Marlowe implemented in Haskell, examples of Marlowe, and describe a tool that allows users to interact in-browser with simulations of Marlowe contracts.
- **SMT-Based Verification of Solidity Smart Contracts,** by Leonardo Alt and Christian Reitwiessner presents a method to perform static analysis checks for Ethereum smart contracts written in Solidity. Since Solidity contracts are compiled into bytecode for the Ethereum Virtual Machine (EVM), the static analysis that the authors propose is integrated in the compiler.

This technique is automatic and readily usable by developers, requiring no additional knowledge of an intermediate representation or language.

- **A Language-Independent Approach to Smart Contracts Verification,** by Xiaohong Chen, Daejun Park and Grigore Rosu, present an approach of using the so-called *language independent formal methods* for the verification of smart contracts. Language independent methods consists of using a sophisticated engine to formally encode operational semantics that can be used to formally derive interpreters, debuggers, symbolic executors, model checkers, etc. In this particular case, the system proposed uses the K-framework to encode the formal semantics of the Ethereum Virtual Machine.
- **Towards Adding Variety to Simplicity,** by Nachiappan Valliappan, Solène Mirliaz, Elisabet Lobo Vesga and Alejandro Russo, considers the smart contract language Spimplicity for the Etherum platform which allows fast analysis of resource consumption. It is argued that by using a categorical semantics, new combinators can easily be added to Simplicity enhancing the structure of corresponding contracts. Moreover, it is argued that the concept of functions should be added to Simplicity.
- **Fun with Bitcoin Smart Contracts,** by Massimo Bartoletti, Tiziana Cimoli and Roberto Zunino gives an introduction to BitML, a Domain Specific Language (DSL) for smart contracts based on process algebra, that compiles into Bitcoin. The computational soundness of the BitML compiler guarantees that the execution of the compiled contract is coherent with the semantics of the source specification, even in the presence of adversaries.
- **Computing Exact Worst-Case Gas Consumption for Smart Contracts,** by Matteo Marescotti, Martin Blicha, Antti Hyvarinen, Sepideh Asadi and Natasha Sharygina, study the problem of calculating the resources needed to execute Ethereum smart contracts. In the context of Ethereum, the resource is called gas, to be paid to the miners that maintain the block-chain, which depends on the execution trace of the contract. This study presents two methods for determining the exact worst-case gas consumption of an Ethereum execution using methods borrowed by symbolic model checking. Additionally, they identify the challenges and sketch potential solutions.
- **Blockchains as Kripke Models: An Analysis of Atomic Cross-Chain Swap,** by Yoichi Hirai, considers the problem of proving the correctness of blockchain artefacts. To this end, the atomic cross-chain swap protocol is studied, a form of epistemic logic is introduced as proof vehicle, the protocol is analyzed and too weak and sufficient assumptions for the protocol to be correct are discussed.

References

1. Ethereum. https://www.ethereum.org
2. Solidity. http://solidity.readthedocs.io/en/develop/introduction-to-smart-contracts.html
3. Hern, A.: $300m in cryptocurrency accidentally lost forever due to bug, November 2017. Appeared at The Guardian https://www.theguardian.com/technology/2017/nov/08/cryptocurrency-300m-dollars-stolen-bug-ether

4. Mix. Ethereum bug causes integer overflow in numerous ERC20 smart contracts (update) (2018). Appeared at HardFork https://thenextweb.com/hardfork/2018/04/25/ethereum-smart-contract-integer-overflow/
5. Nakamoto, S.: Bitcoin: a peer-to-peer electronic cash system. White Paper (2009) https://bitcoin.org/bitcoin.pdf
6. Qureshi, H.: A hacker stole $31M of Ethereum – how it happened, and what it means for Ethereum (2017). Appeared at FreeCodeCamp https://medium.freecodecamp.org/a-hacker-stole-31m-of-ether-how-it-happened-and-what-it-means-for-ethereum-9e5dc29e33ce

Smart Contracts and Opportunities
for Formal Methods

Andrew Miller[1]([✉]), Zhicheng Cai[2], and Somesh Jha[2]

[1] University of Illinois at Urbana-Champaign, Champaign, USA
soc1024@illinois.edu
[2] University of Wisconsin Madison, Madison, USA

Abstract. Smart contracts are programs that run atop of a blockchain infrastructure. They have emerged as an important new programming model in cryptocurrencies like Ethereum, where they regulate flow of money and other digital assets according to user-defined rules. However, the most popular smart contract languages favor expressiveness rather than safety, and bugs in smart contracts have already lead to significant financial losses from accidents. Smart contracts are also appealing targets for hackers since they can be monetized. For these reasons, smart contracts are an appealing opportunity for systematic auditing and validation, and formal methods in particular. In this paper, we survey the existing smart-contract ecosystem and the existing tools for analyzing smart contracts. We then pose research challenges for formal-methods and program analysis applied to smart contracts.

1   Introduction

Smart contracts are programs that run atop of a financial infrastructure, and command the flow of money according to user-defined rules. Today, smart contracts have already been brought to reality on top of publicly deployed cryptocurrencies, most notably Ethereum, which is currently the #2 cryptocurrency, second to Bitcoin [63], and already hosts tens of millions of smart contract programs deployed by users.

On Ethereum today, there have been auction mechanisms to raise capital investment, totalling $1B in the month of 2017 alone. Ethereum contracts have also been used to implement decentralized order books and public auctions. A smart-contract based token exchange, IDEX, is the most widely active used smart contract today, processing $7.5M USD of exchange volume each day[1].

Smart contracts are appealing for many reasons, and seem to show great potential. They essentially provide users with "programmable money" that can be used to automatically enforce agreements between potentially distrusting parties. They can operate on data provided by authenticated sources (such as stock prices, account balances, press releases, etc.). They may even be used to implement decentralized, virtual corporations defined only by the smart contracts

---

[1] https://cryptocoincharts.info/markets/show/etherdelta.

© Springer Nature Switzerland AG 2018
T. Margaria and B. Steffen (Eds.): ISoLA 2018, LNCS 11247, pp. 280–299, 2018.
https://doi.org/10.1007/978-3-030-03427-6_22

programatically governing their behavior. There has been significant demand from within the financial industry, including investments in blockchain technology projects [43]. Though integration with smart contracts with existing financial infrastructure may take years [58].

In cryptocurrencies like Ethereum, smart contracts give end users the full power and expressivity of a Turing-complete language. With such great power can come equally devastating bugs with direct financial consequences. Furthermore, since smart contracts are tied directly to anonymous payment instruments, they are an attractive target for hackers. Recent high-profile disasters involving the TheDAO [59] and the Parity Wallet [36] have highlighted these risks. Attackers have exploited programming bugs to steal approximately $60M USD.

Smart contracts seem to be a compelling motivation for systematic approaches to system validation, and to formal methods and program analysis in particular. Writing a correct smart contract is no easier than writing bug-free code in any other programming language. In fact, smart contract bugs are often harder to fix. For one reason, most blockchain systems are designed for immutability, meaning they do not provide any built-in means to change smart contract code once it is running. It is perhaps no surprise that the recent disasters have led to public interest from the cryptocurrency community in improve verification tools.

In this paper, we provide a background on smart contracts, and in particular the experience over the past few years as Ethereum has brought smart contracts to a wider audience. We argue that not only do smart contracts provide an impetus to improve tooling around formal methods, they also highlight new areas and opportunities for fundamental research in formal methods.

2 Background

Blockchains and Cryptocurrencies. In a nutshell, blockchains are distributed ledgers maintaining a globally consistent log of user-submitted transactions. Blockchains come in many forms, permissioned and permissionless. These are often implemented as open peer-to-peer networks, based on proof-of-work mining. Starting with Bitcoin [63], public blockchains are often used to create a virtual currency. The main idea of a virtual currency is that user accounts are associated with public keys. Where users transfer currency between one another using public key digital signatures.

Smart Contracts in Ethereum. Besides just storing account values, many blockchains, most notably Ethereum, also feature a full-fledged "smart contract" programming languages. In Ethereum, contracts are implemented as a new type of account: ordinary user accounts are associated with public keys, while contract accounts are associated with a fragment of executable code. Users can create a new contract account by publishing a special transaction containing the bytecode for the new contract along with an initial endowment of Ether.

Just like user accounts, smart contract accounts can store and wield a balance of Ether currency. Unlike user accounts, whoever owns the private key determines how the money is spent, the Ether belonging to a smart contract account can only be spent by executing the instructions of the smart contract code. Hence smart contracts can be thought of as programmable money.

The Ethereum blockchain currently stores more than one million contracts. Developers write in a high level language, the most popular of which is Solidity. As a programming model, Solidity smart contracts mostly resemble object-oriented programming. Contracts are defined as a class, including methods and member variables. Users can create an instance object of the class through a contract creation transaction. Once created, contracts are assigned a unique identifier, called its address, which is a 32-byte string such as 0x06012c8cf97BEaD5deAe237070F9587f8E7A266d. Roughly, the address is a hash of the contract's code, and the state of the blockchain prior to its creation. An example of a smart contract written in Solidity is shown in Fig. 1.

3 Smart Contract Disasters in Ethereum

Most Ethereum contracts are used for some financial purpose, such as collecting investment funding [29]. Perhaps their most notable use is for Initial Coin Offerings (ICOs), which have been a successful mechanism for generating investment revenue (more than $1B USD invested in 2017), though these have also drawn the attention of regulators since many have been fraudulent.

ICOs so far have typically made use of a "token" contract, which has emerged as a standard convention. The simple Solidity program in Fig. 1 captures the basic functionality. Tokens have a finite supply, but can be owned by a user, and can be transferred to another user at the owner's discretion. Many ICOs build additional smart contract functionality in addition to the token interface, such as an auction mechanism or a crowd-voting mechanism. Implementation flaws of such smart contracts have already caused several significant disasters in practice. We now tell the stories behind a few of them, and later discuss how they motivated new research questions for formal methods.

3.1 The DAO

The DAO was originally developed as a fundraising platform by a company called slock.it. The idea behind slock.it is the vision of "smart property" as defined by Nick Szabo in his influential 1997 essay on smart contracts [74]. The initial product was a "smart lock," a physical lock that could be applied to bicycles or rental apartments. The lock could be remotely operated by a nearby base station, which also connected to the internet and the Ethereum peer-to-peer network. The opening of the lock could be triggered by a message sent to an Ethereum smart contract. The price for renting a particular bicycle could thus be set by dynamic market.

As ambitious engineers with prior Ethereum experience, slock.it also set out to solve the meta-problem of fundraising. Rather than seeking traditional venture capital funding, and rather than using an existing centralized crowdfunding

```
contract Token {
    mapping (address => uint) balance;

    function transfer(address to,
                      uint      amount) {
        require (balance[msg.sender] >= amount);
        balance[msg.sender] -= amount;
        balance[to] += amount;
    }
    ...
}
```

Fig. 1. Solidity smart contract example.—This excerpt is from an ERC20-compliant "token" contract, which defines a virtual currency that can be transferred between users and traded on exchanges like Etherdelta.

platform like Kickstarter, slock.it developed a multi-purpose Ethereum-based crowdfunding platform, called the Decentralized Anonymous Organization (or The DAO).

The phrase Decentralized Autonomous Corporation (DAC), was first coined by Larimer [51] and expounded on by Buterin [33] as a central motivation for building a flexible programming language on top of Ethereum.

> "Think of a crypto-currency as shares in a Decentralized Autonomous Corporation (DAC) where the source code defines the bylaws" – Daniel Larimer

Token holders would purchase DAO tokens by investing Ether. Token holders would be able to vote on the activities funded by the DAO. Would-be entrepreneurs would submit funding proposals for consideration by The DAO, who would then vote on whether or not to fund the proposal. If accepted, the entrepreneur would pay profits to the DAO, which would be disbursed back to the token holders in proportion to their investment.

The source code for the DAO defined a fairly complex deliberation and decision making structure. For example, in order to mitigate potential hostile takeovers by an investor, the DAO provided a way for a dissenting token holder to exit, or "split" from the DAO, withdrawing their remaining share of the assets. All of this is to say that the DAO's design was ambitious, and experts anticipated that it would have failed for subtle game-theoretic reasons [53]. Instead, the experiment was cut short by a more mundane flaw. The technical cause is interesting, and illustrates some of the challenges in designing smart contracts.

The DAO's Flaw: Re-entrancy Hazards. The technical flaw behind the DAO's failure is essentially due to a unintuitive behavior of method invocation involving untrusted code. The events surrounding the DAO flaw and its exploit are explained in detail by a blogpost by Phil Daian [35]. We illustrate the idea here with a simple example in Fig. 2. When the `ReentrantToken.withdraw` method is invoked, it uses msg.sender.call to invoke the fallback function() method of the caller, transferring the requested Ether. If the caller is AttackContract, then this recursively invokes withdraw again, repeating until gas runs out or the call stack limit 1024 is reached. The Ether is transferred with each call, but the balances field is only updated *after* the recursive call completes, leading to multiple withdrawals.

As it turns out, the attacker was only able to withdraw a portion of the funds from the contract before a team of developers with Ethereum Foundation raced the attacker to withdraw the rest and return them to the original owners [41]. Furthermore, by a stroke of luck (one that defies explanation, involving a subtle design issue with the "split" functionality mentioned above [35]), the attacker's withdrawn funds entered a month-long purgatory, which enabled the Ethereum community to develop a "hardfork" remedy that reverted the theft at last minute [75]. What rules of engagement drive interventions in smart contracts?

```
contract ReentrantToken {
  mapping (address => int64) balances;
  ...
  function withdraw(uint amount) {
    if (balances[msg.sender] >= amount) {
      // The following line transfers control to untrusted code
      msg.sender.call.value(amount)();
      balances[msg.sender] -= amount;
    }
  }
}


contract AttackContract {
  ReentrantToken token = 0x{victimsaddress};

  function startAttack() {
    token.withdraw(100);
  }

  function() payable {
    // Continue the attack, triggering a
    // recursive call
    A.withdraw(100);
  }
}
```

Fig. 2. A toy example of a vulnerable reentrant smart contract (similar to the DAO).

3.2   Parity Wallet Failures

The Parity wallet is an Ethereum smart contract that is provided along with the Parity node, the second most popular Ethereum node software. Although the Parity software supports ordinary user accounts, it also gives the user the option to create a "wallet" account, which creates an instance of the Ethereum smart contract for the benefit of customizability and extra features:

> "The most common use-case are multi-signature wallets, that allow for transaction logging, withdrawal limits, and rule-sets for signatures required."

In Ethereum, each transaction must pay a transaction fee that depends on the amount of resources consumed, including each byte of data, and each opcode executed. Creating a contract means paying for each byte of bytecode. To reduce the costs of creating instances of the same transaction, the Parity wallet makes use of a form of smart contract inheritance.

The idea is that the main portion of the Parity wallet code is uploaded to a single instance, at address `0xbec591de75b8699a3ba52f073428822d0bfc0d7e`, which can be linked to by the individual per-user instances of the wallet. The wallet library defines most of the methods relevant to the wallet, such as "withdraw", while the per-user wallets dispatch to the code contained in the library. This kind of inheritance is achieved in Ethereum through the use of the `delegatecall` opcode, which was added fairly recently to the Ethereum Virtual Machine (EVM). An example illustrating inheritance can be found in Fig. 3.

The `delegatecall` takes in another contract's address as a parameter. The semantics of this opcode instruction runs the code from the target contract, in the context of the calling contract. This essentially achieves the prototype inheritance pattern; *the library is not a superclass, but rather an actual object instance.* As an object instance, methods can be invoked directly on the contract. This fact was overlooked, leading to a disaster totaling in tens of millions of dollars. In particular, while the subclass wallets featured an access control policy whereby only the contract creator can command the contract, the library object itself was uninitialized and had an open access policy. As a result, a random user, who later claimed to be a newcomer to Ethereum, was able to claim ownership of the library and destroy it. At the current time, all instances of this version of the Parity wallet, numbering at least 150 and controlling around $150M USD, are inoperable.

Other Common Bugs in Ethereum Smart Contracts. While the re-entrancy and `delegatecall` bugs are well known and quite severe, there are other classes of bugs that are also relevant to smart contracts (e.g. reliance on poor quality sources of randomness). Atzei et al. [28] provide a taxonomy of common classes of bugs in Ethereum smart contracts.

```
contract Wallet {
  address _walletLibrary = ${hardcoded address};
  ...
  function withdraw(uint amount) {
    _walletLibrary.delegatecall(''withdraw(uint)'', amount);
  }
  ...
}
```

Fig. 3. Prototype inheritance as found in the Parity wallet

4   Research Trends

4.1   Safer Smart Contract Languages

A wide variety of approaches to language design have now been proposed and in some cases tried in practice, as surveyed by Seijas et al. [69]. In Table 1 we provide a summary of such proposals. The simplest path to a better scripting language, taken by Vyper, is to modify the existing Solidity language through syntactic restriction. That is, Vyper is a safer subset of Solidity. Many other smart contract languages use a different programming model, such as functional programming languages, formal logics and automata.

Typed functional programming languages are promising for smart contracts because they are known to be amenable to formal analysis. For example, the Tezos alternative to EVM is called Michelson, and is designed as a typed abstract machine for (mostly) pure functional programs [12], while Liquidity is an Ocaml-inspired functional alternative to Solidity for high level contract programming. At the opposing end of the restrictive-expressive spectrum, the Bitcoin developer community has preferred smart contracts compatible with the existing UTXO model underlying Bitcoin Script [1], and that guarantee a property "reorg safety". Simplicity is a typed functional language for this regime. Phil Wadler has written a comparison of both Michelson and Simplicity, ultimately arguing for Plutus, another alternative typed functional language [76].

Other various programming models have also been proposed, which can be alternatives to EVM. Rholang is build on a core calculus called ρ-calculus (inspired by π-calculus) which provides asynchronous message-passing. Similarly, Scilla is based on communicating automata, while FSolidM is a formally finite-state machine based model for Ethereum. Owlchain, combines timed-automata-language (TAL) and web ontology language (OWL). The formal definitions underlying these models are also expected to simplify formal analysis, though the benefits of these have yet to be seen.

Many blockchain or cryptocurrency projects often differentiate themselves in their smart contract programming language, however several other factors seem to determine how their project evolves. They may differ also by their underlying consensus algorithms, or by the target applications that guide their choices of engineering tradeoffs.

Several proposals have been made for "sharded" blockchains, which achieve better scalability but pose an additional challenges for smart contracts. Instead of a single linearized chain replicated by every node in the blockchain network, the ledger is instead logically divided into separate namespaces, each of which is replicated by only a portion of the nodes. This model underlies Omniledger [48], RScoin [37], Aspen [38], and Scilla [71].

4.2   Program Analysis

As far as we know, there are 11 tools or frameworks attempting to detect various types of vulnerabilities, or give an assistance for programming. The table below (see Table 2) shows their detailed capabilities respectively. Here, we give a summary for them.

From the scale of checking abilities, SmartCheck provides the most types of checking and recommendations, and more serves as a dynamic suggestion-generated system for Solidity source code. Currently, most of its Solidity-related checking is already provided by Solidity IDE [18].

From the view of vulnerabilities, these tools almost cover all possible vulnerabilities mentioned in [4, 24, 28], including safer programming design pattern suggestion. The reentry vulnerability became the most popular one to tackle, and the reason is obvious because this vulnerability resulted in the infamous DAO attack [35].

However, apart from traditional bugs like integer overflow or usage of uninitialized variables, those vulnerabilities shown in contract programming do not have unified definition respectively, or their detection results highly depend on tools' own implementations.

From the view of programming analysis techniques, most of the tools choose static analysis and a majority of them support EVM bytecodes analysis. Securify and Mythril declare supporting on-chain contracts analysis. Porosity does some reverse engineering and provides a prototype for decompilation. Solgraph and Mythril can generate control flow graphs, and Manticore and Maian will generate transactions with inputs for later validation on each vulnerable path. Oyente also has a validation process after symbolic execution analysis. Oyente, Maian and ZEUS provide false-positive analysis, and all of them use manually-tagged data sets, selected from contracts with *verified*[2] Solidity source code.

In order to better describe contracts logic model and specifications, CertiK has its own verification labeling languages, and ZEUS uses an intermediate-level abstract language. Oyente develops their own EVM semantics, EtherLite, and Maian modifies it in their implementation.

Most of those tools are developed in Python, or other languages like Java (SmartCheck), OCaml (Dr.Y), JavaScript (Solgraph) and C++ (porosity). Manticore provides a Python API for analysis of EVM bytecode.

Besides, there are some other efforts in language (Sect. 4.2) or semantics design, which could help with formal verification of smart contracts (see Table 3).

---

[2] Here "verified" means the Solidity source code corresponds to the EVM bytecodes.

Table 1. Languages

Languages	Descriptions (motivation, expressivity, type system, analysis-friendly features, etc.)	Reference
Scilla (intermediate-level) (Zilliqa)	- motivated by achieving expressivity and tractability - based on communicating automata [50] - provide limited translation from higher-level languages (i.e., Solidity) - provide translation into Coq for verification, along with contract protocols, semantics, safety/liveness properties and proof machinery	Paper [71], code [70]
FSolidM (Ethereum, framework, higher-level)	- aims to develop more secure smart contracts - a formal, finite-state machine based model - provide several plugins (i.e., design patterns) to enhance security and functionality, targeting at vulnerabilities as reentry bugs and transaction ordering, or design patterns as time constraint and authorization - primarily for Ethereum, but it may applied on other platforms - provide translation into Solidity	Paper [55], code [54]
Rholang (higher-level, RChain)	- primitively for RChain, but could be used in other settings - focus on message-passing and formally modeled by the ρ-calculus, a reflective, higher-order extension of the π-calculus, which is good for concurrent settings [57]	Code [19]
Vyper (Ethereum, higher-level)	- mainly target at security and auditability - provide the following features: bounds and overflow checking, support for signed integers and decimal fixed point numbers, decidability, strong typing, small and understandable compiler code, and limited support for pure functions - does not support the following features: modifiers, class inheritance, inline assembly, operator overloading, recursive calling, infinite-length loops and binary fixed point - statically typed language	Code [5], doc [27]
Type-coin (Bitcoin)	- a logical commitment mechanism - the logic is linear and not rich to handle complex situations	Paper [34]
Simplicity (Bitcoin)	- type-safety, no unbounded loops, no named variables - no function types and thus no higher-order functions	Paper [66], blog [31]
Michelson (Tezos) (lower-level) (functional)	- a strongly-typed, stack-based language - It doesn't include many features like polymorphism, closures, or named functions - more as a way to implement pieces of business logic than as a generic "world computer" - Programs written in Michelson can be reasonably analyzed by SMT solvers and formalized in Coq without the need for more complicated techniques like separation logic - To provide a straightforward platform for business logic, to provide a readable bytecode, and to be introspectable	Paper [12], web [26]

(*continued*)

Table 1. (*continued*)

Languages	Descriptions (motivation, expressivity, type system, analysis-friendly features, etc.)	Reference
	- Entirely original implementation in OCaml	
	- Isolated economical rules, self-amendable via voting	
	- purely PoS	
	- Blockchain state in a git-like persistent store	
	- Highly functional, defensive coding style for the critical parts	
	- designed with formal certification in mind	
Liquidity (Tezos) (higher-level)(functional)	- It uses the syntax of OCaml, and strictly complies to Michelson security restrictions	code [7], web [65]
Plutus (higher-level) and Plutus Core (lower-level) (IOHK)	- compiled to Plutus Core (lower level), Lisp-like syntax	Code [17], paper [56]
	- a pure functional strictly typed programming language, with user-defined data types and polymorphism	
	- several issues: unbounded integers supporting, non-supporting abstract data types and data constructors	
Owlchain (BOSCoin)	- a decidable programming framework, which consists of the Web Ontology Language and the Timed Automata Language. - OWL is defined as W3C standard, a declarative language that provides decidability	Article [32]
	- separate declaration from processing	
	- TAL, Timed Automata Language, is a new language that is used to create operators. It is a finite state programming environment with two constraints: time limit and pure functions. Timed automata modeling can detect undefined areas (reachability problem) in the code that developers missed. Pure function can eliminate side effects that can occur during development	

Most of proposals relate to functional languages, perhaps due to the advantages to perform static analysis.

For semantics, usually a tool has its own semantics (like Oyente has Ether-Lite). A representative work is [39], because they provide the first complete small-step semantics of EVM bytecodes and formalize it in F*. Also, this paper points out that, though smart contracts are written in a Turing complete language, their computations are bounded by *gasLimit*, thus it becoming a "quasi" Turing-complete language.

4.3   Off-chain Protocols and Cryptography

Off-chain payment channels have emerged as an important topic in smart contracts, in both industry and academia. Once a payment channel is established between two parties, they can send rapid micropayments to each other without

Table 2. Tools and frameworks for analyzing smart contracts

Tool/Framework	Capabilities	Reference
CertiK (Demo)	- target at fully trustworthy blockchain ecosystems in the future - specifications for each function can be expressed using CertiK labels, indicating pre-condition, post-condition and invariants respectively, as comments in Solidity programs	White paper [2]
Dr.Y's Ethereum Contract Analyzer	- a symbolic execution tool, reflecting contract behavior to some point	Code [44]
Maian	- check locked money - detect unchecked suicide or Ether sending - generate inputs to validate through private blockchain	Paper [64], code [8]
Manticore	- detect potential overflow and underflow conditions on "ADD", "MUL" and "SUB" instructions - detect potential uses of uninitialized memory or storage - calculate code coverage - generate inputs which could trigger unique code paths (Solidity source code needed) - Other: offer a Python API for analysis of EVM bytecodes	Article [11], code [9], doc [10]
Mythril	- detect reentry bugs and external calls to untrusted contracts - detect unchecked suicide or Ether sending - check mishandled exceptions (i.e., detect unchecked CALL return value) - check integer underflows - detect usage of "tx.origin" [21] - check dependence on predictable variables (e.g., coinbase, gaslimit, timestamp, number, etc.) - Other: generate control flow graph, blockchain exploration and some utilities - support on-chain contracts analysis	Article [60,61], doc [13], code [62],
Oyente	- detect reentry bugs - check mishandled exceptions (i.e., detect unchecked CALL return value) - check transaction-order-dependency (a.k.a. money concurrency, or front running) - check timestamp dependency - check possible assertion failure (Solidity source code required) - calculate code coverage	Paper [52], web access [16], code [15]
Porosity	- find potential reentrancy vulnerability - support decompilation and disassembly	Code [3], white paper [73], article [72]
SmartCheck (target at Solidity)	- detect reentry bugs - check locked money - detect possibly infinite or impractical loops - detect unchecked low-level call	Code [23], web access [22]

(continued)

Table 2. (*continued*)

Tool/Framework	Capabilities	Reference
	- check integer overflow and underflow, and recommend to use the SafeMath library [14]	
	- check timestamp dependence	
	- Other: more better programming design pattern recommendation	
	- Other: recommendations for standard ERC-20 function usages, and check style guide violation	
	- Other: some checking for recommended Solidity programming style	
Securify	- check reentry bugs	Web access [20]
	- check mishandled exception	
	- check transaction-order-dependency	
	- check insecure coding patterns, e.g., unchecked transaction data length, use of ORIGIN instruction and missing input validation	
	- check unexpected Ether flows, such as locked Ether [68]	
	- check use of untrusted inputs in security operations, i.e., checking whether the inputs to the SHA3 depend on block information (timestamp, number, coinbase)	
Solgraph	- highlight potential unchecked money receiver	Code [67]
	- generate function control flow of a Solidity contract	
ZEUS	- support self-defined policy verification, e.g., reentry bugs, unchecked "send", possibly vulnerable failed "send", integer overflow, transaction state dependency (i.e., usage of "tx.origin"), block state dependency (including all "block" parameters) and transaction order dependency	Paper [47]
	- specification limited to quantifier-free logic with integer linear arithmetic	

any transaction fees. The idea is that the parties send messages to each other in the typical case, off-chain, and only use the smart contract to close. Payment channels are also the building blocks for payment channel networks, which are a highly anticipated scalability proposal for cryptocurrencies.

Payment channels and state channels are multi-faceted protocols, relying not just on the smart contract, but also on a cryptographic scheme involving digital signatures and hash functions, as well as the reconciliation of state stored at different parties. Reasoning about these applications relies on more than just analyzing the smart contract directly.

Off-chain Payment Channels. A smart contract payment channel protocol should provide the following (informal) properties:

Table 3. Language design and model translation

Languages or semantics	Descriptions (motivation, expressivity, type system, analysis-friendly features, etc.)	Reference
SMAC (modular reasoning)	- introduce ECF (Effectively callback free) property for modular object-level analysis - develop online detection algorithm which can apply to Ethereum full node, and monitor non-ECF executions, including the infamous DAO bug	Paper [40]
eth-isabelle (semantics)	- define the complete instruction set of EVM in Lem, a language that can be compiled into Coq, Isabelle/HOL and HOL4 - can prove invariants and safety properties	Paper [46], code [45]
TU Wien F* (2018) (Ethereum)	- present the complete small-step semantics of EVM bytecode in the F* proof assistant - define a number of central security properties, such as call integrity, atomicity, and independence from miner controlled parameters	Paper [39], code [25]
F* (2016) (Ethereum)	- motivated by formal verification - partial semantics for converting Solidity to F*, EVM to F* - show the correspondence between Solidity and EVM to some point	Paper [30]
KEVM (semantics, high-level, Ethereum)	- a complete K Semantics of the Ethereum Virtual Machine (EVM)	Code [6], paper [42]

- (Timing properties.) Payments are processed very quickly (no blockchain transactions), and closure is guaranteed within a predictable time (small number of blockchain transactions).
- (Integrity properties.) If Bob thinks he has received \$X, then he is guaranteed to get at least \$X when the channel closes. And Alice should get back everything except what she has paid.

A payment channel protocol is given in Algorithm 1, comprising a local program for the sender (Alice), a local program for the recipient, and a smart contract program. Alice initially deposits \$$X$ by making an on-chain transaction, into a smart contract running the given pseudocode. Alice can then make numerous micropayments to Bob, by sending signed messages that indicate Bob's latest credit. Each payment can be very fast and efficient, since it requires only point-to-point interactions between Alice and Bob; it does not require any on-chain transaction. At any time, either party can request to "close" the channel, in which case Alice submits her most recent signed message. The smart contract is only activated when the channel closes.

The generalization of a payment channel, a "state channel", allows two or more parties to maintain an off-chain replicated state machine that can be synchronized on demand (or in case of a dispute) with the blockchain.

Algorithm 1. A Smart Contract protocol for Off-chain Payments

Alice and Bob are represented by hardcoded public keys

Local code for Alice (the sender):
1: [Initially]:
2:    credit := X_0 // initial deposit
3: [on input ("pay", X)]:
4:    assert $X \leq$ credit
5:    credit := credit − X
6:    $\sigma \leftarrow$ Sign(X_0 − credit) as Alice
7:    send (σ, X_0 − credit) to Bob
8: [on input ("close")]: send ("close") to the Contract

Local code for Bob (the recipient):
1: [Initially]:
2:    credit := 0
3: [on receiving (σ, credit') from Alice)]:
4:    assert σ is a valid signature on credit' from Alice
5:    assert credit' $\leq$ X_0
6:    if credit' > credit
7:        credit := credit'
8:        $\sigma := \sigma'$
9: [on input ("close")]: send "close" to the Contract
10: [on contract event ("close"):
11:    send ("evidence", σ, credit) to the Contract

Smart Contract Code:
1: [Initially]:
2:    lastKnownCredit := 0
3: [on contract input ("close") from Alice or Bob (only once)]:
4:    within delay $O(\Delta)$:
5:        send (X_0 − lastKnownCredit) to Alice
6:        send (lastKnownCredit) to Bob
7: [on contract input ("evidence", σ, credit)] from Alice or Bob:
8:    assert σ is a valid signature on credit from Alice
9:    assert credit' $\leq$ X_0
10:    if credit > lastKnownCredit
11:        lastKnownCredit := credit

Functionality Model for the Payment Channel. The payment channel protocol above was given an informal specification. To give a precise security definition, an appealing approach is to use the simulation based security framework used by cryptographers. The main idea behind the simulation-based security framework is that instead of expressing properties as indistinguishability games, we provide an explicit program, called an ideal functionality, that exhibits all the properties

---

Algorithm 2. An Ideal Functionality for Off-chain Payments

1: [Initially]
2:     Alice and Bob are represented by hardcoded public keys
3:     credit@A := $\$X_0$ // initial deposit
4:     credit@B := $\$0$
5: [on input ("pay", $\$X$) from Alice]:
6:     assert $\$X \leq$ credit@A
7:     credit@A := credit@$A - \$X$
8:     within $O(1)$ delay:
9:         credit@B := credit@$B + \$X$
10: [on input ("close") from Alice or Bob]:
11:     within $O(\Delta)$ delay:
12:         send at least credit@A to Alice
13:         send at least credit@B to Bob and halt

---

at once. This has the advantage that all the salient security properties of a protocol can be defined in effectively one place.

An ideal functionality for the payment channel protocol is given in Algorithm 2. Note that the functionality is structurally simpler than the protocol (it executes in one location rather than three), and does not contain any cryptography.

It is also easy to see that the functionality exhibits the desired properties. The phrases "$O(1)$ delay" and "$O(\Delta)$ delay" denote the desired time bounds, which would be automatically inferred or written as annotations by the programmer. Here Δ refers to a worst-case bound on the time it takes to submit and confirm a blockchain transaction. Hence the fact that the "pay" command completes in $O(1)$ time reflects the fact that the protocol uses only off-chain messages. The credit@A and credit@B expressions denote the respective local views of Alice and Bob; the functionality explicitly sends a final payment to each consistent with their local views. Note that it is possible for a payment to interleave with channel closure; in this case, Bob may receive more than he expected.

Several Instances of Cryptographic Protocols Where the Smart Contract Acts as a Verifier. OpenVote uses Ethereum as the tallier for a cryptographic, sealed ballot election. Users submit encrypted ballots to the Ethereum blockchain to be tallied, along with a zero-knowledge proof (ZKP) that their vote is correctly formatted (i.e., contains an encryption of just one vote for just one candidate). The use of the Ethereum blockchain in place of an election authority avoids the need to trust any privileged party to carry out the election.

Ethereum has recently included support for the ALT_BN128 elliptic curve, which is used in particular for a generic proof system called zkSNARKs. An example contract is provided where in order to claim a prize, a prover must demonstrate knowledge of a solution to a Sudoku puzzle, but without revealing the solution itself. Further cryptographic applications include privacy-preserving auctions and insurance contracts [49].

In general, it seems likely that many future applications will involve the use of increasingly sophisticated cryptographic primitives within smart contract programs.

5 Challenges and Opportunities for Formal Methods

Smart contracts present three non-traditional challenges to developers, making smart contracts more difficult to implement than code in other contexts.

1. **Composition with untrusted and adversarial code.** Smart contracts are implemented on a distributed system, and are freely accessible by the public. Composition within smart contracts tends to involve untrusted code. The DAO involved transferring control flow to an attacker's smart contract, which carried out the attack. For this reason we would likely want the capability to combine runtime certification with static analysis. We would use static analysis, but may need to write defensive code that provides runtime enforcement of guarantees against untrusted code. Compositional verification technologies are useful here, but the challenge is to write a model E of the environment for the smart contract. Note that E will have to account for other code fragments that the smart contract might interact with and also a model of the underlying infrastructure (e.g. blockchain) that the contract is executing on.

2. **Distributed and asynchronous setting.** Smart contracts are often just one component of a more complicated distributed protocol. Smart contracts often play the role of a "verifier" in a cryptographic protocols. The Ethereum platform enables application developers to make use of built-in primitives, such as hash functions, digital signatures, and now more recently, pairing-friendly elliptic curves, the ingredients for zkSNARK proofs.

   In general, a smart contract protocol may involve local code and custom cryptography, which are just as important to the correct functionality and design of the application of the smart contract itself. However, one challenge here is that the guarantees that the smart contract requires from the cryptographic function will heavily depend on the functionality of the smart contract. Future smart contract programming languages and analysis techniques will need to take this into account.

3. **Economic incentives.** Unlike in traditional software, in the smart-contract setting, many of the desired properties one wishes to establish are *economic*. For example, participants might want to verify that their expected payoff for participating in a contract is non-negative, since otherwise they have little reason to participate. Analyzing a smart contract often involves reasoning about game-theoretic properties like incentive compatibility. Effective tools may need to take this reasoning into account. Formalisms, such as mean-payoff games, might be useful in this context, but verifying properties of these expressive formalisms remains a challenge.

6   Conclusion

This paper surveys the ecosystem of smart contracts, such as various platforms, high-profile bugs, and existing analysis tools. Of course, one can use existing analysis techniques and tools to analyze smart contracts, and one should do so. However, we believe that uniqueness of the smart contracts also brings some unique challenges for the formal-methods community, which will require new techniques and novel research ideas.

References

1. Bitcoin Script Wiki. https://en.bitcoin.it/wiki/Script. Accessed 21 Apr 2018
2. CertiK: building fully trustworthy smart contracts and blockchain ecosystems. https://certik.org/docs/white_paper.pdf. Accessed 28 Mar 2018
3. Decompiler and security analysis tool for blockchain-based ethereum smart-contracts. https://github.com/comaeio/porosity. Accessed 25 Mar 2018
4. Ethereum smart contract security best practices. https://consensys.github.io/smart-contract-best-practices/. Accessed 29 Mar 2018
5. ethereum/vyper - new experimental programming language. https://github.com/ethereum/vyper. Accessed 26 Mar 2018
6. K semantics of the ethereum virtual machine (EVM). https://github.com/kframework/evm-semantics. Accessed 26 Mar 2018
7. Liquidity: a smart contract language for Tezos. https://github.com/OCamlPro/liquidity. Accessed 19 Apr 2018
8. MAIAN: automatic tool for finding trace vulnerabilities in ethereum smart contracts. https://github.com/MAIAN-tool/MAIAN. Accessed 24 Mar 2018
9. Manticore 0.1.7 release - symbolic execution tool. https://github.com/trailofbits/manticore. Accessed 24 Mar 2018
10. Manticore documentation, release 0.1.0. https://media.readthedocs.org/pdf/manticore/latest/manticore.pdf. Accessed 25 Mar 2018
11. Manticore: Symbolic execution for humans. https://blog.trailofbits.com/2017/04/27/manticore-symbolic-execution-for-humans/. Accessed 24 Mar 2018
12. Michelson: the language of smart contracts in Tezos. https://www.tezos.com/static/papers/language.pdf. Accessed 19 Apr 2018
13. Mythril 0.14.9 - security analysis tool for ethereum smart contracts. https://pypi.python.org/pypi/mythril. Accessed 24 Mar 2018
14. Openzepplin/zeppelin-solidity/contracts/math/safemath.sol. https://github.com/OpenZeppelin/zeppelin-solidity/blob/master/contracts/math/SafeMath.sol. Accessed 24 Mar 2018
15. Oyente - an analysis tool for smart contracts, version 0.2.7. https://github.com/melonproject/oyente. Accessed 9 Oct 2017
16. Oyente web access. https://oyente.melon.fund. Accessed 24 Mar 2018
17. Plutus language prototype. https://github.com/input-output-hk/plutus-prototype. Accessed 20 Apr 2018
18. Remix - solidity IDE, v0.4.21. http://remix.ethereum.org. Accessed 28 Mar 2018
19. Rholang. https://github.com/rchain/rchain/tree/master/rholang. Accessed 26 Mar 2018
20. Securify - formal verification of ethereum smart contracts. https://securify.ch/. Accessed 24 Mar 2018

21. Security considerations - pitfalls - tx.origin. https://solidity.readthedocs.io/en/develop/security-considerations.html#tx-origin. Accessed 24 Mar 2018
22. Smartcheck. https://tool.smartdec.net/. Accessed 24 Mar 2018
23. Smartcheck - a static analysis tool that detects vulnerabilities and bugs in solidity programs. https://github.com/smartdec/smartcheck. Accessed 24 Mar 2018
24. Solidity v0.4.21. https://solidity.readthedocs.io/en/v0.4.21/. Accessed 28 Mar 2018
25. The source code of ethereum virtual machine bytecode f* formalization. https://secpriv.tuwien.ac.at/tools/ethsemantics. Accessed 26 Mar 2018
26. Try Michelson. https://try-michelson.com/. Accessed 19 Apr 2018
27. Vyper. https://vyper.readthedocs.io/en/latest/index.html. Accessed 27 Mar 2018
28. Atzei, N., Bartoletti, M., Cimoli, T.: A survey of attacks on ethereum smart contracts (SoK). In: Maffei, M., Ryan, M. (eds.) POST 2017. LNCS, vol. 10204, pp. 164–186. Springer, Heidelberg (2017). https://doi.org/10.1007/978-3-662-54455-6_8
29. Bartoletti, M., Pompianu, L.: An empirical analysis of smart contracts: platforms, applications, and design patterns. In: Brenner, M., et al. (eds.) FC 2017. LNCS, vol. 10323, pp. 494–509. Springer, Cham (2017). https://doi.org/10.1007/978-3-319-70278-0_31
30. Bhargavan, K., et al.: Formal verification of smart contracts: short paper. In: Proceedings of the 2016 ACM Workshop on Programming Languages and Analysis for Security, PLAS 2016, pp. 91–96. ACM, New York (2016). https://doi.org/10.1145/2993600.2993611
31. Blockstream: Simplicity itself for blockchains. https://blockstream.com/2017/10/30/simplicity.html. Accessed 20 Apr 2018
32. BOScoin: Smart contracts and trust contracts: part 3. https://medium.com/@boscoin/smart-contracts-trust-contracts-part-3-6cf76bf5882e. Accessed 21 Apr 2018
33. Buterin, V.: Bootstrapping a decentralized autonomous corporation: part I. Bitcoin Mag. (2013)
34. Crary, K., Sullivan, M.J.: Peer-to-peer affine commitment using bitcoin. In: Proceedings of the 36th ACM SIGPLAN Conference on Programming Language Design and Implementation, PLDI 2015, pp. 479–488. ACM, New York (2015). https://doi.org/10.1145/2737924.2737997
35. Daian, P.: Analysis of the DAO exploit (2016). http://hackingdistributed.com/2016/06/18/analysis-of-the-dao-exploit/
36. Daian, P.: An in-depth look at the parity multisig bug, July 2017. http://hackingdistributed.com/2017/07/22/deep-dive-parity-bug/
37. Danezis, G., Meiklejohn, S.: Centrally banked cryptocurrencies. In: NDSS (2016)
38. Gencer, A.E., van Renesse, R., Sirer, E.G.: Short paper: service-oriented sharding for blockchains. In: Kiayias, A. (ed.) FC 2017. LNCS, vol. 10322, pp. 393–401. Springer, Cham (2017). https://doi.org/10.1007/978-3-319-70972-7_22
39. Grishchenko, I., Maffei, M., Schneidewind, C.: A semantic framework for the security analysis of ethereum smart contracts. arXiv preprint arXiv:1802.08660 (2018)
40. Grossman, S.: Online detection of effectively callback free objects with applications to smart contracts. Proc. ACM Program. Lang. 2(POPL), 48 (2017)
41. Higgins, S.: Ethereum developers launch white hat counter-attack on the DAO, June 2016. https://www.coindesk.com/ethereum-developers-draining-dao/
42. Hildenbrandt, E., et al.: KEVM: a complete semantics of the ethereum virtual machine. http://hdl.handle.net/2142/97207. Accessed 27 Mar 2018

43. Hileman, G.: State of blockchain Q1 2016: blockchain funding overtakes bitcoin (2016). http://www.coindesk.com/state-of-blockchain-q1-2016/
44. Hirai, Y.: Dr. Y's ethereum contract analyzer. https://github.com/pirapira/dry-analyzer. Accessed 25 Mar 2018
45. Hirai, Y.: A lem formalization of EVM and some Isabelle/HOL proofs. https://github.com/pirapira/eth-isabelle. Accessed 25 Mar 2018
46. Hirai, Y.: Defining the ethereum virtual machine for interactive theorem provers. In: Brenner, M., et al. (eds.) FC 2017. LNCS, vol. 10323, pp. 520–535. Springer, Cham (2017). https://doi.org/10.1007/978-3-319-70278-0_33
47. Kalra, S., Goel, S., Dhawan, M., Sharma, S.: Zeus: Analyzing safety of smart contracts. In: NDSS (2018)
48. Kokoris-Kogias, E., Jovanovic, P., Gasser, L., Gailly, N., Syta, E., Ford, B.: OmniLedger: a secure, scale-out, decentralized ledger via sharding (2018)
49. Kosba, A., Miller, A., Shi, E., Wen, Z., Papamanthou, C.: Hawk: The blockchain model of cryptography and privacy-preserving smart contracts. In: 2016 IEEE Symposium on Security and Privacy (SP), pp. 839–858. IEEE (2016)
50. Kuske, D., Muscholl, A.: Communicating automata. http://eiche.theoinf.tu-ilmenau.de/kuske/Submitted/cfm-final.pdf. Accessed 27 Mar 2018
51. Larimer, D.: Overpaying for security: the hidden costs of bitcoin, September 2013. https://letstalkbitcoin.com/is-bitcoin-overpaying-for-false-security
52. Luu, L., Chu, D.H., Olickel, H., Saxena, P., Hobor, A.: Making smart contracts smarter. In: Proceedings of the 2016 ACM SIGSAC Conference on Computer and Communications Security, pp. 254–269. ACM (2016)
53. Mark, D., Zamfir, V., Sirer, E.G.: A call for a temporary moratorium on "the DAO", May 2016
54. Mavridou, A.: Smartcontracts - the FSolidM framework. https://github.com/anmavrid/smart-contracts. Accessed 26 Mar 2018
55. Mavridou, A., Laszka, A.: Designing secure ethereum smart contracts: a finite state machine based approach. arXiv preprint arXiv:1711.09327 (2017)
56. McAdams, D.: Formal specification of the plutus (core) language. https://github.com/input-output-hk/plutus-prototype/tree/master/docs/spec. Accessed 20 Apr 2018
57. Meredith, L., Radestock, M.: A reflective higher-order calculus. Electron. Notes Theor. Comput. Sci. **141**(5), 49–67 (2005). https://doi.org/10.1016/j.entcs.2005.05.016. Proceedings of the Workshop on the Foundations of Interactive Computation (FInCo 2005). http://www.sciencedirect.com/science/article/pii/S1571066105051893
58. Morgan Stanley Research: Global insight: blockchain in banking: disruptive threat or tool? (2016)
59. Morris, D.Z.: Blockchain-based venture capital fund hacked for $60 million, June 2016. http://fortune.com/2016/06/18/blockchain-vc-fund-hacked/
60. Mueller, B.: Analyzing ethereum smart contracts for vulnerabilities. https://hackernoon.com/scanning-ethereum-smart-contracts-for-vulnerabilities-b5caefd995df. Accessed 24 Mar 2018
61. Mueller, B.: Introducing Mythril: a framework for bug hunting on the ethereum blockchain. https://hackernoon.com/introducing-mythril-a-framework-for-bug-hunting-on-the-ethereum-blockchain-9dc5588f82f6. Accessed 24 Mar 2018
62. Mueller, B.: Mythril. https://github.com/ConsenSys/mythril. Accessed 24 Mar 2018
63. Nakamoto, S.: Bitcoin: a peer-to-peer electronic cash system (2008)

64. Nikolic, I., Kolluri, A., Sergey, I., Saxena, P., Hobor, A.: Finding the Greedy, Prodigal, and Suicidal Contracts at Scale. ArXiv e-prints, February 2018
65. OCamlPRO: Liquidity online. http://www.liquidity-lang.org/edit/. Accessed 19 Apr 2018
66. O'Connor, R.: Simplicity: a new language for blockchains. CoRR abs/1711.03028 (2017). http://arxiv.org/abs/1711.03028
67. Revere, R.: solgraph - visualize solidity control flow for smart contract security analysis. https://github.com/raineorshine/solgraph. Accessed 24 Mar 2018
68. Securify: Automatically detecting the bug that froze parity wallets. https://medium.com/@SecurifySwiss/automatically-detecting-the-bug-that-froze-parity-wallets-ad2bebebd3b0. Accessed 24 Mar 2018
69. Seijas, P.L., Thompson, S.J., McAdams, D.: Scripting smart contracts for distributed ledger technology. IACR Cryptology ePrint Archive 2016/1156 (2016). http://eprint.iacr.org/2016/1156
70. Sergey, I.: Scilla-Coq, state-transition systems for smart contracts. https://github.com/ilyasergey/scilla-coq. Accessed 25 Mar 2018
71. Sergey, I., Kumar, A., Hobor, A.: Scilla: a smart contract intermediate-level language. arXiv preprint arXiv:1801.00687 (2018)
72. Suiche, M.: DEF CON 25: Porosity. https://blog.comae.io/porosity-18790ee42827. Accessed 24 Mar 2018
73. Suiche, M.: Porosity: a decompiler for blockchain-based smart contracts bytecode. https://www.comae.io/reports/dc25-msuiche-Porosity-Decompiling-Ethereum-Smart-Contracts-wp.pdf. Accessed 25 Mar 2018
74. Szabo, N.: The idea of smart contracts. Nick Szabos Papers and Concise Tutorials, vol. 6 (1997)
75. Vigna, P.: Cryptocurrency platform ethereum gets a controversial update. Wall Street J. (2016). http://www.wsj.com/articles/cryptocurrency-platform-ethereum-gets-a-controversial-update-1469055722
76. Wadler, P.: Simplicity and Michelson: a programming language that is too simple. https://iohk.io/blog/simplicity-and-michelson/. Accessed 21 Apr 2018

Contracts over Smart Contracts: Recovering from Violations Dynamically

Christian Colombo[2], Joshua Ellul[1,2], and Gordon J. Pace[1,2(✉)]

[1] Centre for Distributed Ledger Technologies, University of Malta, Msida, Malta
gordon.pace@um.edu.mt
[2] Department of Computer Science, University of Malta, Msida, Malta

Abstract. Smart contracts which enforce behaviour between parties have been hailed as a new way of regulating business, particularly on public distributed ledger technologies which ensure the immutability of smart contracts, and can do away with points of trust. Many such platforms, including Ethereum, come with a virtual machine on which smart contracts are executed, described in an imperative manner. Given the critical nature of typical smart contract applications, their bugs and vulnerabilities have proved to be particularly costly. In this paper we argue how dynamic analysis can be used not only to identify errors in the contracts, but also to support recovery from such errors. Furthermore, contract immutability means that code cannot be easily fixed upon discovering a problem. To address this issue, we also present a specification-driven approach, allowing developers to promise behavioural properties via smart contracts, but still allowing them to update the code which implements the specification in a safe manner.

1 Introduction

Smart contracts built on top of blockchain and other distributed ledger technologies (DLTs) have been hailed as a game changer in providing a formal interface through which to regulate interaction between real-world parties. Originally, Szabo [26] conceived the notion of smart contracts as means of automated agreement and regulatory enforcement to the extent that they *"make breach of contract expensive (if desired, sometimes prohibitively so) for the breacher"*—thus allowing for breaches of contract, and yet at a cost. This corresponds closely to the notion of legal contracts which include the possibility of breaches to the extent that they frequently include clauses to regulate what happens in case of violation of other clauses. In contrast, Lessig's [20] dictum of *"code is law"* saw computer code regulating behaviour in an incontrovertible way, and thus, e.g. if the code automatically reroutes 25% of your income to pay taxes, there is no way in which you may breach this 'law' and not pay your taxes.

The term *contract* has been used in different contexts with different meanings, ranging from legal contracts which talk about ideal behaviour agreed upon between the participating parties, to programming language contracts to allow

T. Margaria and B. Steffen (Eds.): ISoLA 2018, LNCS 11247, pp. 300–315, 2018.
https://doi.org/10.1007/978-3-030-03427-6_23

for the specification to be part of the system implementation (e.g. pre- post-conditions in Eiffel [22] and behavioural interfaces [16]). In their current incarnation as adopted on distributed ledger systems such as Ethereum, smart contracts are closer to Lessig's view of code as law, with smart contracts providing executable transactions enforced implicitly by the underlying distributed ledger system and possibly changing its state. They provide an opportunity to execute code affecting global state in a safe manner which would otherwise be impossible without the participation of trusted central authorities or resource managers.

Whether specifications should be executable [13] or not [17] is an old debate in computer science, but what is clear is that a non-executable specification may limit itself to describe *what* the resulting state should look like (or satisfy), while an executable one must also include a description of *how* to achieve such a state. The additional information required for the latter leaves more room for incorrect or mistaken specifications.

This is a crucial issue with the current incarnation of smart contracts: smart contracts do exactly what they say they do, but that might not be what the agreeing parties thought it would do—or for that matter what the developer of the contract thought it would do. This is particularly important since once deployed on the underlying blockchain, smart contracts are immutable and cannot be changed. The only way to support updates to a smart contract is to include the possibility to update the code in its own logic, which goes back to the question of trust. Whether a smart contract is written by one of the parties participating in a transaction, or by an outsider, participating parties may rightfully fear that there might be obscure ways in which others can exploit the contract to their benefit. There have been well-known instances of bugs in smart contracts, for instance, on Ethereum [1].

Although due to the immutable nature of smart contracts one would prefer to use static analysis techniques to ensure correctness at compile-time, such work is still sparse, with most of it aimed at addressing common vulnerabilities rather than business-logic specifications. For instance, Fröwis et al. [12] try to identify control-flow mutability, OYENTE [21] performs reentrancy detection, while Bhargavan et al. [2] transform Solidity into F* on which they perform analysis to identify general vulnerable patterns. Much of this work is performed at the EVM level, partly due to the fact that the semantics of Solidity being only informally described in the language documentation, and effectively pragmatically decided based on what the compiler does. In contrast, there are published formal semantics for EVM bytecode either through direct formalisation or via translation in [15,18]. However, what these approaches do not address are application specific, business-logic properties; perhaps mainly due to issues of scalability, especially because of the data intensive aspects of many smart contracts. In such cases, one may have to resort to runtime analysis of smart contracts.

Runtime monitoring, already a special case of dynamic analysis, admits to a whole family of activities. At the most basic level, one can merely *monitor* or *observe* a system and log information about its runtime behaviour. The next level up is that of *runtime verification,* in which not only is the behaviour observed, but particular behavioural patterns are identified to be undesirable and algorithmically classified to be so. This notion can be taken further by adding on logic to support *runtime recovery* or *reparation*, triggering in the case of undesirable behaviour being observed to make up for it. One can also go another step further, using *runtime enforcement* to ensure that the undesirable behaviour is avoided in the first place, modifying the system's behaviour to ensure it works as expected[1]. In the rest of the paper, we primarily focus on runtime verification and recovery.

The very architecture of blockchain (and similar distributed ledger technologies) in itself provides the monitoring process for free. Each transaction and invocation to a smart contract is immutably recorded on the underlying ledger. The violation detection process itself can be addressed using techniques not too different from those already in use for other software systems. It is worth noting that the ledger architecture does provide an opportunity in injecting online runtime verification into the underlying design—one can design a monitoring-aware DLT in which verification code can be added to the architecture (the DLT implementation itself), ensuring no smart contracts are executed or data written unless verified to be correct. In the rest of this paper, however, we will simply assume that runtime verification is being performed, thus allowing for violations to be identified and captured. Whether this verification is performed in the traditional manner (e.g. injecting code in the smart contract to perform the monitoring and verification), or performed by modifying the underlying architecture is irrelevant.

Even just identifying such violations can be useful in practice—consider a (physical-world) legal contract which stipulates that the parties agree on legal liability whenever the runtime monitor identifies a violation. However, in this paper we concern ourselves primarily with going beyond the monitoring and verification process—looking at the choices and challenges in reacting upon the identification of points of violation, primarily in the form of reparation, but also, enforcement in a limited manner. When runtime verification detects a violation of the specification at runtime, the system is typically instructed on how to react to (i) make up for the violation from the point of view of the system logic (e.g. block an account for safety); and (ii) restore the system state to a sane one (e.g. revert a financial transaction to leave no pending transactions or locked resources). We discuss how one can support such reparations in the context of smart contracts, and show how these notions can be used to extend the existing Solidity runtime verification tool CONTRACTLARVA [10].

However, on normal systems, the detection of a violation also triggers offline behaviour outside of the system—when the system developers try to identify the origin of the bug which led to the violation, fix it and redeploy the updated system. With the immutability of smart contracts, this phase is severely crippled.

---

[1] Needless to say, this terminology has been used in a wide variety of contexts, and not all usages correspond to the neatly compartmentalised descriptions we give. In case of disagreement with our use of terminology, kindly read the rest of the paper replacing the terms with your preferred ones.

One of the contributions of this paper is the proposal of a model-based approach incorporating runtime verification, to support updatable smart contracts in order to address violations discovered post deployment.

In order to be able to illustrate our ideas, in Sect. 2 we give a brief overview of the Ethereum platform[2] and the Solidity smart contract scripting language. In this section, we also show how CONTRACTLARVA specifications can be written, enabling us to propose concrete extensions supporting richer means of handling violation in smart contracts in the following sections. In Sect. 3, we then discuss the challenges of recovery from specification violations both to recover the internal state of the smart contract, but also to make up for the violation from the affected users' perspective. The issue of dynamically addressing bugs discovered post-deployment in the context of smart contract immutability is discussed in Sect. 4. Finally, in Sect. 5, we discuss related work and draw some conclusions.

2   Smart Contracts on Ethereum

Smart contracts and the programming thereof, due to the inherent immutability of blockchains and the critical nature of applications they are used for, requires a different programming mindset [9]. Once deployed a smart contract is there forever. The internal code cannot be changed, and with this in mind, developers tend to use defensive programming techniques to ensure that users cannot exploit bugs or unintended functionality. Ethereum provides for the execution of a 'one world computer', the Ethereum Virtual Machine (EVM) [27], which can be seen as a single computational core which executes function code atomically. What is really happening though, is that every node is computing and storing the same values within the blockchain, and must therefore require computation to be deterministic (since the same result must be computed on every node). Calls to smart contracts are treated as atomic transactions, which often instills a sense of security in programmers since race conditions no longer appear to be an issue. It has been argued that smart contract programming still shares much with concurrent object programming [25] and issues such as reentrancy remain— occurring when calls are made to third party smart contracts that in turn call back the caller smart contract.

The Ethereum platform allows executable smart contracts to be written using the EVM's assembly instruction set, but also provides high-level languages, with the predominant one being Solidity. Once deployed on Ethereum, a smart contract has an associated unique identifier, corresponding to its address and can intrinsically own ether (Ethereum's internal currency) and transfer ether to other addresses (which could be contracts or user accounts). The EVM instruction set is Turing complete, and in order to deal with smart contract functionality which may not terminate or take inordinately long, uses the notion of gas—effectively

---

[2] Since DLTs vary in design and in their take on smart contracts, we particularly focus on the Ethereum blockchain platform [27], even if many of the ideas presented herewith can be extended for other takes on smart contracts and other DLTs.

payment (in ether) for the execution of each instruction step. When the gas allocated to a particular transaction is exhausted, execution stops and the altered state is reverted to the original one upon initiation of the transaction, thus effectively ensuring that (i) all functionality is terminating; and (ii) computationally more expensive functionality is also financially more expensive, thus avoiding possible attempts to overload the Ethereum platform with complex computation.

1. *The casino owner may deposit or withdraw money from the casino's bank, with the bank's balance never falling below zero.*
2. *As long as no game is in progress, the owner of the casino may make available a new game by tossing a coin and hiding its outcome. The owner must also set a participation cost of choice for the game.*
3. *Clauses 1 and 2 are constrained in that as long as a game is in progress, the bank balance may never be less than the sum of the participation cost of the game and its win-out.*
4. *The win-out for a game is set to be 80% of the participating cost.*
5. *If a game is available, any user may choose to pay the participation fee and guess the outcome of a coin toss to join the game. After that, the game will no longer be available to other users.*
6. *The owner of the casino is obliged to reveal the coin tossed upon creating the game within half an hour of a player participating. If the coin matches the guess, the player's participation fee and the game win-out is to be paid to the player from the casino's bank. Either way, the game then terminates.*
7. *If the casino owner does not adhere to clause 6, the player has the right to declare a default win and be paid the participation fee and the game win-out from the casino's bank. At this stage, the game also terminates.*

Fig. 1. A legal contract regulating a coin-tossing casino

In the rest of the paper, we will use a running example of a smart contract to implement a casino which provides a single game that allows for guessing the outcome of a coin toss. The legal contract which we will be using as a running example is shown in Fig. 1. This can be implemented as a smart contract on a platform like Ethereum (with part of the code in Solidity shown in Listing 1), where each party's possible actions are encoded as functions which the respective parties may invoke. The shown `closeBet` function is used by the casino owner to reveal the coin tossed after a player has made a guess, corresponding to clause 6. It is worth remarking on some aspects used in the code which will be used in the rest of the paper.

The `require` function provides a mechanism to ensure that a predicate holds before proceeding with the code. If the predicate does not hold, the whole transaction and execution of the code is abandoned, and the variables are reverted to their original values. This mechanism can also be triggered directly through the Solidity `revert` instruction (which Solidity's `require` uses internally). Reverts are bubbled up to functions calling the failing one, and the only way to stop such a revert chain is through contract communication. Contracts on Ethereum may invoke functions in other contracts through the `call` and `delegatecall` functions which stop the bubbling up of a revert. In addition, delegate calls run the called code from within the caller (i.e. giving access to variables defined in the caller function).

A function call is viewed as a message passed to the contract, accessible through the `msg` variable, and allowing access to information such as the message sender's address: `msg.sender`. A smart contract can transfer any ether owned by the smart contract to an Ethereum address through the `address.transfer(amount)` instruction.

Finally, it is worth noting that `private` variables and functions in Solidity (as opposed to `public` ones), only prevents other contracts from accessing the data directly. However, the data is still visible to anyone outside since it is publicly written on the Ethereum blockchain, so the `hiddenCoin` would have to be encrypted and not simply written to a private variable. One commonly used way is to encode the hidden coin toss by submitting and storing the hash of an odd number if it was heads, and even if it was tails. Upon revealing the actual number, it is easy to confirm that the coin was not changed and whether it was heads or tails (achieved using the function `sameAs`, the implementation of which is not shown).

It is worth noting that contracts may not only call and execute functions in the same contract, but may also have calls to other smart contracts. Solidity provides `call` and `delegatecall` functions as means to execute named functions at a given contract address, with the main difference (of interest to this paper) being that `delegatecall` gives the called contract access to the state of the contract from where the call is made. This allows for delegation of control of state to external contracts.

When an exception is raised within the callee, the `call` function will return a `false` value (and if it was successful, a `true` value). A similar function `delegatecall` allows for calls to external contract functions which execute the external contract function code within the context of the caller's contract and caller's transaction, which will maintain the same values for the `msg.sender`, `msg.value`, and other contract context including the storage used. This can be seen to be the same as though the contract was calling another internal function, although in actual fact the code is stored in an external function.

The code in Listing 1, thus ensures that (i) it is being invoked by the casino owner; (ii) the revealed coin matches the originally given (encrypted) hidden one; and (iii) a player has participated in the game. If all three conditions hold, then the player is given a reward in case of a guess (clause 6). The game terminates after that.

Consider a property which states that the casino owner may not withdraw from the casino's bank leaving less than the required player payout as long as there is an active bet. This property can be expressed as a dynamic event automaton (DEA), the specification language used by CONTRACTLARVA [10] (a runtime verification tool for Solidity contracts), as shown in Fig. 2. DEAs are effectively automata whose transitions are tagged by a triple $e \mid c \mapsto a$, where e is an event, c is a Solidity condition (which has to be satisfied to take the

```
contract Casino {
    .
    .
    address private hiddenCoin;
    .
    .
    function closeBet(uint _shownCoin) public {
        require(msg.sender == casinoOwner);
        require(sameAs(_shownCoin, hiddenCoin));
        require(gameStatus == PLAYER_PARTICIPATED);

        if (matches(_shownCoin, guessedCoin)) {
            player.transfer(participationCost + winout);
        }
        gameStatus = GAME_OVER;
    }
    .
    .
}
```

Listing 1. Part of the smart contract implementing the casino table

transition) and a is a Solidity action (essentially code which is executed upon taking the transition). Both the condition and the action can be left out if not required. The events are of the form: $o :: m : f$, where f is a Solidity function name and parameters, m is the modality which will trigger it, and o is the agent who must call the function for the event to trigger. In turn, the modality can be **start** which triggers as soon as the function is called, or **end** which triggers when the function terminates successfully i.e. without a revert. DEAs also allow a **fails** modality (which will be used later in the paper) which triggers if the function is called but is reverted for any reason other than lack of gas. DEAs are deterministic automata and include identified bad states (marked in black in the figure) which flag a violation if reached at runtime.

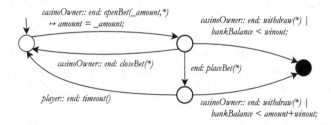

Fig. 2. Property specifying that enough funds must remain in the bank throughout the bet's lifetime.

3   Smart Contract Recovery

Detecting situations where a contract has violated applicable correctness properties is desirable, but dealing with the aftermath of such a discovery might not be straightforward. In the context of software which is not blockchain-based, one approach may simply block the execution of the whole system or of part thereof (e.g. block the users or functionality affected by the issue) until the problem is resolved. In the case of smart contracts though, naïvely blocking the contract from proceeding further would mean locking funds held within it forever, implying the need for more sophisticated recovery code.

Using a custom recovery action to manage such violations allows for comprehensive and customisable handling. For instance, in the casino property example, one might consider an escrow arrangement, in which the casino owner initially pays into the contract an amount which is paid off to the player in case of a violation to make up for the malfunctioning contract. At the most coarse grained level, recovery actions may be generic (any violation fires this recovery), but can be made more specific for particular properties or particular parts of code which trigger the violation (effectively acting similar to typical exception handling). This approach has been adopted by several runtime verification tools e.g. Larva [8] and Java-MOP [4].

While such custom recovery arrangements are convenient in that they provide a specific case-by-case solution to violations, they have the downside of being hard to automate, i.e. procedures have to be customised and coded manually, increasing the complexity of the smart contract. Taking once more the escrow arrangement example, if a contract involves a number of different stakeholders, who has to pay the escrow and how to divide it for each violation becomes substantially more complicated. We now look at a number of alternative approaches to specifying recovery in more compositional ways.

3.1   Checkpointing

One standard way of automating recovery from failure is through the use of *checkpointing* [24], i.e. to save the state of the contract at important points of execution in order to allow reverting back to them when the monitor detects a deviation from the expected behaviour. In the casino example, this would mean that money placed on a bet would automatically be returned to the player. Through the `revert` mechanism, the EVM already provides an underlying notion of checkpointing for its atomic transactions: if a transaction fails half way through, its effects are discarded by returning to the state of the blockchain before the start of the transaction, and this can be used to ensure that calls to a smart contract which cause a property to fail are completely undone, thus guaranteeing that the state is returned to its previous (assumed to be sane) state.

In using reverts to undo execution of a failed transaction on Ethereum, particular care has to be taken due to calls and delegate calls which stop a revert from being bubbled up to the caller.

However, using EVM reverts to handle system state recovery comes with a number of caveats:

Normal vs. exceptional reverts: Since reverts are typically used in the normal logic of the smart contracts (e.g. the assertions in the code shown in Listing 1 may trigger reverts), reverts now play two roles—that of normal exits from the system logic, and that of exceptions due to behaviour which was not expected from the smart contract. Care has to be taken to avoid these from interacting together, particularly since smart contracts may use calls to capture normal (expected) reverts to follow up its behaviour.

Finer grained checkpointing: The basic checkpointing mechanism provided on the EVM does not provide the possibility of fine-grained checkpointing; the checkpoint can only be (implicitly) placed at the start of the transaction. Ideally, one should be able to allow for marking checkpoints and allow for reverting to particular ones. For instance, consider if the casino smart contract were developed by someone other than the casino owner who would benefit from a transaction fee with every attempted withdrawal from the casino bank. In such a case, one may want to ensure that violation of the smart contract property from Fig. 2 should revert the withdrawal from the bank, but still keep the transaction fee. One way of achieving this would be to use named checkpoints (see Listing 2) and reverting to the named checkpoint BEFORE_WITHDRAWAL when that violation occurs. Such a mechanism can be easily implemented using code transformation on the smart contract with the help of explicit calls. The downside of such an approach is that there is even more complex interwinding between the forward and the recovery logic, with checkpoint tags which may have been created purely for recovery appearing in the main code thus violating the often held principle of separation-of-concerns (keeping the normal logic and the verification specification separate). In [6], we had proposed an alternative to this approach in that checkpoints relevant only to recovery are also identified as part of the dynamic analysis. By adding appropriate tagging (e.g. adding a checkpoint tag after the transfer to the developer is specified on the DEA using an action or a checkpoint tagging state), one can still keep checkpoint tags relevant to reparation separate in the specification.

Forward recovery: Whilst reverting to a previous state provides a straightforward way of restoring the state of the smart contract, sometimes one still needs to perform a recovery action *after* recovering the state. For instance, in the casino smart contract, one may want to not only disallow the withdrawal, but also allow the player a default win. Such forward recovery logic can be placed in the smart contract itself, but as argued before, makes more sense in the specification (for instance by tagging the bad state with the code). Figure 3 shows how the specification can be extended with this information, adding another DEA to keep track of the relevant checkpoint upon matching a particular sequence of events.

```
function withdraw(uint _amount) public {
    require(msg.sender == owner);
    ...
    // Pay transaction fee
    developer.transfer(transactionFee);
    // Withdraw specified amount
    checkpoint(BEFORE_WITHDRAWAL);
    casinoOwner.transfer(_amount);
}
```

Listing 2. Named checkpointing for partial reverts

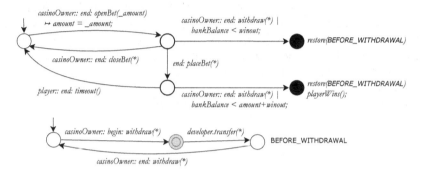

Fig. 3. Extending the property to allow for tagged checkpointing followed by forward recovery—checkpoints being saved upon entering the red state.

3.2   Compensations

The notion of forward recovery after restoring to a checkpoint, as discussed in the previous section, is typically used to make up for earlier behaviour e.g. allowing the player to win is done to compensate for the fact that the player has already (in a previous transaction) committed him or herself to betting in the casino. Although each function call to the EVM is seen as a full transaction, from a higher level of abstraction, sequences of function calls can be seen as long-lived transactions [5,14,24]. Just as in long-lived transactions, previous function calls to the EVM may not always be fully reversible[3], in which case compensation for such functions cannot be feasibly done via checkpointing.

When a global compensation is applied (as in the case of giving a default win to the player), compensations can be easily handled, but when in more complex situations, one usually has compensations gathering as the long-lived transaction advances. The appealing aspect of a compositional compensation mechanism is that each individual action can be assigned a default compensation, i.e. an action which manages the effects of the action being compensated for, and

---

[3] Atomic transactions rely on locking to isolate themselves from external observation—which is impractical with transactions which have a long lifespan. If the environment reacts to intermediate results after which the transaction fails, then the transaction cannot simply be wiped out. Rather, the effects it had on the environment in its lifetime need to be managed. This is done through compensations.

unless specifically changed, the compensation of a sequence of actions results in the execution of the individual actions' compensations in reverse order. Such a mechanism is frequently used on, for instance, payment transaction systems to ensure that the participating entities are compensated for the failing transaction, also in the context of runtime verification [6,7].

For instance, consider a casino scenario in which a player may join either a roulette or a coin-tossing table, where they may place multiple bets. A monitor can be used to ensure that if a player performs an illicit action (e.g. placing more bets than legally permitted), they will be refunded any bets they have placed (less charges, which may depend on the game they are betting on) and their account will be disabled. Figure 4 shows how this can be handled using simplified compensation automata [6]—extending the notation used earlier for transitions to add a compensation u: $e \mid c \mapsto a/u$, where u can either be an action which will be added to the compensation stack or an instruction to clear the compensation stack. When a violation is identified (by a separate monitor), actions are individually removed from the compensation stack and executed.

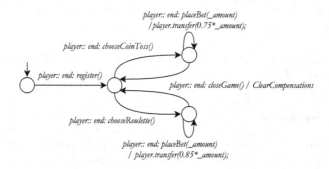

Fig. 4. Monitor-based compensation synthesis.

Since compensations depend on the history of execution, and can very easily lead to substantial increase in space and time execution resources required, this comes with an additional problem when used on platforms such as Ethereum, due to substantial gas consumption increase. A standing challenge is how to constrain the notion of compensations in order to avoid or mitigate this issue.

4 Updating Code

In most software systems, when a violation to a specification is discovered, one important action is to report the problem back to the development team to assess its severity and accordingly report the issue to be eventually addressed in a patch or future release. In hardware verification circles, it has always been recognised that bugs are more serious and costly, as the 1994 Intel FDIV bug [23] had shown, since one cannot cheaply update a chip post-production. In a manner, despite the software nature of smart contracts, their intrinsic immutability shares much with hardware systems. Once deployed, there is no simple manner in which one may update the code.

In order to deal with problems identified post-deployment, the industry has developed a family of design patterns in order to support code updates through having the code of the smart contract refer to updatable references to secondary smart contracts or through means of migrating users from a smart contract to an updated one. Listing 3 shows a code snippet of how this is typically done using the *proxy* or *hub-spoke* pattern. The approach involves the use of an interface contract (with no internal implementation but) with a reference to the current version of the actual contract implementation. Any function calls to the contract are simply passed on as calls or delegate calls (if the data is also stored in the interface contract) to the actual implementation contract. The primary issue with this approach is that each such contract must choose what policy to adopt in order to decide how a version update can be accepted. For instance, in the example shown in Listing 3, the casino owner would be able to unilaterally update the code, but one may adopt more sophisticated approaches, e.g. requiring updates to be decided by a majority vote amongst the current users of the contract.

```
contract Casino {
    address currentVersionOfContract;
    address owner;

    function updateVersion(address _newVersionOfContract) public {
        require(msg.sender==owner);
        currentVersionOfContract = _newVersionOfContract;
    }

    function openTable() public {
        currentVersionOfContract.call(bytes4(sha3("openTable()")));
    }
    ...
}
```

Listing 3. Enabling versioning of smart contracts

In this section we identify a solution to this challenge of enabling smart contract updates in a safe manner, building on ideas from behavioural interfaces [16], monitoring-oriented programming [3] and using dynamic analysis to ensure safety.

The major challenge faced is that unless somehow limited, code updates can be arbitrary and users of the contract have no guarantees that the new contract code will continue to implement the same logic (except for new features or fixed bugs) as the original one they signed up to. We propose a *specification-oriented approach,* in which users initially agree on a specification of how the smart contract is to behave, and set up a smart contract which (i) implements the interface of the contract; (ii) passes on any calls to the public interface to the current version of the implementation available as an external contract; (iii) enables the developer to update the version of the code arbitrarily; but (iv) instruments a monitor to ensure that the specification is adhered to by the current version of the contract. The first three are identical to the design pattern shown in Listing 3, but the fourth is what ensures user confidence in the implementation. No matter how the developer updates their code, the users are guaranteed that any violations to the specification will be captured and acted upon.

Consider, for example, a specification which a user may want to be sure holds in order to trust a casino implementation as shown in Fig. 5 in terms of a DEA. The specification identifies three forms of casino implementation misbehaviour— once a bet is opened by the casino owner and a bet is placed by the user, the three violations identified are if (i) the casino reveals the number which matches the user's guess but insufficient funds are transferred on to the user; (ii) the user calls the timeout after an appropriate amount of time without the number being revealed but not enough funds are transferred to the user; and (iii) the user tries to call a timeout but is stopped from doing so by a revert.

The choice as to whether the proxy should use calls or delegate calls depends on a number of issues, including ones related to monitoring. For instance, if some properties depend on the data stored in the smart contract (e.g. the `openBet` function cannot be called when the balance stored in the state of the smart contract is negative), keeping these parts of the state on the proxy and using delegate calls may be required.

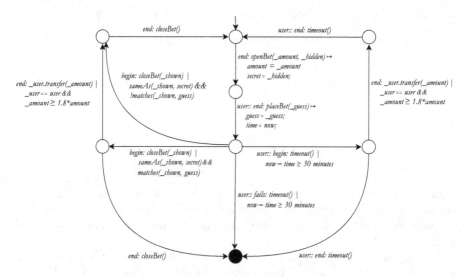

Fig. 5. User-centric casino specification

In order to instrument the specification monitor, we can use CONTRACT-LARVA on the interface contract and the specification to obtain a safely encapsulated behavioural interface as shown in Fig. 6. This will be able to identify any violation at runtime, ensuring we can react accordingly as discussed in the previous sections. In this manner, trust—despite versioning—can be addressed through an immutable behavioural interface, although it remains a major challenge to have a sufficiently detailed behavioural interface which disallows *all* undesirable behaviour.

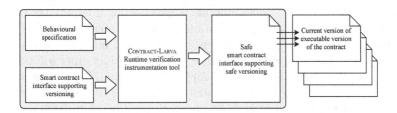

Fig. 6. Building safe behavioural interfaces for smart contracts

This approach borrows much from behavioural interfaces, in that we automatically create a safe, trusted and immutable interface which accesses an untrusted backend and mutable implementation. In a way, the approach also borrows from monitoring-oriented programming [3] in that we are programming the safe interface using monitoring techniques.

5   Conclusions

In this paper we have examined a spectrum of dynamic analysis techniques for making smart contracts safer and more dependable. Although at the surface level smart contracts appear to be normal software, however, there are a number of issues which result in standard runtime techniques to have to be adapted in order to be useful in this context. Clearly, the domain makes static, compile-time analysis even more attractive (or desirable) than for standard systems. However, the sparse literature applying such techniques for smart contracts e.g. [2,21], particularly for business-logic specifications indicates that, at least for the time being, we have to depend on the lower hanging fruit dynamic analysis provides. This brings its own challenges—perhaps most pertinent is that of recovery from violations discovered at runtime. In the domain of runtime verification of general systems, the notion of *healing* has recently been explored in [11], in which the authors classify the solutions into three similar classes as found in our proposal: rollback, preventing further failures and compensation. How these can be adapted for smart contracts is, however, the challenge we have addressed in this paper.

By enriching smart contract programming languages with notions such as checkpointing and compensations, we believe that one could alleviate handling of such violations. Another major challenge is that of the immutability of smart contracts, and the solution we are proposing in order to ensure that the system works correctly but still allow the implementation to be modified follows the conclusions of other work [19], which argued for declarative as opposed to imperative and operational approaches currently used on DLTs such as Ethereum.

We are currently looking at identifying means of deploying many of the ideas presented in this paper on real-world systems. Our tool CONTRACTLARVA has already been applied on a number of smart contracts in order to deploy runtime verification and recovery, but there are still various challenges left to be addressed. It can be argued that our solution to resolve the immutability of smart contracts by making them mutable while ensuring immutability of specifications is nothing but pushing the problem one level up. However, we believe that moving one level of abstraction up, ignoring most implementation details results in lower risk of error. Furthermore, one can consider other solutions currently at the implementation level to support versioning of specifications (e.g. allowing for a specification to be updated by consensus or a majority vote). It will be interesting to see how such an approach would fare on large real-world smart contracts.

References

1. Atzei, N., Bartoletti, M., Cimoli, T.: A survey of attacks on ethereum smart contracts (SoK). In: Maffei, M., Ryan, M. (eds.) POST 2017. LNCS, vol. 10204, pp. 164–186. Springer, Heidelberg (2017). https://doi.org/10.1007/978-3-662-54455-6_8

2. Bhargavan, K., et al.: Formal verification of smart contracts: short paper. In: Proceedings of the 2016 ACM Workshop on Programming Languages and Analysis for Security, PLAS 2016. ACM, New York (2016)

3. Chen, F., Rosu, G.: Towards monitoring-oriented programming: a paradigm combining specification and implementation. Electr. Notes Theor. Comput. Sci. **89**(2), 108–127 (2003)

4. Chen, F., Roşu, G.: Java-MOP: a monitoring oriented programming environment for Java. In: Halbwachs, N., Zuck, L.D. (eds.) TACAS 2005. LNCS, vol. 3440, pp. 546–550. Springer, Heidelberg (2005). https://doi.org/10.1007/978-3-540-31980-1_36

5. Colombo, C., Pace, G.J.: Recovery within long-running transactions. ACM Comput. Surv. **45**(3), 28:1–28:35 (2013)

6. Colombo, C., Pace, G.J.: Comprehensive monitor-oriented compensation programming. In: Proceedings 11th International Workshop on Formal Engineering approaches to Software Components and Architectures, FESCA 2014, Grenoble, France, 12 April 2014, pp. 47–61 (2014)

7. Colombo, C., Pace, G.J., Abela, P.: Safer asynchronous runtime monitoring using compensations. Form. Methods Syst. Des. **41**(3), 269–294 (2012)

8. Colombo, C., Pace, G.J., Schneider, G.: LARVA—safer monitoring of real-time Java programs (tool paper). In: IEEE International Conference on Software Engineering and Formal Methods, SEFM 2009, Hanoi, Vietnam, 23–27 November 2009 (2009)

9. Delmolino, K., Arnett, M., Kosba, A., Miller, A., Shi, E.: Step by step towards creating a safe smart contract: lessons and insights from a cryptocurrency lab. In: Clark, J., Meiklejohn, S., Ryan, P.Y.A., Wallach, D., Brenner, M., Rohloff, K. (eds.) FC 2016. LNCS, vol. 9604, pp. 79–94. Springer, Heidelberg (2016). https://doi.org/10.1007/978-3-662-53357-4_6

10. Ellul, J., Pace, G.J.: Runtime verification of ethereum smart contracts. In: Workshop on Blockchain Dependability (WBD), in conjunction with 14th European Dependable Computing Conference (EDCC) (2018)
11. Falcone, Y., Mariani, L., Rollet, A., Saha, S.: Runtime failure prevention and reaction. In: Bartocci, E., Falcone, Y. (eds.) Lectures on Runtime Verification: Introductory and Advanced Topics. LNCS, vol. 10457, pp. 103–134. Springer, Cham (2018). https://doi.org/10.1007/978-3-319-75632-5_4
12. Fröwis, M., Böhme, R.: In code we trust?—measuring the control flow immutability of all smart contracts deployed on ethereum. In: Garcia-Alfaro, J., Navarro-Arribas, G., Hartenstein, H., Herrera-Joancomartí, J. (eds.) ESORICS/DPM/CBT -2017. LNCS, vol. 10436, pp. 357–372. Springer, Cham (2017). https://doi.org/10.1007/978-3-319-67816-0_20
13. Fuchs, N.E.: Specifications are (preferably) executable. Softw. Eng. J. **7**(5), 323–334 (1992)
14. Garcia-Molina, H., Gawlick, D., Klein, J., Kleissner, K., Salem, K.: Modeling long-running activities as nested sagas. IEEE Data Eng. Bull. **14**(1), 14–18 (1991)
15. Grishchenko, I., Maffei, M., Schneidewind, C.: A semantic framework for the security analysis of ethereum smart contracts. In: Bauer, L., Küsters, R. (eds.) POST 2018. LNCS, vol. 10804, pp. 243–269. Springer, Cham (2018). https://doi.org/10.1007/978-3-319-89722-6_10
16. Hatcliff, J., Leavens, G.T., Leino, K.R.M., Müller, P., Parkinson, M.J.: Behavioral interface specification languages. ACM Comput. Surv. **44**(3), 16:1–16:58 (2012)
17. Hayes, I., Jones, C.B.: Specifications are not (necessarily) executable. Softw. Eng. J. **4**(6), 330–338 (1989)
18. Hildenbrandt, E., et al.: KEVM: a complete semantics of the ethereum virtual machine. Technical report (2017)
19. Idelberger, F., Governatori, G., Riveret, R., Sartor, G.: Evaluation of logic-based smart contracts for blockchain systems. In: Alferes, J.J.J., Bertossi, L., Governatori, G., Fodor, P., Roman, D. (eds.) RuleML 2016. LNCS, vol. 9718, pp. 167–183. Springer, Cham (2016). https://doi.org/10.1007/978-3-319-42019-6_11
20. Lessig, L.: Code 2.0, 2nd edn. CreateSpace, Paramount (2009)
21. Luu, L., Chu, D.-H., Olickel, H., Saxena, P., Hobor, A.: Making smart contracts smarter. In: Proceedings of the 2016 ACM SIGSAC Conference on Computer and Communications Security, Vienna, Austria, 24–28 October 2016, pp. 254–269 (2016)
22. Meyer, B.: Design by contract: the Eiffel method. In: TOOLS (26), p. 446. IEEE Computer Society (1998)
23. Pratt, V.: Anatomy of the pentium bug. In: Mosses, P.D., Nielsen, M., Schwartzbach, M.I. (eds.) CAAP 1995. LNCS, vol. 915, pp. 97–107. Springer, Heidelberg (1995). https://doi.org/10.1007/3-540-59293-8_189
24. Randell, B., Lee, P.A., Treleaven, P.C.: Reliability issues in computing system design. ACM Comput. Surv. **10**(2), 123–165 (1978)
25. Sergey, I., Hobor, A.: A concurrent perspective on smart contracts. In: Brenner, M. (ed.) FC 2017. LNCS, vol. 10323, pp. 478–493. Springer, Cham (2017). https://doi.org/10.1007/978-3-319-70278-0_30
26. Szabo, N.: Smart contracts: building blocks for digital markets. Extropy (16) (1996)
27. Wood, G.: Ethereum: a secure decentralised generalised transaction ledger. Ethereum Proj. Yellow Pap. **151**, 1–32 (2014)

Security Analysis of Smart Contracts in Datalog

Petar Tsankov[✉]

Secure, Reliable, and Intelligent Systems Lab, ETH Zurich, Zurich, Switzerland
petar.tsankov@inf.ethz.ch

Abstract. Smart contracts enable mutually untrusted entities to inter-act without relying on trusted third parties. Despite their potential, repeated security concerns have shaken the trust in handling billions of USD by smart contracts. To address this issue, we have developed SECURIFY, a scalable and fully automated security analyzer for Ethereum smart contracts. A key technical insight behind the design of SECURIFY is that whenever a smart contract violates a security property, it often also violates a simpler property that can be expressed on the contract's data-flow graph. To leverage this insight, SECURIFY symbolically encodes relevant control- and data-flow dependencies in stratified Datalog and uses scalable Datalog solvers to derive key semantic facts about the contract. Then, it inspects the inferred semantic facts to checks a set of compliance and violation patterns, which capture sufficient conditions for proving if a given security property holds or not.

Keywords: Smart contracts · Security analysis · Datalog

1 Introduction

Smart contracts are programs, typically written in Turing-complete languages, which are deployed and executed on top of blockchains (such as Ethereum [9]). As such, they enable mutually untrusted parties to engage in interactions that go beyond basic trading of cryptocurrencies. A nontrivial challenge that must be addressed before the wide-adoption of smart contracts is security: developers often miss critical security bugs [1–5,10] in their smart contracts which, in turn, lead to substantial financial losses. For example, in 2017, two security bugs in a popular multi-signature wallet [5] allowed attackers to steal 30 million USD and, resp., to freeze 280 million USD. To prevent such incidents in the future, it is apparent that effective security checkers for smart contracts are needed.

Challenge. The main challenge in creating an effective security checker for smart contracts is the Turing-completeness of the programming language, which renders automated verification of arbitrary properties undecidable. Most approaches for discovering issues in smart contracts today rely on generic testing and symbolic execution methods. While useful in some settings, these approaches

© Springer Nature Switzerland AG 2018
T. Margaria and B. Steffen (Eds.): ISoLA 2018, LNCS 11247, pp. 316–322, 2018.
https://doi.org/10.1007/978-3-030-03427-6_24

can miss critical violations due to under-approximation. Yet, existing symbolic solutions, such as Mythril [6] and Oyente [13], also produce false positives due to the imprecise modeling of domain-specific elements [12].

Securify. To address the challenges of existing automated symbolic solutions, SECURIFY[1] [14] relies on a novel domain-specific insight. Namely, it is often possible to devise patterns expressed on the contract's data-flow graph in a way where a match of the pattern implies either a violation or satisfaction of the original security property. For example, 91.9% of all calls in smart contracts deployed on Ethereum can be proved free of the infamous DAO bug [3] by matching a pattern stating that calls are not followed by writes to storage. The reason why it is possible to establish this correspondence is that violations of the original property in real-world contracts tend to often violate a simpler property (captured by the pattern).

To leverage this insight, SECURIFY uses two kinds of patterns that mirror a given security property: *(i)* compliance patterns, which imply the property's satisfaction, and *(ii)* violation patterns, which imply its negation. To evaluate these patterns on a specific contract, SECURIFY symbolically encodes the dependence graph of the contract in stratified Datalog [15] and leverages off-the-shelf scalable Datalog solvers to efficiently (typically within seconds) analyze the code.

In the remained of this paper, we illustrate how SECURIFY performs its analysis on a representative example. To read the full technical details of SECURIFY, we refer the reader to [14].

2   Example

In Fig. 1 we show the implementation of a wallet. The code is written in Solidity [7], a popular high-level language for writing Ethereum smart contracts. We remark that this wallet is a simplified version of Parity's multi-signature wallet, which allowed an attacker to steal 30 million worth of USD in July 2017. The wallet has a field owner, which stores the address of the wallet's owner. Further, the contract has a function init, which takes as argument an address _owner and initializes the field owner with it. This function is called by the constructor (not shown in Fig. 1). Finally, the contract has a function withdraw, which takes as argument an unsigned integer _amount. The function checks if the transaction sender's address (returned by msg.sender) equals that of the contract's owner (stored in the field owner). If this check succeeds, the function withdraw transfers

```
contract Wallet {
    address owner;
    function init(address _owner) {
        owner = _owner;
    }
    function withdraw(uint _amount) {
        if (msg.sender == owner) {
            owner.transfer(_amount);
        }
    }
}
```

Fig. 1. A wallet smart contract

---

[1] SECURIFY is publicly available at https://securify.ch.

_amount ether to the owner with the statement `owner.transfer(_amount)`; otherwise, no ether is transferred. The function `withdraw` ensures that only the owner can withdraw ether from the wallet.

Vulnerability. The wallet shown in Fig. 1 has a critical security flaw: any Ethereum user can call the function `init` and store an arbitrary address in the field owner. We recall that a function call in Ethereum is made by sending a transaction with the identifier of the function (e.g., `init`) along with the function's arguments (e.g., an address `_owner`). An attacker can, therefore, steal all ether stored in the wallet in two steps. First, the attacker calls the function `init`, passing her own address as an argument. Second, the attacker calls the function `withdraw`, passing as argument the amount of ether stored in the wallet.

Challenge. The underlying security problem that allows the attacker to steal ether is that the sensitive field `owner` is universally writable by any Ethereum user. This security issue mirrors a more general property [11] stipulating that not all users may write to the field `owner`. This property cannot be checked by observing a single trace (i.e., an execution of a single transaction). To show that the owner `field` is universally writable, we need to prove that all users can send a transaction that modifies the owner `field`, which is impractical due to the enormous space of possible users (concretely, 2^{256} choices).

3   Security Analysis Using Stratified Datalog

In this section, we describe how SECURIFY uses stratified Datalog to discover the security vulnerability in the wallet example shown in Fig. 1. Given a smart contract, SECURIFY first extracts input facts from the contract's code and uses these as an input to a stratified Datalog program, which symbolically captures important data- and control-flow dependencies of the contract, to derive relevant semantic facts about the contract. Then, SECURIFY uses the derived semantic facts to check compliance and violation patterns that imply the satisfaction and, respectively, the violation of a given security property.

3.1   Inferring Semantic Facts

We now describe the main steps performed by SECURIFY to infer semantic facts. In Fig. 2 we depict these steps for our wallet example.

Step 1: Decompile EVM Bytecode. The input to SECURIFY is the Ethereum Virtual Machine bytecode (EVM) of a smart contract. As a first step, SECURIFY decompiles the contract's EVM bytecode into a stackless representation in static-single assignment form (SSA). For example, for the stack expression `push 0x04`, SECURIFY introduces a local variable a and an assignment statement `a = 0x04`. In addition to removing the stack, SECURIFY identifies methods. For example, the method `ABI_00` shown in Fig. 2 corresponds to the method `init` of the wallet contract shown in Fig. 1.

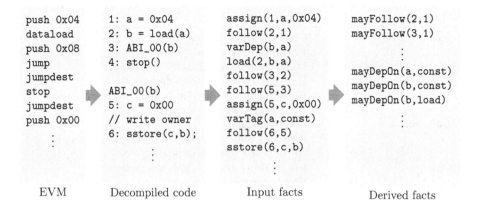

Fig. 2. Deriving semantic facts using stratified datalog

Step 2: Extract Input Facts. Next, SECURIFY extracts input facts from the decompile code. The input facts are of the form `Instr(lab, res, args)`, where `Instr` is an instruction name, `lab` is an instruction's label, `res` is a variable storing the instruction result (if any), and `args` are variables given to the instruction as arguments (if any). For example, the assignment `a = 0x04` at label 1 is encoded to `assign(1,a,0x04)`, and the `sstore` instruction at label 6 is encoded to `sstore(6,c,b)`. Also, for every two labels i and j whose instructions are consecutive in the CFG (either in the same basic block or in linked basic blocks), SECURIFY derives the input fact `follow(i,j)`. For example, SECURIFY derives the input fact `follow(2,1)` for our wallet contract (shown in Fig. 2).

Step 3: Infer Semantic Facts Using Datalog. Using the input facts described above, SECURIFY derives two kinds of semantic facts: *(i)* flow-dependency facts, which capture instruction dependencies according to the contract's control-flow graph (CFG), and *(ii)* data-dependency facts. The derivation of these facts is specified declaratively using stratified Datalog; we refer the reader to [8] for an overview of Datalog. For example, SECURIFY infers `mayFollow` facts which capture whether there may exist an execution where two instructions follow each other. These facts are derived with the following two Datalog rules:

```
mayFollow(X, Y) :- follow(X, Y)
mayFollow(X, Y) :- follow(X, Z), mayFollow(Z, Y)
```

Similarly, SECURIFY infers `mustFollow` facts which capture that for all executions of the contract two instructions must follow each other. Additionally, SECURIFY derives facts of the form `mayDepOn(X,T)`, which capture that the value of a variable X may depend on tag T (where T is either an instruction or a variable), and facts of the form `detBy(X,T)`, which captures that for different values of T the value of X is different. For our example, SECURIFY derives the fact `mayDepOn(b, load)` because the value of the variable `b` depends on the `load` instruction (which returns transaction data).

Category	Security property
Insecure coding	Unrestricted write to storage
	Unhandled exception
	Missing input validation
	Unrestricted contract self-destruction
	Rounding due to division before multiplication
	Unnecessary write to storage
Unsafe transfers	Locked funds
	Rounding affects the amount of transferred funds
	Unrestricted transfer of funds
Unsafe inputs	Unsafe dependence on gas information
	Unsafe dependence on user input
	Delegatecall dependent on user input
	Unsafe call to untrusted contract
Transaction reordering	Transactions affect the amount of transferred funds
	Transactions affect the receiver of funds
	Transactions affect the execution of fund transfer
Reentrancy issues	Write to storage after constant-gas call
	Write to storage after call with unrestricted gas

Fig. 3. Security properties supported by SECURIFY. For details on the properties and code examples, visit https://securify.ch.

3.2   Matching Security Patterns

To check a contract for a specific security property, SECURIFY evaluates a set of compliance and violation patterns defined over the inferred facts described above. In Fig. 3, we list 18 security properties supported by SECURIFY. Based on the outcome of evaluating the patterns, SECURIFY reports: *(i)* a violation, if a violation pattern is matched; *(ii)* a compliance, if a compliance pattern is matched; *(iii)* a warning, if not pattern is matched. Consider the write to the field `owner`. This write is unrestricted as it allows any user to execute the corresponding `sstore` instruction and write to field `owner`. To identify such violations, SECURIFY checks a more general property, which stipulates that an `sstore` instruction is restricted if for some offset `Offset` there is a user that cannot write to it. SECURIFY detects violations of this property by checking if the execution of an `sstore` as well as the value of `Offset` do not depend on the user's address (returned by the instruction `Caller`). This entails that if a user can write to a particular storage offset (e.g., a field) then any other user can also write to it, thereby violating the property. To discover all `sstore` instructions that violate this property, SECURIFY uses the following Datalog rule:

```
unrestrictedWrite(Lab) :- sstore(Lab, Offset, _),
                          !mayDepOn(Lab, Caller),
                          !mayDepOn(Offset, Caller)
```

For our example in Fig. 2, SECURIFY infers the fact `unrestrictedWrite(6)`, which indicates that the `sstore` instruction at label 6 violates the property.

4   Concluding Remarks

We presented the key technical insights behind the design of SECURIFY, a security checker for Ethereum smart contracts. In contrast to other tools, SECURIFY leverages the domain-specific insight that violations of many real-world security properties of smart contracts also violate simpler properties. To check the simpler properties, SECURIFY extracts semantic facts about the contract using existing scalable solvers for stratified Datalog.

Impact. Since its public release, SECURIFY has been extensively used by security experts to perform audits of Ethereum smart contracts. Based on their feedback, we have iteratively extended SECURIFY to support other relevant security properties and to refine the security patterns (to reduce the number of warnings issued by SECURIFY). Our finding was that SECURIFY was particularly helpful in auditing larger contracts, where existing symbolic solutions tend to achieve poor coverage. Overall, we believe SECURIFY is a pragmatic and valuable point in the space of analyzing smart contracts due to its careful balance of scalability, guarantees, and precision.

References

1. Etherdice (2016). https://etherdice.io/
2. King of ether (2016). https://github.com/kieranelby/KingOfTheEtherThrone/
3. theDAO (2016). https://etherscan.io/address/0xbb9bc244d798123fde783fcc1c72d3
   bb8c189413
4. Accidental bug may have frozen $280 million worth of digital coin ether in a cryptocurrency wallet (2017). https://www.cnbc.com/2017/11/08/accidental-bug-may-have-frozen
5. An in-depth look at the parity multisig bug (2017). http://hackxingdistributed.com/2017/07/22/deep-dive-parity-bug
6. Mythril (2018). https://github.com/ConsenSys/mythril
7. Solidity, high-level language for writing smart contracts (2018). https://solidity.readthedocs.io/en/develop/
8. Abiteboul, S., Hull, R., Vianu, V. (eds.): Foundations of Databases: The Logical Level, 1st edn. Addison-Wesley Longman Publishing Co. Inc., Boston (1995)
9. Buterin, V.: Ethereum: a next generation smart contract and decentralized application platform (2013). https://github.com/ethereum/wiki/wiki/White-Paper
10. Bylica, P.: How to find $10 m just by reading the blockchain, April 2017. https://blog.golemproject.net/how-to-find-10m-by-just-reading-blockchain-6ae9d39fcd95
11. Clarkson, M.R., Schneider, F.B.: Hyperproperties. J. Comput. Secur. **18**(6), 1157–1210 (2010)
12. Grishchenko, I., Maffei, M., Schneidewind, C.: A semantic framework for the security analysis of ethereum smart contracts. In: Bauer, L., Küsters, R. (eds.) POST 2018. LNCS, vol. 10804, pp. 243–269. Springer, Cham (2018). https://doi.org/10.1007/978-3-319-89722-6_10

13. Luu, L., Chu, D.H., Olickel, H., Saxena, P., Hobor, A.: Making smart contracts smarter. In: Proceedings of the 2016 ACM SIGSAC Conference on Computer and Communications Security, pp. 254–269. ACM (2016)
14. Tsankov, P., Dan, A., Drachsler-Cohen, D., Gervais, A., Bünzli, F., Vechev, M.: Securify: practical security analysis of smart contracts. In: CCS. ACM (2018)
15. Ullman, J.D.: Principles of Database and Knowledge-Base Systems, vol. 1 (1988)

Temporal Properties of Smart Contracts

Ilya Sergey[1,2,3]([✉]), Amrit Kumar[2,3], and Aquinas Hobor[4]

[1] University College London, London, UK
[2] Zilliqa Research, Singapore, Singapore
{ilya,amrit}@zilliqa.com
[3] Zilliqa Research, London, UK
[4] Yale-NUS College and School of Computing, NUS, Singapore, Singapore
hobor@comp.nus.edu.sg

Abstract. Smart contracts—shared stateful reactive objects stored on a blockchain—are widely employed nowadays for mediating exchanges of crypto-currency between multiple untrusted parties. Despite a lot of attention given by the formal methods community to the notion of smart contract correctness, only a few efforts targeted their *lifetime* properties. In this paper, we focus on reasoning about execution traces of smart contracts. We report on our preliminary results of mechanically verifying some of such properties by embedding a smart contract language into the Coq proof assistant. We also discuss several common scenarios, all of which require multi-step blockchain-based arbitration and thus must be implemented via stateful contracts, and discuss possible temporal specifications of the corresponding smart contract implementations.

1 Introduction

Smart contracts are stateful reactive objects that are stored on a blockchain and serve as mediators for multi-party fund-transferring computations. The last three years have seen a proliferation of smart contracts implementing various decentralised applications (Dapps) on top of the Ethereum blockchain [27]. During this period of ongoing early adoption, the smart contract technology provided by Ethereum has witnessed a number of serious hurdles, manifested by various safety and security vulnerabilities in the deployed implementations and resulting in the losses of USD millions' worth of cryptocurrency [2,9]. Since, once deployed to the blockchain, a contract's implementation cannot be amended, the challenge of identifying the contracts' "good" and "bad" behaviours at the stage of development becomes particularly acute.

In order to ensure the absence of unwelcome outcomes, it is important to be able to reason about safety and liveness of contract executions across multiple transactions and about its possible interactions with other contracts or users. One representative high-level *safety* issue, manifested in multi-transactional contract executions with oracles, is a presence of race conditions, that might leave a contract in an inconsistent state due to unaccounted multiple parties interacting with it in different moments of time, commonly happening while communicating

© Springer Nature Switzerland AG 2018
T. Margaria and B. Steffen (Eds.): ISoLA 2018, LNCS 11247, pp. 323–338, 2018.
https://doi.org/10.1007/978-3-030-03427-6_25

with external oracles [23]. Improperly incentivizing the parties taking different roles in a contract's execution might lead to denial-of-service leaving funds permanently blocked—a violation of an implicitly assumed liveness property (meaning, informally, that *eventually* the funds can be retrieved by a well-behaved party) [3,18]. Detecting such contract instances for the sake of informing the developers, *before* they are deployed, requires techniques for specifying what is considered to be *correct* contract behaviours, and whether a given implementation always adheres to this specification.

In this paper, we make an observation that many behavioural properties of smart contracts that are considered "natural" can be only captured in reference to their *multi-step executions*, by defining relations on a contract's state in different moments of time, thus, corresponding to well-studied temporal properties of programs and state-transition systems [14,21]. We substantiate this claim and demonstrate the utility of temporal reasoning in application to smart contracts by using SCILLA, a recently proposed principled programming model for representing stateful contracts as communicating state-transition systems [24], to express simplified implementations of several classes of popular Dapps. We then sketch the execution semantics of SCILLA smart contracts and use it to define the notion of contract execution traces. Using this trace-based semantics, we then state a number of temporal properties, capturing the notion of particular classes of "well-behaved" smart contracts. Finally, we report on some preliminary results of mechanising the temporal reasoning by encoding SCILLA and its semantics into Coq proof assistant [7].

In this manuscript, we do *not* attempt to design a new set of *temporal logic* connectives for specifying contract properties. Instead, we demonstrate how the natural properties of execution traces can be encoded and proved by means of shallow embedding into Coq's higher-order logic [8], leaving the formal description of the standalone temporal logic for smart contracts as our future work.

2   Overview and Motivation

Let us consider a fragment of the infamous BlockKing contract [1], taken directly from the Ethereum mainnet.[1] Its code in SOLIDITY [26] is presented in Fig. 1. This contract has been a popular testbed for several analyses for smart contracts recently, due to its flawed implementations, prone to concurrency errors [23], commutativity violations [5], and dynamically-determined resource consumption [6]. The defining feature of this contract is interaction with an off-chain oracle service Oraclize by means of calling the `oraclize_query()` function in line 303, so that an oracle can return an expected result by calling the `__callback()` function in line 306. The crux of the problematic behaviour is in the three mutable fields of the BlockKing contract: `warrior`, `warriorGold`, and `warriorBlock`, all of which, after having been set by call to `enter()` in a transaction tx_1, can be later *overriden* by a transaction tx_2 of a competing client of the same contract when executed concurrently.

---

[1] At the moment of this writing, the contract still holds approximately 0.043 ETH.

In this scenario, an oracle's response via `__callback()` might return the value for the value "meant" for the values of the fields set by tx_1 that are no longer present (since they are overriden by tx_2), whereas the sender of tx_2 will enjoy the double reward, "cashing out" both the results of its own game and also when doing so "on behalf" of tx_1 sender's.

```
293   function enter() {
294     // 100 finney = .05 ether minimum payment otherwise refund payment and stop contract
295     if (msg.value < 50 finney) {
296       msg.sender.send(msg.value);
297       return;
298     }
299     warrior = msg.sender;
300     warriorGold = msg.value;
301     warriorBlock = block.number;
302     bytes32 myid =
303       oraclize_query(0,"WolframAlpha","random number between 1 and 9");
304   }
305
306   function __callback(bytes32 myid, string result) {
307     if (msg.sender != oraclize_cbAddress()) throw;
308     randomNumber = uint(bytes(result)[0]) - 48;
309     process_payment();
310   }
311
312   function process_payment() {

        . . .

339     if (singleDigitBlock == randomNumber) {
340       rewardPercent = 50;
341       // If the payment was more than .999 ether then increase reward percentage
342       if (warriorGold > 999 finney) {
343         rewardPercent = 75;
344       }
345       king = warrior;
346       kingBlock = warriorBlock;
347     }
```

Fig. 1. Fragments of the smart contract implementing the BlockKing game.

While multiple ways to identify this problem exist, by employing either concurrency [23], resource [6] or commutativity reasoning [5], we consider this example as an opportunity to provide a "morally correct" specification to the functionality of this game-implementing contract that has to do with identifying the reward by means of taking a random input from an oracle, and transferring this reward to the corresponding player. One way to state the desired property semiformally in the style of Lamport [15] is by means of demanding certain causality between the two *events* in the contract's execution history: entering a game and executing a callback. This can be done as follows:

Property 1 (Correctness of BlockKing payment processing). Any call to `enter()` from a *sender* account a sets the value of the field `warrior` to a, so when the next call to `__callback()` by an oracle takes place, the value of `warrior` is still a.

Obviously, for the given implementation in Fig. 1 does not hold, as they can be violated in the presence of the concurrent transactions. In order to ensure this property, the contract can be fixed by, for instance, enhancing it with a *locking* discipline, prohibiting other players to enter the game before the callback is executed, with the obvious drawback of such a solution that would make the contract prone to DoS attacks. A more clever approach would require one to engineer a register of the players who currently have entered the game but have not got their payments processed.

While fixing the BlockKing contract is not the topic of this paper, this example should make apparent the importance of *temporal* properties of smart contract implementations, relating the effects of events (such as receiving requests and sending funds) taking place at certain *moments of time*, as well as the contract's state at those moments. However, even writing such temporal specification formally for Solidity or EVM contracts is far from trivial, due to (a) intricate control-flow patterns, (b) dependence of one contract's logic on another contract's state and (c) the presence of the implicit execution stack.

To address this specification challenge, we designed of a programming framework for smart contracts and an accompanying semantic formalism that separate and streamline the computation/communication aspects of contracts and allow for natural specifications and verification of safety and liveness properties.

3   The Language and Semantic Model

In order to enable formal reasoning about complex behaviour of stateful smart contracts, we designed SCILLA: a novel intermediate-level programming language for smart contracts [24]. By "intermediate" we mean that we do not expect most programmers to write in SCILLA directly, any more than most programmers write in x86 assembly directly. Instead, the typical path will be to compile a higher-level language to SCILLA and then further to an executable bytecode, very much in a tradition of optimising [20] and verified compilers [16]. SCILLA aims to achieve both *expressivity* and *tractability*, while enabling rigorous formal reasoning about contract behavior, by adopting the following fundamental design principles, based on separation of programming concerns:

Separation Between Computation and Communication. Contracts in SCILLA are structured as *communicating automata*: every in-contract computation (*e.g.*, changing its balance or computing a value of a function) is implemented as a standalone, atomic *transition*, *i.e.*, without involving any other parties. Whenever such involvement is required (*e.g.*, for transferring control to another party), a transition would end, with an explicit communication, by means of sending and receiving messages. The automata-based structure makes it possible to disentangle the contract-specific effects (*i.e.*, transitions) from blockchain-wide interactions (*i.e.*, sending/receiving funds and messages), thus providing a clean reasoning mechanism about contract composition and invariants.

Separation Between Effectful and Pure Computations. Any in-contract computation happening within a transition has to terminate, and have a predictable effect on the state of the contract and the execution. In order to achieve this, we draw inspiration from *functional programming* with effects, drawing a distinction between pure expressions (*e.g.*, expressions with primitive data types and maps), impure local state manipulations (*i.e.*, reading/writing into contract fields) and blockchain reflection (*e.g.*, reading current block number). By carefully designing semantics of interaction between pure and impure language aspects, we ensure a number of foundational properties about contract transitions, such as progress and type preservation, while also making them amenable to interactive and/or automatic verification with standalone tools.

Structuring contracts as communicating automata provides a computational model, known as *continuation-passing style* (CPS), in which every call to an external function (*i.e.*, another contract) can be done as the absolutely last instruction. That is, programming in SCILLA naturally forces the programmer to express the computations with the contract as standalone transitions, performed *atomically*, *i.e.*, without the intermediate interaction with other contracts and relying only on the received messages.

```
1   contract Crowdfunding
2   (owner      : Address,
3    max_block  : Uint32,
4    goal       : Uint32)
5
6   (* Mutable state description *)
7   field backers : Map Address Uint32 =
8       Emp {Address Uint32}
9   field funded  : Bool = False
10
11  (* Transition 1: Donating money *)
12  transition Donate
13  (sender : Address, value : Uint32,
14   tag : String)
15  (* Identifying this transition *)
16  bs ← backers;
17  blk ← & BLOCKNUMBER;
18  nxt_block = blk + 1;
19  if max_block ≤ nxt_block
20  then send {to : sender, amount : 0,
21              tag : "main",
22              msg : "deadline_passed"}
23  else
24      if not (contains(bs, sender))
25      then
26          bs1 = put(bs, sender, value);
27          backers := bs1;
28          send {to : sender, amount : 0,
29              tag : "main", msg : "ok"}
30      else
31          send {to : sender, amount : 0,
32              tag : "main",
33              msg : "already_donated"}
```

```
34  (* Transition 2: Sending the funds to the owner *)
35  transition GetFunds
36  (sender : Address, value : Uint32, tag : String)
37  blk ← & BLOCKNUMBER;
38  bal ← balance;
39  if (max_block < blk) && (sender == owner)
40  then if goal ≤ bal
41      then
42          funded := True;
43          send {to : owner, amount : bal,
44              tag : "main", msg : "funded"}
45      else send {to : owner, amount : 0,
46              tag : "main", msg : "failed"}
47  else send {to : owner, amount : 0, tag : "main",
48              msg : "too_early_to_claim_funds"}
49
50  (* Transition 3: Reclaim funds by a backer *)
51  transition Claim
52  (sender : Address, value : Uint32, tag : String)
53  blk ← & BLOCKNUMBER;
54  if blk ≤ max_block
55  then send {to : sender, amount : 0, tag : "main",
56              msg : "too_early_to_reclaim"}
57  else bs ← backers;
58      bal ← balance;
59      if (not (contains(bs, sender))) || funded ||
60          goal ≤ bal
61      then send {to : sender, amount : 0,
62              tag : "main",
63              msg : "cannot_refund"}
64      else
65          v = get(bs, sender);
66          backers := remove(bs, sender);
67          send {to : sender, amount : v, tag : "main",
68              msg : "here_is_your_money"}
```

Fig. 2. Crowdfunding contract in idealised SCILLA: state and transitions.

3.1 Syntax of Idealised Scilla

We present our examples in *idealised* SCILLA that has a richer syntax than
the original one. For instance, "vanilla" SCILLA does not feature `if-then-else`
statement, and allows for expressions only in A-Normal Form [22].[2]

Figure 2 shows a SCILLA implementation of a crowdfunding campaign à
la Kickstarter. In a crowdfunding campaign, a project owner wishes to raise
funds through donations from the community. In the specific example modelled
here, we assume that the owner wishes to run the campaign for a certain pre-
determined period of time. The owner also wishes to raise a minimum amount
of funds without which the project can not be started. The campaign is deemed
successful if the owner can raise the minimum goal. In case the campaign is
unsuccessful, the donations are returned to the project backers who contributed
during the campaign. The design of the Crowdfunding contract is intentionally
simplistic (for example, it does not allow the backers to change the amount of
their donation), yet it shows the important features of SCILLA, which we elaborate upon.

The contract is parameterised with three values that will remain immutable
during its lifetime (lines 2–4): an owner account address `owner` of type `Address`, a
maximal block number `max_block` (of type `Uint32`, isomorphic to natural numbers
bound by 32-bit depth), indicating a deadline, after which no more donations
will be accepted from backers, and a `goal` (also of type `Uint32`) indicating the
amount of funds the owner plans to raise. The `goal` is not a hard cap but rather
the minimum amount that the owner wishes to raise. What follows is the block
of mutable *field declarations* (lines 7–9). The mutable fields of the contract are
the mapping `backers` (of type `Map Address Uint32`), which will be used to keep
track of the incoming donations and is initialised with an explicitly typed empty
map literal `Emp {Address Uint32}`, and a mutable boolean flag `funded` that indicates whether the owner has already transferred the funds after the end of the
campaign (initialised with `False`). In addition to these fields, any contract in
SCILLA has an implicitly declared mutable field `balance` (initialised upon the
contract's creation), which keeps the amount of funds held by the contract.

The logic of the contract is implemented by three *transitions*: `Donate`,
`GetFunds`, and `Claim`. The first one serves for donating funds to a campaign
by external backers; the second allows the owner to transfer the funds to its
account once the campaign is ended and the goal is reached; the final one makes
it possible for the backers to reclaim their funds in the case the campaign was
not successful.

One can think of transitions as methods or functions in Solidity contracts.
What makes them different from functions, though, is the atomicity of the computation enforced at the language level. Specifically, each transition manipulates
only with the state of the contract itself, without involving any other contracts
or parties. All interaction with the external world, with respect to the contract,

---

[2] For the full specification of SCILLA syntax and runnable contract examples, please,
refer to http://scilla-lang.org.

happens either at the very start of a transition, when it is initiated by an external message, or at the end, when a message (or messages), possibly carrying some amount of funds, can be emitted and sent to other parties.

Each transition can be invoked by a suitable message, which should provide a corresponding *tag* as its component to identify which transition is triggered. It is enforced at the compile time that tags define transitions unambiguously. All other components of the message, relevant for the transition to be executed, are declared as the transition's parameters. For instance, the transition `Donate` expects the incoming message to have at least the fields `sender`, `value`, and `tag`. Each transition will only fire if an incoming message contains an explicit `tag`—a string with the contract transition's name, *e.g.*, code "Donate", which uniquely identifies the code to run upon receiving it.

Every transition's last command, in each of the execution branches, is either sending a set of messages, or simply returning. Messages are encoded as records `{...}` of name : value entries, including at least the destination address (`to`), an amount of funds transferred (`amount`) and a default tag of the function to be invoked (`tag`). All transitions of the Crowdfunding end by sending a message to either the sender of the initial request or the contract's owner. For example, depending on the state of the contract and the blockchain, the transition `GetFund` might end up in either sending a message with its balance to the contract's owner, if the campaign has succeeded and the deadline has passed, or zero funds with a corresponding text otherwise.

The state of the contract, represented by its fields, is mutable: it can be changed by the contract's transitions. A body of a transition can *read* from the fields, assigning the result to immutable stack variables using the specialised syntax x ←`f;`, where `f` is a field name and `x` is a fresh name of a local variable (*e.g.*, lines 16 and 57). In a similar vein, a body of transition can *store* a result of a pure expression e into a contract field `f` using the syntax `f := e;` (as in lines 28 and 66). The dichotomy between pure expressions (coming with corresponding binding form `x = e;` to an immutable variable `x`) and impure ("effectful") commands manipulating the field values, is introduced on purpose to facilitate logic-based verification of contracts, reasoning about the effect of a transition to the contract's state, while abstracting away from evaluation of pure expressions.

In addition to reading/writing contract state, each transition implementation can use read-only introspection on the current state of the blockchain using the "deep read" operation x ←`& BF;`, where `BF` is a name of the corresponding aspect of the underlying blockchain state, *e.g.*, `BLOCKNUMBER`—a number of the block to which the transiation is included. For example, the Crowdfunding contract reads the number of a current block in lines 17 and 37.

3.2 Semantics

We are developing SCILLA hand-in-hand with the formalisation of its semantics and its embedding into the Coq proof assistant [7].[3] We now briefly outline the

---

[3] The mechanised embedding of a subset of SCILLA into Coq is publicly available for downloads and experiments: https://github.com/ilyasergey/scilla-coq.

key components of our formalisation of the trace semantics of SCILLA contracts. We will not explain the entire syntax of our Coq encoding, for which we refer the reader to the accompanying technical report [24].

```
(* In the following definition, a contract automata C is implicit and fixed. *)
Definition step_prot (pre : cstate S) (bc : bstate) (m : message) : step :=
  let CState id bal s := pre in
  let (s', out) := apply_transition C id bal s m bc in
  let bal' := if out is Some m'
              then (bal + val m) - val m' else bal in
  let post := CState id bal' s' in
  Step pre post out.

(* Map a schedule into a trace *)
Fixpoint execute (pre : cstate S) (sc: schedule) : trace :=
  if sc is (bc, m) :: sc'
  then let stp := step_prot pre bc m in stp :: execute (post stp) sc'
  else [::].

Definition state0 := CState (acc C) (init_bal C) (init_state C).
Definition execute0 sc := if sc is _ :: _ then execute state0 sc else [:: Step state0 state0 None].
```

Fig. 3. Contract traces and semantics.

Figure 3 provides Coq definitions of a small-step operational semantics `step_prot` of a contract C by means of executing, for the contract pre-state `pre`, in the blockchain state `bc`, an applicable transition, which is uniquely determined by an incoming message `m`, via `apply_transition`, and changing the contract's state and balance accordingly. The sequence of such changes contributes for a particular *schedule* `sc` of incoming messages contributes an execution traces, as defined by the function `execute`.

3.3 Higher-Order Trace Predicates

With the operational semantics and the definition of traces at hand, we can now proceed to defining trace predicates for specifying relevant contract properties.

We first define a predicate I on a contract state (denoted, in Coq terms, by a "function type" cstate $S \rightarrow$ Prop from the type of states cstate S to propositions Prop) to be a *safety property* if it holds at any state of a contract, that can be obtained as a result of interaction between the contract and its environment, starting from the initial state. The following Coq definition states this formally:

```
Definition safe (I : cstate S → Prop) : Prop :=
  (* For any schedule sc, pre/post states and out... *)
  ∀ sc pre post out,
  (* s.t. triple Step (pre, post, out) is in the sc-induced trace *)
  Step pre post out ∈ execute0 sc →
  (* both pre and post satisfy I *)
  I pre ∧ I post.
```

A safety property means some universally true correctness condition holds at any contract's state, which is reachable from its initial configuration via *any* schedule sc. Typical examples of safety properties of interest include: "a contract's balance is always positive", "a contract's balance equals the sum of balances of its contributors", or "at any moment no money is blocked on the contract". The definition above thus defines safety by universally quantifying over *all* schedules sc, as well as step-triples Step pre post out that occur in a trace, obtained by following sc.

As the next example, let us consider a temporal connective since_as_long p q r, which means the following: once the contract is in a state st, in which (*i*) the property p is satisfied, each state st' reachable from st (*ii*) satisfies a binary property q st st' (with respect to st), as long as (*iii*) every element of the schedule sc, "leading" from st to st' satisfies a predicate r.

The corresponding Coq encoding of the since_as_long connective is given below. We first specify reachability between states st and st' via a schedule sc as the state st' being the *last* post-state in a trace obtained by executing the contract from st via sc:

```
Definition reachable (st st' : cstate S) sc :=
    st' = post (last (Step st st None) (execute st sc)).
```

We next employ the definition of reachability to define the since connective, which is parameterised by predicates p, q and r. The premises (*i*)–(*iii*) are outlined in the corresponding comments in the following Coq code:

```
(* q holds since p, as long as schedule bits satisfy r. *)
Definition since_as_long (p : cstate S → Prop)
                         (q : cstate S → cstate S → Prop)
                         (r : bstate * message → Prop) := ∀ sc st st',
    (* (i) st satisfies p *)
    p st →
    (* (ii) st' is reachable from st via sc *)
    reachable st st' sc →
    (* (iii) any element b of sc satisfies r *)
    (∀ b, b ∈ sc → r b) →
    (* (conclusion) q holds over st and st' *)
    q st st'.
```

Why this logical connective is useful for reasoning about contract correctness? As we will show further, it makes it possible to concisely express "preservation" properties relating contract balance and state, so that they hold as long as certain actions do not get triggered by some of the contract's users.

4   Specifying and Verifying Trace Properties

We now show how the combination of notions of safety and temporal properties presented in Sect. 3.3 allows us to verify a contract, proving that all its behaviours satisfy a certain complex interaction scenario.[4] Specifically, for our Crowdfunding example, let us prove that, once a donation d has been made by a backer with an

---

[4] All definitions, theorems and proofs are in the accompanying Coq development.

account address b, given that the campaign eventually fails, the backer b will be always able to get their donation d back. This can be obtained as the conjunction of the following three properties embodying both safety and temporal reasoning.

Property 1 (No leaking funds). The contract's accounted funds do not decrease unless the campaign has been funded or the deadline has expired.

In our Coq formalisation, this property can be captured via the following definition balance_backed and the accompanying safety theorem, stating that is *always* holds:

```
Definition balance_backed st : Prop :=
  (* If the campaign has not been funded... *)
  ¬ funded (state st) →
  (* the contract has enough funds to reimburse all. *)
  sumn (map snd (backers (state st))) <= balance st.
```

For an arbitrary contract state st, it asserts that if the funded flag is still false in st (*i.e.*, ¬funded (state st)), then the balance of the contract (balance st) is at least as large as the sum of all donations made by the recorded backers (sumn (map snd (backers (state st)))).

```
Theorem no_leaking_funds : safe balance_backed.
```

The second property, which is temporal and it relates several states during the contract's lifetime is informally stated as follows:

Property 2 (Donation record preservation). The contract preserves records of individual donations by backers, unless they interact with it.

To specify this property and state the corresponding theorem we rely on the temporal connective since_as_long defined above and state that, once a backer made a donation, the record of it is not going to be lost by the contract, *as long as* the backer makes no attempt to withdraw its donation.

```
(* Contribution d of a backer b is recorded in the field 'backers'. *)
Definition donated b (d : value) st := get (backers (state st)), b) == d.
```

```
(* b doesn't claim its funding back *)
Definition no_claims_from b (q : bstate * message) := sender q.2 != b.
```

```
Theorem donation_record_preservation (b : address) (d : value):
  since_as_long c (donated b d)
                 (fun _ s' ⇒ donated b d s')
                 (no_claims_from b).
```

By now we know that the contract does not lose the donated funds and keeps the backer records intact. Now we need the last piece: the proof that if a contract is not funded, and the campaign has failed (deadline has passed and the goal has not been reached), then any backer with the corresponding record can *eventually* get the donation back, hence the following property:

```
Theorem can_get_refund id b d st bc:
  (* (a) The backer b has donated d, so the contract holds
         that record in its state *)
  donated b d st →
  (* (b) The campaign has not been funded. *)
  ¬ funded (state st) →
  (* (c) Balance is small: not reached the goal. *)
  balance st < (get_goal (state st)) →
  (* (d) Block number exceeds the deadline. *)
  get_max_block (state st) < block_num bc →
  (* (conclusion) Backer b can get their donation back. *)
  ∃ (m : message),
    sender m == b ∧
    out (step_prot c st bc m) = Some (Msg d id b 0 ok_msg).
```

Fig. 4. A backer can claim back her funds if the campaign fails.

Property 3 (The backer can get refunded). If the campaign fails, the backers can eventually get their refund.

We state the property of interest as theorem `can_get_refund` in Fig. 4. As its premises (a)–(d), the theorem lists all the assumptions about the state of the contract that are necessary for getting the reimbursement. The conclusion is somewhat peculiar: it expresses the *possibility* to claim back the funds by postulating the *existence* of a message m, such that it can be sent by a backer b, and the response will be a message with precisely d funds in it, sent back to b. The theorem, whose proof is only 10 lines of Coq, formulates the property as one single-step, yet its statement can be easily shown to be a safety property, as it is, indeed, preserved by the transitions, and, after the funds are successfully claimed for the first time, the premise (a) of the statement is going to be false, hence the property will trivially hold.

Properties 1–3 deliver the desired correctness condition of a contract: *once donated money can be claimed back in the case of a failed campaign*. It is indeed not the only notion of correctness that intuitively should hold over this particular contract, and by proving it we did not ensure that the contract is "bug-free". For instance, in our study we focused on backers only, while another legit concern would be to formally verify that the contract's owner will be able transfer the cumulative donation to their account in the case if the campaign is *successful*.

5   More Temporal Properties of Common Contracts

We now show two more stateful smart contracts, which commonly occur on Ethereum blockchain, but implemented in SCILLA, informally outlining temporal properties of interest one should aim to prove over their implementations.

```
1   contract SimpleAuction(
2     auctionStart: Uint32,
3     biddingTime: Uint32,
4     beneficiary: Address
5   )
6
7   field ended: Bool = False
8   field highestBidder: Address = 0
9   field highestBid: Uint32 = 0
10  field pendingReturns : Map Address Uint32 =
11    Emp {Address Uint32}
12
13  (* Transition 1: bidding *)
14  transition Bid (sender : Address,
15    value : Uint32, tag : String)
16    blk ← & BLOCKNUMBER;
17    end = auctionStart + biddingTime;
18    after_end = end + 1;
19    e ← ended;
20    if after_end ≤ blk || e
21    then
22      send {to : sender, amount : 0,
23           tag : "main", msg : "late_to_bid"}
24    else
25      hb ← highestBid;
26      if value ≤ hb
27      then
28        send {to : sender, amount : 0,
29             tag : "main", msg : "bid_too_low"}
30      else
31        hbPrev ← highestBidder;
32        prs ← pendingReturns;
33        b = contains(prs, hbPrev);
34        prs1 = b ?
35          let pr = get(prs, hbPrev) in
36          let hs1 = pr + highestBid in
37          put(prs, hbPrev, hs1) :
38          put(prs, hbPrev, highestBid);
39        pendingReturns := prs1;
40        highestBidder := sender;
41        highestBid := value;
42        send {to : sender, amount : 0,
43             tag : "main", msg : "bid_accepted"}

44  (* Transition 2: claiming money back *)
45  transition Withdraw
46    (sender : Address,
47    value : Uint32,
48    tag : String)
49    prs ← pendingReturns;
50    b = contains(prs, hbsender);
51    if b
52    then
53      let pr = get(prs, sender) in
54      let prs1 = remove(prs, sender) in
55      pendingReturns := prs1;
56      send {to : sender, amount : pr,
57           tag : "main", msg : "take_your_money"}
58    else
59      send {to : sender, amount : 0, tag : "main",
60           msg : "nothing_to_withdraw"}
61
62  (* Transition 3: auction ends *)
63  transition AuctionEnd
64    (sender : Address,
65    value : Uint32, tag : String)
66    blk ← & BLOCKNUMBER;
67    e ← ended;
68    t1 = auctionStart + biddingTime;
69    t2 = blk ≤ t1;
70    t3 = not e;
71    t4 = t2 || t3;
72    if t4
73    then
74      send {to : sender, amount : 0,
75           tag : "main", msg : "auction_not_over"}
76    else
77      ended := True;
78      hb ← highestBid;
79      send {to : beneficiary, amount : hb,
80           tag : "main", msg : "highest_bid"}
```

Fig. 5. An Auction contract in idealised SCILLA.

5.1   Properties of Auctions

Figure 5 shows an implementation of a simple auction in SCILLA. Its parameters include the starting block `auctionStart`, a number of blocks `biddingTime` for which it is open for bidding, as well as the address of the `beneficiary`, to which the funds are going to be transferred once the bidding is closed. The mutable fields record the fact whether the auction has `ended`, the latest `highestBidder`, their `highestBid` as well as a mapping of the pending returns, to be reclaimed by bidders who no longer offer the highest bid, but have not yet been reimbursed.

The contract features three transitions. The first one, `Bid` allows anyone to bid for winning in the auction. In case of a higher new bid, the previous `highestBidder` is replaced, simultaneously getting a record in `pendingReturns`, so they could claim their overall bid amount later. The second transition `Withdraw` makes it possible for any previous bidder (who is no longer the highest one) to reclaim the amount of all their previous bids in one transfer. Finally, the transition `AuctionEnd` allows the beneficiary to receive the amount of the highest bid, once the auction has finished.

Even though we encoded this contract in SCILLA, we have *not* formalised and verified any of its properties as we did for `Crowdfunding` in the previous section.[5]

---

[5] That is, there might be bugs in the code, and we invite the reader to find them!

The goal of this smart contract programming exercise is, thus, to *formulate* the desired properties and assess their adequacy. We suggest the following temporal properties for the simple auction contract:

P1. The balance of `SimpleAuction` should be greater or equal than the sum of the `highestBid` and values of all entries in `pendingReturns`.

P2. For any account a, the value of the corresponding entry in `pendingReturns` (if present) should be equal to the sum of values of all transfers a has made during its interaction with the contract.

P3. An account a, which is not the higher bidder, should be able to retrieve the full amount of their bids from the contract, and do it *exactly* once.

Together, a combination of these properties ensure that the contract is not "prodigal", *i.e.*, does not dispense its funds frivolously to the parties who have no right to claim them, neither that it is "greedy", *i.e.*, it does not lock funds forever, so they can be always retrieved [18] (Fig. 6).

```
1   contract RockPaperScissors (
2     player1: Address,
3     player2: Address,
4     owner: Address
5   )
6
7   field p1Choice : String = ""
8   field p2Choice : String = ""
9   field payoffMatrix :
10    Map String (Map String Uint32) =
11    ... (* Omitted for brevity *)
12
13  transition choicePlayer1 (
14      sender: Address,
15      value: Uint32,
16      tag: String,
17      choice: String)
18    if let b1 = tag == "pp1" in
19      let b2 = sender == player1 in
20      b1 && b2
21    then
22      pc ← p1Choice;
23      pm ← payoffMatrix;
24      if (pc == "") && contains(pm, pc)
25      then
26        p1Choice := choice;
27        send {to : sender, amount : 0,
28             tag : "main", msg : "true"}
29      else
30        send {to : sender, amount : 0,
31             tag : "main", msg : "false"}
32    else
33      send {to : sender, amount : 0,
34           tag : "main", msg : "false"}

39  (* choicePlayer2 is similar *)
40
41  transition determineWinner (
42      sender: Address,
43      value: Uint32,
44      tag: String)
45    pm ← payoffMatrix;
46    pc1 ← p1Choice;
47    pc2 ← p2Choice;
48    if not ((pc1 == "") || (pc2 == ""))
49    then
50      let p1cm = get(pm, pc1) in
51      let winner = get(p1cm, pc2) in
52      bal ← balance;
53      if winner == 1
54      then
55        send {to : player1, amount : bal,
56             tag : "main", msg : "Congrats, P1"}
57      else
58        if winner == 2
59        then
60          send {to : player2, amount : bal,
61               tag : "main", msg : "Congrats, P2"}
62        else
63          send {to : owner, amount : bal,
64               tag : "main", msg : "Congrats, Owner"}
65    else
66      send {to : sender, amount : 0,
67           tag : "main", msg : "Not determined"}
```

Fig. 6. A simplistic Rock-Paper-Scissors contract in idealised SCILLA.

5.2   Properties of Multi-party Games

The last contract we consider implements a version of the Rock-Paper-Scissors game and is adapted from the experience report by Delmolino *et al.* [10]. To keep things simple, in this implementation, we do not address a known vulnerability allowing one of the parties to cheat, once they see a result submitted by the competition. The contract implementation is parameterised with identities of `player1` and `player2`, as well as the contract's `owner`. The `payoffMatrix` encodes the outcome of the game depending on the results submitted by both `player1` and `player2`, allowing to unambiguously determine the winner. The transition `choicePlayer1` allows Player 1 to submit their value; `choicePlayer2` is similar and is, therefore, omitted. The transition `determineWinner` can be invoked by anyone and determines a winner based on the payoff matrix with a twist: if the players submitted equal values, the award goes to the contract's owner.

What can we specify about this game? We suggest the following properties:

P1. No other party besides `player1`, `player2`, or `owner` can be awarded the prize, which is equal to the contract's balance remaining constant before then.

P2. Each player can only submit their non-trivial choice once, and this choice will have to be a key from `payoffMatrix` in order to be recorded in the corresponding contract field.

As noticed before, we cannot express a property that would prevent either player from cheating, given that the values of the fields are public, since this property would not hold for this implementation. However, we envision that in a fixed version of the contract [10], one can state it using a knowledge argument over the prefix of an execution history observed so far [12].

6   Related Work

Temporal reasoning about smart contracts has not received much attention to date, but we expect it some to become a popular research direction in the formal methods community. Our proposal on SCILLA [24] was amongst the first one to emphasize the state transition system-like nature of smart contract in order to facilitate reasoning about their behaviours, safety and temporal properties. Other programming language proposals along the same lines of thinking are BAMBOO [4] and OBSIDIAN [19]. That said, none of those languages has been used to provide a framework for formal reasoning about contract executions.

The recently presented tool FSOLIDM [17] proposes a high-level modelling framework for smart contracts based on state automata, targeting verification of automata properties at the level of a model, rather than executable code.

The importance of being able to detect smart vulnerabilities, arising in from violating safety and trace properties, has been realised in the blockchain community, and several automated tools have been recently released to tackle this challenge. Amongst the most related to the ideas we discussed here, the tool by Grossman et al. [11] implements a dynamic analysis of execution traces of smart contracts with the goal to detect DAO-like vulnerabilities [9], manifested by ill-formed reentrancy patterns [25]. ZEUS by Kalra et al. [13] checks contract source for user-defined safety properties; it does not address temporal properties, though. The closest to our proposal is MAIAN by Nikolic et al. [18]. The tool provides a static analysis for detecting bugs, violating certain trace properties, which are expressed as instance of our predicate `since_as_long` (*cf.* Sect. 3.3) for specific precondition p, side-condition r, and a postcondition q.

7   Conclusion

In this position paper we outlined some new avenues for applications of formal methods for reasoning about *temporal properties* of smart contracts. We presented a verification framework, based on the SCILLA smart contract programming language, and sketched a number of critical properties for commonly used smart contracts. We believe that our observations will stimulate research, and allow effective reuse of existing results, tools, and insights for formally specifying and verifying applications built on top of a distributed ledger.

References

1. BlockKing contract (2016). https://etherscan.io/address/0x3ad14db4e5a658d8d20 f8836deabe9d5286f79e1
2. Alois, J.: Ethereum Parity Hack May Impact ETH 500,000 or $146 Million (2017). https://www.crowdfundinsider.com/2017/11/124200-ethereum-parity-hack-may-impact-eth-500000-146-million/
3. Atzei, N., Bartoletti, M., Cimoli, T.: A survey of attacks on ethereum smart contracts (SoK). In: Maffei, M., Ryan, M. (eds.) POST 2017. LNCS, vol. 10204, pp. 164–186. Springer, Heidelberg (2017). https://doi.org/10.1007/978-3-662-54455-6_8
4. Bamboo (2017). https://github.com/pirapira/bamboo
5. Bansal, K., Koskinen, E., Tripp, O.: Automatic generation of precise and useful commutativity conditions. In: Beyer, D., Huisman, M. (eds.) TACAS 2018. LNCS, vol. 10805, pp. 115–132. Springer, Cham (2018). https://doi.org/10.1007/978-3-319-89960-2_7
6. Chen, T., Li, X., Luo, X., Zhang, X.: Under-optimized smart contracts devour your money. In: SANER, pp. 442–446. IEEE (2017)
7. Coq Development Team: The Coq Proof Assistant Reference Manual - Version 8.8 (2018). http://coq.inria.fr/
8. Coquand, T., Huet, G.P.: The calculus of constructions. Inf. Comput. **76**(2/3), 95–120 (1988)
9. del Castillo, M.: The DAO attack, 16 June 2016
10. Delmolino, K., Arnett, M., Kosba, A., Miller, A., Shi, E.: Step by step towards creating a safe smart contract: lessons and insights from a cryptocurrency lab. In: Clark, J., Meiklejohn, S., Ryan, P.Y.A., Wallach, D., Brenner, M., Rohloff, K. (eds.) FC 2016. LNCS, vol. 9604, pp. 79–94. Springer, Heidelberg (2016). https://doi.org/10.1007/978-3-662-53357-4_6
11. Grossman, S.: Online detection of effectively callback free objects with applications to smart contracts. PACMPL **2**(POPL), 48:1–48:28 (2018)
12. Halpern, J.Y., Moses, Y.: Knowledge and common knowledge in a distributed environment. J. ACM **37**(3), 549–587 (1990)
13. Kalra, S., Goel, S., Dhawan, M., Sharma, S.: ZEUS: analyzing safety of smart contracts. In: NDSS (2018)

14. Lamport, L.: "Sometime" is sometimes "not never" - on the temporal logic of programs. In: POPL, pp. 174–185. ACM Press (1980)
15. Lamport, L.: The part-time parliament. ACM TOPLAS **16**(2), 133–169 (1998)
16. Leroy, X.: Formal certification of a compiler back-end or: programming a compiler with a proof assistant. In: POPL, pp. 42–54. ACM (2006)
17. Mavridou, A., Laszka, A.: Tool demonstration: FSolidM for designing secure ethereum smart contracts. In: Bauer, L., Küsters, R. (eds.) POST 2018. LNCS, vol. 10804, pp. 270–277. Springer, Cham (2018). https://doi.org/10.1007/978-3-319-89722-6_11
18. Nikolic, I., Kolluri, A., Sergey, I., Saxena, P., Hobor, A.: Finding the greedy, prodigal, and suicidal contracts at scale. CoRR, abs/1802.06038 (2018)
19. Obsidian (2018). https://mcoblenz.github.io/Obsidian
20. Peyton Jones, S.L.: The Implementation of Functional Programming Languages. Prentice-Hall, Upper Saddle River (1987)
21. Pnueli, A.: The temporal logic of programs. In: FOCS, pp. 46–57. IEEE Computer Society (1977)
22. Sabry, A., Felleisen, M.: Reasoning about programs in continuation-passing style. Lisp Symb. Comput. **6**(3–4), 289–360 (1993)
23. Sergey, I., Hobor, A.: A concurrent perspective on smart contracts. In: 1st Workshop on Trusted Smart Contracts (2017)
24. Sergey, I., Kumar, A., Hobor, A.: Scilla: a smart contract intermediate-level language (2018). https://arxiv.org/abs/1801.00687
25. Sirer, E.G.: Reentrancy woes in smart contracts, 13 July 2016
26. Solidity: a contract-oriented, high-level language for implementing smart contracts (2018)
27. Wood, G.: Ethereum: a secure decentralised generalised transaction ledger (2014). https://ethereum.github.io/yellowpaper/paper.pdf

Temporal Aspects of Smart Contracts for Financial Derivatives

Christopher D. Clack$^{(\boxtimes)}$ and Gabriel Vanca

Centre for Blockchain Technologies, Department of Computer Science,
University College London, London, UK
clack@cs.ucl.ac.uk
http://www.cs.ucl.ac.uk/staff/C.Clack

Abstract. Implementing smart contracts to automate the performance of high-value over-the-counter (OTC) financial derivatives is a formidable challenge. Due to the regulatory framework and the scale of financial risk if a contract were to go wrong, the performance of these contracts must be enforceable in law and there is an absolute requirement that the smart contract will be faithful to the intentions of the parties as expressed in the original legal documentation. Formal methods provide an attractive route for validation and assurance, and here we present early results from an investigation of the semantics of industry-standard legal documentation for OTC derivatives. We explain the need for a formal representation that combines temporal, deontic and operational aspects, and focus on the requirements for the *temporal* aspects as derived from the legal text. The relevance of this work extends beyond OTC derivatives and is applicable to understanding the temporal semantics of a wide range of legal documentation.

Keywords: Smart contract · Distributed ledger · Finance
Semantics · Temporal

1 Introduction

Current research on smart contracts includes a range of use cases, from straightforward automation of relatively simple and relatively low-value business processes to the automation of large and complex legal agreements that have extremely high value and may last for decades. The automation of OTC derivatives contracts lies at the latter end of that range, and substantial research and development in this area have been occurring within universities, investment banks, law firms and financial services trade associations for several years.

Here we use the term *smart legal contract* to refer to a legal contract whose performance is automated on distributed ledger technology, and the term *smart contract code* to refer to the code that automates the legal contract [14]. In some related research the term *smart contract* refers only to the code, yet that definition is problematic in this context since the code itself may not be a legal

© Springer Nature Switzerland AG 2018
T. Margaria and B. Steffen (Eds.): ISoLA 2018, LNCS 11247, pp. 339–355, 2018.
https://doi.org/10.1007/978-3-030-03427-6_26

contract. There are many examples of problems with terminology when computer scientists, lawyers and banking technologists work together [4] and we therefore use a portmanteau definition of the term *smart contract* as follows [3]:

> *A smart contract is an automatable and enforceable agreement. Automatable by computer, although some parts may require human input and control. Enforceable either by legal enforcement of rights and obligations or via tamper-proof execution of computer code.*

The above definition contains key elements for automating OTC derivatives: first, the enforcement of rights and obligations by recourse to a court of law is essential because of the regulatory framework (and the scale of financial risk involved); second, the smart contract code may require human input and control, for example where the code encounters a state that requires human discretion to decide how to proceed or where it is necessary to pause and modify or cancel the code due to changes in the law.

There is an absolute requirement that the smart contract will be faithful to the intentions of the parties as expressed in the original legal documentation; hence our interest in the use of formal methods to validate the smart contract code. There is also a requirement that the processes involved in automating OTC derivatives (including the production of smart contract code and the validation of that code) align with current standardised workflow in terms of how the legal documentation is structured and negotiated. The context of our work is therefore the Smart Contract Templates project [2,3,6] which focuses on alignment with standard practice, including greater standardisation of smart contract code.

Our aim is to derive a formal semantic representation of the set of documents that comprise the legal agreement underlying each individual OTC derivatives transaction. Each transaction will be automated by a separate process (an instance of the smart contract code). Our initial examination of the documentation [4,5] has demonstrated the need for a combined semantic specification, including at least the temporal, deontic and operational aspects of the legal agreement. Once this has been achieved, there are two possible routes for validation: either (i) validation scenarios could be generated from the formal specification and used during verification and validation of the smart contract code;[1] or (ii) a semantic specification of the smart contract code could be checked against the semantics of the legal documentation (perhaps achievable automatically, at least in part).

Here we present early results from our investigation of the temporal semantics of the legal documentation for OTC derivatives.

This paper aims to be accessible not only to academics but also to practitioners such as banking techologists, lawyers, and regulators. Although we present early results from a study of the semantics of legal documentation for OTC

---

[1] For example, "what if?" scenarios might posit a sequence of actions by the parties, or possible changes in the law during the running of the code, together with the required outcome.

derivatives, our observations have much broader implications for the use of formal methods in representing the semantics of many types of legal documentation.

1.1 Standardisation of OTC Derivatives Contracts

OTC derivatives are often purchased as a mechanism for risk management so that the precise form of the purchased derivative will match the purchaser's financial exposures. These derivatives contracts can have substantial value, complexity and longevity,[2] and a firm that purchases a bespoke derivative will need legal clarity and protection relating to the terms of the agreement.

Negotiating the terms and conditions of bespoke derivatives contracts can itself be a lengthy and costly process. This complexity and cost can be improved by increasing standardisation of that process. The International Swaps and Derivatives Association (ISDA) provides a set of legal templates that are commonly used as a known basis for negotiation between counterparties. The primary template is the ISDA Master Agreement, which covers a range of derivatives from "vanilla" interest rate swaps to complex options contracts and which can be used for multicurrency and cross-border transactions.[3]

The Master Agreement contains standard clauses that are generally non-contentious. However, there is a need for customised clauses to be added, and this is achieved using a Schedule template which sets out those areas that are typically customised (and additional clauses may be added). A Credit Support Annex might also be added if the bank requires the firm to provide collateral to reduce its credit risk to the bank.

After these documents have been agreed and signed by the counterparties,[4] they constitute a single agreement and the counterparties may enter into one or more derivatives transactions based on that agreement. Each such transaction is specified using a written or electronic Confirmation document setting out the economic terms for that individual transaction, and that Confirmation document is considered to be part of the overall agreement.[5]

1.2 Smart Contract Templates

The Smart Contract Templates project [2, 3, 6] addresses the process of writing, testing and debugging the smart contract code [3] that will perform a complex OTC derivatives contract in an automated fashion on a suitable technology platform, and how to align that process with the process of using the ISDA document set. In this paper such legal agreements are called "smart OTC derivatives".

Smart Contract Templates provide standardised smart contract code "templates" for the ISDA document set (the Master Agreement, Schedule, Credit

---

[2] Derivatives contracts often last 5 years and can last as long as 30 years.

[3] There are two versions in common use: the 1992 ISDA Master Agreement and the 2002 ISDA Master Agreement.

[4] Derivatives contracts may involve more than two parties.

[5] It may also be possible to attach additional terms and conditions, including additional credit support, to individual transactions.

Suport Annex). The name "template" indicates that the code will leave some terms as yet undefined (example values may be inserted for the purposes of testing and debugging). These templates may be developed and comprehensively verified and validated in advance, and this might include different versions of the code designed to run on different technology platforms.

The workflow for Smart Contract Templates matches that for the institutional workflow as follows:

- A Smart Contract Template will have been developed, tested and debugged in advance for the standard ISDA Master Agreement and Schedule.[6]
- When two or more counterparties establish an agreement, they may negotiate modifications to the Schedule. When the negotiation is complete, a copy will be made of the existing Smart Contract Template and the smart contract code in this copy will be modified—many of the undefined terms in the template will be bound to appropriate values (e.g. the counterparty details), and depending on the extent of the modifications to the legal text, this may require a more or less substantial rewriting of the smart contract code. The overall structure of the code should remain the same, but the code is likely to require further verification and validation. This process should benefit from the fact that the previous template had already been verified and validated. The resulting modified smart contract code should accurately reflect the intentions of the parties under the agreement, but it is not yet ready to run since the parameters for individual transactions are not yet known. Hence, this is still a "template"—here we call it the "agreement template".
- For each new transaction under this agreement there will be a written or electronic Confirmation document. In the simplest case this will do no more than provide value bindings for variables (the "transaction parameters") that are currently undefined in the agreement template.
- A copy of the agreement template is made for each new transaction, and the transaction parameters for a transaction are passed as arguments to the code. Additional parameters might also be passed, for example a unique identifier that can be used to retrieve the original signed legal documents in the case of dispute. The final version of the smart contract code is then instantiated to run on a distributed ledger platform.

2   Validating Smart Contract Code for Smart OTC Derivatives

Many observers have pointed to the need for verification and validation of smart contract code [1,7,9,11]. In particular, [11] highlights five categories of verification and validation for smart contracts. Here we focus on just one of those categories, which we find to be especially problematic—Category 2 "Does the computer program correctly encode the written natural language contract?"

---

[6] For the rest of this paper we assume the 2002 ISDA document set.

Validation may be substantially more difficult than verification. Whereas verification of smart contract code may aim to eliminate error states when the code is run, validation of smart contract code aims to align the semantics of the legal documentation with the semantics of the code (e.g. does it correctly track the rights and obligations of parties, the discharging of obligations, the enforcement of prohibitions, the adherence to temporal aspects, and so on). Understanding the semantics of the legal documentation is non-trivial, since it requires specialist knowledge in the two fields of banking and law; understanding the semantics of the code is similarly non-trivial, since it requires specialist knowledge in computer science. The use of specialist terminology (including cases where common words may have specialist meanings) and implied (unspoken) knowledge has already led to misunderstandings between experts and effective validation may require investment into the training of new staff as hybrid experts in the three areas of banking, law and computer science [4,5].

We have previously stated that a formal semantic specification of the legal documentation must include at least the temporal, deontic and operational aspects of that documentation. Yet that formal specification must itself be validated to determine whether it correctly captures the meaning of the agreement. This will require an expert in law (for example to disambiguate between temporal and non-temporal uses of phrases such as "will", "pursuant to", "after giving effect to" and "after taking into account", or to distinguish between discrete and continuous periods of time as explained below), and also an expert in formal logic. This validation of the specification will be facilitated if the formal specification is similar in structure to the legal text. Three key issues arise:

1. The *separability problem*—the temporal, deontic and operational logics are closely intertwined and very difficult to separate, as explained in [4] and demonstrated further in Sect. 2.2.

2. The *isomorphism problem*—the structure of the semantic specification may be substantially different to the structure of the legal documentation, making it difficult for a specialist in law to understand and verify the semantics.[7]

3. The *canonical form problem*—there may be many different ways to structure the semantic specification for a given legal agreement; specifically there may be no unique normal form ("canonical form"), and this makes it difficult to compare two specifications to see if they are the same.[8]

To achieve the aim of using formal methods to validate smart contract code for a Smart OTC Derivative transaction it will be necessary to create a formal representation of the whole agreement, including the Master Agreement, the

---

[7] For example, a single legal clause may be represented by more than one expression in the formal semantics (perhaps distant from each other), and *vice versa* two or more legal clauses might be represented by a single expression in the formal semantics.

[8] The existence of a unique canonical form (computable in reasonable time) will depend on the logic employed, and the properties of its operators. Where many logics are combined the existence of a unique canonical form may become problematic.

Schedule and the Confirmation. The Schedule and Confirmation may include freshly drafted provisions; thus, it will be necessary not only to represent the legal phrases that exist in the ISDA document set but also to anticipate provisions and constuctions that might appear in freshly drafted legal text.

As a first step, we focus on the 2002 ISDA Master Agreement. To simplify further, we start by exploring just the temporal aspects of the ISDA Master Agreement (though, due to the *separability problem*, we also expect to touch on deontic and operational aspects), resulting in the following structured observations. These are then summarised in Sect. 3.2 as a set of requirements to guide the selection or design of a suitable temporal logic.

2.1   Continuous and Discrete Time

In the 2002 ISDA Master Agreement time is sometimes a continuous quantity, and sometimes discrete.

Continuous Time is a time interval typically used for prohibitions (e.g. a party is prohibited from doing something "at any time"), normally expressed as a range with a start and an end date, and where such a range is not expressed it may be possible to infer a range from the textual context—e.g. the term of the Agreement. Typical relevent phrases in the legal text are:

- "with effect from" may specify the start date of a continuous time range.
- "at all times until X" specifies a continuous range with end date X.
- "so long as" specifies a continuous range that persists for the duration of some other defined time span.[9]
- "to maintain in full force and effect all X" refers to a continuous-time obligation (which might alternatively be modelled as a continuous-time prohibition against doing anything that would negate any X).
- "in the future" generally refers to a time period encompassing all times after the current (according to context, the end date might be the end of the agreement or transaction, or there may be no end date).
- "will survive" generally indicates a continuous time period that continues after the end of the agreement or transaction (according to context).

Discrete Time is by contrast typically measured in days and can be expressed as a single value, an ordered set of values, or a bag of alternative values:

A Single Discrete Time Value is a date representing a day (which might be before the effective date of the agreement, during the term of the agreement, or after the termination of the agreement). Dates may be named, may be referenced via name or context (e.g. "on that date", "on such date", "the date so designated", "the date specified", "the time specified", "the date determined under Clause X"), may be compared for time ordering (e.g. "prior to", "the same day", "after" and "following"), may be counted (e.g. "X days"), that count may be given a

---

[9] Which might be the duration of an obligation.

lower or upper bound (e.g. "at least X days", "no more than Y days"), a date may be defined in relation to another date (e.g. "at least 5 days after X"), a date may be subtracted from another date to give a number of days, and a number of days may be added to or subtracted from a date to give another date.

A named date may have a value that is provided dynamically during performance of the agreement. For example, the Early Termination Date may be "designated" during performance, and a date that is "otherwise agreed" permits a date to be specifed by the parties in some other unspecified way which may be at the start of or during performance of a transaction. A date value can be tested to determine whether or not it was set in the legal text (e.g. using the phrases "is specified in" and "is not specified in"), and whether it has been set during performance of the contract ("has been designated"). Where a designated value replaces a previous value, it is necessary to retain previous values and the reason(s) for the designation(s) in order to support contractual phrases such as "where an earlier Early Termination Date has been designated", "Upon the occurrence or effective designation of", and "in the event of an Early Termination Date which is designated as the result of a Termination Event".

A discrete time value may have a number of associated properties. For example, the property "General Business Day" refers to any day on which commercial banks are open for business. The phrase "the first General Business Day after X" therefore refers to the earliest date Y such that Y occurs after X and where Y has the associated property "General Business Day".[10] Another example property could be "Designated Date" or "Designated Date Due to a Termination Event" (since the text may state that a provision holds if a date has such a property). The author is not aware of any specific discipline relating to the setting and testing of properties of time values within legal text, yet within a formal specification this would be an obvious area for checking correctness (e.g. to ensure that if a property is checked it should be set at some other point in the agreement).

In the legal text, a specified date "has occurred" if the current date (during performance of the agreement) is the same day as or after the specified date. By contrast, the legal phrase "there is" must be interpreted in context; sometimes it refers to the existence of a thing (which is not a temporal property) and at other times it may refer to the current time and may for example establish a reference date for a condition.

A Set of Discrete Time Values is a time-ordered set of discrete dates with a start date and an end date, without duplicates:

– A set may be named and may be specified with certain days missing from the set (e.g. because they lack a given associated property).
– A set may be defined in relation to a date (e.g. "all days within 5 days after X").

---

[10] The property "General Business Day" is described in a generic way so that it could potentially apply to an infinite number of dates, but a property could also be described in a way that it could apply to only a finite number of dates.

- A set of date values may be specified using a constrained universal quantifier (e.g. "all days after event X and before event Y").
- A set of specific date values may be specified using a formula representing repeated dates (e.g. "every first Monday of every month").
- A set of date values may start at the end date of an event (see Sect. 2.2) and continue until Y days later (e.g. "following event X, party A may terminate the agreement with no more than Y days notice").
- "with effect from" may (according to context) specify the start date of a discrete time period (i.e. of a set of discrete time values).

In the legal text, many phrases are used to introduce a set of discrete time values. For example:

- "notice requirement", "applicable grace period" and "applicable waiting period" generally refer to a span of days (a set of discrete time values) where the start and end dates are normally expressly stated.
- "on any day" may indicate a set of discrete dates (especially where it is followed by a qualification of the start or end dates, or both), following which each such day may be referred to using the phrase "on that day" and certain days may be excluded from consideration using a phrase such as "(in each case, other than ...)".
- "next succeeding Scheduled Settlement Date" refers to a set of possible dates (Scheduled Settlement Dates), and selects that date which immediately follows the current date.
- "the time or times specified" is a reference either to an individual date (which could be drawn from a representative bag of date values—see below) or more commonly to a set of relevant specified dates.

A Bag of Alternative Discrete Time Values is a collection of alternative dates, which may contain duplicates, and which arises from phrases that permit a thing to occur on more than one date where two or more of those dates (perhaps specified relative to different events) may be the same. For example, consider the phrase "on or as soon as reasonably practicable following X", which permits an action to occur on date "X" *or* on another date soon after "X" (see also Sect. 2.2 below for a discussion of reasonableness).

A bag of alternative discrete time values represents a single date, but the value of that date is generally only determined dynamically when the contract is performed. This introduces some complexity, since (i) prior to (or after) this date actually means prior to (or after) the date actually chosen rather than prior to (or after) the earliest (or latest) of the alternative dates, and (ii) it is not yet clear whether it might be possible to constuct nested phrases ((prior to (X or Y)) OR (following (P or Q))) and so on. This needs further attention.

2.2   Temporal Aspects of Events, Obligations and Rights

Events (an operational aspect of the agreement), obligations (a deontic aspect of the agreement) and rights, powers or privileges (also deontic aspects) all have associated temporal properties. Thus, it is extremely difficult to separate temporal aspects from deontic and operational aspects (this is the aforementioned *separability problem*).

Events each have a start date and an end date (to support phrases such as "has occurred", "is continuing", and "has ceased", which can also appear in logical conjunction such as "has occurred and is continuing"). The concept of an event can be used quite generally and may include for example (i) actions, such as the giving of notices; (ii) external events, such as the obtaining of judgement on an aspect of the agreement; and (iii) contract states, such as a party being in default, or a failure (e.g. to pay or to deliver). Thus, events may be specified within the agreement, or may be created during the modelling process in order to construct the formal specification.

Any action that has an associated time could be an event, including passive actions such as becoming aware of a fact. For example the phrases "upon becoming aware of" and "when the obligation is ascertained" indicate that becoming aware and ascertaining are events with an associated time. The phrase "the date of the information" may according to context refer to the date of sending or receiving information, both of which are actions.[11]

Defined events may or may not occur during the performance of the agreement. Events also have other associated properties—e.g. "an event of default"—and there may be a total or partial ordering relationship applicable to events (though this is outside the scope of this paper).

In the legal text, a large number of phrases are used to link temporal properties with events. For example:

– "as of the time immediately preceding" or "immediately before" an event X normally means the day before the start date of event X.
– "immediately" normally means either the same day as, or the next day following, the occurrence of an event.
– If an event X "occurs prior to" event Y this is generally taken to mean that the end date of X is prior to the start date of Y.
– "in such event" generally refers to the immediately preceding named event.
– "the occurrence of", "the date as of" and "at such time of being" each refers to an event and may according to context refer to the start date of an event or end date of an event or to the existence of a start date or end date for an event, and must be determined precisely from context.
– "at such time of being" is the time at which an event occurs.
– "upon reasonable demand" specifies the time of an event (a demand) with the proviso that the demand must be reasonable (which may have a temporal aspect such as occurring within or at a reasonable time).
– A "potential event of X" is an event which might become an event with property X (e.g. default) due to further events or the lapse of time.

---

[11] Conceivably this phrase might be used to refer to a date associated with a document, which raises the further issue of associating objects with temporal values.

- An event "would occur" as a result of some action if the action (e.g. performing an obligation, or entering into an agreement) would necessarily lead to the occurrence of the event. This may be difficult to model, e.g. where the action or event is external to the agreement and in one possible future.[12] Similar problems occur with phrases such as "would have been" or "would have been ... if it were not for ...".
- "has taken action X" could be represented by modelling that action as an event (thus it would have a start date and an end date, which are set dynamically during performance of the contract, and which may be the same). If the end date of that event is before the current date (or other reference time according to context) then "has taken action X" would be true.
- "for so long as that is the case" and "for so long as the relevant event or circumstance continues to exist" may both refer to an event, especially where a circumstance or the duration of a conditional can be modelled as an event (for example, given a phrase such as "for so long as the party is unable to receive delivery" would imply that being unable to receive deliery should be modelled as an event with start and end dates).

Applicable law and applicable corporate policies might also be modelled as events in order to support phrases such as "any applicable law ... then in effect", "party's policies in effect at that time"—however, since there might be a very large number of such laws and policies, it might be better to replace such a provision with a call for human input to establish whether the stated condition (relating to law or policy) holds.

It is also important to note that sometimes the word "event" is not intended to refer to a thing that happens during performance of the contract, but rather to the specification of the contract itself and refers instead to the over-riding of one provision by another. For example, the phrase "in the event of any inconsistency" is generally used to refer to an inconsistency between provisions of the agreement rather than a date during the performance of that agreement, and is followed by an indication of which provision should prevail over the other.

Less straightforward references to the temporal aspects of actions and events include the adverbs "timely" and "promptly". These phrases rely on a court of law to apply a post-hoc test of reasonableness. Similar phrases include "as soon as is reasonably practicable" and "as soon as practicable". For the purposes of validation, these adverbial phrases could be set to a global value such as "within 1 day" or "within 2 Local Business Days" (i.e. a set of discrete time values) during simulation of contract performance, to determine the extent to which the agreement might be sensitive to variations in such ambiguous time periods.

Obligations have a start date when the obligation is incurred, a due date, and a discharged date (if the discharged date is after the due date a sanction may be applied). They also have (i) an optional end date at which point the obligation is

---

[12] In the context of the ISDA Master Agreement it might sometimes be preferable to phrase this as a continuous prohibition to engage in an event that generates a Potential Event of Default or Potential Termination Event.

automatically discharged if not previously discharged, and (ii) an ordered set of zero or more "revised due date(s)" (used when an obligation has been deferred or accelerated). It is noted that the triggering of an obligation might also itself constitute an event.

The specification of repeated obligations may require an action to occur "at least X times", "no more than Y times" or "at least X times but no more than Y times" within a certain time interval. Whilst the time interval itself can be expressed as a set, the specification of repeated occurrences is not really a temporal matter. It is an example of how an obligation (deontic aspect) can be linked to repeated actions (operational aspect) within a defined time interval (temporal aspect).

In the legal text, example phrases that link temporal properties with obligations include:

- "the due date" and "when due" both refer to the due date of an obligation.
- "the last payment date" or "the last exchange date" may according to context refer to either (i) the most recent such discharged date (e.g. the date of the most recently made payment), or (ii) from a set of due dates of such obligations to pay or exchange, the date that is latest.
- "satisfying a liability" is generally a synonym for "discharging an obligation". A party "has satisfied" some obligation (e.g. either to another party or to pay tax to an external body) if the current time is after the time that such obligation was discharged. Note that obligations to external bodies may not be precisley expressed in the legal text and may need to be inferred from a provision that refers to the discharge of such an obligation.
- "will be deferred to, and will not be due until" means the dynamic update of an obligation so that its revised due date is set to the stated value.

Rights, Powers and Privileges may apply throughout continuous time, or might become activated by the occurrence of a date or an event. On the occurrence of such a date or event it will be necessary to record that the associated right, power or privilege has been activated, and then also to record the date at which such right, power or privilege was exercised in relation to that date or event. This supports phrases that refer to a delay in exercising a right, power or privilege. Since a triggering event might occur many times, the activation time and exercise time should be recorded in each case.

3   Temporal Representation

Hvitved [8] provides a review of semantic techniques to support formal representation of legal agreements. Our aim is to utilize a formal representation that can combine at least the deontic, temporal and operational aspects of standardised OTC derivatives contracts, and of those technques surveyed by Hvitved the most attractive candidate is the technique developed by Lee [10]. However Lee's representation of temporal aspects needs to be expanded to cover the complexity demonstrated above. Here we briefly discuss Lee's temporal framework and then set out an initial set of requirements for extending the framework.

3.1   Temporal Logic in Lee's Framework

The Rescher and Urquhart temporal logic system [13] is the basis for representing temporal aspects in Lee's framework. Lee calls this the "RU calculus" and explores and extends the use of this system. Pithadia [12] provides an initial critical assessment of Lee's framework.

The Rescher and Urquhart System is based on the temporal operator $R_t\Phi$ that denotes Φ (a formula in conventional first order logic with identity) being realized at time t. Lee rehearses the axioms for R, the total ordering relational operator U, a function $f :: Time \rightarrow \mathbb{R}$, and temporal addition $\oplus$, as follows:

$$R_t(\neg\Phi) \leftrightarrow \neg R_t\Phi$$

$$R_t(\Phi \& \Psi) \leftrightarrow R_t\Phi \& R_t\Psi$$

$$R_{t'}(\forall t\Phi) \leftrightarrow \forall t R_{t'}\Phi$$

$$U_{tt'} \ \ indicates\ that\ time\ t\ precedes\ time\ t'$$

$$f(t \oplus t') = f(t) + f(t')$$

Lee modifies the RU calculus by introducing the day as the basic unit of time and by introducing the concept of time intervals where $SPAN(d, d')$ defines a time span from the beginning of date d to the end of date d', $BEG(d)$ gives the beginning date of a time interval, and $END(d)$ gives the end date of a time interval. Two operations are introduced on time intervals (using Lee's notation, where d is a time interval):

$$RD_d\Phi \leftrightarrow \exists t(t \in d) \& R_t\Phi$$

$$RT_d\Phi \leftrightarrow \forall t(t \in d) \implies R_t\Phi$$

Thus $RD_d\Phi$ indicates that Φ is realized at least once during the time interval d and $RT_d\Phi$ indicates that Φ is realized throughout time interval d. A further operator $RB_D\Phi$ indicates that Φ is realized before day D and is defined in terms of the RD operator using an arbitrary undefined day in the past, which Lee denotes as "_" and we interpret as a "bottom" element "$\perp$":

$$RB_D\Phi = RD_{SPAN(\perp,D)}\Phi$$

Lee further observes that a calendar of dates is an interval scale with no obvious value of "zero" and therefore addition is more complex than represented in the RU calculus; he redefines the operator $\oplus$ to take a date d and a number of days n and return the date that is n days later than d, as follows (where D is the unit "days"):

$$d \oplus nD$$

Lee's Temporal Framework has a number of limitations in the context of smart OTC derivatives, In overview, the most obvious shortcomings are (i) the inability to specify or reason about continuous time; (ii) the inability to specify dates with different properties (such as "Business Day"); and (iii) the inability to specify concisely a set of times with subtle membership rules (such as "the first Friday of every month"). Lee's time intervals provide an implementation of sets (and possibly bags, depending on context) but it is very difficult to specify a time interval with specific dates missing. Whilst it is possible to use a combination of RU calculus operators and Lee's operators to represent phrases such as "action X occurs Y days after event Z" (which could for example be represented as $R_t Z \& (R_{t \oplus Y} X)$), it is difficult to express a provision such as "payments made at a weekend will be processed on the first Business Day of the following week".

Lee's temporal framework could be modified and extended, or could be replaced. However, it is not sufficient to make such a decision based only on an analysis of the temporal aspects. The great advantage of Lee's framework is the way that it combines deontic, operational and temporal aspects. We therefore eschew construction of a formal temporal logic until analysis of the deontic and operational aspects of the ISDA Master Agreement has been conducted. Instead, we provide an initial outline of requirements in the following section.

3.2   Initial Requirements for the Temporal Aspects of a Semantic Framework

Given the *separability problem* relating to the very close coupling between temporal, deontic and operational aspects of legal documents, it is unlikely that a separate temporal logic would be appropriate for formal modelling of smart OTC derivatives. In most cases time is a *property* of deontic and operational aspects (the current time is a notable exception to this observation). However, we can summarise our investigation of the ISDA Master Agreement by setting out some guideline requirements for the expressibility of the temporal parts of the combined logic, as follows:

Requirements for Continuous Time Intervals. It must be possible to express intervals of continuous time with a start and end point denoted by a discrete time value. In general, we would wish to support the following operations:

- create a new continuous time interval with discrete time values for the start and end points (if the end-points are defined to be *outside* the interval, this would give a straightforward representation of an "empty" interval as being one where the start and end points are the same, and it would not be an error to request the start or end point of an empty interval);
- bind a name to an interval;
- create an aggregate collection of intervals (this is one way to implement a union of non-overlapping intervals, since we cannot have an interval result containing gaps);
- get the start or end point of an interval;
- get the intersection of two intervals (perhaps returning an "empty" interval);
- test whether a discrete time value is before the start of such an interval; and

– test whether a discrete time value is after the end of such an interval.

Although in some legal prose a period of continuous time might have a start point that is infinitely in the past (which we denote $T_{-\infty}$), or an end point that is infinitely in the future (which we denote T_{∞}), it is not yet clear whether this is essential or merely lazy drafting. It is an open question as to whether the temporal logic should support such "extreme" values for start and end points of continuous time intervals (nor whether they might be useful for other purposes).

Requirements for Single Discrete Time Values. It must be possible to express single discrete time values, to associate *properties* with a single discrete time value, to keep a history of updates to the time value that is bound to a name, to calculate differences between two dates as a number of days, and to create and use date expressions (including the use of days as relative offset values).

In general, we would wish to support the following operations:

– create a new single discrete time value;
– provide the special single discrete time value that is the *current time*;
– bind a name to a historical list of single discrete time values (and with each such value record when it was bound, who by, why, whether it was bound in the text or during performance, and perhaps some further properties);
– perhaps provide the extreme values $T_{-\infty}$ and T_{∞} mentioned above and to test whether a single discrete time value is one of these two extreme values;
– increment a discrete time value by one day;
– decrement a discrete time value by one day;
– get the difference in days between two discrete time values (though this deserves more attention, since we may need to calculate the number of days with a specified property - e.g. Business Days);
– associate a set of properties with a discrete time value and test a discrete time value to see if it has a stated property;
– apply a predicate to a discrete time value to see if it passes or fails a test;
– provide equality and relational operators to use on two dates;
– create and use date expressions combining any of the above operations.

Requirements for Sets or Bags of Discrete Time Values. It must be possible to express a set or bag of discrete time values where a set or bag has a start and end date and a (possibly discontinuous) collection of valid dates between the start and end dates. It must also be possible to define the members of the set or bag using a generator expression. As with continuous time intervals, if the start and end dates are defined to be *outside* the set or bag this would give a straightforward representation of an "empty" set or bag as being one where the start and end points are the same, and it would not be an error to request the start or end point of an empty set or bag.

In general, we would wish to support the following operations:

- create a new set or bag of discrete time values;
- get the start date or end date of a set or bag;
- test whether a given date is a member of the set or bag;
- get the intersection of two sets or bags, returning a set or bag respectively (which might be empty);
- get the union of two sets or bags, returning a set or bag respectively;
- test whether two sets or two bags are equal;
- bind a name to a set or bag;
- apply a filter to a set or bag, to produce a set or bag (respectively) that may be smaller or equal in size;

3.3 Temporal Requirements Relating to Deontic and Operational Aspects

Each event must have a start date and an end date. In the legal text, it is possible that these dates might be specified in relation to some other dates or as a set or bag of possible dates. However, once the event has started any previous "possible" start time must be updated with the actual start time (and similarly for the end time). Thus when using a temporal logic operator such as $R_t E$ (where E is an event) it is necessary to disambiguate between the "realisation" of the possible and actual start of the event E and the "realisation" of the possible and actual end of that event.

As explained in Sect. 2.2, each obligation has a start date, an optional end date, a due date, and a discharged date. Thus when using a temporal logic operator such as $R_t \Phi$ (where Φ is an obligation) it is necessary to disambiguate between the realisation of the incurring of the obligation, the passing of the end date, the passing of the due date without discharge, or the realisation of the discharge of the obligation. Similarly, rights, powers and privileges have activation times and (perhaps multiple) exercise times and these must be disambiguated.

Where deontic or operational aspects may be repeated a set, minimum, or maximum number of times, there must be a mechanism to express these repetitions.

4   Summary and Conclusion

The legal language used to draft standardised contracts for OTC derivatives is rich and complex. Yet it is essential to have a full and formal understanding of the semantics of the legal documentation in order to validate the associated smart contract code. Here we have presented initial results from an analysis of the temporal language used in the 2002 ISDA Master Agreement for OTC derivatives.

When a formal semantic description of the legal documentation is constructed, it must specify not only the temporal semantics but also the semantics of (at least) the deontic and operational aspects. The *separability problem*—the fact that the temporal, deontic and operational logics are closely interwined—requires a combined logical framework. The results of an analysis of the temporal language used in legal documentation are therefore presented as a set of initial requirements. More work is required to analyse the deontic and operational language, each of which will lead to its own set of requirements. Our final aim is to combine these into a single semantic framework. This is a formidable challenge, yet we envisage that such a framework will be applicable not only to the automation of OTC derivatives but also to the formal understanding of a wide range of legal contracts and statutes.

Acknowledgements. The authors are grateful to UCL students Justin Jude and Mengyang Wu who assisted this work by reviewing logic frameworks and providing supporting tools.

References

1. Al Khalil, F., Ceci, M., O'Brien, L., Butler, T.: A solution for the problems of translation and transparency in smart contracts. Technical report, Government Risk and Compliance Technology Centre (2017). http://www.grctc.com/wp-content/uploads/2017/06/GRCTC-Smart-Contracts-White-Paper-2017.pdf. Accessed 31 Aug 2017
2. Braine, L.: Barclays' smart contract templates. Barclays London Accelerator (2016). https://vimeo.com/168844103/. http://www.ibtimes.co.uk/barclays-smart-contract-templates-heralds-first-ever-public-demo-r3s-corda-platform-1555329/
3. Clack, C.D., Bakshi, V.A., Braine, L.: Smart contract templates: foundations, design landscape and research directions. The Computing Research Repository (CoRR) abs/1608.00771 (2016). http://arxiv.org/abs/1608.00771/
4. Clack, C.D.: Smart contract templates: the semantics of smart legal agreements. In: The Third R3 Smart Contract Templates Summit (2017). https://www.r3.com/slides/third-smart-contract-templates-summit-slides.pdf. Accessed 29 Mar 2018
5. Clack, C.: Smart contract templates: the semantics of smart legal agreements. J. Digit. Bank. **2**(4), 1–15 (2018)
6. Clack, C.D., Bakshi, V.A., Braine, L.: Smart contract templates: essential requirements and design options (2016). https://arxiv.org/abs/1612.04496/
7. Harley, B.: Are smart contracts contracts? Technical report, Clifford Chance (2017). https://www.cliffordchance.com/briefings/2017/08/are_smart_contractscontracts.html. Accessed 31 Aug 2017
8. Hvitved, T.: Contract formalisation and modular implementation of domain-specific languages. Ph.D. thesis, Department of Computer Science, University of Copenhagen (2012). http://www.diku.dk/hjemmesider/ansatte/hvitved/publications/hvitved12phd.pdf
9. ISDA and Linklaters: Smart contracts and distributed ledger – a legal perspective (2017). https://www.isda.org/a/6EKDE/smart-contracts-and-distributed-ledger-a-legal-perspective.pdf. Accessed 31 Aug 2017
10. Lee, R.M.: A logic model for electronic contracting. Decis. Support. Syst. **4**, 27–44 (1988)
11. Magazzeni, D., McBurney, P., Nash, W.: Validation and verification of smart contracts: a research agenda. IEEE Comput. J. **50**(9), 50–57 (2017). Special Issue on Blockchain Technology for Finance
12. Pithadia, H.J.: Capturing language semantics of smart contracts. Master's thesis, Department of Computer Science, UCL (2016)

13. Rescher, N., Urquhart, A.: Temporal Logic. Springer, Wien (1971). https://doi. org/10.1007/978-3-7091-7664-1
14. Stark, J.: Making sense of blockchain smart contracts (2016). http://www. coindesk.com/makingsense-smart-contracts/. Accessed 20 June 2016

Marlowe: Financial Contracts on Blockchain

Pablo Lamela Seijas🆔 and Simon Thompson(✉)🆔

School of Computing, University of Kent, Canterbury, UK
{p.lamela-seijas,s.j.thompson}@kent.ac.uk

Abstract. Blockchains allow the specification of contracts in the form of programs that guarantee their fulfilment. Nevertheless, errors in those programs can cause important, and often irretrievable, monetary loss. General-purpose languages provide a platform on which contracts can be built, but by their very generality they have the potential to exhibit behaviours of an unpredictable kind, and are also not easy to read or comprehend for general users.

An alternative solution is provided by domain-specific languages (DSLs), which are designed to express programs in a particular field. This paper explores the design of one DSL, Marlowe, targeted at the execution of financial contracts in the style of Peyton Jones *et al.* on blockchains. We present an executable semantics of Marlowe in Haskell, an example of Marlowe in practice, and describe the Meadow tool that allows users to interact in-browser with simulations of Marlowe contracts.

1 Introduction

This paper explores the design of a domain specific language, Marlowe,[1,2] targeted at the execution of financial contracts in the style of Peyton Jones, Eber and Seward [16] on blockchains. In doing this, we are required to refine the model of contracts in a number of ways in order to fit with a radically different context.

Consider the following example of an "escrow" contract so that we can explain the motivation more concretely. The aim of this contract, written in functional pseudocode in the style of [16] involves three participants: alice, bob and carol. alice is to pay an amount of money to bob on receipt of goods from her. alice pays the money into escrow controlled by carol.

There are two options for the money: if two out of the three participants agree to pay it to bob, that goes ahead; if, on the other hand, two of the participants opt to refund the money to alice, that is done instead.

This work is part of the Cardano project and is supported by IOHK, https://iohk.io.

[1] Named after Christopher Marlowe, the Elizabethan poet, dramatist and spy, who was born and educated in Canterbury, en.wikipedia.org/wiki/Christopher_Marlowe.

[2] Marlowe is available from https://github.com/input-output-hk/scdsl.

T. Margaria and B. Steffen (Eds.): ISoLA 2018, LNCS 11247, pp. 356–375, 2018.
https://doi.org/10.1007/978-3-030-03427-6_27

The outer primitive When waits until the condition – its first argument – becomes true; in this case, the condition is that either two participants choose refund or two participants choose pay. The second argument of the When is itself another Contract, which is performed after the condition of the When has been met, and it makes the payment if two participants chose pay, otherwise it redeems previous money commitments.

```
(When (Or (two_chose alice bob carol refund)
          (two_chose alice bob carol pay))
      (Choice (two_chose alice bob carol pay)
              (Pay alice bob AvailableMoney)
              redeem_original))
```

We discuss this particular example in more detail in Marlowe in Sect. 3 below; but it already gives us an example of how traditional contracts are fundamentally different from contracts that are meant to be run on top of the blockchain. In the traditional model, enforcement of the contract is the responsibility of the legal system. If alice does not pay the money into escrow, or carol chooses to keep it for herself, then they can be sued for the money (and probably damages), thus providing both legal and financial incentives for compliance. On the other hand, in the decentralised blockchain model, where there is no central authority, the contract needs to be enforced *by design*.

This means that we must require participants to *commit* money to cover all possible expenditure *in advance of the contract executing*. In order to make sure that participants continue to engage with a contract, we ensure urgency by imposing *timeouts*: money is committed for a finite period only. We also impose a timeout when waiting for a participant to make a commitment to ensure that the contract does not become stuck even if one of the participants stops interacting with it.

We make the following contributions in this paper.

- Designing a DSL for financial contracts on blockchains: Marlowe.
- Defining an executable, small-step semantics of Marlowe in Haskell.
- Making Marlowe an embedded DSL in Haskell. This extends the expressibility of the language, as we can use all the facilities of Haskell in defining Marlowe contracts; we achieve this by defining Marlowe as a Haskell data type.
- Developing the Meadow tool that allows users to interact with and simulate the operation of Marlowe contracts and embedded Marlowe contracts.

Having established this model and its semantics we are able to do a number of other things, which we discuss in the paper. We can explore how the language will be implemented on an existing blockchain, such as Cardano, and our model has shown us that we will need to consider how the evolution of a contract interacts with the blockchain, with miners in the case of a 'proof of work'-based chain, and with users participating in contract execution. We can also perform analyses of Marlowe contracts, based on its formal semantics.

In designing a language like Marlowe we are constrained by the blockchain domain, but within that we do have a range of choices. For example, should we

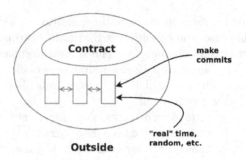

Fig. 1. The context for a contract

base the language on a system with accounts, like Ethereum, or a UTxO-based model as used by bitcoin? We examine this and other choices after introducing the language and examples of its use.

The paper begins in Sect. 2 by introducing the Marlowe model, including the assumptions made in designing it, the types of the principal functions and a description of the DSL as an algebraic type, constructor by constructor. Section 3 revisits the escrow example, and shows how it is described using a combination of Marlowe and Haskell constructs: that is, we use Marlowe as an embedded DSL. Section 4 introduces Meadow, our tool for visualising and interacting with Marlowe contracts. Section 5.1 reflects on the design rationale for Marlowe, showing how it can be supported on a variety of blockchains, and Sect. 5.2 explores how Marlowe can be implemented. Section 6 surveys related work and Sect. 7 enumerates the next steps for the project after drawing some conclusions.

2   The Marlowe Model

The Marlowe domain-specific language (DSL) is modelled as an algebraic type in Haskell, together with an executable small-step semantics. We start by looking at the different types used by the model, and the assumptions about the infrastructure in which contracts will be run. We then we look at the `Contract` DSL itself, and finally we give its semantics in Haskell. Section 3 revisits the "escrow" example using the embedding of Marlowe as a DSL in Haskell.

2.1   The Model Types

A running contract interacts with its environment in two ways, as in Fig. 1.

Observables. First, it will need to observe different kinds of varying quantities including, for example, the current time, the current block number and, random numbers, as well as "real world" quantities like "the price of oil" or "the exchange rate between currencies A and B". As the examples illustrate, observables come both from aspects of the blockchain (e.g. the current block number) and externally. In the latter case, it will be necessary to agree a trusted oracle or beacon giving the value.

Each instance of such an observable will be observed at a particular time and in a particular context. We assume that the system infrastructure ensures that these values are recorded on the blockchain to allow the computation to be repeated for verification purposes.

It is assumed that at each step of the execution of the contract, the values of observables will be available if needed, and these values are (together) given by a value of type OS (for "observable set"), where individual observations are described in a "little language" for that purpose: Observation. Note that these values are not determined by the participants in the contract, but rather by the external environment in which the contract is run.

Inputs and Commitments. On the other hand, at each step there are – potentially, at least – a variety of inputs available from the participants themselves. These include commitments of currency (or "cash"), redemption of commitments, and claims of payments by a participant. Moreover, it is also possible for a participant to input an arbitrary value (which we term a "choice"). The particular inputs at a given step are described by a value of type Input.

While informally we might see a commitment to something as being indefinite, it is important to realise that, on blockchain, a commitment needs to have a timeout so that progress can be forced in a contract. After the timeout period the cash can be refunded through the user creating a transaction to reclaim the cash. Information about the commitments currently in force forms the State, which can be modified at each execution step.

Actions. Payments can be granted by using committed money, but they must be manually redeemed by the recipient, in the same way that cash commitments are redeemed when they expire. The effects of the contract in the blockchain are represented by a list AS of Actions that is derived from the execution of each step of the semantics.

Infrastructure. The model makes a number of assumptions about the blockchain infrastructure in which it is run.

 - It is assumed that cryptographic functions and operations are provided by a layer external to the system, and so they need not be modelled explicitly.
 - We assume that time is "coarse grained" and measured by block number, so that, in particular, timeouts are delimited using block numbers.
 - Making a commitment is not something that a contract can perform; rather, it can request that a commitment is made, but that then has to be established externally: hence the input of (a set of) commitments at each step.
 - The model manages the release of funds back to the committer when a cash commitment expires (see discussion of the stepBlock function below).

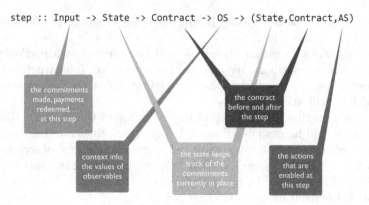

Fig. 2. The `step` function

Computation. Computation is modelled at two different levels.

The `step` function represents a *single computation step* and has this type:

`step :: Input -> State -> Contract -> OS -> (State,Contract,AS)`

which is also illustrated in Fig. 2. The `step` function is total, so that for every contract a result of stepping is defined. However, for some kinds of contracts – commits, redeems or time-shifted contracts – it is possible that performing a step produces the same contract as the result; we call these *quiescent* steps whereas all others *make progress*. We use this distinction in the explanation that follows.

Execution of a contract will involve multiple blocks, with multiple steps in each block. The computation at a single block is given by the `stepBlock` function: this will call the `stepAll` function that calls `step` repeatedly until it is quiescent.

In addition to calling `stepAll`, `stepBlock` will first enable expired cash commitments to be refunded and record, in the state, any choices made at that step. The functions `stepAll` and `stepBlock` have the same type as `step` itself.

2.2   The Contract Type

The type of contracts is given by the following Haskell data type:

```
data Contract =
    Null |
    CommitCash IdentCC Person Money Timeout Timeout Contract Contract |
    RedeemCC IdentCC Contract |
    Pay IdentPay Person Person Money Timeout Contract |
    Both Contract Contract |
    Choice Observation Contract Contract |
    When Observation Timeout Contract Contract
```

Informally, this type provides a `Null` contract, which does nothing. The next three constructs form contracts that do something, and then continue according to another contract (which is one of the components of the original contract). `CommitCash` will wait for a participant to make a commitment, `RedeemCC` allows for a commitment to be redeemed, and `Pay` for a payment between participants to be claimed by the recipient.

The remaining constructors form composite contracts from simpler components: `Both` has the behaviour of both its components, `Choice` chooses between two contracts on the basis of an observation, and `When` is quiescent until a condition – i.e. an `Observation` – becomes true.

Additionally, many of the contracts have timeouts that also determine their behaviour.

2.3 The `step` Function

In this section, we explain the detailed behaviour of contracts by describing how the `step` function operates on each of the constructors of the `Contract` type.

- `Null` is the null contract; it will always be quiescent:

$$\text{step \_ st Null \_ = (st, Null, [])}$$

- `CommitCash ident person val start_timeout end_timeout con1 con2`
  For this contract to make progress,
  - either, before the timeout `start_timeout`, the user `person` makes a cash commitment of value `val` and timeout `end_timeout` with the identifier `ident`,
  - or the timeout `start_timeout` is exceed:

```
step
  commits
  st
  c@(CommitCash ident person val start_timeout end_timeout con1 con2)
  os
  | cexe || cexs = (st {sc = ust}, con2, [])
  | Set.member (CC ident person cval end_timeout) (cc commits)
       = (st {sc = ust}, con1, [SuccessfulCommit ident person cval])
  | otherwise = (st, c, [])
  where ccs = sc st
        cexs = expired (blockNumber os) start_timeout
        cexe = expired (blockNumber os) end_timeout
        cns = (person, if cexe || cexs
                       then ManuallyRedeemed
                       else NotRedeemed cval end_timeout)
        ust = Map.insert ident cns ccs
        cval = evalMoney st val
```

In the first case, a `SuccessfulCommit` action is generated and the contract continues as `con1`; in the second case no action is generated and the contract continues as `con2`. While neither case holds, the contract is quiescent, waiting for the cash to be committed.

If the cash is committed successfully and the timeout `end_timeout` is reached, then it is impossible to further spend the committed cash, and any unspent funds can be reclaimed by `person`. This is enforced by the `stepBlock` function, as noted above.

- `RedeemCC ident con` (`CC` stands for cash commitment.) For this contract to make progress, the creator of the cash commitment with identifier `ident` is allowed to redeem the unspent funds in that commitment; the contract then continues as `con`, and the action `CommitRedeemed` is produced.

```
step commits st c@(RedeemCC ident con) _ =
    case Map.lookup ident ccs of
      Just (person, NotRedeemed val _) ->
        let newstate =
                  st {sc = Map.insert ident (person, ManuallyRedeemed) ccs} in
        if Set.member (RC ident person val) (rc commits)
        then (newstate, con, [CommitRedeemed ident person val])
        else (st, c, [])
      Just (person, ManuallyRedeemed) ->
        (st, con, [DuplicateRedeem ident person])
      Nothing -> (st,c,[])
    where
      ccs = sc st
```

Committed cash can only be redeemed once, and an attempt to redeem it a second time will produce a `DuplicateRedeem` action, continuing as `con`.

If the cash commitment with identifier `ident` has expired, it becomes possible for the remaining funds to be redeemed by the committer; this can be done by the `stepBlock` function processing the appropriate `Input`, and an `ExpiredCommitRedeemed` action will be produced.

Once the commitment `ident` has expired and is redeemed, a `RedeemCC` contract will immediately evolve to `con`.

- `Pay idpay from to val expi con` makes it possible, assuming that sufficient funds are available, for `to` to claim a payment with id `idpay` of `val` from `from` before the timeout `expi`. The contract continues as `con`.

```
step inp st c@(Pay idpay from to val expi con) os
  | expired (blockNumber os) expi = (st, con, [ExpiredPay idpay from to cval])
  | right_claim =
    if ((committed st from bn >= cval) && (cval >= 0))
      then (newstate, con, [SuccessfulPay idpay from to cval])
      else (st, con, [FailedPay idpay from to cval])
  | otherwise = (st, c, [])
  where
    cval = evalMoney st val
    newstate = stateUpdate st from to bn cval
    bn = blockNumber os
    right_claim =
      case Map.lookup (idpay, to) (rp inp) of
        Just claimed_val -> claimed_val == cval
        Nothing -> False
```

By 'available' we mean that sufficient commitments have been made and not yet expired to cover the payment; in this case, the payment uses the currency allocated by the cash commitments made by `from` that expire the earliest. This contract will result in a `FailedPay` action if the funds are not available; otherwise a `SuccessfulPay` action is generated.

– Both con1 con2 enforces the behaviour of both contracts con1 and con2.

```
step comms st (Both con1 con2) os =
    (st2, result, ac1 ++ ac2)
    where
      result | res1 == Null = res2
             | res2 == Null = res1
             | otherwise = Both res1 res2
      (st1,res1,ac1) = step comms st con1 os
      (st2,res2,ac2) = step comms st1 con2 os
```

Because the model is stateful and produces output actions, to make a step, it is necessary to execute a single step of each of the contracts con1 and con2 in sequence: first con1 then con2.

– Choice obs conT conF behaves as either conT or conF depending on the (Boolean) result of obs at the time that the observation is made, conT if it is True and conF if False.

```
step _ st (Choice obs conT conF) os =
    if interpretObs st obs os
        then (st,conT,[])
        else (st,conF,[])
```

– When obs expi con con2 This contract will not progress until obs is True or until the current block number is greater than or equal to the one specified by timeout expi. In case the timeout applies, the contract will continue as con2, if the timeout does not apply and obs is True, then the contract continues as con. Otherwise the contract is quiescent.

```
step _ st (When obs expi con con2) os
  | expired (blockNumber os) expi = (st,con2,[])
  | interpretObs st obs os = (st,con,[])
  | otherwise = (st, When obs expi con con2, [])
```

We look next at an example of Marlowe in action.

3   Marlowe as an Embedded DSL

In this section, we revisit the escrow example that we discussed briefly in the introduction, and show how we can make Marlowe contracts that are easier to write, read, and understand, by embedding them into Haskell code, that is, taking advantage of the fact that Marlowe contracts are implemented as Haskell terms to write Haskell programs that generate Marlowe code, instead of writing Marlowe directly.

We used Haskell because it is the language in which Marlowe is implemented, but it would be easy to embed Marlowe in any other language. It would only be necessary to translate its primitives into a data type in that language. In Meadow we use Fay [5], a subset of Haskell that we discuss in more detail in Sect. 4).

The example we use through this section implements an escrow contract, as first introduced in Sect. 1. The escrow mechanism allows alice to deposit the money into a contract, in a way that the money will only be released when two out of three participants agree on whether bob has indeed given alice the item.

The escrow participant (carol) is supposed to be a neutral third party that will decide in case of dispute. This way, if participants alice and bob are honest, they will just agree on the result of the transaction and carol will not need to do anything. If alice and bob disagree, carol will be able to choose whether the money must go to alice or to bob.

In our implementation we make things more specific: the money paid for the item is 450 ADA, and it must be committed by alice before block 10; it will be refunded to alice if there is no consensus before block 90.

We start by defining some Haskell functions. We can encapsulate identifiers in functions to make the contract more readable. That way we can generate an identifier for the cash commitment:

```
iCC1 :: IdentCC
iCC1 = IdentCC 1
```

An identifier for the payment:

```
iP1 :: IdentPay
iP1 = IdentPay 1
```

And we can create identifiers for all the participants:

```
alice, bob, carol :: Person
alice = 1
bob   = 2
carol = 3
```

We can also create a sub-contract that allows the money from the commitment with identifier IdentCC 1 to be redeemed:

```
redeem_original :: Contract
redeem_original = RedeemCC iCC1 Null
```

Once redeemed, the contract continues as Null since we expect this to be the last thing that is done. Each participant has a say on who deserves the money: either alice deserves a refund, which we represent with the number 0; or bob deserves a payment, which we represent with the number 1. Because there is only one choice to make per participant, we use the same IdentChoice as their participant id. We can define a function that returns an observation that is true if and only if per has chosen the number c for the choice IdentChoice as follows:

```
chose :: Int -> ConcreteChoice -> Observation
chose per c = PersonChoseThis (IdentChoice per) per c
```

Then, we can easily write a function that returns an observation that is True if and only if at least one of the participants per and per' has chosen the number val as follows:

```
one_chose :: Person -> Person -> ConcreteChoice -> Observation
one_chose per per' val = (OrObs (chose per val) (chose per' val))
```

Building on that, we can now write a function that returns an observation that is True if and only if at least two out of the three participants p1, p2, and p3 have agreed in choosing the number c as follows:

```
two_chose :: Person -> Person -> Person -> ConcreteChoice -> Observation
two_chose p1 p2 p3 c = OrObs (AndObs (chose p1 c) (one_chose p2 p3 c))
                             (AndObs (chose p2 c) (chose p3 c))
```

Finally, we can write the escrow contract, thus:

```
escrow :: Contract
escrow = CommitCash iCC1 1 (ConstMoney 450) 10 100
                    (When (OrObs (two_chose alice bob carol 0)
                                 (two_chose alice bob carol 1))
                     90
                     (Choice (two_chose alice bob carol 1)
                             (Pay iP1 alice bob (AvailableMoney iCC1) 100
                                  redeem_original)
                             redeem_original)
                     redeem_original)
                    Null
```

The outermost primitive `CommitCash` allows the `alice` to commit 450 ADA before block 10, with the promise that money will be released on block 100 if they are not claimed before that.

The next primitive, `When`, waits for one of three things to happen:

1. The observation became `True` because two out of three have chosen 0.
2. The observation became `True` because two out of three have chosen 1.
3. The observation remained `False` until 90 was published in the blockchain.

If the third option happens, the money is refunded. Otherwise, there is a `Choice` that will immediately refund the money to `alice` unless two out of three chose option 1; in the later case, `Pay` will give `bob` the opportunity to claim the funds available in the commitment with identifier `iCC1` before block 100 (by using the identifier `iP1` for the claim). If the funds are not claimed before block 100 they will also be refunded to `alice`.

Reflecting on the example, we can see that using Haskell definitions has made the contract substantially more comprehensible. While our current implementation does not do this, it is possible to modify the embedding to support more efficient operation, by preserving *sharing* in the host language. For example, if we were to replace the repeated expression `two_chose alice bob carol 1` by a `where` clause,

```
escrow = ...            (When (OrObs (two_chose alice bob carol 0)
                                     chose_refund)
                         90
                         (Choice chose_refund ...
                               ...
                  where chose_refund = two_chose alice bob carol 1
```

then the repeated computation of the expression could be avoided.

4 Visualising and Interacting with Marlowe Contracts

For Marlowe to be usable in practice, users need to be able to understand how contracts will behave once deployed to the blockchain, but without doing the deployment. We can do that by simulating their behaviour off-chain, interactively stepping through the evaluation of a contract in a browser. We do this in two stages, first transforming an embedded contract (using features of Haskell) to a pure Marlowe contract, and then interactively stepping through that contract.

To achieve this, and to aid Marlowe's take-up usage by people that does not know or are not familiar with its syntax, we have developed Meadow, a web tool that supports the interactive construction, revision, and simulation of smart-contracts written in Marlowe. The tool is publicly available in the url: https://input-output-hk.github.io/scdsl/. In Fig. 3, we provide a screenshot of Meadow in the middle of simulating the execution of the "deposit incentive" contract available in the GitHub repository (in the file: `src/DepositIncentive.hs`) and in the examples section of Meadow (on the bottom right part).

Meadow has been mainly written in Haskell and compiled to JavaScript partially by the Haste compiler [6] and partially by GHCJS [13]; Meadow also relies on the Blockly library [8] for providing a visual editor for smart contracts written in Marlowe. Embedding support in Meadow is provided through a pruned and bundled version of the Fay compiler [5], compiled to JavaScript using GHCJS. All text fields that edit and present Meadow and Fay code are instances of CodeMirror text editor [9].

Blockly's editor allows the user to visualise and edit smart-contracts as interlocking blocks that can be dragged and dropped like pieces of a jigsaw puzzle. Meadow also provides functionality to generate syntactically correct and formatted code (that is displayed in the upper right corner of the application), and to convert the code back to its Blockly representation.

Additionally, Meadow allows the user to use Meadow's Fay embedding from within the browser.

The reason that we chose Fay instead of Haskell for Meadow is a technical one: we wanted Meadow to be run completely inside the browser, because that makes it easy to deploy, since the server is only required to send the page and not to run any Marlowe-related computation. There exist compilers from Haskell to JavaScript but most of them are not easy to bootstrap into JavaScript. Among other reasons, they often rely on the API of the host OS to read and write files.

The Fay compiler, on the other hand, is mostly written in pure Haskell, and it is not hard to compile to JavaScript by using GHCJS. Nevertheless, it does not include a type checker, it relies in GHC's type-checker; and it also tries to read its `Prelude` from disk. We have worked around these issues by disabling typechecking within Meadow embedded editor, and by embedding all the required modules as constant strings in a modified version of the Fay compiler.

In particular, Meadow includes a pruned copy of the Fay compiler, bundled with its Prelude module, its foreign interface, and a module with the definitions of the Marlowe primitives and a function to pretty-print Marlowe contracts. This allows the user to compile and execute, inside Meadow, Fay code that generates and prints a Marlowe contract. When the user opens the embedded editor, the current Marlowe contract is embedded into a template of a Fay program that prints it. The user is able to modify this code in the left panel of the editor and use the advanced functionalities provided by Fay like, for example, bindings, list-comprehensions, turing-complete functions definitions, etc.

When the user clicks the execute button, the Fay code is compiled to JavaScript and evaluated; this causes the Marlowe contract generated by the execution of the code to be written to the panel on the right. Generated contracts can then be sent back to the main screen of Meadow, translated to Blockly, and their execution can be simulated. The embedded editor also allows users to save the Fay code to a file in their computers, to load code from a file in their computers, and to temporarily hide the editor while keeping its contents in memory, even while the compilation and execution process is being carried out in the background.

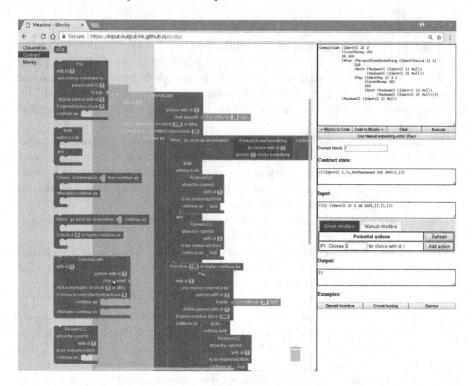

Fig. 3. The Meadow tool simulating the "deposit incentive" contract.

The execution of complete contracts can be simulated block by block by using the panel on the right (see Fig. 4), which includes text fields to view and edit the current block number, the state of the contract, the current inputs, and the outputs from last block.

Additionally, to facilitate the introduction of inputs, Meadow provides two different interfaces:

– The manual interface, provides a template for each of the four possible types of input: commits, redeems, payment claims, and choices.
– The smart interface (shown in Fig. 4), calculates the possible operations that would make sense given the current inputs, state of the contract, block number, and remaining contract; and it provides them in a table with most of the parameters already filled in.

The smart interface is usually more convenient to use than the manual interface since the later provides between 3 and 4 fields for each operation whereas the former "guesses" the possible intentions of the user and usually can input new operations with a single click (except for choices, which still may require the user to input a number).

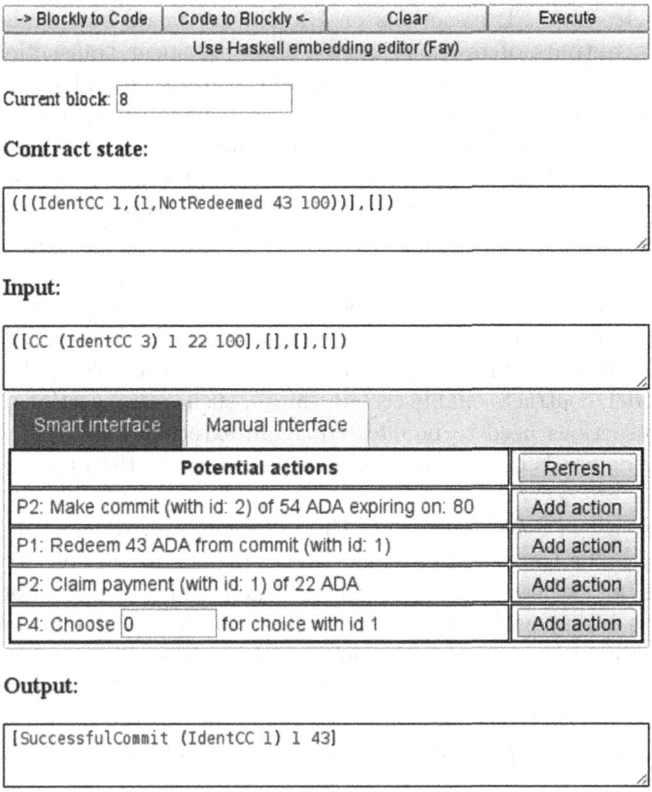

-> Blockly to Code	Code to Blockly <-	Clear	Execute
	Use Haskell embedding editor (Fay)		

Current block: 8

Contract state:

```
([(IdentCC 1,(1,NotRedeemed 43 100))],[])
```

Input:

```
([CC (IdentCC 3) 1 22 100],[],[],[])
```

Smart interface	Manual interface	
Potential actions		Refresh
P2: Make commit (with id: 2) of 54 ADA expiring on: 80		Add action
P1: Redeem 43 ADA from commit (with id: 1)		Add action
P2: Claim payment (with id: 1) of 22 ADA		Add action
P4: Choose 0 for choice with id 1		Add action

Output:

```
[SuccessfulCommit (IdentCC 1) 1 43]
```

Fig. 4. Detail of the interface for contract execution simulation.

In the next section, we re-examine the model and the Marlowe language, looking at possible extensions, alternative design decisions and ways in which we can formally analyse Marlowe contracts.

5   Design and Implementation

Marlowe is defined by its executable semantics, but to be deployed on blockchain it will have to be implemented on an existing distributed infrastructure. We intend to deploy it on IOHK's Cardano infrastructure, but it can be implemented in other systems too, as we explain now.

5.1   Design Rationale

Marlowe abstracts away from a number of concrete details of how blockchains operate. In particular, it is agnostic between UTxO-based systems, such as Bitcoin and Cardano SL, and account-based models such as Ethereum; it can be implemented on "push" or "pull"-based systems, and can be executed on or off-chain.

UTxO and Accounts. Transactions on Bitcoin are made by spending the (as yet) unspent outputs of previous transactions ('unspent transaction outputs' or UTxOs). The chain need not maintain any state, such as the current value owned by any particular participant: such *account* information is implicit and external to the Bitcoin blockchain. On the other hand, the Ethereum model explicitly keeps track of account values, and this information needs to be kept on chain. Of the two, the UTxO model is simpler and requires less support from the implementation of the chain itself.

Interaction Modality. Contracts can be conceived of as acting in two ways. In a *push* model, contracts are seen to make things happen. In the case of blockchain, this would include making payments or transactions take place. Alternatively, in a *pull* model, contracts enable certain things, such as transactions, to happen but the transactions need to be effected by an external actor. The pull model makes fewer demands on the blockchain implementation than the push model.

Layered Design and Sidechains. Some chains have a layered design, in particular Cardano [11]. The Cardano Settlement Layer (SL) is to support settlement of transactions but nothing more complicated, whereas the Computation Layer (or CL) supports more powerful general computations over the chain. Moreover, the Cardano roadmap [3] envisages the possibility of computation taking place, in part at least, on a sidechain rather than on the main chain itself, which may support only the SL. Other off-chain approaches include the Lightning network, overlaid on blockchains (usually Bitcoin) and the channels of æternity [1].

5.2   Compilation

We have designed Marlowe assuming that each contract would be compiled into

- one or more on-chain programs and
- a client side program or interface that has a limited number of choices to be made at each point in time (including an interface for the observables).

The contracts implemented in the Marlowe language have an implicit interface defined for what would correspond to the client side of a distributed application, as shown by the interactive interface. Of course, we probably do not want to give a user a programmatic interface but an actual application with user interface.

A contract written in Marlowe could also be potentially compiled to a smart-contract written in Ethereum. This could be done in two ways: it could be compiled so that a smart contract represents a single instance of the Marlowe contract with a fixed set of participants; alternatively it would be possible to create a generic contract with an extra "instantiate" operation that sets up a new Marlowe contract instance with a given set of participants (set of public keys).

Transactions. In principle, we can directly translate each operation in the model (i.e.: cash commitment, payment claim, choice, or redemption) into a separate transaction in the blockchain. In the Ethereum model this would work in the same way that is simulated by Meadow: several operations can be issued in parallel and the blockchain subsystem will automatically apply them in some order and integrate them into the next block.

Another approach would be to use a UTxO model with continuations in which a UTxO represents a contract. In this model, an operation would correspond to a transaction that spends a UTxO and creates (at least) a new UTxO that represents the contract after the operation.

Usually, in the UTxO model, it is necessary that a UTxO is in the blockchain in order for another transaction to be able to spend it. This could potentially limit the number of operations that can be applied in a single block to one, which would make infeasible the approach of using the same UTxO to represent several instances of the same contract (since it would not scale). On the other hand, it would prevent non-determinism and, with it, it would remove the possibility of race-conditions. A change to the state of a contract before a transaction (and its corresponding operation) is accepted in the blockchain would invalidate the transaction and require the user to issue it again.

Even if we only allow one transaction per block, it would still be possible to combine several transactions off-chain and to issue a transaction that contains several operations. However, that would require an offline protocol independent from the blockchain and it would require participants to collaborate.

Nevertheless, there already exists in Bitcoin a mechanism that allows the combination of several chained transactions within a single block while using the UTxO model, even though it is used to solve a different problem and it is not widely spread yet. This is the case of "child pays for parent", which allows the recipient of an unpublished transaction to issue another transaction that spends the former, with the aim of including enough fees for both transactions to have enough incentive to be included by a miner in a block (in which case both transactions would be included in the same block).

The same mechanism could be used for allowing miners to aggregate several transactions that act as a chain in the same block. The clients would only need to monitor the transaction pool in order to send transactions that can be chained with the existing ones.

Cost. The Cardano platform has a notion of cost, and Marlowe contracts will potentially incur costs of two kinds: The cost of a single transaction execution (e.g. a single Plutus validator), and the cost of the whole contract, which may consist of many transactions.

Even in Ethereum this distinction is important because single contract execution is limited by gas (and is thus finite), whereas the life of the whole contract may be unbounded and consist of an indefinite number of transactions. So far we are assuming contracts defined in Marlowe to be finite in both aspects.

Recording Information on Chain. Inputs and values of observables need to be recorded somehow, and this raises the potential issue about bloating the chain with data. In general, it will only be necessary to store a signed hash value of the observable, and this will keep data usage bounded; but the full information may still need to be posted in case of dispute.

General Computations. If we have contracts that involve, for example, the oil price then we may need to convert a published price in USD into ADA, using a value for the prevailing USD/ADA exchange rate. This will require a computation: in this case, a multiplication. If Marlowe is to be stand-alone then we need to extend it with arithmetic and other operations, but we expect Marlowe to be embedded in a suitable language that provides these facilities.

6   Related Work

Blockchains are executed in a replicated form by parties who cannot be guaranteed not to be hostile, either by directly trying to change the contents of the chain, or through trying to affect other properties of the chain by indirect means (such as swamping honest parties with work). Programming on the blockchain therefore needs to be constrained in some ways, since it has to be amenable to replication or verification within a reasonable time if the security and integrity of the chain are to be preserved. We look at representatives of the main approaches now; we discuss some of these in more detail in an earlier paper [12].

Split Contracts. An early work on smart contracts raises the issue that practical contractual situations may well not be amenable to complete formalisation, hence giving rise to a *split* [14] between an automated part and a non-automated part that mediates, for example, real assets. We can foresee that this approach will be needed for Marlowe too, if it achieves read-world adoption.

Bitcoin Script. One approach to this is to choose mechanisms such as bitcoin script [17] which are manifestly non-Turing complete. A bitcoin script, written in a Forth-like language, is essentially linear: it can branch, but the language contains neither looping constructs nor recursion. It is therefore straightforward not only to see that scripts will terminate, but also to give an accurate estimate of the time taken to execute a script.

Ethereum. On the other hand, the Ethereum system [19] provides a Turing-complete language for the EVM virtual machine, and a higher-level programming language, Solidity, that compiles into EVM code. However, EVM and Solidity programs are constrained *post hoc* by two mechanisms: program execution must be paid for using 'gas' proportional to the effort expended, and a set of *ad hoc* limits on program execution, e.g. on stack size.

Nxt. In Nxt [15], programmability of the system is provided through a "fat" high-level API, which is accessible from Nxt clients through a REST interface. The API provides functionality supporting various kinds of transactions. The core software itself does not support any form of scripting language; rather, users are expected to work with the built in transaction types and transactions that support some 250 primitive operations; these can be "scripted" in a client (only) using a binding to the API, which is available, for instance, in JavaScript.

Multiple Languages. A common feature of many blockchain platforms is that they provide multiple scripting languages. As we noted earlier, Ethereum can be programmed at the EVM level as well as by using the high-level Solidity language. Tezos [7] supports the stack-based, strongly-typed, functional language Michelson, but also provides a high-level language, Liquidity, that compiles into Michelson. Liquidity is also functional and strongly typed, but provides more constructs in a more familiar syntax, namely that of a subset of OCaml.

The æternity system [1] provides multiple languages and VMs [18]: the functional language Sophia (akin to Reason) and the Functional Typed Warded Virtual Machine (FTWVM) for safe "system level programming", the language Varna and the HLM for simple contracts, and a (port of) Solidity and the EVM for compatibility with Ethereum. In a similar way, Cardano provides support for IELE [10], a rational reconstruction of the EVM, and thus for Solidity too.

Domain-Specific Languages. A domain-specific language or DSL is a high-level language designed to work in a specific field or domain. The intention is that because the users will know about the field, the constructs of the language can be designed to be meaningful to them, and also that, because of its nature, the DSL need not include all the features of a general purpose language. Removing this clutter and having the remaining operations directly reflect the application area is intended to make the language more accessible to domain experts who do not necessarily see themselves as programmers.

Stand-alone DSLs have the advantage of providing appropriate, domain-level error messages when things go wrong, but suffer the disadvantage of having to be implemented from scratch. An alternative to this are *embedded* DSLs (EDSLs), which provide a "little language" for the particular domain embedded within a general-purpose host language. This means that parts of the host – such as arithmetical expressions, or list idioms – can be used to extend the expressibility of the DSL. A notable example of this is the financial contracts language described by Peyton Jones and his collaborators [16], which is embedded in Haskell. Marlowe is similar to the DSL in [16] in the use of Haskell embedding, in that the functionality provided is similar, in the use of composable combinators, and in the declarative style that allows users to describe what needs to be enforced and not how. However the two approaches differ in other aspects like the lack of Marlowe's reliance on the legal system for enforcement, its support for multiple party contracts, its explicitness of choices, and its use of a pull model.

Findel. The Findel project [2] examines financial contracts on the Ethereum platform, based on the seminal [16], and the authors note that payments need to be bounded; this is made concrete in our account by our notion of commitments. They take no account of commitments or timeouts as our approach does, but it should be noted that the Ethereum platform is more powerful than the one that we target in this paper.

7   Conclusions and Future Work

In this paper, we have presented Marlowe, a DSL for financial contracts on blockchains, based on earlier work on contracts [16], together with examples of its use. We have seen that to make this operational on blockchain we need to add commitments and timeouts, and to design a semantics that reflects these. As we saw in Sect. 5.1, Marlowe has been designed to make as few demands as possible on the underlying blockchain: it can be implemented on UTxO or account-based blockchains, for example.

We have also presented Meadow, that allows users to interact with and simulate the operation of Marlowe contracts, contributing to the potential adoptability of the system. We have also described the design rationale for Marlowe, and sketched ways in which it can be implemented.

We plan to continue the work with Marlowe in a number of directions. We will continue to develop the core language, for example considering the automation of generation of identifiers for commitments and others. We will then implement this version of Marlowe in Cardano, compiling from Marlowe contracts to on chain contracts and users' wallets, and deploy it in a test network to observe and measure its behaviour in practice.

Building on the operational semantics given here, we will develop analyses of Marlowe contracts – such as to show that contracts cannot generate FailedPay actions in certain circumstances. We will also develop QuickCheck-style property-based testing [4], and properties developed here can become candidates for fully fledged verification in a formalisation of the semantics of Marlowe.

We would like to thank IOHK for supporting us: not only has this led us to work on Marlowe, but we have benefited hugely from collaboration with colleagues including Manuel Chakravarty, Duncan Coutts, Bernardo David, Charles Hoskinson, Aggelos Kiayias, Bruno Woltzenlogel Paleo, Rebecca Valentine and Phil Wadler. We are very grateful to Thomas Arts and colleagues from æternity for their convivial discussions on blockchain and contracts in Göteborg, and to colleagues from the Universities of Kent and Leicester for their comments too.

References

1. æternity: æternity (2018). https://aeternity.com
2. Biryukov, A., Khovratovich, D., Tikhomirov, S.: Findel: secure derivative contracts for ethereum. In: Brenner, M., et al. (eds.) FC 2017. LNCS, vol. 10323, pp. 453–467. Springer, Cham (2017). https://doi.org/10.1007/978-3-319-70278-0_28

3. Cardano: Why we are building Cardano (2017). https://whycardano.com
4. Claessen, K., Hughes, J.: QuickCheck: a lightweight tool for random testing of Haskell programs. In: ICFP 2000, pp. 268–279. ACM (2000)
5. Done, C.: Fay (2012). https://github.com/faylang/fay/wiki. Accessed 14 May 2018
6. Ekblad, A.: Haste (2012). https://haste-lang.org/. Accessed 26 Mar 2018
7. Goodman, L.: Tezos - a self-amending crypto-ledger (2014). https://www.tezos.com/static/papers/white_paper.pdf
8. Google: Blockly (2011). https://developers.google.com/blockly/. Accessed 26 Mar 2018
9. Haverbeke, M., et al.: CodeMirror text editor (2011). https://codemirror.net/. Accessed 14 May 2018
10. IELE Semantics (2016). https://github.com/runtimeverification/iele-semantics. Accessed 26 Mar 2018
11. IOHK: The Cardano Project (2017). https://iohk.io/projects/cardano/
12. Lamela Seijas, P., Thompson, S., McAdams, D.: Scripting smart contracts for distributed ledger technology. Cryptology ePrint Archive, Report 2016/1156 (2016). https://eprint.iacr.org/2016/1156
13. Mackenzie, H., Nazarov, V., Stegeman, L.: GHCJS (2010). https://github.com/ghcjs/ghcjs. Accessed 14 May 2018
14. Miller, M.: The digital path: smart contracts and the third world. In: Birner, J., Garrouste, P. (eds.) Markets, Information and Communication: Austrian Perspectives on the Internet Economy. Taylor and Francis (2004)
15. Nxt (2013). https://nxtplatform.org/. Accessed 26 Mar 2018
16. Peyton Jones, S., et al.: Composing contracts: an adventure in financial engineering (functional pearl). In: Proceedings of the Fifth ACM SIGPLAN ICFP. ACM (2000)
17. Script - Bitcoin Wiki (2010). https://en.bitcoin.it. Accessed 26 Mar 2018
18. Stenman, E.: The æternity system. CODE BEAM SF, March 2018. https://www.youtube.com/watch?v=VXsqvfPIdWg
19. Wood, G.: Ethereum: a secure decentralised generalised transaction ledger. Ethereum Proj. Yellow Pap. **151**, 1–32 (2014)

SMT-Based Verification of Solidity Smart Contracts

Leonardo Alt and Christian Reitwiessner[✉]

Ethereum Foundation, Berlin, Germany
{leo,chris}@ethereum.org

Abstract. Ethereum smart contracts are programs that run inside a public distributed database called a blockchain. These smart contracts are used to handle tokens of value, can be accessed and analyzed by everyone and are immutable once deployed. Those characteristics make it imperative that smart contracts are bug-free at deployment time, hence the need to verify them formally. In this paper we describe our current efforts in building an SMT-based formal verification module within the compiler of Solidity, a popular language for writing smart contracts. The tool is seamlessly integrated into the compiler, where during compilation, the user is automatically warned of and given counterexamples for potential arithmetic overflow/underflow, unreachable code, trivial conditions, and assertion fails. We present how the component currently translates a subset of Solidity into SMT statements using different theories, and discuss future challenges such as multi-transaction and state invariants.

1 Introduction

The Ethereum [6] platform is a system that appears as a singleton networked computer usable by anyone, but is actually built as a distributed database that utilizes blockchain technology to achieve consensus. One of the features that sets Ethereum apart from other blockchain systems is the ability to store and execute code inside this database, via the Ethereum Virtual Machine (EVM). In contrast to traditional server systems, anyone can inspect this stored code and execute functions that can have stateful effects. Since blockchains are typically used to store ownership relations of valuable goods (for example cryptocurrencies), malicious actors have a monetary incentive to analyze the inner workings of such code. Because of that, testing (i.e. dynamic analysis of some typical inputs) does not suffice and analyzing all possible inputs by utilizing static analysis or formal verification is recommended.

SAT/SMT-based techniques have been used extensively for program verification [1,3,5,8,11,12]. This paper shows how the Solidity compiler, which generates EVM bytecode, utilizes an SMT solver and a Bounded Model Checking [5] approach to verify safety properties that can be specified as part of the source code, as well as fixed targets such as arithmetic underflow/overflow, division by zero and detection of unreachable code and trivial conditions. For the user, the main

© Springer Nature Switzerland AG 2018
T. Margaria and B. Steffen (Eds.): ISoLA 2018, LNCS 11247, pp. 376–388, 2018.
https://doi.org/10.1007/978-3-030-03427-6_28

advantage of this system over others is that they do not need to learn a second verification language or how to use any new tools, since verification is part of the compilation process. The Solidity language has requirement and assertion constructs that allow to filter and check conditions at run-time. The verification component builds on top of this and tries to verify at compile-time that the asserted conditions hold for any input, assuming the given requirements.

This paper is organized as follows: Sect. 2 introduces the EVM and smart contracts. Sect. 3 gives a very brief overview of Solidity. Sect. 4 discusses the translation from Solidity to SMT statements and next challenges. Finally, Sect. 5 contains our concluding remarks.

Related Work. Oyente [13], Mythril [7] and MAIAN [15] are SMT-based symbolic execution tools for EVM bytecode that check for specific known vulnerabilities, where Oyente also checks for assertion fails. They simulate the virtual machine and execute all possible paths, which takes a performance toll even though the approach works well for simple programs.

Subsets of Solidity have been translated to Why3 [18], F* [4] and LLVM [10], but the first requires learning a new annotation specification language and the latter two only verify fixed vulnerability patterns and do not verify custom user-provided assertions.

2   Smart Contracts

Programs in Ethereum are called *smart contracts*. They can be used to enforce agreements between mutually distrusting parties as long as all conditions can be fully formalized and do not depend on external factors. Typical use-cases are decentralized tokens which can have a currency-like aspect, any mechanisms that build on top of these tokens like exchanges and auctions or also decentralized tamper-proof registry systems like a domain name system.

Each smart contract has an *address* under which, among other things, its *code*, and a key-value store of data (*storage*) are stored. The code is fixed after the creation phase and only the smart contract itself can modify the data stored at its address.

Users can interact with a smart contract by sending a *transaction* to its address. This causes the smart contract's code to execute inside the so-called *Ethereum Virtual Machine* (EVM), which is a stack-based 256-bit machine with a minimalistic instruction set. Each execution environment has a freshly initialized *memory area* (not to be confused with the persisting storage). During its execution, a smart contract can also call other smart contracts synchronously, which causes their code to be run in a new execution environment. Data can be passed and received in calls. Furthermore, smart contracts can also create new smart contracts with arbitrary code.

Since it would otherwise be easy to stall the network by asking it to execute a complex task, the resources consumed are metered during execution in a unit called *gas*. Each transaction only provides a certain amount of gas, which acts as a *gas limit*. If execution is terminated via the *stop* instruction, any remaining gas is refunded and the transaction is successful. However, if an exceptional condition or this *gas limit* is reached without prior termination, any effect of the transaction is reverted and it is marked as a failure. In every case, the user who requested the execution pays for it with Ethereum's native token, Ether, proportionally to the amount of gas consumed.

A reverting termination can also happen prior to all gas being consumed. This is a special feature of the Ethereum Virtual Machine, which makes the control-flow analysis different from other languages. Whenever the EVM encounters an invalid situation (invalid opcode, invalid stack access, etc.), execution will not only stop, but all effects on the state will be reverted. This reversion takes effect in the current execution environment, and the environment will also flag a failure to the calling environment, if present. Typically, when a call fails, high level languages will in turn cause an invalid situation in the caller and thus the reversion affects the whole transaction.

There is also an explicit opcode that causes the current call to fail, which is essentially the same as described above, but as an *intended* effect. Very briefly, the SMT encoding we will discuss later assumes that no intended failure happens and tries to deduct that no unintended failure can occur. This allows the programmer to state preconditions using intended failures and postconditions using unintended failures.

3   Solidity

Solidity is a programming language specifically developed to write smart contracts which run on the Ethereum Virtual Machine. It is a statically-typed curly-braces language with a syntax similar to Java. The main source code elements are called *contracts* and are similar to classes in other languages. Contract-level variables in Solidity are persisted in storage while local variables and function parameters only have a temporary lifetime. Among others, Solidity has integer data types of various sizes (up to 256 bits, the word size of the EVM), address types and an associative array type called *mapping* which can only be used for contract-level variables.

The source code in Fig. 1 shows a minimal example of a token contract. Users are identified by their addresses and initially, all tokens are owned by the creator of the contract, but anyone who owns tokens can transfer an arbitrary amount to other addresses. Authentication is implicit in the fact that the address from which a function is called can be accessed through the global variable `msg.sender`. In practice, this is enforced by checking a cryptographic signature on the transaction that is sent through the network.

The `require` statement inside the function `transfer` is used to check a precondition at run-time: If its argument evaluates to false, the execution terminates and any previous change to the state is reverted. Here, it prevents tokens being transferred that are not actually available.

In general, invalid input should be caught via a failing `require`. The related `assert` statement can be used to check postconditions. The idea behind is that

```
contract Token {
    /// The main balances / accounting mapping.
    mapping(address => uint256) balances;
    uint256 totalSupply;

    /// Create the token contract crediting 'msg.sender' with
    /// 10000 tokens.
    constructor() public {
        totalSupply = 10000;
        balances[msg.sender] = totalSupply;
    }

    /// Transfer '_value' tokens from 'msg.sender' to '_to'.
    function transfer(address _to, uint256 _value) public {
        require(balances[msg.sender] >= _value);
        balances[msg.sender] -= _value;
        balances[_to] += _value;
    }
}
```

Fig. 1. Example of a token contract.

it should never be possible to reach a failing assert. `assert` essentially[1] has the same effect as `require`, but is encoded differently in the bytecode. Verification tools on bytecode level (as opposed to the high-level approach described in this article) typically check whether it is possible to reach an assert in any way.

We now show how an `assert` can be introduced into the `transfer` function to perform a simple invariant check.

```
function transfer(address _to, uint256 _value) public {
    require(balances[msg.sender] >= _value);
    uint256 sumBefore = balances[msg.sender] + balances[_to];
    balances[msg.sender] -= _value;
    balances[_to] += _value;
    uint256 sumAfter = balances[msg.sender] + balances[_to];
    assert(sumBefore == sumAfter);
}
```

The `assert` checks that the sum of the balances in the two accounts involved did not change due to the transfer. Currently, the `assert` statement is not removed by the compiler, even if the formal analysis module can prove that it never fails.

Note that in the general case, `balances[_to]` can overflow and thus an analysis tool might flag this assert as potentially failing. In this specific example, though, the amount of available tokens is too small for this to happen.

---

[1] As opposed to `require`, `assert` will result in all remaining *gas* to be consumed.

Another important feature that we refer to later in this paper are *function modifiers*. These are Solidity constructs that are used as patterns to change the behavior of functions, and in many cases, to restrict them. Commonly used modifiers are, for example, allowing only the owner of the contract to execute the function, or executing a function if and only if the amount of Ether sent is greater than a certain value. Figure 2 shows a contract using the former, where the execution of function f continues if and only if the original deployer of the contract is the caller. We discuss later how to use modifiers to represent function pre- and postconditions.

```
contract C
{
  address owner;

  // A function using this modifier will be executed only
  // if the require condition holds.
  modifier onlyOwner {
    require(msg.sender == owner);
    _;
  }

  // Create the contract setting the deployer as owner.
  constructor() public {
    owner = msg.sender;
  }

  function f() onlyOwner {
    ...
  }
}
```

Fig. 2. Example of modifiers.

4   SMT-Based Solidity Verification

SMT solvers are powerful tools to prove satisfiability of formulas in different logics which often have the necessary expressiveness to model software in a straightforward manner [1,3,8,11].

We translate Solidity contracts and their functions into SMT formulas using a combination of different quantifier-free theories. We shall name the translated formulas the *SMT encoding* of the Solidity program. The goal of the translation from Solidity to SMT formulas is to verify safety properties from the Solidity program by performing queries to the SMT solver.

4.1 SMT Encoding

The SMT encoding is computed during a depth-first traversal of the abstract syntax tree (AST) of the Solidity program and thus roughly follows the execution order. For now, each function is analyzed in isolation and thus the context regarding the SMT solver (contract storage, local variables, etc.) is cleared before each function of a contract is visited. There are five types of formulas that are encoded from Solidity inside each function. Three of them, *Control-flow*, *Type constraint* and *Variable assignment* are simply translated as SMT constraints. The *Branch conditions* are the conditions of the current branch of execution and thus grow and shrink as we traverse the AST. The last, *Verification Target*, creates a formula consisting of the verification goal conjoined with the previously mentioned constraints, including the current branch conditions, and queries the SMT solver for satisfiability. The different types of encoding are described below.

Branch Conditions. For an if-statement `if (c) T else F`, we add c to the branch conditions during the visit of T. After that, we replace c by $\neg c$ for the visit of F and also remove that when we are finished with the if-statement.

Control-Flow. These constraints model conditional termination of execution. A `require(r)` statement (and similar for `assert(r)`) terminates execution if r evaluates to false, but of course only if it is executed. Thus, we add a constraint $b \to r$, where b is the conjunction of the current branch conditions. Note that due to the implication, we can keep this constraint even when we leave the current branch.

Type Constraint. A variable declaration leads to a correspondent SMT variable that is assigned the default value of the declared type. For example, Boolean variables are assigned false, and integer variables are assigned 0. Function parameters are initialized with a range of valid values for the given type, since their value is unknown. For instance, a parameter `uint32 x` is initialized as $0 \leq x < 2^{32}$ (32 bits), a parameter `int256 y` is initialized as $-2^{255} \leq y < 2^{255}$, and a parameter `address a` is assigned the range $0 \leq a < 2^{(8*20)}$ (20 bytes). The encoder currently supports Boolean and the various sizes of Integer variables.

Variable Assignment. The encoding of a variable assignment follows the *Single Static Assignment* (SSA) where each assignment to a program variable introduces a new SMT variable that is assigned to only once. When a program variable is modified inside different branches of execution, a new variable is created after the branch to re-combine the different values after the branches. We use the if-then-else-function `ite` to assign the value `ite(c, `x_1`, `x_2`)` (if-then-else), where c is the branch condition and x_1 and x_2 are the two SSA variables corresponding to x at the ends of the branches (cf. the ϕ function in SSA).

Verification Target. Every arithmetic operation is checked against underflow and overflow according to the type of the values, and an example is given if there is an underflow or overflow. We also check whether branch conditions are constant, warning the user about unreachable blocks or trivial conditions. The conditions in calls to `assert` represent target postconditions that the Solidity programmer wants to ensure at runtime and are verified statically. If it is possible to disprove the assertion provided that the control flow can reach it (i.e. the current branch conditions are satisfiable), the user is given a counterexample. In contrast, `require` conditions are meant to be used as filters for unwanted input values when they are unknown, for example, in public functions, acting like preconditions for the rest of the scope. Therefore, failing calls to `require` are not treated as errors and are just checked for triviality and reachability.

Figure 3 shows on the left a Solidity sample that requires all five types of encoding, shown on the right, in order to verify the intended properties. Since the variables `uint256 a` and `uint256 b` are function parameters, they are initialized (lines 1 and 2) with the valid range of values for their type (`uint256`). If `a = 0`, the `require` condition about `b` is used as a precondition when verifying the assertion in the end of the function (line 3). The next two assignments to `b` create the new SSA variables b_1 and b_2 (line 4). Variable b_3 encodes the second and third conditions, and b_4 encodes the first condition (lines 5 and 6). Finally, b_4 is used in the assertion check (line 7). Note that the nested control-flow is implicitly encoded in the *ite* variables b_3 and b_4. We can see that the target assertion is safe within its function.

```
contract C
{
    function f(uint256 a, uint256 b)
    {
        if (a == 0)
            require(b <= 100);
        else if (a == 1)
            b = 1000;
        else
            b = 10000;
        assert(b <= 100000);
    }
}
```

1. $a_0 \geq 0 \wedge a_0 < 2^{256} \wedge$
2. $b_0 \geq 0 \wedge b_0 < 2^{256} \wedge$
3. $(a_0 = 0) \rightarrow (b_0 \leq 100) \wedge$
4. $b_1 = 1000 \wedge b_2 = 10000$
5. $b_3 = ite(a == 1, b_1, b_2) \wedge$
6. $b_4 = ite(a == 0, b_0, b_3) \wedge$
7. $\neg b_4 \leq 100000$

Fig. 3. SMT encoding of an assertion check.

As described above, the component performs several local checks during a single run, therefore it is critical that the used SMT solver supports incremental checking. Moreover, we do not abstract difficult operations such as multiplication between variables, and rather try to give precise answers when possible. Therefore we combine various quantifier-free theories, such as Linear Arithmetics, Uninterpreted Functions and Nonlinear Arithmetics. Solidity has integrated Z3 [14] and CVC4 [2] via their C++ APIs. The two SMT solvers are used together to increase solving power. This has been important especially for the programs that require Nonlinear reasoning, since often one solver is able to prove a property that the other cannot. The component is also able to generate smtlib2 [17] formulas in order to interface with additional solvers.

4.2 Specific Examples

Even though the current implementation of the SMT module supports a small subset of Solidity, it can already be used to detect flaws that might be overlooked by the user. We present now a few examples of buggy code that the compiler is able to detect regarding constant conditions, overflow, and assertion checking.

The following loop is infinite because the author of the code forgot to increment the loop variable i. In that case, the user receives a message about the loop's condition being always true for the case where owners.length is not zero.

```
for (uint i = 0; i < owners.length;)
{
    // ...
}
```

Another type of problem that the compiler finds automatically is unreachable code. In the following control-flow expressions, it warns the user that the condition in the else if is unreachable.

```
if (a >= 7) { ... }
else if (a >= 10) { ... }
```

Arithmetic operations should be checked against overflow, especially when parameters of public functions are used. The code below may easily lead to an overflow, which the tool reports with a counterexample. The overflow can be prevented with a require statement.

```
function addFunds(uint256 _amount) {
    // require((_amount + funds) >= funds);
    funds += _amount;
}
```

One of the most important features is the ability to check safety properties statically, by using Solidity's assert. The following example code uses an assert to check the equivalence of two computations, once written using control-flow statements, once as a direct Boolean formula.

```
function f(bool a, bool b) public pure {
    bool c;
    if (a) {
        if (b) c = false;
        else c = true;
    }
```

384   L. Alt and C. Reitwiessner

```
else {
  if (b) c = true;
  else c = false;
}
assert(c != ((a && !b) || (!a && b)));
}
```

Note that the assertion will be reported to fail with the valuation `a = false`, `b = false`, `c = false`. The safe condition would be `assert(c == ((a && !b) || (!a && b)));`.

4.3 Future Plans

We introduce now the features that we intend to implement in the SMT module, as well as discuss arising research problems where we present simple examples that highlight how the new features will work.

Our current implementation plans for the component involve supporting a larger subset of the language, including more complex data structures such as `mapping`. This is especially important for cases such as token contracts, where properties such as funds leakage and wrong balance could be used as targets. The component is meant to be built as a Bounded Model Checker, unrolling loops up to a constant bound and automatically detecting bounds when possible. We also intend to introduce a loop pre and postconditions syntax to help the unbounded case.

Range Restriction of Real Life Values. Some Solidity environment variables have a 256 bit unsigned integer type, although the range of their values is much more restricted in practice. For instance, the UNIX timestamp of the current block in seconds, `block.timestamp` will not exceed 64 bits for the next 500 billion years. To reduce the false positives rate for overflows, it makes sense to restrict the value range for these variables in the SMT encoding. It is an open question how to do this properly, since a straightforward hard cap at some point could create undesired artefacts around that point. Another environment variable that could have a similar behavior is `block.number`.

Revert After Error. Errors are irrelevant if they result in a state change reversion (Sect. 2). The user should be warned about failing checks such as overflow only if they do not result in a state reversion. One popular example is the SafeMath [16] contract which is commonly used to turn wrapping arithmetics into overflow-checked arithmetics:

```
function add(uint256 a, uint256 b) internal pure
      returns (uint256) {
  uint256 c = a + b;
  require(c >= a);
  return c;
}
```

Although the tool detects an overflow in the computation of a + b, the overflow will result in a truncation of c in two's complement and thus any execution that contains the overflow will revert at the **require**. In this case the user should not be warned of the error, since no erroneous cases exist in accepted executions.

Aliasing. In many languages, complex data structures are only assigned by reference, creating two names for the same object and thus changes performed via one name also affect references via the second name. This is of course a big challenge for formal verification and is known as the *aliasing problem*. This is also the case for some aspects of Solidity, but data stored in storage does not have this problem: The structure of storage is determined at compile-time, and all objects are statically allocated; while arrays can grow, their position in storage is fixed at compile-time. Because of that, the aliasing problem is not an issue, as long as we can assume that there are no hash collisions in keccak256 and dynamic arrays are small enough.

```
contract C
{
  uint a;

  constructor () public {}

  function a1() public { a = 1; }
  function a2() public { a = 2; }
  function a3() public { a = 3; }
  function a4() public { a = 4; }

  function plusA(uint x) public view returns (uint) {
    require(x < 1000);
    return a + x;
  }
}
```

Fig. 4. Contract with a storage variable invariant.

Multi-transaction Invariants. One of the most interesting aspects we intend to research and support is multi-transaction invariants. The ultimate goal is to compute invariants for state variables (resident in the contract's storage) considering any arbitrary number of calls to the contract. This would enable these invariants to be used as preconditions whenever they are accessed. Figure 4 presents an example contract with a state variable a which can be assigned differently depending on which public function is called. We can see that if we consider all possible paths, a is never greater than 4, so the invariant $a \leq 4$ holds. Currently, without the discovery of the invariant, the SMT module reports an overflow case in the **return** statement of function plusA. If the invariant is used as a pre-condition of the function, by adding `require(a <= 4)`, for example, no overflow is reported. The SMT component should in the future be able to automatically infer these invariants.

Post-constructor Invariants. A special and restricted case of multi-transaction invariants usage are contracts where a state variable is assigned in the constructor and never modified again. A common example is contract `Token` from Sect. 3. We can see from the constructor that the `totalSupply` of tokens is 10000, which is also the initial amount of tokens given to the deployer of the contract. The only way to move tokens is via the function `transfer`, which decreases a certain amount of tokens from one account, if it owns enough, and increases the same amount in another account. We can modify function `transfer` to use the invariant about state variable `totalSupply`:

```
function transfer(address _to, uint256 _value) public {
    require(balances[msg.sender] >= _value);
    uint256 sumBefore = balances[msg.sender] + balances[_to];
    totalSupply -= sumBefore;
    balances[msg.sender] -= _value;
    balances[_to] += _value;
    uint256 sumAfter = balances[msg.sender] + balances[_to];
    totalSupply += sumAfter;
    assert(sumBefore == sumAfter);
    assert(totalSupply == 10000);
}
```

As we can see, the number of total tokens never changes and the invariant $totalSupply = 10000$ holds in the beginning of any function of the contract. Similarly to the previous example, it is not possible to prove the last assertion without the knowledge about the invariant.

Modifiers as pre and Postconditions. An orthogonal approach to automatically inferred invariants is to provide a good syntax so that Solidity programmers can explicitly state pre and postconditions of functions. Modifiers (Sect. 3) are a natural candidate for that, given their ability to behave as patterns that wrap functions. In the following code, the modifier `safeBalance` states pre and postconditions for the `transfer` function in the `Token` contract (Sect. 3), ensuring that the concrete value of `totalSupply` does not change after a token transfer.

```
modifier safeBalance {
    require(totalSupply == 10000);
    _;
    assert(totalSupply == 10000);
}

function transfer(address _to, uint256 _value) safeBalance {
    ...
}
```

Function Abstraction. If modifiers are used as pre and postconditions as described above, it could be possible to abstract functions based on these modifiers. Let `zeroAccount` be a function from contract `Token` that transfers all the tokens that an account holds to another one of their choice. Function `zeroAccount` should also be sure that the `totalSupply` did not change.

```
function zeroAccount(address _to) {
  transfer(_to, balance[msg.sender]);
  assert(totalSupply == 10000);
}
```

One approach to analyze `zeroAccount` is to abstract function `transfer` by encoding only its modifiers and ignoring its body when trying to prove the assertion. This query is much cheaper for the SMT solver, and in many cases (as it is in this one) it might be enough to prove the assertion.

Effective Callback Freeness. The idea of *Effective Callback Freeness* was recently introduced by [9]. A smart contract C is effectively callback free, if any state change caused by a callback in C can also be caused by an execution that does not have this callback. Straightforward examples include a contract that uses a mutex mechanism to disallow state changes if the function is called as a callback, and the general pattern where all functions perform state changes before they call other contracts. The authors show that most of the contracts deployed on Ethereum have this property. This is a powerful property, since it means that any invariant computed for a contract's state variables still holds even after calling external contracts with unknown behavior. We intend to study how to integrate this approach to our static analysis.

5 Conclusion

We have presented our current work and future plans building an SMT-based formal verification module inside the Solidity compiler. The module creates SMT constraints from the Solidity code and queries SMT solvers to statically check for underflow/overflow, division by zero, unreachable/trivial code, and assertion fails, where require statements are used as assumptions. The programmer receives, in compile-time, feedback with counterexamples in case any of the target properties fail, without any extra effort. The SMT constraints and queries are created using theories that model the Solidity program precisely, therefore the given counterexamples are correct.

The features that are currently under implementation aim at extending the subset of Solidity that is supported, as well as improving error reporting. Future work on the SMT module includes interesting broader research questions, such as computing multi-transaction invariants for state variables, detecting post-constructor invariants, and using modifier-based abstraction for functions.

References

1. Alt, L., et al.: HiFrog: SMT-based function summarization for software verification. In: Legay, A., Margaria, T. (eds.) TACAS 2017. LNCS, vol. 10206, pp. 207–213. Springer, Heidelberg (2017). https://doi.org/10.1007/978-3-662-54580-5_12
2. Barrett, C., et al.: CVC4. In: Gopalakrishnan, G., Qadeer, S. (eds.) CAV 2011. LNCS, vol. 6806, pp. 171–177. Springer, Heidelberg (2011). https://doi.org/10.1007/978-3-642-22110-1_14
3. Beyer, D., Keremoglu, M.E.: CPAChecker: a tool for configurable software verification. In: Gopalakrishnan, G., Qadeer, S. (eds.) CAV 2011. LNCS, vol. 6806, pp. 184–190. Springer, Heidelberg (2011). https://doi.org/10.1007/978-3-642-22110-1_16
4. Bhargavan, K., et al.: Formal verification of smart contracts: short paper. In: Proceedings of the 2016 ACM Workshop on Programming Languages and Analysis for Security, PLAS 2016, pp. 91–96 (2016)
5. Biere, A., Cimatti, A., Clarke, E., Zhu, Y.: Symbolic model checking without BDDs. In: Cleaveland, W.R. (ed.) TACAS 1999. LNCS, vol. 1579, pp. 193–207. Springer, Heidelberg (1999). https://doi.org/10.1007/3-540-49059-0_14
6. Buterin, V.: A next-generation smart contract and decentralized application platform (2014). github.com/ethereum/wiki/wiki/White-Paper
7. ConsenSys: Mythril (2018). github.com/ConsenSys/mythril
8. Donaldson, A.F., Haller, L., Kroening, D., Rümmer, P.: Software verification using k-induction. In: Yahav, E. (ed.) SAS 2011. LNCS, vol. 6887, pp. 351–368. Springer, Heidelberg (2011). https://doi.org/10.1007/978-3-642-23702-7_26
9. Grossman, S.: Online detection of effectively callback free objects with applications to smart contracts. Proc. ACM Program. Lang. **2**(POPL), 48:1–48:28 (2017)
10. Kalra, S., Goel, S., Dhawan, M., Sharma, S.: ZEUS: analyzing safety of smart contracts (2018)
11. Komuravelli, A., Gurfinkel, A., Chaki, S., Clarke, E.M.: Automatic abstraction in SMT-based unbounded software model checking. In: Sharygina, N., Veith, H. (eds.) CAV 2013. LNCS, vol. 8044, pp. 846–862. Springer, Heidelberg (2013). https://doi.org/10.1007/978-3-642-39799-8_59
12. Kroening, D., Tautschnig, M.: CBMC – C bounded model checker. In: Ábrahám, E., Havelund, K. (eds.) TACAS 2014. LNCS, vol. 8413, pp. 389–391. Springer, Heidelberg (2014). https://doi.org/10.1007/978-3-642-54862-8_26
13. Luu, L., Chu, D.H., Olickel, H., Saxena, P., Hobor, A.: Making smart contracts smarter. In: Proceedings of the 2016 ACM SIGSAC Conference on Computer and Communications Security, CCS 2016, pp. 254–269 (2016)
14. de Moura, L., Bjørner, N.: Z3: an efficient SMT solver. In: Ramakrishnan, C.R., Rehof, J. (eds.) TACAS 2008. LNCS, vol. 4963, pp. 337–340. Springer, Heidelberg (2008). https://doi.org/10.1007/978-3-540-78800-3_24
15. Nikolic, I., Kolluri, A., Sergey, I., Saxena, P., Hobor, A.: Finding the greedy, prodigal, and suicidal contracts at scale (2018). CoRR abs/1802.06038. http://arxiv.org/abs/1802.06038
16. OpenZeppelin: SafeMath (2018). github.com/OpenZeppelin/zeppelin-solidity/blob/master/contracts/math/SafeMath.sol
17. SMT-LIB: SMT-LIB (2018). smtlib.cs.uiowa.edu
18. Why3: Why3 (2018). why3.lri.fr

Blockchains as Kripke Models:
An Analysis of Atomic Cross-Chain Swap

Yoichi Hirai$^{(\boxtimes)}$ (iD)

Berlin, Germany
i@yoichihirai.com

Abstract. There is a protocol called "atomic cross-chain swap" that spans across multiple blockchains, but is it really atomic? We analyze the protocol using a modal logic for asynchronous communication. The modal logic allows us to identify some assumptions required for the "atomic" property as logical formulas. We first demonstrate that the atomicity fails without some temporal-epistemic assumptions. We further construct a proof that the atomicity holds with strong enough temporal-epistemic assumptions. In both analyses, we use Kripke models of the modal logic. This is the first analysis of multiple blockchains' interaction using a modal logic.

Keywords: Modal logic · Epistemic logic
Asynchronous computation · Blockchains

1 Introduction

This paper analyzes a concurrent, asynchronous protocol involving multiple blockchains using a modal logic called intuitionistic epistemic logic for asynchronous communication [14].

A blockchain is a singly linked list of data-blobs called blocks. A block contains a cryptographic hash value of the previous block's contents. The hash value serves as the link of the list. A single blockchain is useful for ensuring the integrity of a sequence of blocks because the latest block uniquely identifies the preceding sequence of blocks (assuming no hash collisions).

Today, some proof-of-work protocols (Bitcoin [19] and similar protocols) are spinning concurrent, asynchronous activities into fully sequential histories. These protocols have no fixed number of participants, so the protocols fall out of the traditional distributed protocols (e.g. Paxos [15] and Chandra-Toueg [3]). These blockchain protocols have no termination; they never yield final definite consensus but at most an ever-increasing confidence on one result. This is why these blockchain protocols fall out of scope of some impossibility theorems (e.g. FLP-theorem [9]) regarding distributed consensus. It turns out many people are willing to use such protocols without termination.

Once we start using multiple blockchains for performance reasons (as in Polkadot [25], Plasma [22], or "sharding" aproaches [10,18]), the asynchronous,

© Springer Nature Switzerland AG 2018
T. Margaria and B. Steffen (Eds.): ISoLA 2018, LNCS 11247, pp. 389–404, 2018.
https://doi.org/10.1007/978-3-030-03427-6_29

concurrent reasoning is again required. As an example, this paper analyzes a protocol called "atomic cross-chain swap" [16, 21]. Figure 1 is a concise description of the protocol. In this protocol, two blockchains interact in an asynchronous manner, and they are claimed to establish an atomic swap together. The atomic swap is claimed to either succeed in both blockchains or fail in both.

Such atomicity between asynchronically communicating agents sound dubious to a student of modal epistemic logic, who learns that asynchronous communication never creates a new piece of common knowledge [4]. An atomic swap, if it is atomic as the name suggests, should result in common knowledge. This is because, if the swap atomically succeeds or fails, the result should be known to both parties, and there is no possibility that two parties see different situations, including their epistemic states. As a result, there should be an unlimited nesting of mutual knowledge of the form "X knows Y knows X knows Y knows $\cdots$ that the swap failed." However, in the asynchronous setting, deep nesting of knowledge can be attained only after as many round-trip communication. Since the cross-chain atomic swap does not involve synchronous communication between the two blockchains, there must be some kind of assumptions supporting the "atomic" property. This paper clarifies those assumptions.

Our contributions are:

- defining the syntax (Subsect. 2.1) and the semantics (Subsect. 2.2) of logical formulas for reasoning about the cross-chain atomic swap,
- specifying hashlocks with logical formulas (Sect. 3),
- specifying desired atomicity of cross-chain atomic swaps as logical formulas (Binary-Outcome) and (Weak-Binary-Outcome) in Sect. 4,
- identifying two sets of assumptions that are not enough for the desired atomicity (Propositions 3 and 4), and
- identifying one set of assumptions that is enough for a form of atomicity (Proposition 5).

2   The Logic Used in this Paper

Our task is an instance of the general task of ensuring a desired property (in our case, atomicity) in all possible situations (in our case, protocol executions). If some situations refute the property, we can continue asking if we can restrict the possible situations to regain the desired property. We need a mathematical formalism to express the possible situations, our desired properties, and our assumptions on the possible situations.

We use the approach of mathematical logic [5]. The possible situations are represented as models. Each model contains states that are related temporally or epistemically. Logical formulas express properties of states of models. The syntax of the logic defines what sequence of symbols counts as logical formulas. The semantics of the logic defines which states of models satisfy a logical formula.

We use an extension of intuitionistic propositional logic. Intuitionistic logic originally modeled a mathematician who happens to be an intuitionist. When a proposition φ is known to hold, it holds forever. When the negation $\neg\varphi$ is

The canonical bitcoin atomic swap works as follows: Alice prepares a random secret k with a 20-byte hash H=HASH160(k) and then funds the following contract, in Bitcoin script [2]:

```
IF
  <BKey> CHECKSIGVERIFY
  HASH160 <H> EQUAL
ELSE
  <AKey> CHECKSIGVERIFY
  <ATime> CHECKLOCKTIMEVERIFY
ENDIF
```

Meaning of this contract: A signature from Bob's public key BKey in combination with secret k can spend the money. However as a fallback in case of cancellation, a signature from Alice's public key AKey lets her get a refund, but only after ATime. Bob does not know k, yet. He funds a similar contract on his blockchain using Alice's H value, but with a BTime expiring significantly sooner than ATime:

```
IF
  <AKey> CHECKSIGVERIFY
  HASH160 <H> EQUAL
ELSE
  <BKey> CHECKSIGVERIFY
  <BTime> CHECKLOCKTIMEVERIFY
ENDIF
```

Now, Alice may redeem Bob's contract but in doing so, she must reveal k. Bob can now see k which allows him to redeem Alice's contract. If the deal is called off then Bob is allowed to get a refund at BTime, and then Alice can get her refund after ATime. The above setup is generally perceived as perfectly secure and is being proposed for safe on-chain cryptocurrency exchanges that do not involve a third party.

Fig. 1. A description of a cross-chain atomic swap, cited from [16] with cosmetic modifications.

known, that would also be remembered forever. When neither φ or $\neg\varphi$ is known, according to the intuitionistic interpretation of disjunction $\vee$, the disjunction $\varphi \vee \neg\varphi$ is not known. In other words, whenever $\varphi \vee \psi$ is known, either φ is known, or ψ is known.

This intuitionistic reading of disjunction seems particularly useful for settlement of funds when φ means "Alice obtains the fund" and ψ means "Bob obtains the fund." The settlement should be final, and the finality is already captured by the persistent nature of intuitionistic logic.

Intuitionistic Epistemic Logic for Asynchronous Communication. Modal logic can express the fundamental assumptions about knowledge and time. For instance, the formula $K_A\varphi \supset K_A(K_A\varphi)$ says "if A knows φ, A knows that A knows φ". This formula is named "positive introspection." At first logical formulas look like merely a shorthand for sentences, but the symbolic treatments scale better than English sentences, especially when the modalities are nested.

Intuitionistic epistemic logic [14] was designed to reason about asynchronous communication. The logic can reason about temporal epistemic systems, but it has no explicit temporal modality. The Kripke model [5] of intuitionistic propositional logic is reused as the temporal frame. Originally Hirai [14] used the logic for waitfree communication on shared memory. In this paper we use the logic for asynchronous communication between multiple blockchains.

2.1   Language

Mathematical logic distinguishes syntax and semantics. Logical formulas themselves are just shapes without meaning. A separate criterion dictates when a model satisfies a formula. Of course, certain formulas are never satisfied, and these formulas represent falsehood. However, such interpretations come only after the definition (Definition 2) of semantics.

We first define which sequents of symbols count as logical formulas. The logical formulas contain names of agents and atomic propositions, so we define those first.

An *agent* is one of the four distinct symbols:

$$a ::= \text{Alice}, \text{Bob}, X, Y. \tag{1}$$

They are just distinct symbols, but informally, Alice and Bob are participants of the protocol in Fig. 1, and X and Y are blockchains.

We choose the following set of *atomic propositions*:

$$P ::= D_1, D_2, k, A_Y, B_X. \tag{2}$$

Informally, D_1 holds whenever the wall clock shows more than one day ahead since the beginning of the protocol execution, and D_2 holds whenever more than two days. Also informally, k holds when Alice's secret is publicly visible. A_Y holds when the fund on blockchain Y is available to Alice. B_X when the fund on blockchain X is available to Bob. By introducing the last three atomic formulas, we are effectively assuming that the swaps on blockchains X and Y cannot be reversed. In practice, agents are supposed to ignore contents of too fresh blocks that might be orphaned[1].

Following Hirai [14], a *formula* is syntactically defined as

$$\varphi, \psi ::= \perp \mid P \mid (K_a\varphi) \mid (\varphi \vee \psi) \mid (\varphi \wedge \psi) \mid (\varphi \supset \psi). \tag{3}$$

where symbols a and P are non-terminal symbols from (1) and (2). The symbol $\supset$ stands for implication; a formula of the form $(\varphi \supset \psi)$ says φ implies ψ. Negation $(\neg\varphi)$ is a shorthand for $(\varphi \supset \perp)$. We omit parentheses when there is no ambiguity.

---

[1] A block is orphaned when it belongs to a blockchain that is not considered canonical anymore. This sometimes happens after branching blockchains are formed.

Informal Readings of the Language. BHK-interpretation[2] [24, Chap. 1] is a proof-centric way of reading logical connectives ($\wedge$, $\vee$, $\supset$, $\perp$ and K_a). If one knows what counts as a proof of φ and what counts as a proof of ψ, BHK-interpretation tells what counts as a proof of more complicated formulas: $\varphi \wedge \psi$, $\varphi \vee \psi$ and $\varphi \supset \psi$.

H1. A proof of $\varphi \wedge \psi$ is given by presenting a proof of φ and a proof of ψ.

H2. A proof of $\varphi \vee \psi$ is given by presenting either a proof of φ or a proof of ψ (plus the stipulation that we want to regard the proof presented as evidence for $\varphi \vee \psi$).

H3. A proof of $\varphi \supset \psi$ is a construction which permits us to transform any proof of φ into a proof of ψ.

H4. Absurdity $\perp$ (contradiction) has no proof; a proof of $\neg\varphi$ is a construction which transforms any hypothetical proof of φ into a proof of a contradiction.

Hirai [13] extends the list with one clause about the epistemic modality:

HK. A proof of $K_a\varphi$ is a construction that witnesses agent a's acknowledgment of a proof of φ and also contains the acknowledged proof.

In other words, a proof of $K_a\varphi$ is a proof of φ with a's signature. From a signed proof of φ, one can obtain an unsigned proof of φ, so, the formula $(K_a\varphi) \supset \varphi$ is always satisfied, as we see later in Proposition 7.

The BHK-interpretation explains the logical connectives. We have to interpret the atomic formulas so that we know what count as proofs of the atomic formulas. A proof of k is the secret generated by Alice shown in public. A proof of D_1 and D_2 could be some real-world information only available one day or two days after a certain point in time. A proof of A_Y is an onchain proof that Alice can spend the fund on blockchain Y. A proof of B_X is an onchain proof that Bob can spend the fund on blockchain X. If the cross-chain atomic swap is really atomic, A_Y and B_X both should hold or neither (Sect. 4).

2.2 Models

A model (Definition 1) is a set of states equipped with some relations and functions. We will be using small, finite models to refute the desired atomicity of the protocol (Propositions 3 and 4). We will also be reasoning about arbitrary models to establish the atomicity (Proposition 5).

Definition 1 (Definition 2.3, [14]). *Let A denote the set of agents. A model $\langle W, \prec, (f_a)_{a \in A}, \rho \rangle$ is a tuple with following properties:*

1. *$\langle W, \preceq \rangle$ is a partially ordered set whose elements are called states,*
2. *for each agent $a \in A$, a function $f_a \colon W \to W$ satisfies*
   (a) *$f_a(w) \preceq w$,*
   (b) *$f_a(f_a(w)) = f_a(w)$, and*
   (c) *$w \preceq v$ implies $f_a(w) \preceq f_a(v)$*

---

[2] BHK stands for Brouwer-Heyting-Kolmogorov.

3. *Let* Atom *be the set of atomic propositions and* $\mathcal{P}(W)$ *is the powerset of W.*
   $\rho\colon$ Atom $\rightarrow \mathcal{P}(W)$ *is a function such that each $\rho(P)$ is upward-closed with respect to $\preceq$. In other words, $w' \succeq w \in \rho(P)$ implies $w' \in \rho(P)$.*

Definition 2. *We define a relation $M, w \models \varphi$ (pronounced "the model M at state w satisfies φ") of a model $M = \langle W, \preceq, (f_a)_{a\in A}, \rho \rangle$, a state $w \in W$ and a formula φ. The definition is inductive on the structure of φ.*

(Case $\varphi = \bot$) $M, w \models \bot$ *never holds.*
(Case $\varphi = P$) *for an atomic formula P, $M, w \models P$ if and only if $w \in \rho(P)$.*
(Case $\varphi = K_a\psi$) $M, w \models K_a\psi$ *if and only if $M, f_a(w) \models \psi$.*
(Case $\varphi = \psi_0 \wedge \psi_1$) $M, w \models \psi_0 \wedge \psi_1$ *if and only if both $M, w \models \psi_0$ and $M, w \models \psi_1$ hold.*
(Case $\varphi = \psi_0 \vee \psi_1$) $M, w \models \psi_0 \vee \psi_1$ *if and only if $M, w \models \psi_0$ or $M, w \models \psi_1$ holds.*
(Case $\varphi = \psi_0 \supset \psi_1$) $M, w \models \psi_0 \supset \psi_1$ *if and only if for any $w' \in W$ with $w' \succeq w$, the relation $M, w' \models \psi_0$ implies the relation $M, w' \models \psi_1$.*

Since $\neg\varphi$ is an abbreviation of $\varphi \supset \bot$, the relation $M, w \models \neg\varphi$ holds if and only if no $v \succeq w$ satisfies $M, v \models \varphi$.

Informal Interpretation of the Model. When a state w satisfies a proposition φ, a proof of φ is available in the state. When two states are ordered $v \preceq w$, they are temporarily related. Every proof available in the past state v is also available in the future state w. So, any formula satisfied in v is also satisfied in w (Proposition 6). Such monotonicity is not found in the real world, where people can forget and proofs can be lost. When we analyze cryptographic protocols, it is prudent to assume that attackers do not forget a once-learned secret. The treatment also has shortcomings. Most importantly, our analysis assumes the finality of transactions on blockchains. Nonetheless we will find that more assumptions are necessary.

The state $f_a(w)$ is agent a's latest state seen from w. Every proof in $f_a(w)$ are available in w. Moreover, the proofs available in $f_a(w)$ are all signed by a and made available in w, so, if $f_a(w)$ contains a proof of φ, w contains a proof of $K_a\varphi$. Such situation typically occurs when a sends a message from state $f_a(w)$ and the message arrives in state w. We assume such messages contain all current knowledge of a at $f_a(w)$.

We consider any $f_a(w)$ as a local state of a and thus $f_a(f_a(w))$ is always equal to $f_a(w)$. As a result, $K_a\varphi$ and $K_aK_a\varphi$ are always equivalent (so the property "positive introspection" holds).

Our models can distinguish (a) asynchronous round-trip between Alice and Bob from (b) synchronous communication between them (Fig. 2). In the asynchronous case, if $f_{\text{Alice}}f_{\text{Bob}}f_{\text{Alice}}(v)$ satisfies φ, v satisfies $K_{\text{Alice}}K_{\text{Bob}}K_{\text{Alice}}\varphi$ but not necessarily $K_{\text{Alice}}K_{\text{Bob}}K_{\text{Alice}}K_{\text{Bob}}\varphi$. In the synchronous case, if w satisfies φ, w also satisfies $K_{\text{Alice}}K_{\text{Bob}} \cdots K_{\text{Bob}}\varphi$ with any repetition of K_{Alice} and K_{Bob}.

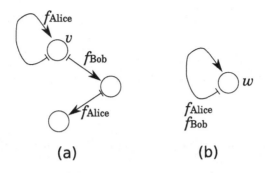

Fig. 2. Kripke models showing (a) asynchronous round-trip and (b) synchronous communication between Alice and Bob. Circles represent the states of models. In (a), the state v contains Bob's message from $f_{\mathrm{Bob}}(v)$, which in turn contains Alice's message from $f_{\mathrm{Alice}}f_{\mathrm{Bob}}(v)$.

3   Common Assumptions

3.1   For the Hashlock on Blockchain X

The cross-chain atomic swap (Fig. 1) is a protocol based on a primitive called "a hashlock." We need to specify the hashlocks using logical formulas.

The most relevant property is a hashlock's ability to settle payments. After a finite amount of time, a hashlock is able to dictate whether the locked fund already belongs to Bob or never. Concretely on blockchain X, after two days, either Bob has obtained the fund and the secret has been revealed ($B_X \wedge k$) or Bob will never get the fund ($\neg B_X$).

$$K_X(D_2 \supset ((B_X \wedge k) \vee \neg B_X)). \tag{X-live1}$$

A hashlock can be unlocked using a secret. On blockchain X, if two days have not passed yet, if Bob provides the secret ($K_{\mathrm{Bob}}k$), Bob obtains the fund (B_X).

$$K_X(D_2 \vee (K_{\mathrm{Bob}}k \supset B_X)). \tag{X-live2}$$

Here, we could not say $(\neg D_2) \supset \cdots$ because that formula is of any relevance only at a state with no future satisfying D_2. The formula $\neg D_2$ is satisfied only when the world ends before two days pass.

The above two properties are about what a hashlock is supposed to do. There is one important thing that a hashlock is not supposed to do. The hashlock grants the fund to Bob only when Bob authenticates himself with the secret k:

$$B_X \supset K_X K_{\mathrm{Bob}}k. \tag{X-safe}$$

3.2   For the Hashlock on Blockchain Y

We can formulate the same properties of the hashlock on the other blockchain. After one day, on blockchain Y, either the fund is given or not given:

$$K_Y(D_1 \supset ((A_Y \wedge k) \vee \neg A_Y)). \tag{Y-live1}$$

Before one day, on blockchain Y, if the hash is known, the fund is given:

$$K_Y(D_1 \vee (K_{\text{Alice}}k \supset A_Y)). \qquad \text{(Y-live2)}$$

Alice cannot obtain the fund on the blockchain Y unless she reveals the hash:

$$A_Y \supset K_Y k. \qquad \text{(Y-safe)}$$

3.3   For the Temporal Ordering of Day One and Day Two

If two days have passed, one day has already passed, too:

$$D_2 \supset D_1. \qquad \text{(Days)}$$

4   Reasoning About Atomicity

4.1   A Failure on Binary Outcome

In general, atomicity states that the protocol cleanly succeeds or fails, without leaving an incomplete success. In our case, the two unlocking events on blockchains X and Y need to succeed both or fail both. One way to express this as a logical formula goes like this; after two days, at least one of the two allowed cases happens:

$$D_2 \supset ((A_Y \wedge B_X) \vee ((\neg A_Y) \wedge (\neg B_X))). \qquad \text{(Binary-Outcome)}$$

However, the already introduced axioms do not guarantee (Binary-Outcome).

Proposition 3. *There is a model that satisfies all of (Y-live1), (Y-live2), (Y-safe), (X-live1), (X-live2), (X-safe) and (Days) at every state, but does not satisfy (Binary-Outcome) at a state.*

Proof. By constructing a model M and a state w (Fig. 3) so that M satisfies all assumptions at every state but w does not satisfy (Binary-Outcome). The state w in Fig. 3 does not satisfy $\neg A_Y$ because there is a future state satisfying A_Y. On the other hand, w does not satisfy A_Y either. So, without looking at B_X or $\neg B_X$, we can conclude that w does not satisfy $(A_Y \wedge B_X) \vee ((\neg A_Y) \wedge (\neg B_X))$. However, w does satisfy D_2. So w does not satisfy the implication (Binary-Outcome). □

Informally speaking, on state w in Fig. 3, two days have passed but neither blockchain has produced visible blocks since the beginning of the protocol.

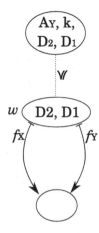

Fig. 3. A model M and a state w for the proof of Proposition 3. Three circles represent the three states of M. Each function f_a is identity whenever not explicitly shown. The $\preceq$ relation holds whenever two states are connected through dashed lines and arrows in a bottom-to-top way.

4.2   A Failure on a Weaker Binary Outcome

We can require that both blockchains contain blocks produced after two days have passed:

$$K_X D_2 \supset (K_Y D_2 \supset ((A_Y \wedge B_X) \vee ((\neg A_Y) \wedge \neg B_X))). \quad \text{(Weak-Binary-Outcome)}$$

This new proposition is strictly weaker than the old one. All states satisfying (Binary-Outcome) also satisfy (Weak-Binary-Outcome), but the inverse is not always the case. For instance, state w in Fig. 3 does not satisfy (Binary-Outcome), but it satisfies (Weak-Binary-Outcome).

Proposition 4. *There is a model that satisfies (Y-live1), (Y-live2), (Y-safe), (X-live1), (X-live2), (X-safe) and (Days) at all states, but does not satisfy (Weak-Binary-Outcome) at some states.*

Proof. By constructing a model M and a state w in it (Fig. 4).   □

Figure 4 demonstrates a lack of communication between the two chains. More specifically, although the hashlock on blockchain Y is unlocked, Bob fails to use the secret revealed on blockchain Y to unlock the hashlock on blockchain X.

4.3   Enough Assumptions for Atomicity

To remedy the situation, we need to assume certain communication between the two chains. Especially, contents on blockchain Y should be read by Bob and transmitted over to blockchain X in a timely manner.

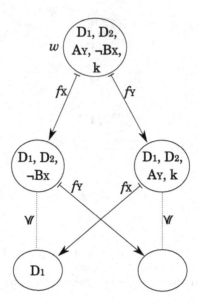

Fig. 4. A model M and a state w for proving Proposition 4. Five circles represent the five states of M. Each function f_a is identity whenever not explicitly shown. The $\preceq$ relation holds whenever two states are reachable following dashed lines and arrows in a bottom-to-top way.

In order to talk about the timing restrictions, we add two more agents in the language: $1\frac{1}{4}$ and $1\frac{1}{2}$ that represent "$1\frac{1}{4}$ (resp. $1\frac{1}{2}$) days from the beginning of protocol execution." In the models, $f_{1\frac{1}{2}}(w)$ is equal to w when the wall-clock time at w is less than one-and-half days from the beginning of protocol execution. Otherwise, $f_{1\frac{1}{2}}(w)$ is a previous state where the wall-clock time is less than one-and-half days from the beginning.

Now we can spell out assumptions; whenever blockchain Y has a record at one-and-quarter days, Bob should have read and submitted the record to blockchain X by one-and-half days:

$$(K_Y K_{1\frac{1}{4}}\varphi) \supset K_X K_{1\frac{1}{2}} K_{\text{Bob}} K_Y K_{1\frac{1}{4}}\varphi. \qquad \text{(Bob-has-chance)}$$

We have defined a set of infinitely many logical formulas where φ is replaced with arbitrary logical formulas.

When blockchain Y contains records at the two-day moment, it also contains witnesses from the one-and-quarter-day moment, saying that the hashlock had already been settled; either Alice had used the secret to unlock the hashock, or Alice would never unlock it:

$$K_Y(D_2 \supset K_{1\frac{1}{4}}((A_Y \wedge k) \vee (\neg A_Y))). \qquad \text{(Y-timed1)}$$

Finally, if Bob ever gets to know the secret, Alice should have opened the hashlock. In other words, Alice does not leak the secret without getting the fund in blockchain Y:

$$K_{\text{Bob}}\mathbf{k} \supset A_Y. \hspace{3cm} \text{(Alice-opsec)}$$

Blockchain X at one-and-half days should allow Bob to unlock the hashlock:

$$K_X K_{1\frac{1}{2}}((K_{\text{Bob}}\mathbf{k}) \supset B_X). \hspace{2.5cm} \text{(X-live1}\tfrac{1}{2}\text{)}$$

When we impose those formulas at every state, the desired weak binary outcome property holds.

Proposition 5. *If a model M satisfies (X-live2), (Y-timed1), (Alice-opsec), (Bob-has-chance), (X-live1$\frac{1}{2}$) at every state, M also satisfies (Weak-Binary-Outcome) at every state.*

Before proving this proposition, we need some preparations.

Proposition 6 (Kripke monotinicity [14]). *$M, w \models \varphi$ and $w \preceq w'$ imply $M, w' \models \varphi$.*

Proof. By structural induciton on φ. □

Proposition 7. *Any model M at any state w satisfies any $(K_a\varphi) \supset \varphi$.*

Proof. For any w' with $w' \succeq w$, we assume $M, w' \models K_a\varphi$ and claim $M, w' \models \varphi$. By the semantics of K_a, $f_a(w')$ satisfies φ. By the definition of a model, $f_a(w') \preceq w'$ holds. By Proposition 6, w' satisfies φ. □

With these two auxiliary propositions, we are ready to continue.

Proof. (of Proposition 5) We take an arbitrary state v in such a model M. And we take an arbitrary state w with $w \succeq v$. We assume $M, w \models K_X D_2$ and $M, w \models K_Y D_2$. It is enough to show that w satisfies $(A_Y \wedge B_X) \vee ((\neg A_Y) \wedge (\neg B_X))$.

Since w satisfies $K_Y D_2$, $f_Y(w)$ satisfies D_2. Since w satisfies (Y-timed1), $f_Y(w)$ satisfies $D_2 \supset K_{1\frac{1}{4}}((A_Y \wedge \mathbf{k}) \vee (\neg A_Y))$. So $f_Y(w)$ satisfies $K_{1\frac{1}{4}}((A_Y \wedge \mathbf{k}) \vee (\neg A_Y))$. That is to say w satisfies $K_Y K_{1\frac{1}{4}}((A_Y \wedge \mathbf{k}) \vee (\neg A_Y))$. By (Bob-has-chance), w also satisfies $K_X K_{1\frac{1}{2}} K_{\text{Bob}} K_Y K_{1\frac{1}{4}}((A_Y \wedge \mathbf{k}) \vee (\neg A_Y))$. In other words, $f_{1\frac{1}{4}} f_Y f_{\text{Bob}} f_{1\frac{1}{2}} f_X(w)$ satisfies $A_Y \wedge \mathbf{k}$ (the positive case) or $\neg A_Y$ (the negative case).

(The positive case) By (X-live1$\frac{1}{2}$), w satisfies $K_X K_{1\frac{1}{2}}((K_{\text{Bob}}\mathbf{k}) \supset B_X)$. In other words, $f_{1\frac{1}{2}} f_X(w)$ satisfies $(K_{\text{Bob}}\mathbf{k}) \supset B_X$. Since $f_{\text{Bob}} f_{1\frac{1}{2}} f_X(w)$ is a future of $f_{1\frac{1}{4}} f_Y f_{\text{Bob}} f_{1\frac{1}{2}} f_X(w)$, by Kripke monotonicity, $f_{\text{Bob}} f_{1\frac{1}{2}} f_X(w)$ satisfies $A_Y \wedge \mathbf{k}$. So, $f_{1\frac{1}{2}} f_X(w)$ satisfies $K_{\text{Bob}}\mathbf{k}$. The same state also satisfies $(K_{\text{Bob}}\mathbf{k}) \supset B_X$. As a result, $f_{1\frac{1}{2}} f_X(w)$ satisfies B_X. By Kripke monotonicity, w satisfies B_X. Also by Kripke monotonicity, w satisfies A_Y.

(The negative case) Since $f_{1\frac{1}{2}} f_X(w) \succeq f_{1\frac{1}{4}} f_Y f_{\text{Bob}} f_{1\frac{1}{2}} f_X(w)$, by Kripke monotonicity, $f_{1\frac{1}{2}} f_X(w)$ also satisfies $\neg A_Y$. Since $f_{1\frac{1}{2}} f_X(w)$ satisfies (Alice-opsec), by the semantics of $\supset$, $f_{1\frac{1}{2}} f_X(w)$ satisfies $\neg K_{\text{Bob}}\mathbf{k}$. Since $f_X(w) \succeq f_{1\frac{1}{2}} f_X(w)$, by Kripke monotonicity, $f_X(w)$ also satisfies $\neg K_{Bob}k$. We claim that w satisfies $\neg B_X$. For that, seeking contradiction, We assume some $x \succeq w$ satisfies B_X. State x satisfies (X-safe), so by the semantics of $\supset$, x also satisfies $K_X K_{Bob}k$. In other words, $f_X(x)$ satisfies $K_{Bob}k$. However, since $f_X(x) \succeq f_X(w)$, this contradicts $f_X(w)$ satisfying $\neg K_{Bob}k$. $\square$

Informal Reading of the Result. We have identified a set of sufficient assumptions that supports the atomicity. We should now reflect on the meaning of these logical formulas, but before that we have to evaluate our choice of the logic. When we modeled the cross-chain atomic swap using intuitionistic epistemic logic, before introducing any axioms, we effectively assumed that all propositions are stable. That is, once they become true, they remain true forever. This stability seems appropriate for the revealed secret k, but questionable for heads of blockchains. For Bitcoin, the head of the chain sometimes jumps to other branches. We discuss approaches to circumvent this problem in Sect. 6.

(Bob-has-chance) is about Bob's ability to read from the blockchain Y and submit the obtained knowledge to the blockchain X, which in turn requires availability of both blockchains. (Alice-opsec) is about Alice's ability to keep the secret when she chooses not to unlock the hashlock. This also requires pre-image resistance of the hash function. The assumptions (Y-timed1) and (X-live2) are about the behavior of the onchain scripts. These two assumptions need to be backed by program analysis. A formal notation of onchain programs like SoK [1] might ease such program analysis.

5   Related Work

Emerson and Clarke [7] already regarded Kripke models as states of communicating processes. They proposed a method for automatically generating finite state machines that represent states of communicating processes. They describe a procedure to decide whether such finite state machines exist for a specification.

Smart Contract Verification. Luu et al. [17] define a lightweight semantics of Ethereum. Nikolic et al. [20] use the same semantics to capture bugs spanning multiple Ethereum transactions. Sergey and Aquinas [23] gave an insight that concurrent reasoning applies to Ethereum contracts' interactions. None of these works treats the interaction of multiple blockchains.

Halpern and Pass's Knowledge-Based Analysis on the Epistemic Property of a Blockchain. Halpern and Pass [12] also analyze the communication ability of a blockchain using a modal epistemic logic. The reasoning framework of Halpern and Pass is based on the tradition of model epistemic logic, admittedly more faithfully than our work is, because their "runs and systems" [8] model has been very popular among computer scientists.

Their focus of attention is different from ours. Halpern and Pass [12] look at a blockchain as a communication medium between agents, and propose a weak form of common knowledge that the blockchain provides. To seek a form of common knowledge, their analysis needs to consider entering and leaving agents. Our analysis never required a global view of all agents.

The difference seems to come from different roles of blockchains. Halpern and Pass seem to regard a blockchain as a mechanism for public attestation of valid contracts between agents. In our analysis, Alice is never interested in Bob's knowledge, or vice versa. The formulas in our analysis do not involve nesting of epistemic modalities like $K_{\text{Alice}} K_{\text{Bob}} \cdots$. The participants are interested to see value transfers recorded on the finalized blocks, but not interested in whether other agents have seen those blocks.

We analyze a situation where multiple blockchains are involved, and, we have identified some synchrony conditions for specific agents (Bob-has-chance), (Y-timed1), (X-live1$\frac{1}{2}$) that are useful for a specific protocol, while Halpern and Pass assume a global parameter to limit delays of all messages.

Hirai's Intuitionistic Epistemic Logic. Hirai [14] characterized waitfree communication over sequentially consistent shared memory using intuitionistic epistemic logic. That work targetted shared memory multi-thread computation. There, a well-known property called sequential consistency was represented as an axiom type[3]. In this paper, we are figuring out desired properties out of Kripke models that reveal missing assumptions (Propositions 3 and 4). Modal logics are useful not only for explaining known properties but for identifying unspecified requirements.

Gleissenthall and Rybalchenko [11] use a more expressive logic with separate temporal modalities and epistemic modalities for characterizing sequential consistency, linearizability and eventual consistency. Their logic is more suitable to express liveness properties (e.g., "if Alice tries to do something infinitely often, she eventually succeeds").

6 Discussion

The biggest remaining problem is the lurking unsoundness with respect to the reality. In our modeling, any satisfied formula remains true in the future. Blockchain developers call our assumption finality. Bitcoin does not provide finality. Sometimes blockchains fork and all branches except one are orphaned. In those cases, a history becomes abandoned. There are three ways to deal with this problem:

1. assume finality and hold agents responsible if they trust blocks too early,
2. model the probability that blocks are final, and
3. model all forking branches.

---

[3] An axiom type is a logical formula with free variables like φ and ψ that can be substituted by any formulas.

Our current treatment is 1. Agents are required to ignore too fresh blocks and only take the contents of older blocks into their knowledge base, and our analysis breaks down when the agents are unluckily not patient enough. Our treatment is in line with the cryptocurrency exchanges' treatment of blockchains. Halpern and Pass [12] talk about probabilistic treatments, which supposedly would support the approach 2. The approach 3 seems not yet explored, but should be an interesting topic for modal logicians.

Another discrepancy is the requirement that agents remember all knowledge. This discrepancy does not matter when a protocol is shown not to work because incomplete memory doesn't work better than complete memory. On the other hand, once a protocol is shown to work, the concrete implementation of the protocol can optimize away irrelevant knowledge.

For more convenience, an automatic decision procedure is desirable that can judge whether a desired property is valid given some assumptions. Is there always a finite model that refutes an invalid property? Moreover, when one develops an on-chain program, their possible behavior should be spelled out automatically as logical formulas.

Our biggest diversion from the traditional treatment of knowledge is the treatment of blockchains as agents. Usually network participants or processes are treated as agents, but not a data structure maintained on the network. Since the semantics of intuitionistic epistemic logic never relies on a global state, we never had to identify a blockchain from a global view point. Given a local w, $f_X(w)$ is blockchain X's state just according to w. If we used the traditional S5 epistemic logic [6], we would define which two states blockchain X can distinguish, but that criterion would assume an undisputed global identification of blockchain X.

The take away for blockchain protocol designers is that, for the atomic cross-chain swap to be atomic, availability and safety assumptions are necessary. For better certainly, merged blocks (e.g. Aspen's checkpoints [10]) will be effective. A merged block belongs to multiple blockchains all at once or none at all. With a merged block, two blockchains can share common knowledge in the same way Alice and Bob share common knowledge in Fig. 2(b).

7   Conclusion

We used Kripke models of intuitionistic epistemic logic to see what kind of assumptions are necessary for "atomic" property of the atomic cross-chain swaps (Propositions 3 and 4). We also showed a set of assumptions is enough for the "atomic" property to hold (Proposition 5). For cross-chain atomic swaps to be atomic, external agents' abilities to read and write blocks within a limited timeframe is crucial. To our knowledge, this is the first analysis of inter-blockchain communication using a modal logic.

References

1. Atzei, N., Bartoletti, M., Cimoli, T., Lande, S., Zunino, R.: SoK: unraveling bitcoin smart contracts. In: Bauer, L., Küsters, R. (eds.) POST 2018. LNCS, vol. 10804, pp. 217–242. Springer, Cham (2018). https://doi.org/10.1007/978-3-319-89722-6_9
2. Bitcoin Wiki: Script (2010–2018). https://en.bitcoin.it/wiki/Script. Accessed 13 Mar 2018
3. Chandra, T.D., Toueg, S.: Unreliable failure detectors for reliable distributed systems. J. ACM **43**(2), 225–267 (1996)
4. Chandy, K.M., Misra, J.: How processes learn. Distrib. Comput. **1**(1), 40–52 (1986)
5. van Dalen, D.: Logic and Structure. Springer, Heidelberg (1994). https://doi.org/10.1007/978-3-662-02962-6
6. van Ditmarsch, H., van der Hoek, W., Kooi, B.: Dynamic Epistemic Logic, 1st edn. Springer, Heidelberg (2007). https://doi.org/10.1007/978-1-4020-5839-4
7. Emerson, E., Clarke, E.M.: Using branching time temporal logic to synthesize synchronization skeletons. Sci. Comput. Program. **2**(3), 241–266 (1982)
8. Fagin, R., Halpern, J.Y., Vardi, M.Y., Moses, Y.: Reasoning About Knowledge. MIT Press, Cambridge (1995)
9. Fischer, M.J., Lynch, N.A., Paterson, M.S.: Impossibility of distributed consensus with one faulty process. J. ACM **32**(2), 374–382 (1985)
10. Gencer, A.E., van Renesse, R., Sirer, E.G.: Short paper: service-oriented sharding for blockchains. In: Kiayias, A. (ed.) FC 2017. LNCS, vol. 10322, pp. 393–401. Springer, Cham (2017). https://doi.org/10.1007/978-3-319-70972-7_22
11. von Gleissenthall, K., Rybalchenko, A.: An epistemic perspective on consistency of concurrent computations. In: D'Argenio, P.R., Melgratti, H. (eds.) CONCUR 2013. LNCS, vol. 8052, pp. 212–226. Springer, Heidelberg (2013). https://doi.org/10.1007/978-3-642-40184-8_16
12. Halpern, J.Y., Pass, R.: A knowledge-based analysis of the blockchain protocol. In: TARK 2017. EPTCS, vol. 251, pp. 324–335 (2017)
13. Hirai, Y.: An intuitionistic epistemic logic for asynchronous communication. Master's thesis, the University of Tokyo (2010)
14. Hirai, Y.: An intuitionistic epistemic logic for sequential consistency on shared memory. In: Clarke, E.M., Voronkov, A. (eds.) LPAR 2010. LNCS (LNAI), vol. 6355, pp. 272–289. Springer, Heidelberg (2010). https://doi.org/10.1007/978-3-642-17511-4_16
15. Lamport, L.: The part-time parliament. ACM Trans. Comput. Syst. **16**(2), 133–169 (1998)
16. Lundeberg, M.B.: Advisory: secret size attack on cross-chain hash lock smart contracts (2018). https://gist.github.com/markblundeberg/7a932c98179de2190049f5823907c016. Accessed 07 Mar 2018
17. Luu, L., Chu, D.H., Olickel, H., Saxena, P., Hobor, A.: Making smart contracts smarter. In: CCS 2016, pp. 254–269. ACM (2016)
18. Luu, L., Narayanan, V., Zheng, C., Baweja, K., Gilbert, S., Saxena, P.: A secure sharding protocol for open blockchains. In: Proceedings of the 2016 ACM SIGSAC Conference on Computer and Communications Security, pp. 17–30. CCS 2016. ACM (2016)
19. Nakamoto, S.: Bitcoin: a peer-to-peer electronic cash system (2008). https://bitcoin.org/bitcoin.pdf. Accessed 20 Mar 2018
20. Nikolic, I., Kolluri, A., Sergey, I., Saxena, P., Hobor, A.: Finding the greedy, prodigal, and suicidal contracts at scale. ArXiv e-prints (2018)

21. Nolan, T.: Re: Alt chains and atomic transfers (2013). https://bitcointalk.org/index.php?topic=193281.msg2224949#msg2224949. Accessed 12 Mar 2018
22. Poon, J., Buterin, V.: Plasma: scalable autonomous smart contracts (2017). https://plasma.io/plasma.pdf. Accessed 07 Mar 2018
23. Sergey, I., Hobor, A.: A concurrent perspective on smart contracts. In: Brenner, M., et al. (eds.) FC 2017. LNCS, vol. 10323, pp. 478–493. Springer, Cham (2017). https://doi.org/10.1007/978-3-319-70278-0_30
24. Troelstra, A.S., Van Dalen, D.: Constructivism in Mathematics: An Introduction, vol. 1. Elsevier, Amsterdam (1988)
25. Wood, G.: Polkadot: vision for a heterogeneous multi-chain framework (2016). https://github.com/w3f/polkadot-white-paper/blob/master/PolkaDotPaper.pdf. Accessed 07 Mar 2018

A Language-Independent Approach to Smart Contract Verification

Xiaohong Chen[1]([✉]), Daejun Park[1,2], and Grigore Roşu[1,2]

[1] University of Illinois at Urbana-Champaign, Champaign, USA
xc3@illinois.edu
[2] Runtime Verification Inc., Urbana, USA

Abstract. This invited paper reports the current progress on smart contract verification with the $\mathbb{K}$ framework in a language-independent style.

1 Introduction and Motivation

Flaws of blockchain programming languages or virtual machines have led and continue to lead to cryptocurrency software bugs that directly translate into significant money loss [1,3,4,6,14]. Formal analysis and verification of blockchain languages and virtual machines is thus very much in need. Traditionally, this is done by giving a formal model of the program-to-verify, either by a manual construction in theorem provers such as Coq [10] or Isabelle [15], or by a translation to some intermediate verification languages (IVL) such as Boogie [2] or Why [7]. Developing program models in theorem provers can be expensive and is only done to mission critical systems, while a translation to IVL may loose program behavior. In either case, a *trusted formal semantics* of the target language together with a proof of correctness of either the program models built in Coq or Isabelle, or the translation to IVL, are required. Such correctness proofs are often done manually on paper and can be expensive. They are also sensitive to the target languages and programs, so small changes on the verification targets require to redo the proofs. Due to the fact that blockchain programming languages are often moving targets and have a rather rapid development cycle, with new versions being released and deployed in a weekly pace, the traditionally program verification approaches are often too expensive to use in practice.

The $\mathbb{K}$ framework [13] adopts a *language-independent* approach to program verification; it was derived from our firm belief that every programming language must have a formal semantics, and that all formal or informal analysis tools for that language should be automatically generated from that semantics in a correct-by-construction manner. Figure 1 illustrates the $\mathbb{K}$ approach. In terms of verification, the *language-independent verifier* is parametric on the semantics of the language, and it takes as input a program and a specification of the program and solves the verification problem (see Fig. 2). Extensive experiments and case studies confirm that this language-independent approach to verification is feasible. For example, [5,11] show that when instantiated with

T. Margaria and B. Steffen (Eds.): ISoLA 2018, LNCS 11247, pp. 405–413, 2018.
https://doi.org/10.1007/978-3-030-03427-6_30

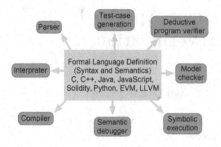

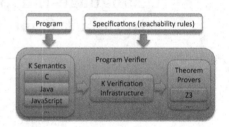

Fig. 1. The $\mathbb{K}$ framework approach to language design and formal verification.

Fig. 2. A language-independent program verifier takes a program and its specification, and verifies it with respect to its formal semantics.

formal semantics of real languages such as C, Java, and JavaScript, the generic $\mathbb{K}$ program verifier is able to check well-known challenging functional correctness properties of heap manipulation programs with mutable data structures, such as AVL trees, read-black trees, and even the Schorr-Waite graph marking algorithm, all implemented in each of C, Java, and JavaScript. Nothing was needed in the generic verifier specific to any of these languages, except for their formal semantics. When it comes to blockchain languages, the advantage of the $\mathbb{K}$ approach is even more significant, as languages and virtual machines in this field change at an unusually high rate and thus there is no need to redo the correctness proofs for either the high-level program models or the translation to IVL. All verification tools are correct-by-construction, and thus are suitable to the rapid development cycle of blockchain languages.

In the rest of the paper, we briefly introduce the $\mathbb{K}$ framework in Sect. 2 and summarize the current progress on blockchain languages and smart contracts verification in Sect. 3. Then we discuss the general workflow of smart contract verification with $\mathbb{K}$ framework in Sect. 4, and conclude with future work in Sect. 5.

2   An Overview of the $\mathbb{K}$ Framework

The $\mathbb{K}$ framework is a rewrite-based executable semantics framework for programming language design and development. It can be regarded as a meta-programming language that defines programming languages. As an example, consider the simple imperative language IMP whose syntax is given in Fig. 3. IMP has arithmetic expressions and the usual assignment, sequential, if-, and while-statements. Arithmetic expressions are used as conditions where zero means false and nonzero values mean true. The complete $\mathbb{K}$ definition of IMP is given in Fig. 4. The definition consists of two modules IMP-SYNTAX and IMP. The module IMP-SYNTAX defines the concrete syntax using the conventional BNF grammar where terminals are in quotes. Production rules are separated by the "|" and ">", where "|" means the two productions (before and after "|") have the same precedence while ">" means the production before has higher precedence (binds

$Exp ::= Id \mid Int \mid Exp + Exp \mid Exp - Exp$

$Stmt ::= Id = Exp; \mid Stmt\ Stmt \mid \{\ Exp\ \} \mid \texttt{if}(Exp)\ Stmt\ Stmt \mid \texttt{while}(Exp)\ Stmt$

$Ids ::= Id \mid Id, Ids$

$Pgm\ \ ::= \texttt{int}\ Ids;\ Stmt$

Fig. 3. The syntax of the language IMP.

tighter) than the ones after. In other words, all the other language constructs bind tighter than the sequential operator in IMP. Categories Int and Id are built-in categories for integers and identifiers (program variables), respectively. Exp is the category for expressions, which subsumes Int and Id and has two productions for plus and minus. Pgm is the category for programs, which is a declaration of a list of program variables (the category Ids) followed by a statement. Ids is defined using $\mathbb{K}$'s built-in list template List, whose second argument is the separating character. In other words, Ids is the category of comma-separated lists of Id's.

Attributes are wrapped with braces "[" and "]". Some attributes are only for parsing purpose while others may carry additional semantic meaning and affect how $\mathbb{K}$ executes programs. The attribute left means left-associative. The attribute strict defines evaluation contexts, so when $\mathbb{K}$ sees the expression $e_1 + e_2$ (and similarly $e_1 - e_2$), it first evaluates e_1 to an integer i_1 and e_2 to an integers i_2 in a *fully nondeterministic* way, and then evaluates $i_1 + i_2$. The attribute strict(1) means if $\mathbb{K}$ sees the if-statement if$(B)\ P\ Q$ it should only evaluates the first argument B to a value v while keeping the other arguments P and Q untouched. Therefore, the two branches of if-statement are *frozen* and will not be evaluated if the condition is not a value. The attribute bracket tells $\mathbb{K}$ that certain productions are only used for grouping, and $\mathbb{K}$ will not generate nodes in its internal abstract syntax trees for those productions. Here, parentheses are used to group arithmetic expressions while curly brackets are used to group program statements. The empty curly bracket "{}" represents the empty statement.

The module IMP defines the operational semantics of IMP in terms of a set of human readable rewrite rules. The category KResult tells $\mathbb{K}$ which categories contain non-reducible values. It helps $\mathbb{K}$ perform efficiently with evaluation contexts. The only category of values here is Int. Configuration is a core concept in the $\mathbb{K}$ framework. A *configuration* of a language holds all information that is needed to execute programs, gathered in *cells*. Simple languages such as IMP have only a few cells, while complex real languages such as C usually have more than one hundred. In $\mathbb{K}$, configurations are defined using a syntax borrowed from the XML format. The configuration of IMP contains two cells: the k cell and the state cell. For clarity, we put all cells in configuration in a top cell: the T cell, but it is not mandatory. The k cell holds the remaining computation (program) that needs to execute and the state cell holds a mapping from program variables to their values in the memory. Initially, the state cell holds the empty map, denoted

```
module IMP-SYNTAX
  imports DOMAINS-SYNTAX
  syntax Exp  ::= Int | Id
                | Exp "+" Exp                          [left, strict]
                | Exp "-" Exp                          [left, strict]
                | "(" Exp ")"                          [bracket]
  syntax Stmt ::= Id "=" Exp ";"                       [strict(2)]
                | "if" "(" Exp ")" Stmt Stmt           [strict(1)]
                | "while" "(" Exp ")" Stmt
                | "{" Stmt "}"                          [bracket]
                | "{" "}"
                > Stmt Stmt                             [left]
  syntax Pgm  ::= "int" Ids ";" Stmt
  syntax Ids  ::= List{Id, ","}
endmodule

module IMP
  imports IMP-SYNTAX
  imports DOMAINS
  syntax KResult ::= Int
  configuration <T> <k> $PGM:Pgm </k> <state> .Map </state> </T>
  rule <k> X:Id => I ...</k> <state>... X |-> I ...</state>
  rule I1 + I2 => I1 +Int I2
  rule I1 - I2 => I1 -Int I2
  rule <k> X = I:Int; => . ...</k> <state>... X |-> (_ => I) ...</state>
  rule S1:Stmt S2:Stmt => S1 ~> S2                     [structural]
  rule if (I) S _ => S requires I =/=Int 0
  rule if (0) _ S => S
  rule while(B) S => if(B) {S while(B) S} {}           [structural]
  rule {} => .                                          [structural]
  rule <k> int (X, Xs => Xs); S </k>  <state> ... (. => X |-> 0) </state>  [structural]
  rule int .Ids; S => S                                [structural]
endmodule
```

Fig. 4. The complete $\mathbb{K}$ definition of the language IMP, consisting of two modules.

as .Map. In $\mathbb{K}$, we use dot "." to denote "nothing", and .Map means the nothing
has type Map. The k cell initially contains a program $PGM:Pgm, where $PGM is a
special $\mathbb{K}$ variable name. To execute an IMP program, say sum.imp, the name of
the source file is passed to $\mathbb{K}$, and $\mathbb{K}$ will parse the source file using the concrete
syntax and associate the result (of category Pgm) to the variable $PGM:Pgm in
the k cell.

$\mathbb{K}$ defines the language semantics in terms of a set of rewrite rules. These
rewrite rules specify a transition system on *configurations*. We point out two
important characteristics of rewrites rules in $\mathbb{K}$. The first important characteristic
of rewrites rules of $\mathbb{K}$ is that $\mathbb{K}$ supports *local rewrites*. In other words, the rewrite
symbol "=>" does not need to appear in the top level, but can appear locally in
which the rewrite happens. Take the lookup rule as an example. Instead of

```
rule <k> X:Id ...</k> <state>... X |-> I ...</state>
  => <k> I ...</k> <state>... X |-> I ...</state>
```
one writes
```
rule <k> X:Id => I ...</k> <state>... X |-> I ...</state>
```

to reduce space and avoid duplicates. The "..." in $\mathbb{K}$ is a shortcut for things that "exist and do not matter and change." The rule says that if the top of the computation in the k cell is a program variable X:Id, and at the same time X binds to the integer I somewhere in the state cell, then rewrite X:Id to I.

The second characteristic of rewrite rules in $\mathbb{K}$ is that $\mathbb{K}$ also supports *configuration inference* and *configuration completion*. The rewrite rules may not explicitly mention all cells in configuration, but just related ones. $\mathbb{K}$ will infer the implicit cells and complete the configuration automatically. For example, instead of

```
rule <T> <k> I1 + I2 => I1 +Int I2 ... </k> <state> M </state> </T>
```

one writes

```
rule I1 + I2 => I1 +Int I2
```

which is not only a lot simpler, but also extensible. If we add a new cell to the configuration, we will not need to modify any of the existing rules.

The rest of the semantics is self-explanatory. The rule for assignment statements X = I:Int; updates the value bound to X in the state cell, as specified in the local rewrite X |-> (_ => I). Here the underscore "_" is an anonymous $\mathbb{K}$ variable; it matches whatever integer that is currently bound to X. After the update, the assignment statement is removed from the k cell, as specified by the local rewrite X = I:Int; =>.. Recall that the dot "." means nothing, and rewriting something to a dot means removing it. Attribute structural means the associated rewrite rule is not counted as an explicit step by $\mathbb{K}$, but an implicit (quite) one. It should not affect how $\mathbb{K}$ executes the programs. The empty statement {} simply reduces to nothing. The last two rules process the declaration list of program variables and initialize their values to zero.

3   Semantics of Blockchain Virtual Machines in $\mathbb{K}$

KEVM. The Ethereum Virtual Machine (EVM) [16] is a low-level bytecode language running on a general-purpose "world computer" built by the blockchain cryptocurrency Ethereum. Small programs called smart contracts are allowed to execute on it, often written in high-level languages such as Solidity (https:// github.com/ethereum/solidity) or Vyper (https://github.com/ethereum/vyper) and then compiled to EVM. To verify smart contracts, a formal semantics of the low-level EVM language was developed [9] using the $\mathbb{K}$ framework, which we refer to as KEVM. As far as we know, KEVM is the first fully executable formal semantics of the EVM language. It is tested against the official 40,683-test stress test suite for EVM implementations that comes with the official C++ implementation of the EVM.

Based on KEVM, the startup Runtime Verification formally verified several smart contracts (https://runtimeverification.com/smartcontract), and the result is available for public access in the spirit of open-source (https://github.com/ runtimeverification/verified-smart-contracts). Since December 2017, a number of smart contracts have been verified with the $\mathbb{K}$ framework; the following is a list of them in chronological order (older to newer):

- Vyper ERC20 Token Contact (https://github.com/ethereum/vyper);
- HackerGold (HKG) ERC20 Token Contract (https://github.com/ether-camp/virtual-accelerator);
- OpenZeppelin's ERC20 Token Contract (https://github.com/OpenZeppelin/openzeppelin-solidity);
- Bihu Smart Contract (https://github.com/runtimeverification/verified-smart-contracts/tree/master/bihu);
- DSToken ERC20 Token Contract (https://github.com/dapphub/ds-token);
- Ethereum Casper Contract (https://github.com/runtimeverification/verified-smart-contracts/tree/master/casper).

A surprising and pleasant observation in the process of the development of KEVM and the verification of smart contracts is that the EVM interpreter automatically generated by $\mathbb{K}$ based on EVM formal semantics is only one order of magnitude slower on average than the official C++ implementation [8]. Since smart contracts are often small programs, the above suggests that KEVM can serve not only as a reference model of the EVM but also as an actual implementation.

IELE. Like EVM, IELE (https://github.com/runtimeverification/iele-semantics) is another virtual machines bytecode language. Unlike EVM, IELE was designed in the spirit of *easier formal verification*, and thus it is significantly different from EVM in various aspects. For example, IELE is a register-based machine, and it supports unbounded integers (as unbounded arithmetics is often easier than bounded arithmetics in verification). IELE was designed purely in a semantic-based style using $\mathbb{K}$, and an automatically-generated virtual machine is derived from its formal semantics, which makes it the first virtual machine whose development and implementation was completely powered by formal methods.

4   Smart Contract Verification

In this section, we briefly discuss the workflow of smart contract verification, taking the open resource of the work of ERC20 verification (https://github.com/runtimeverification/verified-smart-contracts/tree/master/erc20) as a case study example. See [12] for more details.

The ERC20 token contract (abbrev. as ERC20 below) is one of the most popular and valuable smart contracts. An informal standard for ERC20 can be found at (https://github.com/ethereum/EIPs/blob/master/EIPS/eip-20.md), which we refer to as the ERC20 standard. The ERC20 standard essentially defines an API with an informal specification. Figure 5 shows an example of a piece of informal specification of the function `transfer` in the ERC20 standard.

Transfers _value amount of tokens to address _to , and MUST fire the `Transfer` event. The function SHOULD `throw` if the _from account balance does not have enough tokens to spend.

Note Transfers of 0 values MUST be treated as normal transfers and fire the `Transfer` event.

```
function transfer(address _to, uint256 _value) returns (bool success)
```

Fig. 5. The informal specification of the function `transfer` in the ERC20 standard.

```
rule
    <k> transfer(To, Value) => true ... </k>
    <caller> From </caller>                          rule
    <account> <id> From </id>                            <k> transfer(From, Value)
      <balance>                                              => throw ...
        BalanceFrom => BalanceFrom -Int Value            </k>
      </balance> </account>                              <caller> From </caller>
    <account> <id> To </id>                              <id> From </id>
      <balance> BalanceTo => BalanceTo +Int Value        <balance> BalanceFrom </balance>
      </balance> </account>                          requires Value <Int 0
    <log> Log => Log Transfer(From, To, Value)           orBool Value >Int BalanceFrom
    </log>
requires To =/=Int From andBool Value >=Int 0
  andBool Value <=Int BalanceFrom
  andBool BalanceTo +Int Value <=Int MAXVALUE
```

Fig. 6. The formal specification of the function `transfer` in ERC20-K. The rule on the left shows the case when the transfer *succeeds* and the caller is *different* from the receiver. The rule on the right shows the case when the transfer *fails* and the caller is the *same* as the receiver.

The first step of the verification is to take the informal ERC20 standard and *refine* it to a formal specification. The outcome of the refinement, which we refer to as ERC20-K, is a $\mathbb{K}$ definition that captures the complete functionality of the ERC20 API (https://github.com/runtimeverification/erc20-semantics). For example, the above informal specification is divided into four cases in ERC20-K, namely all four combinations of whether the transfer succeeds or fails, and whether the caller is the same as or different from the receiver. Figure 6 gives the formal specification for two of the fours cases. ERC20-K therefore formally specifies the entire ERC20 API and its intended behavior. It is worth mentioning how fast it is to develop such a complete executable formal specification in $\mathbb{K}$: the fully documented ERC20-K took a developer about two weeks to finish, with one week writing the rules and another week revising it, fixing bugs, and writing documentation.

Since smart contracts are compiled to lower-level EVM bytecode, we need to refine the high-level ERC20-K specification further, to an EVM-level formal specification, referred to as ERC20-EVM, which is based on KEVM and takes all EVM-specific details into account. Finally, various smart contracts have been verified with the ERC20-EVM specification and the built-in program verification infrastructure in $\mathbb{K}$. We refer interested readers to [12] as well as our open source project (https://github.com/runtimeverification/verified-smart-contracts) for more experiment details and technical discussion.

5   Conclusion and Future Work

We hope this paper demonstrates that language-independent verification is possible and feasible, and is especially preferable for blockchain languages and smart contracts verification. With only one executable semantics, it suffices to generate all the tools in a correct-by-construction manner, and thus eliminate the need for redundant and error-prone proofs of correctness. In particular, for emerging fields like the blockchain and smart contracts where new languages and programs are released on a weekly or even daily basis, the language-independent approach seems to be the only viable solution. We hope that this wave of blockchain languages and smart contracts verification will raise interest from the community in language-independent semantics frameworks like $\mathbb{K}$ and drives application of the techniques to all languages. As of future work, two sides of research are needed. On the foundation side, a language-independent (program) logic is in need, which allows us to state and reason about any properties of any programs written in any programming languages. On the implementation side, automation of tools is needed.

Acknowledgments. We thank the $\mathbb{K}$ team (http://www.kframework.org/index.php/People) for their sustained dedication and help, as well as to numerous other contributors to the $\mathbb{K}$ framework.

References

1. Atzei, N., Bartoletti, M., Cimoli, T.: A survey of attacks on ethereum smart contracts (SoK). In: Maffei, M., Ryan, M. (eds.) POST 2017. LNCS, vol. 10204, pp. 164–186. Springer, Heidelberg (2017). https://doi.org/10.1007/978-3-662-54455-6_8
2. Barnett, M., Chang, B.-Y.E., DeLine, R., Jacobs, B., Leino, K.R.M.: Boogie: a modular reusable verifier for object-oriented programs. In: de Boer, F.S., Bonsangue, M.M., Graf, S., de Roever, W.-P. (eds.) FMCO 2005. LNCS, vol. 4111, pp. 364–387. Springer, Heidelberg (2006). https://doi.org/10.1007/11804192_17
3. Breidenbach, L., Daian, P., Juels, A., Gün Sirer, E.: An in-depth look at the parity multisig bug (2017). http://hackingdistributed.com/2017/07/22/deep-dive-parity-bug/
4. Buterin, V.: Thinking about smart contract security (2016). https://blog.ethereum.org/2016/06/19/thinking-smart-contract-security/
5. Ştefănescu, A., Park, D., Yuwen, S., Li, Y., Roşu, G.: Semantics-based program verifiers for all languages. In: Proceedings of the 2016 ACM SIGPLAN International Conference on Object-Oriented Programming, Systems, Languages, and Applications (OOPSLA 2016), pp. 74–91. ACM, November 2016
6. Daian, P.: DAO attack (2016). http://hackingdistributed.com/2016/06/18/analysis-of-the-dao-exploit/
7. Filliâtre, J.-C., Marché, C.: The Why/Krakatoa/Caduceus platform for deductive program verification. In: Damm, W., Hermanns, H. (eds.) CAV 2007. LNCS, vol. 4590, pp. 173–177. Springer, Heidelberg (2007). https://doi.org/10.1007/978-3-540-73368-3_21

8. Hildenbrandt, E., et al.: KEVM: a complete semantics of the ethereum virtual machine. In: Proceedings of the 31st IEEE Computer Security Foundations Symposium (CSF 2018). IEEE (2018). http://jellopaper.org

9. KEVM Team: KEVM: semantics of EVM in K (2017). https://github.com/kframework/evm-semantics

10. The Coq Development Team: The Coq proof assistant reference manual. LogiCal Project (2004)

11. Moore, B., Peña, L., Roşu, G.: Program verification by coinduction. In: Ahmed, A. (ed.) ESOP 2018. LNCS, vol. 10801, pp. 589–618. Springer, Cham (2018). https://doi.org/10.1007/978-3-319-89884-1_21

12. Park, D., Zhang, Y., Saxena, M., Daian, P., Roşu, G.: A formal verification tool for ethereum VM bytecode. In: Proceedings of the 2018 ACM SIGSOFT International Symposium on Foundations of Software Engineering (FSE 2018) (2018)

13. Roşu, G., Şerbănuţă, F.T.: An overview of the K semantic framework. J. Log. Algebr. Program. **79**(6), 397–434 (2010)

14. Steiner, J.: Security is a process: a postmortem on the parity multi-sig library self-destruct (2017). http://goo.gl/LBh1vR

15. The Isabelle Development Team: Isabelle (2018). https://isabelle.in.tum.de/

16. Wood, G.: Ethereum: a secure decentralised generalised transaction ledger (2014). Updated for EIP-150 in 2017. http://yellowpaper.io/

Towards Adding Variety to Simplicity

Nachiappan Valliappan[1], Solène Mirliaz[2], Elisabet Lobo Vesga[1],
and Alejandro Russo[1(✉)]

[1] Chalmers University of Technology, Gothenburg, Sweden
russo@chalmers.se
[2] ENS Rennes, Rennes, France

Abstract. Simplicity is a Turing-incomplete typed combinator language
for smart contracts with a formal semantics. The design of Simplicity makes it possible to statically estimate the resources (e.g., memory) required to execute contracts. Such a feature is highly relevant
in blockchain applications to efficiently determine fees to run smart
contracts. Despite being Turing incomplete, the language is capable of
expressing non-trivial contracts. Often, Simplicity programs contain lots
of code repetition that could otherwise be avoided if it had common programming languages features, such as local definitions, functions, and
bounded loops. In this work, we provide the foundations to make Simplicity a richer language. To achieve that, we connect Simplicity's primitives
with a categorical model. By doing so, we lift the language to a more
abstract representation that will allow us to extend it by leveraging category theory models for computations. This methodology facilitates the
addition of local definitions, functions, and bounded loops. We provide
an implementation of Simplicity and its virtual machine in the functional
programming language Haskell.

Keywords: Simplicity · Category theory · Haskell
Functional programming · Blockchain · Smart contracts

1 Introduction

Blockchain technology has emerged as a revolutionary approach for decentralized peer-to-peer networks. The most known deployment of this technology is
Bitcoin [5]. Since its launch in 2009, Bitcoin has spawned a number of alternative crypto-currencies using different optimizations and tweaks (e.g., Litecoin,
Ripple, EOS [9,10]). Among these, Ethereum [12] stands out for its implementation of programmable transactions in the form of smart contracts. Given that
smart contracts are programs, they need to be executed in order to get a result
but without compromising the availability of the whole network. To achieve
that, Ethereum assigns a consumable resource, called *gas*, to the execution of
contracts which is paid by users to the block miners in *ether*—Ethereum's currency [12]. Ethereum uses a Turing-complete computational model, which makes
it challenging to predict the gas required to run contracts.

© Springer Nature Switzerland AG 2018
T. Margaria and B. Steffen (Eds.): ISoLA 2018, LNCS 11247, pp. 414–431, 2018.
https://doi.org/10.1007/978-3-030-03427-6_31

Simplicity [6,7] is a language for smart contracts with a formal semantics that enables "fast" (linear time) static analysis of resource consumption. The operational semantics of Simplicity instructions is given in an abstract machine named *the Simplicity Bit Machine* (SBM). Despite that the language is capable of expressing non-trivial contracts, it can be very cumbersome to actually write one using its minimal constructs. Moreover, the lack of common programming languages features such as local definitions, functions, and loops forces programs to contain lots of code repetition that could otherwise be avoided.

In this work, we show how to interpret Simplicity as a mathematical model from category theory. Once in the territory of category theory, we borrow its results on modeling different computational aspects to extend Simplicity and its virtual machine with functions. By adding functions, Simplicity contracts can account for local definitions as well as bounded loops. We also provide an implementation of Simplicity, the SBM, as well as our extensions in the functional programming language Haskell[1].

Primitive	Description
$iden : A \vdash A$	It is the identity function which simply returns its input.
$unit : A \vdash \mathbb{1}$	It is a unit function which always returns a value of the unit type.
$comp\ f\ g : A \vdash C$	It composes two simplicity functions $f : A \vdash B$ and $g : B \vdash C$.
$pair\ s\ t : A \vdash (B \times C)$	It constructs a product using $s : A \vdash B$ and $t : A \vdash C$.
$take\ t : A \times B \vdash C$	It applies $t : A \vdash C$ to the first component of a product.
$drop\ t : A \times B \vdash C$	It applies $t : B \vdash C$ to the second component of a product.
$injl\ t : A \vdash B + C$	It constructs a coproduct using $t : A \vdash B$.
$injr\ t : A \vdash B + C$	It constructs a coproduct using $t : A \vdash C$.
$case\ s\ t : (A + B) \times C \vdash D$	It is used to pattern match over the coproduct $(A + B)$ in the input. If the coproduct contains a value of type A, then $s : A \times C \vdash D$ is executed, else if the coproduct contains a value of type B, then $t : B \times C \vdash D$ is executed.

Fig. 1. Simplicity's basic functions and combinators

2 Background

Simplicity can be considered a typed functional programming language, where the expressions are essentially built from applying the functions in the language. It therefore consists of base functions and function combinators (or combinators for short). Combinators are dedicated to build more complex functions from

---

[1] Our implementation and accompanying material are available at https://bitbucket.org/russo/isola-additional-material/overview.

simpler ones in a compositional manner. Simplicity has three types: the unit type, written 𝟙, the product type, written $A \times B$, and the coproduct type, written $A + B$. The entire Simplicity's interface is shown in Fig. 1, where $f : i \vdash o$ denotes that the input and output type of function f are i and o, respectively. Simplicity's functions are self-explanatory and therefore we omit discussing them further.

One of the design goals for Simplicity is to enable the estimation of runtime resources statically when executed in a virtual machine. The analysis of runtime resources requires a formal model of the runtime as well as an operational semantics of Simplicity's basic functions and combinators. Observe that the computational power of the language is Turing incomplete (e.g., it lacks loops), which facilitates the estimation of resource consumption—we refer the interested reader to [7] for details.

2.1 The Bit Machine

The Simplicity Bit Machine (SBM) is used to execute Simplicity programs and it consists on an state composed of two stacks of data *frames*: the read stack and the write stack. A frame is a list of cells, where each cell contains either **0, 1** or an undefined value noted as **?**. Each frame has also a cursor, which indicates which cell is to be written or read. The read stack is used to provide the input of the Simplicity function and the write stack is used to write its output. The topmost frame—also called the active frame—contains the input (output) of the current primitive in execution. For instance, in order to execute a Simplicity function $f : A \vdash B$, the active read frame must have a value of type A. After execution, the output value of type B can be found on the active write frame.

Simplicity's types have "finite size", that is, well-typed values have a finite representation in terms of cells. In other words, it is always possible to compute the number of cells required by the input and output of well-typed functions. That is, in terms of number of bits, sizeOf(𝟙) = 0 (as there is only one value), sizeOf($A + B$) = $1 + \max(\text{sizeOf}(A) + \text{sizeOf}(B))$ (where the extra bit is used as a flag to indicate whether the value is of type A or B), and sizeOf($A \times B$) = sizeOf(A) + sizeOf(B) bits. The ability to compute the size from the types plays a crucial role in the operational semantics of Simplicity. From now on, when referring to the *size of a type*, the reader should keep in mind that we are referring to the representation of values of such a type.

The size of the input type is needed to read the exact number of cells which contain the input. Moreover, the size of the output type is required to allocate the amount of needed cells for writing the output of a Simplicity function. The following outlines show how values of a specific type are read or written in the SBM. Note that all the reading (writing) always happens on the active read (write) frame. Below, we briefly describe how SBM behaves when operating with values of different types. The complete operational semantics of the SBM can be found in [7].

▶ To write a value of type $\mathbb{1}$ on the write frame, the SBM writes nothing (as only one value exists). Similarly, to read a value of type $\mathbb{1}$, the SBM reads nothing.

▶ To write a value of type $A \times B$, the SBM writes the value of type A followed by the value of type B on the write frame. Instead, to read a value of $A \times B$, the SBM first computes the size of A and reads that many cells in order to get A. Then, it computes the size of B and reads that many cells in order to get B.

▶ To write a value of type $A + B$, the SBM writes a (cell) flag bit indicating whether the value is A (0) or B (1). After that, it skips any excess cells which may have been allocated (keeping in mind that the value could be A or B), and then writes the available value. This mechanism of skipping ahead is also called *padding*.

Since the resource allocation in the read and write stack is made using the type information (as shown above), and given that the language is Turing incomplete, it becomes possible to do static analysis to compute an upper bound on the runtime resources used by an smart contract. For example, it is possible to estimate the number of cells used by a Simplicity program on both stacks. We refer the reader to [7] for a detailed discussion on static analysis in Simplicity programs.

3 Categorical Semantics for Simplicity

In this section, we establish an unforeseen connection between Simplicity and a branch of mathematics called category theory. Such connection will open the door to apply known results from category theory [3] in order to systematically extend Simplicity and the SBM with new features. We start by briefly describing a specific kind of category: the Bi-Cartesian Categories, or BCCs for short. Then, we show how categories can be used to model Simplicity computations.

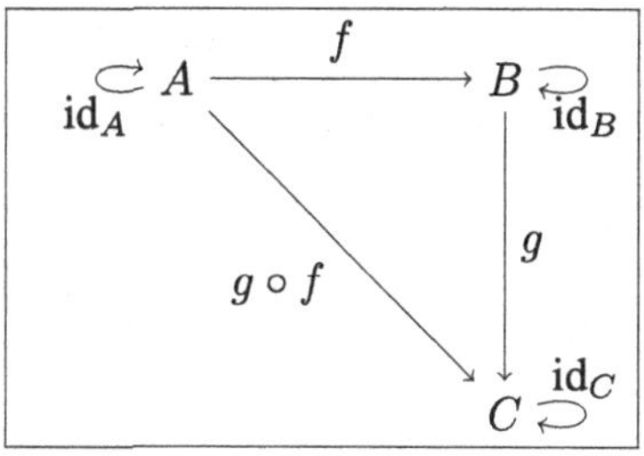

Fig. 2. Identity and composition in a category

A *category* is composed of objects and morphisms between these objects. A simple way to think about it is to consider it as a *graph with certain operations and satisfying certain properties*, where the vertices are the objects and the (oriented) edges the morphisms. Category theory will often characterize the features of the categories, based on the relations between objects and morphisms.

The basic features that a category must have are identity and composition.

▶ *Identity.* For every object A in the category (i.e., every vertex in the graph), there exists an identity morphism (edge) from A to A, noted id : $A \to A$. Since there are many identity morphisms, it is common to identify them by their associated objects, e.g., id : $A \rightarrow A$ is denoted by id_A. For simplicity, while presenting the construction of some categorical features as graphs, we often omit the identity morphisms but recall that they do exist for every object (vertex).

▶ *Composition.* For every two morphisms (edges) $f : A \rightarrow B$ and $g : B \rightarrow C$, there exists a morphism (edge) $g \circ f :: A \rightarrow C$. Furthermore, the composition must be associative, and the morphism id must be the identity for composition, which gives the following equalities: $f \circ (g \circ h) = (f \circ g) \circ h$ and that $f \circ \mathrm{id}_A = \mathrm{id}_B \circ f = f$.

To give an example of a category, let us consider three objects, namely A, B, and C, and two morphisms $f : A \rightarrow B$ and $g : B \rightarrow C$. If we want to place them into a category, we must add an identity morphism for each object and a morphism for the composition of f and g. Figure 2 shows the structure of such a category.

The rest of the section proceeds to describe the remaining features found in BCCs.

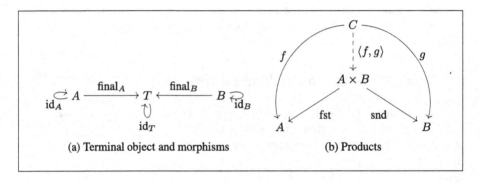

(a) Terminal object and morphisms   (b) Products

Fig. 3. Terminal and products in BCCs

▶ *Terminal Object.* There is an object, we noted it as T, such that for any other object A in the category, there exists precisely one morphism final : $A \rightarrow T$ (also know as terminal morphism). Figure 3(a) shows objects A and B and their corresponding morphisms to the terminal object.

▶ *Products.* For all objects A and B in the category, there exists the product object $A \times B$. Every product object comes equipped with two morphisms fst : $A \times B \rightarrow A$ and snd : $A \times B \rightarrow B$ which project out its components. Importantly, for every two morphisms $f : C \rightarrow A$ and $g : C \rightarrow B$, there exists an unique morphism (represented by a dashed arrow) called *factor*, written $\langle f, g \rangle : C \rightarrow A \times B$, which should fulfill the following equations: $f = \mathrm{fst} \circ \langle f, g \rangle$ and that $g = \mathrm{snd} \circ \langle f, g \rangle$. These equations capture the behavior of factor, i.e., a product element obtained from C is constructed by building an element

A with f and an element B with g. Figure 3(b) introduces objects A, B, C, morphisms $f : C \to A$ and $g : C \to B$, and describes their relation via the product object $A \times B$ and the factor morphism.

▶ *Coproducts.* For all objects A and B in the category, there exists a coproduct object $A+B$. Every coproduct object comes with two morphims, the injections $\text{inj}_1 : A \to A + B$ and $\text{inj}_2 : B \to A + B$. If we have two morphisms $f : (E \times A) \to C$ and $g : (E \times B) \to C$, then there exists a unique morphism called *copair*, written $[f,g] : (E \times (A + B)) \to C^2$. This morphism fulfills the equations: $f = [f,g] \circ \langle \text{id}_E, \text{inj}_1 \rangle$ and $g = [f,g] \circ \langle \text{id}_E, \text{inj}_2 \rangle$. In other words, the copair builds an element of C by using either f or g, depending on either it receives an element of A or B. Figure 4 introduces objects A, B, C and E, morphisms $f : E \times A \to C$ and $g : E \times B \to C$, and describes their relation via the coproduct object $A + B$ and the copair morphism.

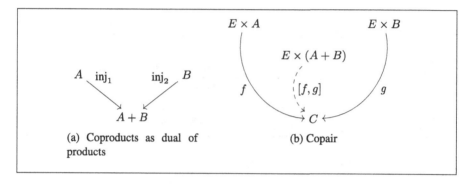

(a) Coproducts as dual of products

(b) Copair

Fig. 4. Coproducts in BCCs

3.1 Simplicity and BCCs

The type signature of BCCs' morphisms and Simplicity's basic and combinator functions look pretty similar. In this section, we describe how to model Simplicity functions using BCCs. Intuitively, the idea is that a function $f : A \vdash B$ will be modeled by a morphism $m : A \to B$. In other words, Simplicity types become objects in BCCs and functions morphisms. For instance, the function *iden* : $A \vdash A$ can be modeled by the morphism id : $A \to A$. The complete translation of Simplicity to BCCs is given on Fig. 5, where we denote $f \rightsquigarrow m$ as the relation "the morphism m models the Simplicity function f".

The most interesting case is the translation of *case s t*. While *case* has type $(A + B) \times C \vdash D$, its closest morphism—copair—has type $(C \times (A + B)) \to D$,

---

[2] In category theory, *copair* is commonly used without the product with E: if $f' : A \to C$ and $g' : B \to C$, then $[f',g'] : A + B \to C$. However, using the morphism containing E will ease the equivalence between morphisms and Simplicity terms.

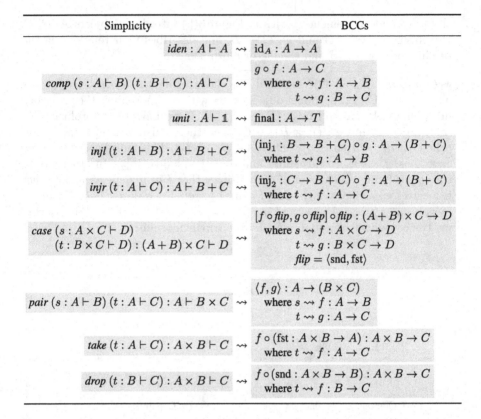

Fig. 5. Translation from simplicity terms to BCCs morphims

hence we cannot use it directly since the type signatures do not align. From category theory, however, we know about the symmetry of products, i.e., $A \times B$ and $B \times A$ are provably isomorphic and therefore there must exist an isomorphism between them. We use one direction of that isomorphism—called *flip* in Fig. 5—to build the corresponding morphism of *case*.

By mapping Simplicity functions into BCCs, the attentive reader could be afraid that we might be introducing or restricting the behavior of Simplicity programs. For example, on one hand, products need to fulfill certain equations in BCCs (recall previous Section). On the other hand, there is no relation stated for Simplicity operators like *pair*, *take*, and *drop*. It is easy to show that Simplicity operators already fulfill all the equations required by BCCs. We refer readers to the accompanying material for the details of the proof.

We have now established the connection between Simplicity functions and BCCs morphisms and we can start adding more features to Simplicity (Sect. 5). Category theory will guide us toward the implementation of user-defined functions. This would be a significant improvement to Simplicity, as it would allow to write simpler and shorter programs.

4   Implementation

In this section, we present another of our contributions: an implementation of Simplicity, its categorical model, and the SBM as embedded domain-specific languages (eDSL) in Haskell [4]. To implement BCCs in Haskell, we need to determine what the objects and morphisms are going to be in Haskell. By doing so, we restrict ourselves to a particular class of BCCs that we call BCCs$_{\text{Hask}}$, where categorical objects are represented with Haskell types.

```
data T
data a :*: b
data a :+: b
```

Fig. 6. Simplicity types

We model both types in Simplicity and objects in BCCs$_{\text{Hask}}$ with the empty types given in Fig. 6. Type T is the unit/terminal, type a :*: b is the product, and type a :+: b is the coproduct. In what follows, we will model the term language of Simplicity and morphisms in BCCs$_{\text{Hask}}$ using *Generalized Algebraic Data Types* (GADTs) [8]. The use of GADTs allows us to directly encode the typing judgements of Simplicity and BCCs$_{\text{Hask}}$ in the constructors. In that manner, the Haskell's type checker ensures that Simplicity functions and BCCs$_{\text{Hask}}$ morphisms are well-typed *by construction*.

4.1   An eDSL for Simplicity

We model Simplicity programs as values of the following GADT parameterized over an input type i and an output type o:

```
data Simpl i o where
    Iden  :: SType a ⇒ Simpl a a
    Unit  :: SType a ⇒ Simpl a T
    Take  :: (SType a, SType b, SType c) ⇒ Simpl a c → Simpl (a :*: b) c
    Drop  :: (SType a, SType b, SType c) ⇒ Simpl b c → Simpl (a :*: b) c
    Injl  :: (SType a, SType b, SType c) ⇒ Simpl a b → Simpl a (b :+: c)
    Injr  :: (SType a, SType b, SType c) ⇒ Simpl a c → Simpl a (b :+: c)
    Comp :: (SType a, SType b, SType c) ⇒
             Simpl a b → Simpl b c → Simpl a c
    Pair  :: (SType a, SType b, SType c) ⇒
             Simpl a b → Simpl a c → Simpl a (b :*: c)
    Case :: (SType a, SType b, SType c, SType d) ⇒ Simpl (a :*: c) d →
             Simpl (b :*: c) d → Simpl ((a :+: b) :*: c) d
```

The type constraint $SType\,a$ restricts the domain of the type variable a. In our case, a type variable a satisfies the constraint $SType\,a$ only if it is instantiated with T, a :*: b or a :+: b, where a and b are simplicity types themselves. The reason for adding this constraint is two fold: first, to ensure that a Simplicity expression cannot be created for some arbitrary Haskell type such as $[Int]$ (as this might break the property that the size of the type can be determined statically), and second, to implement a function $sizeOf$ to calculate the size (in bits) of a Simplicity type—which is used later to run programs on the SBM.

In Haskell, type constraint $SType$ is implemented as a type class, and the Simplicity types which satisfy it are implemented as instances of such a class:

> **class** $SType$ a **where**
> $sizeOf :: a \rightarrow Int$
>
> **instance** $SType$ T **where**
>   ...
>
> **instance** $(SType\ a, SType\ b) \Rightarrow SType\ (a :+: b)$ **where**
>   ...
>
> **instance** $(SType\ a, SType\ b) \Rightarrow SType\ (a :*: b)$ **where**
>   ...

(Ellipsis are used to denote Haskell code that is not relevant for the point being made.) Each Simplicity type instance must provide a definition for the $sizeOf$ function. Recall that the SBM works by allocating cells in the stack frames based on the type information (Sect. 2.1). For brevity, we skip the implementation of $sizeOf$ but it can be found in the accompanying material. Later in Sect. 4.4, we show how to leverage $sizeOf$ to implement the SBM.

4.2   An eDSL for BCCs$_{\text{Hask}}$

In BCCs$_{\text{Hask}}$, we model objects as Haskell types and morphisms as values of the GADT Mph:

> **data** $Mph\ obj\ a\ b$ **where**
> Id $:: obj\ a \Rightarrow Mph\ obj\ a\ a$
> $Terminal :: obj\ a \Rightarrow Mph\ obj\ a\ T$
> Fst $:: (obj\ a, obj\ b) \Rightarrow Mph\ obj\ (a :*: b)\ a$
> Snd $:: (obj\ b, obj\ b) \Rightarrow Mph\ obj\ (a :*: b)\ b$
> Inj_1 $:: (obj\ a, obj\ b) \Rightarrow Mph\ obj\ a\ (a :+: b)$
> Inj_2 $:: (obj\ a, obj\ b) \Rightarrow Mph\ obj\ b\ (a :+: b)$
> $\odot$ $:: (obj\ a, obj\ b, obj\ c) \Rightarrow$
> $Mph\ obj\ b\ c \rightarrow Mph\ obj\ a\ b \rightarrow Mph\ obj\ a\ c$
> $Factor$ $:: (obj\ a, obj\ b_1, obj\ b_2) \Rightarrow$
> $Mph\ obj\ a\ b_1 \rightarrow Mph\ obj\ a\ b_2 \rightarrow Mph\ obj\ a\ (b_1 :*: b_2)$
> $CoFactor :: (obj\ a, obj\ b, obj\ c, obj\ e) \Rightarrow Mph\ obj\ (e :*: a)\ c \rightarrow$
> $Mph\ obj\ (e :*: b)\ c \rightarrow Mph\ obj\ (e :*: (a :+: b))\ c$

This data type is parameterized over a type constraint obj and objects a and b. Each constructor of this data type constructs a morphism in a given BCC$_{\text{Hask}}$. A type constraint $obj\ a$ ensures the type a is indeed an object of the considered BCC$_{\text{Hask}}$, and not some arbitrary Haskell type.

The main difference between $SType$ in $Simpl$ and obj in Mph is that $SType$ is a specific type constraint, while obj is parameterized over. Observe that different instantiations of obj might encode different BCCs$_{\text{Hask}}$. For instance, if obj gets instantiated with $SType$, we obtain a BCC$_{\text{Hask}}$ which models Simplicity in

Haskell (as shown in the next Section)[3]. From now on, we refer to this category as simply BCC_{Hask}.

4.3   A Translation from Simplicity to BCC_{Hask}

The translation from Simplicity to BCC_{Hask} is a Haskell function (named *simpl2mph*) between the eDSLs presented above. In other words, we show how to translate a program $prog :: Simpl\ i\ o$ to a morphism $m :: Mph\ SType\ i\ o$. The constraint *obj* is now instantiated with *SType*, and hence the objects in the BCC_{Hask} are Simplicity types. The translation is essentially a syntactic translation of the rules in Fig. 5—a nice aspect of our approach.

$$simpl2mph :: Simpl\ i\ o \rightarrow Mph\ SType\ i\ o$$
$$simpl2mph\ Iden \qquad = Id$$
$$simpl2mph\ Unit \qquad = Terminal$$
$$simpl2mph\ (Take\ f) \quad = simpl2mph\ f\ \odot\ Fst$$
$$simpl2mph\ (Drop\ f) \quad = simpl2mph\ f\ \odot\ Snd$$
$$simpl2mph\ (Injl\ f) \quad = Inj_1\ \odot\ (simpl2mph\ f)$$
$$simpl2mph\ (Injr\ f) \quad = Inj_2\ \odot\ (simpl2mph\ f)$$
$$simpl2mph\ (Pair\ p\ q) \quad = Factor\ (simpl2mph\ p)\ (simpl2mph\ q)$$
$$simpl2mph\ (Comp\ f\ g) = simpl2mph\ g\ \odot\ simpl2mph\ f$$
$$simpl2mph\ (Case\ p\ q)\ = (CoFactor\ (simpl2mph\ p\ \odot\ flip)$$
$$(simpl2mph\ q\ \odot\ flip))\ \odot\ flip$$

where
$$flip = Factor\ Snd\ Fst$$

As explained in Sect. 3, constructor $Case\ p\ q$ needs an auxiliary morphism $flip$ to use *CoFactor*.

4.4   The SBM

Given the close correspondence between Simplicity's primitives and BCCs' morphisms, the execution of morphisms on the SBM is very similar to the execution of Simplicity functions. A given morphism is translated to instructions of the SBM, which are then executed on the SBM to yield the output.

We start by looking at the SBM interface. The instructions of the SBM are implemented as a Haskell data type (see Fig. 7a). For brevity, we only show some of the instructions here. Type *Bit* is an alias for *Bool* representing a single bit value on the SBM.

---

[3] The encoding of a category using the eDSL for $BCCs_{Hask}$ does not ensure that the category is indeed a BCC. It is the programmers responsibility to ensure this by verifying the existence of constructed morphisms and proving the corresponding laws. The eDSL is simply the "language of BCCs where objects are Haskell types."

```
    data Inst = Nop            1 type Frame = ([Maybe Bit], Int)
         | Write Bit           2 type Stack  = [Frame]
         | Copy Int            3 data Machine = Machine
         | Skip Int            4    { readStack :: Stack
         | Fwd Int             5    , writeStack :: Stack }
         | Read                6 type SBM = State Machine
         ...

        (a) SBM Instructions          (b) SBM components
```

Fig. 7. SBM data types

A list of these instructions are run on the SBM using the function:

$$run :: [Inst] \rightarrow SBM \ (Maybe \ Bit)$$

where output type SBM is a monadic type [11] which encapsulates the stateful behavior of the SBM. This design choice arise from noticing that the evaluation of each instruction may change the state of the SBM, and hence affect the execution of subsequent instructions. More specifically, the SBM type is defined as shown in Fig. 7b line 6, where a value of type $Machine$ (lines 3–5) represents a configuration of the virtual machine at a given moment. The configuration is composed of read ($readStack$) and write ($writeStack$) stacks, which are themselves composed of frames. A frame is a list of cells paired with a cursor. The cursor points to the current cell in the frame and is implemented as an Int representing the index of the current cell. A cell is encoded as a $Maybe \ Bit$, as it can host an undefined value (recall Sect. 2.1). A cell with an undefined value is represented by $Nothing$, otherwise it is a $Just$ value with a Bit.

A given BCC$_{Hask}$ morphism is translated into a list of SBM instructions using the function

$$mph2sbm :: Mph \ Types \ a \ b \rightarrow [Inst]$$

We will look at a few cases of the $mph2sbm$ implementation to illustrate how it works. To understand how to map a morphism $m : A \rightarrow B$ into the SBM, we need to think of it as a Simplicity function $f : A \vdash B$ (recall that we proved that such models are equivalent in Sect. 3.1). In this light, the instructions corresponding to m must assume (before their execution) that the machine is initialized with a configuration where a value of type A is on the active read frame. Post execution of m, the active write frame must contain a value of type B. For example, to execute the morphism id : $A \rightarrow A$, the value of A must be available on the read stack. The expected end configuration is the same value of A on the write stack. That is, we need to copy as many bits as the size of A from the read stack to the write stack. This operation is achieved by using the $Copy$ instruction. To determine the size of A, we use the $sizeOf$ function—where the constraint $SType$ (introduced earlier) on type A comes into action. The implementation of this case is as follows:

$$mph2sbm \ (Id :: Mph \ SType \ a \ a) = [\, Copy \ (sizeOf \ (\bot :: a))\,]$$

(Observe that this definition works for any identity morphism since it is polymorphic in a). To give $sizeOf$ an argument of type a, we must construct a value of that type. For this, we use the value $\bot$ which constructs (or inhabits) every Haskell (and hence Simplicity) type. Notice that Simplicity types are empty data types, and the inhabitant of the type has no significance. We are only interested in the type a as it gives us the corresponding definition of $sizeOf$.

We implement composition as show in Fig. 8. We first allocate memory for the intermediate result of type b, run f (which writes the intermediate result on the active write frame), move the active write frame to the read stack (using $MoveFrame$), and finally run g, which writes the result of type c on the active write frame; having at the end the expected configuration after

$$
\begin{aligned}
mph2sbm \ ((g &:: Mph \ SType \ b \ c) \ \odot \\
(f &:: Mph \ SType \ a \ b)) = \\
& [\, NewFrame \ (sizeOf \ (\bot :: b))\,] \\
& \mathbin{+\!\!+} mph2sbm \ f \\
& \mathbin{+\!\!+} [\, MoveFrame\,] \\
& \mathbin{+\!\!+} mph2sbm \ g \\
& \mathbin{+\!\!+} [\, DropFrame\,]
\end{aligned}
$$

Fig. 8. Implementation of $\odot$

executing ($\odot$). Since the intermediate result of type b is no longer needed, we drop the active read frame (using $DropFrame$). Implementing the compilation of the other morphisms is analogous and can be found in the accompanying material.

5 Adding Functions to Simplicity

In this section, we extend the Simplicity core language with user-defined functions, provide categorical semantics for the extension, and also extend the evaluation model (SBM) to support the extended semantics. To achieve this, we leverage the exposed connection between Simplicity and categorical models (recall Sect. 3). From the latter, we use the concept of *exponential* objects as a guideline to model functions. We briefly introduce what it means for a category to have exponentials and discuss their relation to functions in Simplicity.

▶ *Exponentials.* For objects B and C in a category, an exponential object is a special object (denoted as $B \Rightarrow C$), for which there exists a morphism eval : $(B \Rightarrow C) \times B \to C$. Additionally, for every morphism $f : A \times B \to C$, there must exist a unique morphism curry$(f) : A \to B \Rightarrow C$ such that $f = $ eval $\circ \langle$curry$(f) \circ$ fst, snd$\rangle$. That is, in a category with exponentials, for every morphism $f : A \times B \to C$, there exists a *curried* version of it, i.e., curry(f). Figure 9 shows f and the morphisms involving exponentials— namely curry(f) and eval.

An exponential object is the categorical generalization of the *function type* (→). Operation curry generalizes the construction of a *lambda abstraction*—also known as currying in lambda calculus [1]. The eval morphism generalizes the *application* of a function of type $B → C$ to an argument of type B to return a value of type C.

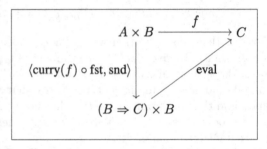

Fig. 9. Exponentials in BCCCs

Exponential objects are implemented by the following data type:

$$\textbf{data } a :⇒: b$$

which represents the exponential object $a ⇒ b$ for some objects a and b. To add the new morphisms, we extend Mph with the new constructors $Curry$ and $Eval$ (see Fig. 10b) as described in Fig. 9. When we include exponentials in a BCC, it becomes a Bi-Cartesian Closed Category or a BCCC.

In Simplicity, $a :⇒: b$ is a function type which expects an argument of type a and returns a value of type b (where a and b are Simplicity types). We add new primitives to Simplicity's eDSL as shown in Fig. 10a. The constructor Lam accepts a Simplicity term whose input and output types are $(a : * : b)$ and c respectively, and constructs a new term $Simpl\, a\, (b :⇒: c)$—where the input is a value of type a and the output is a function of type $b :⇒: c$. The App constructor, on the other hand, accepts a Simplicity term which returns a function of type $b :⇒: c$ and another term which returns a value of type b, and constructs a term which returns a value of type c.

The translation of the newly added Simplicity terms to $BCCC_{Hask}$ (i.e., BCCCs where objects are Simplicity types) is defined as follows:

$$simpl2mph\ (Lam\ f)\ \ = Curry\ (simpl2mph\ f)$$
$$simpl2mph\ (App\ f\ x) = Eval \odot (Factor\ (simpl2mph\ f)\ (simpl2mph\ x))$$

This translation provides the categorical semantics for functions in Simplicity, and hence forms the basis for implementing them.

5.1   Using Functions in Simplicity

Note that the language extension in the previous section does not just enable for functions to be defined, but also treats functions as values. This allows for programming with higher order functions and facilitates some powerful abstractions. For example, functions can be used to introduce *let-bindings* into the language. Let-bindings greatly reduce the duplication of sub-expressions in the language. In the presence of functions, they can be easily encoded using function application as **let** $x = e$ **in** $e' ≡ (λx → e')e$.

Another example of the usefulness of functions is the ability to define a loop combinator. The *loop* combinator (defined below) can be used to repetitively

```
data Simpl i o where
    ...
    Lam :: (SType a, SType b, SType c) ⇒
            Simpl (a :*: b) c → Simpl a (b :⇒: c)
    App :: (SType a, SType b, SType c) ⇒
            Simpl a (b :⇒: c) → Simpl a b → Simpl a c
```

(a) Functions in Simplicity

```
data Mph obj a b where
    ...
    Curry :: (obj a, obj b, obj c) ⇒
            Mph obj (a :*: b) c → Mph obj a (b :⇒: c)
    Eval :: (obj b, obj c) ⇒ Mph obj ((b :⇒: c) :*: b) c
```

(b) Exponentials in BCC

Fig. 10. Implementation of functions and exponentials

apply a Simplicity term to an input value. Term *loop f n* applies f on the input n times. This is possible only when f has the same input and output type, and is hence expected to have the type *Simpl a a*. Symbol n is a Simplicity term of type *SNat* (defined below) which encodes a natural number using using just function abstraction and application—known as *Church numerals* in lambda calculus.

type $SNat = \forall a.\ Types\ a \Rightarrow Simpl\ (a :⇒: a)\ (a :⇒: a)$

```
loop :: Types a ⇒ Simpl a a → SNat → Simpl a a
loop f n = App (App (toLam n) (toLam f)) Iden
    where
        toLam :: (Types a, Types b, Types r) ⇒ Simpl a b → Simpl r (a :⇒: b)
        toLam s = Lam (Drop s)
```

For the Haskell aware reader, note that we use higher-ranked types to define *SNat*—a feature of the Haskell type system which is not available in Simplicity. While this might appear disconcerting, note that this is not a strict requirement to define a *loop* combinator. We could instead encode *SNat* as *SNat a*, removing the explicit quantification ($\forall$) and hence the need for higher-ranked types.

```
zero :: SNat
zero = Lam (Drop Iden)

one :: SNat
one = Lam (App (Take Iden)
          (Drop Iden))
```

Fig. 11. Church numerals

Since the programmer must provide a construction of a Simplicity term of type *SNat* (which always represents a finite number), the loop can only be used for a finite number of iterations. Figure 11 illustrates the construction of some of such natural numbers.

5.2   Implementing Functions on SBM

In this section, we extend the SBM—the primary evaluation model of the Simplicity language—to support higher order functions. To do this, we must implement the translation of *Curry* and *Eval* morphisms to SBM instructions. We start by requiring that an exponential object $a :\Rightarrow: b$ must also be a valid Simplicity type that satisfies the *SType* constraint. Consequently, we must implement an instance of the type class *SType* for the type $a :\Rightarrow: b$, i.e., we need to provide a definition for $sizeOf(a :\Rightarrow: b)$. For that, we need to identify a way to store and retrieve exponential objects in the SBM.

Notice that the serialization of a morphism captured in the exponential $a :\Rightarrow: b$ can be arbitrary long, as the morphisms can be arbitrary complex. As a result, it is not possible to know the number of bits needed to serialize such morphisms only by looking at the type $a :\Rightarrow: b$. This is problematic since the SBM is not meant to manipulate types with arbitrary sizes.

To address this issue, we extend the SBM with a new field responsible to store a list of exponentials. We then represent exponentials in the stack frames as merely pointers (indexes) into such list. We have not yet defined the size of pointers, but we assume them to occupy the amount of bits given by a parameter *sizePtr*—we will see later how to statically compute it. Additionally, we must devise new SBM instructions responsible to execute the *Curry* and *Eval* morphisms, i.e., instructions responsible to create and apply exponentials.

If we follow the philosophy of Simplicity that the input (output) type should indicate the values to be read (write) into the stack, a morphism of the form $Curry\ f :: Mph\ SType\ a\ (b :\Rightarrow: c)$ must be compiled to an instruction that reads a value of type a from the read stack and places the exponential (of type $b :\Rightarrow: c$) in the write frame. In this light, we introduce the instruction *PutClosure* responsible to allocate exponentials:

$$mph2sbm :: Mph\ SType\ a\ b \rightarrow Int \rightarrow [Inst]$$
$$mph2sbm\ (Curry\ (f :: Mph\ Types\ (a:*:b)\ c))\ sizePtr =$$
$$\textbf{let } aSize = sizeOf\ (\bot :: a)\ sizePtr$$
$$\textbf{in } [PutClosure\ (mph2sbm\ f\ sizePtr)\ aSize\ sizePtr]$$

Observe that *mph2sbm* takes the size of pointers as an extra argument as well as *sizeOf*—note that *sizeOf* could be called on a pointer and thus it needs to know its size ($sizeOf\ (a :\Rightarrow: b)\ sizePtr = sizePtr$). The instruction *PutClosure* takes three arguments: the compilation of the curried morphism $f :: Mph\ Types\ (a : * : b)\ c$ ($mph2sbm\ f\ sizePtr$), the amount of bits to be read from the read stack ($aSize$), and the size of pointers ($sizePtr$). When the SBM executes this instruction, it allocates an exponential as the pair composed of f's instructions, paired with the value of type a read from the stack—this semantics is inspired by how Cousineau et al. handle exponentials in the Categorical Abstract Machine [2] as closures. The output in the write stack of *PutClosure* is the pointer to the recently allocated exponential. For instance, Fig. 12 illustrates the effect of running an instruction $PutClosure\ [Read; ...]\ 2\ 4$ under a given configuration of the machine.

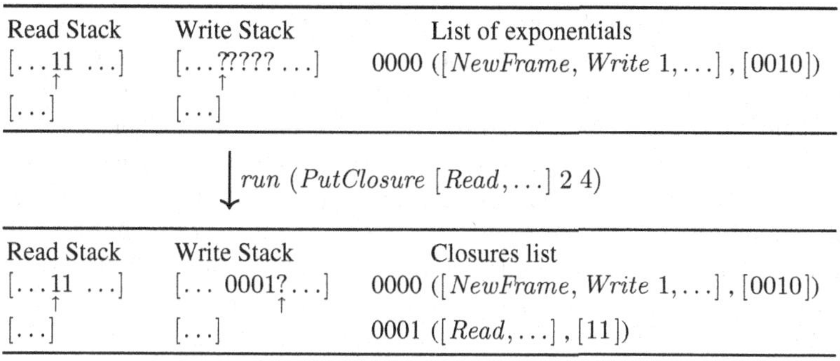

Read Stack	Write Stack	List of exponentials
$[\ldots 11 \ldots]$	$[\ldots ????? \ldots]$	0000 $([NewFrame, Write\ 1, \ldots], [0010])$
$[\ldots]$	$[\ldots]$	

$$\downarrow run\ (PutClosure\ [Read, \ldots]\ 2\ 4)$$

Read Stack	Write Stack	Closures list
$[\ldots 11 \ldots]$	$[\ldots 0001? \ldots]$	0000 $([NewFrame, Write\ 1, \ldots], [0010])$
$[\ldots]$	$[\ldots]$	0001 $([Read, \ldots], [11])$

Fig. 12. Executing *PutClosure* in the SBM

In the same line of reasoning, morphism $Eval::Mph\ SType\,((b :\Rightarrow: c) : * : b)\ c$ should be compiled to an instruction which reads an exponential (i.e., a pointer) together with a value of type b from the read stack and produces a c in the write stack. To achieve that, we introduce the instruction *EvalClosure* in charge of using the exponentials:

$$mph2sbm\ (Eval :: Mph\ SType\ ((b :\Rightarrow: c):*:b)\ c)\ sizePtr =$$
$$[EvalClosure\ sizePtr\ (sizeOf\ (\bot :: b)\ sizePtr)]$$

This instruction takes the size of a pointer ($sizePtr$) together with the size of the value of type b ($sizeOf\ (\bot::b)\ sizePtr$). When executed, *EvalClosure* fetches the exponential via the pointer, and places the value of type b obtained from the read stack as an input to the instructions that constitute the exponential. (There are actually many intermediate steps to reach that configuration and we refer the interested reader to the accompanying material for details.) After the instructions of the exponential get executed, the machine will have a value of type c in the active write frame.

We still need to define $sizeOf$ for the pointers manipulated in the stacks. To know the maximal size (in bits) to encode a pointer, we must know the maximal number of closures existing in a Simplicity program. This number is actually the amount of *Curry* occurrences in the morphism denoting our program. The reader can convince herself that computing this number is a linear traversal in the size of the morphism. Let cc be the number of *Curry* in the morphism, then the maximal size (in bits) of the pointers is $sizePtr = \log_2 (cc) + 1$. Once $sizePtr$ is determined, we can do our translation to SBM instructions by calling $mph2sbm$ with a morphism and $sizePtr$ as a parameter.

5.3   Static Analysis

A notable property of Simplicity is the ability to statically estimate computational resources needed by a program. This is achieved using the underlying evaluation model, i.e., the SBM. In this section, we discuss this property in light of the extensions made to Simplicity and the SBM.

In our model, a given Simplicity program is translated to a BCC_{Hask} morphism using *simpl2mph*, which is then translated to SBM instructions using *mph2sbm*. Consider the problem of estimating the number of instructions executed by the SBM for a given program. In the absence of exponentials, to count the number of instructions, we simply count the number of instructions returned by *mph2sbm*. However, this straightforward approach fails to hold in the presence of exponentials. This is because the instruction *EvalClosure* (introduced for the evaluation of exponentials), cannot be treated as a single instruction. *EvalClosure* contains a pointer to a list of instructions executed by the SBM, which means that it causes several other instructions (including itself) to be executed.

To mitigate this problem, we must also count the number of instructions that are referred to by a pointer of *EvalClosure*. This can be easily calculated in linear time by maintaining an environment which contains the pointers and their corresponding list of instructions as introduced by *PutClosure*.

The static analysis of cell usage described in [7] extends naturally to exponentials since all exponential objects are of a fixed sized *sizePtr* (discussed in the previous section). However, since our storage model has been extended with a list of closures, we must also estimate the maximum size of the closure list. It should be possible to compute an upper bound on the size of the closure list in linear time by maintaining an external environment (as suggested above). Note that since our extensions do not provide a mechanism to define recursion, such as a fix-point combinator, an attempt to perform static analysis in such a fashion must always terminate. However, we have not implemented this static analysis, and leave it as a suggestion for future work.

6   Final Remarks

This work provides a new semantics for Simplicity based on category theory, and extends Simplicity with user defined and higher order functions. Using functions, we have established the foundational and practical basis to enrich the language towards other interesting features such as bounded loops. As long as we stay under a computational model similar to the simply typed lambda calculus, we argue that it is possible to carry out "quick" static analysis to predict resource usage in Simplicity programs. We evaluate our theory by providing an implementation of our results and approach in Haskell. Our hope is to make the language even more useful to develop smart contracts with formal guarantees.

Acknowledgments. This work was funded by the Swedish Foundation for Strategic Research (SSF) under the project Octopi (Ref. RIT17-0023) and the Swedish research agency Vetenskapsrådet.

References

1. Barendregt, H., Dekkers, W., Statman, R.: Lambda Calculus with Types. Cambridge University Press, Cambridge (2013)
2. Cousineau, G., Curien, P., Mauny, M.: The categorical abstract machine. Sci. Comput. Program. **8**(2), 173–202 (1987)
3. Elliott, C.: Compiling to categories. In: Proceedings of the ACM on Programming Languages (ICFP) (2017). http://conal.net/papers/compiling-to-categories
4. Marlow, S.: Haskell 2010 language report (2010). http://www.haskell.org/
5. Nakamoto, S.: Bitcoin: a peer-to-peer electronic cash system (2008)
6. O'Connor, R.: Simplicity: a new language for blockchains. In: Proceedings of the Workshop on Programming Languages and Analysis for Security, PLAS 2017. ACM (2017)
7. O'Connor, R.: Simplicity: a new language for blockchains. CoRR abs/1711.03028 (2017). http://arxiv.org/abs/1711.03028
8. Peyton Jones, S., Vytiniotis, D., Weirich, S., Washburn, G.: Simple unification-based type inference for gadts. In: ACM SIGPLAN Notices, vol. 41, pp. 50–61. ACM (2006)
9. Schwartz, D., Youngs, N., Britto, A., et al.: The ripple protocol consensus algorithm. Ripple Labs Inc White Paper 5 (2014)
10. Swan, M.: Blockchain: Blueprint for a New Economy. O'Reilly Media Inc., Newton (2015)
11. Wadler, P.: Monads for functional programming. In: Jeuring, J., Meijer, E. (eds.) AFP 1995. LNCS, vol. 925, pp. 24–52. Springer, Heidelberg (1995). https://doi.org/10.1007/3-540-59451-5_2
12. Wood, G.: Ethereum: a secure decentralised generalised transaction ledger. Ethereum Proj. Yellow Pap. **151**, 1–32 (2014)

Fun with Bitcoin Smart Contracts

Massimo Bartoletti[1]([✉]), Tiziana Cimoli[1], and Roberto Zunino[2]

[1] Università degli Studi di Cagliari, Cagliari, Italy
bart@unica.it
[2] Università degli Studi di Trento, Trento, Italy

Abstract. Besides simple transfers of currency, Bitcoin also enables various forms of *smart contracts*, i.e. protocols where users interact within pre-agreed rules, which determine (possibly depending on the actual interaction) how currency is eventually distributed. This paper provides a gentle introduction to Bitcoin smart contracts, which we specify by abstracting from the underlying Bitcoin machinery. To this purpose we exploit BitML, a recent DSL for smart contracts executable on Bitcoin.

1 Introduction

Bitcoin and other cryptocurrencies [12,20] allow mutually distrusting parties to securely interact over a peer-to-peer network. Abstractly, Bitcoin can be seen as a decentralized state machine: the blockchain publicly records all the state transitions, and from the sequence of these transitions anyone can infer the state of the machine. The Bitcoin consensus mechanism guarantees that only the transitions which are consistent with the current state can be appended to the blockchain, and that previous transitions cannot be altered or removed.

The main use of Bitcoin so far is that of a cryptocurrency: state transitions record transfers of currency from one user to another one, and the state of the machine associates users to the amount of currency under their control. More in general, Bitcoin also enables various forms of *smart contracts*, i.e. protocols to distribute currency among users according to pre-agreed conditions [4,7,24]. A variety of protocols for lotteries [1,8,10,18], gambling games [17], contingent payments [6], payment channels [14,19,22], and other kinds of fair computations [2,16] witness the capabilities of Bitcoin as a machine for smart contracts.

In practice, the development of Bitcoin smart contracts has been hampered by the absence of convenient abstractions: indeed, existing descriptions of smart contracts require a thorough understanding of low-level features of Bitcoin, like e.g. transactions signatures and scripts.

In this paper we provide a gentle introduction to Bitcoin smart contracts by leveraging BitML [9], a recent high-level, process-algebraic language that compiles into Bitcoin transactions. The computational soundness of its compiler guarantees that the execution of the compiled contract is coherent with the semantics of the source BitML specification, even in the presence of adversaries. We start by specifying in BitML several smart contracts of growing complexity, intuitively describing their behaviour. Then, we show how to execute them on Bitcoin, by exploiting the BitML compiler.

© Springer Nature Switzerland AG 2018
T. Margaria and B. Steffen (Eds.): ISoLA 2018, LNCS 11247, pp. 432–449, 2018.
https://doi.org/10.1007/978-3-030-03427-6_32

2   Contracts

We illustrate Bitcoin smart contracts through a series of examples, without relying on any previous knowledge about Bitcoin. To this purpose we use BitML [9], a formalism which allows to express contracts in a process-algebraic fashion. In Sect. 3 we will show how to effectively execute these contracts on Bitcoin.

Contracts allow two or more participants (denoted as A, B, ...) to exchange their bitcoins ($\textrm{B}$) according to the following workflow:

1. First, a participant broadcasts a *contract advertisement* $\{G\}C$. The component C is the actual contract, specifying the rules according to which the bitcoins can be transferred among participants. The component G is a set of *preconditions* to the execution of C. For instance, G can require participants to deposit some bitcoins, and to commit to some secrets.
2. If all the involved participants accept $\{G\}C$, satisfying its preconditions, the contract C becomes stipulated. Then, participants can interact, following the rules specified by C. According to the actual interaction, the final distribution of bitcoins among participants may vary.

2.1   Direct Payment

Assume that A wants to give $1\textrm{B}$ to B through a contract. To this purpose, A must first declare that she owns $1\textrm{B}$, and that she agrees to transfer it under the control of the contract. This is represented by the following precondition:

$$G \ = \ \textsf{A}\!:\!!\,1\textrm{B} \tag{1}$$

while the actual contract is the following:

$$Pay \ = \ \texttt{withdraw B} \tag{2}$$

We show below a possible computation of $\{G\}Pay$, using the semantics in [9] (which here we slightly simplify to ease the presentation). The configurations of the semantics are the parallel composition (denoted by |) of terms of the form:

- $\{G\}C$, a contract advertisement;
- $\langle C, v\textrm{B}\rangle$, a stipulated contract with a balance of $v\textrm{B}$;
- $\langle\textsf{A}, v\textrm{B}\rangle_x$, a deposit of $v\textrm{B}$ owned by A, and with unique name x;
- $\textsf{A}[\cdots]$, the *authorization* of A to perform some operation.

For instance, we denote with $\textsf{A}[x \rhd \{G\}C]$ the authorization of A to spend the deposit x for stipulating the advertised contract. Other terms needed for more advanced examples will be introduced later.

The initial configuration of our direct payment contract is the parallel composition of $\{G\}Pay$ and a deposit $\langle\textsf{A}, 1\textrm{B}\rangle_x$. The computation proceeds as follows:

$$\langle\textsf{A}, 1\textrm{B}\rangle_x \mid \{G\}Pay \ \to \ \langle\textsf{A}, 1\textrm{B}\rangle_x \mid \{G\}Pay \mid \textsf{A}[x \rhd \{G\}Pay]$$
$$\to \ \langle\texttt{withdraw B}, 1\textrm{B}\rangle$$
$$\to \ \langle\textsf{B}, 1\textrm{B}\rangle_y$$

At the first step, A authorizes to spend the deposit x to stipulate the contract. This move adds to the configuration the authorization $A[x \triangleright \{G\}Pay]$. At the second step, Pay becomes stipulated, since the precondition G is satisfied: indeed, the required $1\dot{B}$ deposit exists, and its spending is authorized by A. After stipulation, the $1\dot{B}$ deposit is assimilated by the contract; both the deposit and the authorization are removed from the configuration. At this point, the contract allows B to withdraw all its balance. When this happens, the contract becomes terminated (disappearing from the configuration), and a new deposit for B is added to the configuration; the deposit name y is fresh.

2.2 Payment from Multiple Senders

In the previous contract, the initial deposit has been provided by a single participant, but more in general, a contract can gather money from multiple participants. For instance, assume A_1 and A_2 want to pay $1\dot{B}$ each to B. We can perform this transfer atomically by using the following precondition:

$$G_2 = A_1 : !\, 1\dot{B} \mid A_2 : !\, 1\dot{B} \tag{3}$$

and the same contract Pay as in (2). Now, to stipulate the contract, both A_1 and A_2 must authorize to transfer their deposits to the contract:

$$\langle A_1, 1\dot{B} \rangle_x \mid \langle A_2, 1\dot{B} \rangle_y \mid \{G_2\}Pay$$
$$\rightarrow \langle A_1, 1\dot{B} \rangle_x \mid \langle A_2, 1\dot{B} \rangle_y \mid \{G_2\}Pay \mid A_1[x \triangleright \{G_2\}Pay]$$
$$\rightarrow \langle A_1, 1\dot{B} \rangle_x \mid \langle A_2, 1\dot{B} \rangle_y \mid \{G_2\}Pay \mid A_1[x \triangleright \{G_2\}Pay] \mid A_2[y \triangleright \{G_2\}Pay]$$
$$\rightarrow \langle Pay, 1\dot{B} \rangle \rightarrow \langle B, 1\dot{B} \rangle_z$$

The contract is stipulated in the third step, which atomically removes the two authorizations and the two deposits from the configuration. Note that, once stipulated, (3) guarantees that B will receive $2\dot{B}$.

A seemingly similar behaviour could be obtained through the parallel composition of two advertisements, where A_1 and A_2 independently send $1\dot{B}$ to B:

$$\{A_1 : !\, 1\dot{B}\} \; \texttt{withdraw B} \mid \{A_2 : !\, 1\dot{B}\} \; \texttt{withdraw B} \tag{4}$$

A remarkable difference between (3) and (4) is that in (4) it may happen that A_1 authorizes the stipulation, while A_2 does not. In this case, B will only get $1\dot{B}$. By comparison, with A_1's authorization alone, the contract using (3) can not be stipulated.

2.3 Procrastinating Payments

Assume now that A wants to stipulate a contract where she commits herself to give $1\dot{B}$ to B *after* a certain date d. For instance, this contract could represent a birthday present to be withdrawn only after the birthday date; or the paying of a rent to the landlord, to be withdrawn only after the 1st of the month. Using the same precondition in (1), A can use the following contract:

$$PayAfter \; = \; \texttt{after}\, 2018\text{-}04\text{-}08 : \texttt{withdraw}\; \mathsf{B} \qquad (5)$$

This contract locks the deposit until 2018-04-08. After then, B can perform action $\texttt{withdraw}\; \mathsf{B}$ to redeem $1\cancel{B}$ from the contract, with no further time limitations. The computations must now record the passing of time: we do this by adding to the configuration a term $t = d_0$, meaning that the current global time is d_0. For instance, a possible computation of $\{G\}PayAfter$ is the following:

$$\langle \mathsf{A}, 1\cancel{B}\rangle_x \mid \{G\}PayAfter \mid t = 2018\text{-}04\text{-}01$$
$$\rightarrow \cdots \rightarrow \langle PayAfter, 1\cancel{B}\rangle \mid t = 2018\text{-}04\text{-}01$$
$$\xrightarrow{\;7\ \text{days}\;} \langle PayAfter, 1\cancel{B}\rangle \mid t = 2018\text{-}04\text{-}08$$
$$\rightarrow \langle \mathsf{B}, 1\cancel{B}\rangle_y \mid t = 2018\text{-}04\text{-}08$$

In the contract $PayAfter$, if B forgets to withdraw, the money remains within the contract. The following contract, instead, allows A to recover her money if B has not withdrawn within a given deadline:

$$PayOrRecover \; = \; \texttt{after}\, d : \texttt{withdraw}\; \mathsf{B} \; + \; \texttt{after}\, d' : \texttt{withdraw}\; \mathsf{A} \qquad (6)$$

where the precondition is the same as in (1), and d, d' are constants such that $d' > d$. The symbol $+$ denotes a *choice* between two mutually exclusive branches: either B withdraws $1\cancel{B}$ after time d, or A withdraws $1\cancel{B}$ after time d'. Note that the contract does not choose internally which of the branches is taken: the actual choice is left to the participants. Technically, $+$ models an *external choice*, taken by the first participant who fires a move on one of the branches. In our specific example (6), before the deadline d no one can withdraw; after d (but before d') only B can withdraw, while after d' both $\texttt{withdraw}$ actions are enabled, so the first one who performs their $\texttt{withdraw}$ will get the money. This contract also models a "limited-time offer", which becomes unavailable after d'.

2.4 Authorizing Payments

Assume that A is willing to pay $1\cancel{B}$ to B, but only if another participant O gives his authorization. With the precondition (1), we can use the following contract:

$$PayAuth \; = \; \mathsf{O} : \texttt{withdraw}\; \mathsf{B} \qquad (7)$$

A computation where O gives his authorization will then proceed as follows:

$$\langle \mathsf{A}, 1\cancel{B}\rangle_x \mid \{G\}PayAuth \rightarrow \langle \mathsf{A}, 1\cancel{B}\rangle_x \mid \{G\}PayAuth \mid \mathsf{A}[x \rhd \{G\}PayAuth]$$
$$\rightarrow \langle \mathsf{O} : \texttt{withdraw}\; \mathsf{B}, 1\cancel{B}\rangle$$
$$\rightarrow \langle \mathsf{O} : \texttt{withdraw}\; \mathsf{B}, 1\cancel{B}\rangle \mid \mathsf{O}[\mathsf{O} : \texttt{withdraw}\; \mathsf{B}]$$
$$\rightarrow \langle \mathsf{B}, 1\cancel{B}\rangle_y$$

The semantics of contracts ensures that `withdraw` B can be performed only if the configuration contains a suitable authorization. In the computation above, this authorization is rendered by O[O : `withdraw` B], added by the participant O at the third step[1]. Of course, there are also computations where O chooses not to provide the authorization.

We can play with authorizations and summations to construct more complex contracts. For instance, assume we want to design an *escrow* contract, which allows A to buy an item from B, authorizing the payment only after she gets the item. Further, B can authorize a full refund to A, in case there is some problem with the item. A naïve attempt to model this contract is the following:

$$NaiveEscrow = A : \textsf{withdraw } B + B : \textsf{withdraw } A$$

If both participants are honest, everything goes smoothly: when A receives the item, she authorizes the payment to B, otherwise B authorizes the refund. The problem with this contract is that, if neither A nor B give the authorization, the money in the contract is frozen. To cope with this issue, we can refine the escrow contract, by introducing a trusted arbiter O which resolves the dispute:

$$OracleEscrow = NaiveEscrow + O : \textsf{withdraw } A + O : \textsf{withdraw } B$$

The last two branches are used if neither A nor B give their authorizations: in this case, the arbiter chooses whether to authorize A or B to redeem the deposit. A variant of the escrow contract where O can issue a *partial* refund is in [9].

Another use case for authorizations is a bet, for instance on a football match. Two players A and B deposit 1Ḃ each, with precondition A : ! 1Ḃ | B : ! 1Ḃ. The winner—determined by a trusted oracle O—can redeem the whole pot:

$$O : \textsf{withdraw } A + O : \textsf{withdraw } B$$

Note that a trusted oracle will only authorize the action corresponding the winner of the football match.

2.5   Splitting Deposits

In all the previous examples, the deposit within the contract is transferred to a single participant. More in general, deposits can be split in many parts, to be transferred to different participants. For instance, assume that A wants her 1Ḃ deposit to be transferred in equal parts to B_1 and to B_2. Using the same precondition in (1), we can model this behaviour as follows:

$$PaySplit = \textsf{split} \left(0.5Ḃ \to \textsf{withdraw } B_1 \mid 0.5Ḃ \to \textsf{withdraw } B_2\right) \qquad (8)$$

The `split` construct splits the contract in two or more parallel subcontracts, each with its own balance. Of course, the sum of their balances must be less than or equal to the deposit of the whole contract.

---

[1] To avoid ambiguities, the BitML semantics decorates contract terms with unique identifiers, referred to in authorization terms. Here we omit them for conciseness.

A possible computation of $\{G\}PaySplit$ is the following:

$$\langle A, 1\dot{B}\rangle_x \mid \{G\}PaySplit \;\rightarrow\; \cdots \;\rightarrow\; \langle PaySplit, 1\dot{B}\rangle$$
$$\rightarrow\; \langle \mathtt{withdraw}\ B_1, 0.5\dot{B}\rangle \mid \langle \mathtt{withdraw}\ B_2, 0.5\dot{B}\rangle$$
$$\rightarrow\; \langle B_1, 0.5\dot{B}\rangle_y \mid \langle \mathtt{withdraw}\ B_2, 0.5\dot{B}\rangle$$
$$\rightarrow\; \langle B_1, 0.5\dot{B}\rangle_y \mid \langle B_2, 0.5\dot{B}\rangle_z$$

We can use `split` together with the other primitives presented so far to craft more complex contracts. For instance, assume that A wants pay $0.9\dot{B}$ to B, routing the payment through an intermediary I who can choose whether to authorize it (in this case retaining a $0.1\dot{B}$ fee), or not. Since A does not trust I, she wants to use a contract to guarantee that: (i) if I authorizes the payment, then $0.9\dot{B}$ are transferred to B; (ii) otherwise, A does not lose money.

Using the same precondition in (1), we can model this behaviour as follows:

$$I : \mathtt{split}\ \big(0.1\dot{B} \rightarrow \mathtt{withdraw}\ I \mid 0.9\dot{B} \rightarrow \mathtt{withdraw}\ B\big)\;+\;\mathtt{after}\,d : \mathtt{withdraw}\ A$$

The leftmost branch can only be taken if I authorizes the payment: in this case, I gets his fee, and B gets his payment. Instead, if I denies his authorization, then A can redeem her deposit after time d.

2.6 Volatile Deposits

So far, we have seen participants using *persistent* deposits, that are assimilated by the contract upon stipulation. Besides these, participants can also use *volatile* deposits, which are *not* assimilated upon stipulation. For instance:

$$G_? \;=\; A\!:\!?\,0.5\dot{B}\,@\,x \mid A\!:\!!\,0.5\dot{B}$$

gives A the possibility of contributing $0.5\dot{B}$ during the contract execution. However, A can choose instead to spend her volatile deposit outside the contract. The variable x is a handle to the volatile deposit, which can be used as follows:

$$Pay? \;=\; \mathtt{put}\ x.\,\mathtt{withdraw}\ B$$

After stipulation, any participant can execute $\mathtt{put}\ x$ to transfer the deposit x to the contract, provided that $\langle A, 0.5\dot{B}\rangle_x$ occurs in the configuration. Unlike the computation in Sect. 2.1, a computation of $\langle A, 0.5\dot{B}\rangle_x \mid \langle A, 0.5\dot{B}\rangle_y \mid \{G_?\}Pay?$ (even after stipulation) is not guaranteed to reach a configuration containing $\langle B, 1\dot{B}\rangle$. Indeed, since x is not paid upfront, there is no guarantee that x will be available when the contract demands it, as A can spend it for other purposes.

Volatile deposits can be exploited within more complex contracts, to handle situations where a participant wants to add some funds to the contract. For instance, assume a scenario where A_1 and A_2 want to give B $2\dot{B}$ as a present, paying $1\dot{B}$ each. However, A_2 is not sure *a priori* she will be able to pay, because she may need her $1\dot{B}$ for more urgent purposes: in this case, A_1 is willing to pay an extra bitcoin. We can model this scenario as follows: A_1 puts 2B̶ as a persistent deposit, while A_2 makes available a volatile deposit x of 1B̶:

$$A_1 : \,! \, 2\text{B̶} \mid A_2 : ? \, 1\text{B̶} \, @ \, x$$

The contract is a choice between two branches:

$$(\text{put } x. \, \text{split } (2\text{B̶} \rightarrow \text{withdraw B} \mid 1\text{B̶} \rightarrow \text{withdraw } A_1)) + \text{after } d : \text{withdraw B}$$

In the leftmost branch, A_2 puts 1B̶ in the contract, and the balance is split between B (who takes 2B̶, as expected), and A_1 (who takes her extra deposit back). The rightmost branch is enabled after d, and it deals with the case where A_2 has not put her deposit by such deadline. In this case, B can redeem 2B̶, while A_2 loses the extra deposit. Note that, in both cases, B will receive 2B̶.

2.7 Revealing Secrets

A useful feature of Bitcoin smart contracts is the possibility for a participant to choose a secret, and unblock some action only when the secret is revealed. Further, different actions can be enabled according to the length of the secret. Secrets must be declared in the contract precondition, as follows:

$$A : \text{secret } a$$

We give the secret a *name*, here a, but we never denote the *value* of the secret itself. A basic contract which exploits this feature is the following:

$$PaySecret \; = \; \text{reveal } a \text{ if } |a| > 1. \, \text{withdraw A} \qquad (9)$$

This contract asks A to commit to a secret of length greater than one[2], and allows A to redeem 1B̶ upon revealing the secret. Until then, the deposit is frozen.

In order to describe computations where participants commit to and reveal secrets, we extend configurations with two new kinds of terms:

- $\{A : a\#N\}$, representing the fact that A has committed to a secret a. The length of a, which is secret as well, is determined by the integer N;
- $A : a\#N$, representing the fact that A has revealed her secret a (hence, she has also revealed its length N).

Running $\{G \mid A : \text{secret } a\}PaySecret$ with a secret of length 2 yields:

$$\langle A, 1\text{B̶} \rangle_x \mid \{A : a\#2\} \mid \{G \mid A : \text{secret } a\}PaySecret \; \rightarrow \cdots$$
$$\rightarrow \{A : a\#2\} \mid \langle PaySecret, 1\text{B̶} \rangle$$
$$\rightarrow A : a\#2 \mid \langle PaySecret, 1\text{B̶} \rangle \; \rightarrow \; \langle \text{withdraw A}, 1\text{B̶} \rangle \; \rightarrow \; \langle A, 1\text{B̶} \rangle_y$$

---

[2] After compiling to Bitcoin, the actual length of the secret will be increased by η, where η is a security parameter, large enough to avoid brute-force preimage attacks.

The `reveal` primitive can be used to design more useful contracts than the one in (9). For instance, we show in (10) how to express a *timed commitment* contract [2,11,15,23], using the same precondition as above. In this contract, A wants to choose a secret a, and reveal it before the deadline d; if A does not reveal the secret within d, B can redeem the 1Ƀ deposit as a compensation:

$$TC = (\text{reveal}\,a.\,\text{withdraw A}) + (\text{after}\,d : \text{withdraw B}) \qquad (10)$$

Only A can choose the first branch, by revealing a. After that, anyone can further reduce the contract, and transfer 1Ƀ to A. Only after time d, if the `reveal` has not been performed, any participant can perform the `withdraw` in the second branch, which transfers 1Ƀ to B. Therefore, before the deadline A has the option to reveal a (avoiding the penalty), or to keep it secret (paying the penalty). If no branch is taken by time d, a race condition occurs: in such case, the first one who fires the `withdraw` gets the money.

Using the precondition A:!1Ƀ | A:secret a | B:!1Ƀ | B:secret b, we can also model a *mutual* timed commitment as follows:

$$TC2 = \text{reveal}\,a.\,C' + \text{after}\,d : \text{withdraw B}$$
$$C' = \text{reveal}\,b.\,C'' + \text{after}\,d' : \text{withdraw A} \qquad (d' > d)$$
$$C'' = \text{split}\,(1\text{Ƀ} \to \text{withdraw A} \mid 1\text{Ƀ} \to \text{withdraw B})$$

The contract $TC2$ can reduce to C' if A reveals a; otherwise (after d) B can redeem 2Ƀ. If A reveals, then B can choose not to reveal. Doing so, however, B will lose his deposit, since, after d', A can withdraw the 2Ƀ deposited in the contract. Instead, if B reveals, the 2Ƀ are split between A and B. Any participant (either A or B) who behaves honestly is guaranteed to learn the other participant's secret, or to gain 1Ƀ as compensation—in this sense the protocol is fair. Note that d' must be sufficiently greater than d, to avoid the attack where A waits until the very last moment to reveal her secret, so making it difficult for B to respect the deadline.

2.8   Lotteries and Other Games

Now that we have introduced all the primitives of BitML, we can combine them to construct more advanced contracts. For instance, consider a multiparty lottery where n players put their bets in a pot, and a winner—fairly chosen among the players—redeems the whole pot.

We model a lottery similar to the one in [2,3], for two players A and B who bet 1Ƀ each. The contract preconditions are the following:

$$A:!3\text{Ƀ} \mid A:\text{secret}\,a \mid B:!3\text{Ƀ} \mid B:\text{secret}\,b \qquad (11)$$

where the deposit of each player includes the 1Ƀ bet, plus a 2Ƀ collateral used as compensation in case of dishonest behaviour. The contract is the following:

```
split ( 2Ƀ → reveal b if 0 ≤ |b| ≤ 1. withdraw B  +  after d : withdraw A
      | 2Ƀ → reveal a. withdraw A  +  after d : withdraw B
      | 2Ƀ → reveal ab if |a| = |b|. withdraw A
            + reveal ab if |a| ≠ |b|. withdraw B )
```

The balance is split in three parts. Player B must reveal b by the deadline d; otherwise, A can redeem B's collateral (note that this is a timed commitment, similar to the one in (10)). Similarly, A must reveal a. To determine the winner we compare the lengths of the secrets, in the third part of the split. The winner is A if the secrets have the same length, otherwise it is B. Checking that b's length is either 0 or 1 is needed to achieve fairness: indeed, B can increase his probability to redeem 2Ḃ in the third part of the split by choosing a secret with length $N > 1$. However, doing so will make B lose his 2Ḃ deposit, so overall B's average payoff would be negative. A rational B would then choose a secret of length 0 or 1. Similarly, a rational A must choose a secret of length 0 or 1, otherwise she decreases her probability to be the winner. When both lengths are chosen in $\{0, 1\}$, both A and B can collect their collateral back, and they have a $1/2$ probability to win the lottery, provided that at least one of them chooses the length of the secret uniformly.

We also show a variant of the two-players lottery which requires no collateral, similarly to [8,18]. The preconditions just require the 1Ḃ bets and the secrets, while the contract is the following, where $d' > d$:

```
reveal b if 0 ≤ |b| ≤ 1.( reveal a if |a| = |b|. withdraw A
                         + reveal a if |a| ≠ |b|. withdraw B
                         + after d' : withdraw B )
   + after d : withdraw A
```

Here, B must reveal first. If B does not reveal his secret by the deadline d, or the secret has not the expected length, then A can redeem 2Ḃ. Otherwise, A in turn must reveal by the deadline d', or let B redeem 2Ḃ. If both A and B reveal, then the winner is determined by comparing the lengths of their secrets. As before, the rational strategy for each player is to choose a secret length 0 or 1, and reveal it. This makes the lottery fair, even in the absence of a collateral.

Using similar insights, we can craft contracts for other games. For instance, consider *Rock-Paper-Scissors*, a two players hand game where both players choose simultaneously a hand-shape, and the winner is decided along with the following rules: rock beats scissors, scissors beats paper, and paper beats rock.

We model the game for two players A and B who bet 1Ḃ each, and represent their moves as secrets of length 0 (rock), 1 (paper), and 2 (scissors). We define the following boolean predicate to determine the winner:

$$w(N, M) = (N = 0 \wedge M = 2) \vee (N = 2 \wedge M = 1) \vee (N = 1 \wedge M = 0)$$

The contract preconditions are as in (11), while the contract is the following:

```
split(
  2Ḃ → reveal b if 0 ≤ |b| ≤ 2. withdraw B  + after d : withdraw A
 | 2Ḃ → reveal a if 0 ≤ |a| ≤ 2. withdraw A  + after d : withdraw B
 | 2Ḃ → reveal ab if w(|a|, |b|). withdraw A
      + reveal ab if w(|b|, |a|). withdraw B
      + reveal ab if |a| = |b|. split (1Ḃ → withdraw A | 1Ḃ → withdraw B))
```

The contract is split in three parts, each with a balance of 2Ḃ: the first two parts allow the players to redeem the collaterals by revealing their secrets in time (similarly to the first version of the lottery), while the third one computes the winner. The winner is A if $w(|a|, |b|)$, and B if $w(|b|, |a|)$. If a and b have the same length (i.e. , they represent the same move), then there is a tie, so the bets are given back to the two players. Notice that if a player chooses a secret of unexpected length, then it may happen that the 2Ḃ in the third part of the split remain frozen. However, in such case the dishonest player will pay a 2Ḃ penalty to the other one. A zero-collateral version of *Rock-Paper-Scissors* can be obtained similarly to the second version of the lottery.

3   From Contracts to Bitcoin Transactions

In this section we show how to execute on Bitcoin the contracts in Sect. 2. We start by providing some minimal background on Bitcoin. A transaction represents a transfer of bitcoins, and the sequence of all transactions is stored in a public, append-only data structure called *blockchain*. When a new transaction T is appended to the blockchain, it redeems bitcoins from one or more transactions already on the blockchain. For the aims of this paper we abstract from the fact that, in Bitcoin, there exist some transactions (so-called *coinbase*) which generate bitcoins from nothing, and that transactions are grouped into blocks.

The simplest Bitcoin transaction, which transfers 1Ḃ to participant A, can be represented as follows, using the notation in [5]:

T_A
in : T
wit : w
out : $(\lambda x.\mathsf{versig}_A(x), 1\dot{B})$

The transaction T_A is a record with three fields. The field in points to another transaction T, which must occur before T_A on the blockchain. The field out is a pair, whose first element is a boolean predicate (called *script* in the Bitcoin jargon), and the second element is the amount (1Ḃ) deposited in T_A. To append T_A to the blockchain, T must contain at least 1Ḃ. The script specifies the condition under which a subsequent transaction T' can redeem the 1Ḃ in T_A, transferring it to T'. In our case, the script requires a signature x of A on T'. To evaluate the script, the formal parameter x will be instantiated to the value of the wit field (called *witness*) of T'. In the previous figure, the witness w in T_A is the actual parameter used to evaluate the script in T, the transaction referred by T_A.in. If such evaluation yields true, then T_A can be appended to the blockchain, redeeming 1Ḃ from T. That sum is now under the control of A, since she is the only participant who can provide the needed witness in T'.

To execute a BitML contract, the involved users first translate it into a set of Bitcoin transactions, using the compiler in [9]. Then, they append one or more of these transactions to the Bitcoin blockchain. Intuitively, appending a transaction corresponds to a step of the contract execution, and so it may require users to perform the corresponding actions, like e.g. revealing a secret or providing an authorization. To compile contracts we will often exploit more advanced features of Bitcoin transactions than the above-mentioned ones, like e.g. that of collecting bitcoins from many inputs, and splitting them between many outputs. Further, we will often use more complex output scripts, and we will specify time constraints on when a transaction can be appended to the blockchain[3]. We will illustrate these features along with the examples where they are needed (see [5] for details).

3.1 Direct Payment

Recall the contract advertisement $\{A:!\,1\cancel{B}\}$ withdraw B from Sect. 2.1. By exploiting the BitML compiler, A and B construct the following transactions:

T_{init}	T'_B
in : T_A	in : T_{init}
wit : sig_A	wit : $\mathsf{sig}_A\ \mathsf{sig}_B$
out : $(\lambda\varsigma_0\varsigma_1.\,\mathsf{versig}_{AB}(\varsigma_0\varsigma_1),\,1\cancel{B})$	out : $(\lambda\varsigma.\,\mathsf{versig}_B(\varsigma),\,1\cancel{B})$

where $\mathsf{versig}_{AB}(\varsigma_0\varsigma_1)$ is a shorthand for $\mathsf{versig}_A(\varsigma_0) \wedge \mathsf{versig}_B(\varsigma_1)$, and sig_A represents A's signature on the enclosing transaction (similarly for sig_B).

In BitML, the stipulation of the contract starts with the following step:

$$\langle A, 1\cancel{B}\rangle_x \mid \{G\}Pay \;\rightarrow\; \langle A, 1\cancel{B}\rangle_x \mid \{G\}Pay \mid A[x \rhd \{G\}Pay]$$

In Bitcoin, to perform this step the participants generate T_{init} and T'_B (which initially have an empty wit field), sign them, and exchange the signatures. After that, they insert the signatures in the wit fields as shown in the figure above. Crucially, the signature on T_{init} is broadcast by A only *after* B's signature has been received and verified. In this way, when T_{init} is put on the blockchain, starting the execution of the contract, A knows all the needed signatures to redeem it with T'_B later on. This guarantees that, after the contract starts executing, it can be run until completion. In BitML, A's signature on T_{init} is rendered as the authorization term $A[x \rhd \{G\}Pay]$.

The second computation step in BitML is the following:

$$\langle A, 1\cancel{B}\rangle_x \mid \{G\}Pay \mid A[x \rhd \{G\}Pay] \;\rightarrow\; \langle \texttt{withdraw } B, 1\cancel{B}\rangle$$

In Bitcoin, this corresponds to appending T_{init} to the blockchain. This transaction redeems $1\cancel{B}$ from T_A (displayed before at page 10)—the concrete counterpart of the BitML deposit $\langle A, 1\cancel{B}\rangle_x$. Note that, since both A and B know the witness of T_{init}, any of them can append such transaction.

The last computation step in BitML is the following:

$$\langle \texttt{withdraw } B, 1\cancel{B}\rangle \;\rightarrow\; \langle B, 1\cancel{B}\rangle_y$$

---

[3] The BitML compiler always produces *standard* Bitcoin transactions, by exploiting the BALZaC tool (https://github.com/balzac-lang/balzac). This is crucial, since the Bitcoin network currently discards non-standard transactions.

where y is a fresh name. In Bitcoin, this corresponds to appending to the blockchain the transaction T'_B, which redeems 1β from T_{init}. After that, 1β is under B's control, since the script of T'_B only requires B's signature. The unspent transaction T'_B corresponds to the BitML deposit $\langle \mathsf{B}, 1\beta \rangle_y$.

3.2 Payment from Multiple Senders

Recall $\{G_2\}Pay = \{\mathsf{A}_1 : !\,1\beta \mid \mathsf{A}_2 : !\,1\beta\}\,\texttt{withdraw}\ \mathsf{B}$ from Sect. 2.2. Assume that the deposits of A_1 and A_2 are provided by two transactions $\mathsf{T}_{\mathsf{A}_1}$ and $\mathsf{T}_{\mathsf{A}_2}$ similar to the transaction T_A at page 10 (but for the script). Although the initial deposits are more than one, we still use a single transaction T_{init} to gather them, by exploiting the fact that Bitcoin transactions can have multiple inputs. The compiler produces the following two transactions:

T_{init}
in : $0 \mapsto \mathsf{T}_{\mathsf{A}_1}$, $1 \mapsto \mathsf{T}_{\mathsf{A}_2}$
wit : $0 \mapsto \mathsf{sig}_{\mathsf{A}_1}$, $1 \mapsto \mathsf{sig}_{\mathsf{A}_2}$
out : $(\lambda\varsigma_1\varsigma_2\varsigma.\,\mathsf{versig}_{\mathsf{A}_1\mathsf{A}_2\mathsf{B}}(\varsigma_1\varsigma_2\varsigma), 2\beta)$

T'_B
in : T_{init}
wit : $\mathsf{sig}_{\mathsf{A}_1}\ \mathsf{sig}_{\mathsf{A}_2}\ \mathsf{sig}_\mathsf{B}$
out : $(\lambda\varsigma.\,\mathsf{versig}_\mathsf{B}(\varsigma), 2\beta)$

Transaction T_{init} has two inputs: the one at index 0 points to $\mathsf{T}_{\mathsf{A}_1}$, while the other points to $\mathsf{T}_{\mathsf{A}_2}$. Consequently, it is possible to append T_{init} to the blockchain only if both $\mathsf{T}_{\mathsf{A}_1}$ and $\mathsf{T}_{\mathsf{A}_2}$ are still unredeemed on the blockchain. To this purpose, T_{init} needs to provide two witnesses, one for each input. In BitML, $\mathsf{T}_{\mathsf{A}_1}$ and $\mathsf{T}_{\mathsf{A}_2}$ are represented as deposits, say $\langle \mathsf{A}_1, 1\beta \rangle_x$ and $\langle \mathsf{A}_2, 1\beta \rangle_y$, and communicating the two signatures on T_{init} corresponds to providing the authorizations $\mathsf{A}_1[x \triangleright \{G_2\}Pay]$ and $\mathsf{A}_2[y \triangleright \{G_2\}Pay]$. As before, these signatures are exchanged only after all the other signatures have been exchanged and verified. Once the contract is stipulated, its execution proceeds as in Sect. 3.1.

3.3 Procrastinating Payments

To deal with time constraints, we exploit the absLock field of the Bitcoin transaction: namely, setting $\mathsf{T}.\mathsf{absLock} = d$ prevents T from being appended to the blockchain before time d. For instance, recall $PayAfter$ from (5). The BitML compiler produces the following two transactions:

T_{init}
in : T_A
wit : sig_A
out : $(\lambda\varsigma_0\varsigma_1.\,\mathsf{versig}_{\mathsf{A}\mathsf{B}}(\varsigma_0\varsigma_1), 1\beta)$

T'_B
in : T_{init}
wit : $\mathsf{sig}_\mathsf{A}\ \mathsf{sig}_\mathsf{B}$
out : $(\lambda\varsigma.\,\mathsf{versig}_\mathsf{B}(\varsigma), 1\beta)$
absLock : d

In this way, even if after stipulation all the participants know all the witnesses, T'_B cannot be appended to the blockchain until time d, and as a consequence, B cannot use the 1β in T'_B before such date.

Recall now *PayOrRecover* from (6). The transactions obtained by compiling it are similar to the previous ones:

T_{init}
in : T_A
wit : sig_A
out : $(\lambda\varsigma_0\varsigma_1.\,\text{versig}_{AB}(\varsigma_0\varsigma_1),1\dot{B})$

T'_B
in : T_{init}
wit : $\text{sig}_A\,\text{sig}_B$
out : $(\lambda\varsigma.\,\text{versig}_B(\varsigma),1\dot{B})$
absLock : d

T'_A
in : T_{init}
wit : $\text{sig}_A\,\text{sig}_B$
out : $(\lambda\varsigma.\,\text{versig}_A(\varsigma),1\dot{B})$
absLock : d'

The main difference with (5) is that now there are two transactions, T'_B and T'_A, that can redeem T_{init}. However, since T_{init} cannot be redeemed twice, only one of them can be appended to the blockchain: appending T'_B corresponds to executing the left branch of the choice, i.e. $\texttt{after}\,d : \texttt{withdraw B}$, while T'_A corresponds to the right branch, i.e. $\texttt{after}\,d' : \texttt{withdraw A}$.

3.4   Authorizing Payments

As seen in the previous examples, to implement contract stipulation participants must exchange and verify their signatures on the Bitcoin transactions generated by the compiler. However, in case of contracts with authorizations, some signatures can be provided only during the execution of the contract, after stipulation. For instance, compiling *PayAuth* in (7) results in the following transactions:

T_{init}
in : T_A
wit : sig_A
out : $(\lambda\varsigma_0\varsigma_1\varsigma_2.\,\text{versig}_{ABO}(\varsigma_0\varsigma_1\varsigma_2),1\dot{B})$

T'_B
in : T_{init}
wit : $\text{sig}_A\,\text{sig}_B\,[\text{sig}_O]$
out : $(\lambda\varsigma.\,\text{versig}_B(\varsigma),1\dot{B})$

where the square brackets around sig_O in T'_B indicate that such signature does *not* need to be exchanged at stipulation time. Providing such signature at run time corresponds to the following computation step in BitML:

$$\langle O : \texttt{withdraw B},1\dot{B}\rangle \rightarrow \langle O : \texttt{withdraw B},1\dot{B}\rangle \mid O[O : \texttt{withdraw B}]$$

Only after O's signature on T'_B is made public, it is possible to append such transaction to the blockchain, transferring $1\dot{B}$ to B.

3.5   Splitting Deposits

Bitcoin transactions can have multiple outputs: in this case, whoever redeems the transaction must specify *which* output it is redeeming. This feature is exploited to compile the $\texttt{split}$ construct of BitML. For instance, compiling *PaySplit* from (8) produces the following transactions:

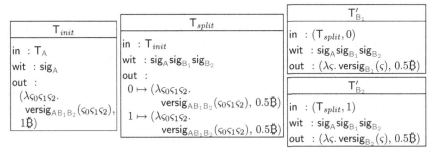

As usual, T_{init} gathers A's deposit and starts the contract. Then, appending T_{split} to the blockchain splits the contract balance between two different outputs, indexed with 0 and 1. In BitML, this would correspond to the computation step:

$$\langle PaySplit, 1\dot{B} \rangle \; \rightarrow \; \langle \texttt{withdraw } B_1, 0.5\dot{B} \rangle \mid \langle \texttt{withdraw } B_2, 0.5\dot{B} \rangle$$

where the two contracts in the parallel composition can be executed independently (as usual in process calculi). Similarly, the two outputs of T_{split} can be independently redeemed by T'_{B_1} and T'_{B_2}. The in field of these transactions specifies, besides the input transaction T_{split}, also the index of the output they want to redeem. Appending T'_{B_1} corresponds, in BitML, to the step:

$$\langle \texttt{withdraw } B_1, 0.5\dot{B} \rangle \mid \langle \texttt{withdraw } B_2, 0.5\dot{B} \rangle \; \rightarrow \; \langle B_1, 0.5\dot{B} \rangle_y \mid \langle \texttt{withdraw } B_2, 0.5\dot{B} \rangle$$

3.6 Volatile Deposits

Recall Pay? from Sect. 2.6, where A uses a volatile deposit x and a persistent one. Assume that the Bitcoin counterpart of x is a transaction T_x, from which A can redeem 0.5$\dot{B}$ by providing her own signature. The BitML compiler outputs:

T_{init}		T_{put}		T'_A	
in : T_A		in : $0 \mapsto T_{init}, 1 \mapsto T_x$		in : T_{put}	
wit : sig_A		wit : $0 \mapsto sig_A\,sig_B, 1 \mapsto sig_A$		wit : $sig_A\,sig_B$	
out : $(\lambda\varsigma_0\varsigma_1.versig_{AB}(\varsigma_0\varsigma_1), 0.5\dot{B})$		out : $(\lambda\varsigma_0\varsigma_1.\,versig_{AB}(\varsigma_0\varsigma_1), 1\dot{B})$		out : $(\lambda\varsigma.\,versig_A(\varsigma), 1\dot{B})$	

The transaction T_{init} gathers the persistent deposit, stored in T_A. The transaction T_{put} has two inputs: T_{init}, which can be redeemed with the signatures of both A and B, and T_x, which can be redeemed with A's signature only. Since all these signatures are exchanged before stipulation, any participant can append T_{put} to the blockchain—provided that T_x is still unspent. Instead, if T_x has been spent, the contract gets stuck, and the deposit within T_{init} is frozen.

3.7 Revealing Secrets

Recall $PaySecret$ from Sect. 2.7. In the stipulation phase, A commits to a secret (named a) and to its length N, by publishing the term $\{A : a\#N\}$. In Bitcoin, this corresponds to choosing an actual bitstring s_a for the secret, and broadcasting its hash $h_a = H(s_a)$. To ensure that s_a cannot be recovered by brute force, even when N is small[4], we let the actual length of s_a be $\eta + N$, where η is a public security parameter, large enough (e.g. , $\eta = 128$). In this way, the other participants cannot infer s_a (assuming H to be preimage resistant), nor its length. Further, A cannot later on reveal a different secret or a different length (assuming collision resistance). The BitML compiler generates the transactions:

T_{init}	T_{reveal}	T'_A
in : T_A	in : T_{init}	in : T_{reveal}
wit : sig_A	wit : $sig_A [s_a]$	wit : sig_A
out : $(\lambda\varsigma x.versig_A(\varsigma) \wedge$ $H(x) = h_a \wedge \|x\| > \eta + 1, 1\text{B})$	out : $(\lambda\varsigma. versig_A(\varsigma), 1\text{B})$	out : $(\lambda\varsigma. versig_A(\varsigma), 1\text{B})$

Transaction T_{init} collects A's deposit, and its output script requires two witnesses: a signature ς of A on the redeeming transaction, and a bitstring x whose hash $H(x)$ is equal to h_a; further, x must be longer than $\eta + 1$ bits, to satisfy the condition $|a| > 1$ in the reveal $\cdots$ if. These witnesses are provided by T_{reveal}, where the square brackets around s_a indicate that the secret can be provided *after* stipulation. Broadcasting the secret and appending T_{reveal} to the blockchain correspond to the following two BitML steps (which assume $N > 1$):

$$\{A : a\#N\} \mid \langle PaySecret, 1\text{B} \rangle \rightarrow A : a\#N \mid \langle PaySecret, 1\text{B} \rangle \rightarrow \langle \text{withdraw } A, 1\text{B} \rangle$$

Note that, once the transaction T_{reveal} is on the blockchain, everyone can read the secret in its wit field. After that, appending T'_A corresponds to the step:

$$\langle \text{withdraw } A, 1\text{B} \rangle \rightarrow \langle A, 1\text{B} \rangle_y$$

Recall now $TC = (\text{reveal } a. \text{withdraw } A) + (\text{after } d : \text{withdraw } B)$, the timed commitment contract in (10). As before, we assume that A commits to a secret s_a by broadcasting its hash h_a. Further, we assume that A and B generate other two key pairs, (k_{sA}, k_{pA}) and (k_{sB}, k_{pB}), and share their public parts. The transactions obtained by the compiler are the following:

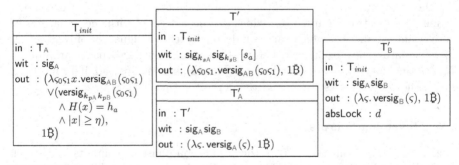

---

[4] The reason why BitML allows secrets to have small lengths is to make it easier to write some contracts, like e.g. those in Sect. 2.8.

The transaction T_{init} can be redeemed in two ways, according to the two clauses in the disjunction of its output script: either with the signatures sig_A and sig_B, or with the signatures $\text{sig}_{k_{sA}}$ and $\text{sig}_{k_{sB}}$ *and* the secret value s_a.

In the first case one can use the transaction T'_B, which however can be appended only after time d, because of the time constraint specified in its absLock field. Appending T'_B corresponds to the following step in BitML (where $d' \geq d$):

$$\langle TC, 1\ddot{B}\rangle \mid t = d' \;\rightarrow\; \langle B, 1\ddot{B}\rangle_y \mid t = d'$$

In the second case, one can use the transaction T', by filling its wit field with the secret s_a revealed by A. Doing this corresponds to the following computation steps in BitML (which can be performed at any time):

$$\{A : a\#N\} \mid \langle TC, 1\ddot{B}\rangle \;\rightarrow\; A : a\#N \mid \langle TC, 1\ddot{B}\rangle \;\rightarrow\; \langle \texttt{withdraw}\,A, 1\ddot{B}\rangle$$

After that, anyone can append the transaction T'_A to the blockchain to transfer $1\ddot{B}$ under A's control. Once T' is on the blockchain, it will be no longer possible to append T'_B, since both transactions want to redeem T_{init}.

4 Related Work and Conclusions

We have illustrated Bitcoin smart contracts from a programming languages perspective, by exploiting the BitML calculus [9]. Although BitML can express many of the smart contracts appeared in the literature [4], there exist some contracts which can be executed on Bitcoin but are not expressible in BitML. This is the case e.g. of *contingent payment* contracts, where a participant A promises to pay B for a value x satisfying a predicate chosen by A (e.g. , x is a prime factor of a given large number). Contingent payments can be implemented in Bitcoin similarly to timed commitment contracts: A pays a deposit, which is taken by B after revealing a preimage of $H(x)$ which satisfies the predicate. An off-chain protocol [6] (which exploits zero-knowledge proofs) is used to guarantee that $H(x)$ is indeed the hash of a value x satisfying the predicate (note that, in the Bitcoin scripting language, one can only check trivial predicates, like e.g. equality). Another kind of contracts which are not expressible in BitML are those for which one cannot pre-determine a *finite* set of transactions, or of signatures, before executing the contract. This is the case, e.g. , of crowdfunding contracts [4], where participants invest some money until a given threshold is reached. Here, we do not statically know neither the number of participants, nor their identities, so it is not possible to statically produce (and pre-sign) a set of transactions, as required by BitML. To the best of our knowledge, the existence of negative results on the expressiveness of Bitcoin contracts is still an open question

Only a few other languages for Bitcoin contracts have been proposed so far. TypeCoin [13] is an high-level language which allows to model the updates of a state machine as affine logic propositions. Users can "run" this machine by putting transactions on the blockchain, with the guarantee that only the legit updates can be performed. A downside of [13] is that liveness is guaranteed only by assuming cooperative participants, i.e. , a dishonest participant can make the others unable to complete an execution. Note instead that in BitML, honest participants can always make a contract progress, regardless of the behaviour of the environment. Cooperation is incentivized by punishing misbehaviour with penalties, like e.g. in the lottery of Sect. 2.8. The other works we are aware of, IVY[5], BALZaC[6] and Simplicity [21], replace the Bitcoin scripting language with more high-level languages, through which they simplify writing the transactions needed in a smart contract (e.g. , by providing static checks to determine if a transaction can redeem another one, etc.). Compared to these approaches, BitML completely abstracts from Bitcoin transactions, in this way allowing for more elegant specifications of contracts (compare e.g. the lotteries in Sect. 2.8 with those in [3,8,18]), and paving the way towards automatic verification.

Acknowledgments. This work is partially supported by Aut. Reg. of Sardinia projects "Sardcoin" and "Smart collaborative engineering".

References

1. Andrychowicz, M., Dziembowski, S., Malinowski, D., Mazurek, Ł.: Fair two-party computations via Bitcoin deposits. In: Böhme, R., Brenner, M., Moore, T., Smith, M. (eds.) FC 2014. LNCS, vol. 8438, pp. 105–121. Springer, Heidelberg (2014). https://doi.org/10.1007/978-3-662-44774-1_8
2. Andrychowicz, M., Dziembowski, S., Malinowski, D., Mazurek, L.: Secure multiparty computations on Bitcoin. In: IEEE S & P, pp. 443–458 (2014)
3. Andrychowicz, M., Dziembowski, S., Malinowski, D., Mazurek, L.: Secure multiparty computations on Bitcoin. Commun. ACM **59**(4), 76–84 (2016)
4. Atzei, N., Bartoletti, M., Cimoli, T., Lande, S., Zunino, R.: SoK: unraveling Bitcoin smart contracts. In: Bauer, L., Küsters, R. (eds.) POST 2018. LNCS, vol. 10804, pp. 217–242. Springer, Cham (2018). https://doi.org/10.1007/978-3-319-89722-6_9
5. Atzei, N., Bartoletti, M., Lande, S., Zunino, R.: A formal model of Bitcoin transactions. In: Financial Cryptography and Data Security (2018)
6. Banasik, W., Dziembowski, S., Malinowski, D.: Efficient zero-knowledge contingent payments in cryptocurrencies without scripts. In: Askoxylakis, I., Ioannidis, S., Katsikas, S., Meadows, C. (eds.) ESORICS 2016. LNCS, vol. 9879, pp. 261–280. Springer, Cham (2016). https://doi.org/10.1007/978-3-319-45741-3_14
7. Bartoletti, M., Pompianu, L.: An empirical analysis of smart contracts: platforms, applications, and design patterns. In: Brenner, M., et al. (eds.) FC 2017. LNCS, vol. 10323, pp. 494–509. Springer, Cham (2017). https://doi.org/10.1007/978-3-319-70278-0_31
8. Bartoletti, M., Zunino, R.: Constant-deposit multiparty lotteries on Bitcoin. In: Brenner, M., et al. (eds.) FC 2017. LNCS, vol. 10323, pp. 231–247. Springer, Cham (2017). https://doi.org/10.1007/978-3-319-70278-0_15
9. Bartoletti, M., Zunino, R.: BitML: a calculus for Bitcoin smart contracts. In: ACM CCS (2018)

---

[5] https://ivy-lang.org/bitcoin.
[6] https://blockchain.unica.it/balzac/.

10. Bentov, I., Kumaresan, R.: How to use Bitcoin to design fair protocols. In: Garay, J.A., Gennaro, R. (eds.) CRYPTO 2014. LNCS, vol. 8617, pp. 421–439. Springer, Heidelberg (2014). https://doi.org/10.1007/978-3-662-44381-1_24
11. Boneh, D., Naor, M.: Timed commitments. In: Bellare, M. (ed.) CRYPTO 2000. LNCS, vol. 1880, pp. 236–254. Springer, Heidelberg (2000). https://doi.org/10.1007/3-540-44598-6_15
12. Bonneau, J., Miller, A., Clark, J., Narayanan, A., Kroll, J.A., Felten, E.W.: SoK: research perspectives and challenges for Bitcoin and cryptocurrencies. In: IEEE S & P, pp. 104–121 (2015)
13. Crary, K., Sullivan, M.J.: Peer-to-peer affine commitment using Bitcoin. In: ACM Conference on Programming Language Design and Implementation, pp. 479–488 (2015)
14. Decker, C., Wattenhofer, R.: A fast and scalable payment network with Bitcoin duplex micropayment channels. In: Pelc, A., Schwarzmann, A.A. (eds.) SSS 2015. LNCS, vol. 9212, pp. 3–18. Springer, Cham (2015). https://doi.org/10.1007/978-3-319-21741-3_1
15. Goldschlag, D.M., Stubblebine, S.G., Syverson, P.F.: Temporarily hidden bit commitment and lottery applications. Int. J. Inf. Sec. 9(1), 33–50 (2010)
16. Kumaresan, R., Bentov, I.: How to use Bitcoin to incentivize correct computations. In: ACM CCS, pp. 30–41 (2014)
17. Kumaresan, R., Moran, T., Bentov, I.: How to use Bitcoin to play decentralized poker. In: ACM CCS, pp. 195–206 (2015)
18. Miller, A., Bentov, I.: Zero-collateral lotteries in Bitcoin and Ethereum. In: EuroS&P Workshops, pp. 4–13 (2017)
19. Miller, A., Bentov, I., Kumaresan, R., McCorry, P.: Sprites: payment channels that go faster than lightning. CoRR abs/1702.05812 (2017). http://arxiv.org/abs/1702.05812
20. Nakamoto, S.: Bitcoin: a peer-to-peer electronic cash system (2008). https://bitcoin.org/bitcoin.pdf
21. O'Connor, R.: Simplicity: a new language for blockchains. In: PLAS. ACM (2017)
22. Poon, J., Dryja, T.: The Bitcoin lightning network: scalable off-chain instant payments (2015). https://lightning.network/lightning-network-paper.pdf
23. Syverson, P.F.: Weakly secret bit commitment: applications to lotteries and fair exchange. In: IEEE CSFW, pp. 2–13 (1998)
24. Szabo, N.: Formalizing and securing relationships on public networks. First Monday 2(9) (1997). http://firstmonday.org/htbin/cgiwrap/bin/ojs/index.php/fm/article/view/548

Computing Exact Worst-Case Gas Consumption for Smart Contracts

Matteo Marescotti[1]([✉]), Martin Blicha[1,2], Antti E. J. Hyvärinen[1],
Sepideh Asadi[1], and Natasha Sharygina[1]

[1] Università della Svizzera italiana (USI), Lugano, Switzerland
{matteo.marescotti,martin.blicha,antti.hyvarinen,
sepideh.asadi,natasha.sharygina}@usi.ch
[2] Faculty of Mathematics and Physics, Charles University, Prague, Czech Republic

Abstract. The Ethereum platform is a public, distributed, blockchain-based database that is maintained by independent parties. A user interacts with Ethereum by writing programs and having miners execute them for a fee charged on-the-fly based on the complexity of the execution. The exact fee, measured in gas consumption, in general depends on the unknown Ethereum state, and predicting even its worst case is in principle undecidable. Uncertainty in gas consumption may result in inefficiency, loss of money, and, in extreme cases, in funds being locked for an indeterminate duration. This feasibility study presents two methods for determining the exact worst-case gas consumption of a bounded Ethereum execution using methods influenced by symbolic model checking. We give several concrete cases where gas consumption estimation is needed, and provide two approaches for determining gas consumption, one based on symbolically enumerating execution paths, and the other based on computing paths modularly based on the program structure.

1 Introduction

Algorithms for reaching consensus in a distributed environment have recently found applications in financial transactions based on distributed, public databases. One of the most famous applications of such systems is the Bitcoin platform. The idea is generalized to executing programs in [17] and has then been applied to other blockchains [12,13], most notably to the Ethereum platform that provides a Turing-complete execution environment where participants run programs in the form of *smart contracts* [4].

Smart contracts resemble *classes* in programming languages such as Java, C++, or Python, in that they contain data fields, called *storage*, and program code, called *functions*, which in turn have variables with a scope local to the functions. They differ from traditional programs in that, once deployed, a smart contract cannot be changed and will be publicly available. The contracts are commonly associated with monetary value, and therefore programming errors in contracts might have financial implications to the contract participants. As a result, the correct behaviour of contracts is of high interest to the participants.

© Springer Nature Switzerland AG 2018
T. Margaria and B. Steffen (Eds.): ISoLA 2018, LNCS 11247, pp. 450–465, 2018.
https://doi.org/10.1007/978-3-030-03427-6_33

The execution of the Ethereum platform is carried out by *miners* that mine the transactions between a contract participant and a contract for a fee. The fee is based on the cost of the transaction as specified by the execution environment, in an abstract quantity called *gas*. A participant specifies the price he or she is willing to pay for a unit of gas, and provides an amount of money for the transaction. The miner then keeps the price of the actual gas used in the transaction from the amount as a compensation for mining the transaction, and returns the rest. In the whole Ethereum platform the daily gas costs sum up to roughly 500'000 USD at the moment of writing, and therefore even small changes in gas consumption can have a big cumulative effect.

In general the cost of a transaction depends on the unknown state of the platform, and therefore it is useful to talk about transaction's worst-case gas consumption. Ethereum provides a Turing-complete execution environment, and therefore computing the worst-case consumption is undecidable.[1] We address the central challenge of computing the exact worst-case gas consumption of a transaction through highly efficient methods adapted from symbolic bounded model checking [3] and using efficient SMT solvers [2,7,10,16]. The gas consumption of a transaction is of interest to contract participants for several reasons. In the following, we identify three cases in which computing gas consumption can help in making Ethereum more efficient.

- The Ethereum protocol imposes an upper limit for the amount of gas that a transaction may consume. As a result, if the execution cost of a function increases over time, it may happen that at a certain point a transaction of a program can no longer be carried out [1]. Computing the gas consumption helps identifying such programming errors.
- A reliable gas estimation helps a participant to place a price on the unit of gas in line with the utility of the transaction. An amount that turns out to be insufficient to carry out the transaction results in the participant losing the money without executing the transaction, while an overestimated gas consumption makes the transaction less appealing to a miner and therefore less likely to be executed.
- An approach for computing the exact worst-case gas consumption can be used as an aide to the developer for comparing semantically equivalent smart contracts with respect to their gas consumption. If the tool can show that one implementation has a lower gas consumption than others, the developer can choose to deploy the implementation with the lower gas consumption.

We define the *gas consumption paths* (GCPs) for Ethereum, and exhaustively examine all GCPs of a function using symbolic methods. The paths are identified in the high-level language Solidity, and projected to the low-level assembly code EVM currently used in Ethereum. This approach has several advantages: Due to the combination of high and low-level representations we are able to be precise on the execution paths while maintaining exactness of the gas consumption. The

---

[1] The protocol imposes, however, a maximum gas consumption for a block, making the computation in principle decidable.

approach is independent of the low-level representation, where gas consumed by the instructions might depend on protocol version, different compilers might produce different code, and even the assembly language is subject to change.

We suggest two algorithms for studying the GCPs. Both use techniques influenced by symbolic model checking [3] to enumerate all paths that can have different gas consumption. The first, Gas Consumption Path Enumeration, collects all constraints that affect the gas consumption, evaluates all combinations of them one-by-one, and simulates those that are satisfiable. The second, Function-Oriented Gas Consumption Path Enumeration constructs GCPs for each function as explicit *cost-equivalence classes*, which are reused through variable renaming to recursively construct more cost-equivalence classes for calling functions. We outline in addition how both algorithms can be parallelized. Both algorithms are capable of computing the exact worst-case behaviour assuming that the underlying bounded model checking formula exactly describes the contract behaviour and that the EVM and Solidity gas consumption paths have one-to-one correspondence.

Related Work. The `solc` compiler for the Solidity language provides a gas consumption estimate as part of the compilation. However, the estimator assumes concrete values for transaction parameters and the Ethereum state, therefore merely providing a lower bound for the worst-case gas consumption.

The tool GASPER [5] analyses Ethereum smart contracts compiled into the low-level EVM bytecode and is capable of identifying certain constructs that are costly and can be simplified to equivalent, less costly programs. While some technologies used in GASPER, such as SMT solvers and symbolic computation, are similar to ours, we identify two important differences: We propose to work on the higher-level Solidity language, and our goal is to estimate the worst-case gas consumption instead of identifying code that can be optimized.

Incorrect gas consumption values for EVM instructions enable DoS attacks on Ethereum based on frequently executing under-evaluated instructions. In [6], the authors propose an emulation-based framework to automatically adjust the gas prices of EVM instructions based on measuring their resource consumptions. As part of the emulation the approach measures the gas consumption of functions based on control and data flow, but the emulation is based on random sampling and therefore is bound to be incomplete for all but the simplest contracts. Our approach instead guarantees the completeness of the gas consumption measurement through symbolic computation and could therefore be used for improving the precision of the approach.

Correctness aspects of smart contracts other than gas consumption have been studied using symbolic methods. For instance Oyente [14] extracts the control flow graph from the EVM bytecode of a contract, and symbolically executes it in order to detect some vulnerability patterns, although it is neither sound nor complete. Zeus [11] is a framework for verification of Solidity smart contracts using abstract interpretation and symbolic model checking. The tool works by converting Solidity to LLVM bit code, and verifying reachability properties using the SeaHorn model checker [9].

2 Preliminaries

The *Ethereum Virtual Machine* (EVM) is a distributed-consensus-based computer running in the Ethereum blockchain [4]. EVM executes *smart contracts*, programs written in a stack-based byte-code providing a small set of low-level instructions. Smart contracts can be seen as entities that contain scoped program functions which operate on contract-wide storage that is persistent over function calls, and local variables that are only visible inside a function. We define a function in Ethereum, both in EVM byte-code and in solidity, as $f(v)$ where f is the name of the function, and v is the set of function's formal parameters. When clear from the context, we omit v. The storage, denoted by an array $\mathbb{S}$, is the set of storage variables that the function may access. Accesses to storage are denoted by $\mathbb{S}[i]$ where i is an integer.

Table 1. Some EVM instruction costs [18]. The second half of the table lists examples of instructions whose cost depends on the context in which they are executed and the arguments provided.

Instruction	Gas	Description
JUMPDEST	1	Indicates a valid jump destination
POP	2	Pop from the stack
PUSHn	3	Push an n-bit item to stack
ADD/SUB	3	Arithmetic Operation
LT/GT/SLT/SGT/EQ	3	Arithmetic comparisons
MLOAD/MSTORE	3	Memory operations
MUL/DIV/MOD	5	Arithmetic Operations
JUMP	8	Unconditional jump to a location at the top of the stack
JUMPI	10	Conditional jump to a location at the top of the stack
SLOAD	200	Load from storage
CALL	700	Call a contract transaction with zero-valued arguments
CALLVAL	9,000	Call a contract transaction with non-zero valued arguments
SSTORE	5,000	Store a zero, or non-zero when previous value is non-zero
SSTORE	20,000	Store a non-zero when previous value is zero
SSTORE	15,000	Added to refund counter when storing a zero and previous value is non-zero.

While smart contracts correspond to concepts such as instances of Java classes, they differ in an interesting way in some respects. For instance, once deployed in Ethereum, smart contracts become publicly visible and the contract code cannot be changed. Anybody can interact with EVM through *transactions*, i.e., creating smart contracts or calling their functions, by paying a *miner* that will carry out the transaction.

The complexity of a transaction is measured in its *gas consumption*. Each EVM instruction has an associated gas consumption, a measure that relates the instruction to its storage or execution cost. See Table 1 for examples of some costs. In addition to instruction-specific costs, certain instructions and declarations affect the size of the memory local to a function, called the *active memory* [18]. Let a and b be the sizes of the active memory in bytes, respectively, before and after executing an instruction. The possible change incurs a cost or a refund defined as

$$\Delta C_{mem}(a,b) = 3 \cdot (a - b) + \left\lfloor \frac{a^2}{512} \right\rfloor - \left\lfloor \frac{b^2}{512} \right\rfloor.$$

To execute a transaction through a miner, a user provides a price he or she is willing to pay for a unit of gas in a currency called Ether, and the total amount of Ether that the transaction may consume. Assuming no errors are encountered while running the transaction and the amount paid for the actual gas consumption is sufficient, the transaction is carried out successfully. If carrying out the transaction requires more gas than what is provided, the execution is terminated without a refund.

Due to the memory model of EVM, in some cases the cost of an instruction depends on arguments of the instruction or the state of the contract when executing the instruction. For example:

- The instruction SSTORE writes into contract storage. The operation is costly in particular if a non-zero value is written to a storage location that previously contained a zero value. The EVM execution model contains a *refund counter* which is used for rewarding the user for executing instructions that make EVM less expensive. This is reflected in the case where SSTORE instruction writes a zero value to a location that previously held a non-zero value, resulting in a refund.
- The instruction cost of the instruction pair CALL and CALLVAL depend on their arguments. The instructions are used to call a transaction in another contract. While technically two different instructions, they can be interpreted as a single instruction from the perspective of a higher-level language. In this case the cost of a transaction depends on whether the values of the arguments passed in the call are zero.

The cost of a complete transaction in EVM is in part defined by the flow of control dictated by the EVM state, arguments, and the function code. Due to argument and environment dependence of instruction costs, the control flow graph is not sufficient for determining the transaction cost. We generalize the control flow graph to a *gas consumption graph* by adding new edges and nodes based on the instruction argument and environment dependence in a natural way, and call paths in the gas consumption graph *gas consumption paths* (GCP). All executions of a function that follow the same gas consumption path consume therefore equal amount of gas. Our approach aims at identifying a GCP that maximizes the gas consumption over all GCPs. Instead of working directly on EVM bytecode, we base the analysis on the higher-level Solidity language, arguably the most popular language for writing smart contracts at the time. Therefore we generalize the concept of GCPs to Solidity GCPs. These are not in general the same for instance due to low-level optimizations available for EVM. As a result we do not attempt to compute the gas consumption on the Solidity code, but instead compute exact EVM gas consumption using concrete executions that are guaranteed to cover all Solidity GCPs.

We assume that the Solidity GCPs cover also all EVM GCPs. We want to emphasise this methodological choice as a potential threat to the validity of the results, and will reflect it in the theorems on correctness in the next sections.

To identify potentially different GCPs we employ bounded-model-checking techniques [3] together with SMT solvers [2,7,10,16], by operating on the static single assignment (SSA) level of Solidity where loops have been unwound up to a given limit. The approach can be made complete by increasing the unwinding limit since the Ethereum protocol imposes a maximum gas consumption for a transaction.

3   Gas Consumption Path Enumeration

We present an algorithm for enumerating symbolically Solidity GCPs based on the unwound SSA representation of smart contracts. While the number of GCPs is in general exponential in the size of the unwound SSA representation, due to the symbolic representation the algorithm runs in polynomial space.

We first give the translation of a Solidity contract to an unwound SSA (USSA) form in Fig. 1 for an example program adapted from [8]. For brevity, Fig. 1(a) uses a pseudo-code resembling the Solidity language instead of the actual Solidity language.[2] The contract consists of functions f and g, where g calls f. Function g writes to the storage variable z and uses the solidity msg.sender.transfer function here abstracted simply as transfer(z). Function f does operations on its arguments inside a loop, stores the result into a local variable, and returns the result after the computation.

The search for GCPs is done on the USSA form, given in Fig. 1(b). The form consists of a sequence of *guarded assignments* having the form $c \rightarrow b = e(x)$ or $c \rightarrow b =^s e(x)$, where c is a conjunction of Boolean-valued expressions, and $e(x)$ is an operation over variables x. We distinguish between assignments where the left side of the equality is a variable in memory ($=$) and a storage location ($=^s$) since depending on the values these have different costs (see Table 1). Similarly the costs of some instructions depend on their arguments. For this purpose we define the function ArgCond that maps an instruction to its cost condition. For

---

[2] For a compilable Solidity contract see Fig. 2.

$$x_1 \geq y_1 \wedge y_1 \geq 0 \rightarrow z_1 =^s x_1 + y_1; \tag{1}$$

```
int z;
func g(x, y):
  if (x >= y)
    if (y >= 0)
      z = x + y
      transfer(z)
  z = f(x, y)

func f(a, b):
  int i = 0
  while (i < a + b):
    if (i < a):
      i = i + a
    else:
      i = i + b
  return i
```

$$x_1 \geq y_1 \rightarrow \texttt{transfer}(z_1); \tag{2}$$

$$true \rightarrow \mathbf{f}_{a_1} = x_2; \tag{3}$$

$$true \rightarrow \mathbf{f}_{b_1} = y_2; \tag{4}$$

$$true \rightarrow \mathbf{f}_{i_1} = 0; \tag{5}$$

$$(\mathbf{f}_{i_1} < \mathbf{f}_{a_1} + \mathbf{f}_{b_1}) \wedge (\mathbf{f}_{i_1} < \mathbf{f}_{a_1}) \rightarrow \mathbf{f}_{i_2} = \mathbf{f}_{i_1} + \mathbf{f}_{a_1}; \tag{6}$$

$$(\mathbf{f}_{i_1} < \mathbf{f}_{a_1} + \mathbf{f}_{b_1}) \wedge (\mathbf{f}_{i_1} \geq \mathbf{f}_{a_1}) \rightarrow \mathbf{f}_{i_3} = \mathbf{f}_{i_1} + \mathbf{f}_{b_1}; \tag{7}$$

$$(\mathbf{f}_{i_1} < \mathbf{f}_{a_1} + \mathbf{f}_{b_1}) \rightarrow \mathbf{f}_{i_4} = \texttt{ite}((\mathbf{f}_{i_1} < \mathbf{f}_{a_1}), \mathbf{f}_{i_2}, \mathbf{f}_{i_3}); \tag{8}$$

$$(\mathbf{f}_{i_1} \geq \mathbf{f}_{a_1} + \mathbf{f}_{b_1}) \rightarrow \mathbf{f}_{i_5} = \mathbf{f}_{i_1}; \tag{9}$$

$$true \rightarrow \mathbf{f}_{i_6} = \texttt{ite}((\mathbf{f}_{i_1} < \mathbf{f}_{a_1} + \mathbf{f}_{b_1}), \mathbf{f}_{i_4}, \mathbf{f}_{i_5}); \tag{10}$$

$$(\mathbf{f}_{i_6} < \mathbf{f}_{a_1} + \mathbf{f}_{b_1}) \wedge (\mathbf{f}_{i_6} < \mathbf{f}_{a_1}) \rightarrow \mathbf{f}_{i_7} = \mathbf{f}_{i_6} + \mathbf{f}_{a_1}; \tag{11}$$

$$(\mathbf{f}_{i_6} < \mathbf{f}_{a_1} + \mathbf{f}_{b_1}) \wedge (\mathbf{f}_{i_6} \geq \mathbf{f}_{a_1}) \rightarrow \mathbf{f}_{i_8} = \mathbf{f}_{i_6} + \mathbf{f}_{b_1}; \tag{12}$$

$$(\mathbf{f}_{i_6} < \mathbf{f}_{a_1} + \mathbf{f}_{b_1}) \rightarrow \mathbf{f}_{i_9} = \texttt{ite}((\mathbf{f}_{i_6} < \mathbf{f}_{a_1}), \mathbf{f}_{i_7}, \mathbf{f}_{i_8}); \tag{13}$$

$$(\mathbf{f}_{i_6} \geq \mathbf{f}_{a_1} + \mathbf{f}_{b_1}) \rightarrow \mathbf{f}_{i_{10}} = \mathbf{f}_{i_6}; \tag{14}$$

$$true \rightarrow \mathbf{f}_{i_{11}} = \texttt{ite}((\mathbf{f}_{i_6} \leq \mathbf{f}_{a_1} + \mathbf{f}_{b_1}), \mathbf{f}_{i_9}, \mathbf{f}_{i_{10}}); \tag{15}$$

$$true \rightarrow \mathbf{f}_{ret_1} = \mathbf{f}_{i_{11}}; \tag{16}$$

$$true \rightarrow z_2 =^s \mathbf{f}_{ret_1}; \tag{17}$$

(a) Pseudo-solidity

(b) USSA approximation (bound = 2)

Fig. 1. Converting a contract into a USSA

instance, $ArgCond(a + b) = \emptyset$, and $ArgCond(\texttt{transfer}(x)) = \{x = 0\}$. The cost implied by ΔC_{mem} only depends on the control flow path and therefore requires no special treatment.

The pseudo-code of the enumeration-based algorithm is given in Algorithm 1. The algorithm takes as input an entry point function $f(v)$ and constructs the USSA starting from f, in-lining recursively all functions called from f (line 1). The USSA is then traversed to construct a set of Boolean expressions C by adding each conjunct from each guard c of the USSA assignment in lines 4–9. Additional Boolean expressions are added to C for each storage assignment $=^s$ (line 7), and for each instruction whose cost depends on its arguments (line 9). The function $pre(x_i) = x_{i-1}$ maps a USSA variable x_i to its previous instantiation. In case x_i is the first instantiation (i.e., $i = 1$), $pre(x_i)$ is a "fresh" variable not appearing in the USSA.

In the second phase the algorithm exhaustively queries the SMT encoding of the USSA form for each Boolean combination of expressions from C and obtains values for v and $\mathbb{S}$ that cover these cases in case of satisfiability. The cost of each value combination for v and $\mathbb{S}$ is then queried by simulating the transaction, and the highest gas estimate is returned as the exact worst-case bound.

Input   : Entry function f; unwind limit n
Output: A set of Boolean expressions C
1 Let $U =$ the USSA form starting from f unwound up to n
2 Let $C = \emptyset$
3 **foreach** *guarded assignment* $a \in U$ **do**
4   Let $c_1 \wedge \ldots \wedge c_k$ be the guard of a
5      $C = C \cup \bigcup_{i=1}^{k} \{c_i\}$
6   **if** a *is of form* $c_1 \wedge \ldots \wedge c_k \to y =^s e(x)$ **then**
7         $C = C \cup \{(e(x) = 0) \wedge (pre(y) = 0), (e(x) \neq 0) \wedge (pre(y) = 0)\}$
8   **end**
9      $C = C \cup \mathrm{ArgCond}(e(x))$
10 **end**
11 **foreach** *truth value combination for the elements of* C **do**
12   **if** $C \wedge U$ *is satisfiable* **then**
13   Measure the gas consumption of f on environment corresponding to the satisfying truth assignment
14   Update the maximum if necessary
15   **end**
16 **end**

Algorithm 1. Enumeration-based algorithm to compute GCPs of a function f.

Example 1. Running Algorithm 1 on the USSA form on Fig. 1(b) gives

$$C = \{x_1 \geq y_1, y_1 \geq 0, (x_1 + y_1 = 0) \wedge (z_0 = 0), (x_1 + y_1 = 0) \wedge (z_0 \neq 0), z_1 = 0,$$
$$\mathbf{f}_{i_1} < \mathbf{f}_{a_1} + \mathbf{f}_{b_1}, \mathbf{f}_{i_1} < \mathbf{f}_{a_1}, \mathbf{f}_{i_6} < \mathbf{f}_{a_1} + \mathbf{f}_{b_1}, \mathbf{f}_{i_6} < \mathbf{f}_{a_1},$$
$$(\mathbf{f}_{ret_1} = 0) \wedge z_1 = 0), (\mathbf{f}_{ret_1} = 0) \wedge z_1 \neq 0)\},$$

where the first two constraints $x_1 \geq y_1$ and $y_1 \geq 0$ and the whole of the second row constraining the local variables of the functions $f_{i_j}, f_{a_j}, f_{b_j}$ come from the if-conditions; the conjunctive constraints $(x_1 + y_1 = 0) \wedge (z_0 = 0), (x_1 + y_1 = 0) \wedge (z_0 \neq 0)$ come from the argument and environment dependency of SSTORE (see Table 1), and the constraint $z_1 = 0$ comes from the argument dependency of CALL and CALLVAL, that is, $\mathrm{ArgCond}(\mathtt{transfer}(z_1))$; and the third row comes similarly from the argument and environment dependency of SSTORE.

The constraint set C is then provided to an SMT solver together with an SMT representation of the USSA form. Each combination of truth values for the constraints in C is queried from the USSA form, resulting in the worst case $2^{11} = 2048$ SMT queries. Note that due to the incremental implementation of SMT solvers in practice the number of queries might be (exponentially) smaller, depending on the order of the queries. In certain scenarios also the input v of the function might be known, reducing the number of queries to a fraction of the worst case.

From the results of the satisfiable queries the algorithm will extract concrete values for v and $\mathbb{S}$, which are then used for computing exact gas consumptions for the corresponding gas consumption paths.

The USSA form presented in Fig. 1 does not acknowledge the invariant $z \geq 0$, and is therefore more permissive than the original contract. Obtaining such *contract invariants* is non-trivial and out of the scope of this paper. To obtain exact worst-case gas consumption, contract invariants need to be conjoined to the USSA.

By construction of Algorithm 1 and the definition of GCPs, we immediately have the following theorem:

Theorem 1. *Given a function f, assuming a USSA for f that exactly describes the contract behaviour, and that there is a one-to-one mapping between the Solidity and the EVM code, Algorithm 1 return the worst-case gas consumption of f.*

4   Function-Oriented GCP Enumeration

In this section we present an algorithm for *Function-Oriented GCP Enumeration* (FGCP), an approach to computing GCPs that prunes locally the immediately unsatisfiable gas consumption paths. The basic GCP Enumeration presented in Sect. 3 in-lines every function call and computes GCPs from the encoding of the whole program. The function-oriented approach computes the paths gradually, starting from the low-level instructions and refining the set of GCPs discovered so far in a recursive manner. We expect local pruning of GCPs to be particularly efficient for contracts that call a given function multiple times, since the approach is able to reuse previously computed, function-specific GCPs.

To present the function-oriented approach, we change slightly the notation used in Sect. 3. We introduce *cost equivalence classes* that extend the notion of cost condition from a single instruction to a block of instructions and user-defined functions. The cost equivalence classes capture the conditions under with a function behaves differently with respect to gas consumption. They correspond exactly to the GCPs of the function. We use the term function to refer to both low level instructions, such as arithmetic operations, and user-defined functions, since cost-equivalence classes do not distinguish between the two. We do not distinguish between $=$ and $=^s$, but instead introduce a separate function SSTORE that is used for updating the storage $\mathbb{S}$. Finally, we introduce a separate function-oriented version of the static single assignment form, called FSSA, that is based on guarded function calls instead of guarded assignments.

Definition 1 (Environment). *Given a function $f(v)$ and storage $\mathbb{S}$, the environment of an execution of f is an evaluation υ for v and σ for $\mathbb{S}$.*

Given a function f and its environment, the execution of f is deterministic and results in a new storage state.

Definition 2 (Cost-equivalence class). *Given a function $f(v)$ and storage $\mathbb{S}$, a cost-equivalence class is a formula representing environments $\varphi(\mathbb{S}, v)$, such that the cost of executing f on any environment satisfying φ is the same.*

Algorithm 2 computes a set of cost-equivalence classes for the input function $f(v)$. Note that the set of classes computed by the algorithm is not guaranteed to be the minimal, namely there may be different classes representing executions with equal costs.

We define with $\mathbb{C}$ the map from function to a set of its cost-equivalence classes, such that every environment satisfies exactly one formula. Thus, given a function $f(v)$, the cost equivalence classes of f is the finite set

$$\mathbb{C}[f(v)] = \{\varphi_1(\mathbb{S}, v), \ldots, \varphi_n(\mathbb{S}, v)\}$$

such that $\bigvee_{i=1}^{n} \varphi_i$ is a tautology and for all $i \neq j, \varphi_i \wedge \varphi_j$ is unsatisfiable.

Initially, all the basic functions are defined in $\mathbb{C}$ having their classes inserted manually following their cost specification. For instance, in Ethereum storing a value in the storage is performed by the operation SSTORE, which cost depends on both the value and the storage location [18]. In particular, setting a storage location from zero to a non-zero value costs more than all the other cases. Thus, according to the EVM gas consumption specifications, $\mathbb{C}[\text{SSTORE}(l, v)] = \{(\mathbb{S}[l] = 0 \wedge v \neq 0), (\mathbb{S}[l] \neq 0 \vee v = 0)\}$.

Algorithm 2 assumes that $\mathbb{C}$ contains all the functions in the input function's call tree. Such functions are both basic functions and user defined functions for each of which a previous execution of the algorithm created its classes. We assume there is no recursion.

Definition 3 (FSSA: Function-oriented SSA). *Given a function $f(v)$ and its USSA representation, the FSSA representation is a list of guarded function calls, one for each function call in f and having the form $c \rightarrow g(l \mapsto v_g)$ where $l \supseteq v$ are the local USSA variables representing the inlining of the call mapped*

Input   : A FSSA $f(v)$, the cost-equivalence classes $\mathbb{C}$.
Assume: Every function in f is in $\mathbb{C}$.
Initially: $\mathbb{C}[f] \leftarrow \{\top\}$.
1 Let $Tr_f(\mathbb{S}, v)$ the USSA of f, having local SSA variables l.
2 **foreach** $c \rightarrow g(l \mapsto v_g)$ *in* f **do**
3   **with** Tr_f **compute**
4          $\pi(\mathbb{S}, v) :=$ path constraint of the call $g(v_g)$.
5          $M(\mathbb{S}, v, v_g) :=$ the mapping from v to v_g of the call $g(v_g)$.
6   **end**
7   Let $s = \emptyset$
8   **foreach** $\varphi(\mathbb{S}, v)$ *in* $\mathbb{C}[f]$ **do**
9   **if** $\neg\pi \wedge \varphi$ *is* SAT **then** $s \leftarrow s \cup \{\neg\pi \wedge \varphi\}$;
10   **foreach** $\psi(\mathbb{S}, v_g)$ *in* $\mathbb{C}[g]$ **do**
11   Let $\varphi'(\mathbb{S}, v) = \pi \wedge \varphi \wedge M \wedge \psi$
12   **if** φ' *is* SAT **then**
13                  $s \leftarrow s \cup \{\varphi'\}$
14   **end**
15   **end**
16   **end**
17      $\mathbb{C}[f] \leftarrow s$
18 **end**

Algorithm 2. The FGCP algorithm to compute the set $\mathbb{C}[f]$ of cost equivalence classes of f.

to the arguments v_g *needed for executing g, and* $c \in l$ *is the USSA guard of the call.*

The FSSA provides the necessary information for building the *call specific* mapping M on line 5 of Algorithm 2. In particular, M maps the current call site to the previously computed cost-equivalence classes of the callee. Therefore M enables building the cost-equivalence classes of a callee function g (from Definition 2 defined over its variables v_g), in terms of v. A new cost-equivalence class in terms of the caller variables is built by conjoining M and ψ in line 11, resulting in a formula defined over $\mathbb{S}$ and v. Such operation is always possible because the USSA provides a formula for computing USSA local variables l in terms of v. Then, a simple rewriting following each FSSA call $l \mapsto v_g$ will therefore build the new class in terms of v. An example of FSSA is given in Fig. 2.

Theorem 2. *Given a function* f, *assuming that the USSA formula* Tr_f *used in Algorithm 2 exactly describes the contract behaviours and that the EVM and Solidity gas consumption paths have one-to-one correspondence, Algorithm 3 returns the maximum gas consumption of* f.

Theorem 2 ensures that the size of each classes set in $\mathbb{C}$ is finite, and that every possible behaviour is considered. This proves termination and completeness of the algorithm.   ·

Proof Sketch. The property that every environment satisfies exactly one class in $\mathbb{C}$ is an invariant during the execution of Algorithm 2. The property is maintained inductively. In line 11 the algorithm creates the new classes φ' for f from the classes ψ of the callee g. Each φ' is mutually exclusive provided that all ψ in $\mathbb{C}[g]$ are mutually exclusive, because every ψ appears in the conjunction. Furthermore, the disjunction of s is a tautology meaning it is complete, if the disjunction of all ψ in $\mathbb{C}[g]$ is also complete. The models excluded by π being in the conjunction in line 11, are considered by the class $\neg\pi$ added to s in line 9.   □

Input   : A function $f(v)$, the cost-equivalence classes $\mathbb{C}$.
Output : The maximum cost c.
1 Let $c = 0$
2 **foreach** $\varphi(\mathbb{S}, v)$ *in* $\mathbb{C}[f]$ **do**
3 | Let $\sigma(\mathbb{S}), v(v) =$ an environment in φ
4 | Let c' the cost of executing $f(v)$ with storage σ
5 | **if** $c' > c$ **then** $c \leftarrow c'$;
6 **end**
7 **return** c
Algorithm 3. The algorithm to compute the maximum gas consumption.

Algorithm 3 computes the costs of every cost-equivalence class and returns the maximum. Definition 2 ensures that every environment satisfied by the same equivalence class has the same cost. Thus, on line 3 the SMT solver is queried for a model of each class φ, which is guaranteed to be satisfiable by line 13 of Algorithm 2. We split the environment in two parts: σ assigning storage locations' values, and v assigning values to the input argument $\boldsymbol{v}$. Then on line 4 the function f is executed on the specific environment and the cost of such execution is returned. If the cost is higher than the current maximum, on line 5 the current maximum is updated to the new value.

4.1 Parallelization Opportunities

Often the complexity and intrinsic sequentiality of model checking algorithms prevent parallelization. This results in missing the opportunity to exploit the modern hardware infrastructures, increasingly directed toward higher degrees of parallelism. Algorithms 1, 2 and 3 are immediately suitable for parallelization.

Due to the worst-case exponential number of SMT queries that Algorithm 1 needs to perform we believe that the part most profiting from parallelization is the evaluation of truth assignments and simulating the execution on the block starting at line 11. Since the USSA form U remains the same over the queries, the parallelization may be enhanced with a clause-sharing scheme similar to [15].

Algorithm 2 can be parallelized by asynchronously executing the building of all formulas and SMT queries inside the **foreach** at line 8. Each independent process can safely execute line 13 because inserting a new formula in the set s affects neither the future nor running executions. Executing line 16 and proceeding to the next function call can be done as soon as all independent executions are terminated. Algorithm 3 can be easily parallelized with using the MapReduce paradigm by defining proper *map* and *reduce* procedures. In this particular case the procedure *map* maps classes to their costs, while reduce compares the costs in order to compute the maximum.

5   Example

In this section we provide the example contract C, and we simulate the execution of Algorithms 2 and 1 on C.

5.1   Function-Oriented GCP Enumeration

The contract in Fig. 2 uses two basic functions, namely ADD and STORE. Following the Ethereum gas specification we define

$$\mathbb{C}[\text{ADD}(x,y,r)] = \{\top\}, \text{and}$$
$$\mathbb{C}[\text{SSTORE}(l,v)] = \{(\mathbb{S}[l] = 0 \land v \neq 0), (\mathbb{S}[l] \neq 0 \lor v = 0)\}.$$

The execution of Algorithm 2 on $\mathbf{g}(u)$ and $\mathbb{C}$ will result in the classes

$$\mathbb{C}[\mathbf{g}(u)] = \{M_7 \land (\mathbb{S}[l] = 0 \land v \neq 0), M_7 \land (\mathbb{S}[l] \neq 0 \lor v = 0)\}.$$

```
1   contract C {                                1   f(bool c, int z):
2      int a;                                   2       c → g(z ↦ u)
3      function f(bool c, int z)                3       c → ADD(z ↦ x, 1 ↦ y, z₁ ↦ r)
4      {                                        4       c → g(z₁ ↦ u)
5         if (c)                                5
6         {                                     6   g(int u):
7            g(z);                              7       ⊤ → SSTORE(id(a) ↦ l, u ↦ v)
8            z = z + 1;                         8
9            g(z);                              9   ADD(int x, int y, int r):
10        }                                    10       ⊤ → r = x + y
11     }                                       11
12                                             12   SSTORE(int l, int v):
13     function g(int u)                       13       ⊤ → S[l] = v
14     {
15        a = u;
16     }
17  }
```

Fig. 2. Left: an example contract with two functions. Right: the encoding to FSSA. Lines not representing an implication are only intended to show which function the following implications refer to. The macro `id()` returns the storage id of the variable.

where $M_7(\mathbb{S}, u, l, v) := (l = \mathrm{id}(a) \wedge v = u)$. Note that M_7 describes the mapping of the specific function call in line 7 of the FSSA in Fig. 2, which is the only function call in $\mathbf{g}$, having path constraint $\pi := \top$. The transition relation $Tr_{\mathbf{g}}$ of $\mathbf{g}$ is

$$Tr_{\mathbf{g}}(\mathbb{S}, u) := \mathbb{S}[\mathrm{id}(a)] = u.$$

After simplifying, the classes of $\mathbf{g}$ are

$$\mathbb{C}[\mathbf{g}(u)] = \{(\mathbb{S}[\mathrm{id}(a)] = 0 \wedge u \neq 0), (\mathbb{S}[\mathrm{id}(a)] \neq 0 \vee u = 0)\}.$$

We now consider an execution of Algorithm 2 on $\mathbf{f}(c, z)$, a function with 3 FSSA guarded calls at lines 2, 3 and 4 of Fig. 2 right, all having $\pi := c$. The USSA transition relation of $\mathbf{f}$ is

$$Tr_{\mathbf{f}}(\mathbb{S}, c, z) := c \to (\mathbb{S}[\mathrm{id}(a)]_1 = z \wedge z_1 = z + 1 \wedge \mathbb{S}[\mathrm{id}(a)]_2 = z_1),$$

and the mappings for each function call in $\mathbf{f}$ are

$$M_2(\mathbb{S}, c, z, u) := (u = z),$$
$$M_3(\mathbb{S}, c, z, x, y, r) := (x = z \wedge y = 1 \wedge r = z + 1), \text{and}$$
$$M_4(\mathbb{S}, c, z, u) := (u = z + 1).$$

The resulting classes for $\mathbf{f}$ are

$$\mathbb{C}[\mathbf{f}(c, z)] = \{ \neg c,$$
$$c \wedge \mathbb{S}[\mathrm{id}(a)] = 0 \wedge z \neq 0 \wedge z \neq -1,$$
$$c \wedge \mathbb{S}[\mathrm{id}(a)] = 0 \wedge z = 0,$$
$$c \wedge \mathbb{S}[\mathrm{id}(a)] = 0 \wedge z = -1,$$
$$c \wedge \mathbb{S}[\mathrm{id}(a)] \neq 0\}.$$

Algorithm 2 computes a total of 5 classes. This set is not the minimal because both classes $\mathbb{C}[\mathtt{f}]_3$ and $\mathbb{C}[\mathtt{f}]_4$ cause exactly one write from zero to non-zero, resulting in the same cost. The minimal set would then be of size 4. However, by trivially combining all the cases, the total number of combinations is 16. The proposed algorithm is therefore able to reduce the number of possible classes consistently with respect to trivial enumeration, keeping the size of $\mathbb{C}$ reasonable.

5.2   Symbolical GCP Enumeration

The USSA form for contract C in Fig. 2 is

$$c_1 \rightarrow g_{u_1} = z_1;$$
$$c_1 \rightarrow a_1 =^s g_{u_1};$$
$$c_1 \rightarrow g_{u_2} = z_1 + 1;$$
$$c_1 \rightarrow a_2 =^s g_{u_2};$$
$$a_3 = \mathtt{ite}(c_1, a_2, a_0);$$

Running Algorithm 1 on the USSA gives the set

$$C = \{c_1, (a_0 = 0) \wedge (g_{u_1} = 0), (a_0 \neq 0) \wedge (g_{u_1} = 0),$$
$$(a_1 = 0) \wedge (g_{u_2} = 0), (a_1 \neq 0) \wedge (g_{u_2} = 0)\}.$$

The size of the set is five, resulting in the worst case $2^5 = 32$ SMT queries.

6   Summary and Future Work

In this paper we have presented a solution to the problem of estimating the gas consumption for Ethereum smart contracts based on techniques inspired by bounded model-checking techniques.

We have defined a *gas consumption path* which extends a program path in a natural way taking into account the fact that the same operation consumes different amount of gas depending on the values of its arguments and the current environment. We have presented two different algorithms to identify gas consumption paths of a given function. For each gas consumption path we are able to obtain, using SMT solver, the state of the environment that forces the execution to take the given path. Finally, we can use the functionality provided by EVM to compute the exact gas consumption of the function under the obtained state of the environment.

The main application is in computing the worst-case gas consumption that provides useful insights for the developers and may lead to uncovering a flaw in the design of the smart contract or may provide useful information when choosing between two alternative implementations. Worst-case gas consumption is of interest also for a user who wants to call a method of a contract with certain arguments, but the state of the environment is not known.

As a next step we plan to implement the presented algorithms on top of the EVM framework APIs. The implementation will serve us to compare and evaluate our proposed approach on real-world smart contracts.

Acknowledgement. This work has been supported by the SNSF project 166288. The authors would like to thank Leonardo Alt for the useful discussions about Solidity language and compiler, and Michael Huth for his insights into distributed ledger systems.

References

1. GovernMental's 1100 ETH jackpot payout is stuck because it uses too much gas (2017). https://www.reddit.com/r/ethereum/comments/4ghzhv/governmentals_1100_eth_jackpot_payout_is_stuck/
2. Barrett, C., et al.: CVC4. In: Gopalakrishnan, G., Qadeer, S. (eds.) CAV 2011. LNCS, vol. 6806, pp. 171–177. Springer, Heidelberg (2011). https://doi.org/10.1007/978-3-642-22110-1_14
3. Biere, A., Cimatti, A., Clarke, E., Zhu, Y.: Symbolic model checking without BDDs. In: Cleaveland, W.R. (ed.) TACAS 1999. LNCS, vol. 1579, pp. 193–207. Springer, Heidelberg (1999). https://doi.org/10.1007/3-540-49059-0_14
4. Buterin, V., et al.: A next-generation smart contract and decentralized application platform. White paper (2014). https://github.com/ethereum/wiki/wiki/White-Paper
5. Chen, T., Li, X., Luo, X., Zhang, X.: Under-optimized smart contracts devour your money. In: IEEE 24th International Conference on Software Analysis, Evolution and Reengineering, SANER 2017, Klagenfurt, Austria, pp. 442–446 (2017)
6. Chen, T., et al.: An adaptive gas cost mechanism for ethereum to defend against under-priced DoS attacks. In: Liu, J.K., Samarati, P. (eds.) ISPEC 2017. LNCS, vol. 10701, pp. 3–24. Springer, Cham (2017). https://doi.org/10.1007/978-3-319-72359-4_1
7. Cimatti, A., Griggio, A., Schaafsma, B.J., Sebastiani, R.: The MathSAT5 SMT solver. In: Piterman, N., Smolka, S.A. (eds.) TACAS 2013. LNCS, vol. 7795, pp. 93–107. Springer, Heidelberg (2013). https://doi.org/10.1007/978-3-642-36742-7_7
8. Fedyukovich, G., D'Iddio, A.C., Hyvärinen, A.E.J., Sharygina, N.: Symbolic detection of assertion dependencies for bounded model checking. In: Egyed, A., Schaefer, I. (eds.) FASE 2015. LNCS, vol. 9033, pp. 186–201. Springer, Heidelberg (2015). https://doi.org/10.1007/978-3-662-46675-9_13
9. Gurfinkel, A., Kahsai, T., Komuravelli, A., Navas, J.A.: The SeaHorn verification framework. In: Kroening, D., Păsăreanu, C.S. (eds.) CAV 2015, Part I. LNCS, vol. 9206, pp. 343–361. Springer, Cham (2015). https://doi.org/10.1007/978-3-319-21690-4_20
10. Hyvärinen, A.E.J., Marescotti, M., Alt, L., Sharygina, N.: OpenSMT2: an SMT solver for multi-core and cloud computing. In: Creignou, N., Le Berre, D. (eds.) SAT 2016. LNCS, vol. 9710, pp. 547–553. Springer, Cham (2016). https://doi.org/10.1007/978-3-319-40970-2_35
11. Kalra, S., Goel, S., Dhawan, M., Sharma, S.: ZEUS: analyzing safety of smart contracts. In: NDSS (2018)
12. Lundbæk, L.N., Beutel, D.J., Huth, M., Kirk, L.: Practical proof of kernel work & distributed adaptiveness (2017). https://www.xain.io/pdf/XAIN_Yellow_Paper.pdf

13. Lundbæk, L.-N., Callia D'Iddio, A., Huth, M.: Centrally governed blockchains: optimizing security, cost, and availability. In: Aceto, L., Bacci, G., Bacci, G., Ingólfsdóttir, A., Legay, A., Mardare, R. (eds.) Models, Algorithms, Logics and Tools. LNCS, vol. 10460, pp. 578–599. Springer, Cham (2017). https://doi.org/10.1007/978-3-319-63121-9_29

14. Luu, L., Chu, D.H., Olickel, H., Saxena, P., Hobor, A.: Making smart contracts smarter. In: Proceedings of the 2016 ACM SIGSAC Conference on Computer and Communications Security, pp. 254–269. ACM (2016)

15. Marescotti, M., Hyvärinen, A.E.J., Sharygina, N.: Clause sharing and partitioning for cloud-based SMT solving. In: Artho, C., Legay, A., Peled, D. (eds.) ATVA 2016. LNCS, vol. 9938, pp. 428–443. Springer, Cham (2016). https://doi.org/10.1007/978-3-319-46520-3_27

16. de Moura, L., Bjørner, N.: Z3: an efficient SMT solver. In: Ramakrishnan, C.R., Rehof, J. (eds.) TACAS 2008. LNCS, vol. 4963, pp. 337–340. Springer, Heidelberg (2008). https://doi.org/10.1007/978-3-540-78800-3_24

17. Szabo, N.: Smart contracts (1994). http://www.fon.hum.uva.nl/rob/Courses/InformationInSpeech/CDROM/Literature/LOTwinterschool2006/szabo.best.vwh.net/smart.contracts.html

18. Wood, G.: Ethereum: a secure decentralised generalised transaction ledger. Ethereum Proj. Yellow Paper **151**, 1–32 (2014)

Industrial Day

Digital Transformation Trends: Industry 4.0, Automation, and AI
Industrial Track at ISoLA 2018

Axel Hessenkämper[1], Falk Howar[2(✉)], and Andreas Rausch[3]

[1] Hottinger Baldwin Messtechnik GmbH, Darmstadt, Germany
[2] Dortmund University of Technology and Fraunhofer ISST, Dortmund, Germany
falk.howar@tu-dortmund.de
[3] Clausthal University of Technology, Clausthal-Zellerfeld, Germany
andreas.rausch@tu-clausthal.de

1 Topic and Goal

The industrial track at ISoLA 2018 provided a platform for presenting industrial perspectives on digitalization and for discussing trends and challenges in the ongoing digital transformation. The track continued two special tracks at ISoLA conferences focused on the application of learning techniques in software engineering and software products [3], and industrial applications of formal methods in the context of Industry 4.0 [5]. Topics of interest included but were not limited to Industry 4.0, industrial applications of formal methods, and applications of machine-learning in industrial contexts.

Industry 4.0. Since the "Umsetzungsempfehlung für das Zukunftsprojekt Industrie 4.0" was published in 2012, industries and enterprises are trying to define and implement their Industry 4.0 and digitalization strategy [4]. The past years are embossed by papers, conferences, speeches, tracks and all kinds of information. But what is Industry 4.0 and what does that mean for businesses of tomorrow? The early history teaches us that a lot of money is spent and a lot is said but the real change is missing! Who will make the race towards Industry 4.0 and the digitalization? How will companies with long mechanical background look like in 5–10 years from now?

Formal Methods. The adoption of formal methods in industrial contexts has a huge potential for reducing the effort that is necessary for developing systems and for making systems more save and more secure (e.g., model-based approaches or automated verification techniques). However, the transfer of results of academic research in many instances is not straightforward: Developed methods are abstract and generic and have to be concretized and tailored to concrete problems. Is it possible to identify best practices and structured methods for applying formal methods in practice?

Machine Learning. We are entering the age of learning systems! On the one hand, we are surrounded by devices that learn from our behavior [1]: household appliances, smart phones, wearables, cars, etc. On the other hand, man-made systems are becoming ever more complex, requiring us to learn the

T. Margaria and B. Steffen (Eds.): ISoLA 2018, LNCS 11247, pp. 469–471, 2018.
https://doi.org/10.1007/978-3-030-03427-6_34

behavior of these systems: Learning-based testing [2, 6, 7], e.g., has been proposed as a method for testing the behavior of systems systematically without models and at a high level of abstraction. Advances in both areas raise the same questions cornering properties of inferred models: *How accurate are the descriptions that can be obtained of some behavior?* and: *How can we reason about and assure the safety of such systems?*

The industrial track aimed at bringing together practitioners and researchers to explore the practical impact and challenges associated with the trends sketched above.

2   Contributions

The track featured three contributions with accompanying papers and two invited talks. Contributions focused on Industry 4.0, automated synthesis of workflows and factory layouts. The invited talks reported on applications of machine-learning techniques in automotive systems.

The first contribution *"GOLD: Global Organization aLignment and Decision - Towards the Hierarchical Integration of Heterogeneous Business Models"* by Barbara Steffen and Steve Bosselmann [9] (in this volume) presents a multi-perspective framework for supporting organizations in analyzing their business strategy in the context of Industry 4.0 at multiple levels and discusses technological requirements as well as challenges for the development of modeling tools that support hierarchical integration of analyses and models, allowing to converge on an organization-wide aligned business strategy.

The second contribution *"Automatic composition of rough solution possibilities in the target planning of factory planning projects by means of combinatory logic"* by Jan Winkels, Julian Graefenstein, Tristan Schäfer, David Scholz, Jakob Rehof, and Michael Henke [10] (in this volume) presents an automated approach for generating meaningful alternative factory floor plans at an early stage of the planning process. The method enables an efficient planning process in terms of time and cost: With the help of a constraint-based variant compilation on the basis of previously defined target and frame parameters as well as information on the factory system, various possible solution variants for target planning are generated through combinatory synthesis. A specific use case scenario is used to evaluate the presented methodology.

The third contribution *"A Methodology for Combinatory Process Synthesis: Process Variability in Clinical Pathways"* by Tristan Schäfer, Frederik Möller, Anja Burmann, Yevgen Pikus, Norbert Weißenberg, Marcus Hintze, and Jakob Rehof [8] (in this volume) develops a structured method for the industrial application of combinatory process synthesis for the automated generation of workflows. The presented approach is based on the Design Science Research principles. The approach is evaluated in an industrial case study, in which combinatory process synthesis was used for generating workflows in a hospital.

References

1. Bosch, J., Olsson, H.H.: Data-driven continuous evolution of smart systems. In: Proceedings of the 11th International Symposium on Software Engineering for Adaptive and Self-Managing Systems, SEAMS 2016, pp. 28–34. ACM, New York (2016)
2. Hagerer, A., Hungar, H., Niese, O., Steffen, B.: Model generation by moderated regular extrapolation. In: Kutsche, R.-D., Weber, H. (eds.) FASE 2002. LNCS, vol. 2306, pp. 80–95. Springer, Heidelberg (2002). https://doi.org/10.1007/3-540-45923-5_6
3. Howar, F., Meinke, K., Rausch, A.: Learning systems: machine-learning in software products and learning-based analysis of software systems. In: Margaria, T., Steffen, B. (eds.) ISoLA 2016. LNCS, vol. 9953, pp. 651–654. Springer, Cham (2016). https://doi.org/10.1007/978-3-319-47169-3_50
4. Kagermann, H., Wahlster, W., Helbig, J.: Umsetzungsempfehlungen für das zukunftsprojekt industrie 4.0: Deutschlands zukunft als produktionsstandort sichern. Abschlussbericht des arbeitskreises industrie 4.0, acatech - Deutsche Akademie der Technikwissenschaften e. V., München, April 2013
5. Margaria, T., Steffen, B. (eds.): ISoLA 2016. LNCS, vol. 9953. Springer, Cham (2016). https://doi.org/10.1007/978-3-319-47169-3
6. Meinke, K., Sindhu, M.A.: Incremental learning-based testing for reactive systems. In: Gogolla, M., Wolff, B. (eds.) TAP 2011. LNCS, vol. 6706, pp. 134–151. Springer, Heidelberg (2011). https://doi.org/10.1007/978-3-642-21768-5_11
7. Raffelt, H., Merten, M., Steffen, B., Margaria, T.: Dynamic testing via automata learning. Int. J. Softw. Tools Technol. Transf. **11**(4), 307–324 (2009)
8. Schäfer, T., et al.: A methodology for combinatory process synthesis: process variability in clinical pathways. In: Margaria, T., Steffen, B., (eds.) ISoLA 2018. LNCS, vol. 11247, pp. 472–486. Springer, Heidelberg (2018)
9. Stefffen, B., Bosselmann, S.: GOLD: global organization alignment and decision - towards the hierarchical integration of heterogeneous business models. In: Margaria, T., Steffen, B., (eds.) ISoLA 2018. LNCS, vol. 11247, pp. 504–527. Springer, Heidelberg (2018)
10. Winkels, J., Graefenstein, J., Schäfer, T., Scholz, D., Rehof, J., Henke, M.: Automatic composition of rough solution possibilities in the target planning of factory planning projects by means of combinatory logic. In: Margaria, T., Steffen, B., (eds.) ISoLA 2018. LNCS, vol. 11247, pp. 487–503. Springer, Heidelberg (2018)

A Methodology for Combinatory Process Synthesis: Process Variability in Clinical Pathways

Tristan Schäfer[1(✉)], Frederik Möller[1], Anja Burmann[2],
Yevgen Pikus[2], Norbert Weißenberg[2], Marcus Hintze[3],
and Jakob Rehof[1,2]

[1] TU Dortmund University, August-Schmidt-Straße 4,
44227 Dortmund, Germany
{Tristan.Schaefer,Frederik.Moeller,
Jakob.Rehof}@tu-dortmund.de
[2] Fraunhofer ISST, Emil-Figge-Straße 91, 44227 Dortmund, Germany
{Anja.Burmann,Yevgen.Pikus,
Norbert.Weissenberg}@isst.fraunhofer.de
[3] Fraunhofer IML, Joseph-von-Fraunhofer-Straße 2-4,
44227 Dortmund, Germany
Marcus.Hintze@iml.fraunhofer.de

Abstract. Combinatory Process Synthesis (CPS) is a special case of software synthesis that can be used to manage variability by synthetizing target-specific processes from a repository of components. While conducted CPS research mainly addresses formal aspects of algorithm engineering, no structured methodology is available that enables the broader industrial application. This study addresses this gap and proposes a procedural model for CPS. The presented research bases on the Design Science Research principles. A case study in the healthcare sector shows the successful applicability of the elaborated procedure.

Keywords: Combinatory Process Synthesis · Clinical pathways
Business process modeling · Design Science Research · Variability modeling

1 Introduction

Combinatory Process Synthesis (CPS) as introduced by Bessai et al. proved to be able to synthesize variable processes based on a domain-specific repository of components [1]. It uses a type theoretical foundation to determine valid compositions of components and generates business processes according to a target type expression.

Its transfer to unexploited domains requires an intelligent repository design and is hitherto not accessible for a general application initiated by a specific need arising from potential users. Domain-independent and beneficial utilization of CPS thus requires a structured conceptual framework to guide potential users through the domain transfer. Within this work, the authors suggest such an artifact. The Design Science Research Methodology (DSRM) offers a procedural model for deriving such a conceptual method [2] and is thus followed in this work. We furthermore identify the specific need

T. Margaria and B. Steffen (Eds.): ISoLA 2018, LNCS 11247, pp. 472–486, 2018.
https://doi.org/10.1007/978-3-030-03427-6_35

for a powerful process-modeling tool within a variability inherent application domain, the healthcare sector. In order to evaluate the proposed framework, we exemplarily apply it to the identified field.

The introduction of Diagnosis Related Groups (DRGs) as the medium for reimbursement in the US healthcare sector in the 1980s marked a paradigm shift. Previously hierarchically structured organizations transformed towards operational and process-oriented caretaking. Different challenges emerged in this transformation, such as the need for reducing incurred costs per case, increasing efficiency, and at the same time sustaining, standardizing and increasing the quality of their care delivery [3]. This favored the adaptation of industrial process modeling methods by the healthcare sector to actively steer all activities orchestrated around the recovery of the patient economically, but also to ensure the best possible treatment according to current scientific evidence (evidence-based medicine EBM) [4].

One inherent characteristic and the major challenge in modeling clinical processes, while taking into account medical decisions, is process variability. The treatment process must be adjusted according to patient-specific conditions, needs, and complications. These variations are either known at admission to hospital, e.g., a pregnant patient cannot go through radiological diagnostic imaging like a non-pregnant patient. Variations like complications during surgery or infection with multi-resistant germs in the clinic may also arise while the process is running. The capability of a process-modeling notation to respect and illustrate these variations is crucial when aiming for a high penetration rate in real operation in the hospital. In fact, as also pointed out in [5] the effective handling of process variability is an essential requirement to further advance the digitalization in the healthcare sector.

Research in the field of variability modeling involves techniques to express and resolve variability [6]. The application of CPS in outlining patient-specific process steps throughout a hospital may improve process transparency, planning capability of individual therapy and resource utilization and thus the quality of care delivery. In this paper, we propose a structured methodology for transferring the capabilities of CPS to a new application domain and conduct CPS in synthesizing treatment paths in hospital processes. The authors see the focus on a domain-specific use case as a starting point for further use cases [7]. The results can achieve higher potential for generalizability by broadening the base of application domains [8]. In the following, the authors present the usage of Combinatory Process Synthesis (CPS) to generate process variants according to a configuration in the form of a semantic type. Section 2 introduces related work necessary for the understanding of clinical processes, current modeling approaches, Combinatory Process Synthesis and its applicability in the mentioned field. Following, Sect. 3 outlines the research design. Section 4 develops the procedural model. Section 5 presents the use case. Lastly, Sect. 6 discusses the results.

2 Related Work

2.1 Business Process Modeling with BPMN 2.0

A business process is a particular instance of a business transaction consisting of a linked set of activities [9] and represents the transformation of input factors to output factors [10]. Transferred to the application domain of hospital processes, business processes are referred to as clinical pathways. Hospitals derive clinical pathways from medical guidelines and enrich these with organization-specific information and requirements, e.g., equipment, documentation, responsibility, time or costs. This channels latest medical evidence into local structures [11]. Clinical pathways (also known as critical pathways, care maps or collaborative care pathways) are set up in multidisciplinary teams and thus sequence all necessary actions, goals and essential elements surrounding the treatment of a specific pathological condition. The effects of the implementation of clinical pathways are varying across different studies. For instance, the meta-analysis by Rotter et al. primarily identified relevant reductions of in-hospital complications, improved documentation, a reduction of the length of stay as well as of the hospital costs [12].

The BPMN 2.0 is a declared ISO standard [13] and has been established to be the leading industry standard for business process modeling [14–16]. It provides an XML schema and is supported by various execution engines. There is a clear modeling toolkit for professionals of all areas involved in the development of clinical pathways [17].

Still, BPMN 2.0 poses weaknesses in its applicability towards clinical pathways. Various additions and extensions, such as adding color schemes for representing the role of the information [17] or the inclusion of evidence-based medical decision activities [18], address these issues. However, the modeling process of clinical pathways still remains time-consuming and resource-intensive [19].

Due to the significance of the standard, the research in this paper will focus on business process modeling of clinical pathways with BPMN 2.0. Bessai et al. demonstrated that the corresponding XML scheme is well suited for use in Combinatory Process Synthesis [1].

2.2 Process Synthesis

Several aspects can differentiate approaches in the field of synthesis of process descriptions and workflow code. A synthesis method is characterized by specification of the underlying domain, the synthesis strategy and the definition of search space. Various forms of process synthesis can be found that attend special challenges or tasks. Planware [20, 21] is a project that uses synthesis to produce domain-specific scheduling algorithms. The synthesis strategy is a graph-based compositional approach, which relies on concepts taken from category theory. The specification of the synthesis goal is formulated using higher-order logic, and the corresponding compositional result specification can be translated into runnable code. The approach in [22] addresses the particular problem that specifications usually require a formal expression which is not comprehensible to end-users. Instead, graphical notation is introduced which describes the data flow of the process. This initial workflow specification is enriched with further domain knowledge and translated into temporal logic. The synthesis algorithm eventually uses a path search technique to generate process models that comply with the specification. A technique involving the iterative refinement of the user intent is proposed in [21]. The specification and process model are expressed in temporal logic. The results of a path search algorithm are transformed into a BPMN-like graph by using process mining techniques. In [23], temporal business rules are transformed into finite state automata that enable for the synthesis of a BPEL service composition by using ontology-based substitution of service variability points. Ontologies are also used in [24] to achieve runtime flexibility for software engineering processes in combination with ADEPT [25, 26]. The specification of the problem space can also be achieved by definition of a Domain-Specific Model [27].

2.3 Combinatory Process Synthesis CPS

Combinatory Process Synthesis (CPS, [1]) is a synthesis framework for BPMN 2.0 processes. It makes use of the Combinatory Logic Synthesizer (CL)S [28] to perform the component-based software synthesis by solving the inhabitation problem. A program is constructed by identifying an applicative composition of software components that conform to a target specification. These components (combinators) represent programs, data or process fragments that are organized in a repository. This repository (denoted as Γ) also contains a type assumption for each combinator and is an essential input for the synthesis algorithm. The synthesis uses a combinator's type to determine which elements can be applied to each other and how variability points can be resolved.

The basic idea of the type-based synthesis is following the propositions-as-types correspondence [29, 30]. Combinators and their type assumptions can be considered as axioms of a system. In this particular case, the aim of inhabitation is finding applicative compositions of software components that match the target type specification.

Informally speaking, the inhabitation algorithm is a top-down search strategy. It analyzes combinators that produce the result when applied to a corresponding argument list where the required arguments can also be the result of inhabitation. The formal foundation of (CL)S is the combinatory logic with intersection types, which are denoted σ, τ and defined as follows:

$$\sigma, \tau ::= a \,|\, \alpha \,|\, \omega \,|\, \sigma \to \tau \,|\, \sigma \cap \tau$$

The type constants, ranged over by $a, b, c, \ldots$, can be native types (i.e., types of the underlying programming language) or textual semantic descriptions. ω is a unique type constant that is linked to subtyping. The type variables $(\alpha, \beta, \gamma, \ldots)$ are placeholders that will be replaced with type constants according to a substitution map. Type expressions further involve functions $(\to)$ or intersections $(\cap)$. A combinator with the function type $Integer \to String$ can be applied to an argument of type $Integer$ and yields a $String$. Intersection types, on the other hand, can be used to express feature vectors. A combinator described by the semantic type $ReadValue \cap SensorA$ is affiliated with a read result from $Sensor\ A$.

Figure 1(a) contains a simplified, informal representation of a combinator with two variability points that are affiliated with the semantic types $TypeA$ and $TypeB$. Any suitable combinators with types or subtypes of $TypeA$ resp. $TypeB$ can be inserted by the inhabitation algorithm. Valid process instances will be constructed as illustrated in Fig. 1(b). The use of type taxonomies and type variables further supports the comprehensive specification of complex combinators. In addition to the type signature, implementation details can be provided for combinators.

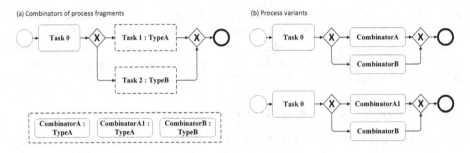

Fig. 1. Process combinator, process variants

3   Research Design

This paper presents a procedural model and a related set of deliverables for Combinatory Process Synthesis. As the proposed artifact is a typical result of design-oriented research efforts, i.e., a model, the authors follow the Design Science Research paradigm [31]. DSR is an increasingly essential and accepted research paradigm in information systems research. One stream of research focuses on the design and development of novel IT-artifacts [32]. Peffers et al. propose the Design Science Research Methodology (DSRM) outlining a procedural model consisting of six activities (*Identify Problem & Motivation, Define Objectives of a Solution, Design and Development, Demonstration, Evaluation,* and *Communication*), which the authors use as a guide [2] (see Fig. 2).

As of now, there is a lack of structured and well-designed methodology to assist the execution of CPS. Especially scientists who have no educational background in theoretical computer science and mathematical logic need a structured methodology to use the advantages of combinatorial process synthesis. The scope of this paper covers the design of a procedural model, i.e., a sequence of activities and corresponding deliverables necessary to conduct CPS. The development of the methodology follows the principles of Method Engineering, which provides a concept of methods consisting of

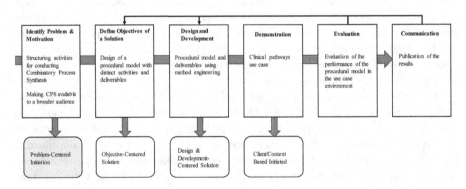

Fig. 2. The Design Science Research process as proposed by Peffers et al. [2]

five core-elements, namely *Activities, Deliverables, Roles, Techniques,* and *Meta-Model* [33]. Subsequently, the authors demonstrate the procedural model using a concrete use case from the domain of clinical pathways. Lastly, the authors evaluate the procedural model by the performance in the use case [31].

Focusing on one specific case allows for intensive analysis of the artifacts performance in the application domain [34] and assists with the generation of complex solutions [35]. A generalization of the results requires additional use cases in different domains [36]. Through their complex nature, clinical pathways provide ample opportunity for leveraging and demonstrating the benefits of Combinatory Process Synthesis.

4   A Methodology for Combinatory Process Synthesis

The procedural model for Combinatory Process Synthesis describes the synthesis-based development lifecycle of process variants and is a result of the Design Science Research paradigm. It consists of seven development activities that are illustrated in Fig. 3.

The first step is a thorough **analysis of the underlying process**. The result of this task is accurate process documentation that may consist of process requirements, restrictions, but also textual or model descriptions.

The activities summarized in the **specification phase** aim to establish a domain representation that is suitable for the synthesis framework. The **definition of semantic types** captures type-based semantic descriptions of process fragments and primarily refers to type constants. Detailed knowledge of the domain is a requirement for a precise characterization of process fragments that can also be expressed by forming comprehensive intersection types.

With the semantic types at hand, the subtyping relation between the types is established in the form of a **type taxonomy**. The inhabitation algorithm will consider subtyping according to the type rule ($\leq$):

$$\frac{\Gamma \vdash e : \tau \quad \tau \leq \tau'}{\Gamma \vdash e : \tau'}(\leq)$$

The type judgment $\Gamma \vdash e{:}\ \tau'$ (i.e., the term e has the type τ' under the type assumptions in Γ) is valid under the premises $\Gamma \vdash e : \tau'$ and $\tau \leq \tau'$. In this case, any inhabitant of $\Gamma \vdash ?{:}\ \tau$ will also be a result of the question $\Gamma \vdash ?{:}\ \tau'$. As a consequence, the use of a taxonomy allows for generalization and specialization of the semantic process descriptions.

The **definition of the combinators** involves the type signature and the implementation. The algebraic signature determines the result type of the combinator and its input arguments that will be resolved by the inhabitation algorithm. Only if inhabitants could be determined for these arguments, the combinator can yield the result type when used in an applicative composition. The semantic alignment of workflows can be expressed by the combinator's implementation, e.g., by using template code for BPMN 2.0 processes. The contained variability points can be substituted with process

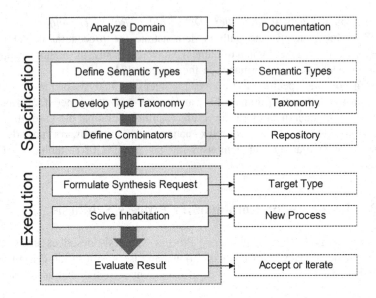

Fig. 3. Procedural model and corresponding deliverables for CPS

fragments that are determined by inhabitation. While other approaches to express process variability [37, 38] incorporate the adaption of base processes by deleting, inserting or modifying process segments, the (CL)S inherently uses substitution in accordance with combinatory logic.

The **execution phase** starts with the **formulation of the synthesis request**. The main aspect of this task is the definition of the target type. As the process variant is constructed from this type, it can be considered as the configuration step in the lifecycle of process variants [39]. Context-awareness can be established by using auxiliary functions that compute the target type by analyzing the process context. For instance, the patient record can be analyzed to derive mandatory process features in the form of a type expression. A selection of relevant repositories should also be considered at this point in the development process. Some requests only involve certain combinators that can be summarized in repositories according to their features. For instance, different repositories could be established for separate departments or families of clinical pathways. That way, it is possible to effectively limit the number of combinators (i.e., the search space) and thus reduce the run-time of the algorithm. For that reason, it is advised to set up smaller repositories that need to be explicitly involved in the inhabitation request. It is possible to form the union of repositories which is defined as follows:

$$\Gamma_1 \cup \Gamma_2 = \{x\ :\ \sigma | x\ :\ \sigma \in \Gamma_1 \vee x\ :\ \sigma \in \Gamma_2\}$$

The **execution of the inhabitation algorithm** is eventually performed to synthesize new process descriptions. The final step of the CPS approach is the evaluation of the results. In case of a BPMN 2.0 definition, a resulting XML markup can be validated against the BPMN 2.0 scheme and executed in a BPM system to discover specification errors. A detailed evaluation should be performed in cooperation with expert users. This addresses potential misunderstandings between the developer and the expert user during the analysis task.

5   Process Variability in Clinical Pathways

A general clinical pathway starts with the admission to hospital. After hospitalization, the patient undergoes inpatient diagnostic, therapy, and stationary aftercare. Outpatient care and therapy supplied before hospitalization or after discharge from the hospital are not part of the clinical path itself. Every step on this path contains several sub-processes, which are required to adapt accordingly to the individual pathology and pre-existing conditions of the patient. It also includes capabilities and capacity of the care-supplying hospital. Following, Fig. 4 exemplifies the execution of the methodology presented in Sect. 4 through the excerpt 'surgery' of the clinical pathway 'spinal surgery' provided by Reuter [40]. Next, the predefined phases of the introduced procedural model in Sect. 4 will be successively executed, and the corresponding phase's outcomes will be presented.

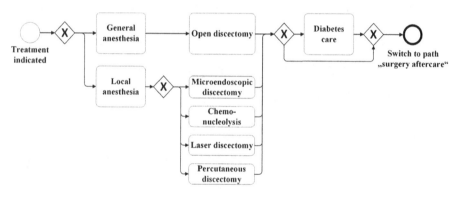

Fig. 4. Process mapping of the use case (BPMN 2.0)

The path-excerpt is the result of the **domain analysis** and displays the clinically relevant variability points as XOR-gateways. Namely, these are the kind of anesthesia, surgery and the optional diabetes treatment. The **semantic type definition and taxonomy development** produced the semantic layer outlined in Fig. 5. Minimal invasive surgical procedures are summarized under the type *sp_minimal_invasive*. They can be performed under local anesthesia whereas an open discectomy requires general anesthesia. Additionally, the type constants *diabetes_proc* and *nodiabetes_proc* were introduced.

Due to the taxonomy, a synthesis request like $\Gamma \vdash ?: sp\_minimal\_invasive \cap diabetes\_proc$ is possible and will yield four process variants. A more general synthesis

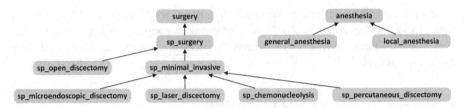

Fig. 5. Type taxonomy of spinal surgeries

request $\Gamma \vdash ?$: *diabetes_proc* returns a list of any processes that are suitable for diabetes patients, without selecting a particular surgery method.

Listing 1 shows the Scala implementation of the SpinalSurgeryProc combinator. The inhabitation algorithm determines valid substitutions for the arguments anesthesia_task and surgery_task. The process fragments are implemented as XML literals and have the native type scala.xml.Elem. The semantic type value is contained in the trait SpinalSurgerySemanticType.

```scala
@combinator object SpinalSurgeryProc
    extends SpinalSurgerySemanticType {
  def apply(anesthesia_task:Elem, surgery_task:Elem):Elem ={
    <process id="spinal_sugery_process "
            name="Spinal Surgery Process">
      <startEvent id="startevent_ssp" name="Start" />
      <endEvent id="endevent_ssp" name="End" />
      {anesthesia_task}
      {surgery_task}
      <sequenceFlow id="flow_start_anesthesiaTask"
          sourceRef="startevent_ssp"
          targetRef="anesthesia_task" />
      <sequenceFlow id="flow_anesthesiaTask_surgeryTask"
          sourceRef="anesthesia_task"
          targetRef="surgery_task" />
      <sequenceFlow id="flow_surgeryTask_end"
          sourceRef="surgery_task"
          targetRef="endevent_ssp" />
    </process>
  }
}
```

Listing 1. Scala Implementation of the SpinalSurgeryProc Combinator

Figure 6 partly illustrates the **definition of combinators**. The combinator SurgeryDiabetes shown in Fig. 6(a) will add a diabetes activity to the surgery subprocess. The dashed rectangle represents an input parameter named surgery_subprocess. It will be substituted by a term of type $\alpha \cap$ *nodiabetes_proc* which is resolved by the inhabitation algorithm. The type variable α represents the different surgical kinds. A representation of the repository structure is shown in Fig. 7.

Every surgical procedure is affiliated with a certain type of anesthesia, which can be roughly distinguished to be general or local anesthesia. A corresponding type

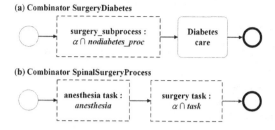

Fig. 6. Combinators (a) surgery_diabetes and (b) spinal_surgery_process

expression can specify valid compositions of surgery and anesthesia kinds. The combinator SpinalSurgeryProcess is illustrated in Fig. 6(b) and creates task sequences according to the following semantic type expression:

$$
\begin{aligned}
&(local\_anesthesia \rightarrow sp\_laser\_discectomy \cap task \rightarrow \\
&\quad sp\_laser\_discectomy \cap nodiabetes\_proc) \cap \\
&(local\_anesthesia \rightarrow sp\_chemonucleolysis \cap task \rightarrow \\
&\quad sp\_chemonucleolysis \cap nodiabetes\_proc) \cap \\
&(local\_anesthesia \rightarrow sp\_microendoscopic\_discectomy \cap task \rightarrow \\
&\quad sp\_microendoscopic\_discectomy \cap nodiabetes\_proc) \cap \\
&(local\_anesthesia \rightarrow sp\_percutaneous\_discectomy \cap task \rightarrow \\
&\quad sp\_percutaneous\_discectomy \cap nodiabetes\_proc) \cap \\
&(general\_anesthesia \rightarrow sp\_open\_discectomy \cap task \rightarrow \\
&\quad sp\_open\_discectomy \cap nodiabetes\_proc)
\end{aligned}
$$

The expression states that a task described by $sp\_open\_discectomy$ can only be composed with a task corresponding to $general\_anesthesia$ (note that only the last two lines concern $general\_anesthesia$). The type expression can be simplified by introducing a new variable β. It describes the four minimally invasive surgery tasks that can be aligned with a $local\_anesthesia$ task. With the new variable at hand, the following semantic type can be used instead:

$$
\begin{aligned}
&(local\_anesthesia \rightarrow \beta \cap task \rightarrow \beta \cap nodiabetes\_proc) \cap \\
&(general\_anesthesia \rightarrow sp\_open\_discectomy \cap task \rightarrow \\
&\quad sp\_open\_discectomy \cap nodiabetes\_proc)
\end{aligned}
$$

Figure 8 shows two process variants that can be retrieved by the solving the inhabitation for the questions $\Gamma \vdash ?$: $sp\_open\_discectomy \cap diabetes\_proc$ and $\Gamma \vdash ?$: $sp\_laser\_discectomy \cap nodiabetes\_proc$. Eventually, domain experts positively validated several produced clinical pathways regarding workflow integrity. Following our procedural model for CPS, all synthesis results were accepted without the need for additional iterations of the specification phase.

$\Gamma = \{$

    SurgeryTaskOpen :
        XmlElem ∩ sp_open_discectomy ∩ task
    SurgeryTaskPercu :
        XmlElem ∩ sp_percutaneous_discectomy ∩ task
    SurgeryTaskLaser :
        XmlElem ∩ sp_laser_discectomy ∩ task
    SurgeryTaskMicro :
        XmlElem ∩ sp_microendoscopic_discectomy ∩ task
    SurgeryTaskChemo :
        XmlElem ∩ sp_chemonucleolysis ∩ task
    AnesthesiaTaskLocal :
        XmlElem ∩ local_anesthesia
    AnesthesiaTaskGeneral :
        XmlElem ∩ general_anesthesia
    SurgeryDiabetes :
        (XmlElem → XmlElem) ∩ (α ∩ nodiabetes_proc → α ∩ diabetes_proc)
    SpinalSurgeryProc :
        (XmlElem → XmlElem → XmlElem) ∩
        (local_anesthesia → β ∩ task → β ∩ nodiabetes_proc) ∩
        (general_anesthesia → sp_open_discectomy ∩ task →
        sp_open_discectomy ∩ nodiabetes_proc)

$\}$

Fig. 7. Repository structure for spinal surgeries

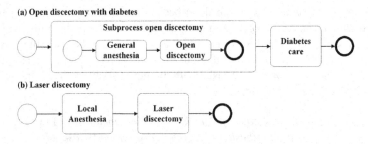

Fig. 8. Process variants (a) open discectomy with diabetes and (b) laser discectomy

6   Discussion Limitations and Conclusion

The conducted procedural model addresses a gap of the practical application of Combinatory Process Synthesis for enabling process variability. To the best of our knowledge, the available research focusses on theoretical formalization, algorithmic implementation and complexity of Combinatory Process Synthesis, but not at the explicit procedural model for the application in the field. The elaborated procedural model is a result of the systematic application of the Design Science Research principles. The model specifies seven steps required for the application of the process synthesis in a new domain. A case study evaluation in the healthcare sector has produced the expected clinical pathways. Concretely, successively execution of the procedural steps yields the case-specific semantic types, taxonomies, and combinators.

The gap between theory and practice could be bridged by a close collaboration of the research areas type theory, digital business engineering, and healthcare. The combinators were implemented according to this specification and the synthesis yields the desired specialized process variants. Thus, the use case can be considered to be successful.

However, there is still a need for extended tool support to enable the technique to be applied in an industrial context. The specification task could benefit from diagram editors for combinators and type definitions. Moreover, the approach should be used incorporated with a suitable BPM system that allows for dynamic deployment of synthesis results.

The research presented in this paper requires the consideration of **limiting factors**. Using BPMN 2.0 guarantees the utilization of a well-established and domain-independent standard for process modeling. However, the single-case study deals explicitly with clinical pathways, which are an object of interest from the healthcare sector and thus are subject to domain-specific constraints. In future research endeavors, the presented research might act as a starting point for subsequent case studies in various application domains. That would enable the construction of a larger scale multiple case study enabling the empirical analysis of application domain transferability.

It is worth noting that the synthesis approach offers several advantages regarding process model quality [41]. Generally, in real-world settings process models tend to become increasingly large and complex. As a result, it raises maintenance and development to a new challenging level. However, the process synthesis approach reduces the required effort for achieving a desired degree of flexibility. Concretely, the substitutable process variability points enhance the reuse of process fragments and substitution variables on several granularity levels. The synthesis request constraints the scope of constructed processes. It reduces the size and complexity of process models and increases the degree of transparency. For example, a clinical pathway contains diabetes treatment activity only if a patient has diabetes. The configuration of process variants can be accomplished by formulating adequate target types. The synthesis approach supports process model evolution because modifications are limited to the corresponding domain specification. The changes can be propagated to all affected process variants by reinitiating the synthesis.

Future research will address techniques that enable an automated end-to-end process synthesis. That involves automated decomposition of business processes, detection of process variants and workflow synthesis with particular regard to soundness.

The integration of electronic case records is of particular interest for subsequent studies. The patient's data can be used to determine the result type that will be part of the synthesis request. A user interaction model can help to translate the medical expert's intent to type expressions.

As pointed out in [5], process flexibility is particularly necessary for the healthcare sector. Thus, the synthesis-based runtime adaption of business processes will be investigated. The BPMN 2.0 and the corresponding BPM systems do not offer the features to support the dynamic instantiation of synthesized process fragments fully. However, the workflow management systems YAWL [42] and ADEPT2 [43] offer process flexibility support that might be suitable for a late binding approach based on combinatory process synthesis. The use case discussed in this paper could be extended to show the applicability of this approach. It should be possible to generate valid process instances according to the process context (e.g. patient records) and thus allow for synthesis-based process adaptions at runtime.

Another major research aspect could be the enhancement of CPS with planning capabilities. As an initial approach, time-dependent repositories could serve as an indicator for contemporary ressource availability. For instance, the contained combinators can represent medical staff or equipment. These ressources are not taken into account in the process synthesis when the corresponding combinators are removed from the repository. Purging and allocating of ressource combinators could be automatically performed by the synthesis framework in cooperation with the corresponding BPM system upon instantiation or termination of tasks or process instances.

Acknowledgment. The research project presented in this paper stems from the Center of Excellence for Logistics and IT (http://www.leistungszentrum-logistik-it.de/, last accessed: 04. 09.2018) located in Dortmund.

References

1. Bessai, J., Dudenhefner, A., Düdder, B., Martens, M., Rehof, J.: Combinatory process synthesis. In: Margaria, T., Steffen, B. (eds.) ISoLA 2016. LNCS, vol. 9952, pp. 266–281. Springer, Cham (2016). https://doi.org/10.1007/978-3-319-47166-2_19
2. Peffers, K., Tuunanen, T., Rothenberger, M.A., Chatterjee, S.: A design science research methodology for information systems research. J. Manag. Inf. Syst. **24**, 45–77 (2007)
3. Busse, R.: Diagnosis Related Groups in Europe. Moving Towards Transparency, Efficiency and Quality in Hospitals. McGraw Hill Open University Press, Maidenhead (2011)
4. Sackett, D.L.: Evidence-based medicine. Semin. Perinatol. **21**, 3–5 (1997)
5. Reichert, M., Pryss, R.: Flexible support of healthcare processes. In: Combi, C., Pozzi, G., Veltri, P. (eds.) Process Modeling and Management for Healthcare, pp. 35–66. Taylor & Francis Group, London (2017)
6. Rosa, M.L., van der Aalst, W.M.P., Dumas, M., Milani, F.P.: Business process variability modeling. A survey. ACM Comput. Surv. (CSUR) **50**, 2 (2017)
7. Yin, R.K.: Case Study Research: Design and Methods. Sage Publications, Beverley Hills (2008)
8. Lee, A.S., Baskerville, R.L.: Generalizing generalizability in information systems research. Inf. Syst. Res. **14**, 221–243 + 315 (2003)
9. Broy, M.: From actions, transactions, and processes to services. In: Kordon, F., Moldt, D. (eds.) PETRI NETS 2016. LNCS, vol. 9698, pp. 13–19. Springer, Cham (2016). https://doi. org/10.1007/978-3-319-39086-4_2
10. Aguilar-Savén, R.S.: Business process modelling. Review and framework. Int. J. Prod. Econ. **90**, 129–149 (2004)

11. Kinsman, L., Rotter, T., James, E., Snow, P., Willis, J.: What is a clinical pathway? Development of a definition to inform the debate. BMC Med. **8**, 31 (2010)
12. Rotter, T., et al.: Clinical pathways: effects on professional practice, patient outcomes, length of stay and hospital costs. Cochrane Database Syst. Rev. CD006632 (2010)
13. ISO: Information technology – Object Management Group Business Process Model and Notation 35.020 Information technology (IT) in general. ISO/IEC 19510:2013 (2013)
14. Chinosi, M., Trombetta, A.: BPMN: an introduction to the standard. Comput. Stand. Interfaces **34**, 124–134 (2012)
15. Muehlen, M., Recker, J.: How much language is enough? Theoretical and practical use of the business process modeling notation. In: Bellahsène, Z., Léonard, M. (eds.) CAiSE 2008. LNCS, vol. 5074, pp. 465–479. Springer, Heidelberg (2008). https://doi.org/10.1007/978-3-540-69534-9_35
16. Aagesen, G., Krogstie, J.: BPMN 2.0 for modeling business processes. In: vom Brocke, J., Rosemann, M. (eds.) Handbook on Business Process Management 1. IHIS, pp. 219–250. Springer, Heidelberg (2015). https://doi.org/10.1007/978-3-642-45100-3_10
17. Müller, R., Rogge-solti, A. (eds.): BPMN for healthcare processes. CEUR-WS.org (2011)
18. Braun, R., Schlieter, H., Burwitz, M., Esswein, W. (eds.): BPMN4CP: design and implementation of a BPMN extension for clinical pathways. In: 2014 IEEE International Conference on Bioinformatics and Biomedicine (BIBM) (2014)
19. Scheuerlein, H., et al.: New methods for clinical pathways-business process modeling notation (BPMN) and tangible business process modeling (t.BPM). Langenbeck's Arch. Surg. **397**, 755–761 (2012)
20. Blaine, L., Gilham, L., Liu, J., Smith, D.R., Westfold, S.: Planware-domain-specific synthesis of high-performance schedulers. In: Proceedings of 13th IEEE International Conference on Automated Software Engineering, pp. 270–279 (1998)
21. Becker, M., Gilham, L., Smith, D.R., et al: Planware II: synthesis of schedulers for complex resource systems (2003)
22. Lamprecht, A.-L., Naujokat, S., Margaria, T., Steffen, B.: Synthesis-based loose programming. In: 2010 Seventh International Conference on the Quality of Information and Communications Technology (QUATIC), pp. 262–267 (2010)
23. Yu, J., Han, Y.-B., Han, J., Jin, Y., Falcarin, P., Morisio, M.: Synthesizing service composition models on the basis of temporal business rules. J. Comput. Sci. Technol. **23**, 885–894 (2008)
24. Grambow, G., Oberhauser, R., Reichert, M.: Semantically-driven workflow generation using declarative modeling for processes in software engineering. In: Proceedings of EDOCW 2011, pp. 164–173. IEEE Computer Society (2011)
25. Dadam, P., Reichert, M.: The ADEPT project: a decade of research and development for robust and flexible process support. Comput. Sci.-Res. Dev. **23**, 81–97 (2009)
26. Reichert, M., Dadam, P.: ADEPT flex—supporting dynamic changes of workflows without losing control. J. Intell. Inf. Syst. **10**, 93–129 (1998)
27. Roser, S., Lautenbacher, F., Bauer, B.: Generation of workflow code from DSMs. In: Proceedings of OOPSLA 2007 (2007)
28. Bessai, J., Dudenhefner, A., Düdder, B., Martens, M., Rehof, J.: Combinatory logic synthesizer. In: Margaria, T., Steffen, B. (eds.) ISoLA 2014. LNCS, vol. 8802, pp. 26–40. Springer, Heidelberg (2014). https://doi.org/10.1007/978-3-662-45234-9_3
29. Curry, H.B.: Functionality in combinatory logic. Proc. Natl. Acad. Sci. **20**, 584–590 (1934)
30. Howard, W.A.: The formulae-as-types notion of construction. HB Curry Essays Comb. Log. Lambda Calc. Form. **44**, 479–490 (1980)
31. Hevner, A.R., March, S.T., Park, J., Ram, S.: Design science in information systems research. MIS Q. Manag. Inf. Syst. **28**, 75–105 (2004)

32. Carlsson, S.A., Henningsson, S., Hrastinski, S., Keller, C.: Socio-technical IS design science research: developing design theory for IS integration management. Inf. Syst. e-Bus. Manag. **9**, 109–131 (2011)
33. Gutzwiller, T.A.: Das CC RIM-Referenzmodell für den Entwurf von betrieblichen, transaktionsorientierten Informationssystemen. Physica-Verlag HD, Heidelberg (2013)
34. Gerring, J.: What is a case study and what is it good for? APSR **98**, 341–354 (2004)
35. Eisenhardt, K.M., Graebner, M.E.: Theory building from cases: opportunities and challenges. Acad. Manag. J. **50**, 25–32 (2007)
36. Flyvbjerg, B.: Five misunderstandings about case-study research. Qual. Inq. **12**, 219–245 (2006)
37. Hallerbach, A., Bauer, T., Reichert, M.: Capturing variability in business process models: the Provop approach. J. Softw. Evol. Process. **22**, 519–546 (2010)
38. Kumar, A., Yao, W.: Design and management of flexible process variants using templates and rules. Comput. Ind. **63**, 112–130 (2012)
39. Hallerbach, A., Bauer, T., Reichert, M.: Managing process variants in the process lifecycle (2008)
40. Reuter, C.: Modellierung und dynamische Adaption klinischer Pfade auf Basis semantischer Prozessfragmente. Shaker, Aachen (2012)
41. Weber, B., Reichert, M., Mendling, J., Reijers, H.A.: Refactoring large process model repositories. Comput. Ind. **62**, 467–486 (2011)
42. van der Aalst, W.M.P., Ter Hofstede, A.H.M.: YAWL: yet another workflow language. Inf. Syst. **30**, 245–275 (2005)
43. Reichert, M., Rinderle, S., Kreher, U., Dadam, P.: Adaptive process management with ADEPT2. In: 2005 Proceedings of 21st International Conference on Data Engineering, ICDE 2005, pp. 1113–1114 (2005)

Automatic Composition of Rough Solution Possibilities in the Target Planning of Factory Planning Projects by Means of Combinatory Logic

Jan Winkels[1]([✉]), Julian Graefenstein[2], Tristan Schäfer[1],
David Scholz[2], Jakob Rehof[1], and Michael Henke[2]

[1] TU Dortmund, Otto-Hahn-Str. 12, 44227 Dortmund, Germany
{Jan.Winkels,Tristan.Schaefer,
Jakob.Rehof}@tu-dortmund.de
[2] TU Dortmund, Leonhard-Euler-Str. 5, 44227 Dortmund, Germany
{Graefenstein,Scholz,Henke}@lfo.tu-dortmund.de

Abstract. Increasing competition, stronger customer focus, shorter product lifecycles and accelerated technological developments imply that companies are faced with the challenge of adapting their own production to the circumstances at ever shorter intervals. The factory planning project is becoming increasingly complex, but there is less and less time available for adaptation. Particularly in the initial planning phase, targets are defined without reliable planning information for the further course, which have far-reaching consequences for the outcome of a successful planning. This paper shows a possibility to generate meaningful solution alternatives at an early stage of the target planning in order to enable an efficient planning process in terms of time and costs. With the help of a constraint-based variant compilation on the basis of previously defined target and frame parameters as well as existing information on the current factory system, various possible solution variants for target planning are to be created. A specific use case scenario was used to develop and test the presented methodology. By comparing combinations of the most diverse possible solutions, the use of a combinatory logic approach enables the first rough and plausible solution variants to be generated automatically, on the basis of which the detailed planning process for achieving the determined solution variant can be created. This way, planning bottlenecks due to the wrong choice of variants as well as large time expenditure for the creation of solution variants can be avoided.

Keywords: Automatic composition · Combinatory logic · Factory planning
Target planning

1 Introduction

When initiating a new factory planning project, it is assumed that the status quo of the factory system is not suitable for future requirements. Due to changing framework conditions and influencing factors which directly affect companies, the factory system

© Springer Nature Switzerland AG 2018
T. Margaria and B. Steffen (Eds.): ISoLA 2018, LNCS 11247, pp. 487–503, 2018.
https://doi.org/10.1007/978-3-030-03427-6_36

has to be adapted in order to remain competitive. In a first step, it is necessary to determine which target state has to be achieved. Correspondent with the company's goals, project objectives are developed to provide a specific framework under certain conditions for the future planning project [1].

However, the strategically oriented goals from the management level cannot be transferred directly to an operative project planning. Figure 1 shows the different levels of influences and responsibilities which are involved in a factory planning project. Each level has different topics to deal with which cumulates in specific information relevant for the following level. For example, a legal guideline might be the restriction to use different materials because of ecological concerns. These materials were used before by the company and now have to be replaced with other materials that follow these new legal guidelines and laws. An example for an objective of the corporate management might be to address a wider range of wealthier range of customers which accepts a much higher price for a product that fulfills certain ecological requirements. In order to follow these objectives of the strategic management in combination with the legal guidelines that have to be followed, the operational management, the level of "Solution variants", uses these cumulated information formulated by every preceding level to consider different solution variants. The last level is responsible for generating a planning process workflow based on the solution variants worked out before which transfers the chosen variant in specific tasks.

An intermediate stage is required in which the management compares the corresponding goals with the strategic corporate goals and defines specific objectives for the planning project in cooperation with the project management [2].

The target planning phase is intended for this purpose in the context of several factory planning procedures [3–5]. Within this first planning phase, individual planning scenarios are worked out which can fulfill the respective objectives and other framework conditions. However, the task of target planning is not responsible for developing implementation measures for the solution variants. These implementation measures are considered by the factory planning procedures to be developed in the following, rather operationally shaped planning phases [2, 5].

It is a requirement of the target planning to consider possible developments and future scenarios in order to develop suitable solution variants [6]. However, such solution variants are initially developed on a very rough basis. They are elaborated with the help of creative methods such as brainstorming or scenario techniques and are based on fuzzy information and knowledge [5, 6]. On the one hand, this is necessary in order to start the development of implementation measures and the general planning process as soon as possible in order to be able to begin with the implementation of the adaptation as quickly as possible. On the other hand, at this early stage a detailed elaboration of the problem definition is not possible due to missing or insufficient and, as already mentioned, fuzzy information [7]. This fast and less detailed and therefore very vague procedure brings along the danger of ending up in a planning dead-end and thus inefficiently working on the whole planning project [8].

If the percentages of cost responsibility of the respective planning phases are considered in a classical factory planning procedure (see Fig. 2), it becomes apparent that the target planning phase occupies half of the total financial volume. This means that decisions made in the target planning phase have a strong influence on the financial

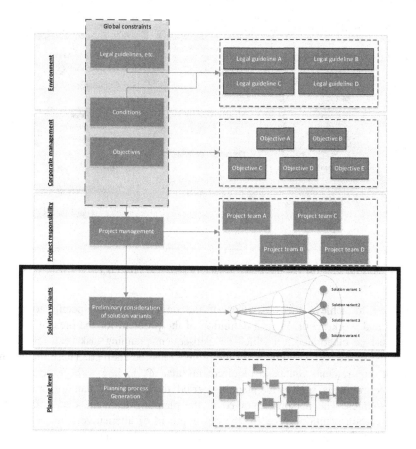

Fig. 1. Levels of responsibility in factory planning

dimension of the whole planning project. As mentioned before there are several factory planning procedures which consider the target or goal planning as a very first step of the whole planning procedure. In this early phase, however, decisions can be adjusted to avoid possible financial damage, which could occur later in the planning process. The decisions of the target planning thus have a significant influence on the successful completion of the project, as it lays the foundation for further procedures.

The objective of the target planning is to develop suitable rough solution variants based on different framework conditions and performance targets for the factory system. These variants are to serve as a guideline and orientation for successful planning. They specify a planning direction with corresponding tasks, which are further detailed in the following planning steps and phases. This first planning phase lays the foundation for the ongoing planning project and is a necessary basis for further decisions made in the following planning phases. Classical planning procedures in factory planning follow the principle of rough approximations to fixed specifications and also make it clear that the results of target planning are on a low level of detail [3, 5, 11].

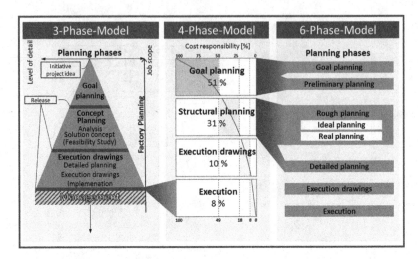

Fig. 2. Cost responsibility in factory planning projects [3, 9–11]

In order to achieve the objectives of the target planning, specific topics are addressed and worked out. First, a definition of the problem for the present planning project must be elaborated, on which the subsequent planning tasks can refer to. In addition, the framework conditions for the project must be clarified. These include not only legal requirements, but also requirements that are in line with corporate management requirements, such as the planning period, the budget for planning or available human resources. The persons involved in the planning team are decisive, as they provide a certain solution space for the development of alternative solution variants based on their individual knowledge and background. This can result in a restricted number of variants because of their individual creativity and knowledge.

Based on the objectives set by the company's management and the identified framework conditions, options of action for formulating solution variants can now be developed. Options for action represent individual aspects of a solution variant, which result as a combination in a possible scenario for achieving the defined targets. The solution variant created by the project team and then agreed on by the management is the aforementioned intermediate stage between the strategic and operative level and the basis for the more detailed planning in the following planning phases (see Fig. 3). An example of a solution variant could be to increase the output of the production system by changing the existing layout. Therefore the layout has to be changed in a way that several segments have to be rearranged because of additional machines and the shift schedule might be necessary to reconsider etc. The details concerning in which way the goals and tasks will be achieved and processed and how to develop the necessary information will be part of the following phases.

Figure 3 shows on the left side the classic approach of formulating and considering several solution variants which then results in evaluating and choosing a specific variant which seems to be the best possible option for the planning project. As mentioned before several information and framework conditions are considered to derive

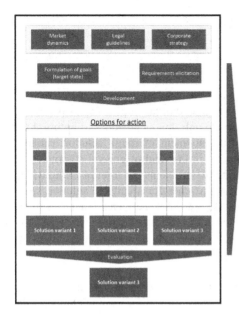
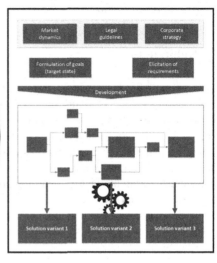

Fig. 3. Classic and new approach for generating solution variants [10]

options of actions. These options of action will then be combined to form individual solution variants based on the creativity and knowledge of the participating project members. There is a vast number of possible variants that can be formed out of the options for action, which cannot be handled in its entirety by some participants on their own. Because of the huge variety of possible combination of options, it might be too complex to formulate every existing solution for the specific project by hand. The process of combining several options for action to a specific solution variant is very hands-on and therefore the variants have a high risk of creating mistakes and future problems in the ongoing planning process.

To optimize this process of formulating solution variants and in combination with that to reduce the risk of failure and possible, high costly problems for the whole planning project the planning phase of target planning needs to be reconsidered in the way this phase is handled. Therefore, the method of combinatory logic will be used to accelerate the generation of high quality and reliably working solution variants, which is illustrated on the right side of Fig. 3. This paper will show the benefits of a fast, reliable and automated generation of solution variants with the help of combinatory logic based on a specific use case. With the help of combinatory logic, it will be possible to reduce influences of individual creativity and knowledge of all participants in order to reduce the possible problems that come with these factors. This will also improve the following planning process as it points out specific intermediate planning tasks, which can be used to generate an optimized planning process workflow for the whole project. Section 2 summarizes related work for the research fields factory planning and software synthesis. The synthesis is performed by making use of the Combinatory Logic Synthesizer (CL)S that is outlined in Sect. 3. These preliminaries are followed by a description of the use case, selected implementation details and a discussion of the results.

2 Related Work

Little attention has been paid so far to the research field of target planning as part of the wider field of factory planning [6, 12]. There are only few approaches to optimize the phase of target planning and therefore the development of rough solution variants. Approaches that are more specific can be found in the field of general corporate and strategic planning. Some recent works describe the problems of target planning within the context of factory planning and present approaches for a suitable solution space management along the factory planning process, as well as the scenario analysis in the target planning and the maturity level management of factory planning itself [6, 8, 13]. However, only a few other approaches were developed which specifically address the target planning as part of the factory planning and therefore try to improve and optimize this planning phase.

The phase of goal definition and variant formation represents a small part of the whole factory planning process and does not receive the necessary attention as the percentage of cost responsibility suggests (see Fig. 2). Within the scope of corporate and strategic planning there are more specific approaches which clarify the classification of the target planning of a factory planning project as a link between strategic corporate planning and the operative implementation of the planning project [4, 14, 15]. In addition, it becomes clear that creativity techniques such as the already mentioned scenario technique, SWOT analysis, brainstorming and cognitive methods are being used to an increasing extent for the development of solution variants [16–19]. It also emerges from the strategic planning that the focus of academic research is on the interaction of the responsible planners with adjacent disciplines and not on the optimization of developing solution variants as a main aspect [19, 20]. New approaches for the automatically supported development of solution variants are not in focus. Approaches for the automated compilation of planning tasks within the scope of factory planning have already been shown, but not yet specifically transferred to the field of target planning [21]. In the area of software engineering, however, there are quite a number of approaches that also use the combinatory logic approach like it is shown in this paper, but not with a specific application reference to the field of factory planning.

There are various approaches to the problem of software synthesis that can be distinguished by Search Space, User Intent and Search Technique. These aspects form the *dimensions in program synthesis* [22, 23].

The program to be synthesized contains domain relevant code. Thus, the dimension of search space is strongly connected to the research field of domain modeling. Accordingly, the specification of the search space can be achieved by using a Domain-Specific Model [24]. The development of these models is usually supported by domain specific modeling tools. The additional design effort for these tools can be compensated by the CINCO meta modeling framework [25–27]. Its applicability has been shown by the development of DIME [28]. The user intent is a formulation of the desired program. Common formalisms to express its properties are temporal logic [29–31], first-order logic [32] or higher-order logic [33]. Moreover, synthesis can be performed according to a set of input/output examples [34, 35]. The search technique determines how the synthesis algorithm is looking for the target program within the search space. There are several approaches that incorporate constraint solving [36], the use of semantic reasoners (i.e. a graph-based search technique) [37] or neural networks [38].

Synthesis can be a powerful technique to support planning tasks, yet only a few studies deal with automated code generation in this domain. The work in [39] demonstrates the synthesis of domain-specific hierarchical task network (HTN) planning software. Planware [40, 41] is a system to synthesize algorithms that produce optimal domain-specific schedules. The synthesis of workflows can also be considered as a part of planning synthesis. The concept proposed in [29] enables for the iterative refinement of the domain specification until a suitable process can be generated. In [37], automated runtime flexibility for software engineering processes is provided by incorporating a semantic reasoner and ad-hoc changes of process instances featured by AristaFlow [42]. As opposed to these studies, the approach for target planning presented in this paper is formally sound and complete. It is particularly well suited to handle synthesis tasks with an emphasis on features and it produces a list of possible solutions that can be further analyzed by experts.

The component-based software synthesis is a powerful technique which can formalize variability in product lines by making use of feature models. Feature modeling and Software Product Lines (SPL) [43–45] are closely related topics that represent individualization and standardization of software. They both contribute to shortening development life cycles of software products by facilitating the reuse of software while comprehending a systematic management of software product families. Research resulted in the programming paradigm feature oriented software development which is supported by comprehensive development environment [46].

Variability modeling is a well developed research topic in the context of business process modeling and still receives continued attention. In 2017, an overview to existing approaches in this field was given in a comprehensive survey by La Rosa, van der Aalst et al. [47].

3   Combinatory Logic Synthesizer

The Combinatory Logic Synthesizer ((CL)S, [48]) is a framework to compose software components or data structures according to their type signature. In this paper, (CL)S is used to form rough solution possibilities for target planning. Thus, its formal foundation will be outlined in this section to provide the reader with an elementary understanding of the theoretical background.

The framework determines a result term in the form of an applicative composition in compliance with combinatory logic. Applicative terms are defined as $e ::= x | (e\,e')$, where x ranges over a denumerable set of variables. The type system of (CL)S is based on intersection types [49].

Type expressions are denoted σ, τ and defined as follows:

$$\sigma, \tau ::= a \,|\, \omega \,|\, \alpha \,|\, \sigma \to \tau \,|\, \sigma \cap \tau$$

Type constants are ranged over by a, b, c, ... and they can be programming language types (native types) or textual descriptions (semantic types). The special type constant ω is the root element of the subtyping relation. Type variables are ranged over by α, β, γ, ... and they are substituted with type constants according to a substitution map. This map is part of the domain specification (i.e. not part of type expressions) and will be used to resolve type variables prior to the computation of an inhabitant. Additionally, type expressions can contain function types ($\to$) and intersections ($\cap$).

(CL)S performs the software synthesis by solving the type theoretic problem of inhabitation. It is often abbreviated as $\Gamma \vdash ? : \tau$ and asks if a term with type τ exists under the type assumptions stated in Γ. The propositions-as-types correspondence [50, 51] connects the type theory with programs. According to the propositions-as-types correspondence, a proof term M for the type judgement $\Gamma \vdash M : \tau$ must be a program or data structure that conforms to the target type τ. Thus, solving the inhabitation problem can be interpreted as type-directed software synthesis.

The synthesis is not building code from scratch but making use of software components held in a repository Γ. The components are also referred to as combinators as they will be composed in a combinatory way. The repository is a finite set that contains a type assumption for each combinator: $\Gamma = \{(x_1 : \tau_1), \ldots, (x_n : \tau_n)\}$ with $x_i \neq x_j$ for $i \,/ = j$ where $x_1, \ldots, x_n$ represent combinator names and $\tau_1, \ldots, \tau_n$ are the corresponding type assumptions. During inhabitation, the combinator's type is used to determine which elements can be applied to each other in order to satisfy the target type. The current inhabitation algorithm is proven to be complete and enumerates all inhabitants.

In addition to the type signature, implementation details can be provided for combinators. They can contain programs, data, data fragments or functions. Moreover, variability points can be inserted and described with the type expression. The use of type taxonomies and type variables further supports the comprehensive specification of complex combinators. An algorithm to decide the inhabitation problem for intersection types is described in detail in [52].

The component-based synthesis with intersection types can be classified according to the *dimensions in program synthesis* [22]. Domain knowledge can be expressed by the semantic layer and corresponding combinator implementation. The search space is defined by well-formed applicative compositions of available combinators. The inhabitation algorithm represents the search strategy and the user intent must be supplied as a target type expression.

(CL)S has been used to synthesize BPMN 2.0 business process descriptions in interaction with the Combinatory Process Synthesis framework (CPS, [53]), showing that the synthesis approach is suitable to generate structured data. Recent research puts the emphasis on language independent code generation using meta code generation [54]. For this study, the Scala based version of the (CL)S was used[1]. The underlying

---

[1] The source code of the (CL)S framework is available at https://github.com/combinators/cls-scala.

formalism extends the Bounded Combinatory Logic (BCL, [52]) by introducing n-ary type constructors and demanding the use of substitution maps for type variables. Compared to BCL, this results in higher expressiveness while type variable mappings require a more precise specification.

4 Specific Industrial Use Case for Testing the Approach

To build a test model and to review the developed code, a real planning scenario of a company in the manufacturing industry was used as a basis.

The planning impulse was triggered by the company management. Due to a changing customer structure with correspondingly different products and sales figures, the production system had to be changed. First, framework conditions and targets were formulated at the level of corporate management in order to set a direction for the final design of the planning. The main points were:

- No changes to existing production lines.
- Employees will not be laid off or hired.
- The property or the existing built-up area will not be changed.
- The factory hall is not extended.
- A certain sales figure must be produced with the existing manufacturing equipment.

Further information on these framework conditions and targets were provided in order to be able to develop rough solution variants according to these specifications. First, a sales volume could be determined that differed from the previous one. The demands by the customer of each individual product are to be more volatile than before, which requires increased flexibility for the new system. Likewise, the changed product variants result in increased storage requirements in order to be able to cover the correspondingly greater variety of products.

The goals and general conditions set by the corporate management led to the decision that the biggest variable that would fulfill the requirements and goals was the planning of a new logistics concept. The number of employees as well as the existing structure of the building and production lines should remain unchanged. It was checked whether the production lines and the respective equipment were technically capable of manufacturing the new products. As this could be guaranteed, the focus was on logistics as a variable to be changed. Storage types as well as the conveying means including the corresponding connections to the respective operating means of the production lines had to be redesigned. After it was decided that a new rough logistics concept should be developed, all relevant parameters were identified in order to be able to meet the targets with the new concept (see Fig. 4). The main parameters were the capacity of the storage types, the needed space in the layout and the costs of each logistic element. Based on these parameters three rough solution variants could be generated, which differed in the financial expenditure along other specifics.

For the algorithm, individual parameters, such as type of storage like Kanban racks or high rack store, as well as conveying equipment such as classic forklifts or automated guided vehicles were identified and analyzed. These parameters were subdivided into small groups with their individual attributes such as cost rates, area requirements or capacities, so that these values could be transferred into a form that can be processed by the algorithm (see Fig. 4). With this breakdown of individual solution elements, individual options for action could be broken down into many smaller elements. This should allow a more diverse generation of solution variants without being limited by the planner and the solution space of his participating personal. In addition, the respective attributes of each element should allow a more detailed compilation according to specific criteria such as costs or used space in the factory.

5 Implementation and Experimental Results

In this section, we will use the previously presented use case as a practical framework for evaluating our approach to automated composition of factory configurations. The scenario is well suited to illustrate process synthesis because it is well-structured and contains inherent variability. The inputs for the CL(S) are available as an accompanying download[2]. It is the aim to use the synthesis algorithm described in Sect. 3 to automatically show which configuration options can be used for the use case and under which conditions they can be implemented. In order to be able to map the variability and the numerous different configuration possibilities in the present scenario, the scenario was converted into a feature model. Feature models are originally a representation of all occurrences of a software product line (SPL). An SPL is a collection (or family) of related programs that are based on a common software kernel but differ in features. A "feature" is defined as a "salient or distinguishable user-visible aspect, quality or characteristic of a software system" [55]. Feature models are visualized through feature diagrams and used throughout the product line development process. The model defines the features, their characteristics, as well as their dependencies, which are reflected in the diagram.

In addition, the models can have other constraints, which can be represented in additional documentation (tables, etc.). A concrete incarnation of a member of an SPL is called a feature configuration. A configuration is only allowed if it does not violate any constraints described in the model. The concept of the software product lines has been adapted to the present work and its underlying scenario. It will be introduced and used as a production product line (PPL) at this point. In our scenario, different variants of individual components of the material flow are considered as features. Different transport systems for example represent different factory features. Configuration is allowed if at least one feature is selected from all the required components and global constraints such as the budget limit are not violated. The scenario model is shown in Fig. 4.

The model shows the existing variation possibilities. For example, it is possible to combine different transport systems. Each system has individual characteristics, such as specific costs, throughput or floor space requirements.

In the next step, the feature model was transformed into combinators for synthesis. The individual combinators are shown in Fig. 5. The name of the combinator follows

---

[2] https://james.cs.tu-dortmund.de/smjawink/CLS-FactoryConfig.

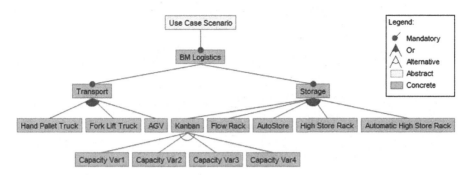

Fig. 4. Feature model

the "prefix" + "name of the feature to be selected" structure. Possible prefixes are "storage-Selector" and "transportSelector" to indicate the corresponding branch of the Feature Model Tree. The combiner for selecting an AutoStorage system is therefore called "storage SelectorAutoStore". In principle, there is a combiner for each entry in the feature tree whose signature can be filled in by various forms of its child nodes. As a result the existing combinator "configuration" needs an expression of the transport and storage selector to be able to be executed. This is equivalent to the entry BA-Configuration in the Feature Model.

Note the two combinators addTransport and AddStorage, which are intended to increase the number of transport or storage systems used. For instance, if you want to use 2 Forklift trucks, the combinator selectTransport (ForkLift) would be executed twice and then combined with the addStorage combinator to form a transport system. With this construction, however, there is a problem: Since the constraints are not checked until after the synthesis algorithm has been completed, it can theoretically happen that the addStorage combinator could be back-interchanged infinitely, resulting in an infinite number of solutions. To prevent this, the maximum depth of the resulting tree grammar in the implementation has been limited.

The inhabitation is executed with a call of the form:

```
lazy val resultsFromRequests: Results =
Results.add(Gamma.inhabit[Form]('FactoryConfig
('AutoStore)).
```

This means that the algorithm is asked if it is possible to generate a solution that meets the required specifications from the given repository Γ. In the example above, the use of an AutoStore system is explicitly specified. For the experiment in the present scenario, no restrictions of this kind were specified in order to enable as many possible solutions as possible. All other constraints were taken directly from the given scenario in order to make the solutions applicable to it.

The solution set is then displayed in a web interface where the user can view and evaluate the solutions. The web interface displaying the solutions of the experimental run can be seen below.

$\Gamma = \{$

configuration:	(String $\rightarrow$ String $\rightarrow$ String $\rightarrow$ Form) $\cap$
	(Title $\rightarrow$ NameTransport(a) $\rightarrow$ NameStorage(b) $\rightarrow$ OrderMenu)
storageSelectorKanban1:	(String $\rightarrow$ String) $\cap$
	(NameTransport(a) $\rightarrow$ NameStorage(Kanban1))
storageSelectorKanban2:	(String $\rightarrow$ String) $\cap$
	(NameTransport(a) $\rightarrow$ NameStorage(Kanban2))
storageSelectorKanban3:	(String $\rightarrow$ String) $\cap$
	(NameTransport(a) $\rightarrow$ NameStorage(Kanban3))
storageSelectorKanban4:	(String $\rightarrow$ String) $\cap$
	(NameTransport(a) $\rightarrow$ NameStorage(Kanban4))
storageSelectorFlowRack:	(String $\rightarrow$ String) $\cap$
	(NameTransport(a) $\rightarrow$ NameStorage(FlowRack))
storageSelectorAutostore:	(String $\rightarrow$ String) $\cap$
	(NameTransport(a) $\rightarrow$ NameStorage(Autostore))
storageSelectorHighRackStore:	(String $\rightarrow$ String) $\cap$
	(NameTransport(a) $\rightarrow$ NameStorage(HighRackStore))
storageSelectorAutoHighRackStore:	(String $\rightarrow$ String) $\cap$
	(NameTransport(a) $\rightarrow$ NameStorage(AutoHighRackStore))
transportSelectorHandPallet:	(String $\rightarrow$ String) $\cap$
	(Title $\rightarrow$ NameTransport(HandPallet))
transportselectorForkLift:	(String $\rightarrow$ String) $\cap$
	(Title $\rightarrow$ NameTransport(ForkLift))
transportselectorAGV:	(String $\rightarrow$ String) $\cap$
	(Title $\rightarrow$ NameTransport(AGV))
combineStorage:	(String $\rightarrow$ String $\rightarrow$ String) $\cap$
	(NameStorage(a) $\rightarrow$ NameStorage(a) $\rightarrow$ NameStorage(a))
combineTransport:	(String $\rightarrow$ String $\rightarrow$ String) $\cap$
	(NameTransport(b) $\rightarrow$ NameTransport(b) $\rightarrow$ NameTransport(b))
ConfigTitle:	String $\cap$ Title

$\}$

WF = { {a $\rightarrow$ AGV}, {a $\rightarrow$ HandPallet}, {a $\rightarrow$ ForkLift}, {b $\rightarrow$ AutoHighRackStore}, {b $\rightarrow$ HighRackStore}, {b $\rightarrow$ Autostore}, {b $\rightarrow$ FlowRack}, {b $\rightarrow$ Kanban1}, {b $\rightarrow$ Kanban2}, {b $\rightarrow$ Kanban3}, {b $\rightarrow$ Kanban4}
}

Fig. 5. Combinator repository overview

In the use case scenario, the following configuration was chosen as the solution: As a transportation system, an AGV System was selected, the storage system was an AutoStore rack. As Fig. 6 shows, this solution also appears in the solution set of the algorithm (solution number 5 of 24 in total). In addition, further alternative configurations can be seen.

These generated solutions differ in terms of various measures, such as the capacity or the number of employees required per shift. For instance, the usage of a forklift truck as a transportation appears to be much cheaper, but also offers a smaller amount of transportation capacity per hour. Which configuration is selected at the end also depends on how the responsible persons weight the individual parameters and which personal preferences they have and fits best to given case.

This shows that our approach does not only provide all possible solutions, but also evaluates them directly with regard to important key figures. This way, the responsible persons not only directly see which options are available, but can also directly see their pros and cons and thus make a quick and well-founded decision.

Requests:

Solutions:

Fig. 6. Inhabitants of the experimental run

6   Conclusion and Outlook

It has been shown that plausible and useful solutions for target planning can be obtained with our approach. By offering a large number of different solutions and a large variability of different aspects of the solution, planners can make quick and reliable decisions based on the generated proposals and thus advance the planning process. Further, it is possible to support the following more detailed planning process by giving specific directions based on the chosen solution variant. Therefore the possible solution space for the whole detailed planning process can also be reduced so that a more precise planning process can be generated afterwards.

In order to further improve the technology and its benefits, various points of dependences are conceivable. Of course, the first starting point to consider is to support more complex decisions and other aspects of the planning process such as the ressource planning or the layout planning through the procedure. In addition to that, other areas where planning workflows are needed to manage complex planning projects could be addressed with the approach shown in this paper. An example would be the management of the construction of a new hospital building where a great amount of different information and dependences are interconnected with each other. It is necessary to be able to handle this complex kind of project and our approach would be beneficial in automatically generating sufficient planning workflows based on our produced solution variants.

The currently still hard-coded combinator repositories are also to be dynamized in the future. The development of a parser that automatically generates the combinators from a domain model is conceivable. In combination with modern domain modeling tools such as DyWA [25], it would be possible for users without programming knowledge to design repositories and execute inhabitation requests.

Another starting point is to improve the quality of the solutions offered. By adding feedback loops and using machine learning methods, the tool aims to gain knowledge of generated solutions which were considered good and practicable. In the best case scenario, it should be able to learn which possible configurations are the best for certain requests.

Acknowledgement. The study presented in this paper was partly funded by the GRK 2193 (www.grk2193.tu-dortmund.de/de/) and the Center of Excellence for Logistics and IT (www. leistungszentrum-logistik-it.de/) located in Dortmund.

References

1. Brankamp, K.: Zielplanung. In: Eversheim, W., Schuh, G. (eds.) Produktion und Management 3. Gestaltung von Produktionssystemen. Hütte, pp. 9.31–9.39. Springer, Heidelberg (1999). https://doi.org/10.1007/978-3-642-58399-5
2. Both, P.V., Rexroth, K.: SIAS – Konzeption eines planungsunterstützendenWerkzeuges für die Zielplanung. In: Knoll, M., Oertel, B. (eds.) Dienstleistungen für die energieeffiziente Stadt, pp. 109–130. Springer Spektrum, Heidelberg (2012)
3. Aggteleky, B.: Fabrikplanung. Werksentwicklung und Betriebsrationalisierung, 2nd edn. Hanser, München (1987)
4. Pawellek, G.: Ganzheitliche Fabrikplanung. Grundlagen, Vorgehensweise, EDV-Unterstützung, 2nd edn. VDI-Buch. Springer, Berlin (2014)
5. Grundig, C.-G.: Fabrikplanung. Planungssystematik - Methoden - Anwendungen, 5th edn. Hanser, München (2015)
6. Baumeister, M.: Fabrikplanung im turbulenten Umfeld. Methodik zur Zielplanung einer Fabrik unter Berücksichtigung eines turbulenten Unternehmensumfeldes und der übergeordneten Unternehmensziele. Zugl.: Karlsruhe, Univ., Diss., 2003. Forschungsberichte aus dem Institut für Werkzeugmaschinen und Betriebstechnik der Universität Karlsruhe, vol. 115. Inst. für Werkzeugmaschinen und Betriebstechnik, Karlsruhe (2002)
7. Hawer, S., Ilmer, P., Reinhart, G.: Klassifizierung unscharfer Planungsdaten in der Fabrikplanung. ZWF (2015). https://doi.org/10.3139/104.111339
8. Hilchner, R.: Typenorientiertes Lösungsraum-Management in der Fabrikplanung. Zugl.: Aachen, Techn. Hochsch., Diss., 2012, 1st edn. Edition Wissenschaft Apprimus, vol. 2012,13. Apprimus-Verl., Aachen (2012)
9. Schulte, C.: Logistik. Wege zur Optimierung der Supply Chain, 7th edn. Vahlens Handbücher der Wirtschafts- und Sozialwissenschaften (2016)
10. Eversheim, W., Schuh, G. (eds.): Produktion und Management 3. Gestaltung von Produktionssystemen. Hütte. Springer, Heidelberg (1999)
11. Kettner, H., Schmidt, J., Greim, H.-R.: Leitfaden der systematischen Fabrikplanung. Hanser, München (1984)
12. Rexroth, K., Brüggemann, T., Both, P.V.: Methodology of target and requirements management for complex systems concerning the application field of an energy-efficient city. In: Schrenk, M. (ed.) REAL CORP 2009: cities 3.0 - smart, sustainable, integrative. Proceedings of 14th International Conference on Urban Planning, Regional Development and Information Society; Beiträge zur 14. Internatinalen Konferenz zu Stadtplanung, Regionalentwicklung und Informationsgesellschaft; [strategies, concepts and technologies for planning the urban future; 22–25 April 2009, Centre de Disseny de Sitges, Catalonia, Spain; Tagungsband], pp. 353–359

13. Krunke, M.: Reifegradmanagement in der Fabrikplanung. Dissertation, RWTH Aachen (2017)
14. Girmscheid, G.: Projektabwicklung in der Bauwirtschaft - prozessorientiert. Wege zur Win-Win-Situation für Auftraggeber und Auftragnehmer, 5th edn. VDI-Buch (2016)
15. Welge, M.K., Al-Laham, A., Eulerich, M.: Strategisches Management. Grundlagen - Prozess - Implementierung, 7th edn (2017)
16. Wilson, I.: Strategic planning isn't dead—it changed. Long Range Plan. (1994). https://doi.org/10.1016/0024-6301(94)90052-3
17. Glaister, K.W., Falshaw, J.R.: Strategic Planning. Still Going Strong? Long Range Plan. (1999). https://doi.org/10.1016/s0024-6301(98)00131-9
18. Frentzel, W.Y., Bryson, J.M., Crosby, B.C.: Strategic Planning in the Military. Long Range Planning (2000). https://doi.org/10.1016/s0024-6301(00)00040-6
19. Wolf, C., Floyd, S.W.: Strategic planning research: toward a theory-driven agenda. J. Manag. (2016). https://doi.org/10.1177/0149206313478185
20. Liedtka, R.M.D.O.J., Jacobs, D.C., Heracleous, L.: Strategizing through playful design. J. Bus. Strat. (2007). https://doi.org/10.1108/02756660710760971
21. Graefenstein, J., Scholz, D., Henke, M., Winkels, J., Rehof, J.: Intelligente Orchestrierung von Planungsprozessen. ZWF (2017). https://doi.org/10.3139/104.111696
22. Gulwani, S.: Dimensions in program synthesis. In: Proceedings of the 12th International ACM SIGPLAN Symposium on Principles and Practice of Declarative Programming, pp. 13–24 (2010)
23. Gulwani, S., Polozov, O., Singh, R.: Program synthesis. Found. Trends® Program. Lang. **4** (1–2), 1–119 (2017)
24. Roser, S., Lautenbacher, F., Bauer, B.: Generation of workflow code from DSMs. In: Proceedings of the 7th OOPSLA Workshop on Domain-Specific Modeling (2007)
25. Naujokat, S., Lybecait, M., Kopetzki, D., Steffen, B.: CINCO: a simplicity-driven approach to full generation of domain-specific graphical modeling tools. Int. J. Softw. Tools Technol. Transf. (2017). https://doi.org/10.1007/s10009-017-0453-6
26. Naujokat, S., Neubauer, J., Margaria, T., Steffen, B.: Meta-level reuse for mastering domain specialization. In: Margaria, T., Steffen, B. (eds.) Leveraging Applications of Formal Methods, Verification and Validation: Discussion, Dissemination, Applications, pp. 218–237. Springer, Cham (2016). https://doi.org/10.1007/978-3-319-47169-3_16
27. Steffen, B., Naujokat, S.: Archimedean points: the essence for mastering change. In: Steffen, B. (ed.) Transactions on Foundations for Mastering Change I. LNCS, vol. 9960, pp. 22–46. Springer, Cham (2016). https://doi.org/10.1007/978-3-319-46508-1_3
28. Boßelmann, S., et al.: DIME: a programming-less modeling environment for web applications. In: Margaria, T., Steffen, B. (eds.) ISoLA 2016. LNCS, vol. 9953, pp. 809–832. Springer, Cham (2016). https://doi.org/10.1007/978-3-319-47169-3_60
29. Awad, A., Goré, R., Thomson, J., Weidlich, M.: An iterative approach for business process template synthesis from compliance rules. In: Advanced Information Systems Engineering, pp. 406–421 (2011)
30. Yu, J., Han, Y.-B., Han, J., Jin, Y., Falcarin, P., Morisio, M.: Synthesizing service composition models on the basis of temporal business rules. J. Comput. Sci. Technol. **23**(6), 885–894 (2008)
31. Lamprecht, A.-L., Naujokat, S., Margaria, T., Steffen, B.: Synthesis-based loose programming. In: 2010 Seventh International Conference on the Quality of Information and Communications Technology (QUATIC), pp. 262–267 (2010)

32. Alur, R., et al.: Syntax-guided synthesis. Form. Methods Comput.-Aided Des. (FMCAD) **2013**, 1–8 (2013)
33. Srinivas, Y.V., Jüllig, R.: Specware: formal support for composing software. In: International Conference on Mathematics of Program Construction, pp. 399–422 (1995)
34. Le, V., Gulwani, S.: FlashExtract: a framework for data extraction by examples. In: ACM SIGPLAN Notices, pp. 542–553 (2014)
35. Feser, J.K., Chaudhuri, S., Dillig, I.: Synthesizing data structure transformations from input-output examples. In: ACM SIGPLAN Notices, pp. 229–239 (2015)
36. Solar-Lezama, A., Tancau, L., Bodik, R., Seshia, S., Saraswat, V.: Combinatorial sketching for finite programs. ACM Sigplan Not. **41**(11), 404–415 (2006)
37. Grambow, G., Oberhauser, R., Reichert, M.: Semantically-driven workflow generation using declarative modeling for processes in software engineering. In: Proceedings of EDOCW 2011, pp. 164–173. IEEE Computer Society (2011)
38. Parisotto, E., Mohamed, A.-R., Singh, R., Li, L., Zhou, D., Kohli, P.: Neuro-symbolic program synthesis. arXiv preprint arXiv:1611.01855 (2016)
39. Ilghami, O., Nau, D.S.: A general approach to synthesize problem-specific planners. University of Maryland, College Park, Department of Computer Science (2003)
40. Becker, M., Gilham, L., Smith, D.R., et al.: Planware II. Synthesis of schedulers for complex resource systems (2003)
41. Blaine, L., Gilham, L., Liu, J., Smith, D.R., Westfold, S.: Planware-domain-specific synthesis of high-performance schedulers. In: Proceedings of 13th IEEE International Conference on Automated Software Engineering, pp. 270–279 (1998)
42. Reichert, M., et al.: Enabling Poka-Yoke workflows with the AristaFlow BPM Suite (2009)
43. Pohl, K., Böckle, G., van der Linden, F.J.: Software Product Line Engineering – Foundations, Principles, and Techniques. Springer, Heidelberg (2005). https://doi.org/10.1007/3-540-28901-1
44. Apel, S., Batory, D., Kästner, C., Saake, G.: Feature-Oriented Software Product Lines. Springer, Heidelberg (2013). https://doi.org/10.1007/978-3-642-37521-7
45. van Gurp, J., Bosch, J., Svahnberg, M.: On the notion of variability in software product lines. In: Proceedings of Working IEEE/IFIP Conference on Software Architecture, pp. 45–54 (2001)
46. Thüm, T., Kästner, C., Benduhn, F., Meinicke, J., Saake, G., Leich, T.: FeatureIDE: an extensible framework for feature-oriented software development. Sci. Comput. Program. **79**, 70–85 (2014)
47. Rosa, M.L., van der Aalst, W.M.P., Dumas, M., Milani, F.P.: Business process variability modeling: a survey. ACM Comput. Surv. (CSUR) **50**(1), 2 (2017)
48. Bessai, J., Dudenhefner, A., Dücke, B., Martens, M., Rehof, J.: Combinatory logic synthesizer. In: 6th International Symposium on Leveraging Applications of Formal Methods, Verification and Validation, ISoLA 2014, Corfu, Greece, 8–11 October 2014, pp. 26–40 (2014). https://doi.org/10.1007/978-3-662-45234-9_3
49. Coppo, M., Dezani-Ciancaglini, M.: An extension of basic functionality theory for lambda-calculus. Notre Dame J. Form. Log. **21**, 685–693 (1980)
50. Curry, H.B.: Functionality in combinatory logic. Proc. Natl. Acad. Sci. **20**(11), 584–590 (1934)
51. Howard, W.A.: The formulae-as-types notion of construction. To HB Curry: Essays Comb. Log. Lambda Calc. Formalism **44**, 479–490 (1980)
52. Dücke, B., Martens, M., Rehof, J., Urzyczyn, P.: Bounded combinatory logic. In: Proceedings of Computer Science Logic, CSL 2012, pp. 243–258. Schloss Dagstuhl (2012)

53. Bessai, J., Dudenhefner, A., Düdder, B., Martens, M., Rehof, J.: Combinatory process synthesis. In: Proceedings of 7th International Symposium on Leveraging Applications of Formal Methods, Verification and Validation: Foundational Techniques, ISoLA 2016, Imperial, Corfu, Greece, Part I, 10–14 October 2016, pp. 266–281 (2016). https://doi.org/10.1007/978-3-319-47166-219

54. Bessai, J., Düdder, B., Heinemann, G., Rehof, J.: Towards Language-Independent Code Synthesis (2018)

55. Kang, K.C., Cohen, S.G., Hess, J.A., Novak, W.E., Peterson, A.S.: Feature-oriented domain analysis (FODA) feasibility study. Technical Report CMU/SEI-90-TR-021, SEI, Carnegie Mellon University, November 1990

GOLD: Global Organization aLignment and Decision - Towards the Hierarchical Integration of Heterogeneous Business Models

Barbara Steffen[1] and Steve Boßelmann[2]($\boxtimes$)

[1] Rotterdam School of Management, Rotterdam, Netherlands
barbarasteffen@gmx.net
[2] TU Dortmund University, Dortmund, Germany
steve.bosselmann@cs.tu-dortmund.de

Abstract. The so-called fourth industrial revolution (Industry 4.0) is changing the landscape in the manufacturing industry. Although recognized as an essential factor to preserve competitiveness, organizations are still figuring out drivers, enablers and barriers as well as suitable business models to pave the way for innovations in fields such as highly customized products or exponential technologies. The central challenge for a successful adoption of Industry 4.0 is not primarily the required technology, but the emergence and aggregation of a common view and sound models focusing on paramount aspects like quality, customer perception and margins. We argue that available solutions for modeling business strategies fail at providing sufficient guidance for organizations in analyzing opportunities and driving innovations due to their narrow nature as well as missing combination and aggregation possibilities. In contrast, we outline a multi-perspective framework to support organizations in analyzing their context at multiple levels and discuss technological requirements as well as challenges for the development of modeling tools that support hierarchical integration of analyses and models as well as different perspectives to converge on an organization-wide aligned business strategy.

Keywords: Global organization alignment & decision framework
Global organization alignment & decision tool
Hierarchical integration of heterogeneous business models
Multi-level business modeling · Industry 4.0 context · B-2-B market

1 Introduction

Today SMEs in the manufacturing industry serving the global B-2-B market while producing in western countries (in the following addressed as SMEs) are trapped. First, "increased competition due to globalization and therefore increased commoditization of products" [20] necessitates that SMEs fully satisfy

© Springer Nature Switzerland AG 2018
T. Margaria and B. Steffen (Eds.): ISoLA 2018, LNCS 11247, pp. 504–527, 2018.
https://doi.org/10.1007/978-3-030-03427-6_37

the customers' needs and differentiate themselves from their price-driven competition. As superior quality and increased productivity measures are not enough they are forced to find novel ways to the balancing problem of economies of scale and scope [2]. Second, they cannot handle the steadily increasing complexity of their products and supply chains due to their customers' rising demands [9]. Especially, the integral quality constraint i.e., the requirement that the newly bought equipment must adhere to the existing infrastructure, processes, and products already in place [21] characterizes most deals in the B-2-B market and asks for invasive product or machine modifications.

To survive in this complex setting SMEs have to offer single unit customizations or solutions as standardized or mass customized offers fail to adequately meet the individual customer expectations [11]. Evanschitzky et al. [8] defined solutions as "individualized offers for complex customer problems (...) whose components offer an integrative added value by combining products and/or services so that the value is more than the sum of its components". Solutions make it possible to offer a 'worry-free' customizable mix of products and services that fully satisfy the customer's specific needs. In this context the supplier is highly dependent on the customer and enters specific investments prior to the transaction. This supplier-side burden due to the exploding diversity of the effective product portfolio leaves only low profit margins in comparison to the incurred additional effort [13]. For the suppliers this means handling more product and machine variations in smaller lot sizes, which significantly decreases the standardization potential and positive scalability effects. Thus, it is not surprising that these invasive single piece customizations/solutions typically only benefit the customer directly, while the supplier faces major cost and effort investments which can be hardly compensated with the indirectly gained advantages [12].

To stay competitive in the manufacturing industries, e.g., automotive, product and plant industry, Industry 4.0 acts as essential enabler to make this diversification economically worthwhile [2]. This is further confirmed by the observation that Industry 4.0 is currently moving from a 'Schrittmacherkonzept' (pace maker concept) to a 'Schlüsselkonzept' (key concept) [10]. In other words, it advances from a movement one can invest in to gain competitive advantage to a movement one has to invest in to prevent suffering e.g. severe competitive disadvantages.

Typical definitions of Industry 4.0 are rather vague, like the following two: Industry 4.0 is "the comprehensive transformation of the whole sphere of industrial production through the merging of digital technology and the internet with conventional industry" by Angela Merkel, the German Chancellor [4], and Industry 4.0 is "the introduction of Internet technologies into industry" by Drath and Horch [6]. Common to both definitions is the underlying implication that the novel aspect of Industry 4.0 is not so much the technology itself, but rather that it combines existing technologies in a new way.

Currently, there is no common understanding of the final impact Industry 4.0 will have nor in which directions the organizations must transform. It is predicted that the Industry 4.0 wave creates "disruptive technologies [...] [which] will enable productivity gains and new business models, and fundamentally alter the competitive landscape" [5]. SMEs are confronted with many opportunities accompanied by challenges and risks, e.g. extensive investments and invasive changes. However, the biggest risk is to ignore the need for change as it will eventually wipe them out of the market [3]. Thus, the overwhelmed SMEs have to find their strategy in the uncertain context surrounding Industry 4.0. Today, this often leads SMEs to pursue rather incremental adaptations with apparently limited risk, which is itself rather risky: the SMEs may miss out on major business opportunities that could provide competitors with unfair advantages and thereby endanger their own market position. Thus, it is business critical for SMEs to take informed decisions and to establish a winning path that exploits the Industry 4.0 hype. The difficulty of this task lies in the required alignment of the mindsets of the disparate stakeholders involved, in particular experts in manufacturing, business, and IT, to deliver competitive Industry 4.0 business models.

In addition, especially SMEs as compared to OEMs struggle considerably with successfully adapting the applications and technologies offered by Industry 4.0 as they miss the resources and manpower to experiment with ideas and opportunities that go beyond their existing products and processes. This lack disqualifies them from becoming early adopters, as they cannot risk investing into potentially failing emerging technologies [9]. Thus, the concrete pressing question is how to reap the benefits without incurring too large risks.

The successful adoption of Industry 4.0 asks organizations to rethink their strategy and requires a comprehensive top-down driven corporate transformation. The top-management will have to set a new direction, translate it into a vision of the future organization, and guide a consistent and aligned organization-wide implementation. Here, organizations are missing clear strategic directions, and a vision for a value-driven business model which has the potential to establish a competitive advantage. This underlines the demand-pull for a strategic framework that guides the organizations' decision-making process to make the right decisions regarding which Industry 4.0 topic to address and how to stepwise implement it.

Several frameworks and tools already support business analysis and business modeling from various individual perspectives. However, to our knowledge none of such frameworks and tools try to establish a coherent multi-perspective decision making support, and the corresponding available tools, like the Business Model Canvas (BMC) [19], hardly provide any sophisticated guidance.

This paper aims at introducing the concept of a multi-perspective, interactive framework which shall support organizations in analyzing their context and provide them with an initial prototypical navigation tool that directs them through the nontransparent Industry 4.0 landscape along their path to developing a context specific and fitting organizational strategy. This framework, called the GOLD Framework for Global Organization aLignment and Decision, aims at the analysis of an organization's situation in a top-down fashion, uncovering several opportunities and strategic directions while ensuring that no relevant business or technical aspects are neglected or analyzed in a wrong way. The motivation for GOLD arose in a case study for which the first prototype was developed. In this case study we concretized the requirements and tested the GOLD Framework's usability and functionality.

2   Case Study

The case organization is a SME with an international footprint offering products/solutions in different markets and industries. The analysis focused on a niche in the infrastructure monitoring market. This newly addressed market was chosen as pilot project for the SME's Industry 4.0 adoption. Throughout our interviews we heard statements like "the cloud has a major potential, but entering the market is challenging due to the wind park market's conservative nature. No one dares to be the first adopter" as was stated by an Engineering Services Sales Manager. A member of direction of a scientific association for management and consulting added "organizations are paralyzed in the decision-making process. They identified the need to act, but are afraid of the barriers, potentially adopting the wrong technology and failing at a successful implementation, doing more harm than good". This hesitation is not unsubstantiated as a Software developer and PhD Student confirmed that "Industry 4.0 offers many possibilities not yet adopted in the industry. But the possibilities come with risks like increased security challenges".

Thus, this cautious attitude stands for a widespread general 'trap' between risk and opportunity costs in the generally conservative manufacturing industry. Here, the organizations prefer the traditional cost-driven approach over a value-driven approach which inevitably would lead to more radical business model adaptations. The cost-driven approach aims at ensuring a profit contribution with the aim to at least cover all incurred costs. It is customary for business models to get incrementally adapted instead of radically revolutionized. The cost-driven approach promotes technology-pushes as organizations do not need to orientate themselves at the environment and customer needs. Thus, this approach feels safe and familiar, explaining why many competitors went for it. However, this form of Industry 4.0 adoption only buys limited time and does not cover and satisfy the successful adoption of Industry 4.0 in the long run. To stay sustainably competitive organizations must dare taking the risky step of disruptive and radical changes to both the business model and internal processes to fully exploit the potential of the Industry 4.0 transformation.

Unfortunately, the strategic frameworks and models available to managers, as guidance for their thinking and approach, are merely described concepts. So, it is not surprising that SMEs feel left alone without proper guidance explaining the SMEs' traditional approach and stagnation. For example, Porter's Five Forces [7] model shows several dependencies and interdependencies explaining the power relations present in the market. It states that organizations need to be aware of all the different parties involved to make educated decisions regarding their bargaining power, to actually understand their role and possibilities, and eventually to be able to make the right decisions when forming their strategy and entering business deals. However, Porter's model does not provide any guidance regarding where to get the necessary information from, how to interpret it and how to adapt the organization's strategy accordingly. Further, Porter does not provide any clear guidance regarding how to connect his own different models (e.g. Porter's Five Forces, Porter's Diamond Model and Porter's Value System) to a coherent framework ensuring that the organization considers all important aspects simultaneously. Instead, all these models are rather meant to be thought stimulators. Sadly, this phenomenon of just hinting at 'important' business concepts and aspects without practical guidance applies to most frameworks and models.

However, a systematic strategy analysis is needed for companies and organizations to survive in today's fast developing environments.

2.1   Vision of the GOLD Framework

This paper aims at conceptualizing a comprehensive strategy modelling that comprises the corporate, the business, and the project level together with their inherent interdependencies, and complemented by an ontology-based tool support that actively guides its users through the modelling process. Such active support is particularly important for the proposed multi-level modelling, which by its own nature requires the cooperation of experts of the different levels and in order to globally enforce (dynamically introduced) constraints for guaranteeing overall consistency. The envisioned result is a living multi-level strategy modelling scheme, the GOLD Framework. It incorporates the most important frameworks and models (e.g. Porter's Five Forces, the BMC, and the Value Proposition Canvas) and connects them in a consistent fashion throughout the organization's vertical and horizontal levels. It also aggregates all the requirements and constraints in a comprehensive ontology to provide just-in time modelling support and feedback. It will support both the line of command and the direction of feedback by including cooperative business analyses, aggregating diverse inputs, and guiding the subsequent decision and realization process. As this integrated framework is no longer restricted to the modelling level, it can also support the implementation and operation phases through automatic evaluation and control, e.g. for just in time target-performance comparisons. Of course, these benefits require major organizational changes, and a (meta-) modelling effort that comprises all the involved levels and that imposes some inter-level standardization. The subsequent concrete modelling and implementation for new business scenarios should, however, become much easier and much less error prone. Moreover, if set up adequately, the imposed standardization should not lead to prohibitive constraints. The goal is to derive from a given holistic and consistent strategy a system of level-specific, connected strategy modelling schemes which together cover the intended strategy in a consistent fashion, and therefore form a sound basis for the subsequent strategy implementation.

2.2   The GOLD Tool's Envisioned Functionalities

A first step in the direction of integration and support was made by the Business Model Developer (BMD), a tool inspired by the BMC that offered several advantageous abilities compared to the plain templates [1]. First, it is active, meaning that it can suggest specific modelling entities, restricts the occurrence of possible mistakes and actively supports the process of developing a strategy with recommendations throughout all aspects and levels of the company. Thus, the tool is able to control the user on basis of rule-based regulation. Second, several kinds of links between the fields can be programmed with different meanings, this way drastically increasing its abilities to express dependencies and traceability compared to the original templates. Third, it can be customized to different forms of templates including the original BMC, adapted versions, a mix of them, or completely different models.

The goal is to turn strategy modelling from a business-level activity into a comprehensive process that adequately aligns the required corporate-level, business-level, and project-level activities throughout the entire process of innovation, from the modelling of the ideas to the eventual operation phase. This should be additionally guided by consistency rules and just in time target-performance comparisons.

The envisioned GOLD Tool's main goal is to be holistic, enforce organization-wide alignment and automatically share and provide information/knowledge to allow for educated decisions. It allows the managers in charge to clearly define different kinds of strategy modelling schemes as well as interdependencies both between the fields of a given strategy model as well as between fields of different strategy models. This potential will be further exploited to model the required (multi-level) relationships for expressing consistency rules, target-performance comparisons, and other causal relations useful to provide snapshots for continuous auditing.

The envisaged GOLD Tool with its established transparent global perspective can significantly reduce the risk of misconceptions, communication errors, and failing assumptions by functioning as an early warning system. It also provides the required communication infrastructure to solve revealed problems and support a holistic strategy development.

3   Preliminary Results

In the following, the structure and the use of the GOLD Tool will be explained along the steps managers would take when using it. The pre-suggested structure offers guidance of how to start and how to look at the organization and its environment. It can be adapted if wished, but it ensures that the organization does not necessarily have to start from scratch.

Figure 1 shows the overview of the initial structure of the GOLD models, which embodies a rough vertical abstraction hierarchy of six different levels. The levels depicted from top to bottom describe in diagrams the organization (level 1), the market situation (level 2), an overview of the different industries (level

3), each separate industry (level 4), the industries' target segments (level 5), and their individual target customers (level 6). This hierarchical view is compact yet precise: it summarizes visually the corporate-, business-, and project level of the organization and the business line(s) under discussion. It helps managers orientate themselves by providing a general overview of the organization's different fields of operation while depicting how the different parts are connected.

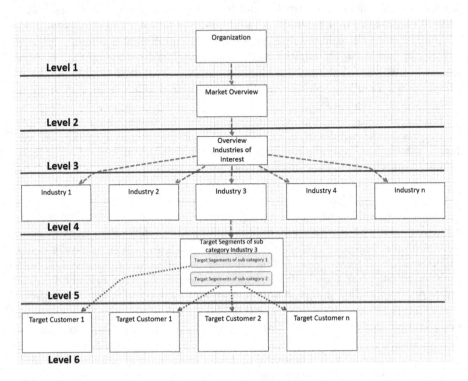

Fig. 1. GOLD tool overview with its 6 levels

3.1   GOLD Tool Application to the Case Study

The general structure of the tool and its diagrams will be described in parallel with its application to the case study, which shows (partially) instantiated diagrams, illustrating its concrete use.

Figure 2 in fact shows the full 6 level model hierarchy for a selection of the diagrams of the case study. Here we see that at each level the diagrams can include one or more purely descriptive fields (like in Level 1, Organization), depicted as light blue components, or also model diagrams, like e.g. the Market description (Level 2), that includes the Organization's main Market diagram, which is the Porter Five Forces diagram of Fig. 3.

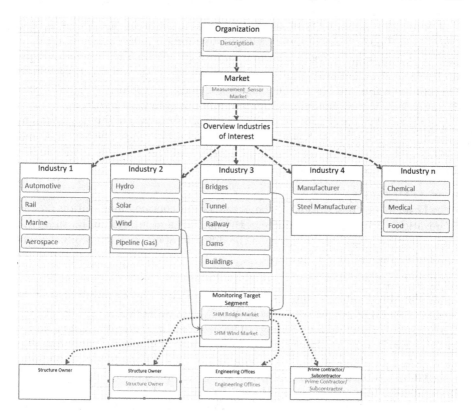

Fig. 2. Case study's 6 levels of the overview hierarchy in the GOLD tool (Color figure online)

Level 3 and 4 are in this case kept completely descriptive: they consist of the Industries of Interest diagram and of a description of each division of this company, matching their Industry categories (here kept anonymously). These are the branches for which this company produces its technologies, components, and systems. Each industry is subdivided in segments as depicted by the Sub-industry depiction.

Level 5 is instantiated in the case study only for the Monitoring Target Systems technology, which concerns Sub-industry C of Industry 2 and Sub-industry A of Industry 3. Both markets are subject to Infrastructure Monitoring, therefore there are specific diagrams for the Infrastructure Monitoring A market and the Infrastructure Monitoring B market.

For each of these markets, there are level 6 refinements concerning the specific target segments to that market. While Fig. 2 only depicts the Structure Owner segment for the Infrastructure Monitoring B market, addressing single owners, it shows three different target customers for the Infrastructure Monitoring A market: again the Structure Owners, but also Engineering Offices and Prime Contractor/Subcontractors, for which individual sub-diagrams exist.

Already this overview level shows how such a hierarchy provides a robust structure, while simultaneously allowing customization in the choice of what to refine and how, e.g. by descriptions or with diagrams, and that it encourages the creation of an ontology capturing the terminology and the relations of the "things" (divisions, markets, technologies, segments, et cetera) that play a significant role in the organization's business and operations structure.

Levels 1 and 2 concern the corporate-level considerations of the organization, levels 3 and 4 describe the business-level of interest in the specific analysis, and levels 5 and 6 detail the project level specifics of the business model under discussion and the units involved in its realization.

Level 1: Organization

In Level 1, the description of the organization contains information on the organization's structure, including e.g. the number and location of its sites, the sites' tasks, the employees in charge of the different operations, its product portfolio and its competitive advantage.

Level 2: Market

On the Market level managers describe the market the organization is operating in. Initially they may limit themselves to those markets relevant to the current analysis (incremental modelling). The high-level market situation is appropriately described in its strategic context by means of Porters' Five Forces diagram. In fact, the Organization's main market(s) tile connects to such a diagram: in the GOLD Tool the navigation to sub-models happens by clicking on the blue tiles that refer to a new connected 'page', in this case Fig. 3.

At modelling time, the manager can simply select the Porter Five Forces tile, drag and drop it onto the canvas at the appropriate level (Level 2 in this case), and rename it to the specific market analysis of concern. By clicking on it, the overview of Porter's Five Forces model appears, showing the empty but structurally correct and complete model. The organization can use this predefined framework and fill it out at need, as shown in Fig. 3. E.g. for the case study the model was instantiated by the experts to reflect the situation of the market it is operating in.

Business-Level: Levels 3 (Industries of Interest) **and 4** (Specific Industry Description).

These levels define the industries the organization is doing business with, before describing specific target segments and target customers in Levels 5 and 6. The same Porter Five Forces diagram template can be used at the single industry level to get a more detailed overview of the organization's different fields of operation.

Obviously, managers may not be interested in filling out all different tiles by themselves and therefore it is envisioned to connect the tool with other tools, like e.g. proper modules of SAP, acting as extensive and important source of organizational and operational information. Further, if the organization has defined information at one 'place', this 'place' can be connected via edges to other 'places' on different 'pages' e.g. depicting different models and frameworks. Thus,

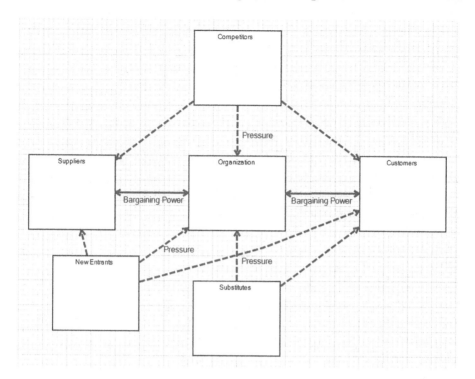

Fig. 3. Porter's five forces - market overview and power division (Color figure online)

among the connected 'places' alignment and up-to-datedness of information can be ensured.

In this case study, the company has simply described the areas in which it is active, basically providing a taxonomy of its broad and detailed areas of activity. For the specific question under consideration the analysis was concentrated on Levels 5 and 6, where we find again a wealth of diagrams.

Level 5: Target Segments

At Level 5, the target segments can be described in several different ways, depending on the kind of analysis and the degree of detail it requires. Here we see the power of the flexibility of the GOLD Framework coupled with the rigour of the GOLD Tool: while the framework provides a harness of top-down hierarchy and a methodology linked to a collection of models and diagrams, the tool manages the freedom to pick and choose the case-appropriate model for the specific analysis at hand. In case of need, it is also possible to design new models, as shown in the case study at this level.

Level 5 is instantiated in the case study only for the Monitoring Target Systems technology, which concerns Sub-industry C of Industry 2 and Sub-industry A of Industry 3. Both markets are subject to Infrastructure Monitoring, therefore there are specific diagrams for the Infrastructure Monitoring A market and for the Infrastructure B market.

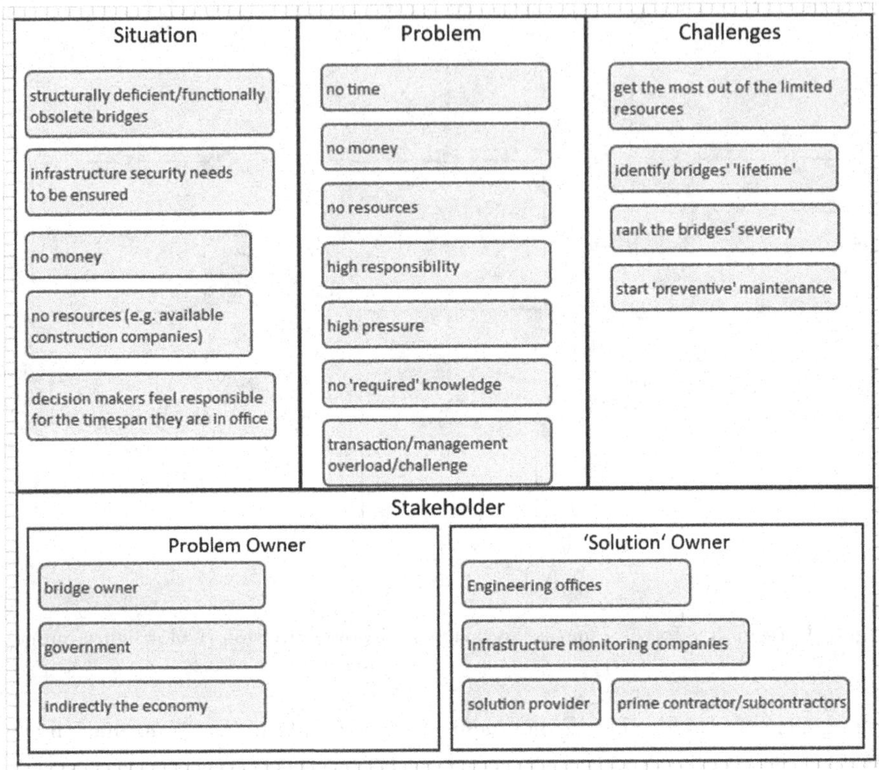

Situation	Problem	Challenges
structurally deficient/functionally obsolete bridges	no time	get the most out of the limited resources
infrastructure security needs to be ensured	no money	identify bridges' 'lifetime'
no money	no resources	rank the bridges' severity
no resources (e.g. available construction companies)	high responsibility	start 'preventive' maintenance
decision makers feel responsible for the timespan they are in office	high pressure	
	no 'required' knowledge	
	transaction/management overload/challenge	

Stakeholder

Problem Owner	'Solution' Owner
bridge owner	Engineering offices
government	Infrastructure monitoring companies
indirectly the economy	solution provider · prime contractor/subcontractors

Fig. 4. Case study's infrastructure market overview (custom model type)

The Infrastructure Monitoring market description diagram is shown in Fig. 4. It is a new diagram custom-designed for the case study team. The organization was interested in a situational depiction of the characteristics of this specific market together with the potential opportunities for the company, with the aim of identifying untapped opportunities that may ideally be low hanging fruits or solvable with the use of more advanced IT. Working in a mind-set and layout similar to the various canvas models, the structure of this model arose from the needs discussed with the company experts: its 'What layer' (top) depicts the characteristics of this specific market (fields Situation, Problem and Challenge), and its 'How layer' (bottom) hints at the potential opportunities for the company (fields Problem Owner and Solution Owner). This new canvas model proved very effective in summarizing the necessary information, and useful as a communication basis for discussions with top-management and the engineering groups. The descriptions also contribute to the ontology of the case study.

Level 6: Individual Target Customers

For each of the Level 5 markets there are one or more level 6 refinements concerning the target segments specific to that market. The Infrastructure Monitoring B market consists in this example only of the Structure Owner segment, and it is not further refined. The Infrastructure Monitoring A market is the actual market under detailed analysis, and has multiple segments of target customers: again the Structure Owners, but also Engineering Offices and Prime Contractor/Subcontractors, for which there are individual sub-diagrams. Note that these target customers already appeared as "Solution Owners" in Fig. 4. The segment Infrastructure Monitoring Companies is not further considered as it comprises the company itself and its competitors, none of which is a target.

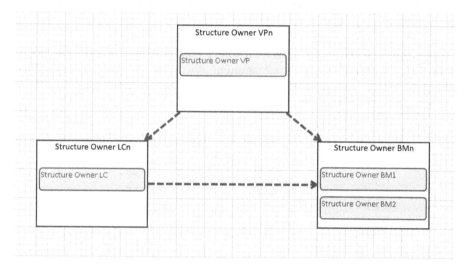

Fig. 5. Overview target customer - infrastructure monitoring a (custom model type) (Color figure online)

When clicking at the blue tile Structure Owner in Fig. 2, the model depicted in Fig. 5 pops up. Figure 5 is another self-created diagram. It provides an overview of the different information the organization possesses on a specific target customer segment, in this case the Infrastructure owners (Structure Owner). It connects information from the Value Proposition Canvas [18] with the Lean Canvas [16] and the BMC, all three materialized in corresponding models.

Figure 6 depicts the Value Proposition Canvas, Fig. 7 shows the corresponding Lean Canvas and Fig. 8 the related BMC. It is suggested to use these three models in this specific order as the Value Proposition Canvas allows for an in-depth understanding of the customers, their problems the organization has to find a fitting solution for, by exploiting its unfair advantage and the specific jobs-to-be-done and the pains and gains customers are experiencing. This information is particularly interesting and crucial for hypothesizing the customers' main problems, which are the starting point for the Lean Canvas. In the Lean

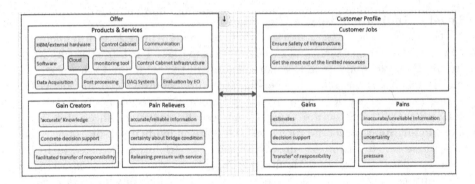

Fig. 6. Value proposition canvas - infrastructure monitoring a - market owners (Color figure online)

Canvas, based on the hypothesized customer problems the organization has to find a fitting solution, by exploiting its unfair advantage and developing a unique value proposition leading to a competitive advantage. Once the Lean Canvas is coherent, it is advised to develop several BMCs.

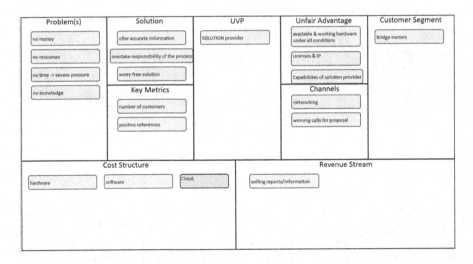

Fig. 7. Lean canvas - infrastructure monitoring a - market owners (Color figure online)

Most fields of the Lean Canvas and BMC are identical, as Maurya used the BMC as foundation for the Lean Canvas. Those fields of the BMCs will be in a future release automatically filled in by the GOLD Tool to ensure that all models of the framework are consistent. All changes made to 'things' that are identical (by copy or links) will be automatically kept aligned tool-wide. Further, the GOLD Tool will guide the user in filling out those frameworks correctly by making concrete suggestions of what to enter, using the ontology harvested in previous models of the same organization or division. For example, if managers already defined the organization's key partnerships somewhere else, then such entries are re-proposed everywhere where key partnerships need to be defined. This reuse automatically prevents inconsistencies, avoids managing duplicates and ensures by design a higher coherence of the information in the organization's ontology.

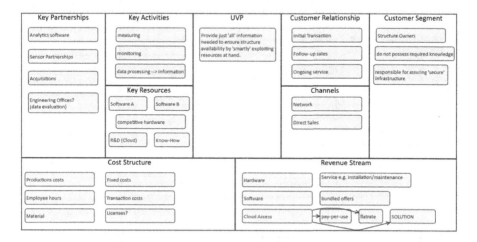

Fig. 8. Business model canvas - infrastructure monitoring a - market owners

3.2   GOLD Tool Outlook

Further, in future it is envisaged that some models will be connected with external tools, e.g. the Lean Canvas and BMC to be connected to cost models in Excel. This integration may allow changes throughout the business model developing process in the cost structure and revenue stream to trigger automatic updates and changes to the financial forecasts of the models. Later, if the organization starts to implement those models the actual data can be entered, this way enabling continuous target-performance comparisons.

The blue tiles represent a special way to ensure consistency: they refer directly to new models and, instantiated or not, they are 'standards' which can be used and re-used on any other page (no reuse is permitted in their own page: there is no self-inclusion of elements).

For example, we see the blue Cloud tile occur in both Figs. 6 and 7: they both open the Product Composition diagram in Fig. 9.

This diagram summarizes the product offerings envisioned by the company's team as a consequence of their analysis. Based on different cloud platforms, on different levels of processor power, storage dimensions, versions of a visualization app, and the possible add-on of an analytics engine, different packaged products were defined, whereby only the offer on Project-Report-Basis includes the Analytics Software service.

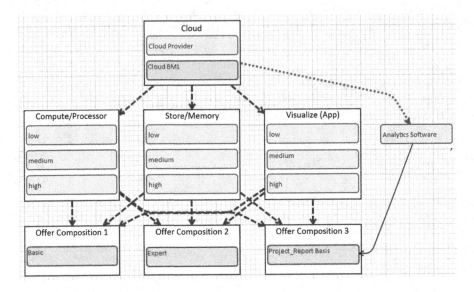

Fig. 9. Case study's cloud idea/service overview (Color figure online)

Over time the GOLD Tool will become a quite extensive analysis suite comprising all of the organization's main information and knowledge. A role-based view will be implemented to prevent overwhelming employees with too much information and/or them getting access to information they do not possess the clearance for. This role-based view approach will provide every employee with access to exactly the information and knowledge needed to perform their tasks. Additionally, it will be possible to show the information at different levels of abstraction, with different levels of aggregation in the reporting. The top-management is mostly just interested in overviews of all the key data of their different branches. They can explore 'the deeper level' of information and knowledge by data drill down, as all data is linked, however they are not distracted by it in first instance. The middle managers will have as default view a constant overview of the business units and projects they are responsible for, while the employees will have direct access to all the 'raw data' with which they work daily.

4 Technical Perspective

The development of a software product to support something as tangible as business modeling touches many aspects. Modeling guidance by means of predefined components and applicable rules are one thing. Being able to apply model analysis and comparison is another crucial factor, particularly in supporting business model innovation. In this section we focus on the requirements mainly from a technological perspective towards a simplicity-driven, structured approach to domain-specific business modeling that has been conceived to overcome the drawbacks of the mere generic solutions currently available.

The current version of the GOLD tool, i.e. the implementation of a software product supporting the GOLD framework, is developed with the *CINCO SCCE Meta Tooling Framework* [17] that facilitates the development of domain-specific graphical modeling tools in a rigorous model-driven fashion. Following the XMDD paradigm (*Extreme Model-Driven Design*) [15] the development process puts the domain expert (typically a non-programmer) in the center of the development process. Though the GOLD tool is significantly more sophisticated, its development benefits from the achievements made so far with the development of the Business Model Developer [1]. The focus during development lies on simplicity for the user, as the notion of simplicity has been identified as a driving paradigm in information system development [14].

In the following, both the already implemented as well as the envisioned features of the GOLD tool are broken down into specific aspects of tool development.

4.1 Domain-Specific Modeling

Models in general consist of components that represent entities from the respective area of application. In terms of business models these are business-related entities that make up the terminology of the "things" that play a significant role in the organization's business and operations structure. In the following, these "things" will be referred to as "business items". The type of these business items heavily depends on the actual application domain. As an example, business models related to hospitals address very different business items compared to models related to car manufacturing. Although both domains might be served by means of generic components, a domain-specific modeling environment significantly improves the modeling efficiency by serving the respective modeler with well-known concepts, i.e. the terminology they are used to. This typically results in effective support in the creation of meaningful models.

Structure via Taxonomies. Currently, there are virtually no domain-specific solutions that guide the creation of business models for specific business fields or application domains. Instead, available tools pursue a mere generic approach based on unspecific model components. As an example, the actual components to fill the Business Model Canvas are generic notepads that hold textual labels manually created by the modeler. We argue that this is not to be excused by arguments regarding design freedom or boosting creativity. Even the most simple drawing programs provide shapes and powerful editing tools instead of leaving the user with only a freehand tool, a blank canvas and some good advice on how to succeed. We argue that useful components and editing tools rather push effectiveness instead of limiting creativity and domain-specific solutions in the context of business modeling would cause the same positive effect.

In contrast to a generic approach, we facilitate a domain-specific setup of the modeling environment by means of building a taxonomy of modeling components. This taxonomy is achieved by collecting and characterizing the business items derived from the concepts in the organization's terminology. It can be created and maintained in different ways.

- In a distinct customization step typically preceding the actual model design phase. Different stakeholders with different disciplinary backgrounds might be involved, spanning domain experts, application experts, business strategists, etc.
- Manually in the modeling environment by means of extending and maintaining the taxonomy on demand.
- Automatically, by means of collecting items that are used throughout the different models and presenting them to the modeler in a live-updated view.

The latter option might additionally make use of knowledge discovery techniques and this way may become a very powerful tool, especially if the GOLD framework grows, e.g. towards a multi-user, multi-organization platform. In such an environment the automatic discovery of modeling components can enable reasonable recommendations tailored towards the specific domain to enhance the overall modeling experience. But even a manually maintained taxonomy of business items would mean a huge achievement in enhancing organization-wide knowledge management.

The taxonomy of modeling components, i.e. the outcome of the domain-specific setup, is going to be referred to as the library of "building blocks". That they are well-structured by means of characterization paves the way for many of the envisaged features of the GOLD framework, as this characterization can be interpreted as static types from a programming perspective.

Modeling Guidance. Available solutions in the field of business modeling, both pen-and-paper-based approaches as well as software-based model editors, lack support for the model design process itself. These tools provide a blank canvas to start with but do not convey the required knowledge on how to actually fill it. Step-by-step guides that put design steps in a meaningful order are outsourced to theoretical training courses or not to be found at all. This means an initial hurdle in terms of investment upfront before creating the first model, although many modeling tools have been conceived with brainstorming and innovation in mind. However, attending courses might extend the mindset of the participants but does not add guidance to the modeling tool of choice.

The GOLD tool comes with canvas-specific guidance by means of a wizard that guides through useful, ordered steps to fill the respective canvas in a meaningful manner. We have already introduced this feature with the Business Model Developer on a per-canvas basis. We now envisage to integrate and extend it by means of supporting hierarchical models, thereby relying on the per-canvas solution on each respective hierarchy level.

4.2   Canvas Customization

Besides the tailoring of the modeling environment towards a specific domain by the creation of building blocks the layout of the canvas is another aspect that might be domain-specific. Applying our modeling tool in practice and evaluating the feedback we experienced that business professionals are really interested in re-designing the canvas they work with. Hence, the further development of the GOLD tool introduces custom canvases. This not only allows the user to rename or move specific tiles but also to delete them or invent completely new ones from scratch. As various communities have created custom canvases for specific purposes, already, we provide them with explicit tool support for integrating their ideas to build a comprehensive modeling environment.

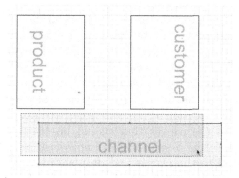

Fig. 10. Tile arrangement for a custom canvas (from [1])

Tile Arrangement. The crafting skills that are needed to build a custom layout are rather little sophisticated as it all comes down to arranging tiles and giving them a name. Therefore, the model editor supports the creation of various shapes, reaching from rectangles over circles or ellipses to complex polygonal shapes (cf. Fig. 12). Figure 10 shows a screenshot of a simple arrangement of tiles in the creation process of a custom canvas layout.

Building a custom layout is an activity that is not typically part of the actual business design process but rather takes place in a preceding customization phase, along with the initial definition of building blocks to create a domain-specific setup. It is more like creating the meta model of a specific canvas to be added to the modeling environment. We might even consider a dedicated role in the overall design process to lead the customization process. However, as there is no specific reason for not adding a custom canvas on demand, the GOLD tool is envisaged to support both possible approaches.

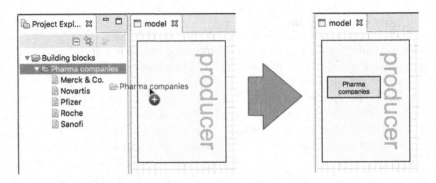

Fig. 11. Definition of containment rules (from [1])

Templating. Having created and properly arranged the tiles to form a custom layout, it will be available for the business modelers to utilize it. However, its creator might be particularly interested in defining what is allowed to be inside each respective tile of the canvas. To do so, they can make use of the structure that arises from the library of building blocks that are part of the domain-specific setup. In order to allow or forbid the usage of specific building blocks, their type (i.e. the classification within the respective taxonomy) can be linked to the specific tiles of the canvas that should be constrained. The editor of the GOLD tool makes this a specifically simple task as the type of building blocks can be dragged to the canvas and dropped on the respective tile. This triggers the creation of a node in the tile that represents this exact type. Figure 11 shows a screenshot with an example, in which a collection of building blocks (in this case companies) is linked to a tile labeled "producer". The created node is interpreted as a containment rule, which specifies that all building blocks inside the referenced collection can be used to fill the respective tile at model design time.

The creation of custom canvases along with the specification of containment rules results in the definition of so-called "templates". This action is typically not part of the actual business model design, but rather takes place in a preceding customization phase. At runtime, the model editor of the GOLD tool is capable of providing a modeling environment based on the template definition. With this, users are able to create business models based on the respective template (generally referred to as "instantiation") and fill the provisioned tiles with building blocks according to the specified containment rules. These rules either become part of the general canvas validation, i.e. error and warning messages are generated in case of rule violation, or they can even be enforced by means of suppressing the creation of forbidden nodes completely. This supports the modeler in two ways, through the enforcement of structural correctness of the models as well as through additional guidance for the modeler by means of validating the model semantics. The latter helps at avoiding models that, even though structurally correct, lack soundness or are just not meaningful.

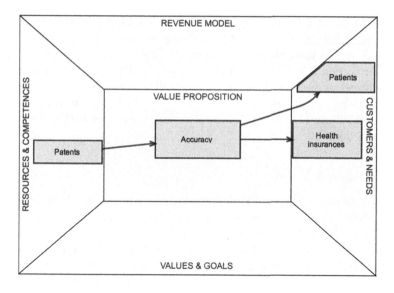

Fig. 12. Example of a custom canvas (from [1])

Scenario Validation. With the overall templating approach, sophisticated canvas layouts can be defined already. Figure 12 shows a layout based on polygonal shapes. However, in terms of constraining the use of the template in terms of how it is to be filled, we have just scratched the surface. We recently established a scenario-based approach with extended containment constraints by means of, for example, cardinalities as well as attribute value checks. Users can link templates with so-called "scenarios" that represent a specific instantiation of the template that is intended to either be enforced or avoided. Scenarios are created using the items as well as their types from available taxonomies, i.e. the library of building blocks.

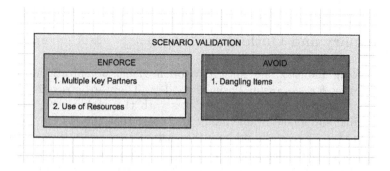

Fig. 13. Scenarios to be enforced or avoided

Figure 13 shows how easy scenarios are linked with a specific template. The graphical model of a template contains a dedicated validation area. This is where those files from the workspace that contain the scenario descriptions are dragged to in order to link it with the current template. Both types of scenarios, those to be enforced as well as those to be avoided, are interpreted as rules to be validated at the runtime of the canvas editor. This means warnings and errors are generated during the design of models based on the respective template in case of rule violation.

4.3   Aggregated Views

As the complexity of the GOLD Tool grows, the integration of the support for different views on the models becomes mandatory. The multi-level approach of the GOLD Framework naturally involves various stakeholders in the design process, each of them having different skills, knowledge, roles and responsibilities within the organization. Some information might only be relevant for a few users, or even for a single user. We strive to integrate the concept of personalized, aggregated views to the GOLD Tool, in multiple variations. On the one hand, the visibility of information and data held by a specific model might be customized towards specific user roles. On the other hand, information from submodels can be collected and displayed in the parent model in an aggregated fashion. Parts of one model might even be filled with information from submodels. However, the data is to be updated in a live fashion as the models evolve. That way, information and data is kept accurate and visualized for those users that really want or need to see it.

The definition of views is facilitated by the rigorously structured approach of the GOLD Tool, based on determined model layouts filled with well-defined building blocks. Additionally, the realization of a model interface concept can help to define exactly which information is provided by a specific type of model to be read externally and used from, for example, parent models. The final step is to integrate a role concept in order to leverage role-based views, up to real personalization.

5   Summary and Outlook

SMEs adopting Industry 4.0 must develop a global organizational strategy paving the way for successful business models. They are struggling to couple their 'manufacturing' core competences with the enabling IT technology to a compelling and incontestable unfair advantage that allows for unique value propositions that successfully address the customer segments they are serving (illustrated on the left-hand side of Fig. 14). This silo-driven approach must be bridged internally allowing for a more in-depth customer understanding. The GOLD Framework and Tool are envisioned to guide and support the organization in bridging the gap between the silos of manufacturing, IT and business (see the GOLD Effect shown at the right-hand side of Fig. 14). GOLD's global approach of analyzing the external and internal world of the organization in a controlled and ordered manner allows for finding and defining coherent and consistent strategies, processes and business models. It aims at guiding all the involved stakeholders via hierarchical collections of analyses from different perspectives to converge on an organization-wide aligned business strategy. Only with this internally and externally driven orientation and alignment will SMEs be able to master the Industry 4.0 adoption and translate it into a competitive advantage.

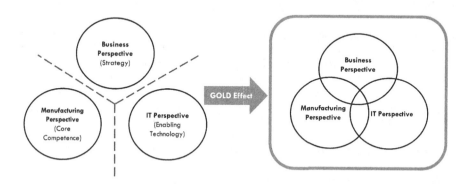

Fig. 14. Envisioned GOLD effect

The impact of the proposed GOLD Framework and Tool has the potential to go far beyond the mere design phase for competitive business models. In fact, once the strategic direction is set, the envisaged GOLD Tool with its established transparent global perspective can significantly reduce the risk of misconceptions, communication errors, and failing assumptions by functioning as an early warning system e.g. based on systematic target-performance comparisons.

To our knowledge the GOLD approach is the first systematic attempt to go beyond the known perspective-specific frameworks and tools to establish a coherent, tool-supported multi-perspective decision support system. In a sense, this is achieved at the meta level, as the GOLD Framework and Tool can be regarded as orchestrators of already existing frameworks as colorfully illustrated in Chap. 3 Preliminary Results. In fact, adequately linking well-known frameworks allowed to aggregate global knowledge for the top-management to take informed decisions regarding the organization's short-term and long-term strategic direction.

The results found in this work clearly show limitations in size, scope and depth, especially regarding the validation of the GOLD Framework and GOLD Tool. This paper explored a global flavor of the current situation in the manufacturing industry in the context of Industry 4.0. This context could be successfully established as a source of knowledge to deduce requirements for the GOLD Framework and GOLD Tool. This broad perspective inevitably leaves room for further investigation in three main dimensions:

- to validate the general need and usability of the framework and tool in small scale proof-of-concepts (**Technology and Industry**),
- to elaborate on the technological potential via a running prototype implementation and user feedback at several organizations (**Technology and Scale**).

A careful analysis of this potential requires a fully established setup at some organization and has therefore to wait until an installation at some adequate early adaptor has reached the required state.

References

1. Boßelmann, S., Margaria, T.: Domain-specific business modeling with the business model developer. In: Margaria, T., Steffen, B. (eds.) ISoLA 2014. LNCS, vol. 8803, pp. 545–560. Springer, Heidelberg (2014). https://doi.org/10.1007/978-3-662-45231-8_45
2. Brettel, M., Friederichsen, N., Keller, M., Rosenberg, M.: How virtualization, decentralization and network building change the manufacturing landscape: an industry 4.0 perspective. Int. J. Mech. Aerosp. Ind. Mechatron. Eng. **8**(1), 37–44 (2014)
3. Consulting, C.: Industry 4.0 - the capgemini consulting view - sharpening the picture beyond the hype. Accessed 22 Sept 2018
4. Davies, R.: Industry 4.0 Digitalization for productivity and growth. WGMB GmbH (2017)
5. Digital, M.: Industry 4.0 how to navigate digitization of the manufacturing sector. https://www.mckinsey.com/business-functions/operations/our-insights/industry-four-point-o-how-to-navigae-the-digitization-of-the-manufacturing-sector. Accessed 22 Sept 2018
6. Drath, R., Horch, A.: Industrie 4.0: Hit or hype? [industry forum]. IEEE Ind. Electron. Mag. **8**(2), 56–58 (2014). https://doi.org/10.1109/MIE.2014.2312079
7. E Porter, M.: The five competitive forces that shape strategy **86**, 23–41 (2008)
8. Evanschitzky, H., Wangenheim, F., Woisetschläger, D.: Service & solution innovation: overview and research agenda introduction **40**, 657–660 (2011)
9. Faller, C., Feldmüller, D.: Industry 4.0 learning factory for regional SMEs. Procedia CIRP **32**, 88–91 (2015). https://doi.org/10.1016/j.procir.2015.02.117. 5th Conference on Learning Factories
10. Fink, D., Knoblach, B.: Von disruptiven geschäftsmodellen zur digitalen transformation (2017)
11. Fließ, S.: Kundenintegration, pp. 223–247. Springer Fachmedien Wiesbaden, Wiesbaden (2015). https://doi.org/10.1007/978-3-8349-4681-2
12. Hildebrand, V.G.: Individualisierung als strategische Option der Marktbearbeitung. Deutscher Universitätsverlag, Springer Fachmedien Wiesbaden (1997). https://doi.org/10.1007/978-3-663-01519-2
13. Jacob, F., Kleinaltenkamp, M.: Leistungsindividualisierung und -standardisierung, pp. 601–623. Gabler Verlag, Wiesbaden (2004). https://doi.org/10.1007/978-3-322-91260-2
14. Margaria, T., Steffen, B.: Simplicity as a driver for agile innovation. Computer **43**(6), 90–92 (2010). https://doi.org/10.1109/MC.2010.177
15. Margaria, T., Steffen, B.: Service-orientation: conquering complexity with XMDD. In: Hinchey, M., Coyle, L. (eds.) Conquering Complexity, pp. 217–236. Springer, London (2012). https://doi.org/10.1007/978-1-4471-2297-5

16. Maurya, A.: Running Lean: Iterate from Plan A to a Plan That Works, 2nd edn. O'Reilly Media Inc., Sebastopol (2012)
17. Naujokat, S., Lybecait, M., Kopetzki, D., Steffen, B.: CINCO: a simplicity-driven approach to full generation of domain-specific graphical modeling tools. Softw. Tools Technol. Transf. (2017). https://doi.org/10.1007/s10009-017-0453-6
18. Osterwalder, A., Pigneur, Y., Bernarda, G., Smith, A., Papadakos, T.: Value Proposition Design: How to Create Products and Services Customers Want. Business Planning. Wiley, Hoboken (2014)
19. Osterwalder, A., Pigneur, Y.: Business Model Generation (2013)
20. Sharma, A., Iyer, G.R.: Are pricing policies an impediment to the success of customer solutions? Ind. Mark. Manag. **40**(5), 723–729 (2011). https://doi.org/10.1016/j.indmarman.2011.06.002. Service and Solution Innovation
21. Weiber, R., Ferreira, K.: Transaktions- versus Geschäftsbeziehungsmarketing, pp. 121–146. Springer Fachmedien Wiesbaden, Wiesbaden (2015). https://doi.org/10.1007/978-3-8349-4681-2

Author Index

Printed in the United States
By Bookmasters